Henning Kronstam

Florida A&M University, Tallahassee
Florida Atlantic University, Boca Raton
Florida Gulf Coast University, Ft. Myers
Florida International University, Miami
Florida State University, Tallahassee
University of Central Florida, Orlando
University of Florida, Gainesville
University of North Florida, Jacksonville
University of South Florida, Tampa
University of West Florida, Pensacola

Henning

University Press of Florida

Gainesville/Tallahassee/Tampa/Boca Raton

Pensacola/Orlando/Miami/Jacksonville/Ft. Myers

Kronstam

Portrait of a Danish Dancer

Alexandra Tomalonis

With an Afterword by Ellen G. Levine, M.D.

Copyright 2002 by Alexandra Tomalonis
Printed in the United States of America on acid-free paper

07 06 05 04 03 02   6 5 4 3 2 1

Frontispiece: An official portrait of Kronstam with his Royal and
State decorations. Courtesy of Mydtskov.

Library of Congress Cataloging-in-Publication Data
Tomalonis, Alexandra.
Henning Kronstam: portrait of a Danish dancer / Alexandra
Tomalonis; with an afterword by Ellen Levine.
p. cm.
Includes bibliographical references (p.) and index.
ISBN 0-8130-2546-x (alk. paper)
1. Kronstam, Henning. 2. Ballet dancers—Denmark—
Biography. 3. Choreographers—Denmark—Biography. I. Title.
GV1785.K744 T66 2002   2002020447

The University Press of Florida is the scholarly publishing
agency for the State University System of Florida, comprising
Florida A&M University, Florida Atlantic University, Florida
Gulf Coast University, Florida International University, Florida
State University, University of Central Florida, University of
Florida, University of North Florida, University of South
Florida, and University of West Florida.

University Press of Florida
15 Northwest 15th Street
Gainesville, FL 32611-2079
http://www.upf.com

For my mother, Millicent Tomulonis, with deepest gratitude

La danse, c'est une question morale.
—George Balanchine

Contents

Preface

Like its subject, this book has changed form and character several times. It was originally intended to be a study of Henning Kronstam's roles, then became an artistic biography, a biography, and finally a portrait.

I first approached Kronstam in the spring of 1993 and asked if he would be interested in working with me on a book about his roles. I had met him three years earlier; although I had been very interested in the Royal Danish Ballet and the ballets of Bournonville since I first saw them in 1976, I was unable to travel to Copenhagen until the spring of 1990. Kronstam had just staged *Giselle* and I thought it an exceptional production because of its poetry and dramatic cogency. During several subsequent visits, I was equally impressed with other ballets in his charge—*La Sylphide, Napoli, Onegin, Theme and Variations*. Whether they were his productions or ballets he had merely rehearsed, each had a directorial style that distinguished it from the other works in the company's repertory. I was especially intrigued because, even though I watched the rehearsals, I couldn't figure out how he did it. There was a mystical symbiosis between Kronstam and the dancers that produced miracles and that left the Royal Theatre with him. Kronstam had a reputation—partly deserved—for being a difficult and private man. Sensing that he would not be open to a biography, I proposed a book about his roles. I would interview him about the ballets he was preparing and write about what I saw in rehearsals and on stage.

I began to suspect that the gods would not smile favorably upon this project when, two days after Kronstam had agreed to my proposal, he vanished from the Theatre. The explanation given by the company's management was so inconsistent with what I had observed that I became curious and decided to try to find out what had really happened. After ignoring several letters, Kronstam finally wrote me and we agreed to start working on the book in January 1994. I never asked him what had happened at the Theatre, partly because I did not want to start from his side of things, and partly because he was mired in a severe depression much of the time I knew him. One of the ways he coped with his illness was to avoid discussion of painful or unpleasant matters. He was just beginning to be able to discuss the situation at the Theatre when he died.

Since I could not watch Kronstam coach his roles, the book evolved into an artistic biography, although I was handicapped by the fact that I had barely seen him dance. I came to know him as a dancer through the eyes of other dancers and through watching the few snatches of film that are available, mostly in private hands. The second section of the book, in which I discuss his major roles in detail, is primarily drawn from interviews with him, which are left, as much as possible, in his voice.

After Kronstam died, in May 1995, the book changed yet again, as there were too many gaps or unanswered questions to make a biography as complete as I would have wished. There were questions I had not known to ask, dates, motivations, and explanations that will never be known. At the beginning, Kronstam had wanted to restrict the book to his artistic life. During our last interviews, a few weeks before he died, he decided that two aspects of his life that he had always kept secret were important to the book and agreed to their inclusion. He suffered from an illness that he went to great lengths to conceal and that affected all aspects of his career and his life. He had begun to talk about it, but there were still many things I did not know. This aspect of his life has been reconstructed with the help of a psychiatrist, Dr. Ellen Levine, who has written an afterword.

This, then, is a portrait rather than a formal biography. There are a few gaps, mostly dates and places where Kronstam worked during summers and dates of several incidents in his private life that cannot now be ascertained. There are several people whom I wanted to interview who could not be found, a few who declined, some who died during the course of the project before being interviewed, and several friends who could never be identified—there was only a description or a first name.

The book is written by an American for American readers. The Danish ballet world, especially Kronstam's world, is very different from the American one. That is precisely one of the things that attracted me to Kronstam and the Danish tradition, and it must be borne in mind when one confronts something that contradicts everything one has ever been taught about ballet (such as the fact that boys have to begin studying ballet at eight or nine while girls can start as late as eighteen because their bodies are more flexible). I have tried to understand the Danish point of view and present it for American readers. I hope I will not offend Danes in doing this, and that I have interpreted their beautiful tradition as accurately as could be expected from a foreigner. The book is also written for those who inhabited Kronstam's world. I hope the Danish dancers, especially *"Hennings børn"* (Henning's children), will understand that some of the material here that seems to violate Kronstam's privacy was necessary in order to tell his story fairly. Although the end of his life was difficult, he had great courage and an indomitable spirit and there was always a strong pulse of optimism coursing beneath the surface.

Notes on Sources

Unless otherwise noted, all the quotations attributed to Henning Kronstam come from three interview sessions with him in January 1994, August 1994, and April 1995, and from many telephone interviews and conversations between February 1994 and May 1995.

All other quotations are from interviews I conducted with dancers and other associates, as well as Kronstam's friends and members of his family. References are given only for quotations from print sources or other interviews, or if the identity of a source is not obvious from the text. I owe an enormous debt of gratitude to the artists, friends, and family who gave so generously of their time and memories: Nina Ananiashvili, Ib Andersen, Niels Balle, Ann Barzel, Peter Bo Bendixen, Henrik Bering Liisberg, Jessie [Kronstam] Birger-Christensen, Mogens Boesen, Jens Brenaa, Jette Buchwald, Claudia Cassidy, Rudi van Dantzig, Johnny Eliasen, Erling Eliasson, Sorella Englund, Eliot Feld, Flemming Flindt, Vivi Flindt, Carla Fracci, Tommy Frishøi, Rose Gad, Franz Gerstenberg, Ingrid Glindemann, Serge Golovine, Kenneth Greve, Ann-Kristin

Hauge, Bjarne Hecht, Linda Hindberg, Jan Holme, Tove Holme, Nikolaj Hübbe, Mette Hønningen, Mona Jensen, Lis Jeppesen, Boel Jørgensen, Una Kai, Niels Kehlet, Patricia Klekovic, Mette-Ida Kirk, Fred Konrad, Janne Kronstam, Torben Kronstam, Alexander Kølpin, Niels Bjørn Larsen, Anne Grethe Lassen, Peter Ernst Lassen, Larry Long, Murray Louis, Adam Lüders, Thomas Lund, Anna Lærkesen, Bruce Marks, Peter Martins, Alexander Meinertz, Beppe Menegatti, Margaret Mercier, Poul Rolf Meurs-Gerken, Henriette Muus, John Neumeier, Kjeld Noack, Margrethe Noyé, Benedikte Paaske, Viveka Paulsen, Stephen Pier, Yuri Possokhov, Kirsten Ralov, Lloyd Riggins, Jerome Robbins (by letter), Heidi Ryom, Silja Schandorff, Margrethe Schanne, Peter Schaufuss, Lise Scherfig, Lene Schrøder-Hansen, Antoinette Sibley, Kirsten Simone, Ulla Skow, Glen Tetley, Ingryd Thorson, Julian Thurber, Helgi Tomasson, Violette Verdy, Karin Vikelgaard, Edward Villella, Arne Villumsen, Arlette Weinreich, Stanley Williams, Annemari Vingård, Anne Wivel, and Richard Wolf.

All newspaper and magazine articles, contracts, and correspondence are from Kronstam's own collection, now in the possession of his nephew and heir, Torben Kronstam, or the Drama Collection of the Royal Library, Copenhagen. Kronstam kept no diary but had saved two drawers and one suitcase full of clippings. He was not an archivist, and many of the clippings are undated. Because newspaper dance reviews are often placed on the lower half of the page, the paper's name was often cut off as well; dates and newspaper names are given, when known, in the text.

I have enough Danish to read through the clippings as well as books on Danish ballet and garner facts, and some of the translations of simple texts, or a few phrases, are my own. For longer or more complex texts I was dependent on others, and I am extremely grateful to Alexander Meinertz, Bjarne Hecht, Lene Schrøder-Hansen, and Birgitte Engelbrechtsen, who translated dozens of Danish newspaper clippings, letters, and contracts.

Kronstam also kept a large file of contracts and other correspondence. There were very few personal letters, and these were mostly letters from admirers, or thank you notes from dancers he had coached. While at first this seemed a minimal archival record, these papers proved to be invaluable in verifying things he told me and checking stories that came up in interviews. There were a few times Kronstam claimed poor memory in order to avoid answering a question, but I never caught him in a lie.

Several other works were of enormous help in writing this book. First and foremost, Tobi Tobias's 1983 interviews with Kronstam for her "Oral History of the Royal Danish Ballet and Its Bournonville Tradition" provided information that would have otherwise been lost. Two works of Erik Aschengreen were also very helpful: his list of Kronstam's roles published in *Les saisons de la danse* in 1976, which provided an outline for my research; and his entertaining and informative history of the Royal Danish Ballet from 1948 to 1998, *Der går dans,* which helped place many events in context and give the Danish view of things.

I owe a deep debt of gratitude to many people: first and foremost Henning Kronstam, for working with me during what must have been the most difficult period in his life, for his candor, and for all he taught me. His story would not have been brought to print were it not for the tireless efforts of my agent, Laura Langlie. For this, and for her unwavering faith in this project, I owe her an enormous debt. I am also very grateful to my editors at the University Press of Florida, Meredith Morris-Babb and Gillian Hillis, for their care and guidance, and the designer, Louise OFarrell.

Dancers were unfailingly generous with their time and memories, and I am extremely grateful to everyone I interviewed for the book, even those not directly quoted here. Several people endured multiple interviews and were helpful in other ways. Kirsten Simone showed me her private collection of films of Kronstam's dancing, which enabled me to understand Kronstam's gifts as a dancer. Kenneth Greve gave me access and introductions to friends of Kronstam's outside the Theatre. Ib Andersen, Bjarne Hecht, Nikolaj Hübbe, Margaret Mercier, and Arlette Weinreich, each with extraordinary memories, answered far more than their share of questions and were invaluable in helping me place events in context.

Dr. Kay Jamison was very helpful in answering questions about Kronstam's condition. I am extremely grateful to Dr. Ellen Levine, who provided invaluable guidance in helping me present as accurate a picture as possible of Kronstam's health as well as a psychological autopsy as an afterword. Dr. Levine traveled to Copenhagen to meet with several people who had known Kronstam so as not to be dependent on my view alone, listened to taped interviews with him, and was willing to go over material countless times as new insights were discovered.

I thank those who read the manuscript in various stages and provided corrections and suggestions: Mary K. Baumgartner, Elizabeth Liebman, Michael Popkin, Lene Schrøder-Hansen, and Leigh Witchel. George Jackson not only read the manuscript but has answered endless questions about Danish ballet and ballet history in general from the time I began writing, more than twenty years ago. I am grateful to colleagues who answered questions, usually on very short notice, including Joan Acocella, Erik Aschengreen, Mary Cargill, Robert Greskovic, Majbrit Hjelmsbo, Knud Arne Jürgensen, Alan M. Kriegsman, Alastair Macaulay, Lewis Segal, and Tobi Tobias. Alexander Meinertz has provided information and assistance that made many parts of this book possible, allowed me access to his research on Vera Volkova, read several chapters more than once, and constantly goaded me to do better. I also thank Torben Kronstam for granting me access to his uncle's papers, and Majbrit Hjelmsbo for her hospitality and for checking many facts and sources. Of course, any errors in facts or conclusions are mine alone.

I am also grateful to several directors of the Royal Danish Ballet—Frank Andersen, Peter Schaufuss, Johnny Eliasen, Maina Gielgud, and Aage Thordal-Christensen—for allowing me access to rehearsals, classes, and performances between April 1990 and January 2000. Marianne Hallar and Lilo Skaarup at the Royal Theatre's library were very helpful in finding the photographs for this book and in working out a way for me to have copies of them. I thank all the photographers who allowed me to use their work, especially Morten Mydtskov Rønne at the Mydtskov studios, who made so many of his family's photographs of Kronstam available to me, and John Johnsen, whose photos from the 1970s give a rare glimpse of Kronstam in live performance, as well as David Amzallig, Marianne Grøndahl, and Claus Poulsen. Several photographs in Kronstam's collection were without identifying information. There were a few photographs from the 1950s and 1960s where no address for the photographer could be found, despite concerted efforts, but I thank those photographers as well. I am grateful, too, to the Danish newspaper *Politiken,* which was kind enough to allow me to reprint substantial portions of an important interview with Kronstam before he took over the directorship of the Royal Danish Ballet in 1978. Finally, I am extremely grateful for three generous donations, from Elizabeth Liebman, Queen Margrethe and Prince Henrik's Fund, and Queen Ingrid and King Frederik's Fund, which helped cover the costs of the photographs in this book. My mother, Millicent Tomalonis, has supported my writing in every way possible. To her, as well as the many friends and colleagues who listened to my book stories, I am extremely grateful.

Part one

The Making of an Artist

In *Napoli*, Act III. Photo: Mydtskov. Private collection.

As dancer, artistic director, ballet director, and teacher, Henning Kronstam, who died yesterday, became perhaps the most influential person in the Royal Ballet during the past fifty years.
—Erik Aschengreen, *Berlingske Tidende*,
    May 29, 1995

He was the glue that held the company together. He was the reason it maintained its international reputation as long as it did.
—Ib Andersen

One

Henning Kronstam and His World

Henning Kronstam was a dancer of uncommon beauty, musicality, and grace. He was tall—six foot one—and darkly handsome, with a virile elegance and a body ideally suited to ballet. The long, strong thighs gave his jump its power; the foot, with its high arch, gave that power an eloquent sensitivity. The hands were especially beautiful, alive with implied movement even in repose; the open, mobile face, with its enormous brown eyes, easily reflected a thousand emotions.

Kronstam was a superb technician, but what separated him from the other great male dancers of the age was his unparalleled dramatic range. Unlike most stars, who cannot shed their egos and thus remain ever themselves, Kronstam became the character he was dancing. He transformed himself into a role the way Merlin changed himself into an owl. The transformations seemed infinite.

He danced poets and princes, sad clowns and mad priests, the heroic, the wounded, and the depraved.

He was, above all, a creature of the theater. As a teenager, he had toyed with the idea of becoming an actor and never lost his delight in the magic of the stage. He is pictured as a child on the cover of Allan Fridericia's *Harald Lander og hans balletter* (Harald Lander and His Ballets). He is nine and stands, finger in mouth and eyes wide with wonder, watching the ballet master gesture from his high director's chair. For Kronstam, like many theater children, being on stage was both serious work and as natural as play. He retained his child's eagerness in adulthood, throwing himself into his roles like a boy who had tumbled into a storybook.

Kronstam danced at the apex of a golden age of Danish male dancing and was one of three Danish men of his generation who achieved international fame. Erik Bruhn, six years older, with an impeccable classical technique and controlled dramatic fire, was a golden zephyr, breezing in for a month or two to dance a few roles, then flying away again. Flemming Flindt, two years younger than Kronstam, was a virtuoso dancer with a dramatic stage presence. Bruhn left Copenhagen for New York, Flindt for London and Paris. It was expected that Kronstam too would leave, especially after his success on the company's first American tour in 1956.

Kronstam never left Denmark, he said, because he couldn't match his repertory anywhere else. More important perhaps, he loved Copenhagen and its Royal Theatre. He danced at the height of the ballet boom, the age of Nureyev—and Nureyev and Bruhn are the stars other dancers invariably compare with Kronstam—but Kronstam was not chiefly motivated by fame or money. He wanted stage time, new roles, and the chance to work with interesting choreographers. He got those chances by remaining open, professionally innocent, and—the word most often used to describe him by other artists—humble. He thrived in the repertory theater system. Violette Verdy, New York City Ballet's French ballerina who danced with Kronstam early in both their careers, remembered that even at twenty-one, when they first danced together, "he wanted to serve an institution and he was already institutional in his discipline. If he had left he would have had to compromise in some ways, and he wanted to keep clean, because he was a class act." She also observed that Kronstam didn't have to leave to attract choreographers, because "they all came to him, came to this Prince of Denmark."

Part of serving a ballet institution is passing on what one has learned, and that was a responsibility Kronstam took very seriously. Verdy described him as "a high priest of an aristocratic art, a celebrant," and that is how he approached his work as an *instruktør* (director-producer) as well as a dancer. He celebrated classical dancing and he celebrated the individuality of the dancers with whom he worked. He had a special talent for making the old look new. "He would show you the steps—oh, you would hear drum rolls. He would take out the steps and they would be gold," said Nikolaj Hübbe, now a star of the New York City Ballet, who learned many of his early roles from Kronstam.

As much as he was the Royal Danish Ballet's high priest, Kronstam was also its master craftsman. At a time when ballet in much of the world had become mass produced, with dancers learning roles from videotapes or a notator who had never danced the part, Kronstam taught his dancers the steps, musical phrasing, mime or gesture, as well as the spirit behind them. Great dancers do not always make great coaches or directors, but Kronstam did, and his productions had a vitality, wealth of delicate detail, unerring sense of atmosphere, and sheer stagecraft only a rare few could match.

Craftsmanship is very much a part of Danish culture; Danish furniture, beautifully designed and exquisitely made, is still a source of national pride. Ballet in Denmark was made with the same care until the 1990s, when administrative changes at the Royal Theatre turned that institution's priorities from art to efficiency, with predictable results. While Kronstam's story is interesting for its own sake—he was a great dancer and a complex personality who worked with the major artists of his day—it is also important in the history of ballet because he was so significant to the Royal Danish Ballet and its traditions and held so many of its secrets.

Denmark, a small Scandinavian kingdom with a population of only five million, is an unlikely world power in ballet. The Royal Danish Ballet, the country's only classical company, is located in Copenhagen, the nation's intimate, cosmopolitan capital where 25 percent of the population resides. It is one of the three great European ballet companies that can trace its roots to the eighteenth century.[1] The Danish court had acquired a dancing master during the Renaissance, as had the courts of many other European kingdoms, and Copenhagen's Royal Theatre has had a ballet master and small cadre of dancers from its first season, in 1748. Because of the smallness of its population and its

Kronstam as the Drum-
mer in David Lichine's
Graduation Ball, performance shot, 1965. Private
collection.

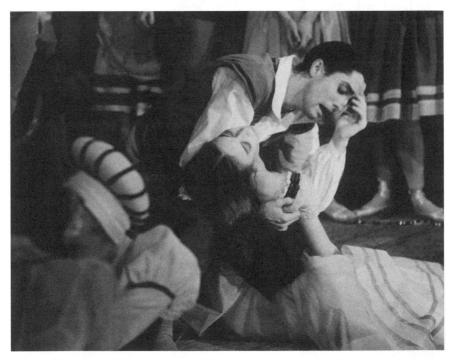

The death of Giselle. Kronstam as Albrecht, with Anna Lærkesen, 1967. Photo:
Mydtskov. The Royal Theatre, Copenhagen. By permission of Det kongelige Teaters
bibliotek og arkiv.

As Apollo, with Mette Mollerup as Terpsichore, 1957. Photo: Mydtskov. The Royal Theatre, Copenhagen. By permission of Det kongelige Teaters bibliotek og arkiv.

As Jean in Birgit Cullberg's *Miss Julie*, with Kirsten Simone, 1959. Photo: Mogens von Haven. Private collection.

As the Don in Yuri
Grigorovich's staging of
Don Quixote, 1982.
Photo: Erik Petersen for
Politiken. Private collec-
tion. By permission of
Polfoto.

In Murray Louis's
Hoopla, 1976. Photo:
John Johnsen. The Royal
Theatre, Copenhagen.
By permission of Det
kongelige Teaters
bibliotek og arkiv.

As James, with
Margrethe Schanne, in
La Sylphide, performance
shot, New York, 1965.
Photo: Fred Fehl. Univer-
sity of Texas at Austin. By
permission of University
of Texas at Austin.

In Bruce Marks's
Asylum, 1971. Photo:
John Johnsen. The Royal
Theatre, Copenhagen.
By permission of Det
kongelige Teaters
bibliotek og arkiv.

coffers, Danish ballet would have diminished in importance shortly thereafter, as had happened in Germany and Sweden, but for an incredibly lucky accident.

In the summer of 1792 a French dancer, Antoine Bournonville, lingered in Copenhagen toying with the affections of a young Danish danseuse while waiting to sail to Stockholm to dance for the Swedish king. Antoine was all too successful; impending fatherhood and marriage to his "little Jensen" led him to stay in Copenhagen and dance for the Danish king instead. Antoine believed that being a ballet dancer was "the most glorious career in the world" and, in 1820, sent his youngest son, August, to study in Paris with the greatest dancer of the day, Auguste Vestris. August Bournonville came home to Denmark after several successful years dancing in Paris and London, became the company's star dancer and ballet master in 1830, at the age of twenty-five, and one of the greatest choreographers who ever lived. He remained with Copenhagen's Royal Theatre, with a few years off, until 1877, choreographing fifty ballets and numerous divertissements, directing plays and operas, and training four generations of Danish dancers.

Bournonville wrote the libretti for his ballets (he called them "ballet poems"). They are as vivid as movie scripts; you can dance them in your mind as you read them. His subjects included fairy tales, domestic comedies, and heroic stories taken from Danish history and mythology. With his eye for character and detail, Bournonville was the Jane Austen of ballet, and his works, peopled by nineteenth-century sylphs, trolls, brave soldiers, and virtuous maidens, and based on early-nineteenth-century values of beauty, simplicity, and harmony, were the bones and sinew of the Royal Danish Ballet for more than a century after his death.

There were dozens of good choreographers in nineteenth-century Europe. Every city large enough to have an opera house had at least one. But only two created a body of works that are still danced: Bournonville and Marius Petipa, the Frenchman who choreographed *Swan Lake* and *The Sleeping Beauty* for the czar's Maryinsky Ballet. Of the more than four hundred ballets created during the Romantic era, only around two dozen are still danced in anything resembling their original form, and eight of these are by Bournonville. His ballets endured because they continued to challenge dancers and please audiences. More important for the Royal Danish Ballet's survival as a first-rate classical institution, keeping Bournonville's ballets alive insured that dancers of successive generations maintained the highest technical standard, as well as the ability to tell stories through dancing.

Drama has long been a Danish interest and a Danish specialty, and theater was long at the center of Copenhagen's cultural life. In the early and mid-nineteenth century, Denmark enjoyed an artistic flowering now known as the Danish Golden Age, and the Royal Theatre at Kongens Nytorv (the King's New Square) was at the center of it.[2] Everyone who was important to Copenhagen's intellectual life had some connection with the Theatre. Hans Christian Andersen wrote plays for it after failing to gain entrance to its world of the three arts as an actor, a singer, or a dancer. Søren Kierkegaard went to the Theatre regularly and wrote about it often. It was the entrance of Bournonville as Mephistopheles in his own ballet, *Faust,* Kierkegaard wrote in his diary, that gave him an understanding of the demonic.[3] When Kierkegaard wrote, "the knights of infinity are ballet dancers," it was the dancers of this Theatre who inspired the metaphor, and the philosopher's famous "leap of faith" very probably was suggested by a Bournonville grand jeté en avant.[4] It was Copenhagen's Royal Theatre that first produced Ibsen's plays, considered too controversial for his native Norway. Both Johanne Louise Heiberg, Denmark's greatest actress and the theater chief who made the decision to produce them, and Betty Hennings, the first Nora in Ibsen's *A Doll's House,* had begun their careers in the ballet school. In Copenhagen, theater and the ballet have long been intertwined.

Significantly, it has always been called the Royal Theatre, never the Royal Opera House, as is common in other European cities. The Royal Theatre is the home of all the performing arts: drama, opera, ballet, and music. The Royal Symphony Orchestra plays for ballet and opera performances. Until the 1960s the other three branches mingled, sharing programs and personnel, and the Danish ballet audience has always been a theater audience. Often a ballet would share the bill with a play, and many Danish plays contain dances. Actors would take mime roles in ballets, members of the opera chorus would sell lemons and ribbons in ballet crowd scenes, and ballet dancers would carry spears and bash tambourines in operas. Many of the operas and plays—and nearly every Bournonville ballet—had roles for children and older people, so Copenhageners were accustomed to seeing their entire society on the stage.

The Royal Theatre's audience is drawn predominantly from the educated middle class. Good democrats, the Danish royal family pays an annual subscription fee for the royal box and takes an unusually active interest in the ballet. The Theatre is just a few blocks from Amalienborg Palace and the current Queen, Margrethe II, attends ballet performances frequently—not for show, or to "support the arts," but because she actually likes it.[5] Queen Margrethe (a talented designer and translator whom tour guides tout as "the only reigning monarch capable of earning her own living") designed the costumes for a recent production of Bournonville's *A Folk Tale*. Her father, King Frederik IX (known as the Sailor King and famous for his tattoos), would conduct *Napoli*, his favorite Bournonville ballet, on occasion. Sometimes he would send champagne backstage on *Napoli* nights with instructions for each tarantella dancer to drink a glass before dancing, perhaps on the theory that one dances with more spirit when inspired by champagne.

The present Theatre is not the same building in which Bournonville spent most of his career, although he did work there during his last three years as ballet master and restaged his works then in repertory for the more expansive dimensions of the new house. The old theater, which stood on a site adjacent to the present one, was replaced by a larger building in 1874. The new Theatre is made of sandstone. Dirt and pollution have blackened it; it was scrubbed in 1991 and once again glows softly, a giant, soft candle illuming Copenhagen's dark winters. Everything about the Royal Theatre is welcoming. Outside, on either side of the stairs, are statues of two of Denmark's greatest playwrights (Ludvig Holberg, the leading eighteenth-century dramatist, whose deft comedies are still performed; and Adam Oehlenschläger, the nineteenth-century poet and father of Danish Romanticism, whose tragedies, alas, are not). The lamps outside glow red when the house is sold out; smoke puffs from the rooftop on premiere nights. Inside, on the lobby walls and up the stairs, there are paintings and sculptures of Danish theatrical personalities. The auditorium seats only eleven hundred.[6] There is an enviable intimacy between artist and audience, which is very much a part of the Royal Theatre experience for those on both sides of the proscenium.

This was the world Henning Kronstam entered as a child, and it quickly became the center of his existence. He lived in and for the Theatre; his private life was arranged so that he could devote his energies completely to his work. "You had the feeling the real world didn't mean very much to him," observed American choreographer Eliot Feld, who created a ballet for Kronstam in 1971. For

Kronstam, ballet *was* the real world. Ballet was how he organized his mind, the spyglass through which he viewed the universe. His reading consisted primarily of biographies of dancers or actors and the literary works on which the ballets in his repertory were based. His music collection contained mostly operas and ballets; he learned about music, especially twentieth-century music, from the ballets in which he danced.

An artist's dedication is often seen as obsession, and that can be suspect in a society where peer pressure to conform is constant. Danes prize harmony above all else and both obsession and great talent are threats to that harmony. During the Golden Age, there was a brief, heady rebellion by men of genius—Oehlenschläger called them the Rare Few—but that was a short-lived experiment. Since Denmark's gentlemanly revolution in 1848 (which ended the absolute monarchy; *that* King Frederik locked the city gates every night when he went to bed at nine and slept with the keys by his pillow), being different has been looked upon with suspicion, and being "special" is an offense punishable by ridicule or ostracism. It simply isn't done. The resentment of anyone extraordinary is so pervasive in Danish society that it even has a name: Jantelov, or Jante's Law, after issues raised in Aksel Sandemose's popular novel from the 1930s, which both exposed and named the problem and its chilling effect on individuality and personal ambition.[7] There are actually ten laws and every schoolboy can recite them: "Don't think you are anything. Don't think you are as much as us. Don't think you are smarter than us. Don't think you are better than us. Don't think you know more than us. Don't think you are more than us. Don't think you're any good. Don't laugh at us. Don't think anybody cares about you. Don't think you can teach us anything." Simply put, being special, or trying to be special in any way, violates Jantelov. The corollaries—If you were special, you wouldn't be here. If you're from somewhere else, you must be great. If you're so good, why don't you leave?—are obvious, and especially troubling to artists. Jantelov is probably as responsible as any factor in the decision of many Danish dancers to leave. But Kronstam was utterly, happily, proudly Danish, and he learned to live within Jantelov's constraints. Being a star without acting like one, dominating a performance without upstaging anybody, working hard without seeming too eager, never claiming credit for what he had accomplished—Kronstam made dozens of such adaptations in both his professional and his private life.

One of the most costly of these adaptations was that Kronstam chose to remain apart from his fellow dancers socially. He attended company parties and, especially as a young man, went out drinking with other dancers to wind down after performances. But there was always a barrier between Kronstam and his colleagues that no one managed to cross. He wanted to work at the Theatre throughout his life and planned his career around that goal. He understood company politics all too well. "We're like a family," he said. "We all love each other and we all fight each other." Especially as he began to assume responsibility for coaching, casting, and staging ballets, he did not want to give the appearance of favoritism, nor do anything that would feed gossip or provoke a scandal. (He was justly famous for never having had a romantic liaison with anyone at the Royal Theatre, an accomplishment that will probably never be equaled, especially by a star dancer and ballet master.) He kept his private life absolutely private. Friends from one part of his life were often unaware of the very existence of other friends. He settled down when still in his teens and lived quietly for over forty years with a man fourteen years his senior, known to the ballet world only as Franz.

Of course, Kronstam's remoteness added to the aura of mystery that surrounded him. References to his "Hamlet quality" would crop up in reviews, and Glen Tetley, an American choreographer who worked with Kronstam several times, was undoubtedly not the only person who thought, "He was a Gothic mystery. I imagined him living in Elsinore." Nikolaj Hübbe felt it too. "I always wanted to have a relationship with him outside the Theatre, but I didn't know how. He is such a mystery man. He used to take a bus home. I thought, 'Henning Kronstam on the bus? No. He has wings and flies home. His Pegasus is waiting for him on top of the roof.'"

To the dancers it seemed as though Kronstam walked out of the Theatre and was swallowed by the darkness. Colleague after colleague tells of never visiting his home, never sharing coffee after rehearsals, never having a personal conversation with him. Stanley Williams, whom Kronstam described as his closest friend during his first decade with the company, said they had good times together and shared a few laughs, but that they seldom discussed personal matters. "He was a very private person," Williams said, "and from the very beginning, he was utterly focused on the career." Kronstam gave few interviews during that career. He avoided hobnobbing with Danish critics because he felt Copenhagen was so small that it was better to keep a distance, and especially after he became the company's director, in 1978, he retreated into his home.

It was somehow fitting that he lived the last thirty years of his life in a spacious flat on the far side of Copenhagen's beautiful lakes—remnants of the moat that had formed the outer fortification of the city for centuries.[8] It was whispered that he lived a troubled life. A photograph by Serge Lido taken in his dressing room captures Kronstam's Hamlet side. There he sits, brainy and doomed, sweat dripping from the long, handsome face, the picture of a tormented artist. (Or an exhausted dancer. Kronstam said simply, with a smile, "I had just come from class.")

Yet he had a mischievous side and a mellow side and a sweetness spiced with dry wit. Most days he was optimistic. Often he could be downright cheery. He was a constant chameleon; the protective coloration would change depending on the circumstances, but the man remained the same. At base he was even-tempered. He seldom raised his voice in rehearsals, although colleagues describe his moods as completely unpredictable; he could be supportive one day, hard to please the next. He was a perfectionist, set others the same high standards that he set for himself, and believed that if he had not done something perfectly, then he had failed. There was no middle ground. Not surprisingly, dealing effectively with pressure was often a struggle. It was difficult to concentrate "on those days when everything is crashing in on you," he said. Some days he was pulled tight as a wire, the energy pouring out of him, although he seemed more agitated than excited or ecstatic. Two days later he could be like a big, sad, hibernating bear roused suddenly from sleep, unable to do much more than sit and brood. Then someone would tell a joke and he would smile and make a wry comment. In an instant the melancholia seemed an unwelcome, temporary visitor rather than an inherent condition, although the acute passivity remained. He was reserved and aloof, as though encased in a palpable plastic bubble, yet he could also be warm and sensitive, and his dancers adored him.

During the last few months of his life, Kronstam's world was reduced to the few blocks around his home. He would go for walks, chat with neighbors, and eat at neighborhood cafés. He was no longer part of the Theatre but he was still a dancer and he took his performance opportunities where he could find them. One afternoon in April, a few weeks before he died, he stopped for lunch at one of the cafés a block or so from his house.

A little girl stood by the window. Bored, she held onto the back of a chair, rocking it back and forth. An old man—her grandfather, or perhaps a guardian—sat at the table behind her, staring impassively at the people walking by the lakes on a chilly spring afternoon. When Kronstam walked in the child looked up and instantly recognized a playmate. She was tiny, about four years old, with dimples and masses of black curls. "Ah, a little gypsy girl," he said, delighted. Her response was to giggle and flirt. He loomed over her but she was fearless. "No," she said, putting her hand on the back of the chair he was about to take. "This is *my* chair." With a bow and an utterly serious smile, Kronstam said, "Then I shall have this chair," and reached to take the adjacent one. "No! That is *my* chair," she said, doubling over with the giggles, and staking claim, one by one, to every chair within reach. He countered her, chair for chair, entering completely into her world, as though the veteran of a thousand little girls' tea parties. They played their game until the old man said something to the child in Turkish and she stopped in mid-giggle. Kronstam and the little girl looked at each other, and it was impossible to tell who was the more disappointed. The child obediently returned to her guardian's side. Kronstam ordered lunch and began to reminisce about the war—it was the fiftieth anniversary of the end of World War II, and war stories filled the newspapers and theaters that spring—and about learning to dance in wartime Copenhagen.

Suddenly, my mother got it into her head that
my brother and I should take dancing lessons.
—Henning Kronstam, "Oral History"

Two

A Wartime Childhood

Henning Kronstam came to ballet the way dozens of little boys did in the 1940s: his mother made him take ballroom dancing lessons and he was snatched away by the ballet teacher. At the beginning of the 1942–43 school year, when Denmark had been occupied by the Nazis for nearly three years and it seemed as though the war would drag on indefinitely, Meta Kronstam decided to send her two sons to dancing school so that they would learn proper social behavior and grow up to be civilized. "This war won't last forever," she told them. "It will all be over one day, and you must know how to behave." So Henning, eight, and his older brother, Allan, eleven, went once a week to Ruth Strøm Nielsen's dancing school to learn the waltz and the polka and peacetime manners.

There was no reason to suspect that either boy would grow up to be a professional ballet dancer. There were no dancers on either side of the family as far as anyone knew. When Henning Anker Wad Kronstam was born in Copenhagen on June 29, 1934, the second son and third child of Liv Kjellman Kronstam and Meta Thomsen-Andersen Kronstam, his father was a stockbroker, his mother a department store mannequin.[1] The family lived in comfortable circumstances in Østerbro, a neighborhood of townhouse apartments just east of the central city. Their apartment on Ourøgade was about a block from Fælledparken, Copenhagen's version of Central Park, with tennis courts, swimming pools, and playgrounds hidden behind hedges; endless soccer fields; and acres of flowers, trees, and meandering woodland paths. Kronstam remembered that this was his only home until he was sixteen and the family moved next door to the Royal Theatre. His older sister, Jessie, however, remembered that the family moved "every year." Both were right. The Copenhagen phone directory lists "K. Kronstam, prokurat," at several addresses in the 1930s before the family moved to Ourøgade 35 in 1939, when Kronstam was four.[2]

The family name is Swedish. Liv Kjellman Kronstam, who called himself by the more Danish name Kjeld, had been born in Denmark of a Swedish father and Danish mother; he was their only child. Kronstam knew little about his father's family other than that they were poor and that his grandfather had emigrated to the United States sometime in the 1920s, leaving his family behind. Kronstam had only a shadowy memory of his paternal grandmother: "She went a little mad and entered a home for old people. She didn't like my mother because she thought that my mother stole my father away from her. So we went to see her, but it was not very pleasant." The family was closer to Meta's parents. Jensine and Anders Thomsen-Andersen had a little house on the outskirts of Østerbro, where the boys had their gardens. Jensine died during the winter of 1943, when many Danes either starved or froze to death during the Nazi Occupation. Anders was a craftsman.[3] He had been a soldier in the 1880s, a fact of which Kronstam was quite proud. He remembered his grandfather as a "strong, beautiful man" who had a way with women and who lived until he was ninety.

Kronstam inherited his wavy brown hair and soft brown eyes from his mother; the rest of the family were Nordic blonds. Like her husband, Meta was an only child. She was beautiful, charming, adventurous, and willful. Before she married, Meta Thomsen-Andersen had worked as a clerk in Illum's, Copenhagen's fashionable department store, located on Strøget (the walking

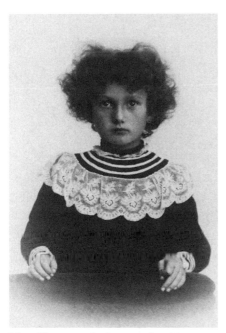

Meta Thomsen-Andersen, about ten years old. Private collection.

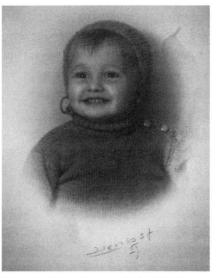

Henning Kronstam as a baby. Private collection.

Anders Thomsen-Andersen as a soldier in the 1880s. Private collection.

street that runs for more than a mile through the Old City), a few blocks from the Royal Theatre. After her marriage, when she was offered the chance to become a mannequin, modeling high-fashion clothes at Illums, Meta eagerly accepted, putting her four-year-old daughter in the care of her parents. Thinking the name Meta old-fashioned and stodgy, she rechristened herself Mitse (pronounced Mitzi), which she thought was more appropriate for the fashion world, and performed her modeling duties with theatrical flair. She seems to have had an untapped dramatic talent. When the family dined out, Kronstam remembered that his mother "always made sure to make an entrance," and she was a vivacious hostess at family parties.

Kjeld and Meta Kronstam had very different natures. "My mother was sanguinic and my father was phlegmatic and I am bits of both of them," their younger son said, Balanchine's ballet *The Four Temperaments* having been a recent topic of discussion. "My father was very proper, like an English banker. Everything had to go square. Dinner always had to be on the table on time. My mother was flamboyant. She gave wonderful parties. She arranged everything, the invitations, the flowers, and she was a very good cook."

By all accounts Henning was his mother's favorite and, by his own admission, "a little bit spoiled. I was always 'Mama's little baby.'" Mother and son were very close, and it seemed obvious to his friends and other family members that Meta favored her handsome, imaginative younger son. When his mother was in a sociable mood, Henning was her favorite companion. When he was very small she would dress him in his company best and take him to the fashion shows at Illum's to show him off to her friends. Some afternoons he would find her waiting for him when he came home from primary school, all dressed up in *her* company best, and they would take the tram into the center of town to a *konditori* (combination bakery and coffee shop), where she would meet her friends and Henning would eat tea cakes. "She had to get out," Kronstam said. "She had to be with people."

The streets around Ourøgade were full of children, and the Kronstam boys played with them in the apartment's courtyard when the weather was warm enough, but Kronstam's best friend as a child was his brother, Allan. "We played everything together. We had toy horses and cows and little houses, and we would sit in front of the window and build farms. We had toy soldiers and a little toy theater. When it was warm we would go to the courtyard and play hide and seek and other games with the children who lived nearby. When Allan was

Allan (left) and Henning
Kronstam, ages 11 and 8.
Private collection.

older he got a Tekno set [a forerunner of Lego]. I helped him build things, but
I never cleaned it up. He had to do that. After the war we got motors for our
bicycles and rode around. They weren't real motorbikes, just our old bikes with
the motors put on them. We were very much a pair of brothers."

In many ways his was a normal, middle-class childhood. Summer vacations
were spent with the family at the shore or on a farm that took in paying guests,
where the boys could run free in the country and play with the animals. The
children's birthdays were celebrated with parties and there must have been
some social pressure for them to be popular, for Kronstam remembered that
his classmates "all came home to my parties. Children from the best families."
There is a photo in his family album of a birthday party where Kronstam looks
very solemn in his white shirt and tie, wearing the traditional cone-shaped hat.

Christmas was a festive family holiday, although the proper Hr. Kronstam
refused to dress up as Father Christmas, as was the custom in many Danish
homes. The whole family, with the addition of Jessie's fiancé, the Thomsen-
Andersens, and some neighbors whom the children addressed as Aunt and
Uncle out of courtesy, gathered in the Kronstams' flat to sing songs and share
Christmas dinner. Kronstam retained a love of Christmas his entire life, and
that love was rooted in happy memories. "Christmas was always very good. In

The Kronstam family at Easter. Fru Kronstam is second from left; her father, Anders Thomsen-Andersen, second from right. Kjeld Kronstam sits at the head of the table; Allan is to his right; Henning, about age 10, to his left. Jessie Kronstam and her fiancé are standing behind Henning. The other guests are neighbors. Private collection.

Denmark, the children get their gifts the evening before Christmas, and that is when you have the holiday meal. We would have goose or duck and we always ate at home; we never went out. There was always a Christmas tree, with candles, and we danced around the tree and sang all the songs. There were always beautiful presents for us. On those Christmases during the war, in 1942, '43, '44, and '45, you needed people around you, and we always had them."

Of course the war and the invasion of Denmark by the Nazis on April 9, 1940, changed everything, and the war was the source of Kronstam's most vivid pre-Theatre memories. "One of the first things I remember clearly is when the German planes came in over Denmark in 1940. We heard airplanes at about five o'clock in the morning. My father woke up and saw the size of the planes, and he called us to come see and we said, 'No, this is not possible.' We had an agreement with Germany that they wouldn't invade. It couldn't be true. But the Germans came and they were here for five years.

"In the beginning Germany said that they didn't want war with us; they just wanted to take care of Denmark. Then slowly it changed. They took all our food, because the Germans were hungry; we were like a supermarket for them. Then our Resistance started. Jessie's fiancé was in the Resistance for three years—he was in the group that rounded up the Danish Nazis at the end of the war—but we didn't talk about that at home. I didn't know it. I think Father would have known it, and my sister, of course, but I didn't know anything. The Occupation affected everybody in Denmark. There were ration cards, and we couldn't get this and we couldn't get that. I had wooden shoes; we couldn't get leather. If you had a bicycle you could have the rubber put under your soles, but I didn't have one so I was in wooden shoes. The Germans took everything we had. There is still an animosity in the people who went through that. There is that still."

The war was not discussed at home. "At least it wasn't when I was there. I was very excitable,[4] and I think they felt that I shouldn't hear about politics. We listened to the BBC every evening, even though it was forbidden, so we would know what was really happening, instead of just hearing the German lies. We knew there were Danes who collaborated with the Germans, but if we had said anything bad about them, then someone in our family would be taken and shot. So we didn't. Allan and I were forbidden to talk to the German soldiers. My father said, 'Don't talk to them. If they ask you about something, say, "I don't know."' The family spent most of the war in Copenhagen, but during the General Strike in 1943, Kjeld Kronstam sent his wife and children to the country.

Kronstam remembered the day when the Jews who had not already left for a neutral country were rounded up. "There were Jews on our street, people we had known all our lives—blond Jews, Danes. The Nazis came and they were taken and made to stand in open cars with their hands behind their heads. We didn't have the yellow star here because King Christian said, 'If the Jews have to wear the yellow star, then I will wear one too.'"[5]

One incident in particular stood out: the humiliation of the collaborators at the end of the war. Kronstam witnessed this and identified strongly with the victims, instinctively recoiling from mob behavior. "For the young German soldiers it was Heaven to come here and not be sent to Russia or Poland. They just loved to be here. I think what was done after the war to the poor girls who had affairs with German soldiers was terrible. I saw that and it was horrible. They shaved their heads and made them run naked through the streets with the cross on their backs. Since then I've always hated it when the mob takes after one person and persecutes them. I get so sick because that was one of the things I remember very strongly. That was in '45, so I was eleven. That always comes back to me when I think about that time."

Suddenly it was over. On May 4, 1945, "it was on the radio that Germany had dropped the occupation of Denmark, Norway, and Holland. The next day, the whole city went wild. It was an explosion, a complete explosion of the whole town. Everybody was out in the street. Everybody was putting their last candle in the windows. The trams were filled with people standing on the roof, and everybody was just screaming.[6] My brother went into town because he was older, but my mother wouldn't let me go. The only thing I thought about was that my father had said to me, 'The day the war is over, you can get a bicycle.' And he kept his promise. He bought me a bicycle the next week."

The war caused disruption in nearly all phases of daily life, even in that of a schoolboy. Kronstam had started primary school at the very beginning of the Occupation and had to change schools several times because the Germans would commandeer the school building to use as a barracks. After each move the classes would get larger, and Kronstam's parents became worried about his education. He was an intelligent child and a quick learner, but he found school-work boring and was jarred by the constant relocations. He later thought that one of the reasons his parents allowed him to attend the ballet school at the Royal Theatre was because there were only four classrooms there, and they thought that would be the one place the Germans wouldn't try to take over.[7] So in a sense the war was twice responsible for Kronstam coming to ballet.

The dancing lessons with Ruth Strøm Nielsen lasted only two months. Kron-stam loved it but Allan rebelled. "All the girls were on one side of the room, and we boys were on the other, and Allan couldn't bring himself to walk across the floor and bow to the girl and ask her to dance. He said to my parents, 'No, I won't do it.' I loved it, but I said I would stop too because he did. But the teacher had noticed that I learned the steps quickly and loved it, and she said to the ballet teacher, 'Come down and see that boy.' The teacher came down and watched me, and she called my mother and told her that I should take ballet lessons."

The teacher, Jonna Beitzel, had danced in the corps de ballet at the Royal Theatre in the 1930s. She was always on the lookout for promising boys for her ballet class, which then had but two, among thirty girls. Kronstam agreed to try it. He learned his first classical steps from Beitzel, studying with her until

Ruth Strøm Nielsen's Dancing School, 1945. Kronstam is the boy on the left. Private collection.

April 1943, when she suggested that he audition for the ballet school at the Royal Theatre. Neither parent knew anything about the Theatre; both were innately suspicious. "My father said, 'Never,' but my mother said, 'They won't take him, so let him try. Let him go to the audition.' They hadn't been to the Royal Theatre, ever. They didn't know what it was about. But I was determined to do it." The basis for his determination was not just a love of ballet. Despite his and his sister's recollection that Kronstam had been the favorite child and was doted on by their mother, his teacher's interest was novel enough to spark ambition. "It was the first time anybody had said I was good at anything," he said. "It was as if somebody had given me a degree. They were saying, 'He has a talent for something.'" The desire to please remained Kronstam's most powerful incentive, and the need to work hard for the approval, often of a single person, drove him throughout his career.

Kronstam had never been to the Royal Theatre, and the only idea he had of theatrical dancing was that in the old pantomimes at Tivoli Gardens, which, like most Copenhageners, the family visited every summer. "It was something to do on a Saturday. You would see a pantomime, and go on a few of the rides, and have chocolate and cakes." The mischievous Harlekin was Kronstam's favorite pantomime character and he enjoyed watching his antics, although nothing he saw at Tivoli's beautiful little Peacock Theatre inspired him to become a dancer. However, although he had no context in which to place it, he had always loved to dance. "I couldn't just walk somewhere. I always chasséed down the street, or from the tram up to the house. Everybody on the street thought, 'Well, that boy is crazy.' But I had to do something like that."

Jessie remembered that her little brother had danced around the house, with or without music, before he had ever heard of ballet, and, from a very early age, entertained family and guests without any hesitancy or shyness. As a very small boy he had been given a toy theater: a model of the Royal Theatre, accurate down to the naked cherubs on the front curtain, and the famous "Ei Blot Til Lyst" (Not for pleasure only) inscribed above the stage. The little theater had scenery and cardboard characters on sticks. Before entering the ballet school, Kronstam had played with the toy by himself, making up plays and taking all the parts, assuming a distinct voice for each. After he became a "ballet child," his mother thought his play should be more serious, and she bought him little books of dramas for children and helped him stage them and act them out.[8]

In April 1943, Kronstam, accompanied by his mother, went to the yearly audition at the Royal Theatre. There were three hundred and twenty children there, about forty of whom were boys. The girls were examined first, so the boys had a long wait before they were taken to Gamle B (Old B), the studio in which Bournonville had once worked, near the men's dressing rooms on the Theatre's fourth floor. Kronstam's first action at the audition was predictive of the modest competitiveness that would characterize his career. He ran to the back of the room (standing in the front would have been showing off), grasped the barre, and placed his feet firmly in fifth position.

The school's two teachers, Leif Ørnberg and Karl Merrild, conducted the audition. First the teachers looked at the children's bodies to see if the legs and the back were straight and the proportions of the body were those of a classical dancer. Next the children were asked to perform a few simple steps to see if they could follow directions. Finally a waltz, a polka, and walking in a circle tested their musicality. Fourteen of the three hundred and twenty, four of the forty boys, moved to the next phase: an examination by a doctor for general health and to see if the children had asthma or were allergic to theater dust, among other environmental perils. Those who passed the physical were notified that they had been accepted and were instructed to report to the Theatre on the twelfth of August.

Kronstam's parents didn't make a fuss about his acceptance, although he sensed that his mother was proud. "She had seen those three hundred and twenty children, and knew it was something special that I had been chosen." The children in the courtyard were puzzled, and he didn't quite know how to explain it to them. "All I remember is that I told them I was going to go to a school where I would learn to be a Harlekin."[9]

"It was a good childhood," he said once, in a satisfied tone. For the most part, it probably was. Like his father, Kronstam liked things "to go square," and he wanted to remember people and events in their best light. But the good childhood was not entirely a blissful time of birthday parties and dancing lessons. Sometimes a curtain over the past would part for a moment and a very different picture could be glimpsed, though only glimpsed. Characteristically, Kronstam told few tales, and left only clues. Talking about his mother, he once said, "My mother was very warm, but she was up and down, up and down." Another hint came when he described his mother's enjoyment of family parties: "New Year's Eve was wild. My mother decorated the room so beautifully. My mother was often ill and had to lie in bed for a couple of days, but when she had to do something special, then she would perform."

Sometimes the illness was serious enough to prevent Meta Kronstam from taking care of her children: "When my mother was ill, my father would take us for walks, or to the Deer Park or on trips to Helsingør."[10] Often, his sister had to assume the role of a parent, and Kronstam thought "those years were so difficult for her because of my mother's illness." Jessie told him one story that says much about how Kjeld Kronstam handled his parental responsibilities. When her mother was ill, Jessie had to care for her little brothers, a task that she at times, quite naturally, resented. When Kronstam was an infant and Allan about four, Jessie, then fourteen, would be tempted to go with her friends and shorten the mandatory hour-long walk Hr. Kronstam insisted she take with the boys every afternoon. As a check, Hr. Kronstam would prescribe an exact route for Jessie to travel; it would be the same one he took on the tram in the morning to his office. He wrote down what was in the shop windows on the way and had Jessie recite this information to him at dinner to make sure that she had followed orders.

A picture in Kronstam's photo album brought back a less pleasant story. It was taken on the day of Jessie's wedding, as the family was walking into the church. They're a glum lot. Kjeld Kronstam looks worn, withdrawn, and very thin; Henning, then about twelve, is on the verge of tears. "I am unhappy because I am wearing my mother's coat. She made it over for me. We were very poor. It was right after the war. You can see how thin my father is; we didn't have very much to eat in the last years of the war." He paused. "And he had just been released from prison, and so he was dead inside." Kjeld Kronstam had been caught up in a financial scandal, one that ruined many businessmen accused of speculating and profiteering during the war.

Kronstam remembered his father's arrest vividly; he had been eleven, Allan, fourteen. "There was a pounding on the door at three in the morning. The police came and took my father. Allan and I were left alone because my mother was in the psychiatric hospital. I remember the last thing my father said was, 'Allan, you must take care of Henning.'" The experience must have been traumatic for both boys; Kronstam's grades were markedly lower for one grading period of this year, indicating not only that he was disoriented but also, perhaps, that he missed his father's strict discipline. Later, the boys were told that their father had done nothing wrong but had covered for his boss at the brokerage firm, who had. He was eventually released, but it was a devastating experience for the whole family. Kjeld Kronstam changed jobs, going from stockbroker to real estate agent. "There was more money in that, and he needed it to pay for my mother's treatments." Meta Kronstam's illness had gotten worse as she grew older, which placed an increasing emotional and financial strain on her husband. "He did everything he could for her," Kronstam said, in one of the few times he spoke with emotion about his family. "He loved her very much. I know that."

Meta Kronstam was hospitalized for depression several times when Kronstam was growing up.[11] She was given shock treatments, which terrified her. She dreaded them and it took her several days to recover from each therapy session. After Jessie left home Kronstam often had to take care of her during those times. Meta suffered from manic-depression, or bipolar illness, a genetically linked mental disorder that results from a chemical imbalance in the brain. The manic-depressive experiences uncontrollable mood swings, tossing from manic highs, where inhibitions are lowered and the person has unlimited energy, to black depressions, where the patient is sapped of strength and often can do little but lie on a bed in a darkened room. Although manic-depression is popularly labeled a mental illness because it affects behavior and the cognitive processes, it is of physical rather than psychological origin.[12] Shock therapy can often end the depressive cycle. A regular dose of lithium (which repairs the chemical imbalance) is a more effective treatment, but that therapy was in its experimental stages in the 1940s; more modern mood-stabilizing drugs had yet to be invented.

Her illness sheds light on the two conflicting pictures of Meta: at times the proper housewife and mother, worried about her children's schooling and manners, at times the flamboyant woman who loved parties and "had to get out and be with people." Kronstam knew the name of his mother's illness, but he did not completely understand it, either as an adult or a child. "My mother was always very happy, except when she had those manic-depressive things," and "the manic-depression got worse when she got older, first when Jessie left home, and then Allan left, and then I left." Statements such as these indicate that Kronstam believed his mother suffered from a psychological malady triggered by events in her life, not realizing that her "ups and downs," although they could very well have been worsened by environmental influences, would have occurred in some form without them. Children, who are the centers of their own small universe, often think themselves responsible for anything that goes wrong. Kronstam was a sensitive boy and must have been confused and frightened by the unpredictable changes in the moods and behavior of the mother he adored.

It is easy to understand the attraction that the Royal Theatre would hold for such a child. The ballet classes provided not only an outlet for physical energy, but were a substitute for the stability and constancy lacking in his home life. Ballet is an art of rules, and morning class, which begins the day for every dancer regardless of rank throughout his or her career, is like morning prayers. Despite its difficulties, it is a comforting, repetitive ritual. A dancer strives for total control over the body, and this must have been an anchor for someone with so little control over many other aspects of his life. Ballet soon became the physical and emotional center of Kronstam's existence.

In the 1940s anything smacking of a psychological disorder was considered shameful, so Meta's illness could not be mentioned outside the home. By the time he entered the Royal Theatre, Henning Kronstam already had secrets. By the age of nine he had a public face. Former classmates remember him as a very well-behaved child, shy, quiet, maybe a little lonely, maybe a little sad. The easily excitable, imaginative little boy who danced from the tram up to the house and chattered incessantly about the Theatre at home was seldom seen at Kongens Nytorv.

Henning was very well mannered and the teachers loved him. He could charm them. He would turn his brown eyes to them and look very sweet, and it was easy for him. We girls did his homework.
—Kirsten Simone

If Kirsten Simone tells you she was doing her homework during those two hours, then that's nonsense. She was down in the street eating ice cream.
—Henning Kronstam

 Three

The Boy Who Practiced Dying

When Henning Kronstam came to the Royal Theatre in the summer of 1943, its school was a wondrous and magical place. It bore no resemblance to an ordinary school. There were academic classes in "reading and writing and counting and things like that," but the teachers for the Læseskole (Reading School) came there after they had finished teaching in the ordinary public schools, so classes began at one o'clock in the afternoon, coinciding with the Theatre's rehearsals, and rehearsals always took priority. From the moment they walked through the door, the children's real world was the stage. Nearly every ballet, opera, and play in the Royal Theatre's repertory had roles for children, and, from his first season, Kronstam was on stage once or twice a week. "I loved it," he said. "From the very beginning I just loved it."

The children's domain was the Theatre's fifth floor. There were four classrooms and separate dressing rooms and lunchrooms for boys and girls. The atmosphere was homey. The wife of the Theatre chief sat at a window over-looking the street and waved to the children as they came in each morning. The boys had an old man to look after them, named Mr. Plaum; the girls were watched over by his wife. "He would smack us when we were naughty and watch to make sure we ate our lunch."

A child's day began at nine in the morning with a one-hour dancing class. The dancing was first, as it had been since Bournonville's day. In many other schools, the dancing class is in the afternoon, after academic lessons, but Bournonville believed that children should be taught dancing early in the morning, when they were fresh, and this most sensible tradition has contin-ued. Bournonville died in 1879, but he was still very much a presence in his school and his company sixty years later. He left no training system, no sylla-bus, but his pupils created one, using many of his steps in their own classes, partly because Bournonville was a genius at putting steps together in interest-ing ways and this was a good way to remember them, and partly in an attempt to preserve the style. Bournonville had been the Danish ballet's master teacher and choreographer for nearly fifty years and was the company's link to Paris, the wellspring of classical dancing. His pupils realized that no one among them was his equal and so did not try to compete with him. His steps, his style, and his aesthetic remained the standard in Copenhagen. The company kept the Bournonville classes in the same way shipwrecked colonists kept the ritu-als of home, and for the same reason: through regular and diligent practice and in the faith that one day they would be rescued and their children would be considered civilized.

At first this collection of the old master's steps was done informally. In the 1890s, Hans Beck, the dancer and ballet master who did the most to save Bournonville's ballets, arranged the steps, and some variations from his bal-lets, into six classes. These classes, known today as the Bournonville Schools, were danced by both pupils and dancers until the 1930s, when Harald Lander became ballet master and began to experiment with Russian training, but the children danced the six Bournonville Schools exclusively until 1949, when Karl Merrild, one of Beck's pupils and a star in the early part of the century, retired. The classes were not danced in sequence (Monday's class on Monday, Tuesday's on Tuesday). Instead the children would dance Monday's class for three or four days; after some measurable progress had been demonstrated

Kronstam (far left, in plus
fours) at 12, playing bob
in the boys' room at the
Royal Theatre School. Mr.
Plaum is in the back-
ground. Private collection.

they would move on to Tuesday's class, eventually making their way through
the week. Although today's teachers find the idea of children as young as six
dancing adult combinations absurd—if not lethal—the system worked. Most
of the greatest dancers Denmark has yet produced came out of it.

There were only two classes at the Ballet School in those days. The children
were divided by age; boys and girls were taught together. The little children,
aged six through ten, were taught by Leif Ørnberg (1904–1977), a sturdy,
princely blond who was the Danish ballet's first Apollo (and the uncle of Peter
Martins, the Danish-born dancer who now heads the New York City Ballet).
Karl Merrild (1889–1973), a tall, thin man who had been both a virtuoso and an
accomplished character dancer, taught the older children, aged eleven through
fifteen. At sixteen the children finished their academic schooling and became
aspiranter (apprentices) for two years. Aspirants were treated as probationary
adults. They took class every morning with the company and a special aspirants' class, taught by Harald Lander, the ballet master of the company, every
afternoon.[1]

Kronstam saved his *karakterbog*,[2] so there is a record of his progress. The
first comment on his dancing, signed by Ørnberg, was "hard working"; his
mark was the equivalent of a B+. The next year there is a comment for the first
term only, again signed by Ørnberg: "Henning is clever, but has trouble remembering." The 1945–46 school year's comments are unsigned, but would
have been by Karl Merrild. There is no grade. The comments are "making an
improvement" and "progressing." On the Reading School side of the page, the

teacher has written, and underlined in red, "*Urolig i timerne*," which, loosely translated, means that Kronstam had trouble keeping quiet during lessons. Merrild's comments on his dancing in the 1946–47 year were: "He needs a more measured energy," "Can work with unlimited strength and will," and, finally, "Go for it!" The old man evidently had both a keen eye and a sense of humor.

Ørnberg, whom Kronstam remembered as a "kind man and a good teacher, for his time—in the Bournonville style," gave strict Bournonville classes, which Kronstam felt had given him a strong foundation in technique. Ørnberg was a German sympathizer and his politics brought the war inside the classroom. A "Hippo" (Hilfspolizist, a Danish Nazi guard) sat in Ørnberg's room as he taught as Ørnberg was afraid the pianist, who was virulently anti-German, would attack him during class. Ørnberg was arrested after the war and had to leave the Theatre. In the cruel euphoria that erupted in Copenhagen that spring, the young men in the company, some of whom had been in the Resistance, went to Ørnberg's dressing room the day the Germans were marched out of Copenhagen, took his things, and threw them out the window.

The younger class was then taken by Børge Ralov (1908–1981), the company's reigning male star and the first dancer accorded the rank of first solo dancer.[3] Ralov did not teach the Bournonville Schools but gave a class of his own devising. The war was over and a new wind began to blow on Kongens Nytorv. "Ralov had these swinging arms and stretches and things like that. I think he had studied in Paris with [Serge] Lifar. He had been out in the 1930s, like Hans Brenaa, like Niels Bjørn [Larsen]." "Getting out" was a Danish dancer's greatest ambition. During the 1920s and 1930, dancers left to study abroad, in Paris, London, New York, Madrid—even Russia. During the war, of course, "getting out" was not a possibility, and the enforced artistic claustrophobia would have severe consequences for the company when the war was over.

When he was twelve Kronstam moved up to Karl Merrild's class of five boys and twelve girls and returned to Bournonville.[4] Like other teachers of his time, Merrild "worked with a stick. He had a good eye for everybody. Suddenly he would come running through the row and then [whack]. 'What was that you did there?' But he had some crazy ideas too. Crawling on the floor, and things like that. In the middle of the barre, he had us going down, first on one knee, then the other knee. Walking backward on the knees, walking forward on the knees, hanging upside down from the barre. I think he had seen gymnastic

Kronstam, 10, in Børge Ralov's class. Kronstam is the taller boy at the back wall. Of this group, only the boy behind him, Poul Klipmann, also got into the company. Private collection.

classes somewhere and thought, 'Maybe I will try that.' At the end of the barre the girls would put on pointe shoes. They were doing the cancan up on pointe, while we boys would do Russian folk steps."

Kronstam liked the Bournonville Schools—most of them. "We loved the Wednesday class because that's the pretty one. We hated Thursday. It's dull. It was all plié, developpé forward, slide. Down. Plié. Up. Slide. Back. Long, long, long adage. It was all to build up our strength. But there are many things in the Wednesday class that are very beautiful. And we liked the Saturday class, of course, because you got to jump out the door at the end." Merrild had collected some steps he remembered that were not in the six classes, and he made it into a Sunday class. "On special days, if it was your birthday, or something like that, he would say, 'It's your birthday today, so you choose which class we will dance.' And some days we would say, 'Oh, can we have the Sunday class?' And then we did all the steps that we loved. They were the steps that Merrild re-membered from his classes with Christian Christiansen."[5]

Merrild told his pupils stories as he taught. The Bournonville Schools are mostly collections of small variations, little dances. Each one had acquired a nickname over the years, usually the name of a dancer who excelled in a particular variation, or whose memory had preserved that variation. "That's how I had an idea of the dancers who had come before me. Merrild would tell us about them when we danced their variations."

Merrild taught with a sharp tongue as well as a stick and was not above using sarcasm to make his points, which caused him to be feared by many of his pupils. "If you were a little bit too much of a star, he would bite on you and he would kick you in the head," Kronstam said. Once, when Kronstam was standing at the side, waiting for his turn to dance, Merrild thought he wasn't paying sufficient attention and called him "Dreamer." The name stuck for a while, until Merrild came up with a better one. "I was fooling with my hair, or something, when the other group was dancing, and he ran over to me and gave me a whack and yelled, 'You are Gregers Werle! You are Gregers Werle!' And then he always called me that." Kronstam hadn't seen Ibsen's *The Wild Duck* at the time. When he did, years later, he remembered the comment. Gregers Werle is "always doing crazy things and thinking very much of himself, and I thought, 'Oh, you bitch of a man.' But he got it out of me. I have to say that." Merrild also gave Kronstam some practical advice, telling the boy that he should watch carefully during rehearsals and learn all the parts. That way, when someone was injured or had to be replaced for some other reason, Kronstam would be ready to dance the role.

Merrild was a passionate Bournonvillean and had no truck with foreign ways. One evening, during a performance of *Napoli,* Erik Bruhn, already a virtuoso dancer, immensely popular and freshly returned from triumphs abroad, danced the second man's solo in the last act's pas de six. Bruhn changed the choreography, adding showier steps and doing four pirouettes instead of the two called for by the choreography. Star dancers had been embellishing their variations for centuries everywhere but in Copenhagen. There Bournonville, who loathed gratuitous virtuosity, wouldn't allow it; his disciples kept this as an article of faith. To Merrild's mind Bruhn had imposed foreign vulgarity on Bournonville. The audience cheered but Merrild was so upset that he rose in his seat, shouted, "This is a disgrace. It's all wrong!" and stalked out of the Theatre. Merrild retired from teaching shortly afterward, although he continued to attend performances. He lived on Tordenskjoldsgade, the street that runs by the stage door, and Kronstam would pass him now and then on his way to class or performances. Merrild, perhaps seeing something of himself in the tall young dancer, would often stop and say kindly, "I see you're getting along well, Henning."

The daily one-hour dancing class was the only dance education the children had. There were no partnering classes, no separate pointe work classes for the girls, who started dancing on toe at eleven or twelve, when they entered Merrild's class. Kronstam remembered that they weren't given any instruction, or even proper shoes, and "they were all on their knuckles. Some survived, but we had a lot of girls with claw feet."[6] There were no character dance classes. The children learned polkas and mazurkas and czardas as they danced them, in ballets like *Petrushka* and *Coppelia*.[7] Merrild taught ballroom dancing each November in preparation for the school's Christmas ball. Kronstam enjoyed the ball: "Some of the girls hated it because there were about fifteen boys and thirty-two girls, and the tall girls had to march in with each other, holding hands. I always had a good time."

Every spring there was a ballet examination and the children prepared for it for months; their promotions, their futures, depended on how well they had mastered the material. The teacher would decide which class they would dance, and they would practice it. During the exam they were required to dance the steps from memory, without the teacher cueing them. Older children would also dance solos from the Bournonville repertory. Kronstam's first exam solo was the male variation from the pas de trois in *The King's Volunteers on Amager*, one of the most difficult in the repertory and a very ambitious choice for a child of twelve. ("I don't know what it looked like, but it was fun to try it.") The examination "was in the old studio. They brought in three golden chairs— they looked more like thrones to us—and put them in front of the mirror. And there sat the chief of the Theatre, Mrs. Borchsenius, and Mr. Lander.[8] They would be sitting there, watching us. The little ones did very little. The older ones did a barre and then the center work. Then we had Bournonville pas de deux and pas de trois. And then we bowed and we went out."

Promotion could not be taken for granted. Several children were dismissed each year, sometimes because of physical problems, sometimes because it became evident that the child lacked the talent or personality for a career as a dancer. Parents were given reports through the school year, but the most important decision—whether the child should return the next year—was communicated only indirectly. "Some got letters that they might try us one year more, but they weren't sure that the talent was big enough, and some got letters that they shouldn't come back next year. That was the only comment we got. We waited until around the fifth of June and if we hadn't had a letter, then we knew that we were in. I never got a letter."

Exams were for dancing only. Kronstam said, rather proudly, that he had never had to take an exam while in the Reading School. Nor did he learn very much while in the Reading School. "There were about fifty children in the school, spread over ten grades. The early grades always had full classes, but at the end, when we went to the seventh, eighth, ninth, tenth grade, there were only about two in each grade, so we couldn't sit there half asleep. But we didn't learn much because each classroom would have two or three grades in it, so you were always waiting for the little ones to catch up."

The subjects were standard elementary school fare: religion, reading, writing, arithmetic, natural history, history, and geography. Kronstam began studying English and German when he was eleven; French was added three years later. Kronstam's *karakterbog* shows that he nearly always received the equivalent of A− and B+, and, except for being chastised for making noise, the comment was usually "hard working and clever" (a joke to his family, as he never did homework). His best subjects, the A minuses, were religion and geography; *religion* at that time meant Bible history, and it was taught as heroic stories rather than theology.[9] Kronstam was the only boy in a class of five. The girls were Mona Kiil (later Jensen), Lizzie Rode, Viveka Segerskog, and Kirsten Simone. Mona, who liked to draw, took care of Kronstam's nature study homework. Kirsten, who entered the school the summer after the war, could be counted on for math and, later, German grammar. Kronstam maintained that the girls helped him not because he was lazy but because he was in so many rehearsals that "there was no time for it."

Between the early-morning dancing lessons and the afternoon academic classes there was a long lunch break and what was supposed to be a two-hour study period so the children could do their homework. Kronstam thought of it as a two-hour recess. "We had one hour's training in the morning, then two hours to run in the streets and eat ice cream. Then four hours of the academic school, and then we had the Theatre to ourselves. Nobody could see if we stayed in the Theatre, nobody could see if we played hide and seek in the basement, or what we did. We went all over, to the room where they built the sets, and the room where they painted the sets—the painters just loved us. We went to the costume room, where they sewed the costumes. You wouldn't believe some of the names that are sewn in some of those costumes.[10] The children today don't have the same freedom. They have to get out of the Theatre at such and such a time, and they can't get back in again."

In warm weather, they roller-skated. Copenhagen is very flat and during the war there were no cars, so the streets were roller rinks. The children would skate up Bredgade (Broad Street) to what is now Churchill Park, and around by the harbor and the statue of the Little Mermaid (a dancer, of course—Ellen Price de Plane, the Sylphide of her generation). After the war there were new pleasures in addition to the long-coveted bicycle. American movies, banned during the war, were very popular, especially the war pictures. ("The Germans took such a beating in those films. We all loved them.") Copenhagen, which despite the deprivations of the Occupation had survived the war in better condition than most other European cities, began to return to normal. There were goods in the shops again. There was, once again, chocolate. "When the war was over we would queue up to buy chocolates, or oranges and bananas. We hadn't had them all those years during the war. There were always queues outside those shops. We would buy chocolate at one place and then run and stand in the next queue and then the next queue to buy some more."

In colder weather they were confined indoors and the pent-up energy often erupted in fights. "It was more like wrestling, really. The older boys had too much time in those two hours, so it was, 'Who should we get today?' They would chase us around the fifth floor. They would get one of the little boys down on the floor and then sit on his chest. Which hurts." Kronstam came in for his share of pummeling, although he said he wasn't singled out.[11] When he was the victim, however, he had his protectors. "The girls in my class always ran after the boys and pulled them off me if they tried to beat me up," he said, without a shred of shame.

Kronstam's real work was done in rehearsals and on the stage. There were few boys in Kronstam's age group, so he was used in nearly all the operas and plays as well as the ballets, although he missed out on some cherished parts, like the children's dance in *Elverhøj* (the Danish national play), because he was too tall. Unlike many other theater children, he was not thrilled at the mere prospect of being on stage. From the beginning he "wanted to be used," as he often put it. Being part of the crowd was not enough for him, even if it meant putting on makeup and a costume, even at nine. His first appearance, shortly after he entered the school, was in the last act of *A Folk Tale*. "All I did was stand there, holding an opera chorus woman by the hand, and wave a branch." He was more excited at being cast in *Aïda* as one of the little "Negro boys," because there he had a real dance. The boys blacked up with burnt cork, which was much more fun to put on than to take off. When the opera was over the boys ran as fast as possible up to their dressing room to be scrubbed clean in a big steel tub. There was only one tub and the water quickly cooled, so the smallest and slowest boys had a cold, gritty time of it.

Kronstam danced children's parts in the Bournonville ballets, of course. *Napoli* teems with children, and Kronstam started in this ballet as one of the little altar boys who walks across the stage in the first act. Like all Danish ballet children, he stood on the bridge and watched the last act's famous pas de six and tarantella.[12] When he was a little older he became a fisher boy in *Napoli's* first act, which he found great fun, "because you got to run around." Children did not dance in the last act in the 1940s; their little dance was added later by Hans Brenaa. When Kronstam was eleven, however, he was chosen to sit on top of the cart and wave the Italian flag as Gennaro, Teresina, and Mama go off after the wedding, and he thought that was terrific.

He was also chosen for a small, but very special part in *Far from Denmark*. As the children could choose which class they wanted to dance on their birthdays, Danish kings could choose what ballet they would like to see danced on theirs. *Far from Denmark* was King Christian X's favorite, and he chose it to celebrate his seventy-fifth birthday, shortly after the end of the war. The old King had been a unifying symbol during the war. His daily unescorted horseback rides through the city during the Occupation had been an act of real courage, as were his threat to wear a yellow star if Jewish Danes were forced to do so and his yearly Christmas card to Copenhagen's chief rabbi. The performance was as much a patriotic celebration as a birthday. The second act of *Far from Denmark* takes place on board a Danish frigate anchored off the coast of Argentina (which Bournonville, who also spent little time in the Reading School, fancied was part of the Caribbean). Sailors mass on the deck; honored visitors are piped aboard. Kronstam was one of the little cadets, the one who impulsively kneels and kisses the Danish flag as the national anthem is played. It is a moving moment in any performance, but on that occasion it symbolized much more than Bournonville could have imagined.

Another important children's part is the reel in the first act of *La Sylphide*, and Kronstam was the center boy during his first season at the Theatre. In the reel, the children are part of a group, but they're in the front line and dance the same steps that the grown-ups do, so it is a responsible part. Unfortunately, the picture in his scrapbook of the reel was ruined because he had a crush on Viveka Segerskog that year and had cut her image out of the photo, wearing it on a string around his neck until it fell apart. ("I cut Viveka out because I was so much in love with her that I had to carry her with me. She was so pretty, and she was so sweet and funny.")

The children also took part in rehearsals with the company, another valuable learning experience. Until 1950 most of the ballets in the repertory were the work of Harald Lander, and Lander conducted most of the rehearsals, both of his own ballets and of the Bournonville productions. Lander had revived and revised the core Bournonville repertory in the 1930s, assisted by Valborg Borchsenius, who had been Hans Beck's partner around the turn of the century and an exemplary interpreter of Bournonville maidens. Some dancers say Lander invited Borchsenius to help him stage the ballets, others maintain that the old lady marched into the rehearsal room and insisted on helping because she was afraid that Lander would modernize the style. Everyone agrees that Borchsenius (who had actually met Bournonville once, passing him on the stairs when she was a ballet girl of seven and he was an old, old man) is the very fragile link by which the Bournonville style, as well as the actual steps and gestures, were preserved. Borchsenius was not a great director or coach; she was a conservator with a remarkable memory. She had innumerable scraps of paper from her dancing days on which she had scribbled the steps from the solos or corps dances, as well as the mime speeches. She kept these in a sewing basket that never left her side. During rehearsals, Kronstam remembered, she would say, "Wait. That is wrong," and rummage through the basket until she found the right piece of paper. "Aha!" she would say, triumph in the small, pinched voice. "It is with the right finger, not the left."[13]

Lander eventually persuaded Borchsenius to write down what she remembered, and the result is the now famous Borchsenius Notebooks, which, along with the Schools, make up the Bournonville bible. They represent the choreography and mime in the Lander-Borchsenius stagings of the 1930s. Dancers of that era, notably Hans Brenaa, the most important stager after Borchsenius, could remember a brief passage that wasn't in the Notebooks, but for the most part the Notebooks contain the consensus versions and are how ballets first danced more than 150 years ago could still be danced in Copenhagen.

The Bournonville ballets had retained their popularity through the war because Copenhageners turned to the Theatre as an escape. "They liked to come because it reminded them of the good old days," Kronstam said. The only political ballet was Harald Lander's *Spring,* which was considered rebellious because it was set to music by the Norwegian composer Edvard Grieg, and because of its politically suggestive content. "There was a pas de deux for Margot Lander and Børge Ralov, and, in the middle of it, some people came in and barred the door and put a lock on it. Then Margot Lander came out dressed all in black and danced a solo. And everybody knew what that meant." Since there were no words, it couldn't be censored as a ballet about Nazi repression. One of the beauties of ballet is that there are always people who can be convinced that it doesn't mean anything.

The war affected the Royal Theatre as it affected everything in Copenhagen. Performances were at five in the evening because there was an eight-thirty curfew. Classes ended at four and there wasn't time for the children to get home, eat, and return to the Theatre. The Theatre's canteen was closed, so the Theatre administration made an arrangement with Brønnum's, the famous old restaurant across the street from the Theatre, to feed the children and have them ready to go onstage at five. After performances, dancers chaperoned the children on their tram rides home. "There was a lady who lived in Gentofte [a few stops up the tram line from Østerbro], and she would put me on the tram and put me off at my stop. There could be raids in those trams, if the Germans suddenly thought that somebody was hiding there." Some nights the performance would be over so close to curfew that the children would be driven home through the dead, black streets in police cars.

As a small boy Kronstam appeared on stage about twice a week. When he was a little older and was used in ballets, plays, and operas, it could be up to five times a week. He said his parents were supportive. "They could see my eyes were like this," he said, making his eyes bigger, if that were possible. "Already they could see that the Theatre was taking over very much in my mind."[14] He talked about the Theatre endlessly at home, telling his parents stories. "Lies, really. Things I made up about what happened at the Theatre, and they would listen and listen, and then they would say, 'All right, Henning, that's enough. Now you go to your bed.'" Kronstam said that his parents were encouraging and interested in what he was doing, but never pushed him. His sister thought that his mother was theater-mad and very much wanted to have a child on the stage. The attention Kronstam received exacerbated the sibling rivalry with his older brother Allan, who had a mathematical rather than theatrical bent. "It wasn't so much fun for Allan when Henning would come home with all his stories about the Theatre," said Kronstam's nephew, Torben, translating for his mother (Jessie), who confirmed Kronstam's perception that Allan had always been jealous of him.

Kronstam's artistic education was completely in the hands of the Theatre; literature and the arts had little place in the Kronstam home. Both boys took piano lessons, Henning for only two years because practicing bored him. The only music he heard at home was popular music; he said his taste for classical music was developed completely in the Theatre. As for literature, his father read little but the paper, his mother, novels. Much of Kronstam's reading as a child was related to his career. "I always showed them what I was reading. They were amazed when I started reading *Macbeth* and things like that. They'd say, 'You are reading what? By who?'"

Kronstam's first role of any real importance was as Macduff's son in *Macbeth* when he was ten.[15] Bodil Ipsen, one of the most respected directors of the time, staged the production. Karin Nellemose, a noted actress, was Lady Macduff. The ballet side of the house provided several dancers, including the young Fredbjørn Bjørnsson as Fleance, as well as the three witches, one of whom, Gerda Karstens, was the ballet's leading mime. This was the first time his parents came to watch him on stage "because that was something they should see. That was a real role." Kronstam saved the script from that production. The play was in archaic Danish (presumably analogous to Shakespearean English) and Kronstam had written the contemporary Danish equivalent under many of the words. Even at ten, he needed to understand what he was saying.

His next big part came two years later, in Kaj Munk's play *Niels Ebbesen*. "That came after the war. It was about the time when the Germans occupied all of Jutland, a long time ago. I was in that play, too, so I read it. Munk was killed during the war. The Germans came for him one night and woke him up and drove him out into the country. They shot him and threw his body out of the car and into a ditch."

Niels Ebbesen was a farmer during that earlier German occupation (Munk's play could not be performed during the war, for obvious reasons). Kronstam

These two photos show that two sides of Kronstam's stage persona—the beautiful, sensitive, melancholy hero and the lighthearted boy with a delightful sense of humor—were present from his first roles. Kronstam, 10, with Karin Nellemose as Lady Macduff, in *Macbeth*. Photo: Mydtskov. Private collection.

Kronstam, 12, with Mogens Wieth, in *Niels Ebbesen*. (The little girl's identity could not be ascertained.) Photo: Mydtskov. The Royal Theatre, Copenhagen. By permission of Det kongelige Teaters bibliotek og arkiv.

played Niels's son Ebbe and had one big scene. When talking about his roles, Kronstam often went back and forth between the first and third person, an indication of how much he identified with the characters he played: "I was the oldest boy, the one who liked the German soldier. That boy was at an age where he had to ask questions. Why this and why that. 'Why can't I talk to the German soldier?' I [Ebbe Ebbesen] thought the soldier was so handsome, and I wanted to talk to him. I had such a slash from my father—the man playing my father. His father hit him. And that was that." The Theatre toured *Niels Ebbesen*, taking the play to Norway, and thus providing Kronstam with his first taste of life on the road, but no lasting memories.

Kronstam liked being in the plays because he was treated seriously. It gave him a chance to see another way of working, with words rather than steps, and to watch the process of theatrical production. "They really worked with you. The placement on the stage, the blocking, that was interesting. If you were in a ballet as a child, then you are one on a line, or two lines, and you would do the same steps as everyone else. But in a play what we had to do was individual, and you had personal instruction. They would say, 'This was no good today,' or whatever. They treated you like a professional. I felt it was an honor to be in these productions." Kronstam was cast as Cleopatra's younger brother in *Caesar and Cleopatra* but he had a growth spurt and lost the role to a smaller child "because they needed a small boy to sit on the throne. I had to learn a lot of lines for that one," he said, with a lingering twinge of regret.

There was no formal instruction in makeup at the Theatre in those days. "When we were children, we had some of the aspirants help us. One day Mr. Lander told them, 'You have to choose a boy each and help him with his makeup.' We were about ten, eleven years old. And I had a dancer called Ole Suhr. He was an aspirant then. He did my first makeup. This is the character you see in the *Peter Grimes* pictures, just darkening the eyebrows, following the line of the brow. Before that, I had just looked at the others and copied them. Otherwise, when we were trolls in *Peer Gynt* or things like that, they'd give us some green paint to put on our faces, and that was fun. One thing I learned then, which they don't do any longer: you have to put makeup on the back [of the neck]. I don't know why they never do that. Because in *Napoli*, they're all brown here [on the face], then it just stops."

The mime part of John, the fisherman's apprentice, in Benjamin Britten's opera, *Peter Grimes*, was Kronstam's biggest child's part. It was produced in the

Kronstam, 13, in *Peter Grimes*. Photo: Mydtskov. Private collection.

fall of 1947, when he was thirteen. The production was an important one for the Royal Theatre, part of the artistic blossoming made possible by the end of the war. The opera's repertory was very traditional in those days: *Aïda, La Bohème, Carmen. Peter Grimes* was new music, and by an Englishman. The opera's director said, in a newspaper interview, that he had chosen Kronstam because of his "large, expressive brown eyes." John is killed in the opera, and his death scene must tug at the heart. It did. One reviewer wrote, "Henning Kronstam is already skilled in both movement and mime," and described Kronstam as "looking just like the original illustration for Dickens's Oliver Twist." The death scene was much rehearsed. Kronstam's sister remembered that Kronstam would come home every day with a new version and try it out on his family. "Should I die with my eyes open? Should they be closed?" Everyone would discuss it and suggest which gesture or expression was the most effective.

Kronstam became something of a child star after these performances.

Flemming Flindt, two years younger, remembered, "That was really a big thing here." Kirsten Ralov, ten years older than Kronstam and later his assistant during his time as ballet master, saw the opera when she was a young dancer and still remembered it vividly fifty years later. "I thought of Henning so much when the opera revived *Peter Grimes* this year, and I saw the little boy," she said in 1994. "When Henning did it, it was a big part, but now it doesn't look like such a big part. I kept wondering what the difference was. It was Henning. That was the difference." Colleagues would make similar comments about Kronstam throughout his career. While perhaps not very evocative to those who did not see the performance, Kronstam was one of those rare artists who would draw the eye even when standing still, an ability evident even in childhood.

Kronstam's success in *Peter Grimes* got him noticed backstage too. Margot Lander, the reigning ballerina, graciously allowed him to fetch tea for her and her friends one afternoon. Børge Ralov singled him out for similar honors, asking him to go to the canteen and buy him his afternoon porter (a strong Danish beer) or go down to the street and buy him a newspaper.[16] "He would often ask the boys to get his paper. And after you'd brought it to him he'd look at it, and if he thought you'd been reading it he'd give you a whack and say, 'You read my paper. No money for you today.' He wasn't being mean. It was just dancers' nerves." The greatest compliment of all came from Valborg Borchsenius. The seventy-seven-year-old guardian of the Theatre's traditions trudged up the five flights of stairs from the stage to the boys' dressing room one night after a performance of *Peter Grimes* to tell him: "You were very good tonight, boy."

The attention made him think that acting might be a more rewarding career than dancing. It was on stage in *Peter Grimes,* he said, that he first felt the magic of the theater. He was not, and never would be, attracted merely by the glamour of it or the spectacle of it, but by the emotion of it. On stage, dying in *Peter Grimes,* he felt a connection with the audience, felt them respond in sympathy to his character. He yearned to be part of something, to contribute to the success of a production, and during these years he was searching for his proper place. He responded to praise not simply because he liked the attention, although no doubt that was part of it, but because the praise was guidance. A teacher said he was a good dancer, so he wanted to try dancing, even though he wasn't quite sure what it was. Now people were saying that he was a good actor and he seriously considered changing to acting as a career. "I didn't really have a sense of dancing from the classes. It was just steps. I couldn't see the meaning behind it."

There was meaning in *Peter Grimes,* and the notion of becoming an actor was real enough to be given voice. There is an article about *Peter Grimes* in his scrapbook that ends, "It is Henning Kronstam's dream, when he is no longer a pupil at the ballet school, to become a real actor." The Theatre's acting school would not admit students under the age of eighteen, so he faced a long wait. But the thought had been planted and, although he continued his studies, he had the idea—sometimes in the back of his head, sometimes in the front—that he wanted to become an actor, a "real actor."

When I started to grow I was all arms and legs.
I was Bambi on ice.
—Henning Kronstam

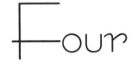

The Lander Years

Adolescence is especially difficult for dancers. In addition to the confusions that bedevil all teenagers, dancers have to deal with physical changes that affect their profession. A child may have a growth spurt or suddenly stop growing. As the body changes the dancer has to make adjustments in technique to compensate. Kronstam grew fast. He was nearly full-grown at fourteen and reached his full adult height—six foot one—at sixteen. A constantly shifting center of gravity made turning especially difficult, and he felt that he was awkward. "Every summer I would come back and be five centimeters taller," he remembered, "and I'd have to learn how to turn all over again."

The growing pains were compounded by the fact that Kronstam literally had a foot in two worlds. Still a child in Royal Theatre terms, until he would become an aspirant at sixteen, he was treated as a child for most of the day—

Third row: From left: Kronstam (age 14); Mrs. Plaum; Ole Fatum, Lizzie Rode. Karl
Merrild is in the center, Kirsten Simone is to his right, Mona Jensen to his left, then
Fritzy Koch and Viveka Segerskog. Flemming Flindt is in front of Simone. Mr. Plaum,
wearing the beret, is at the far right. Second row: second from left, Agneta Segerskog.
First row: seventh from left, Karin Vikelgaard, tenth from left, Solveig Østergaard.
Photo: E. Poulsen. Private collection.

and, of course, at home—but his talent, and his rapidly maturing body, earned
him adult treatment professionally. Soon after *Peter Grimes* he began to dance
with the men, as a man, in the corps de ballet. The pride he felt in being given
adult responsibilities was tempered by the anxiety he felt in assuming them.
As they did throughout his career, curiosity, ambition, and a desire for adventure conquered the fear. Kronstam would be a risk taker all his life and he took
his first professional chances during this period.

The years immediately following the end of the war were a time of growing
pains for the company as well. The Royal Danish Ballet was about to lose its
innocence and its confidence, though it too thought only of impending adventure. The dancers had been locked in Copenhagen for five years. Forays to London and Paris to study with new teachers and see new ballets had been impossible during the war, and five years is a long time in the life of a young dancer.
Because of its athletic component, dancers need to measure themselves
against the best, whoever and wherever the best may be. International contact
is essential to maintain international standards.

As soon as it was practical after the war, Danish dancers started to "get out,"
to travel and see what had happened while they had been shut in. While time

had stood still at Kongens Nytorv, in London, New York, and Paris, choreographers like Frederick Ashton, George Balanchine, Antony Tudor, and Roland Petit were creating exciting new ballets, with new subjects and built on new ways of moving. In London, a newly arrived Russian émigrée named Vera Volkova offered technique classes far more advanced than any then available in the West. Several of the company's young men took her classes and came home singing her praises. Volkova had a studio across the street from the Sadler's Wells (later the Royal) Ballet, and many Sadler's Wells dancers would sneak across to take her classes. She coached several Sadler's Wells dancers and guided Margot Fonteyn in two of her great classical roles: Aurora in *The Sleeping Beauty* and Odette/Odile in *Swan Lake*. Volkova was an inspired and inspiring teacher and the Danish men urged Harald Lander to bring her to Copenhagen as a guest instructor. Danish dancers had been trained in a method codified in the 1890s; the world had changed in fifty years. To be able to dance the new ballets, the nature and the aesthetic of the Royal Danish Ballet would have to change. "Getting out" opened a Pandora's box whose temptations, pleasures, and demons still trouble the Danish ballet. Pride in Danishness and a simultaneous eagerness to acquire everything that isn't Danish as quickly as possible have been in conflict ever since.

From the Golden Age to the war years the company's repertory had been dominated by Bournonville ballets, or imitation Bournonville ballets made by his successors. The old formula of a good story told through lots of characters, with a little tasteful virtuoso dancing in places appropriate to the plot, still pleased, but the audience was getting tired of seeing the same dozen or so ballets danced repeatedly. No one yet questioned the formula, questioned Bournonville's "Choreographic Credo," with its emphasis on the importance of beauty and good taste, or that classical ballet should be the basis of the repertory. When Diaghilev's Ballets Russes stormed through Europe in the years just before World War I, with its new music and new artists and ballets packed with wild and glorious dancing, the clamor for new ballet increased. But the Danes did not want new Russian ballets; they wanted new Danish ones. Like most audiences, they wanted their ballet to be up-to-date, but they wanted it to look like what they were used to.

The great Ballets Russes choreographers Mikhail Fokine and George Balanchine came, in turn, to Kongens Nytorv, attracted by its reputation among Europe's ballet elite as a great classical institution. Both staged a few of their works and excited the dancers—though not the audience—and neither stayed longer than two seasons. Three of Fokine's ballets (*Petrushka, Chopiniana,* and *Prince Igor*) did remain in the repertory for decades, but audiences preferred Emilie Walbom's Danish versions of the Russian ballets.[1] Her *Dream Pictures,* reminiscent of Fokine's *Carnaval,* but set to Danish polkas and waltzes with a Biedermeier air, was more suited to Copenhagen taste.

Hans Beck resigned as ballet master in 1915, probably because he refused to give in to pressure to internationalize. After Beck's resignation, a succession of his pupils took over leadership of the company; none were choreographers, although each fashioned at least one ballet. After ten years with Gustav Uhlendorff, during which time photographs show that the dancers' classical technique had deteriorated badly, the directorship changed hands every year, the Theatre's conductor even having a turn at the helm. The company badly needed a strong leader, and the appearance of Harald Lander promised renewal and stability. Lander had a strong personality and enormous energy. He was only twenty-seven but he had been out in the world, studying in Spain and Russia.

As a dancer, Harald Lander specialized in Russian and, especially, Spanish dance. His first ballet, *Gaucho,* was a hit. It looked like a Ballets Russes ballet, with its exotic location (Argentina), character dancers (lots of castanets and stomping boots), and a story with a hint of sex in it. But there was a Danish feel to it too. Lander's genius was finding the common ground between the old (Bournonville) and the new (the Ballets Russes). He created dozens of ballets, using this formula, each with good parts for everybody, another Bournonvillean characteristic. Most important, Lander had authority and confidence. When he became ballet master he took over, declared himself leader, and got to work. He was the leading character dancer and his wife, Margot, was the company's ballerina. He taught company class and choreographed most of the ballets in the repertory, as well as several for plays and operas. Only one of his ballets (*Etudes*) is still danced and Kronstam said that, seen in retrospect, Lander's ballets were provincial, but, at the time, he was greatly revered. Critics of the day called the Lander period the company's third great flowering.[2]

Some Danes assert that Lander intended to ignore the Bournonville repertory and replace it with his own ballets. Although he is now thought of as a Bournonville savior, most of the serious works (among them *The Valkyries, Valdemar* and *The Lay of Thrym*) disappeared during this time. It is usually said

Harald Lander rehearsing
Børge Ralov and Margot Lander
in Gamle B (Old B), the studio
where Bournonville had
worked and Kronstam had his
audition. On the wall is a photo
of Hans Beck and Valborg
Borchsenius in *Napoli*. Private
collection.

that this is because the audience found these ballets old-fashioned, but it is at
least as likely they lost their effectiveness because Lander was incapable of
staging them properly; his talent was for light comedy, not the heavy history
and tragedy ballets from Bournonville's late career. Lander retained and mod-
ernized eight ballets, speeding up their action by cutting some of the mime
scenes and putting some of the dances on pointe. While this modernization
was applauded by some, those who remembered Beck's stagings were ap-
palled, writing that Lander had damaged the style, introducing foreign elements that had nothing to do with Bournonville, and had destroyed the atmosphere of the ballets. "His dances are not Nordic. They come from the world,"
wrote George Wiinblad of the new, improved version of Bournonville's grand
mythological ballet, *The Valkyries*. The costumes and sets were acceptable, "but
the style, the style! It has nothing to do with Bournonville or Hartmann [the
composer]. . . . In the Greek pictures [scenes], the style is straight out of Trudi
Schoop!"—which is to say it was cartoonlike.[3] Trudi Schoop, trained in the ex-
pressionist modern dance of Central Europe, directed a mime company that

was very popular in those days, and her pieces were mostly comic, and very broad. Since its inception, there has been a tension within the Danish Ballet between the dancers of the royal court and those of the popular theater (and their spiritual descendants) who joined together in 1748 to form the ballet company. From Bournonville's time through Beck's, at least, the former, the French neoclassical school of ballet, dominated. In Lander's time the popular theater style was ascendant, and it is probably for this reason that most of the Bournonville ballets that survived the Lander regime are comic and Romantic ones rather than the grand historical and mythical ballets.

Lander is described as a dictator who allowed only his own choreography to be performed, but an examination of the repertory of the time shows that several choreographers, all Danish, were represented, including Birger Bartholin, Nini Theilade, Emilie Walbom, and Børge Ralov. That Lander's managerial style was dictatorial, however, is undisputed. Lander was as feared as he was respected, and there were grumbles by nascent choreographers about their lack of opportunity, but he was in his forties, vigorous and productive, and it was impossible to imagine the Royal Danish Ballet without him.

At the end of the war, when Kronstam was one of the children on *Napoli*'s bridge, the Royal Danish Ballet had fifty dancers, led by its stars, Børge Ralov and Margot Lander. Ralov was a demi-caractère dancer who excelled in dramatic parts. He was noted for his impassioned Gennaro, the Italian fisherman hero of *Napoli;* Albrecht in *Giselle;* and the title part of the lovelorn puppet in Fokine's *Petrushka.* Margot Lander's great role was Svanilda, the naughty heroine of *Coppelia,* but she was also a superb Giselle and a deliciously sexy Birthe, the troll fiancée in *A Folk Tale.* Not to mention a scamp of a Broom in Harald Lander's *The Sorcerer's Apprentice.* Her dancing sparkled, she was witty and sophisticated, yet her humility kept her adorable and she was beloved by the Danish audience. When she retired she had three farewell performances, giving her public a last memory of all her great roles. On the last evening the King rose in his box and spoke a tribute to her, an event unique not only in Danish history but in that of dance.

The company was full of strong characters. Gerda Karstens and Niels Bjørn Larsen led a contingent of gifted mimes. Svend Erik Jensen was a virtuoso as well as a strong mime; Frank Schaufuss—extremely tall for a dancer of his time at six foot three—was developing along the same line. Hans Brenaa was the company's champion turner, a superb partner, and a cavalier, at that time, very interested in the Russian style of dancing. In those days, dancers remained in the company as active members until they retired at fifty, and there were a half-dozen mature men who excelled in character parts. There was also a young generation on the rise: Poul Gnatt, handsome and dramatic; Fredbjørn Bjørnsson, handsome and sweet; and Erik Bruhn, only twenty in 1948, but already possessing a beautifully pure classical technique. Among the women, in addition to a dozen personable beauties in the corps de ballet, were four young ballerinas: Mona Vangsaae, a lovely long-limbed lyric blonde; Margrethe Schanne, a tiny, birdlike jumper who held exclusive rights to the part of La Sylphide for twenty years; Kirsten Ralov, who excelled in both dramatic and virtuoso roles; and Inge Sand, a dimpled devil of a comic who succeeded Margot Lander in the role of Svanilda.

Almost everyone in the company seemed to be related or married to someone else. Frank Schaufuss's sister Kate was in the corps; he was married to Mona Vangsaae (their son Peter later led the company briefly; their daughter Puk became one of the Theatre's leading actresses). Kirsten Ralov was Poul Gnatt's sister. She had been married to Børge Ralov for a time and, although she later married Fredbjørn Bjørnsson, she kept her first husband's name. Kjeld Noack, a corps member who often danced solo roles, was the consort of Margrethe Schanne. Dancing was a good living and a respectable career for men, and it was not uncommon for married dancers to enroll their children in the school. Friendships and feuds extended across generations. For good and ill, the Royal Danish Ballet was a family.

In 1948, probably as a concession to the dancers' demands for novelty, Lander invited Léonide Massine, one of the important choreographers of the Ballets Russes, to stage two of his ballets. In the teens and early twenties, Massine's sophisticated character ballets had been all the rage. During the thirties, he had been the most celebrated choreographer in Europe. He had pioneered the "symphonic ballet," setting choreography to an already composed symphonic score, and adding characterization, symbolism, and hints of a story. During the war, he worked in New York, had a few failures, and his star began to fall. New York was tiring of Russian ballet and becoming intrigued by the new classicism of George Balanchine, the psychological dramas of Antony Tudor, and American-flavored works by Jerome Robbins and Agnes de Mille. Massine, then in his early fifties, returned to Europe. In Copenhagen, his works would be new.

Massine was the first of many international choreographers who cast Kronstam in their ballets. The Russian staged two of his most popular works, *Symphonie Fantastique* and *Le Beau Danube*, for the Royal Danish Ballet. Both ballets were well suited to the company. *Le Beau Danube* was a frothy comedy set to a selection of Strauss waltzes. A slice-of-life work about an afternoon in a park, *Le Beau Danube* wove the adventures of characters named the Dandy, the Hussar, and the Street Dancer into a slight story that generated a variety of pleasant moods. *Symphonie Fantastique,* to the Berlioz symphonic poem of the same name, was a dramatic ballet, a fantasy about the opium-induced dreams, fears, and torments of an artist. While *Le Beau Danube* was a merry ballet, easy for audiences to like, *Symphonie Fantastique* (known in Copenhagen by its subtitle, *Episode af en Kunstners Liv* (Episode from the Life of an Artist) was something totally new. It "surprised and impressed" the audience, wrote Henry Hellssen after the premiere. Hellssen's masterful review, which relates the action to the music and describes the décor as an active part of the ballet, shows that the Bournonville aesthetic, the very way of looking at dancing as a moving painting and a drama with music as its script, was still intact as late as 1948, although the new generation of critics who would come to power after 1950 and dominate Danish ballet for the next several decades had different experiences and different tastes.

Helissen, writing in *Berlingske Tidende,* gave Kronstam his first review as a dancer. The ballet opened with a tableau of the Poet's Beloved (Mona Vangsaae) surrounded by her admirers. "The first gentleman was Henning Kronstam," he wrote. "Dear God, one says to oneself, is this an illusion from *Peter Grimes* where he was the fisherman's mistreated boy? What is the poor child doing here? Henning Kronstam seems happy among the adults. But he is still a baby" (February 4, 1948). The premiere of *Symphonie Fantastique* came four months after *Peter Grimes,* and he was still thirteen.

Kronstam was indeed happy among the adults and enjoyed working with Massine and his wife, Tatania. During this period he was a quiet observer, keeping to the edges of the studio, watching and listening with everything he had. The rehearsals with Massine were the first time Kronstam had the chance to use his English, as that was the language in common between the Russians and the Danes. Not all of the Danish dancers were fluent, however, and there were some amusing misunderstandings. One day, in a rehearsal, Massine was demonstrating a phrase to one couple, then turned to another and said, "Now you do the opposite." "So the dancer took the girl and put her on his shoulder," Kronstam recalled, "because he thought Massine had said 'up and sit.'"

Kronstam started in *Symphonie* as a member of the corps. "I was billed as an understudy for everything. But then Erik [Bruhn] suddenly had an engagement and Kjeld Noack was moved over to do Erik's part as the Shepherd in the third movement and that left the leading man in the Waltz, and there was nobody for that. And Massine said, 'I want the young man.' I had never lifted a girl before and there were lifts and lifts and lifts." There were no partnering classes in the school at that time—Bournonville's ballets have no lifts or intricate partnering; he believed that men and women should dance eye to eye, as equals—and Kronstam had never had a partnering class and never had to turn or lift a woman. "She must have been thirty or something," he said of that first partner, adding, almost inaudibly, "and I was so shy." He watched what the other men did and copied them, but he needed more practice. "Kirsten Simone was very good to me in that way because she offered to work with me every morning before class, and we practiced turns and lifts and finger turns for fifteen or twenty minutes every morning."

Kronstam always learned steps quickly and impressed Massine enough during rehearsals to earn the part of the Street Sweeper in *Le Beau Danube*. The Street Sweeper has a tiny solo at the beginning of the ballet, then becomes part of the crowd. It wasn't a big role, but it was his first solo.

The Massine experiment was a success. Both dancers and audience had been excited by the experience. Shortly afterward Lander—whether inspired or threatened by the competition—began work on what would be his most famous and enduring ballet, *Etude*. A pure dance work with dancing as its subject, *Etude* presented Margot Lander as a prima ballerina attended by two cavaliers and supported by the entire company (plus a few pupils) in the corps de ballet. *Etude* was the first Danish "tutu ballet," and an attempt by Lander to translate the new neoclassical style of ballet as he had once adapted Ballets Russes style ballets to native tastes and talent. Kronstam, still thirteen, was again an understudy for the corps. *Etude* underwent several revisions (even its name changed; it is now known as *Etudes*) and it is difficult to see in contemporary performances the gentler, smaller ballet that Lander made in 1948. It is also difficult to imagine a thirteen-year-old getting through it; technically, *Etude* was a killer. However, Kronstam learned several corps parts and even got to dance a small solo. The series of brisés in the finale, now danced by a group of men, was originally a solo, and Kronstam danced it several times. "They had to take out the air turns for me, but aside from that I danced what you see today," he said.

Margot Lander danced the first performances of *Etude,* and the ballerina role was built on her personality—her belovedness—and her technique. She was the opposite of the grand prima ballerina; she danced on a human scale. She was also thirty-eight and past her prime as a technician and there was a tall young girl in the corps named Toni Pihl, whose pure classical technique and long line intrigued Lander. He saw in her his ballerina of the future. Lander gave Toni special classes every afternoon, exploring what she could do, what a ballerina could do. They learned together. Lander became more and more fascinated, and *Etude* began to change. Toni Pihl, then only seventeen, was given the leading role. One afternoon, the story goes, Lander said to Margot during a rehearsal: "Margot, don't you think it's time you retired?" It was a humiliating, public dismissal, but Margot graciously complied. She got her three farewell performances and her salute from the King, and Toni got *Etude*—and Harald. In 1950, Toni Pihl was made solo dancer and married Harald Lander (who had been divorced from Margot since the early 1940s).

The rapid rise of Toni Pihl did not sit well with the company's ballerinas, who had been waiting for Margot Lander's retirement for years and had expected to divide her repertory among them. Kronstam, even though a child, sensed the political side of the situation: "Toni was not a star at that time. He [Lander] was building her. She took special classes in the afternoon with him, and I think that the *Nutcracker* pas de deux was the first thing she did. Then other roles came, and when Margot Lander left, Toni got *Etude.* And that was when Mona Vangsaae and Kirsten Ralov and Margrethe Schanne started to think, 'What is this?' There was Toni, an eighteen-year-old, getting Mr. Lander's star role. I remember when she got the role, they said, 'That's not proper. It should be one of the ballerinas doing that role, and not a young corps de ballet girl.'"

Margot Lander's farewell performance was in 1949, a fateful year for the Royal Danish Ballet. Despite its popularity, Lander decided to scrap Massine's *Symphonie Fantastique* after only half a season. He had the sets painted over and used the flats for his staging, with Borchsenius, of *Salut for August Bournonville,* a series of divertissements including several solos and duets that had not been danced for decades and that would have otherwise been lost. However, historic preservation was not the dancers' priority, and *Salut* was seen as a reactionary move. Was Lander throwing down an aesthetic gauntlet, rejecting Massine's expressionism in favor of Bournonville's classicism? Or was he forcing his own supremacy, saying, in effect, "We do not need Massine, or any other foreigner. Denmark has Bournonville, and Denmark has me." Perhaps it was a bit of both, but, along with the casting of Toni Pihl in *Etude*, the retrograde *Salut for Bournonville* exacerbated the discontent in the company. Borchsenius died that year, Karl Merrild retired, and Hans Beck, no longer an active presence at the Theatre, would die in 1950; the last vestiges of the Beck era at Kongens Nytorv were over.

Kronstam was in the corps de ballet in *Salut* too (dancing in the wedding waltz in *A Folk Tale*), and in the corps of nearly every ballet in the repertory. He was also cast in new works when Lander invited several Danish, though not Royal Danish, choreographers to create for the company. He danced in Birger Bartholin's *Symphonie Classique* and was one of three fighting Capulets in Bartholin's small-scale Tchaikovsky *Romeo and Juliet*. Bartholin was a Dane who came from "outside the walls"; he had not been trained at the Royal Theatre's school. He had danced with Ida Rubenstein in the 1920s, where he had become a friend of Frederick Ashton, also in the Rubenstein company at that time. After returning to Copenhagen, Bartholin established a school and choreographed several ballets for the Royal Theatre.

Another wandering Dane was the beautiful Nini Theilade, who had worked with the great filmmaker Max Reinhardt and had created roles in Massine's *Nobilissima Visione, Seventh Symphony,* and *Bacchanale* with the Ballet Russe de Monte Carlo. Theilade had made a ballet (*Psyche*) for the company in 1932 and returned to create two works in 1950. Kronstam was in both. He was one of six couples in her classical *Schumann Concerto* and was cast in her expressionistic *Metaphor,* which he remembered as being "about a woman's suffering. We were five men and we did something with sticks." He understudied Børge Ralov, the ballet's leading man, and was astonished when Theilade told him she wanted him to dance the part the following season.

Taking part in rehearsals, or even watching them, was much more fun than sitting in school. One afternoon Kronstam saw Hans Beck, now nearly ninety, take Erik Bruhn in a rehearsal of "the yellow pas de deux" in Bournonville's *The Kermesse in Bruges*. That variation had been made for Hans Beck when he was eighteen, not by Bournonville, who was then retired, but by a French ballet

A rehearsal of Nini Theilade's *Metaphor*. From left: Ole Palle Hansen (kneeling), Kronstam (holding a stick over his head), Fredbjørn Bjørnsson, Mona Vangsaae, Poul Vessel, Nini Theilade (in trousers), Kaj Lund, Anker Orskov, Ole Suhr (kneeling), Søren Weiss. Private collection.

master, Gustave Carey. Bournonville had seen Beck dance it at his debut in 1879; afterward he was heard to say, "I could return to the Theatre to make something for that boy." Three days later Bournonville fell dead in the street on his way home from church and his comment cloaked Beck like a benediction for the rest of his career. In those days roles were treasured, usually danced in each generation by a single dancer, who, in turn, taught the role to his successor. Beck had taught the role to Svend Erik Jensen, who had taught it to Bruhn. Now, Beck came to watch this promising young dancer, not much more than eighteen himself. It would be Beck's last time in the Theatre too.

Kronstam and his classmates watched rehearsals as often as they could manage it. "We would sneak down and sit in the back of the Theatre and watch and then tell them up in the school that we had been in rehearsal. We put oil on our faces so that it was dripping down and we would stand on our hands outside the classroom door until the face got really red. Then we would stand at the door and say, 'Just finished. Can we have a break?'"

By the 1949–50 season Kronstam was needed for so many rehearsals that he was rarely in class and Lander took him out of the Læseskole. The theater chief wrote a letter to Kronstam's parents asking them to send him to private tutors for English, French, and German lessons, which they agreed to do, and an hour of language classes, at eight o'clock every morning, was added to his schedule. He still took the children's technique class every morning (now taught by Hans Brenaa, Merrild having retired), and he took Lander's company class immediately afterward, as well as the special afternoon class for aspirants, also taught by Lander. It was an honor, and a thrill, to take class with the grown-ups, but Lander was a strict teacher and, Kronstam said, "It took enormous courage to take his classes."[4] Whatever it took for Kronstam to summon up the courage to get through those classes was worth it, for it was in Lander's class, he said, that he began to acquire professional discipline.

Kronstam was taking so many classes it is hard to imagine how he had the time, much less the energy, for anything else, but, despite being given every encouragement by Lander, he had not given up his dream of becoming an actor. In addition to his other lessons and performance responsibilities, he began to take acting lessons. "I was becoming uninterested. I didn't like the academics, and we had Lander's classes in the morning and he was very strict. We were always doing his ballets, and the ballets were the same, and I began to lose interest in dancing."

Still too young for the Theatre's drama school, Kronstam began reading plays privately with an actor named Martin Hansen. "I knew he took private pupils, and I asked my mother to call him and ask him if he would take me for lessons. He said, 'He's too young. I can work with him, but he can't come to audition for the school until he is eighteen.' He was the actor who always played the nice man, or the young prince, or a good son, parts like that. I liked him because he had the most beautiful way of speaking. It was so clear, his way of speaking Danish." Kronstam would meet with Hansen about once a week. "We just went through plays. He would give me some plays to go home and read, and then I would come back and he would hear how I would make that person, that character." Kronstam continued the lessons with Hansen until the winter of 1951, when a new teacher would renew his interest in ballet.

Kronstam was listed in the 1949–50 souvenir book as an aspirant, a season ahead of his classmates, although he did not receive his official appointment until July 1, 1950, two days after his sixteenth birthday. This meant that he was now an apprentice member of the company and would earn a small salary, but in practical terms, there was little change in either his routine or his status in the company.

In Denmark at that time, the two aspirant years were devoted to concentrated professional education. It was the perfect training system to prepare the young dancers for the company's repertory. After dancing the Bournonville Schools for ten years, the dancers had the steps in their muscles, minds, and bones; they could dance them as soon as they heard the music. In the process they had not only mastered basic classical technique but had learned a hearty chunk of the Bournonville repertory by heart. They had danced in the Bournonville ballets since childhood and had absorbed the style and the atmosphere of the company without being conscious of it. Now, as aspirants, they took a special mime class every morning, in which they learned all the mime speeches in the Bournonville ballets and studied the important roles in the repertory.

Valborg Borchsenius had taught the mime classes for the past twenty years but had died in 1949. The class was now taken by Gerda Karstens, one of the most extraordinary artists ever produced by the Danish ballet. Those who saw her still maintain she was the greatest of all Madges, the witch in *La Sylphide*, and she performed grotesque, dramatic, and comic parts with equal imagination and verve. Karstens revolutionized the acting style of the Danish ballet through her mime classes. During the 1920s, she had studied at the Theatre's acting school, where Stanislavsky Method was taught. She brought much of what she learned to her classes and the pupils she trained between 1950 and her retirement in 1956 not only infused the traditional repertory with her spirit but found her approach invaluable when they encountered contemporary ballets with psychological content in the coming decades.

Karstens was very different from Borchsenius, who had taught by rote, insisting that her pupils copy the gestures exactly and making sure they knew the words that accompanied them, but never getting inside the characters. Borchsenius had invited Kronstam to take her class during his unofficial aspirant year, and, as much as he honored the old lady, he found it dull. "In Mrs. Borchsenius's class, everything was from the outside, just copying," he said.

Karstens gave the students exercises that today would be called structured

Gerda Karstens as Madge.
Photo: Mydtskov. The Royal
Theatre, Copenhagen. By per-
mission of Det kongelige
Teaters bibliotek og arkiv.

improvisations. The only one Kronstam could remember was having to mime
the contents of a letter. "She would tell us who we were—a young boy, a priest,
a sailor—and the pianist would play some music, We wouldn't know what the
music would be, and we would have to show in mime what was in the letter. It
would have to match our character and be on the music, and everybody would
have to understand what we were 'reading.'"

The bulk of the work of the mime class was learning the ballets. Karstens's
classes were like rehearsals; she produced the mime sections of each Bournonville ballet in turn. "We would take a ballet like *La Sylphide* and work on it until
we knew it, probably for six weeks. Then we would do another ballet. I learned
the whole Bournonville repertory from Gerda Karstens."

Sometimes the children would learn the roles they were most likely to
dance as adults, sometimes Karstens gave them roles "out of type" to stretch
their range. Kronstam danced James in *La Sylphide,* but not Gurn, a demi-
caractère role. Other roles were the stupid, uncouth brother, Geert, in *The Kermesse in Bruges;* and, in *A Folk Tale,* both the good and the bad troll brothers
(Viderik and Diderik, respectively; he preferred the sly, thuggish Diderik). He
also learned *Folk Tale*'s hero, Junker Ove, and the young naval lieutenant,

Wilhelm, from *Far from Denmark,* a part he would dance two years after leaving the mime class. He learned Gennaro, the hero of *Napoli,* whose mimed monologue lamenting the loss of his beloved is the most powerful mime speech in the extant repertory.

By the time they were appointed aspirants the ballet children were completely absorbed in the world of the Theatre. Those who weren't usually dropped out and chose a less difficult, less all-consuming life. With two classes in the morning, another at four in the afternoon, rehearsals every day between the two classes, and dancing in ballets or operas as many as five nights a week, there was time for little else. It was hard to maintain friendships outside the Theatre, and the young dancers were friends as well as classmates out of necessity. Even as a child Kronstam was reserved and apart from the others, but he was also beginning to exhibit leadership characteristics. Even at this age he seemed aware of his place in the company. Several dancers remember small kindnesses—Kronstam comforting a crying child or taking a frightened little girl's arm and walking her across a bridge. The priest who conducted Kronstam's confirmation classes sensed this, as well as something reckless about the boy, for he gave him a warning: "You are a leader. Take care of yourself."

Kronstam's first friend in the Theatre was Ole Fatum, a boy slightly younger than Kronstam. The two would go for walks together and explore the town during their "homework" period. "Otherwise," Kronstam said, "I would go out with the girls and eat ice cream." He ate so much ice cream, and chocolates the girls brought him, that he started to gain weight. Lander wrote to Kronstam's mother telling her to watch what her son ate, which mortified him. "So for two years I threw away my lunch and all I ate was one egg, one apple, one tomato, and milk."

Kronstam was the only boy in a class of five girls in the Reading School and had always been a handsome child. The girls vied for his attention; the chocolates were bribes. Classmate Mona Jensen claims she gave Kronstam his first kiss during a school outing when he was nine and she ten. They sat under a tree during a break, kissed, and solemnly vowed eternal love. Jensen remembered that Kronstam had written, "Henning and Mona kissed each other on this day," and buried the paper under the tree. His crush on Viveka Segerskog began soon afterward, when they danced together in the reel in *La Sylphide.*

By the time Kronstam was a teenager the games played in the Theatre's basement carpet room during the empty hours between the end of classes and beginning of the evening performances had become more adult. "Ole and I would go there with the girls and get them out of their clothes so we could see how they were made," Kronstam said. Not all the girls, he insisted. Some of them you wouldn't think to ask, but others could be persuaded to do more than undress. "You have to experiment. Otherwise, how do you know what you will like?" he said of these experiences.

Kronstam had been experimenting in a different way outside the Theatre, however, since he was eleven. "One day I was riding home from school on the tram, and a man was looking at me, and I knew what he wanted. He met me at school the next day," was all he would say about his first sexual encounter, but it was not an isolated incident. "I would go out in the evenings. I would tell my parents that I was riding my bicycle. Sometimes a man would call my house and my father would get so angry." His parents made a few attempts to question him, but he evaded their probing. When he was older he began going to Copenhagen's gay bars, enjoying the attention he got and proud of the fact that he could easily pass for eighteen.

Kronstam had been living the life of a boy/man for so long it is understandable why he began sexual experimentation so early. He had to play a man on stage and his prowling was partly motivated by his need to know how to act older than he was. His theatrical existence was schizoid. An example is a curious double bill of two Lander works, *The Shepherdess and the Chimney Sweep,* a children's ballet from the Hans Christian Andersen tale, and *Bolero,* a very nonchildren's ballet to Ravel's *Bolero* in which Mona Vangsaae seduced a crowd of undulating men, one of whom was Kronstam. In the children's ballet, he played the role of the Hundred-Year-Old Chinaman.

Bolero was suggestive for its day, and Lander cast Kronstam in several similar parts, perhaps because he was tall and dark, perhaps to give him experience. In Manuel de Falla's opera *La Vida Breve,* which Lander staged in 1950, Kronstam had to stand at the top of the stairs, hold one of the corps dancers in a passionate embrace, and kiss her for twenty minutes. "She was a nice lady," he said, "but twenty minutes is a long time to kiss anybody." It was obvious from the way he told the story that he had been embarrassed by the request. "Of course it was a test on Mr. Lander's part," he said.

Despite the embarrassment, the ambivalence, and the nights in the bars, during this time he was still at least somewhat interested in girls. Around the

Kronstam, 16, center, as the Hundred-Year-Old Chinaman in Harald Lander's *The Shepherdess* (Kirsten Petersen) *and the Chimney Sweep* (Flemming Flindt). Private collection.

time of his confirmation, in October 1949 when he was fifteen, he began to court Kirsten Simone. "I won't say we had an affair," he said, "But I would give her bracelets and earrings and things like that." Simone was as beautiful a girl as she is a woman and was sweetly stunning in her confirmation dress, a photo of which was in Kronstam's photo album. "I remember after the confirmation, my brother-in-law came over to me and said, 'Who is that girl? She is beautiful!' and I said, 'That is Kirsten.' My family had heard about Kirsten, but he had never seen her. And my brother-in-law said, 'You should marry her. She is the most beautiful girl here.' And she was, because she was so pure and so innocent in that white dress." During this period Kronstam's reading expanded from books and plays directly related to his work to novels. "I would read love books. Oh, I loved that. On my holiday I would go to Fælledparken with a blanket, and just lie there in the sun and read love stories."

In the spring of 1951, Kronstam went to Tivoli one morning and his life changed forever. "I saw him," Kronstam said, "and I looked at him, and I just knew." The man was Franz Gerstenberg, twice Kronstam's age and a baron. Kronstam thought he was very handsome, "like a movie star. He looked just

like Leslie Howard." They spent the day together. "The next morning at breakfast I said to my mother, 'I have a friend, and he has a car. Should I phone him?
We could drive up the coast to Helsingør.' And she said yes and so we did." Fru
Kronstam was quite impressed with her son's titled friend and liked him, besides. She approved of the new friendship, despite the age difference. According to other family members, none of them realized that there was anything
more to the relationship than friendship. Kronstam, however, was equally certain that both parents knew exactly what was going on from the beginning.

At first Gerstenberg was not particularly interested in the much younger
man, but Kronstam was persistent. Margrethe Noyé, who had known Gerstenberg since he was fifteen and remained a friend of both men all their lives, first
met Kronstam early in their friendship. Noyé and Gerstenberg were sitting in
a café when a handsome young man came over to talk to them. Noyé remembered Kronstam as "a cheerful, happy, friendly boy," who was very sweet, very
polite. The three talked for a while, then Kronstam left. Gerstenberg told Noyé

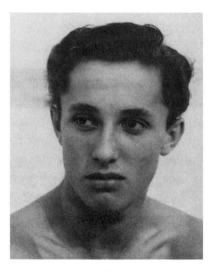

Kronstam, 14. Studio shot taken by
an unknown photographer friend.
Private collection.

Kronstam, 16, dancing with his
mother, "the New Year's Eve before I
met Franz." Private collection.

a bit about his young friend, saying that he thought the age difference was too great and that he didn't think that the two had much in common. Gerstenberg had no interest in ballet and knew nothing about theater life. That same summer, Noyé also met Kronstam's family, whom she described as "cold and greedy people. Henning was completely different, not like them at all."

Despite Gerstenberg's misgivings, Kronstam was in love, and his persistence eventually won out. "I was only sixteen, but there was no doubt. He came to my seventeenth birthday—I met him May 4th, and I was seventeen at the end of June and he came to the dinner. My father made a speech and said how it was so nice to see me grow up, and we are here to celebrate my son's seventeenth birthday, and Franz got so pale and practically fell out of his chair because I was forbidden. I had told him I was eighteen and I looked it, so he had believed me."

Kronstam seems to have understood and accepted his homosexuality very early and was positive that his parents understood that the two were more than friends. "I think my parents knew that I was different from the moment of my birth. I think they were happy I had found someone to stay with. They were glad that I would settle down. And they liked Franz then. We played bridge together and some nights, when we played too late for him to go home, my mother made up a bed for him in my room."

Gerstenberg, who had the title of baron but not the fortune with which it is associated, was the editor and advertising manager of several business publications. Although thirty-two, he lived with his mother, with whom he was very close. Gerstenberg was an only child. His father had walked out on the family the morning of his silver wedding anniversary, "leaving Agnes to cope with the guests," as Kronstam put it. Agnes Gerstenberg and Kronstam became good friends. "I loved his mother. She was such a sweet lady," he said, and there were several cards and notes from her among his correspondence. Fru Gerstenberg had a summerhouse in Asserbo, a dark log house hidden in the Danish forest, and the two young men spent many days there that first summer with members of both families.

It was a busy summer. Kronstam had an engagement in July with a little group Lander had put together to dance in the parks around Copenhagen and Oslo. Before that tour, Kronstam and Gerstenberg drove to Nice for a short vacation, accompanied by Fru Kronstam. It was Kronstam's second trip through France; he and his mother had taken a holiday there in 1947, and the

Kronstam, 17, at the summerhouse.
Private collection.

Franz Wilhelm Gerstenberg when Kronstam first met him. Private collection.

bombed out cities remained a strong memory. Four years later Europe was
beginning to recover, and Fru Kronstam, who loved traveling, was eager to see
how it was changing. The trip was not without problems. "I think we were a
little too wild for her. We would go out every night drinking, and she would stay
in her room. She went back home before we did, but it was all very friendly."
The wildness included gambling. Kronstam and Gerstenberg ran out of
money, and Gerstenberg went into a casino to try to win enough to prolong
their stay. Kronstam, too young to go in, waited outside until Gerstenberg came
out with his winnings.

After Kronstam returned from Nice, he left almost immediately for the tour
with Lander. There were only three other dancers: Jan Holme, Tove Leach (the
woman from the top of the stairs in *La Vida Breve*), and Toni Lander. He now
realized that Lander was grooming him as a partner for Toni, and he was, of
course, very happy at that realization. The tour was neither rigorous nor artistically challenging, just something for the dancers to do to make money and
break up the tedium of the ten-week summer holiday. They were one of three
acts on a bill, dancing a divertissement Lander had created for the occasion.

What stood out in his mind about that tour was that Lander—a stern man,
not known to be chummy with his dancers, especially aspirants—was kind to

him, telling the boy that he could learn the *Nutcracker* pas de deux next season, and would perform the virtuoso showpiece with Toni. This was an extraordinary opportunity. Erik Bruhn had had a sensational success with *Nutcracker* the previous season. Bruhn had left the company (presumably, at the time, for good), and Lander was essentially telling Kronstam that he would be Bruhn's successor.

In his photo album there is a small white object that looks and feels like a blob of cotton. "Oh, that is a flower Mr. Lander gave me," Kronstam said. "It was one day when we were in Norway. It was a beautiful day and Toni and Mr. Lander went out walking in the mountains. And when he came back he gave me that flower. He was very kind to me." Lander talked to Kronstam for a while, giving him advice that was no doubt well intentioned. Lander had apparently been aware of, and worried about, the boy's homosexuality for some time. He told Jan Holme, "The time has come for Kronstam to choose between men and ballet." Now, Lander warned the young dancer that leading an openly homosexual life would hurt his career. "'I don't care what you do in your bed, Henning,' he told me, 'but if you want a good career, you must marry. Why don't you marry that pretty little girl with the long blonde braids, and then you can do what you like.' He meant Kirsten. He knew we were friends." Kronstam considered Lander's advice but decided that, as he put it, "It wouldn't have been fair to her." Kronstam and Simone remained friends throughout their careers, though the relationship was complex and became rather strained in later years. In the 1950s and 1960s, however, they danced together frequently both at home and abroad, and sometimes went on holiday together (with Gerstenberg, of course, and it did not help that he and Simone did not get along). "We might as well have gotten married," Kronstam once grumbled goodnaturedly. "We spent more time together than most married people do."

The summer of 1951 was a magical time, the kind of summer youth deserves, when love and happiness seem infinite and all things are possible. Kronstam was seventeen. He was happy, he was in love, and he felt secure in his relationship with his family. Mr. Lander, who had led the Danish ballet for twenty years and was now at the height of his power, had taken an interest in him and had chosen him as a partner for the young woman who was about to become the company's ballerina. Everything in his life was perfect. What could possibly go wrong?

It was Vera who changed me into a dancer.
—Henning Kronstam

ive

Vera Volkova and the Making of a Dancer

After the summer parks tour Kronstam returned to Copenhagen for a few more weeks' vacation, and Harald Lander went in search of the legendary Russian teacher Vera Volkova. He found her in Milan; she had left her London studio to become artistic director of the ballet company at La Scala. Volkova agreed to come to Copenhagen that autumn for three months as a guest teacher. His mission accomplished, Lander returned home to start rehearsals for the new season. He was met at the railroad station by the theater chief, Henning Brøndsted, and the church minister,[1] who told him they had some serious matters to discuss. During the summer holidays, charges of artistic and moral misconduct had been lodged against Lander. The impossible had happened. Lander was out. He came to the Theatre one Sunday to get his things and left. The Lander Scandal, one of the most troubling chapters in the history of the Royal Danish Ballet, the repercussions of which reverberate in Kongens Nytorv to this day, had begun.

The dancers' dissatisfaction with Lander's directorship had built steadily during the five years since the end of the war. However, Lander was so powerful it seemed impossible that he could be unseated. Theatre regulations required that Lander would have to be found guilty of a crime, or at least some immoral conduct, to be dismissed. During the summer of 1951 forces outside the Theatre—perhaps acting independently, perhaps nudged by unhappy dancers—handed the anti-Lander faction a gift. Several female dancers complained to friends about actions by Lander that would today be called sexual harassment. In the end there were several charges, the most serious of which were that Lander had made unwelcome advances to underage girls and that he had covered up the rape of one of the company's women by a dancer. Three men—a dancer, a music publisher, and the dance critic for *Kristeligt Dagblad* (The Christian Daily)—brought the complaints to the attention of the Theatre's administration. The church minister was High Church and very conservative, and he was incensed.

The case exploded in the tabloids and there was much speculation about backstage life at the Royal Theatre. Dancers wrote letters to the editor. One such letter, signed by most of the company, demanded that Lander go; another, signed by the rest, insisted that he stay. Erik Bruhn, now a guest artist and thus free to speak his mind, gave several interviews, all anti-Lander, and wrote a letter to the editor in which he laid out the anti-Lander position on artistic matters. Bruhn was still very young (only twenty-two), but he had begun to make a career abroad, which gave him much more credibility than any mere stay-at-home Danish dancer.

By all accounts life backstage during this period was absolute hell. The division was deep and the handful of dancers who didn't choose sides were detested by both factions. Poor Toni Lander stayed through it all, taking class every day and even performing, until her husband's case was settled. After an administrative hearing, Lander was dismissed with a reduced pension. He left, taking his ballets with him, undoubtedly confident that the company would collapse without them and he would soon be asked to return. While he waited he staged Bournonville ballets and his own *Etudes* abroad and, although he eventually became a ballet master and choreographer at the Paris Opera Ballet, seems never to have stopped plotting and planning to get back into the Royal Theatre.

Niels Bjørn Larsen was appointed to lead the company. He was probably chosen because he had experience outside Denmark (he had toured with Trudi Schoop's mime troupe in America and Europe during the 1930s) and had choreographed several ballets and directed small touring companies over the years. Larsen had modest ambitions as a choreographer, but he had a balanced temperament and was a good "daily man," as Kronstam put it, by which he meant that Larsen had the patience for the day-to-day tedium of managing a dance company housed in a state theater. Larsen had not instigated any aspect of the scandal, although he was on the anti-Lander side after it erupted.

Of course, the pro-Lander faction viewed Larsen as a traitor and made his life difficult, constantly challenging his authority. The Danish critics, who regarded Lander as a great choreographer, were united against Larsen as well. Dancers who survived this period say that the critics used Larsen as a political football in their fight to get Lander reinstated. For several years they pounced on anything Larsen did as a director and declared it a disaster. There are dancers today who still feel their careers were blighted by critics who attacked them as a way to make Larsen's directorship look incompetent.

For an ambitious seventeen-year-old who had been promised the world only two months ago it was an especially confusing time. "The company was turned upside down," Kronstam said with a rueful laugh forty years later, "and all I could think of was that I wouldn't get to dance *Nutcracker* with Toni." At first, Kronstam was sympathetic to Lander. "Lander was very strict. So if he gave you, 'Today, this was really wonderful,' you felt like, 'Ah! He has given me a jewel.' So when the whole scandal happened, I was very much in doubt about which side I should stand on. It was Vera who helped me out of that."

Despite fights in and out of the newspapers and dirty looks tossed about backstage, life, of course, went on. The season's repertory had been planned by Lander the year before but, as it consisted mostly of Lander works that were no longer available, Larsen had to scramble to find new ballets. Larsen had never been a classical dancer; he was, by talent and inclination, a character dancer and mime. Company class was now taught by Stanley Williams, who had been Lander's assistant, and Hans Brenaa, who had studied in Paris with Lubov Egorova during the thirties and—he was famous for this—brought back the secret of spotting to Copenhagen.[2] Brenaa was the company's cavalier (the dancer who supports the ballerina in classical pas de deux), and a superb turner. "Hans could turn," said Kronstam, "and the ladies loved him. He was so charming and lovable on stage. Børge Ralov couldn't partner, so in *Coppelia*, and ballets like that, Hans would partner Margot Lander in the adagio, and then Børge would dance the solo." But neither Williams nor Brenaa had Lander's authority or stature, and the most pressing need was not only for a choreographer but also a teacher and coach, a ballet master in the technical sense of the term. Ironically, Lander's final act—the engagement of Vera Volkova—ensured that the company would survive without him.

Volkova walked into the hornet's nest that was the Royal Danish Ballet in November 1951 to fulfill her three-month contract as a guest teacher. She remained until her death, twenty-three years later. Along with Franz Gerstenberg, she would become the most important person in Henning Kronstam's life. "I remember the first day she came," he said. "I was very disciplined from Lander's morning class, so Hans [Brenaa] put me right there in front of her, and there she sat. Didn't say a word, didn't give anything away. From the day she started teaching she took us back to the beginning, because what we were doing had become a bit sloppy. She really started us like little children. Some of the older dancers didn't like it. That's why Børge Ralov left her classes. He said, 'Am I going to start all over again?'" The way the men of the company treated Volkova in the early years is a prime example of the *gadedrenge* (street boy) behavior that seems to boil silently under the surface in this company, erupting during times of weak leadership, a by-product of Jantelov, some say, when "ordinary people" have a chance to strike back at "the Rare Few." The men talked and acted up in class and refused to take instruction from Volkova, sometimes openly insulting her. Occasionally the situation was so unpleasant that Volkova would storm down to the theater chief's office and get him to come up and restore order.

Vera Volkova, ca. 1951. Photo: Mydtskov. Private collection.

Starting over was exactly what Volkova had in mind. She had been born in St. Petersburg in 1904, making her an exact contemporary of George Balanchine and Frederick Ashton. She had begun lessons too late to become a leading dancer; from the beginning, however, it was obvious that she had an extraordinary gift for teaching. She studied with both Maria Romanovna (mother of the great ballerina Galina Ulanova) and Agrippina Vaganova, who had codified and refined the Russian methods of teaching classical ballet in much the same way that Hans Beck had done in Copenhagen, although Vaganova was more systematic.

The spider web of connections among ballet dancers is always fascinating, Volkova's especially so. The most basic was that Romanovna's teacher had been a Swede named Christian Johansson, whose teacher had been a Dane named August Bournonville. In a very real sense, Volkova brought Bournonville's standards of classical dancing back to Copenhagen. A second strand of the web was that Vaganova used Volkova and a young dancer named Alexander Pushkin as the models on which she worked out her now celebrated Vaganova syllabus—the pedagogical system for teaching the Russian style of classical ballet that Vaganova devised, which has by now virtually conquered the world. Pushkin stayed in Leningrad and became a legendary teacher. Among his pupils were Rudolf Nureyev (who later came to Copenhagen to study with Volkova), Yuri Soloviev, and Mikhail Baryshnikov.

It is the third strand that is the most eerie. In the 1920s Volkova had toured Japan and China with two young men. One was George Goncharov, who settled in Singapore and would become the first teacher of a little girl called Peggy Hookham, who grew up to be Margot Fonteyn; the other was Serge Toporov, who died in the purges during the early Stalinist era and of whom Volkova was immensely fond. Volkova told Kronstam and several others that Toporov bore a striking resemblance to the tall Danish boy who was told to stand "right there in front of her" that first morning in Copenhagen.

Volkova married an Englishman, the painter Hugh Williams, and came to London in 1936, where she opened a studio. By the early 1940s, she had become an enormous influence on the dancers of the Sadler's Wells Ballet, many of whose dancers took her classes, and its great choreographer, Frederick Ashton. She was not only an inspiring teacher but an extraordinary coach, and she seemed to have met (and acquired the phone numbers of) everyone of importance in ballet. Volkova was the first truly international-level artist on staff at Kongens Nytorv since Bournonville, and her influence on the company is incalculable.

Volkova was also the first woman to hold real power in Danish ballet; she changed the teaching methods, she coached dancers in roles, she lured the greatest choreographers of the day to Kongens Nytorv. A small, determined woman with dark hair and sad, dark eyes, she had a strong personality and did nothing to soften it. "She was very firm when she came. She was very Russian, very disciplined. But during those first three, four months she was here, she got everybody very warm and very close to her," Kronstam said. In his "Oral History," Kronstam explained "very Russian": "She could be very, very angry. And when she really got angry she was like a furioso. She was really mad. But everybody knew what she wanted, what she was heading for. There was no fiddling around about it, no. . . . She wanted this and that, and everybody would know it by watching what she was doing. Giving extra tuition to certain dancers and things like that. She couldn't care less for the rest. If they had no talent? Whoosh—[*snapping sound*]—out. I don't care."[3]

There is no question that Volkova changed the company's way of dancing. Some say she cleaned up bad habits that had crept in over the decades and brought the dancers' technique up to contemporary international standards (Kronstam held to that opinion); others that she destroyed much of what was uniquely Danish about the company's dancing. "She came, of course, with the Russian style; what we see now at the Vaganova Institute is close to a lot of the things she did. But she had been in England and she had some Cecchetti with her too. And she . . . slowly started to learn the Bournonville repertory that we needed, so all her classes had much more batteries [i.e., petite batterie] than when she started, quick, fast little batteries, especially for the girls. And she brought steps from the Bournonville repertory into her style, and at the end she was sort of a mixture of Cecchetti, Russian, and the Bournonville, what she thought we needed in the Bournonville style."[4]

Her decision to stay had an immediate effect on Kronstam's career. "It was when Vera came that I knew I wanted to be a dancer," he said. His dreams of becoming an actor vanished in an instant. Volkova touched his arm to make a correction and, as he had said of his first meeting with Gerstenberg, "I just knew." Kronstam responded to Volkova's interest, but, more than that, he respected her knowledge and her discipline. "She was supposed to be here for three months. That was it. But then she said that she wanted to have the afternoon classes with the aspirants. I always liked to be told what I have to do, and she started on all our faults, slowly working them out. She gave good classes and she made it make sense. Before Vera, I didn't understand the sense of what I was doing."

As a mature dancer, Kronstam was famous for, among other things, his plush landings from jumps; he credited this to Volkova's teaching. "Lander was not a bad teacher. The only thing he didn't give me was a good plié. Vera had me doing plié, plié, plié every morning. Vera gave me my plié. If I had kept on with Mr. Lander, I would have been finished at twenty-seven. My knees would have been gone." Kronstam demonstrated an aspect of both the technical and poetic aspects of Volkova's teaching: "The plié is essential because it is the landing from a jump that is so beautiful. It is not enough to hang in the air; you have to come down. And you should not come down with a bang. It is beautiful to hang in the air and then"—he turned his hand into a glider, made a half-circle with it in the air, then brought it down for a landing, oh so quietly, with a gentle "whoosh."

Volkova had a great influence on other dancers, especially four young women—Kirsten Simone, Mette Mollerup, Ruth Andersen, and Kirsten Petersen (later Kirsten Bundgaard). She was more than willing to work with the dancers already in the company, and those who were open to what she could teach them benefited greatly. Fredbjørn Bjørnsson, already a solo dancer, took class with her. Kronstam remembered hearing older dancers grumbling, asking "who does that Russian woman think she is, giving a correction to a dancer as great as Fredbjørn Bjørnsson?" But because he *was* a great dancer, Bjørnsson welcomed her guidance. Stanley Williams learned much from Volkova, and Erik Bruhn, always in and out of the company, studied intensively with her when he was in Copenhagen.

Bruhn was Kronstam's boyhood model. "I remember my brother came with me and watched from the wings when Erik danced *Nutcracker,* because I had been talking about it at home and saying, 'Oh, this is so wonderful. You have to come see it. You'll never see anything like it.' Erik was the one who let me see what dancing could be—not as an artist, but as a dancer," Kronstam said. "When Vera came, when we did the center work in class, she told me, 'Stay behind him. Watch him.' If you stand behind somebody when you are dancing, your eye will take it in. Erik had beautiful port de bras. Deep and rich. And he had a nice open turnout, and nice attitude pirouettes. Beautiful jumps. Light, light, light. He had already danced a lot of roles before Vera came, but she helped him a great deal."

Despite Volkova's attention, Kronstam's course in the company was not smooth after Lander's ouster. Although Lander had clearly been grooming Kronstam for solo roles, he was still an aspirant, and his career was put on hold by the new regime. One of the by-products of the Lander Scandal was that dancers challenged Larsen in ways they would never have dared challenge his predecessor. They especially complained about the allocation of roles. Kronstam had been given many roles by Lander and the guest choreographers who came to the company between 1948 to 1951, and several men a few years older than the young aspirant thought that those parts should have been theirs. They complained, and Kronstam lost roles. He did not hold this against Larsen. "They were so against him and he had so many problems, he had to give them something," Kronstam said. So, despite Nini Theilade's wishes, he never got to dance the star role in *Metaphor,* and he was cast in few new parts during Larsen's first seasons.

Kronstam suffered from another side effect of the Lander Scandal. So much had been written and said about the morality, or immorality, of ballet dancers that the Theatre administration worried about public perceptions. Anything having to do with sex, or what would today be called lifestyle choices, made them nervous. Kronstam began to be taunted "for the life I was leading." The Royal Danish Ballet had always been aggressively heterosexual. There were only two other gay men in the company at the time, and some of the men were determined there would not be a third. Kronstam was publicly discreet about his relationship with Gerstenberg, but almost everyone backstage knew about "Henning and his baron." The young men all ate lunch together, and there was a vulgar, locker room tone to their conversation. "We were all men in the company at that time," as Jan Holme, a dancer about ten years older than Kronstam (and his good friend) put it, reflecting the attitude toward homosexuals prevalent in the company. Volkova noticed that Kronstam was avoiding the lunchroom (she had already put a stop to his apple-egg-and-tomato diet) and, upon learning the reason, asked Stanley Williams, a slightly older dancer and fine teacher, to befriend Kronstam. "Stanley and I ate lunch in his dressing room, and talked about ballet and beautiful things," Kronstam said. The two quickly became good friends. They were both reserved as people, serious as artists, and absolutely obsessed with ballet.[5]

Other problems were less easily solved. Some dancers spread rumors about Kronstam's life outside the Theatre. "Kjeld Noack said that I entertained at parties, that I would be naked and painted all over with gold paint, and be carried in on a platter," Kronstam said. "It was so silly because I've always been a modest person. I would never have done anything like that." Noack was a few years older than Kronstam and the two men were often considered for the same roles, as they were the same lyrical Type although Kronstam was much the taller man.[6] They also shared a dressing room, which made the situation even more difficult. "We ended up being good friends, though, despite all that nonsense at the beginning," Kronstam, who always wanted to smooth things over, added.

As the result of a more vicious rumor, Kronstam became involved in a police investigation. An elderly man who was known to frequent gay bars had been found dead in his apartment, and someone (Kronstam later found out, after Gerstenberg investigated, that it was the ambitious father of a slightly younger rival) wrote on the walls of several of the city's public toilets, "If you want to know what happened to X, ask Henning Kronstam." Kronstam had to go to the police station for questioning. "My father got a letter from the police one morning at breakfast, and he said, 'Henning, you must deal with this yourself.' So I went to the police station and they showed me photographs of the dead man, five photos. He hadn't been strangled or anything. He had just died. But the policemen laughed, saying 'What did you do to him? Did you kill him with your beauty?' I didn't know him. I had never seen him before."

Since his father had refused to help him, he turned to Gerstenberg, who convinced the police that Kronstam was not involved in the situation in any way and, more important, somehow managed to keep the story out of the newspapers. If this matter had become public Kronstam's career would have been over before it started, even though he had been falsely implicated, which is why the mischief had been made in the first place. Gerstenberg saved Kronstam's career, which was tantamount, he said, to saving his life. In later years Kronstam would often explain that he stayed with Gerstenberg because the older man had been "so helpful to me in my career when I was young." This is what he meant.[7]

A second encounter with police fractured Kronstam's relationship with his family. One afternoon Kronstam was called to the theater chief's office and told that the police wished to question him.[8] He was escorted to a police station; Gerstenberg was already there, though he was held in another room. Kronstam later learned that his mother had called the police, telling them that

Gerstenberg was having an affair with her underage son. "Luckily, Franz was very clever, and we had planned for this. So we both had the same story. We said we had done nothing, that we were waiting until I came of age. Franz was in one room and I was in another, and they kept questioning us. But we stuck to the story and they had to let us go." Kronstam believed that some of the men in the company had telephoned his mother and warned her that the relationship with Gerstenberg threatened his career. "I think she became frightened and that's why she did what she did." That thought was in retrospect; at the time he was angry. He went home (the family had moved to a flat at 16 Tordenskjoldsgade, on the same street as the Theatre and just a few yards from the stage door, the year before) and found that his mother had thrown a few things that Gerstenberg had left there out into the street. There was an ugly scene. Fru Kronstam—perhaps shocked (as her daughter, Jessie, thought) at learning that Gerstenberg and her son were lovers; perhaps frightened (if Kronstam's perceptions were accurate) that others would discover what she suspected—told Kronstam he must choose between his family and his friend. Gerstenberg, terrified at losing Kronstam, threatened to kill himself if Kronstam didn't leave with him. Kronstam, only seventeen, had a terrible choice to make in an instant. "She adored me," he said of his mother, "but I had to pull away from her." He chose Franz.

Kronstam moved in with Gerstenberg and his mother, Agnes, until the two men found an apartment of their own. At the Theatre, Volkova provided both moral and practical support. Gerstenberg would usually meet Kronstam at the Theatre at the end of the day. On one occasion Kronstam's brother-in-law showed up at the stage door and tried to get Kronstam to go with him. Volkova intervened. "No," she said firmly. "Henning is going with Franz."

When Kronstam first talked about this period of his life, he told the story as if little time elapsed between his leaving home and his mother's death. In fact she died six years later, in late summer 1957. In subsequent retellings Kronstam mentioned some contacts with the family after he left home. "I remember my mother came to my eighteenth birthday party," he said, and he also recalled that his family attended several of his performances. There was at least one friendly meeting. One day as Kronstam was going into the Theatre he ran into Kirsten Simone, all dressed up and on her way out. He asked her where she was going and she replied that his mother had telephoned and invited her to tea. Kronstam said, "You're not going there without me," then turned around and accompanied her. Simone remembered the meeting as quite pleasant, with no visible tensions, and that Fru Kronstam had been very nice to her.[9]

Despite the occasional contacts Kronstam perceived that the relationship had been permanently breached. He found it difficult to talk about this period, saying only, "It was very unpleasant. They got a lawyer and we got a lawyer." The family did continue to communicate. Among Kronstam's papers there were several notes congratulating him on this or that performance, usually signed "Mor og Far" (Mother and Father), though obviously written by his mother. The tone is warm and loving; there is no sign of strain. There is one rather formal letter from Hr. Kronstam "on the occasion of your coming of age," which asks "if it is not time we resume normal family relations." In Kronstam's mind, at least, apparently it was not.

Whether Kronstam withdrew from his family solely because of its attitude to the relationship with Gerstenberg and his mother's actions or also because of the increasing demands of his career is impossible to determine now. What is clear is that he felt estranged. His relationship with his brother was permanently damaged, and he was never fully reconciled with his mother. Only his grandfather, now nearly ninety, opened his heart to him. "When Franz and I were pushed out of the house, my grandfather called and said, 'You can come to me any time.' And we came. And he said, 'You can have a *snaps* each and you sit and talk, and I don't care what you do. And I think that Meta is very stupid.'"

A clue to the depth of Kronstam's psychic separation from his family lies in a sentence in the brief biography in the souvenir book for the Royal Danish Ballet's first American tour in 1956. "His grandfather, General Heinrich von Gerstenberg, had been ambassador to Imperial Russia during the last great days of the ballet and there was strong enthusiasm for the ballet in his family," it reads.[10] Gerstenberg was his family now, and a life-size portrait of that balletomane grandfather who had watched Christian Johansson's Russian pupils dance hung on the sitting room wall throughout their life together.

On March 24, 1952, Kronstam finally made his official debut.[11] The first ballet Larsen brought into the repertory was a lighthearted work that suited the company's talents, if not its mood: David Lichine's *Graduation Ball*. Volkova had urged Larsen to have two casts for this production (which was not the company's usual practice), one for the established dancers, another for the youngsters. Kronstam danced the bravura role of the Drummer in the second cast.

Graduation Ball is about the end-of-term party at a girl's boarding school in turn-of-the-century Vienna; the music is, of course, by Strauss. A nearby boy's military school is invited, and the students put on a show. Young love runs its course, hearts are broken in a night, and the Old General and the girls' Headmistress almost kiss under an enormous moon. It's slight and, when the Danes danced it, fun, although the ballet was killed in the 1970s by campy performances by other companies.

The Drummer dances in the divertissement. His short, forceful solo is full of difficult steps and was unlike anything Kronstam had yet danced. "Lichine was the first one that dared to take me for something like that. All the others had used me for lyrical things, beautiful things. But Lichine said, 'No. That boy has sex too.'" Kronstam had to fight to master both the steps and the swagger the part required, but, "Lichine kept keeping on me. He would say, 'We have a break, ten minutes. I just keep Drummer Boy. [*He snaps his fingers.*] Are you warm, Drummer Boy?' And we would work and work." Kronstam had particular trouble with a series of double air turns, a step he had just learned, and thus almost lost the role. Years later, he told Nikolaj Hübbe, who was having problems of his own with double tours, that the role had nearly been given to the understudy, Kjeld Noack. "But I was determined I was not going to lose a part to Kjeld Noack," he told Hübbe, "and so I worked until I got it."[12]

The air turns were made more difficult by the fact that the Drummer wore hard leather boots "with heels, real heels, like they wear in *Coppelia*," he said. These were inflexible, and did not allow the dancer to feel the floor. "Oh, the boys today are such babies," Kronstam said, with a laugh. "They have to have soft boots now. Ever since they saw Ib [Andersen, who left to dance with the New York City Ballet in 1980] wear those soft boots, they all said, 'Oh, can't we have those too?'"

Another problem—shared by every man who's danced the role—is that the Drummer has to twirl his drumsticks several times during the solo. "I had to learn that too, and you feel so stupid when you finish that last double tour, and you twirl your sticks—because you have to end BAM! like that, and with a big flourish—and nothing happens. So you just stand there like a fool and smile. That happened a lot. But it was a wonderful solo. I just adored it. I had such a good time with it; I danced it for ten years."

There was a short interview with Kronstam and five other young dancers in the newspaper around the time of this performance.[13] In it, Kronstam was asked if he wasn't a bit too tall to be a ballet dancer. His reply—"I think I have stopped growing now. I am 181 centimeters. Frank Schaufuss, who also dances the Drummer, is two centimeters taller than I."—indicates that his height was still a worry; the men of the Royal Danish Ballet were considerably shorter than that at the time. He was also asked if he had been surprised about being cast in the role, and his response is rather blustery, like the character he was dancing. "I simply didn't believe that it would happen. . . . When I understood that it was serious [that I would dance the role], I was delighted and astonished—and nervous! I think that the Drummer is just right for me, but Christ, I was nervous, until the day came—then I could push it away." The interview ends with his assessment of his performance, a simple, "And so it went," which is both a joke and a nod to Volkova. She very rarely praised her dancers. Unless a performance was extraordinary, she would stick her head in the dressing room afterward and say, simply, "It went." Kronstam's comment, that he "pushed the nerves away," is significant, as this is the way he tried to handle nerves, and other problems, throughout his life.

The Drummer was Kronstam's only new role that season. In the spring of 1952 the American choreographer John Taras, who was then ballet master with the Grand Ballet de Marquis de Cuevas, was invited to stage his *Design with Strings*. Called *Variationer* (Variations) in Copenhagen, this was a small work for two men and four women that was very popular in the 1950s. Taras wanted Kronstam to dance the male lead but was told that this was impossible because the boy was still only an aspirant; Kronstam was allowed only to understudy the second man's role. Taras taught him both parts anyway, telling him, "You'll dance both of them some day." The lyrical ballet was neither a particularly difficult technical nor stylistic challenge, but once again, Kronstam had been noticed by a visiting choreographer, and Taras was very important to Kronstam in the early years of his career by choreographing on him and introducing him to other choreographers.

Kronstam's second aspirant year was drawing to a close, and he began to prepare for the final exam. He and Kirsten Simone were learning the *Paquita* pas de deux, a very difficult showpiece in the grand Russian style. That year was the first time the aspirants had been given anything other than Bournonville to dance. "You can see the changes Vera had made already," Kronstam said. "The year before, I had danced the first solo from *Napoli*. Now, Vera had us doing Petipa." Photos from those rehearsals show how well Volkova had

Kronstam as the Drummer in *Graduation Ball* at his debut in March 1952.
Private collection.

Kronstam and Kirsten Simone in the
Paquita pas de deux; graduation, 1952.
Private collection.

succeeded in making Kronstam and Kirsten Simone into a partnership. "It did
not take very long before Vera started matching Kirsten and me. She came in
November and the exam was in May. Already by then she had seen that we
were a match in our height and our line. She wanted to make a couple out
of us."

The examinations were no longer danced before gods seated on golden
thrones. That was in the old days; everything was democratic now. In addition
to Larsen and Volkova, Brøndsted, Henning Rohde (then the secretary of the
Royal Theatre), Stanley Williams, and the head of the dancer's union (Svend
Karlog), all watched the exam. Kronstam was not pleased with his performance; Simone remembered that he had danced very well. What happened
afterward, however, had nothing to do with dancing.

During the postexamination discussions, strong opinions were voiced that
Kronstam should not be taken into the company. Some of the men did not

want him because he was homosexual; the Theatre administration was skittish about another scandal. The official reason—Volkova told him all this later— would be that Kronstam had not danced as well as they had expected at the exam. As the men argued, Kronstam's career was in real jeopardy. Then Vera Volkova stood up, took her newspaper, folded it, and whacked Henning Rohde over the head with it, shouting, "If you throw that boy out then I will leave too." Larsen also stood up for Kronstam: "That didn't matter to me," Larsen said. "Henning was a good dancer, and he should have gotten into the company." He did, and was appointed ballet dancer July 1, 1952, two days after his eighteenth birthday.[14]

When the company broke up for the long summer holiday, Kronstam and Gerstenberg went to the summerhouse. Very shortly thereafter, when Kronstam turned eighteen and their relationship could be legal, they bought a house in Hellerup, a Copenhagen suburb of big houses with gardens. They lived there for ten years. Despite his youth Kronstam was happy to settle down. He needed a stable home and that, above all, is what Gerstenberg gave him. Gerstenberg organized Kronstam's life so that the young dancer could concentrate all his energies on his dancing. He hired the housekeepers, invested their money, and managed the pair's finances. They stayed together for forty-two years. "He was everything to me," Kronstam said, three months after Gerstenberg's death in the spring of 1994. "Father, brother, friend, everything. And they had to understand that I needed somebody like that."

Gerstenberg was by far the most controversial figure in Kronstam's life. To some he was a charming, witty man, absolutely devoted to Kronstam. To others he was overbearing and manipulative and had ruined Kronstam's life by first seducing him and thereafter treating him cruelly. Gerstenberg *was* charming, and clever, and a financial wizard. He could be coarse, and he enjoyed shocking people. He liked to talk and often bragged about money more than good taste allowed. He acted as a watchdog, screening calls and callers, and guarding Kronstam against distractions as well as the attentions of numerous admirers of both sexes.

What few people understood—only Volkova and one or two others—was how much Kronstam needed Gerstenberg's care, and why. By now it was already evident to some that Kronstam had inherited his mother's manic-depression. Margrethe Noyé said that she had always known Kronstam was manic-depressive, adding, "It was obvious. He was different, morning to night." In its

Gerstenberg and Kronstam at home, 1950s. Private collection.

early stages, the illness seemed more of an imbalance in energy than of mood. Kronstam would work to the point of exhaustion, unable to pace himself. "Vera went to Franz and said, 'You take care of that boy.' Franz was always very ambitious for me, so he listened to what she said. Vera always knew when I had to get away and rest, and she would go to Franz and say, 'You had better take him away for a few weeks.'"

The physical aspect of their relationship ended after only two years, possibly because Gerstenberg could not fulfill the dual role of lover and guardian. "We talked about it," Kronstam said, "and agreed that we would stay together and take care of each other." Kronstam understood the arrangement but was not happy with it, and it's likely that his affection for ballets like *Romeo and Juliet* and *Cyrano,* and other stories of frustrated and unrequited love stemmed from his own situation. Although Kronstam had at least one other serious relationship and innumerable dalliances, Gerstenberg remained at the center of his life. Friends remember that Kronstam would periodically try to break away from Gerstenberg, but he never went through with it. The reasons were quite complicated. He was bound to the older man by love, by the sense of obligation for Gerstenberg's help in that terrible early scandal, and by need. As Kronstam's illness progressed with time and the increasing pressures of his career, Gerstenberg's care would help Kronstam manage his "ups and downs," as he preferred to call his illness. Without Franz—or "someone like that"—it is unlikely that Kronstam would have been able to have so successful a career in such a physically and emotionally demanding art, and much of Kronstam's life was a paring away of distractions or anything that would interfere with the intense focus he gave to the Theatre. Several people who knew both men said that Gerstenberg took advantage of this need to keep Kronstam, constantly telling the younger man that he would not be able to survive without Gerstenberg's support.

Although nearly everyone in the Theatre was aware of Kronstam and Gerstenberg's relationship, Copenhagen as a whole was not. Kronstam accepted his homosexuality, in the sense that he did not fight it or try to hide it, but he was not proud of it and always felt like an outsider. Like his father, Kronstam wanted very much to be "proper," and it was not proper for two men to live together in 1952. Kronstam called Gerstenberg Farbrør (father's brother, one of the Danish words for uncle) until the end of his life. He went to parties either alone or with a female friend because "going with Franz wasn't allowed." He lived a very private life, giving few interviews and inviting few people into his home. Partly this was because he was reserved by nature and protective of his privacy, and partly because his home was a sanctuary, the only place where he could relax and be himself. But the secrecy was also because Kronstam, from the beginning, knew exactly what kind of artist he wanted to be. Unlike most theatrical people, who make sure they are always in the news, attending film and gallery openings and other important social events ever ready with a good quote, Kronstam kept his private life private and restricted his performances to the stage. He did not want to assume a concrete personality in the public's mind because he wanted to be free to show a hundred different personalities on the stage. "I always tried to hold something back," he said. "I always wanted there to be some mystery."

I had the good luck to dance at a time
when there were great choreographers.
—Henning Kronstam

Six

The Pepper Boy in the Sugar Bowl

It is an irony that the career of this most Danish of dancers was so inextricably
linked with foreigners. It was the guest choreographers—Balanchine, Taras,
Ashton, Petit, Birgit Cullberg—who would give Kronstam his first big roles.
During his first two and a half years as a company member, he was cast in very
few roles in the Danish repertory. In addition to the political aspects already
mentioned—that several older dancers who had felt passed over by Lander in
Kronstam's favor had successfully pressed the new director, Niels Bjørn
Larsen, for his roles—Larsen preferred small, quick, demi-caractère dancers,
commenting that Kronstam had been "a good dancer, but not so good a mime"
(a singular opinion), explaining, "he was not demi-caractère." Kronstam would
likely have been given the few classical roles then in the Danish repertory eventually, but in his teenage years, he danced mostly in the corps. Had Vera

Volkova not come to Copenhagen, with her eye for classical dancers and her contacts with the era's major choreographers, it is likely that Kronstam would have followed his childhood ambition and transferred to the Theatre's drama department.[1]

But Volkova did come and Kronstam stayed, and with her he "worked like a devil."[2] The hard work was soon rewarded. By the time he was twenty he had made his breakthrough and within two years he would be established as a leading dancer. Many of the roles he danced in these early years remained the core roles in his repertory; they will be discussed in more detail in part 2 and given only the briefest of summaries here. However, the minor roles, as well as several important events in his professional and personal life, shed light on Kronstam's development as an artist. Lessons learned during this period, on stage and off, were important not only to his education as a dancer but his future as a ballet master. "I was never one of those who left the room when I wasn't actually in the rehearsal," as he put it. "I was always watching."

In the autumn of 1952, during Kronstam's first season as a company member, Volkova persuaded George Balanchine to come to Copenhagen and stage *Symphony in C*. It is surprising that Balanchine would agree to give the company this ballet; it was quite new, having been created for the Paris Opera Ballet (where it is called *Le Palais de Cristal*) only four years earlier. It was a ballet worthy of Paris, requiring virtuoso soloists and a strong corps de ballet. Volkova took the theater chief, Henning Brøndsted, to see the ballet when New York City Ballet was on tour in Europe and urged him to acquire it. Balanchine agreed to come to Copenhagen to cast "the Bizet," as dancers usually refer to *Symphony in C*.

Balanchine chose Kronstam as a "side boy" for the first movement and began rehearsals. "He came in on a Saturday," Kronstam said, "and asked Schanne and Schaufuss, Eva Plaun, Mette Mollerup, Kjeld Noack, and me to come in for rehearsal the next day. It was the first movement and he thought that it should be very brilliantly danced." (Margrethe Schanne and Frank Schaufuss were the first movement's leading couple; Mona Vangsaae and Børge Ralov did the second movement; Inge Sand and Erik Bruhn, the third; and Kirsten Ralov and Stanley Williams led the fourth.) Balanchine then turned the rehearsals over to an assistant, Vida Brown.

Symphony in C was popular with the audience and well received by the critics—the third movement, with its exuberant jumpers, was the favorite[3]—and, as Volkova had hoped, the ballet remained in the repertory. Kronstam soon replaced Ralov in the second movement, and later danced the leading male role in the first movement as well.

Kronstam worked with Volkova on this, as on nearly every ballet he danced. He also took her afternoon aspirants' class (in addition to his morning company class) until he was twenty-four. Volkova gave him strength and polished his technique, but probably the most important thing he got from her was his sense of weight. The Danish style under Lander had been very light, very demi-caractère, and Kronstam, who was by physique as well as temperament a danseur noble, had adapted his body to this in his early training.[4] He had an unusual speed and lightness for so tall a man, but Volkova wanted to give him the weight needed to dance the Petipa repertory as well. She did this by working on his plié, stressing the importance of feeling the floor, pushing down into the floor, not escaping from it. This not only prepared Kronstam for the Prince roles, but it was this sense of weighted movement that is at least partly responsible for his later success in modern-dance roles.

Volkova also took charge of Kronstam's artistic education, suggesting books for him to read, mostly biographies of other dancers or theater people; he was especially intrigued by Isadora Duncan, who he thought "had led a fascinating life!" He read Hans Beck's memoirs, as well as those of Ulla Poulsen and Clara Pontoppidan (a Danish dancer and actress respectively). There were several copies of Richard Buckle's magazine, *Ballet*, from the early 1950s on his shelves.[5] Kronstam spoke of Volkova's guidance in an interview in *Information* by "m" in January 1957. After saying that the most difficult time for him at the company was when he was sixteen or seventeen, because "the older ones were always standing in my way!" he said: "Here is where Madame Volkova was invaluable. She takes particular care of all the young, those who are in the middle, between the children's school and the adult positions, and are neither fowl nor fish: She took her time to talk with us—and she gave me other ballet people's memoirs to read. And so I could see that they had all felt the way I did."

Volkova also urged him to start visiting museums, so this was how he and Gerstenberg would spend their Sundays. He was listening to music on his own, becoming especially interested in opera and chamber music; according to longtime friend Lene Schrøder-Hansen, he hated jazz. During this period he wrote a review entitled "Couldn't We Get a Couple of Hours of Late Night

Music," in which he critiqued a week's worth of programming on Danish radio. His comments show that his aesthetic judgment and sense of humor were
already evident:

> I expected a lot from *Tourist in the Copenhagen of Christian IV,* which was
> announced as a picture by Harry Kaae and hung by Viggo Clausen. The idea
> seemed to have possibilities, but unfortunately, in my view, these went awry.
> The painting was hung very loosely, and as the program progressed, it fell
> completely apart. It was very hard to stay focused, despite a few good passages.
>
> You get a lot more out of the half-hour Sunday programs, *Visit in Old
> Copenhagen,* by Peter Linde. These give a much different picture of the times
> and open your eyes to many interesting details of the monuments and architec-
> ture of the city in an inspiring way, and it does so without those humorous
> interruptions which *Tourist in the Copenhagen of Christian IV* had, and which I
> could have done without.
>
> Saturday night, Wilmer Sorensen had a program called *Light Saturday,* with
> something for everyone and well put together. Time and again, you are sur-
> prised by the ability of that magician, Wilmer Sorensen, to put a program
> together that caters to the whole family. It was light without being ridiculous
> and it was nice to be without the applause of the studio audience, which has
> become the norm on Saturday programming. This can be very distracting, as
> the applause often is for passages meant for the eye and therefore not under-
> stood by listeners.
>
> How wonderful to see how elegantly Wilmer Sorensen includes an aria by
> Mozart in a light Saturday program. It is possible that many listeners, normally
> fearful of turning on a Mozart program, were led in this way to the first step in
> understanding the beauty and worth of classical works. This was a program that
> made you forget that you were tied to the radio by duty on a warm June night. A
> light program, but not too light. Bravo. . . .
>
> *The Fall of a Tyrant* was on *Radio Theatre of the Week,* a program I had looked
> forward to praising. Everyone worked hard from 8:20 to 10:00 P.M., but in
> consideration of the writer and the director, I will refrain from commenting on
> this program.
>
> Finally a little sigh. All winter long I and many others have to work night after
> night in a poor attempt to give the audience an enriching night in the theater.
> But when we, tired, return home for a cup of tea before bed, all that's left to hear
> on the radio is the last notes of the Danish national anthem. Night workers also
> have a need for a couple of hours of programming. It could be gramophone
> programs of some seriousness if the personnel's contracts give them the right
> to leave early, or if it's because of neighbors—well. Night listeners just tune to

foreign stations anyway, where you can always find programming until 1:00 or 2:00 A.M. And by the way, a radio can be turned to a level where it is enjoyable to you without annoying others.

In addition to supervising his artistic education, Volkova also saved Kronstam from the army. There is universal conscription in Denmark and young men are required to serve two years in the armed services. Kronstam's older brother had done his service, so Kronstam knew what army life would be like. "If I had marched for two years in those boots," he said, "my feet would have been ruined." He registered for the draft but sought a deferment, which was apparently easy to get. Volkova's theory was that if the young men kept postponing their service until the last possible minute, there was a good chance they'd have an injury serious enough to allow them a permanent deferment, which is what happened in Kronstam's case. Despite his pride in his grandfather's military service, Kronstam did not regret missing a taste of military life. "I asked the sergeant what I would do in the army," Kronstam said, "and he told me, 'We'll have you peeling potatoes.'"

Kronstam got his first chance in a big role at the beginning of his second season, the autumn of 1953, and it was, in his words, "my disaster." It was also

Kronstam and Simone in the pas de deux from *The Nutcracker,* 1953. Photo: Mydtskov. The Royal Theatre, Copenhagen. By permission of Det kongelige Teaters bibliotek og arkiv.

his baptism by fire into the wicked ways of ballet politics, as the critics used his performance as an opportunity to make a frontal assault on Larsen's directorship. The ballet was Harald Lander's *Nutcracker* pas de deux, the one Lander had taught Kronstam three years earlier and that the young dancer had expected to dance the year the Lander Scandal temporarily derailed his career.

After the company returned from its highly successful first visit to London in the autumn of 1953, Volkova coached Kronstam and Kirsten Simone (who had danced the pas de deux the year before with Erik Bruhn) in the duet and urged Larsen to let them perform it. The debut was finally scheduled, at the end of a very long evening following a five-act play by the nineteenth-century playwright (and powerful theater chief) Heiberg, a curious double bill. As soon as the casting was announced there were rumblings by those angry that Volkova would dare stage what they considered "Lander's ballet." Hugh Williams remembered that there was so much anxiety backstage that the theater chief feared his administration would be threatened if Kronstam did not dance well. Williams said that the performance went so well, in fact, that Brøndsted's wife turned to Williams and Volkova with a satisfied nod and gave a thumbs-up at its conclusion.[6]

That was not how the critics saw it and their opinions were delivered in unusually strong language. Danish reviews of this period were written for a general readership; there was very rarely any detailed critical analysis, especially regarding technique, and even more rarely anything resembling an overt personal attack. After the Lander Scandal, however, reviews were very political. Erik Bruhn felt he was a victim: "When I got back [to Copenhagen] in 1952, my role in the Lander affair had obviously harmed my reputation and people were out to get me. For one whole year the press treated me abominably. They wrote that I was the most horrible and inartistic dancer. They wrote I was star conscious. They said, 'Who does this twenty-three-year-old dancer think he is?' And they pointed out the names of younger dancers, saying that I had better watch out or I would be out of the ballet business quicker than I thought. If I had taken all that abuse seriously, I would be dead by now."[7] Kronstam was one of the "younger dancers" the critics were using to get at Bruhn, but for *Nutcracker* they turned on him as well, attacking Larsen's directorship, but attacking Kronstam too, and the reviews seem all the more harsh because he was so young. Passages from several reviews are quoted here to show how heated the ballet politics of this period were and what a firestorm one pas de deux had ignited. Larsen even had to give an interview defending his actions, with the headline "The Young in Ballet Shall Have Their Chance." Beneath the barbs, there are some interesting descriptions of Kronstam as a dancer.

"Not Defensible" was the headline on Harald Engberg's review in *Politiken* (one of Copenhagen's leading newspapers, politically centrist and intellectual), which said, in part: "Henning Kronstam is so appealing and talented a dancer that one should not expose him as a partner in a virtuoso act. He cannot present a ballerina. . . . There are beautiful lines in his long jumps, but they skim closely to the floor. The two partners became each other, like youth becomes youth, but there was no *ballon* in their movements, and certainly no style as a whole. It was irresponsible. And the ballet master should have seen that."

Bent Schønberg, in *Ekstra Bladet* (one of several Danish tabloids, although Schønberg was a respected, if rather gossipy, critic), wrote that Kronstam

> can be complimented for having acquired more restrained facial expressions [than his predecessors] and for his entrechats. Unfortunately, this is where the words of praise run out. Not even first-night nerves can explain the many weaknesses in the dancer that this demanding pas de deux revealed in a most dumbfounding way. His partnering was insecure and in several instances damaged the ballerina. His jumps had no élan and his tours en l'air did not finish in clean positions. Sadly, nothing here gave promise of great things in any near future. On the contrary, one must assume that Kronstam will have to work hard, and for a long time, before accepting a task as demanding as this one again.

According to Allan Fridericia, the critic of the communist paper *Information*, whose taste for Soviet culture was not limited to ballet, "The technique was on a high, though far from convincing, level. Mostly it was the dancer's looks that made you believe in his future. Henning Kronstam is masculine; he has a well-shaped, tall, and beautiful figure. The feet are uniquely fine and shaped in a high arch that leads one's thoughts to Poul Gnatt. Henning Kronstam has much to learn. His movements lack emotion and in several places the jumps seemed low, without elevation. It was really only at the beginning of the coda that one saw the dancer jump high." The comments about the low jumps are quite probably a misunderstanding of the kind of sophisticated dancing Volkova was restoring to Kongens Nytorv. The critics were used to a hard-sell approach, where the dancer expended as much visible effort in his first seconds on stage as he did in the last, while Volkova was teaching a more modulated sense of dynamics. Likewise, Engberg's complaint about the lack of ballon, so essential to Bournonville style, indicates he was unaccustomed to seeing weightier Russian jumps.

Fridericia ended his review with a not-so-veiled attack on Larsen and Volkova, noting that no stager for the pas de deux was credited on the poster, a departure from tradition. "It becomes more and more obvious why the Royal Theatre prefers this particular procedure. There is no stager. . . . The performance borders on the scandalous, and the procedure harms the young people like Kirsten Simone and Henning Kronstam. I have no doubt that their dancing could have been different had there been a director who would not have put them on stage until giving them artistic confidence, enthusiasm, and discipline in the dance."

Writing in *Berlingske Tidende* (Copenhagen's other leading newspaper, this one more establishment and pro-business), "nls" (possibly Nils Schiørring) had a different, though equally harsh, view. First, commenting on the placement of the pas de deux at the very end of a long evening: "That could have made another man run amok, but he took it rather well. He is a handsome man to look at. He has a handsome figure, beautiful posture, and manly movements. Those are not bad qualities and one would like to see them promoted at the ballet. But the art needs more than this, including mind and temper. Neither in his interaction with Simone nor in his solo did he express experience, and even less fantasy. Even if, for a mere second, his dancing did have momentum, technically it did not go beyond discipline."

As will often happen in this story, the backstage view differs markedly from that on the printed page. Kronstam was unhappy with his performance, saying he was so focused on the technical side of the role that there "was no nuance to it," but others thought that the reviews were overly negative. Larsen said that Kronstam had no trouble with the steps, "he just didn't know how to sell it." Arlette Weinreich (a dancer who later worked with both Brenaa and Kronstam directing ballets), who had seen the performance and remembered it though she had been only a schoolgirl, said, "Henning hadn't learned how to smile yet. He was like this [miming mechanical, like a toy soldier]."

As fate would have it, Kirsten Simone, who has many films of her roles, has one of the adagio from this performance. It shows two very talented and mature young dancers. Although it is not a warm performance, and both were a bit overcareful, Simone never lost her center, Kronstam presented her beautifully, and Fru Brøndsted's thumbs-up to Volkova seems quite justified.

Kronstam, always extremely sensitive to criticism, said he weathered the storm by ignoring the critics and listening to Volkova. Later, when he was artistic director, dancers would comment that Kronstam always listened to his own voice in determining whether a performance went well or not. No matter how glowing the reviews were, or how loud the applause, if a performance was not up to standard, he would know it; conversely, if a first-rate performance was ignored or panned, he would stand behind it. It is likely that he learned this valuable lesson, as well as a lifelong mistrust of critics, from the *Nutcracker* experience.

Kronstam danced in three relatively unimportant ballets during these two and a half years: in the corps of Frank Schaufuss's *Idolon* (The Idol; set to Tchaikovsky's *Serenade for Strings*); as a coolie in Børge Ralov's *Kurtisanen* (The Courtesan; which Erik Aschengreen wittily describes as "an erotic ballet without eroticism");[8] and as an artist in Birger Bartholin's *Parisiana* ("we were atmosphere," as Kronstam put it.) In May 1954, Kronstam inherited the second movement of *Symphony in C* from Børge Ralov. At that time stars still owned roles and could decide when they no longer wished to dance them. ("He did three or four performances and then he wrote to me and said, 'Henning, be good to Mona. She's too much for me,'" Kronstam said.)

Kronstam was an unscheduled substitute for the African Chief in the 1787 Vincenzo Galeotti ballet *The Whims of Cupid and the Ballet Master*, standing in for an injured Svend Karlog, a much older man. "I did my own makeup and I thought I was quite wonderful. The King was really *evil* at that time, with human bones hanging from his belt," Kronstam remembered. "But Svend Kragh[-Jacobsen] wrote that it was a scandal to send a young boy down to do that role, so maybe [the makeup] wasn't as good as I thought."

At the beginning of the 1954–55 season Kronstam was a last-minute substitute again, filling in for two very different dancers in Larsen's *Lunefulde Lucinda* (Capricious Lucinda), a lighthearted work inspired by a 1796 Galeotti ballet. The ballet was a series of vignettes that showed the many moods of Lucinda (Inge Sand), and Kronstam was in two scenes, dancing Harlekin (for Anker Ørskov, with Solveig Østergaard) that showed her in a happy mood, and Neptune (for Frank Schaufuss, with Mona Vangsaae) that showed a more romantic side. "It was light but Niels Bjørn wanted something edible for the audience,"

Kronstam said. The critics felt that the ballet would have been suitable for Tivoli's Pantomime Theatre but was not weighty enough for the Royal Theatre.

In January 1955, John Taras came to Copenhagen to stage Balanchine's *Søvngængersken* (The Sleepwalker; now known in the United States as *La Sonnambula*) and chose Kronstam as the Poet, giving the Royal Danish Ballet one of its most popular works and Kronstam his first starring role. Larsen had seen the ballet danced by the de Cuevas company and "knew right away that this

Kronstam with Margrethe Schanne in *La Sonnambula;* from a 1956 calendar. Photo: Mydtskov. Private collection.

would be a good ballet for us," Kronstam said. It was a dramatic ballet with lots of dancing and—one of the most important criteria for a Danish ballet master—good roles for several soloists. Kronstam and his Sleepwalker, Margrethe Schanne, gave exceptional performances, and the rest of the cast included Børge Ralov as the Baron, Mona Vangsaae as the Coquette, Inge Sand and Fredbjørn Bjørnsson as the Negro couple, and the eighteen-year-old Flemming Flindt as Harlequin.

Kronstam was admired by the critics as well as his fellow artists in this role, which he danced for twenty years. He felt he had achieved a breakthrough, not only in the sense that it advanced his career but also that he learned from working with Taras "how to hold the stage while standing still." This is one of the main images dancers remember from his performances. Ib Andersen, who saw Kronstam dance the role in the early 1970s, said, "His entrance was the most amazing thing. Actually there was no entrance; he just appeared, and even though he was standing still, you couldn't take your eyes off him. There was almost a glow about him."

Two months later Frederick Ashton came to Copenhagen to choreograph *Romeo and Juliet* for the company. This was the first full-evening work created for the Danish ballet in decades and, some would say, the most important ballet made on it in the entire twentieth century. Expectations were high and everybody wanted to be in it. Mona Vangsaae and Frank Schaufuss had scored a big success in Bartholin's very popular chamber version of the story to the Tchaikovsky score two years ago, and there was a faction that thought they had a right to the same roles in the new ballet. Others, who considered Margrethe Schanne the company's prima ballerina, felt the ballet should be hers.

According to Hugh Williams there was no doubt, from the moment Ashton laid eyes on Kronstam, that this would be his Romeo. Volkova brought Ashton in to watch class on a Sunday. Some of the dancers were absent, as they were dancing out of town with Inge Sand's group. When they returned and learned they had missed what was essentially an audition, they asked for a chance too. Ashton watched class Monday morning as well, but he didn't change his mind. His Juliet would be Mona Vangsaae because of her long lines and sweet lyricism, and his Romeo would be Henning Kronstam, only twenty and still in the corps.

Kronstam learned of it by reading the cast list on the company bulletin board: "There, out of the clear blue sky, on the wall: Romeo, Henning Kron-

Frederick Ashton re-
hearses Mona Vangsaae
and Kronstam in *Romeo
and Juliet,* 1956. Photo:
Mydtskov. The Royal
Theatre, Copenhagen.
By permission of Det
kongelige Teaters
bibliotek og arkiv.

stam." It was not a popular decision. Larsen again was pressured but, according to Williams, backed Ashton's choice, as did Volkova, of course. Frank
Schaufuss was so upset at not being given Romeo that Ashton, who cast him
as Mercutio, told him that when the ballet was finished, if he didn't like the role
he wouldn't have to dance it. Part of the lore surrounding the seven weeks of
rehearsals for the ballet are tales that Ashton was so nervous that he vomited
every morning on his way to the studio from his room at the Hotel
D'Angleterre, across the square from the Theatre. It is usually assumed that he
was worried about the way work was progressing, but it was instead the backstage intrigues that made him ill. The only one Kronstam chose to remember
was that the Theatre's dressmaker, a close friend of Schanne, was so furious
that she had not been cast as Juliet that he refused to make the dresses for the
ballet unless the casting was changed. The Theatre hired another dressmaker.

Despite the nerves and the intrigues, the ballet was a success and, as Erik
Aschengreen would later write, "For Henning Kronstam, Romeo was a tri-

umph."[9] The audience was unusually enthusiastic; on opening night there were nine curtain calls, an unprecedented event, as curtain calls were not allowed in the Royal Theatre at that time except on benefit nights as a matter of law (stemming from a court scandal centuries earlier). Vangsaae was overcome by emotion at the audience response and told Kronstam in the wings, "You will probably live it again, but I will never have another night like this."

The 1954–55 season was important to Kronstam not only because of the Poet and Romeo, but also because it is when he began to make appearances away from the company as a guest artist. In the summer of 1955 he took part in a festival devoted to opera and opera ballets in Aix-en-Provence. He had agreed to this engagement before Inge Sand invited him to dance with her Soloists of the Royal Danish Ballet at Jacob's Pillow, and so missed being part of the group that introduced Bournonville and Danish dancing to North America, although he would later dance with the troupe in Europe and Latin America.

In Aix, Kronstam danced in two opera ballets choreographed by John Taras, who had arranged the invitation: *The Marriage of Figaro*, and *Orpheus and Eurydice*, partnering Colette Marchand in the former and Violette Verdy in the

The curtain call, opening night, *Romeo and Juliet*. Mona Vangsaae and Kronstam are in the front row. Private collection.

Kronstam and Violette Verdy in John Taras's *Orpheus and Eurydice*. Performance shot, 1956. Private collection.

latter. Kronstam and Gerstenberg stayed with Verdy and her mother in a house Mme. Verdy had found. Verdy is one of the few people who seemed to like Gerstenberg, finding him "very polite, very gentlemanly, and very protective of Henning," and said they all got along well. Verdy's assessment of Kronstam as a dancer is particularly interesting because it is a pure snapshot of him as a very young dancer, unspoiled by subsequent images, as Verdy did not often see him dance in later years: "He was an absolutely beautiful dancer, one of the best I have ever seen by any standard, even with the Danes. Technically, he was able to do absolutely anything, of course, but he also had a feminine quality in the sense that his line and the softness of his dancing was also very beautiful, and that gave his dancing a more complete feeling. He wasn't just doing macho tricks."

The two rehearsed in Toulon and Verdy remembered Kronstam as very disciplined and very obedient, very much "a product of a great academy." Kronstam remembered there had been a ruckus over the costumes. In *Orpheus,* he wore the costume of an eighteenth-century danseur noble, with garters, plumed helmet, and tonnelet (a skirt modeled on the ancient Roman toga).

Verdy was in twentieth-century ballerina garb, slightly adapted to the time period of the opera, but her tutu was stiff and belled out when she turned. "My
skirt had pleats," Kronstam said, "and fell beautifully when I danced. Mama
Verdy was furious and wanted Violette's costume changed, but they wouldn't
do it, so the afternoon of the premiere she got out her scissors and cut pleats
into Violette's skirt." Mme. Verdy was the prototypical ballet mother and famous for doing anything that would help her gifted daughter. Verdy's skirt
now moved beautifully.

Kronstam's part in *Marriage of Figaro* was in a divertissement, danced with
the French ballerina Colette Marchand. After Taras left, Kronstam said March-
and changed the choreography. "There's no reason that it should be so difficult," she told him.

Kronstam felt that his stay in Aix did a great deal to form his taste and
"awaken my love of beauty," as he put it. "Just being in that city, seeing beauty
every day. It was the whole atmosphere, the audience. I had never seen anything like this." The festival also introduced him to someone who would later
be important to his career: Ruth Page, the glamorous and eccentric choreographer who headed the Chicago Opera Ballet. She and her husband, Tom Fisher,
had a villa in St. Tropez, and Taras drove down there one Sunday and told Page
she had to see Kronstam. She did and would later sign him as a guest star for
her company.

In August the Royal Danish Ballet went to the Edinburgh Festival, where
Kronstam received excellent notices, especially for *Romeo* and *Sonnambula.*

Volkova had lured Jerome Robbins to Copenhagen to stage a ballet for the
1955–56 season. Kronstam had been invited to dance at the wedding of Grace
Kelly and Prince Rainier in Monaco that year, as had Toni Lander, Margrethe
Schanne, and Flemming Flindt. However, the Theatre would not let him go
because Robbins was coming to stage *Fanfare,* and they presumed the young
dancer, who now was the only male soloist with a strong technique left at
home, would be needed.[10] To Kronstam's disappointment there was no role for
him in *Fanfare.* According to Kronstam, Robbins explained, "No one told me
about you, Henning." "He came to do *Fanfare,*" Kronstam said, "and all he
wanted to do was *Afternoon of a Faun* for me."

Kronstam's new roles that season were the Poet in *Chopiniana* and Wilhelm, the almost faithless young lieutenant in Bournonville's *Far from Denmark. Chopiniana*[11] added yet another poet to his growing gallery of sensitive

young men. Fokine had set the ballet during his stay in Copenhagen in the 1920s (along with *Petrushka* and *Polovetsian Dances*). Reviews of *Chopiniana* give an interesting picture of Kronstam as a dancer at this time, and also provide insight into the way Danish critics viewed ballet during this period. It was still enough of a rarity for a Danish male dancer to wear tights that a reviewer would take note of the costume, as this review by "mumme" indicates:

> Fokine's lovely little divertissement, *Chopiniana,* is the playground for the new hope of the ballet at the moment. . . . Yesterday, Henning Kronstam took over the male role.
>
> The young dancer has caliber and calm. He looked beautiful in classical tights and he showed that he can do more than be just an effective background to the floating sylphs. In his solo dancing, he made one happy by his forceful jumps, and in his dances with Kirsten Simone and Inge Sand he became a beautiful part of the whole. (February 13, 1956)

Kronstam was constantly compared to Bruhn in the first decade of his career. Under the headline "New Signs That He Will Take the Inheritance from Erik Bruhn," in *Berlingske Tidende,* "nls" wrote:

> The very young and promising dancer of the ballet, Henning Kronstam, jumped in last night to perform Fokine and Ralov's *Chopiniana,* a courageous and a beautiful jump, considering the glory that surrounds the part from its previous owner, Erik Bruhn [who danced the part at his] royal good-bye. But Kronstam is a proud jumper. Boldly he put all precautions aside and placed himself beautifully in the not too easy aims of the task. . . .
>
> He is naturally suited to the male solo, dancing amid the white flutter of Sylphs in the woodsy atmosphere, simply by his classical stature—he is a stately young man—and in the harmonic calm of his style. Add to that, in the Mazurka and in the Waltz with Kirsten Simone, the virile strength and beauty of his plastique, still slightly dormant and only barely matured, but all the more promising. His partnering is characterized by sensitivity, and his jumps by inspired flight. As a mime, however, he doesn't let one know of any experience of either the music or the dancing. This impenetrable nostalgia though surrounded by so many lovely girls—is this serious dancing really [supposed to be] this inhumanely serious? It is, however, written that the part must be like this. It is an ironclad act of male loneliness in a white world of girls, a pepper boy in the sugar bowl, and there too Kronstam fits in as a spoon for a bowl.

"F.D." indicated that Kronstam had matured as a technician: "Last night, Henning Kronstam danced the male solo part in *Chopiniana* for the first time.

Kronstam with Kirsten Simone in Fokine's *Chopiniana*. Photo: Mydtskov. The Royal Theatre, Copenhagen. By permission of Det kongelige Teaters bibliotek og arkiv.

And, as was to be expected, Kronstam superbly became a part of the unreal romantic atmosphere that inhabits the production of Fokine's famous divertissement at Kongens Nytorv. His lyrical appearance and wiry ease become the part, and his superlative technique makes him capable of performing it with a great sense of naturalness" (February 13, 1956).

Anne Chaplin Hansen wrote more of Kronstam's interpretation than his jumps: "Kronstam gave all his melancholic Weltschmerz in this melodic moonlight where Sylphs float, play birds, and flirt with Chopin performed by orchestra. Fine style, plastique and sensitivity, this is the specialty of Kronstam, from his young Poet in *Sonnambula* to Prokofiev's *Romeo,* and in *Chopiniana* he reaches nothing less than an idealization of himself, an oversensitive flight which is revealed to perfection in the enchanting waltz with Kirsten Simone" (February 13, 1956).

Bournonville's merry *Far from Denmark* is set in a completely different world from *Chopiniana*'s haunted glade. *Far from Denmark* is Bournonville's "American" ballet, inspired by Louis Moreau Gottschalk's "Negro Dance," which Bournonville thought would make a charming ballet. He initially had difficulty figuring out how to get Danes to the New World but, as Denmark had colonies in the Caribbean, he decided to bring them by sea.[12] The ballet's hero, Wilhelm, is a young lieutenant whose ship is anchored in the waters off Argentina. There he meets an enticing señorita, flirts with her and forgets, for a few moments, that he is engaged. Just in time, he remembers his true love and does not stray. The ballet was popular through much of the twentieth century, partly because of its Negro Dance (Bournonville was proud to point out that they were *servants,* not slaves, and that Denmark was the first country in the world to abolish slavery) and other character dances—Eskimos, Red Indians, Chinese—and partly because of two rare "breeches parts," where the company's youngest ballerinas-to-be take the roles of two (male) cadets.

Wilhelm was Kronstam's first leading Bournonville role, and he was praised for his mime. He attributed this to his work with Gerda Karstens in the aspirant mime classes. "I remember they had a beautiful notice [i.e., review] about it," Kronstam said in his "Oral History," "and they said it was fantastic to see a young man in one of his first roles walk on the stage and do all that mime." In gratitude, Kronstam cut out the review and sent it to Karstens with flowers.[13] In another cast, he danced the Chinese dance, with its many jumps from a deep plié, alternating both roles with Stanley Williams. He also danced the virtuoso pas de trois in Bournonville's *La Ventana* with Inge Sand and Kirsten Ralov.

In the summer of 1956, Kronstam again took part in the Aix-en-Provence festival, this time dancing in a Taras opera ballet, *Platée,* with French ballerina Janine Monin. This was a Harlequinade to a seventeenth-century score by

Kronstam with Mette Mollerup in the Zouave Galop from Emilie Walbom's *Dream Pictures*. On tour in Ireland with the Inge Sand group. Photo: James O'Callaghan. Private collection.

Kronstam with Kirsten Ralov (left) and Inge Sand (right) in the pas de trois from Bournonville's *La Ventana*, 1956. Private collection.

Rameau, and the French critic André-M. Alautzen wrote that Kronstam was "la future grande étoile mondiale" (the future world superstar), a quote that was picked up by the Danish press.

Although many expected that Kronstam would be promoted immediately after his performances in *La Sonnambula* and *Romeo and Juliet,* he was not given the rank of solo dancer until halfway through the season, on January 1, 1956.[14] He was twenty-one. By this time the critics had begun to accept him. What Bent Schønberg wrote in May 1956 is very far from what he had written in the fall of 1953: "Another positive experience in the performance was Henning Kronstam in *Søvngængersken* and the Bournonville ballet [*The Kermesse in Bruges,* where Kronstam danced the "gold" pas de deux]. Here too one is faced with a gifted artist who continues to develop rapidly. His mime is excellent and his looks are in such perfect synch with the two roles he portrays. It is more than sad that we will lose Bruhn again, but it's a great comfort to know that we will keep Kronstam."

In September 1956 the Royal Danish Ballet made its first tour to North America, appearing in twelve cities,[15] traveling by train from one city to the next. The previous summer English and American critics had been invited to the company's summer festival, where they had been charmed by the company and had written glowing reviews. Thus expectations were high, and so was the pressure. New York, especially, would not be an easy success. Every city has its politics. In the 1950s, in addition to an ongoing battle between the native modern dance and what some Americans still considered foreign ballet, there was a division between fans of the Ballets Russes and Ballet Theatre, with their emphasis on stars, story ballets, and an extrovert performing style, and the followers of George Balanchine and the "no star" New York City Ballet, with its repertory of contemporary, often pure dance, ballets. The two major critics, John Martin and Walter Terry, had gone to the Copenhagen festival the preceding spring and were very enthusiastic about the season, but they also expected Erik Bruhn to be the star, and, at the last minute, Bruhn learned that Ballet Theatre would not let him dance with his home company in New York.

This gave Kronstam an enormous opportunity. He would have danced the Poet and Romeo in any case, but Bruhn's absence gave him his chance at James in *La Sylphide.* Børge Ralov was still the company's senior dancer, but he was in his forties (and did not dance James). Ralov would dance *Petrushka,* and Gennaro in *Napoli,* but otherwise the New York season was Kronstam's. Oddly, it was his ascension to a comparatively small role that brought this fact home to him. "When I learned that I had been cast as the center boy in ballabile [in *Napoli*], well, that was Erik's role and that was when I knew that they were pinning the whole season on me," he said.

Kronstam made his debut as James on opening night of the company's season at the Metropolitan Opera House in New York in a double bill of *La Sylphide* and *Graduation Ball* (in which he danced the Drummer). Walter Terry's review makes Kronstam's performance seem an extraordinarily finished debut: "Dash and brio, however, were appropriate to [the Sylph's] Scottish lover and young Henning Kronstam soared in dazzling leaps, led a Scottish ensemble dance with vigor and invested his mime with force and emotional urgency" (*New York Herald Tribune*, September 1, 1956).

The company was generally well received throughout North America. It was admired for the dancers' appealing personalities and its ensemble spirit. Even the stern Russian émigré critic Anatole Chujoy, writing in *Dance News*, liked the company (except for its production of *Petrushka*, which he felt had gone badly astray). There is, however, a condescending tone in some of the reviews. Martin called *Napoli* "pure theatrical corn, but heartwarming" (*New York Times*, September 19, 1956). Several critics found *La Sylphide* old-fashioned and of only historical interest.

To some, the company was charming but clung to a hopelessly outmoded tradition. In addition, several critics mistook the understated, pure classical dancing of the Danes for weak technique. One wrote that Kronstam danced the extremely difficult solo in *La Ventana* well, but "it certainly wasn't taxing." The notion that the company was merely a museum, clinging desperately to its Romantic past because it had no present, was a view widely held by American (and British) critics, which the Danes naturally resented; it also had an unfortunate influence on the company's development. The British and American companies were new, their traditions barely decades old, and there may well have been an undercurrent of resentment beneath the condescension. Four contrasting reviews present differing American attitudes.

T. H. Parker saw the Danish repertory in purely commercial terms—a view that must have seemed curious to Danish readers.

> One may easily believe that at home, the Royal company is loved nostalgically as the keeper of a national art which is almost a legend. And for foreigners who think of Denmark and Hans Christian Andersen as inseparable, Romanticism

will of course have permanent allure. In both cases, the Danish Ballet may feel it is making a contribution to audiences, and receiving a return contribution at the box office.

As has been remarked by others, however, the Royal Danish Ballet appears to feel that its devotion to the wellsprings of dance is exactly what gives it its particular distinction, not to say salability. To widen its views and activities would make it just another European company and force it into the rat-race of competition. At the same time, it is fundamentally a sound troupe and it seems too bad that it should dwell like a recluse in the cloisters of the past entirely. (*Hartford Courant*, October 7, 1956)

Herbert Whitaker saw the good in the old and the new:

[*La Sylphide*] a quaint old legend, besmacking of a bygone theatre as well as of a discarded literature. But last night this work became as true as any story in today's newspaper. The Royal Danish dancers, under the direction of Frank Schaufuss and Hans Brenaa, who have carried over the Bournonville choreography from Harald Lander, know how to make *La Sylphide* true within its tradition, so that we can sit rapt as Danish audiences have for 120 years.

The performing of this miracle of conviction is the work of the whole company, all sharing easily and confidently in the tradition, but naturally the two leading interpreters must supply the chief magic. This Margrethe Schanne and Henning Kronstam did generously.

Miss Schanne, the Sonnambula of the opening night, here again exhibited amazing gifts of technique, creating in the lovelorn Sylphide a figure of airy grace, a creature of delicacy in mind and form, with no more stamina than a moth, to be burnt away in a moment of flame.

Mr. Kronstam, the Poet of the preceding night, is again a worthy partner to Miss Schanne, making the fickle Scottish lover wildly sincere and a true slave of passion. His dancing, as his miming, was always excellent and he will understand the compliment when we say that he made us forget his great predecessor in the role—Erik Bruhn—while he was on the stage. (*Globe and Mail*, September 17, 1956)

Walter Terry, who seems to have understood the Danish style and traditions as well as, if not better than, any of his colleagues, wrote in his opening-night review: "It is impossible not to love those splendid Danish artists who perform with bubbling, sparkling friendliness, who dance as if they were in love with dancing and all who shared their enthusiasm. The Royal Danes, however, do far more than bubble and project their undeniable charm. They have a great and unique tradition of ballet and they manage, by some miracle, to preserve that tradition while investing it with contemporary vitality and present technical skill" (*New York Herald Tribune*, September 17, 1956).

John Martin of the *New York Times* took a middle view, combining an appreciation of the tradition with a suggestion that change was in order: "On many sides, these developments [foreign choreographers and the work of Volkova] are now being greeted with misgivings. It is feared that the characteristic Bournonville flavor will ultimately be lost and the Danish ballet will become simply one more European company. This is a risk that cannot be ignored, to be sure, but it must be taken. You cannot live in the past, no matter how great a past it may have been" (September 28, 1956).

The mixed message—that the company upheld proud traditions only it could bring to life (heard in Denmark as "they should dance only Bournonville") yet was completely out of date and needed to become more contemporary (heard as "replace Bournonville with new works that are modern and hence inherently superior")—would have a profound effect on the Danish ballet in years to come.

Despite reservations about the company's future, the tour was very successful. In New York, according to both the *Times* and the *Herald Tribune,* the company sold out every performance in its two-week run at the Metropolitan Opera House, and there were usually standing-room patrons. The Danish ballet seduced its audience, and, for a brief time at least, it became a real threat to the established order of things. Had the company returned to New York as frequently as did England's Royal Ballet, the development of ballet in America, and in Denmark (not to mention Kronstam's career), might have been quite different. The ebullience and personal magnetism of the dancers, their affinity for drama, their ensemble spirit, and, above all, the many strong and talented male dancers were all eye-openers. Neither America nor England had men of such a high caliber. Dancers like Fredbjørn Bjørnsson and Stanley Williams were admired for their virtuosity, but Kronstam received the lion's share of attention, partly because of his gifts, but also because he danced what, by American standards, were the star roles. (Bjørnsson danced Franz in *Coppelia* and Børge Ralov was Gennaro in *Napoli* and *Petrushka,* but these roles were not considered as important as James or Romeo.) It was Kronstam who made the Americans realize that the Danish ballet was a great classical institution. Erik Bruhn could no longer be seen as an anomaly, a uniquely gifted individual, but rather, like his younger countryman, the product of a great tradition and school.

Martin singled Kronstam out in a *New York Times* Sunday piece, writing under the heading "The Case of Kronstam":

> Perhaps the outstanding illustration of that [the encouragement by the company of individual talent] is to be found in the case of Henning Kronstam. Only recently elevated to the rank of soloist, he quite swept everything before him during the recent New York season. He was not only a superb Romeo (Frederick Ashton chose him out of the ranks for the role when he was creating the ballet last year as guest choreographer), but he also stepped into the traditional *La Sylphide* with such authority as to challenge the memory of even Erik Bruhn's fine performance of it in Copenhagen. *Chopiniana* is possibly too abstract for him to get his teeth into, and the Drummer Boy in *Graduation Ball* (his first solo role) has been danced with more flash and humor by others. But his Poet in *La Sonnambula* is sensitive, high-strung, and commanding.

Martin continued, giving one of the most complete descriptions of Kronstam as an artist in this period:

> He is handsome, tall, admirably in command of his body; his technique is strong, with notable elevation, and a line that is lyric without being weak. He has an intuitive dramatic sense, reacting automatically to the scene about him, and allowing his feeling to show in his face without a trace of mugging. At present he is inclined to lack variety, but he is only twenty-two and has little experience to draw upon. Obviously he has everything in his favor, and if before he is thirty he is not one of the great male dancers of his time, it will be very surprising indeed. (October 7, 1956)

There are dozens of similar assessments in Kronstam's collection of clippings, but undoubtedly one of the sweetest, and most honest, reviews he ever received was in the December 1956 edition of the *New York Ballet Club Newsletter*. Nan Smith wrote a brief "Tribute to the Danes," hoping they would return, and ending: "Speaking for myself, I enjoyed most of all the dancing of Henning Kronstam and of the company's repertory I preferred those ballets in which he had an opportunity to shine."

I've never been able to stop halfway when I've
started anything. If I had chosen another profession, I think I would have been in some sort
of university course by now. I must master a
field in order to exist.
—Henning Kronstam, interview, January 1957

Seven

Firestorms and Breakthroughs

The North American tour had been closely reported in the Danish press and
when Kronstam returned he was greeted as a hero. Perhaps partly because he
had received such an enthusiastic reception abroad, perhaps partly because
that reception had bolstered his confidence, he was no longer judged merely
promising. After a performance of *Chopiniana* shortly after the company's return, Svend Kragh-Jacobsen wrote: "The ensembles had a confident line and
among the soloists one especially noted Henning Kronstam, who seems to
have had the greatest personal success in the USA. He had clearly grown with
experience and now filled the part of the youth with sheen in his pure and
beautiful dancing" (*Berlingske Tidende,* November 1956).

In the 1956–57 season, with both Bruhn and Flindt away, Kronstam was, as
he modestly put it, "all alone in the repertory." Until this point he had made his

reputation in the Young Lover roles and was seen as the company's Romantic or lyrical hero. While this was probably his natural employ, Kronstam was eager, from the very beginning of his career, to extend his range. Again luck favored him, and in the next four years he danced a variety of big roles in quick succession, the first being George Balanchine's Apollo.

The New York City Ballet had danced at the Royal Theatre while the Danish ballet was in New York, and at the end of the tour, Tanaquil Le Clercq, one of the company's leading ballerinas and George Balanchine's wife, became ill with polio. Le Clercq and Balanchine remained in Denmark while the company continued its tour. Balanchine was understandably distraught and spent time with Volkova when he wasn't at the hospital, cooking special meals for Le Clercq in Volkova's kitchen. Volkova, thinking Balanchine needed to work, suggested he "do a little something" for the company. He came and watched class and said, "All right. I will do *Apollo* for the tall, dark boy." Balanchine saw something wild beneath Kronstam's calm, disciplined exterior and brought that out, calling him a "black panther."[1] ("I was very pumped up from the American tour," was Kronstam's laconic explanation.) Kronstam was a very pagan Apollo. Kirsten Simone has a film of the first solo, shot in the early 1960s; although it is silent, you can hear the music by watching Kronstam dance. He dances like a wild young god praying in a pagan grove, the classical veneer barely masking an inner energy and power.

Balanchine also set *Serenade* for the company and told Kronstam he would have liked him to dance in that ballet as well. "One day in the showers—we were both in the showers, Mr. B and I, and he said, 'Honestly, Henning, I'd rather have you do *Serenade* as well.' The Elegy. But the direction didn't allow it. It was too much to put on me, at that age. He said, 'You should dance in all my ballets, Henning.'"

Shortly after Apollo came another god, Orpheus, in a ballet called *Myte* by a fellow dancer, Ole Palle Hansen. Although the costume was one of Kronstam's most fetching, the ballet was judged a naive first effort. He next danced Siegfried in a one-act version of *Swan Lake* staged by Frank Schaufuss, who had planned to dance the Prince with his wife, Mona Vangsaae, as Odette, until they had a fight one day in rehearsal. Kronstam remembered Schaufuss sticking his head out the door of the studio, yelling, "Who wants to be the next Swan Queen?" Apparently there were no takers. Schaufuss withdrew; Vangsaae danced with Kronstam. Although he would later dance a great deal with Kirsten

George Balanchine conducting a stage rehearsal of *Apollo,* 1957. From left: Mette Mollerup, Kirsten Petersen (bending), Mona Jensen, Mercedes (the dresser), Kirsten Simone, Balanchine, Kronstam. Private collection.

Simone, Anna Lærkesen, Vivi Flindt, and Mette Hønningen, at the beginning of his career Kronstam was consistently paired with the company's senior ballerinas, Margrethe Schanne or Mona Vangsaae. He admired Schanne though he did not especially like her, but he enjoyed the partnership with Vangsaae immensely, thinking her sweet and beautiful, and expressing tender feelings toward her years later.

Toward the end of the season Kronstam added another of the great prince roles to his repertory when Ninette de Valois and Peggy van Praagh came to Copenhagen to stage *Sleeping Beauty*—another of Volkova's acquisitions, though not a long lived or popular one. The production was considered dull by some, and the costumes (in sixteenth-century Spanish style by André Delfau)

hideous. Kronstam danced with both Schanne and Kirsten Simone (who had
her own breakthrough as Aurora in the second cast) and was recognized by the
critics as an ideal Desiré. His beautiful solo in the third act, choreographed by
Ashton for Michael Somes to the Gold Fairy music in an earlier London production, was all style and flying ronds de jambe.

By the end of this season, although Kronstam was still only twenty-two, he
was established as a leading dancer. He gave several interviews during this
period and was asked in each if he was going to leave. The response was always

Kronstam with Kirsten Simone in *Myte*, 1957. Photo: Mydtskov. The Royal Theatre,
Copenhagen. By permission of Det kongelige Teaters bibliotek og arkiv.

that, although he had had foreign offers, he would stay in Denmark as long as he continued to be given challenging opportunities. His answers indicate that even at such an early age he was aware of more than his own career and had given thought to what was unique about his company. Asked what distinguished the Royal Danish Ballet from others, he replied: "its homogeneity and drama." And always the emphasis was on the importance of the school and proper training.

One lengthy interview that he gave to "m" of *Information* in January 1957 has several revealing passages. The interviewer asked: "Is there any way the audience can evaluate ballet—apart from feeling good due to the beauty of the movements, and the relationship between the dancing and the music?" Kronstam's reply indicated he already listened more to his colleagues than to either critics or audience:

> Some can, of course—including some of the critics. But it is not a lot of them, which is why I've always been fairly at ease with newspaper reviews, whether they were ones of praise or criticism. When I get to my dressing room after a performance, I know very well if I did something bad—and then it doesn't matter if the papers praise it to the skies. And if at a premiere I know that I've danced the way the choreographer wanted me to, well, then I can't really care if the critics write that I got the intent all wrong.
>
> No, the criticism that counts is the one coming from one's colleagues. When I've performed Apollo and the old great ones come up afterward and approve of my performance, then I know it's right. They're in a position to dissect what happens on stage.

He spoke about his career, about staying in Copenhagen, and expressed what is nearly every dancer's preference for created roles over existing ones, although it is interesting that his reason is not the often-stated one of not liking to be compared to earlier interpreters, but rather of wanting to be part of the creative process:

> One always wants to learn from the big guns, but now they're coming here. Before, the dancers would always travel to Volkova to learn more, but we've got her now; at the moment we've got Balanchine and we've had Taras and Ashton. . . . It has been a great experience to dance for Balanchine [the interview took place around the time of the *Apollo* premiere]. But my greatest ballet experience was *Romeo and Juliet*. Balanchine had *Apollon Musagetes* all ready,[2] when he came here. All I could do was go into the role and see how close I could get to what he had intended. But *Romeo and Juliet* was created while we worked on it.

Ashton discussed how to do a certain detail with us; in a way he built it for Mona Vangsaae and me. One contributed in creating a role.

The final question was if he had considered choreographing a ballet, something Kronstam never did. This answer too is revealing, for it touches on his disciplined focus, the way he would push away everything that wasn't the task at hand, as well as his perfectionism and what he felt about the communication between dancer and audience: "Not yet, anyhow. It is far too strenuous to advance so quickly for one to think of anything other than dancing. Talent is all very good—and it's that which makes ballet an experience for the audience—but what's the use, if the body cannot follow your real intentions? The audience doesn't see what one thinks, only that which one is capable of translating into the dance."

Kronstam danced the third solo in *Napoli* for the first time in May 1957 and there was a short news article about what must have been an extraordinary rehearsal:

> When the last act of *Napoli* is performed tomorrow night at the gala performance at the Royal Theatre in honor of Queen Elizabeth and Prince Philip's visit to Denmark, there will be a new solo for the outstanding first dancer of the Royal Theatre, Henning Kronstam. When Henning Kronstam had completed the solo brilliantly and in such a way that it left everybody who saw it at the rehearsal yesterday afternoon breathless, the entire corps de ballet broke into spontaneous applause, the greatest honor any dancer could want.
>
> Henning Kronstam once again danced the great solo and it was now the King's adjutant who saw the rehearsal who spontaneously had to stand up and clap. In other words, the chosen few who will be at the Theatre for this historic event tomorrow night will have an experience out of the ordinary in every way.[3]

The Royal Theatre's annual festival gave spectators a concentrated view of the repertory and the dancers and often provoked editorials criticizing the company's direction. Svend Erichsen tried to take a positive view in May 1957, while noting that the constitution of the company had changed radically, from being centered on a small cadre of male soloists, to ballets with a female corps and a single male star.

> In spite of all this, it shows, however, that it is possible to create wonderful performances with the female dancers who are available, supplemented with Henning Kronstam in a leading role. This in spite of the fact that Kronstam is still a weak mime. He looks good as long as he keeps his face steady. When he

moves it, one thinks that he's going for the grotesque and one is insulted when one finds out that it is in all seriousness.

The secret of our fine ballet performances is the great foreign choreographers and directors—Ashton, who created *Romeo and Juliet,* Balanchine with *Apollon Musagète*—this is where we reach the heights. One might add *Sonnambula,* staged by Taras after the choreography by Balanchine, and even smaller things, such as [Anton] Dolin's *Pas de Quatre,* and Robbins's *Fanfare.* It would be much too hard to make comparisons with the number of Danish stagings. Let it suffice to say that *Swan Lake,* alongside its pony, *Kermesse,* is the low point of the Festival.

It looks as if ballet management understands the situation. The engagement of more foreign directors indicates this. It is not possible to invent or conjure up Danish choreographers and directors and the young male dancers that we miss. But one can make amends by getting the finest of artists from America, England, and France to come here. This is the path that has been chosen, and it's the one that must continue. (Svend Erichsen, May 1957)

When he came home from vacation at the end of the summer of 1957, Kronstam faced one of the most serious crises of his life, one that cast a shadow over his life from that day forward. "They didn't know where I was," he said, "but they held the funeral until I came home. My father met me at the airport. I don't remember him ever holding me before. He embraced me and said, 'Come, let us bury her together.'"

Kronstam's mother, who had been in and out of psychiatric hospitals for years, had walked away from the hospital after yet another round of shock treatments, gone into the woods, and committed suicide by taking an overdose of pills. She left a note only for her youngest son and died with his photograph on her breast. He kept her last letter, creased and yellowed, in his room for the rest of his life and, from its condition, he had read it often. In the letter, which began "Dear Little Henning," his mother's childhood name for him, and ended, "Love, Mother," Meta Kronstam wrote that she understood what Franz Gerstenberg meant to her son and that she knew that he would never have had a career without the older man. This was probably meant as an apology, but mother and son had never been reconciled and Kronstam blamed himself for his mother's death for the rest of his life. Since his siblings did as well, family gatherings were often painful and strained.

It was a difficult start for the new season. He went to Volkova for comfort and said she was very kind and had helped him enormously simply by listening. Years later he got up the courage to ask his father if he thought he was responsible for his mother's death. "He said, 'Henning you must never think that. She was afraid of growing old.'" In addition to feeling guilty, which his father's words did not assuage, Kronstam knew he had inherited his mother's illness and believed that he too was fated to be a suicide. It seems that Kronstam was usually able to "push this aside," as he did his preperformance nerves, through a tremendous act of will, but both the guilt and the fear were with him, at least in the back of his mind and, like twin demons, would strike him during the depressive periods of his illness.

Kronstam seemed outwardly untouched by his mother's death and consoled himself with work. In the 1957–58 season Kronstam added another major creation, the role of Nilas in Birgit Cullberg's *Moon Reindeer,* and photographs show how much he had matured, physically and emotionally. This was a ballet based on a Norse legend about a beautiful woman who turned into a reindeer every evening and the hunter who pursued the reindeer and loved the woman. Again, Kronstam was paired with Vangsaae ("She was the only woman in the company who could wear a unitard," he said). *Moon Reindeer* had a strong story and good roles for several dancers. He was given a very different role that season in *Whims of Cupid,* where he was cast against type as the awkward Quaker man—a total contrast to Romeo, and the fact that he was again paired with Vangsaae made it even funnier.

The other new ballets that season were judged to be workshop level, not ready for the main stage, and neither Mona Vangsaae's *Spektrum* (in which Kronstam danced a duet with Vangsaae and then ran off with Stanley Williams) nor Frank Schaufuss's slight *Opus 13* (to music of Richard Strauss in which Kronstam danced a duet with Schanne), found favor with the public either. Both Bruhn and Flemming Flindt (who had left almost as soon as he joined the company and was now dancing with London Festival Ballet) were in Copenhagen as guests, and Kronstam had to share the role of James in *La Sylphide,* although he kept the roles he had originated—the Poet, Romeo, and Apollo. Bruhn danced only a few performances of both *La Sonnambula* and *Romeo and Juliet.*[4] As "F.D." wrote in May 1956: "[Bruhn's] Romeo had a superficiality that tilted the performance. The shimmer of young love that Henning Kronstam finds such beautiful expressions for were very much lacking in Bruhn's performance. [Bruhn] often impressed by his blinding technique and his handsome appearance, but only rarely had the ability to move [the spectator]."

Kronstam with Mona Vangsaae in Birgit Cullberg's *Moon Reindeer,* 1957. Photo: Mydtskov. The Royal Theatre, Copenhagen. By permission of Det kongelige Teaters bibliotek og arkiv.

Another review of Bruhn's Romeo, "More Bruhn Than Romeo," illustrates a major difference between Bruhn and Kronstam that was already apparent. By that time, Bruhn had developed a very precise stage persona—the perfect classical Prince—and was most effective in roles where he could be himself. In contrast, Kronstam was never himself, adapting to the style and character of each ballet he danced, which was one of the main reasons choreographers were so interested in working with him. Kirsten Ralov reflected on this difference, saying that she thought this was, in part, why Bruhn chose a career away from his home theater: "Erik felt that he didn't get enough, and that was because Erik was so special, and especially when people looked at him here. He was a Prince, the golden boy. They would never give him any good chances, which Henning got because Henning looked different. Henning could look ugly, Henning could look small, and big, and they would give him the other parts. And Erik was not satisfied because he didn't want to do the Prince roles all the time. He wanted to go away and be offered other jobs. Henning didn't have to do that."

Kronstam did leave to do other jobs from time to time, although he never left the company completely. In the summer of 1958 he went to Edinburgh, this time with Kirsten Simone. He worked with Taras again and, for the first time, with John Cranko, creating roles in new ballets by each. Taras made a simple, abstract ballet, *Octet,* rather along the lines of *Variations for Four.* In Cranko's *Secrets,* Kronstam played a bored husband who dallies with a young woman (Simone); Carla Fracci was the wife. Kronstam was later told by a close friend of Cranko's that *Secrets* had been a rough sketch for *Onegin.* "Not the story," he said, "but the atmosphere." Fracci remembered this time with obvious pleasure. "We were so young. It was fun, and an exciting time for all of us. And exciting for John [Cranko] too, to discover three young dancers." Fracci would later invite Kronstam to dance *Giselle* with her in Rome, and Cranko to dance with his new company in Stuttgart, but neither *Octet* nor *Secrets* was of lasting value.

Noël Goodwin reviewed both ballets for *Dance and Dancers:* "Kirsten Simone from Denmark, all blonde and pink as candy floss, looked and danced adorably as the Sweet Young Thing (in Cranko's *Secrets*), and the Italian dancer Carla Fracci, flashingly dark, and scarlet and eloquent, made a fine contrast as the so-understanding Wife. Henning Kronstam found it difficult to look a bored husband while supporting her through some complicated lifts (why not drop her and be done with it?) but otherwise—and especially in an attractive pas de trois with the two girls—danced with the consummate style of the fine artist he has become."

Goodwin found Taras's *Octet* negligible: "Henning Kronstam worked hard to justify it and his fluent elegance was again admirable to watch. Simone lacked a matching fluidity of line as the principal girl, and the six supporting dancers were hampered by horrid costumes as they appeared and disappeared in various permutations of numbers, contriving sometimes to keep the principals apart, sometimes to bring them together, but all to no apparent purpose."

These performances had been the tentative beginnings of what would be called the Edinburgh International Ballet, but the company was unable to raise the necessary funds to continue. Immediately after the performances in Edinburgh, Kronstam and Simone went to the Nervi Festival with Inge Sand's group. Peter Williams wrote:

> All of the numbers were very well done, but quite outstanding was the selection of dances from the second act of *La Sylphide,* danced by Kirsten Simone and Henning Kronstam. Simone's youth and delicacy made her a very plausible Sylphide, even if, at the moment, she lacks the mature style of a Margrethe Schanne or a Markova. She was charming in this act's many touching moments. Since I last saw him, Kronstam has developed into one of the outstanding male dancers of our time. Always possessing a noble presence, he once tended to be rather soft on the stage. Today his personality and his technique have hardened and he uses his height to its best possible advantage and covers the stage in a way I have seen from very few of our contemporary male dancers. His breadth of movement and his ease are a joy to watch. (*Dance and Dancers,* September 1958)

Back home in Copenhagen, the 1958–59 season produced several ballets, none of which, apparently, was a joy to watch, and Kronstam was in most of them. One, by Fredbjørn Bjørnsson, called *Lykke paa Reise* (The Happy Journey)—about a tour bus guide (Kronstam) and four female passengers, all of whom fell in love with him and one of whom (Simone) married him—was considered so naive that it had no place on the stage of the Royal Theatre, and the management of the company was again severely taken to task in the press for allowing this ballet to be staged.

The repercussions from the Lander Scandal had never completely subsided, and the state of the repertory caused the matter to erupt again. Shortly before the 1956 North American tour Frank Schaufuss had been appointed acting ballet master after Larsen had accepted the director's post at Tivoli's Pantomime Theatre.[5] Schaufuss was a Lander man (and a rather rough individual), and the crisis soon boiled over. Forces in both the government and the Copenhagen arts world had been trying to find a way to bring Lander back to Copenhagen since he had been dismissed. They believed that he was a great choreographer, that he had been unfairly treated—they knew the morals charges, even if true, were merely a ruse to get rid of him—and they thought the company was not being properly directed. Lander, of course, wanted his job back. Once during his exile he had invited Volkova to meet with him at D'Angleterre one evening for drinks and had asked her to leave the company because she was the only person holding up the directorship. He proposed that if she left the company would fall apart, as there would be no one with her contacts or her teaching ability at the Theatre. He promised he would bring her back and together they would direct a great company. Volkova refused.[6]

Now the Theatre management proposed inviting Lander back merely to stage his ballets—not, they promised, to be ballet master. The dancers were divided but there were many more anti-Lander than pro. The situation became so heated that the pro-Lander dancers split off from the dancers' union, forming one of their own. For a time they refused to take Volkova's class, and Hans Brenaa did a class for the anti-Volkova dancers. Volkova seriously considered leaving; Kronstam, of course, was her staunch defender.

Kronstam was now the vice chief of the dancers' union, and involved in the negotiations and turmoil that followed. "I don't know why the critics were so much for Lander," he said. "It must have been *Etudes* because the other ballets were rather naive." The dancers opposed to Lander took their position on artistic rather than moral grounds. "If Lander came back, we were afraid we would go back to having only his ballets," Kronstam explained.

The story of the second Lander affair, in essence a failed coup, is laid out with remarkable clarity in Erik Aschengreen's *Der går dans*. In brief summary, the matter involved Parliament, the Danish Supreme Court, the state ombudsman, a review of the original case against Lander, a protest by the dancers that they could not be forced to work with Lander, and the threatened resignation of the Theatre's top management. Various compromises were suggested, the most ludicrous being that, since the dancers refused to work with Lander in the studio, Lander could sit in the auditorium and call out instructions to the dancers on the stage. At one point there was a serious discussion about firing all the anti-Lander dancers and replacing them with French ones. A commentary in a Norwegian paper found this absurd and questioned why the critics, government, and theater management were all so insistent on bringing Lander back, pointing out that he had choreographed only one good ballet while in Denmark and nothing of substance since leaving it.

Though all of this was covered, with varying degrees of accuracy and hysteria, in the daily press, the company went on working and Aschengreen makes the point that the performances on stage gave no hint of the turmoil behind the scenes.[7] The crisis blew up in December 1958, shortly before the premiere of Cullberg's *Miss Julie*, when the dancers learned that Schaufuss had been in Paris negotiating with Lander not, as they had been told, to set a program of ballets, but to return as ballet master. There was another uproar, as the dancers were incensed that they had been so misled. Schaufuss was suddenly released from his contract as ballet master, although he remained as a dancer.

The troubles were not over. A month later, in January 1959, the dancers were told they could lose their jobs if they refused to work with Lander. The principal dancers, including Kronstam, were fired on the morning of Kronstam's debut as Albrecht in Erik Bruhn's staging of *Giselle*. They danced anyway. Kronstam was paired with Margrethe Schanne and had a success (with reservations, as he was thought as yet too young for the role). Kronstam did not receive much help from Bruhn, he said. (He would work with Bruhn again later on the role, with happier results.) One account of the performance captures the atmosphere in the Theatre that night. In reading the final comment, one must remember that Danes have developed irony to a high art form:

> To dance the way the ballet danced last night in *Giselle*, and not least in *Miss Julie*, that is, to dance in world class, is in itself an achievement. To do it when one is under such pressure as the ballet must feel in the present situation is nothing less than an achievement.
>
> A full house applauded this achievement the way it was deserved. Throughout the whole of this uniquely beautiful ballet evening, applause could be heard again and again that were more than warm and probably rather demonstrative in character. It started immediately after the curtain rose on *Giselle*, and when two of the twelve [fired] principal dancers, namely Niels Bjørn Larsen and Henning Kronstam, appeared on stage, and it continued throughout the performance, at times as rhythmic salutes to Henning Kronstam as well as Margrethe Schanne, who danced the title role. It culminated when that man's man, Erik Bruhn, appeared himself in the character of Jean, the servant, in *Miss Julie*. By then, the applause was so strong and long that it almost stopped the performance. It was with a sense of joy and anxiety and anticipation that the audience followed this Swedish masterwork, which the Royal Danish Ballet performs in a way no other company anywhere in the world can surpass.
>
> The Theatre's directors, Henning Brøndsted and Henning Rohde, were seated in the orchestra and rejoiced over the triumph of the ballet.

Eventually a compromise was reached between management and dancers. The dancers would permit Lander to come and stage his ballets, and the Theatre management (who had withdrawn their resignations) swore that there would be no more behind-the-scenes double-dealing. Henning Rohde would become the administrative leader of the company and would consult with a triumvirate: Erik Bruhn, who would teach at the school; Niels Bjørn Larsen, who would run the ballet from day to day; and Vera Volkova as both teacher and artistic advisor, although she was never officially granted that title. In an exasperating anticlimax, once he had permission to come, Lander suddenly found he was too busy to get away from the Paris Opera, where he was then employed as a ballet master. The political situation settled down eventually, although the wounds from the battle lingered. Schaufuss, though relieved of his duties as ballet master, taught company class after Bruhn left. He was not highly regarded as a teacher. In Kronstam's papers were several rough drafts of a letter he wrote to the theater chief, passionately pleading for a change.[8]

Dear Mr. Brøndsted,

Today I have had a conversation with Mr. Rohde, to whom I have very strongly protested the temporary change in the male classes, where Frank Schaufuss has been given three classes a week. I protested in the fall of 1958 to Mr. Rohde when Frank Schaufuss gave himself the job as teacher for the men, and my protest was followed up by the whole male corps before Frank Schaufuss's resignation as ballet master, December '58. I must, at this point, underline that Schaufuss, whatever good things you can say about him, has absolutely no talent as a teacher. He has now again been appointed as temporary teacher for the men, but Mr. Rohde has not discussed this with the other teachers of the company, and I find that unconscionable. Mr. Rohde seems to have forgotten my protests from two years ago and was very surprised to hear that Frank Schaufuss was so unable, and he apologized strongly that he hadn't sought advice from the other teachers. The end of my conversation with Mr. Rohde was that he very clearly promised me that when Stanley Williams returns they will revise the class schedule, which would first and foremost be approved by Mme. Volkova and Stanley Williams.

I apologize for this letter, but I thought it necessary for Mr. Brøndsted to be kept informed about what is going on at the ballet, and to make you aware that you can expect a protest from the union through Mr. Jacobi [lawyer to the dancers' union].

After *Giselle*, Kronstam danced in two more Cullberg ballets, *Medea* (with Schanne) and *Miss Julie* (with Kirsten Petersen), taking the role of Jason in the former ballet and Jean in the latter. Several critics commented on how virile

Kronstam's performance as Jason was. Aschengreen later wrote, "Both [Margrethe Schanne as Medea and Kirsten Simone as Kreusa] wanted Henning Kronstam, whose Jason was the most handsome male figure he had created, perfect in stature, and for this occasion wearing a dark beard, which gave him a strong and virile expression. The style was that of Cullberg, a mix of classical and modern, which demanded a strong technique."[9]

Jean, the butler who is mistreated and eventually rapes his mistress, was another strong character. This was Kronstam's first "nasty" role, and it became one of his specialties. Dancing with Kirsten Petersen, he was second cast to Bruhn, who had his own breakthrough in this role, delivering a cruel and brilliant performance; previously, Bruhn had been admired more for his technical prowess than his acting ability. To the surprise of some, Kronstam was able to put aside his Romantic Lover and be convincing in the brutality of the part. Jørgen Budtz-Jørgens (in *Berlingske Aftenavis*) goes into some detail, and shows how Kronstam was already able to develop a character: "Henning Kronstam brought out the underdog and the proletarian of the handsome male, Jean, excellently, from the slick hairdo parted in the middle to his servile stare and devoted servant's posture that perhaps he still underlines too stiffly. Also, the contrast between Jean's predatory lust, which contains so much contempt for the fine miss when she offers herself to him, and his healthy sensual joy in the maid Kristin, were both finely expressed in his interpretation of the part. Together they danced the two strongly sensual sections of *Miss Julie* with a passion and an artistic security that were equally dazzling."

Jean was one of Kronstam's most admired roles. He had a fan who saw every performance, a wealthy woman known as "the last person to live in an apartment at Kongens Nytorv" (which is now all commercial property). "She would leave a note for me at the stage door sometimes and invite me to come over after the performance for a drink. And we would have a sherry, and we would talk." Asked what they talked about, and why he thought she had done this, Kronstam replied, in his deadpan fashion, "Well, I think she wished that her butler were a little bit more like Jean."

During the late 1950s, Kronstam and Kirsten Simone began what was to be a long partnership as guest artists. Kronstam not only enjoyed dancing with Simone but traveling with her. They got along well, they had fun together, and, probably most important to him, she was thoroughly professional and a hard worker. He didn't have to worry about a partner's preperformance nerves or

Kronstam with Kirsten
Petersen in Cullberg's
Miss Julie, 1958. Private
collection.

ballerina temperament. They danced together with Inge Sand's group, at Dame
Margot Fonteyn's annual charity matinee for the Royal Academy of Dancing, on
the *Firestone Hour* and *Bell Telephone Hour* on American television, and on several long American tours with Ruth Page's Chicago Opera Ballet.

Kronstam and Simone received a government grant to spend some time in
Venice, taking classes and sightseeing (the Danish government believes in the
broadening effects of travel and encourages it among their artists). They also
danced the pas de deux from *Sleeping Beauty* at a gala program in Tivoli.
Simone tells a story about their partnership dating from these performances
that says much about their relationship at that time. Kronstam was often nervous before performing a solo with multiple pirouettes, so "to put him in a
good mood," she would give him a wink during a moment in the adagio when
she was facing him, with her back to the audience. In return he would steady
her nerves by looking at her intently and firmly holding her hand.

It was during these performances at Tivoli that Kronstam sustained his first major injury. "The first thing that happened to me was a car accident. I was on a bike, and a car drove into my right foot. [Dancers remembered that Kronstam told them at the time he had been distracted, thinking about steps for class.] That was the year I was doing Tivoli. It was the second year in *Sleeping Beauty,* the summer of 1959.

"I went to the hospital and they opened the wound here, which they had to sew. I was in the hospital for two days and then I went back, and Kirsten and I worked slowly up again and we danced *Sleeping Beauty* in Tivoli. Twice a day. I danced a long time without having any trouble with it, but that meant that my demi-plié was a little shorter on this leg than on that leg. Nobody could see that, but I knew it."

In April 1959, Kronstam was invited to dance with Svetlana Beriosova in John Cranko's *The Lady and the Fool* to be filmed for British television. This may have been another of Volkova's ideas, as she thought Beriosova would be the

Kronstam as the Toreador in Roland Petit's *Carmen*. The women are, from left to right: Viveka Segerskog, Karin Vikelgaard, Marianne Walther, Arlette Weinreich. Photo: Associated Press, Copenhagen. By permission of Worldwide Photos.

perfect partner for Kronstam, as David Blair would be for Simone, and she hoped to arrange exchanges and guest appearances to this effect. However, the English dancers' equity union did not want a foreign guest star and blocked Kronstam from dancing. The headlines in the Danish press, in rapid succession, were: "Kronstam Til England," then "Kronstam Ikke Til England" ("Kronstam to England," "Kronstam [will] not [go] to England"). Volkova's wish to have Beriosova and Blair appear with the Royal Danish Ballet and dance with her two favorite pupils was never fulfilled.

Kronstam had another breakthrough the following season in his first big comic role, as the Toreador in Roland Petit's *Carmen*. Volkova knew Petit and his wife, the ballerina Renée Jeanmaire (also known as Zizi), because Jeanmaire had taken her classes in London and she had arranged for Petit to bring *Carmen* to Copenhagen. "Of course, I hated it that I didn't get to do Don José," Kronstam said. "But Zizi saw right away that Kirsten [Simone] and Flemming [Flindt] hated each other and she went screaming to Roland that they would be perfect." This was another time when the company's ballerinas competed for the leading role. Kronstam remembers Schanne nonchalantly performing Giselle's solos during the few minutes' break in class between barre and center work, taken so that the women may put on their pointe shoes. But Carmen is a turning role, and Simone was the best turner in the company. There was a lot of backstage muttering that she was "too blonde" and "wouldn't dare put on the black wig," but she did and had a triumph, as did Flindt.

Kronstam at first thought that the Toreador would be a meaty role, as he was familiar with both the opera and novel (he had not yet seen the ballet). He was nonplussed to find that it was only a four-minute comic solo. "Well, I had to do something about that," he said. He did. When Kronstam danced the Toreador, it was not a small role. Petit pushed him to make his performance bigger, bringing him out of his shell. "Roland would sit in the Theatre and scream at me during dress rehearsals, 'Bigger, Kronstam. Move!'" It worked. His Toreador—in his words, "a dance caricature," an outrageously arrogant man overwhelmed with his own beauty and fame—stopped the show, and Flindt and Simone's intense performances in the leading roles made this one of the hits of the Danish repertory for the next decade.

Kronstam's performance is preserved on the film *Black Tights,* a collection of Petit ballets (Renée Jeanmaire and Petit dance Carmen and Don José; Kronstam is the Toreador; and Fredbjørn Bjørnsson the red-haired thief). There were newspaper reports of "two Danish stars in Paris," showing Kronstam and Bjørnsson, dressed in business suits, leaping about the Champs Elysées.

Kronstam danced in two relatively minor ballets that season as well, as the Bridegroom in Alfred Rodrigues's *Blood Wedding* and in Birger Bartholin's *The Shadow*, based on the Hans Christian Andersen story of the Learned Man (Kronstam) who cannot escape his Shadow (Frank Schaufuss). *Blood Wedding* was not a hit, although Kronstam had some affection for it, as he thought it was a good story, with strong roles, and a good balance of dancing and acting. *The Shadow* was another ballet where he had to create a character without dancing a step. He succeeded, but it wasn't a good ballet and didn't last long in the repertory.

That season Kronstam had to substitute for Flemming Flindt, two years younger and a rising star, in a Hans Brenaa ballet, *Harlekins Millioner*, a revised version of Emilie Walbom's production of Petipa's *Harlequin's Millions*. The role of Harlekin had been created for Flindt and was a demi-caractère role built on pirouettes, which presented Kronstam with a difficult technical challenge. "There was a big variation—everything was pirouettes. And that was not my strongest," Kronstam said. "But then Flemming had a crash on his leg, or something like that, and I had to learn it. That was a big test for me, to do a big variation of just pirouettes. Attitudes and attitudes and arabesque." It was Stanley Williams who taught him to turn, he said. "Vera couldn't get me to do it. I had a very high arch, and I was always doing my pirouettes all the way up there [on high demi-pointe]. We started, all of us, to get up, because Erik had been doing that. Stanley was so quiet and so patient. He took me after class. Just simple, simple, simple: two or three pirouettes, from second [position], from fourth, from fifth. He always said, 'Go for the ending. Don't do one, two, three [*voice trails off*]. Do one, two, three [*voice snaps crisply*].'"

Their hard work paid off and, although the impish Harlekin was not Kronstam's métier, he mastered the role. Aschengreen wrote of his performance: "The bubbly, the high-spirited and the harlequinesque was not the thing for this romantic, elegiac lover, but of course he could dance the part."[10]

By the end of the 1959–60 season, Kronstam was twenty-five and a mature dancer. He had established himself in a wide range of roles, from the Romantic Lover to the classical Prince and the neoclassical Apollo and was beginning to build the gallery of dramatic portraits for which he was to be famous: the hunter, Nilas; the brutal butler, Jean; the pompous Toreador. He had also learned, from the more mediocre ballets in which he had danced, how "to make something out of nothing," a phrase that comes up again and again when dancers talk about Kronstam. Criticisms of him as a mime—either that he was too blank, or grotesquely expressive—are very rare after the Toreador and Jean.

His social life during this period is buried in the mists of time. "We had dinner parties and I always did the cooking," he said. "I liked to cook." (In fact, one of his ambitions at the time was to open a restaurant on Capri when he retired.) But, aside from Frederick Ashton and Jerome Robbins (on separate occasions) there's no record of the guests. It's likely his circle of friends, outside the company, were mainly friends of Gerstenberg.

By this time he was quite close to Volkova. "Before, it was just working together in the studio. But when the second scandal with Lander happened, we became closer. This is when we went to her home at three o'clock in the night to talk. We talked about the ballets we were doing, and the ballets we wanted to do, and what would be good for the company. Not so much about technique, because Hugh and Franz were there, always, and they would be bored to death if we were sitting there talking about tendus." These conversations were among the most important lessons in his training as a future ballet master.

A letter from Vera Volkova that year is interesting in its portrait of the times, as she knew everyone in the ballet world:

8 July 1959

Dear Henning,

I find New York fascinating, but exhausting. I will tell you all about it when I see you in Copenhagen. I finished my work and after the last class the pupils got a few bottles of champagne and we drank it from paper cups. I never tried that before.

Now I am doing all the things I was not able to do before. Went to Boston, Harvard University, have seen four plays, including *West Side Story* and *Raisin in the Sun*, acted entirely by Negroes. I am meeting Hugh in England on the 16th July and we expect to be back in Copenhagen on the 25th.

A week later.

Never finished the letter. Went to "Jacob's Pillow."

Before Robbins left for Europe, I watched some of his rehearsals. He asked me how you were and told me that he still is waiting for an "official" invitation to come to us and stage a ballet. It was very tempting for me to sign him just then with the date and all. But I was relieved to learn that he is not angry after all this mess with Frank Schaufuss and Henning Rohde. Tonight I am going to dinner with George Balanchine.

I also have seen Fred Ashton in London. He is free to revive *Romeo* for us, anytime between January and June.

Kenneth MacMillan is free from April to July and also is willing to come.

Everybody is expecting us here in 1960. It is so important to have a good season this year and at least one good ballet, preferably by an American choreographer. So Robbins is just the man. But as neither Erik [Bruhn] nor I are given the authority to act, I was unable to make definite arrangements.

All my love to Frantz [*sic*] as well as yourself.

Kronstam and Gerstenberg often dined with Volkova and Hugh Williams at D'Angleterre after performances, as Kronstam could not eat before a performance. They were frequently joined by two neighbors, Jytte Abildgaard and her mother. Abildgaard was the heiress to a pharmaceutical fortune and helped Kronstam (and, later, other young dancers) by funding his trips abroad. She remained a friend of Kronstam's to the end of his life. For years she accompanied Gerstenberg to the ballet. Jytte and her mother also frequently vacationed with the two men, often picking up the bill.

Kronstam was very close to three fellow dancers—Stanley Williams, Fredbjørn Bjørnsson, and Ole Fatum. The four often went out drinking Saturday nights to unwind from the week's work. Danish drinking is a story all its own. The Danes have nearly as many varieties of beer as the French have wine, graduating in potency from the relatively innocent bubbly gold familiar to Americans to mighty concoctions resembling melted tar. A high tolerance for alcohol was a measure of manhood for Kronstam's generation; some dancers even drank at the Theatre during rehearsals. Both Kronstam and Bruhn astonished their fellow dancers by downing large quantities of alcohol in the evening, then showing up in class the next morning in impeccable condition. The rules were quite clear, although unwritten: do what you want on your own time, but maintain discipline and decorum at the Theatre. When he had been a pupil in the school, Kronstam remembered seeing one teacher come in drunk; Lander admonished the teacher sternly, and Kronstam never forgot that lesson. He was, even as a young man, very disciplined. "Stanley and I would go drinking in the bars," he said, "and it would be three o'clock in the morning and I'd say, 'I'm sorry, but I have to go get some sleep. I have class tomorrow.'"

The 1960s were a time of enormous change in ballet. Modern dance had matured, and some, in Europe as well as America, felt that classical ballet was outmoded and modern dance was its successor. There was another audience, however, hungry for ballet, and air travel opened up a world of opportunities that previous generations of dancers could not have imagined. Kronstam stood at the edge of that world, one of the most gifted, and handsome, young stars in ballet. In the summer of 1955, "He was *the* young one," as Violette Verdy put it. By 1960, Kronstam faced a choice: stay in Copenhagen and continue to be guided by Volkova and expand his range, continuously challenged by new roles and new choreographers, or become a traveling guest star, playing the handsome Prince or sensitive Romantic Lover.

An examination of Kronstam's central roles, as well as his approach to creating and maintaining them, shows as clearly as anything how he faced that choice and what he chose.

Part two

The Roles

I saw him in *La Sonnambula*, and I remember
thinking, would those people doing the divertissement get the hell out of the way so I could
see the Poet sitting on that bench?
—Eliot Feld

The Poet: Balanchine's *La Sonnambula*

The Poet in George Balanchine's *La Sonnambula* was not only Kronstam's first
leading role and his breakthrough into the top ranks of the Royal Danish Ballet
at the age of twenty, but in many ways it remained at the core of his repertory.
There was a bit of the Poet in many of the roles he later danced. Kronstam
made his debut in the part on January 9, 1956, and danced the role for twenty
years, the last time in 1976 on the occasion of his twenty-fifth-anniversary jubilee. He chose the role as his farewell as a classical dancer.

It is a Romantic and dramatic, rather than bravura, role. Balanchine's Poet,
an innocent, the artist who is apart from the world, comes to a very worldly
party. He is at first seduced by the Host's mistress, who is the personification
of earthly love, but when left alone he sees a lovely, mysterious Sleepwalker,
the wife of the Host, whom he instantly recognizes as the other half of his soul.

As this is a Romantic ballet, of course this love cannot be realized, and the hero is killed by the Host.

La Sonnambula's Poet is one of the very few true danseur noble roles created in the twentieth century. There are social dances in the first scene and two pas de deux, the second containing an extremely difficult backbend—as the Poet sinks to his knees and bends, yearns, backward, his arms first encircling the Sleepwalker's body, then opening to let her pass—that is rarely performed smoothly. In addition *La Sonnambula* is a ballet of atmosphere and the Poet must be a dancer who can create and sustain both character and mood with very little incident to support him.

At the heart of the ballet are the two pas de deux, the first with the Coquette, the second with the Sleepwalker. In the duet with the Coquette, the Poet is the passive one, she, the seductress. In the guise of a social dance, Balanchine created a dance of seduction, with the two teasing, resisting, escaping, and returning to each other. In the second duet the partners barely touch. The Sleepwalker is insensible, unseeing. The Poet gently moves her limbs and tries to wake her, tries to stop her as she bourrées past him with her useless, lighted candle. "He is trying to get into her," Kronstam said repeatedly. At one point, as the music crests, she bends to him and they almost kiss, but she rises again and continues on her restless walk. The sleepwalking state becomes a metaphor for any barrier between two people. There must be a sense that the two are destined for each other, that the Sleepwalker is as drawn to him as he to her, yet it must be extremely subtle. As Kronstam danced it, the Poet, caught by something so real, yet unfathomable, is desperate to communicate with the Sleepwalker. This desperation, as well as his awe and wonder, were beautifully caught in the live performance shots by John Johnsen that accompany this chapter.

The Night Shadow, as it was originally called, was created in 1946 for the Ballet Russe de Monte Carlo and received its premiere at New York's City Center on February 27, 1946. Nicholas Magallanes danced the role of the Poet; Alexandra Danilova was the Sleepwalker; Maria Tallchief, the Coquette; and Michel Katcharoff, the Host. The ballet, often called simply *Night Shadow,* was renamed *La Sonnambula* when the work entered the repertory of the New York City Ballet in 1960. The ballet was taken into the repertory of the Ballet de Marquis de Cuevas in 1948, and the Royal Danish Ballet and the Dutch National Ballet in 1956. In Denmark it was called *Søvngængersken (The Sleep-*

walker) and was the second ballet of that name in the Danish repertory, the first being August Bournonville's staging of Jean Aumer's ballet in 1829.

The ballet became one of the company's staples for the next two decades. *La Sonnambula* received 192 performances in Copenhagen between 1956 and 1976 and was frequently included in the company's foreign and Danish tours.[1] From his first performance, Kronstam was considered definitive as the Poet. Although several other men danced the role, Kronstam was always in the first cast. After he retired in 1976, the ballet left the repertory and was not revived until the 1992–93 season.

Although Kronstam felt his early performances were rather tentative, most of the critics wrote as though it were a mature portrayal. The most poetic, and detailed, review was Svend Kragh-Jacobsen's:

> Margrethe Schanne was like the loveliest nocturnal dream, floating and light in her flowing garments, almost not corporeal as she glides on the tips of her toes into her night walk. Her big pas de deux with Henning Kronstam was the high point of the evening. The dance is wonderfully shaped with the rise of his love and his despair at not being able to make the beautiful sight come to life. This is fantastically expressed in the variations, where he pushes her from him, pulls her toward him, leads her in circles and curves, kneels, pleads, and tries to stop her. But she passes him, evades his arms; she is untouchable. This is where Schanne's poetic dance art culminated, and Henning Kronstam, who from his entrée had shown himself as a born moonstruck lover of Romanticism marked by noble dignity, became one with her in the dancing. He was an excellent partner but furthermore he was completely his own person as the unhappy-happy victim of the magic of love. In his first pas de deux with the Coquette, he even showed us that a young and hasty, hot-headed love is part of his register. (*Berlingske Tidende*, January 10, 1955)

Bent Schønberg wrote in *Ekstrabladet:*

For Henning Kronstam, the night meant a breakthrough as a spirited and soulful dancer. It is doubtful if today there is any other artist at the Royal Theatre who can make as deep an impression as he. He had a rare poetry that one seldom sees. He created and maintained a Werther-like figure from the first moment he appeared on stage.

Kronstam danced with three different Sleepwalkers over the years: Margrethe Schanne, Anna Lærkesen, and Kirsten Simone. "Schanne had an enor-

Kirsten Petersen as the Coquette, Kjeld Noack as the Host, and Kronstam as the Poet in Balanchine's *La Sonnambula*, 1956. Photo: Mydtskov. The Royal Theatre, Copenhagen. By permission of Det kongelige Teaters bibliotek og arkiv.

Kronstam and Margrethe Schanne in *La Sonnambula*, 1956. Photo: Mydtskov. The Royal Theatre, Copenhagen. By permission of Det kongelige Teaters bibliotek og arkiv.

mous stage presence, and she was in the long skirt, so you didn't see the bulky legs. She was strong on pointe. She was always extraordinary.

"Anna was this mysterious person that you couldn't get in touch with. The big shock with Anna was when she carried me out, not because she's strong, but because nobody believed that she liked me. With Schanne and with Kirsten, there's something that touches me, there's something, there's something. But with Anna, there was absolutely nothing, until she just turned around and said, 'Come.' And walked out.

"Kirsten was, of course, beautiful, with that long blonde hair. She didn't have great success at the beginning because she didn't have the role in her, but she became fine in it. She was twenty at that time, as I was, and she didn't get a proper chance until later."

Much was made of the final moments of the ballet, when the Sleepwalker carries the body of the Poet back to the tower. In the Danish version, the Sleepwalker's final walk, after she returns to the courtyard, is halted by the body of the Poet. Rather than stepping over him and walking back to the tower, as has been done in other productions, she stops and the entertainers in the ballet's divertissement pick up the body and place it in her arms. She then turns and walks in a semicircle around the stage before disappearing into the tower. Schanne was a small woman, barely five feet tall. The contrast in size was striking and the duet was a much commented on novelty. Schanne was interviewed shortly after the premiere by one of the Danish tabloids, under the headline "Sympathy of the Audience Is Worth More Than Any Title!": "Henning Kronstam, who is my partner for the first time in this role, and who has been lovely to work with, weighs more than 138 pund [69 kg.; 152 lb.], but it's easy anyway. He finds my balance and—as is well known—sleepwalkers have supernatural powers. The same thing is the case for me in this task, since one becomes one's part completely."

On the 1956 American tour, Kronstam seemed to grow as the Danes danced across the country, from around 150 pounds (an accurate estimate) on the East Coast, to a very inaccurately estimated 180 pounds a few days later in the Midwest. Some American reviewers barely mentioned anything else about the ballet. One example is J. Dorsey Callaghan's review, "Crowd Carried Away by Ballerina's Feat," in the *Detroit Free Press*: "Some 4,500 persons who attended the opening night of the Royal Danish Ballet Thursday at Masonic Temple are going to have a job on their hands. They know by first hand evidence that a mere slip of a woman weighing not much more than 100 pounds walked off the stage with a 180-pound man in her arms, and never batted an eyelash in the doing. But they won't be able to sell it. No one will believe it, and I for one won't blame them. It just can't be done, but Margrethe Schanne, one of the solo dancers of the Royal Danish Ballet, turned the trick in her sleep."

Another review from that first North American tour caught more of the poetry of the piece:

> The entire company is involved in his hauntingly staged ballet of so many and such quickly shifting moods. Its principal figures are Henning Kronstam as the poet in search of beauty and Margrethe Schanne as the night shadow, or death, in whose icy arms he finds the object of his quest.
>
> In addition to being superb dancers, Kronstam and Miss Schanne are clearly deeply sensible of the meanings of their characters; he as handsome as poets are supposed to be, she a wraith with the supernatural strength to leave the stage carrying such a giant of a man in her arms.

Anna Lærkesen remembered that most evenings, after the performance, when they were in the wings and she had put him down, Kronstam would turn to her and say, softly, "Thank you," and she found this quite moving, but the actual performance was more elusive. She could say only that this "was also one of the roles where I felt we had a wonderful rapport together. But it's about things that you can't explain."

Kronstam's first Coquette was Mona Vangsaae, and photographs show that she brought out rich undertones in the role that are often ignored today. She was neither flirt nor courtesan but a grand, kept lady, and there was a wisdom and understanding as well as sexual allure in her face.

Vivi Flindt took the part in the revivals of the 1970s and remembered the performances a decade earlier, which she had watched as a child: "Henning was beautiful in it, in his pale blue. Tall, poetic, vulnerable, loving. Absolutely stunning. I was totally enthralled by his performance. I remember, as a child, I would draw pictures. I always drew the Coquette and him, never the Sleepwalker, because that kind of personality has never attracted me. I always thought that they were very beautiful, but they were not reality to my character. It was always the other person. She had the drama and she took the revenge.

"When later I realized that I had to dance this role, I was in Heaven. We never discussed anything, Henning and I. Just the lifts and the positions, and he helped me because he had been told exactly from day one how it was. You

Kronstam with Vivi Flindt as the Coquette in the 1970s. Photo: John Johnsen. The Royal Theatre, Copenhagen. By permission of Det kongelige Teaters bibliotek og arkiv.

could sit on that bench with Henning, sitting there and looking into his eyes for twenty minutes, and acting, and playing the game with the fan. He never took his eyes away, not for twenty minutes. So much happened. Not a word was spoken and yet everything took place. He produced a kind of a contact where he opened up a certain part of his soul that there were no words to."

Dancers repeatedly said that they felt a special rapport with Kronstam that went beyond words, that they communicated completely on a nonverbal level. These perceptions are accurate, for Kronstam's relationship with every dancer seems to have been special, each in a different way. One of his favorite partners was Sorella Englund, who danced the role of the Coquette with Kronstam when she was very young. Englund said that in rehearsals, "We didn't talk. I think I have always had with Henning some very strange, completely nonverbal contact. He said very little directly and instead he took me somewhere, and I was able to follow. It sounds so strange. It was not normal, but with a complete understanding. Complete understanding. There were no words that we needed to say. It was the same when he was directing something. He never said any-thing."

Sorella Englund's first performance as the Coquette did not go smoothly. During the divertissement, the Poet and the Coquette continue their seduction while seated on a bench behind the performers. Englund was in the second cast and suddenly realized, sitting there looking at Kronstam, that they had never rehearsed this section, and she had no idea what to do. Kronstam's inten-sity flustered her. "I should have been the strong one in that scene, but he was so strong, so I just couldn't—I was too young and too afraid of him. He really shocked me, and it taught me a lot. Because the next time I knew that as he is so strong, I really had to do something here." But at her debut, "the whole pas de deux afterward was very shaky because I was just paralyzed by this man," Englund said. "And he looked like he enjoyed it a little bit, I must say," she added with a laugh.

Kronstam's concentration was legendary at the Theatre, noticed even by very young dancers. Arne Villumsen danced in the divertissement in the 1970s and remembered how Kronstam prepared for the performance while waiting in the wings: "Every time he did *Sonnambula,* I remember him stand-ing, three or four minutes before he went onstage. I was doing the pastorale and I wasn't on the stage then, so we were looking. He was standing right in front of where he was supposed to go in. Just standing there, going into him-self. He was shut away."

Kronstam considered this ballet, and his work with Taras, very important to his development as an artist. "It is a difficult role because he has very little to dance. He is just standing there, all alone on the stage when the guests leave, and with the focus of fourteen hundred people on him. So there I think I learned what it meant to fill the stage.

"It was a role that was so close to my personality at that time. He's a fragile person. He's easily conquered by the Coquette, and when he sees the Sleep-walker, it's a soul that he has a contact with. She is so serene and so light, after all the noise of that party. And he doesn't understand why he has to die for it, because there are so many beautiful things he could write. These are all things that John [Taras] said to me a long time ago, in 1955: 'You have to think, in the last minute, of all the beautiful things you would have said to the world before you just—stumble over.'"

Kronstam was always aware of the role of the other characters in a ballet, as

The death of the Poet. Behind Kronstam, from left: Flemming Halby, Adam Lüders (as Harlequin), Frank Andersen. Photo: John Johnsen. The Royal Theatre, Copenhagen. By permission of Det kongelige Teaters bibliotek og arkiv.

well as his own. "The Sleepwalker is kept in the tower because she is his daughter, or a virgin bride, or something like that. She's never been let out, and has never been to parties. She is always closed in. Her whole desire is to meet other people. And to him [the Poet], she is the dream of his poetic writing, or his painting, or whatever he is. The first one, the Coquette, she is human life. You can paint her like this: boom, boom, boom, boom, and there she is. But the Sleepwalker is indescribable for him, and he cannot get in touch with her. It's a much bigger drama than where they just play with it, and say, 'Oh, well. She can't see. Take the light up and down.' Much bigger.

"Of course the Coquette is very important too. All the girls who get the Coquette say, 'Oh, do I have to do that one? Why don't I get the Sleepwalker?' But she is so important because she is building up the drama. The Coquette has to have a coolness about her. Because sometimes it's done like: 'Well, tonight I am just one of those whores. Kiss my hand.' She is happy for [the Baron's] big house, his big parties. She is happy for all the jewels she gets, and everything else. But she doesn't have him as a husband because that one is up there in the

The Poet senses the
Sleepwalker. Photo: Bent
Mortensen. Private col-
lection.

tower. The Baron is an old man and she sees a young, handsome man and he
is different, and that is what attracts her. Then, of course, if she can get him by
her seductiveness—maybe she doesn't even want him, but she wants to try it."

From his first entrance, it must be clear that the Poet is not of the same
world as the guests at the party. "When he comes in, he just looks around, and
somebody is coming to say hello, and he doesn't know what to do. Maybe
somebody in the party invited him, and he doesn't know anybody. And then he
sees a very beautiful woman and she seems like she wants to talk to him. And
that's what gets his interest there. Of course, she goes further and she tries to
seduce him. But she is not heartbroken when she is taken out by the Baron.

"And then he just stands there and says, 'Well, what was this?' Until he
hears that SCREAM from the tower—and that's in the music. And it should

With Kirsten Simone as the Sleepwalker, 1970s. Photo: John Johnsen. The Royal Theatre, Copenhagen. By permission of Det kongelige Teaters bibliotek og arkiv.

With Anna Lærkesen as the Sleepwalker, 1970s. Photo: John Johnsen. The Royal Theatre, Copenhagen. By permission of Det kongelige Teaters bibliotek og arkiv.

With Kirsten Simone, 1970s. Photo: John Johnsen. The Royal Theatre, Copenhagen. By permission of Det kongelige Teaters bibliotek og arkiv.

be seen in his back that it is as though somebody has caught him, or some-thing like that. And it is her spirit, which is a spirit that works with his—yin and yang. That's what it is.

"The pas de deux is to wake her up, to get through to her. And she is just impossible. He gets more and more desperate, and not more and more play-ful—which I saw Lloyd [Riggins] do one evening [in 1993]. I went to him and I gave him such a hell. He was laughing at the part when she puts her leg out, and then he puts one arm, and then the other arm [on the ground in front of her leg to stop her]. He laughed at her, like it's fun, it's play. I said, 'Lloyd, this is not fun. You are trying to stop her. It's like Giselle. You want to get into this person. You want to understand. You want to talk to her.' 'Oh, I never thought about it like that,' he said. I said, 'Well, please do!' It's a beautiful role."

While some dancers have a fixed idea of a role and keep to that idea as they mature, Kronstam deliberately aged his characters as he aged. In this case, age brought a richer pathos to the ballet. Rather than the tragedy of a young artist slain before he can begin his life's work, the tale of unfulfilled promise that Kronstam danced at twenty, his portrayal of the Poet when he was in his late thirties and early forties deepened to something at once individual and univer-sal. His older Poet was a man who had never fulfilled that early promise, never found his muse. Perhaps he is acclaimed—he must have been, to have been invited to such a gathering—but he has yet to create a truly great work. The Sleepwalker thus represented not just an unconsummated love, but an unworshipped muse, and the notion of an artist in maturity, cruelly cut down seconds after he finally opened his soul and could realize his full potential, was immensely poignant.

The opportunity to grow up in a part, to develop it, was one of the reasons that Kronstam chose to remain in Copenhagen rather than launch a jet set career. "I did *Sonnambula* for twenty years. Then you really get into the role, and you really know what it's all about. But now, with five performances, maybe with two casts, I think it's mad. The audience gets cheated and the dancers get cheated because they never get the feeling of owning the roles."

It is often said that a dancer finds something new in a role each time he or she dances it, but Kronstam had a different idea: "You don't find new things in the ballets," he said. "You find new things in yourself because it's yourself that changes."

Equal to [Kirsten Simone's] grand and fugitive
passion was Kronstam's delicately shaded
Romeo, the perfect Renaissance princeling,
noble, ecstatic and doomed.
—John Percival

Nine

Romeo: Ashton's *Romeo and Juliet*

There had been two prior productions of *Romeo and Juliet* in the Royal Danish Ballet's repertory, one a five-act dramatic pantomime by Vincenzo Galeotti in 1811, the other a one-act version to Tchaikovsky's suite by Birger Bartholin in 1952. The latter, starring Mona Vangsaae and Frank Schaufuss, was very popular, and it was probably not the Theatre's original intention to look for a replacement. But Volkova wanted a ballet by Ashton, and it was through her auspices that the British choreographer came to Copenhagen to create *Romeo and Juliet*. Volkova went to London to discuss it with Ashton, and he proposed either *Sylvia* or *Romeo*.[1] He had wanted to choreograph *Romeo* for the Royal Ballet, but Ninette de Valois, who was director of England's Royal Ballet at that time, decided she did not want two ballets by Prokofiev in the repertory (Ashton had choreographed Prokofiev's *Cinderella* in 1948).

Kronstam did not know very much about Ashton before he met him in the rehearsal room. "I'd read that he had done ballets for Margot Fonteyn in London, and bits and pieces, but we didn't know much, really. Vera [Volkova] knew him because he had been working in her class. He couldn't work in Ninette de Valois's class because she was too strict, but Vera always said if there's any possibility that anybody has choreographic talent, let them do their own little businesses, as long as they don't disturb the class. And so Fred was there in the back, doing his stuff, whatever he liked to do."

The Prokofiev score had already been produced in Czechoslovakia and, more famously, in Russia, but Ashton's was the first postwar Western version. He created it without having seen Leonid Lavrovsky's production, and although he followed Prokofiev's libretto, Petipa was his model. Ashton's *Romeo and Juliet* was not at all expressionistic but a classical ballet with variations and formal suites of dances. Ashton created the ballet in seven weeks of rehearsal. Nearly every dancer who's worked with Ashton found that the choreographer built the roles from his dancers, rather than imposing his steps on them, and Kronstam was no exception. "Fred used all my qualities, as he has done with everybody. That's why there are so many arabesques in *Romeo and Juliet,* because Mona was best in arabesques. I remember he said at one rehearsal, 'Can't you show me something other than an arabesque?'

"He started with the madrigal, the first little pas de deux in the beginning of the ballroom scene. We slipped away from the party and we left. Then he went on with my entrance variation, and then Mona's. And then he must have done the balcony pas de deux. But he had to know me, he had to know my abilities, how much I could jump, and if I could do a double saut de basque into arabesque, things like that. I know he went to classes and performances. Sometimes he would come to Vera's afternoon class, and I know he saw my *La Sonnambula.*" (On another, less guarded occasion, Kronstam said, with a laugh, "He was watching me any chance he could get.")

Ashton worked by showing the steps. "He would say, 'Can you do something like this?'" Kronstam remembered, elaborating: "And then he did his steps. And then I said, 'Well, what do you mean?' He said, 'Well, up in the air, and both legs, and end in high arabesque. Stupid boy!' And then I understood. He couldn't show it at that time, really. What was he? At the end of his forties?

Kronstam as Romeo in
Frederick Ashton's
Romeo and Juliet, 1956.
Photo: Mydtskov. The
Royal Theatre, Copen-
hagen. By permission of
Det kongelige Teaters
bibliotek og arkiv.

So he marked it. He still could mark the steps. And especially Juliet. He loved
to do Juliet!

"He was very correct about it. The boys' dance, he knew exactly what he
wanted for that. But with the pas de deux, it was a little different. 'Couldn't you
do it once more?' And 'Couldn't you do it twice a little different?' Or 'Could you
raise your arm a little more, and could you use a little more back,' and things
like that."

The dances for the corps were not universally admired; the Danish dancers
called those in the second act "flag hell." "All the big group dances, especially
the townspeople, were mostly made on Flemming Flindt and Ole Fatum. He
said, 'What can you do? Show me? Oh, I'll use five of those, and then I'll do five
to that side, and five to the other side.' He was not deeply interested in the
corps de ballet. But the lyricism, the poetry, of Shakespeare's words really came
out in Ashton's ballet."

Ashton did not discuss the play with the dancers. "He used the words,
Shakespeare's words, and then I would go home and read how they came into

the context of the story. He had had them in his head probably for a year, you know. So to him, it was natural. He would just say, 'Well, now you hear the lark.' And then Juliet says, 'No, 'tis a nightingale.' And then I had to go home and I had to start reading the whole story over again, and figure out what he meant." Kronstam had not read or seen the play before Ashton came to Copenhagen. When he did read it, he read it in English; Fredbjørn Bjørnsson gave him a copy shortly after the casting had been announced. Kronstam said he had no models for his characterization (apparently he had not found either Schaufuss's or Bruhn's Romeo in the Bartholin version useful). "All I had was the movie with Laurence Harvey, who was beautiful in it. That was in the cinemas about a month before we had the opening night."

Otherwise, Ashton gave Kronstam everything he needed in rehearsals. "He was very sensitive. He was not so much interested in the brilliance of the dancing. In that triple dance for the three boys, he wanted to show me off in what I could do the best. He made that dance for the nine men with Kjeld Noack [as Paris] in the middle. Otherwise, the ballet was more lyrical. It was like one long pas de deux all the way through. You didn't follow so much the tragedy of the two families fighting and all of that. You followed the tragedy of two young lovers who couldn't get out to have each other."

If Ashton used "all our qualities," one of Kronstam's best qualities, even at that early age, was his musicality. "Fred told me that he never worked on the beat of the music. He always worked on the melody. But it didn't matter whether you were on one or on four, as long as you were with the music."

The ballet's duels presented a special challenge. Unlike Russian dancers, the Danish men had not been trained in fencing while at school. An old fencing teacher was brought in to help stage the fights. "Ashton told him what he wanted, that he wanted the corps de ballet to move to this side, and then the dancers come up here, and then the corps de ballet moves back, and they're falling down the stairs, and things like that. He [the fencing teacher] was there to explain the fencing manner. Sometimes Ashton had an idea and wanted this and that, but the fencing master said, 'No, you have to do it this way.' He was not very theatrical, the one we had at that time."

The duels were very violent. "It was fencing, fencing, fencing, fencing, sticking, running up the stairs, fencing on the stairs, running down again, stick him [Tybalt] in his stomach, and then he had to roll down, and then he crawled forward on his knees, and rose up, fell down, and died." There were mishaps. "Niels Bjørn [as Tybalt] was hurt one evening. We were about seven steps up and I gave him such a bang on his shoulder with my sword that he fell down the stairs and broke his arm. He crawled forward with a broken arm [*mimes graphically*] and he raised himself up and he gave a scream, and he fell down on the floor, and was lying still until the curtain went down."

Kronstam seems to have relished the fights. He scoffed at the notion that it was difficult to fight fiercely, yet carefully, to separate fighting from play-acting. "We are Danes. We are different. We just go into it and we fight. We don't hold back. We don't think about what can happen. We work it up, we rehearse it, and then we do it full out. So there is nothing playful about it. It really goes like a fight."

The rehearsals went very smoothly. Kronstam could remember only one scene that gave Ashton difficulty, the one with Romeo and Juliet in Friar Law-rence's cell. "That was his big problem because it's such beautiful music; it's reminiscent of the balcony scene. And he just couldn't figure out what to do because all Mona was doing was a little bourrée, and she did an arabesque, and she was standing, and he said, 'Oh, you must do something else. This is too much. The music is too strong.'

"Otherwise, I don't remember that there was any problem. And he didn't have a fit. Not one. A lot of choreographers have fits because they are fright-ened that their work is not good enough, and the dancers forget it from day to day, and things like that. Ashton didn't have one fit. After rehearsals, he went over to the [Hotel] D'Angleterre and was sitting with Stanley Williams, having a scotch—but only one. And he said, 'This was this day's work. Tomorrow is another day.'"

Ashton did give Kronstam guidance on makeup. Kronstam had fended for himself since that brief tutorial around the time of *Peter Grimes* until *La Son-nambula*. "Then [John] Taras came, and at the first dress rehearsal I had my usual makeup. He said, 'Everything is very good, but we have to do something about your makeup.' So he came up to my room, and we went with a pale, pale face, bigger mouth, bigger eyes, eyebrows, everything he changed, so I looked—weird. And that lasted a couple of years because that was how he made it, and I thought it was glorious." Kronstam came to the *Romeo* rehearsals with the pale, pale face and big mouth and eyes, "But Fred said, 'No, don't use that for Romeo. You do something more standard or you don't do any makeup at all.' He put a wig on me for the first performances. Which he took off."

Looking back on those weeks, Kronstam said that working with Ashton had been enjoyable, "but while you're working, you don't think so much about that. You just meet every day, and try to be as fresh and as clear and remember everything that he said yesterday, and go into it. It was really after the premiere that I realized that he had made a masterwork."

Kronstam's Romeo was highly praised. Svend Kragh-Jacobsen, whose judgment counted most in Denmark at this time, wrote: "The ballet put the definitive exclamation mark after the name of Henning Kronstam. In him, our ballet now has a young Romantic dancer with excellent dancing skills and rare plastic beauty. His growth in the past season is as impressive as it is joyous. He's now completely in the first rank, exactly that much wanted but rarely found complement to our world dancer Erik Bruhn, who has just returned and who will later alternate with him in the role" (*Berlingske Tidende,* May 20, 1956).

As had happened with *The Nutcracker,* however, political undertones can be detected in several reviews. It is hard to read Harald Engberg's remarks in his review of the second performance for *Politiken,* without seeing a little dig at

The ballroom scene, 1956. Left to right: Mercutio (Stanley Williams), Romeo (Kronstam), and Benvolio (Ole Fatum) enter the ballroom scene. The women left to right: Aase Bonde, Ruth Andersen, Mette Mollerup, Kirsten Simone, Elisabeth Envoldsen, Elin Bauer. Photo: Mydtskov. The Royal Theatre, Copenhagen. By permission of Det kongelige Teaters bibliotek og arkiv.

Volkova—were Lander still at Kongens Nytorv, the young male dancers would have a proper model—and a wink to the rumors then being spread by his rivals about Kronstam's homosexuality. "Henning Kronstam has now learned to close his mouth, but when will come the time when we don't see our dancers copying Lifar and Petit? They seem 'girly,' and as it is through their masculinity that they rise above the dance artists from abroad, one sincerely has to wonder why not one living soul at the Theatre to this day has been able to set them straight."

Allan Fridericia, reviewing the opening night's performance in *Information,* seems to be one who had thought the leading roles should have gone to Margrethe Schanne and Frank Schaufuss, and also questioned Kronstam's manliness: "The choice of title roles is not entirely successful. It is still a misunderstanding to let the very young Henning Kronstam dance with Mona Vangsaae. To yours truly, it was very hard to believe in their love, something that was underlined by Kronstam's lack of masculinity."

It seems unlikely that Kronstam, who was consistently praised for being virile and masculine at the *Nutcracker* debut the preceding season, had suddenly become effeminate. It is possible that some critics confused lyrical and Romantic men[2]—the Poet and Romeo—with effeminacy. There is a suspicion of elegance running through some Danish reviews. These gave Kronstam a complex and he worried for years that he was not masculine enough on stage. "Franz and Hugh and people like that would tell me not to worry about it, but I did," he said. When he began dancing in America, critics constantly referred to the "virility" of his dancing, and the earliest comparisons were to Igor Youskevitch, one of the most masculine dancers of the age. Dancers, and those who knew Kronstam from boyhood to later in life, say he was never effeminate.

On another battlefront, there had been much speculation that Ashton had intended the role of Romeo for Bruhn, who was performing in New York and could not get away. In an undated interview with "mark," Ashton was asked if he had expected to work with Bruhn: "Yes, if I were to be totally honest, but his stay in the U.S. drags on more than expected. Instead Henning Kronstam dances the male part and he does it to my great satisfaction. This is also the case with Mona Vangsaae as Juliet." Ashton may well have assumed that Bruhn would be Romeo, as he thought Schanne might have been Juliet, since those were the two dancers whose names and reputations he knew. However, once Ashton saw the company, there was no talk about Kronstam being second choice, or in any way a disappointment to him. The reviewer "pinoc" alludes to this issue, this time in Kronstam's favor: "By looks, the young dancer, Henning Kronstam, is the perfect image of the romantic lover, something he already had indicated in *Sonnambula*. Apparently he's one of the dancers that Ashton knows how to shape because one has never seen him dance better than last night. At the performance during the Edinburgh festival, the Royal Romeo will be taken by Erik Bruhn. He will be able to dance it with great technical promise, but not with the lyric sensitivity that Henning Kronstam radiates."[3]

Nils Schiørring did not find Kronstam's poetic movement effeminate and, with "pinoc," praises Ashton as a coach as well as a choreographer: "Henning Kronstam towered over all of them as Romeo. Not only does he have the age of Romeo, he also has his poetry. He danced so wonderfully, purely, and beautifully, and with such devotion. He has grown even more after his remarkable performance in *Sonnambula*. Almost all his little faults seem gone, and Ashton's direction showed itself to be triumphant."

Despite the praise, as he had of his Poet, Kronstam thought his Romeo had been merely sketched at that first performance: "Surely I must have been blank, very weak and blank, in the beginning. It changed, definitely. Because then came all these other roles, and I got more sure about myself on the stage. I dared more. I read more about the story."

The *Romeo and Juliet* story, that "of the two young people who just wanted to get out and have each other" remained one of Kronstam's favorites throughout his career. He never tired of stories of lovers separated by an insurmountable barrier, whether in *Romeo and Juliet*, in Petit's *Cyrano de Bergerac*, or Glen Tetley's *Firebird*. Undoubtedly Kronstam's own troubles with his family and an unblessed love made it easy for him to understand the ballet, and he had a great affinity with the character. He discussed who Romeo was, and described the ballet from Romeo's viewpoint.

"I certainly understood him. Ashton wanted us to show the characters, and Romeo was romantic, dreaming. Tybalt was catlike, mean. And Mercutio was strong and handsome and wanted to fight. Romeo didn't know who he was, really. He had his friends, and they were young boys. And he was more romantic than the others.

"The rest of the story is so easy because then comes the marriage and then come the fights, first between Tybalt and Mercutio and then between Romeo and Tybalt. And then it's very natural, if you're moved in your spirit, which I

The bedroom scene, 1965. Kronstam and Simone. Photo: Mydtskov. The Royal Theatre, Copenhagen. By permission of Det kongelige Teaters bibliotek og arkiv.

was when I did the role, always, then you cannot help feeling hate for that
Tybalt who did it [killed Mercutio]. Even though it's an accident, you have to
have revenge for it."

The tomb scene, where Romeo danced briefly with what he thought was
Juliet's dead body, caused a bit of a stir and was considered by some to be un-
seemly, if not obscene. Compared to later versions, it is quite tasteful, but it
was a new idea in 1956. Kronstam said emphatically, "There was *nothing* obscene about that scene. I just took her off the coffin, I brought her forward, put
her on her pointes, laid her on my knee, put her on my left leg and embraced
her, raised her up, looked at her one side and the other side, lifted her, and I put
her back on the coffin. And today? What are they doing today? No, no. That was
just—sometimes critics have to say something. But Ashton was more erotic in
it, even though it was very lyrical. He went a little further with us than he had
done with the English ballet, I think. He dared to do more. All this kissing and
all those things, he did that much later in his career in England. Romeo was a
fighter. They were all fighters. Right from the start of the ballet, everybody
fights. Even the girls fight, even in Ashton's very civilized version."

Like the Poet, Kronstam's Romeo changed over the ten years he danced it. "It changed as my own personality changed. I swear, I never gave a performance where I didn't give everything I had in me. Every night I would be on my knees asking God that I would give a good performance. So naturally, it grows. I don't think you can do a ballet like that for ten years and still be interesting in it without really being deeply involved in the role."

Romeo and Juliet was performed 111 times in Copenhagen and frequently on tour at home and abroad.[4] Kronstam felt, however, that the ballet was not very well cared for. "We had the premiere in the opening of the Festival in May," he said, "and it was on for two or three performances, and then we had to open with it in Edinburgh in August. And that was tough.

"Niels Bjørn [Larsen] was in charge of the company at that time, and he kept the ballet up. Fred came up to Edinburgh, just to see that it looked all right. But it was not on the level that it had been. It could never be, after two months' holiday. You've got to have the proper rehearsal time, and we had to rehearse *La Sylphide* and *Folk Tale,* all these ballets too. And Ashton's ballets have to be nursed because otherwise he says, 'Oh, who cares. My old stuff.'"

When the company brought *Romeo and Juliet* to Edinburgh, it ran into British ballet politics. Ashton was not popular with all the British critics, some of whom found him old-fashioned and dull. A rather nasty review by Cecil Smith in August 1955 had the subheading: "Beguiling, But Where Are the New Ideas, Mr. A?"

> Mona Vangsaae was an entrancingly pretty Juliet—demure and winning, but never sentimental or pretty-pretty. Henning Kronstam's tall, lithe figure and naturally manly bearing made him an ideally romantic Romeo.
>
> Mr. Ashton owes a debt of gratitude to the Danes. They made his ballet seem better than it really is.
>
> The steps and figures and grouping were, of course, always slickly professional, for Mr. Ashton knows his business thoroughly. In a superficial way they always looked well.
>
> But there was little inner dramatic impulse in the material he gave the dancers. And I think I should drop dead with shock if he ever had a really fresh dance idea nowadays.

"L.G.," however, felt that "Ashton has improved on Shakespeare": "Opposite her is Henning Kronstam, the perfect Romeo, expressively tender as he wins her love, virile in combat, dignified in grief at the death scene. Not yet at his

In the crypt with Mona Vang-saae, 1956. Photo: Mydtskov. The Royal Theatre, Copenhagen. By permission of Det kongelige Teaters bibliotek og arkiv.

In the crypt with Kirsten Simone, 1965. Photo: Mydtskov. The Royal Theatre, Copenhagen. By permission of Det kongelige Teaters bibliotek og arkiv.

full powers as a dancer, he gives promise of greatness. His bearing is noble and he partners beautifully. To the character he brings sensitivity and insight, and his dance with the body of his supposedly dead love is one of the most moving moments seen on a stage. Romeo is a masterpiece, and the Danes add to its luster" (*Evening Dispatch,* August 27, 1955).

When Bruhn did dance the role, he was judged disappointing. "F.D." wrote: "*Romeo and Juliet* with Erik Bruhn was one of the festival ballets that had been the most anticipated. But the performance, which took place last night to a sold-out house, was far from successful. Erik Bruhn disappointed, surprisingly, by insecurity and a failing memory, and his Romeo thus was facile and that gave the performance a list. The sparkle of young love that Henning Kronstam finds such beautiful expressions for in his Romeo was very much missing in Bruhn, who often impressed by his blinding technique and his beautiful appearance, but who only rarely managed to move the spectator."

This was the first ballet in which Kronstam had received better reviews in a role than his older rival, and he must have been pleased, but he was also very sympathetic to Bruhn, who he felt hadn't really been given "a proper chance" at the role. "He didn't feel at home in it because it wasn't made on him. And he had only two weeks' rehearsal, and not with Ashton. Erik had a more strict way of dancing than I had. I was more melting into it, and there was more flow to it—which Ashton liked." He added, almost as an afterthought, "And besides, he'd seen me in it," by which Kronstam meant he had similar experiences with roles Bruhn had created and had felt intimidated after seeing another dancer so well suited to a role and may have assumed that Bruhn reacted in the same way.

One thing that seemed to puzzle Kronstam about Bruhn was why the older man had been a rather late developer as an actor because "he was such an intelligent boy." This point came up several times in the interviews for this book, Kronstam saying that it was such a shame that Bruhn hadn't had Gerda Karstens for mime class rather than Borchsenius (whom Bruhn mentions—in John Gruen's *Erik Bruhn, Danseur Noble*—as being an uninspiring teacher). Kronstam referred to "Erik's book" again in the context of *Romeo and Juliet.* It is worth recounting here, as it also explains one aspect of Kronstam's working method.

"I don't know if Erik ever sat down and read *Romeo and Juliet* and found words to use because that's what I have done for all of my dramatic roles. Cyrano, and *The Lesson,* and *Romeo and Juliet* and everything. Sat down and read to find out, 'This is a word I can use here,' and 'This is a word I can use there.' That makes movement sense. Because if you do that, then you have something to think in your mind when you're on stage so you don't look blank. Maybe Erik was thinking too much of his presence. I don't know what. He was wonderful, and he was a lovable person, and we ended up being very good friends. We were, of course, competitors, but we ended up being very good friends."

Ashton's *Romeo and Juliet* remained in the repertory for nearly a decade. Whoever was the company's ballet master, either Larsen or Frank Schaufuss, was responsible for rehearsing it, and Kronstam felt that neither man really understood how to cast or stage the ballet. Kronstam, and Volkova, wanted Ashton to come to Copenhagen again and rehearse the work. It has been suggested that Ashton could not make the time to come, but in Volkova's letter to Kronstam in 1959, in which she wrote of meeting Ashton in London, she

Left to right: Benvolio (Flemming Ryberg), Romeo (Kronstam) and Mercutio (Tommy Frishøi), 1965. Photo: Mydtskov. The Royal Theatre, Copenhagen. By permission of Det kongelige Teaters bibliotek og arkiv.

mentioned that he had told her he could come to work on the ballet "any time within the next six months." Why this did not happen remains a mystery.

The greatest *Romeo and Juliet* mystery, however, is why the ballet disappeared from the repertory after 1965. Because Flemming Flindt did not schedule it during his directorship, and because he also dropped the other Ashton work in the repertory, *La Fille mal gardée,* which had only been performed for one season, it has been assumed that this was Flindt's choice. According to Larsen, however, the truth is not so simple. Apparently, Ashton, director of England's Royal Ballet in 1965, wanted to acquire *La Sylphide* and asked for someone to come from Copenhagen to stage it, but Flindt refused, saying it was one of the company's signature pieces and he couldn't let it out of repertory. Ashton, as a tit for tat, then withdrew the rights for the Royal Danish Ballet to perform *Romeo and Juliet.*[5]

When the company danced the Prokofiev score again, it was John Neumeier's production in 1974. Kronstam directed this production until 1993. He liked the drama of the Neumeier version and thought it suited the Danish audience better than the Ashton, but he retained his love of Ashton's ballet for its lyricism and its poetry. He also used much of what he had learned from Ashton while directing the Neumeier. "I know where the music matches the poetry in the play because I remember what he told me," Kronstam said in a 1991 interview. "The boys are always asking me, 'How do you know that's where the lark is?,' and I say, 'I know because I got it from Ashton.'"

But the gift he was most grateful for was how deeply Ashton believed in him. "I said the other day he was in love with me. He wasn't in love, but he was infatuated with me, the way choreographers get sometimes with dancers. He was fascinated by me and by what he could get out of me. He was always telling me, 'Henning, believe you are the best dancer on that stage. Do whatever you like to do, and I'll instruct the others about it.' He gave me confidence, which was what I needed. I was not a principal dancer. I was just corps de ballet, just coming out of the aspirants' class. So I think that was what meant the most to me, that he believed in me so much that he gave me such a big role. And then that we would continue the friendship for such a long time."

It was that long friendship—the two corresponded, their paths crossed a few times professionally, and Kronstam stayed with Ashton when he visited London—that led to the revival of first the balcony pas de deux, and thus, indirectly, the entire ballet in the early 1980s. Kronstam repaid his debt to Ashton by giving Ashton the confidence that his ballet could be revived and that there was an interest in its revival. "Ashton was like a lot of other choreographers. He said, 'It won't last. It will only last a couple of years, and that's it.' So when I took the pas de deux to New York, and then Peter Schaufuss took the ballet on again, he said, 'Oh! Why do you do my old stuff?'"

The balcony pas de deux from *Romeo and Juliet* was the Royal Danish Ballet's contribution to the gala celebrating the Metropolitan Opera's hundredth anniversary in New York in 1984. "Jane Hermann called me and asked us to come and said to bring the *Coppelia* pas de deux. But I said no, because it's a bad pas de deux and it doesn't have a coda. I said I would bring the *Romeo and Juliet* pas de deux, and I called Fred and asked him, and he said, 'Well, all right, Henning, if you can remember it.'

"Fred said that he didn't remember *Romeo*. He said he definitely didn't remember a step of it. But when I came [to the Met] with Arne [Villumsen] and Lis [Jeppesen], I insisted that he have the last rehearsal with them. We went into the room and they started the pas de deux and right away he knew what was going on. Especially Lis. He was very enchanted with Lis, and he wanted her to do the first night in London. But then she got sick and couldn't do it. But he remembered. He said, 'Is that right, Henning? Is that how you did it?' I said, "Yes, it is.' 'All right. But then I think a little more—a little more passion.' I don't think he could ever have enough passion."

During the interviews for this book, Kronstam watched a videotape of the balcony scene from the telecast of the Met gala and commented on what he saw. This brief interview is given here in its entirety:

Q: Before we leave Ashton, could I play you the videotape of the balcony pas de deux from the telecast of the Met gala and see if watching it makes you remember anything else?

Kronstam: Sure. [Tape begins.] This is the New York Met version. Lis is standing alone—now, the stairs were much higher, and there were no flowers around. It was a bare stage. But what I love is that it is so simple.

Q: Her arm movements, did that—

Kronstam: It's shivering. Like you can't fall asleep. She just cannot find rest, you know. It's like, "What's happened to me?" It has to be an expectation, freezing, but almost like a fever at the same time, from meeting this boy for the first time. [Romeo enters.] This is typical Ashton, you know. This is all breathing. We

Two moments from the balcony pas de deux with Kirsten Simone, 1965. Photos: Mydtskov. The Royal Theatre, Copenhagen. By permission of Det kongelige Teaters bibliotek og arkiv.

breathe together. You don't get that that much from Lis, but that's what it's supposed to be.

Q: [Romeo's solo begins.] Could you tell me what you remember about the solo?

Kronstam: We had a little foyer, the old foyer that was in the old Theatre, before it was rebuilt, and that's where we did his variation. He would have an idea about what was going to be done, but he did it on me, and whatever I could do, like the double sauts de basque into arabesque, the big kick, he used. He used all my épaulement—there was much more épaulement!—and plié pas de bourrée, and those pas de flêche, going down. Plié, pas de bourrée, attitude, stay, and plié pas de bourrée, stay. He marked it, and I did it, and it was done in fifteen minutes.

Q: Was the phrasing—

Kronstam: The phrasing was much stronger.

Q: And you said the other day that the dancing should be sharper?

Kronstam: Definitely. A double pas de basque en tournant really has to be [snaps fingers]. And end in arabesque. And stand. And that's what he wanted.

Q: How do you keep it in the style? How do you make it sharp, but keep it smooth and creamy at the same time?

Kronstam: Because you know where to stop. You know which position—again, I come back to the plié. You've done your double sauts de basque, and you continue your plié. The position is there, but the plié can continue while you're lifting your leg so it looks very harmonious.

Q: Did he give you any direction or lines, that sort of thing?

Kronstam: No, no. He didn't. It's a love declaration to Juliet. And that, I understood. [Tape continues.] The beautiful thing about it [the pas de deux] is, it's so simple.

Q: Yes. All the other choreographers would have Juliet being—

Kronstam: Oh! Turned around, and twirled around, and things like that. You can't get anything more simple than this. Just promenade, coupé—Now, this is what he called dancing on coals. Because he wanted her to do attitude piqué, piqué, attitude piqué, piqué, and Mona was doing it sort of, one, two, three, four; one, two, three, four. And he said, "It shouldn't be like that. It should be like you are walking on burning coals. So that means that every lift of the leg should be like you've burned yourself."

Q: Rehearsing Apollo, in one of the variations Balanchine told Peter Martins that it should be like "walking on hot coals."

Kronstam: No, that wasn't Balanchine. That was Ashton.

Q: Apparently Balanchine used the same image for Apollo.

Kronstam: Wait—yes. I know which part he means. It's the beginning of the last variation. I remember Balanchine showed me the whole variation, and I did it, and he was amazed that I could do it the way he wanted it the first time. And he said, "How can you do that?" And I told him because Ashton did it for Juliet, and said it was to be like dancing on hot coals. It's the last variation, just before the last pirouette down on the knee.

Q: Ashton was always quoted as saying the eyes are very important.

Kronstam: Very. He said to me, "Don't smile. If you want to smile, smile with your eyes. But don't give me any grin." Brought up in the Bournonville style at that time, you naturally had it. But he said, "If you smile with your eyes, then your face will change." And this is another thing that I use in coaching, because some of the young boys say, "Well, I can't smile because I'm too nervous." And I say, "Well, I don't care. Your eyes have to smile. Your eyes." And the minute your eyes start smiling, your face lifts. And if your eyes are dull, forget it.

Q: [Tape continues.] In the pas de deux, Juliet is almost leading, in a way. She's the one who takes the arabesque, and he has to come and support her. Did that just happen, or was that part of his plan?

Kronstam: Don't forget that Mona was thirty-five and I was twenty.

Q: And the little flutters with the feet, is that the heart beating?

Kronstam: Yes. Oh—that's Freddie! The way Lis runs to him? Fred stopped the rehearsals when we did it the first time, and then he went into Juliet, and he grabbed Arne's hands.

Q: That's more than a wave good-bye, that last gesture.

Kronstam: That's morning. That's the dawn coming up. There was the kiss, and then it was suddenly that the dawn was coming, and then jump over. [Tape ends.]

Q: What do you think of *Romeo and Juliet* as a ballet?

Kronstam: It had wonderful roles. It was weak in the corps de ballet, especially the townspeople. Not so much the ball; the ball was rather powerful. He was interested in the main figures. He was interested in Romeo and Juliet, who were the main thing for him, and then Mercutio and Tybalt, the mother, the nurse. It was all the things that you would read in the play. You don't read about the peasants.

Most of all, I remember his James. I was one of
the kids in the reel, and we would stand down
in the wings and watch. We were almost crying
every time. I don't remember any other
Jameses; I only remember Henning.
—Arne Villumsen

Ten

James: Bournonville's *La Sylphide*

The role of James, the doomed, impetuous hero of Bournonville's *La Sylphide,*
is the most treasured part for men in the Danish repertory. It is rich in both
dancing and dramatic opportunities, and Kronstam's dark good looks and
masculine sensitivity suited it perfectly. He danced James for fourteen years,
from 1956 to 1970, and by the early 1960s had become definitive in the role.
With his airy jump, effortless beats, and spacious, musical dancing, he was
technically brilliant. More important, perhaps, Kronstam's warmth and humanity made his audience sympathetic to the plight of the young man who
chases his dream, and drew them into the world he created on stage. Sorella
Englund, the magical, sensual Sylph of the 1970s, first saw Kronstam's James
when she joined the company as a teenager. "We would stand in the wings
every night that he danced, all the young girls and boys, and we would cry. His

tragedy was that he was longing for something so much, but he didn't even really know what it was. At the end, he was completely broken. Completely. He gave everything on the stage. Nothing was false. It was as if it were his own life we were watching."

Glen Tetley also remembered Kronstam's James: "From the very first moment when the curtain went up and I saw him sitting in that chair, I knew it was going to be a very special James. A very dark, brooding, haunted and, of course, eloquent and elegant figure. Henning not only brought flight to his roles, he brought this sense of gravity and weight, to make the characters in his roles fully fleshed.

"So he was a wonderful contrast [to the Sylph]. The ballet demands that. It can't be just danced with the steps, if there isn't a deep, romantic sensual quality about it of being in love with the unattainable, not just in the stereotyped, poetic fashion, but with every atom of your being."

James is the prototypical Romantic hero, as *La Sylphide* is the prototypical Romantic ballet. Bournonville brought his version of *La Sylphide* to Copenhagen in 1836, four years after the original Opera production had dazzled Paris and belatedly introduced Romanticism to ballet. *La Sylphide* also began the era of the ballerina, when pointework caught the public's fancy, elevating the status of female dancers and decimating the ranks of their now nearly superfluous male colleagues. Bournonville left Paris at the beginning of the pointe shoe revolution and continued his career as a dancer at home in Copenhagen, and so neither ballerinas nor toe shoes ruled at Kongens Nytorv. Bournonville based his libretto for *La Sylphide* on the Paris version, although he used a different score and the steps were his own. Bournonville was the first James and his sixteen-year-old pupil, Lucile Grahn, was his Sylph.

The story of *La Sylphide* is both simple and complex, as the best ballet stories are. The Sylphide is a lovelorn, woodland fairy who appears to James on the morning of his wedding as he dreams in his chair. Infatuated by her beauty, James deserts his mortal bride, Effy, and follows the Sylph into the forest. There, she dances with him, but will not let him touch her. James sees Madge, a witch, who gives him a magic veil that, she tells him, will win the Sylph. However, when James wraps the veil around the Sylph's shoulders, her wings fall off and she dies. Effy marries Gurn, James's rival, as Madge had predicted. Madge has taken her revenge for an old quarrel, and James, having lost both his real and his dream lover, dies in despair.

James presents an extraordinary challenge to the dance actor. In the first act, he must be in love with Effy and ready for marriage, yet torn by doubts and dreams. In the second, he has perfect happiness within his grasp, then loses it in a heartbeat. In the last three minutes of the ballet alone, James experiences love, passion, grief, betrayal, guilt, anger, fear, and despair. Kronstam's beautiful, expressive face, his ability to change moods in an instant, and the rich tone of his dancing made him unforgettable in this role.

The French tired of *La Sylphide* long ago, but Bournonville's production has been danced in Copenhagen nearly continuously since its premiere. It was a Danish exclusive until the 1960s, when the ballet entered the repertory of American Ballet Theatre; now, many ballet companies have productions, and the role of James has always lured male stars. Erik Bruhn had had a great success in the role, first in Copenhagen and later in New York, dancing with Carla Fracci at American Ballet Theatre. Bruhn, a pure classical dancer, was intensely dramatic and a powerful performer, but Kronstam's dark, sensual Romanticism made him the more believable James for many. Bruhn danced the role in New York through the 1960s but stopped dancing James in Copenhagen after Kronstam became established in the role there. Flemming Flindt, two years younger than Kronstam, was also a noted James, and some preferred him to either Bruhn or Kronstam as he was earthier, less noble, and thus appealed to those who felt that James was more peasant than laird. James was also a favorite of Rudolf Nureyev, who learned the role from Bruhn and danced it frequently, mostly with the National Ballet of Canada. He was an exciting James, romantic in a wild, Byronic way, but he never mastered the light, fleet Bournonville style. His ardent, overly emphatic dancing (with Fracci) is captured, in part, in the film *I Am a Dancer*. Nureyev worked at James throughout his career, and it was the ballet he chose to dance on his return to St. Petersburg in 1989.

In Copenhagen, several able dancers followed Kronstam as James in the 1970s, although none erased his memory. The next James-most-likely was Peter Martins, whose blond good looks and granite technique presaged a James in the Erik Bruhn mold, but Martins danced only a few performances before flying away to his own world of dreams at the New York City Ballet. Kronstam did not have a true successor in the role until Arne Villumsen made his debut as James in 1979. Kronstam coached Villumsen, as he did three other notable young Jameses in the late eighties and early nineties: Alexander Kølpin, Nikolaj Hübbe, and Lloyd Riggins.

Kronstam watched *La Sylphide* from the wings from his first season at the Theatre, when he was cast as one of the children in the reel. The only Sylph he remembered clearly was Margrethe Schanne, who owned the role, dancing it exclusively from 1945 until her retirement in 1965, and he watched her for thirteen years before dancing with her. She had several partners and Kronstam saw all of them, learning, as he did so, both choreography and characterization and trying out interpretations in his imagination as he decided what kind of James he wanted to grow up to be.

The first James was Børge Ralov, the company's reigning male star. A demi-caractère dancer, Ralov was a great Gennaro in Bournonville's *Napoli* but was ill suited to James, and danced the role for only a single season. He was succeeded by Poul Gnatt, whom Kronstam greatly admired. "That was one of the first times I saw a man lying right there on the stage, and the tears were running out of his eyes. Poul was a very strong James. He was a hero, but he was a man at the same time.

"After Poul, I saw Erik [Bruhn], who was beautiful. His James became very different later on, but in the beginning he was so blond and so beautiful that he was almost fading out. He danced like a dream, but I thought he was too pale. I also saw Serge Golovine, and he was very French and very Romantic, though not in the poetic way. He was Romantic in a wild way, and that was the way I decided to go. Of course, it changed later, but at first I wanted it to be very much an adventure."

Kronstam began his adventure as James under what sound like terrifying circumstances: He made his debut in the role on the opening night of the company's first American tour, at New York's Old Metropolitan Opera House in September 1956, at the age of twenty-two. His Sylphide was Schanne; his Madge, Niels Bjørn Larsen, also making his debut. Kronstam said he got the chance because the company was short on men in general, and Jameses in particular. Gnatt had left a few years before; Bruhn was then appearing with American Ballet Theatre and barred by contract from dancing with his home company. Kronstam had learned the steps from watching the ballet and the mime scenes in Gerda Karstens's classes. He was coached by Hans Brenaa, who polished his style and, as he put it, "relaxed me in the role." The part is technically demanding. James leads a vigorous Scots reel (and, in some productions, dances a classical solo) in the first act and has three solos, full of quick, beaten steps, jumps, and double air turns, in the second. Kronstam,

As James in the first-act
reel, *La Sylphide*, 1956.
Private collection.

brought up in the style, found the actual dancing relatively easy: "If you've
learned the style, and it's natural for you to dance the Bournonville steps, then
it's very enjoyable to do the variations. The first act variation is a joy to do."[1]
The characterization was another matter; he worked on it throughout his fourteen years as James.

Many of the Americans watching Kronstam's debut found *La Sylphide* interesting, if a bit old-fashioned, and responded warmly to the Danish genius for
creating characters. Both John Martin of the *New York Times* and Walter Terry of
the *Herald Tribune* had visited Copenhagen the preceding spring to see the then
annual Festival of Music and Dance, and so they were prepared for the
company's approach to ballet, so different from New Yorkers' usual fare of
Balanchine's neoclassical works or the lavish story ballets danced by British
and Soviet companies. Martin wrote: "Young Henning Kronstam is [the Sylphide's] lover and does a brilliant job of it. He is handsome, believable and technically excellent."

The audience approved, as well. The Copenhagen daily *Berlingske Tidende* reported that "the reel nearly caused an ovation" and that there was constant applause during Kronstam's second-act solos. "It was Kronstam's debut, and he was simply beautiful. Since Erik Bruhn could not dance here, the ballet could not have given New York a more excellent James than Kronstam. That was the Danish opinion yesterday, and it is the American judgment today."

When Kronstam danced his first James at home in November, he received mixed reviews. In *Berlingske Tidende*, "nls" wrote:

> Henning Kronstam, the new handsome central figure of the ballet has become [Schanne's] partner as James, again placed in one of Erik Bruhn's most celebrated parts, one that he covers finely and daringly in the dancing, outstanding in the jumps of the second act and, furthermore, dramatic with a virile stature, air, and a very Scottish profile. It is impressive that the very young dancer, who has advanced so rapidly, almost forced to the front line of the ballet, has managed to defend and fully complete this very demanding task for the ballet's American tour. The audience recognized his success last night with great applause.

The Danish audience treated the performance as a triumphant homecoming for Kronstam, who had been the clear hero of the American tour, and stamped loudly (stamping on the Royal Theatre's wooden floor is the preferred way for the Danish audience to show its affection, and is much more exciting than the endless "bravos" during the Ballet Boom in New York.) Another reviewer, however, felt that Kronstam was too forceful, guessing correctly that he was building his characterization on Golovine's:

> There are still the changes in casting from the American tour that are presented as novelties to the Danish audiences. Thus, Henning Kronstam showed us his James in *La Sylphide* yesterday. He gave the few dance variations all of his physical handsomeness in mighty and high jumps and double turns in the air. As a dramatic role, however, his whole performance is too strained. His acting is so eager that it is impossible for any poetic atmosphere to be created around the character and an elegiac, Romantic James must be the natural possibility for Kronstam. Perhaps Golovine's irresistible hearty fellow has been his ideal, but for such an expression of a young, virile temperament a slim physique and a big mouth full of smiles is both too little and too much. (Unsigned review, November 1956)

The complaint that Kronstam was not Romantic enough would arise again in other Bournonville roles (most notably when he later danced Gennaro in

Napoli). The critics expected him to be a lyrical Romantic dancer, after the Poet and Romeo, and seemed disappointed when he did not fulfill that expectation.

Several critics noticed a difference in Kronstam after the American tour. Bent Schønberg wrote: "As James, Henning Kronstam shows elevation that astounded. What development is this artist not undergoing?" And "B" gave praise with a sense of humor: "Any soundly thinking James would prefer her to all other Sylphs, even if Scottish sport socks can make even the most imperial-looking ballet legs look like poles, Henning Kronstam was the most handsome and most highly sensitive James in memory and close to overshadowing the memory of Erik Bruhn, and that is as high as you can get." This is one of the earliest indications that Kronstam (still only twenty-two) was not merely a good dancer when Bruhn was not available.

La Sylphide also opened the company's second tour of America (which began in Los Angeles and bypassed New York) in September 1960. *Berlingske Tidende* could again report on the critical reaction with pride. In Chicago, it

Arlette Weinreich as Effy, Henning Kronstam as James, and Flemming Halby as Gurn in the first act of *La Sylphide,* 1965. Photo: Mydtskov. The Royal Theatre, Copenhagen. By permission of Det kongelige Teaters bibliotek og arkiv.

noted that Claudia Cassidy, "the U.S.A.'s most feared ballet critic," had received the company with "a nearly unheard of enthusiasm and warmth."

Cassidy was particularly enthusiastic about Kronstam and is one of the few
critics to have consistently valued his dancing and understood the uniqueness
of his range. (In Chicago, Kronstam followed James with his Toreador in
Roland Petit's *Carmen*.) "While Miss Schanne is a delightful dancer of great
lightness and skill, Mr. Kronstam as the young Scot is a showstopper. He rivals
the best in his field. Taller than most men in ballet, handsome in a dark, lean
romantic style, his technique is extraordinary in its supple strength, with what
seem to be effortless entrechats and cabrioles. He is a danseur noble, but not a
stuffy one. Just stick around for *Carmen* and see the job he does in almost nothing flat on a conceited popinjay named Escamillo."

Kronstam danced James (again with Schanne) in his second New York appearance, in 1965. Walter Terry wrote in the *Herald Tribune:* "As for Mr. Kronstam, he gave us a vivid portrait in dance of a wildly romantic, tender and ador-
ing youth, utterly ensorcelled by the Sylphide. The virtuosity was glorious, the
Bournonville style faultless, making Kronstam the best of all Jameses." Clive
Barnes, the new dance and theater critic for the *Times,* disagreed. Barnes wrote
about Kronstam as though he were a tyro, mistakenly calling him "a James new
here." He went on to say that the thirty-one-year-old dancer "acted with a boyish
ardor that needed a bit more solidity, even stolidity, to convince; he seemed too
flamboyant, too extrovert. Also, his mercurial dancing lacked the effortless
magisterial qualities brought to the role by Erik Bruhn and Flemming Flindt."
(Kronstam remembered this with a rueful laugh: "They changed my performance from the evening to the matinee because Clive Barnes couldn't go in the
evening, and then he hated me.")

Back in Copenhagen, Kragh-Jacobsen wrote several later reviews of Kronstam's James, here with Margrethe Schanne:

> There was great dancing here from Margrethe Schanne and Henning Kron-
> stam, who seemed to have found each other in the most beautiful dancing,
> where she is the creature of the moonlight and he is the Romantic youth in love.
> At the end, though, he's also the man who has to pay with his life for his
> dangerous infatuation with the beautiful woodland creature, who has to die as
> well because she has dared to leave her world and has exposed herself to the
> revenge of the witch.
>
> Both dancers have both the spirit and the style in their hearts and in their

legs. They show a simplicity of the characters that may be naive but that is not in the least bit comic. On the contrary, it's noble simplicity that animates them. In their dances of the first act, both are perfect. Schanne has come to emphasize from the first act, and she is right to do so, the tragic motifs of her anxiety and fears that things cannot go well. But she is touchingly happy for her James, and Kronstam performs the character with a passion in his acting that is absolutely eruptive in the despair of the final scene. That both of them give shape to the steps exquisitely, one hardly needs to mention.

Last night was pure joy because they interpreted Bournonville so wonderfully and so right.

Of Kronstam's first performance with Anna Lærkesen, Kragh-Jacobsen wrote: "Henning Kronstam is today our best James. He's brilliant as a dancer, even if in a week from now he will probably be even more pure doing his tours en l'air, and he owns a richness of expressions for the heartache of poor James. He is—as Bournonville describes him in his program notes from 1836— *grillefænger* [lit., excited by an idée fixe] in the confusion visibly created in him by the declaration of love from the spirit of the air. He and Lærkesen are a leading couple that any company would lick their lips for."

On most days, Kronstam loved James the best of all his roles. After he stopped dancing the part, he worked with Hans Brenaa, who kept the ballet in repertory, sometimes staging the ballet himself, usually assisting Brenaa, until Brenaa's death in 1988, when Kronstam took over the staging until he left the Theatre. Every new James—or Sylphide, or Madge, or Effy, or Gurn—gave him the chance to rethink the ballet. Every detail, from James's rudeness to Madge, to his mother's fears, to the silence of the forest, had been thought through. Kronstam talked about James for over an hour in an interview for this book in January 1994. He usually answered questions thoughtfully, if rather laconically, but *La Sylphide* unleashed a torrent of words, as though fifty years of thoughts about James and his world had been suddenly given voice. He talked about the characters, who they were and why they behaved as they did. He told the story of the ballet from the inside, from James's point of view. He danced the steps with his hands, as grounded dancers often do, and mimed not only James, but the other parts as well. His level of intensity equaled that of a performance and, as he was ill at the time, it must have required an enormous effort; he was exhausted the following day. His comments were obviously colored by his experiences as a coach in addition to his memories as a dancer, and he sometimes seemed to blend his own life with that of James.

"James can be a man who is so infatuated with the Sylph that he abandons everything to follow her. Or he can be a Romantic soul who is looking for the beauty of life and he sees that more in the Sylphide than in a household. Or he can be very impulsive. That's why all the dancers I've coached have been different, because they all approach it in different ways, and that's why I think James is the most interesting of all the Bournonville heroes. James has his doubts, and he has his fears of what he is going to do, but he cannot help himself. Or, if you do it differently, it's that he wants to get away. It's not that he is unhappy; it's because he wants to get out. That's another approach.

"If I were to play the role now, I think James has felt the Sylphide before, but this is the first time that he has seen her. She materializes for him so that he will be able to see her. Before, when he has been hunting in the woods, he has often thought, 'What was that?' because he has felt her presence. She has been watching him from the time he was a little child until he was a grown man. He has always had a feeling that she was there, but he has never seen her. When she materializes on the wedding day, James says [in mime], 'You, here? But what are you doing here?'[2] He becomes frightened, frightened of himself and of what he sees. During the reel, he is afraid he sees something that the others can't see. Suddenly she appears again, up there at the top of the stairs. He sees her, but everyone else continues dancing. So perhaps he thinks, 'Maybe I'm going crazy.' Then she gets stronger and stronger and more and more tempting. When she comes to take the ring, right before the marriage ceremony, that's real. The Sylph has become real. She takes the ring out of his hand, and he knows she is real because she takes the ring."

Four women—the Sylph; Effy, James's fiancée; Anna, his mother; and Madge, a witch—play important roles in the ballet, and Kronstam was very sure of their personalities, as well as that of James.

"At the beginning, the Sylphide is quiet and doesn't want to disturb him when he is asleep in the chair. And then she says, 'Well, I'm here.' She is still frightened; she doesn't know how far she can go. She gets a little more daring the second time, when she comes in through the window, and she starts clapping her little hands, and dancing and showing off to arouse him. The third time she comes is while Effy is putting on her wedding veil and she takes the ring. And there she shows that she wants him very much.

"Whether the Sylph is real or a dream is up to the audience. I think that she can materialize, or she can disappear. This is the strange thing about her. To

James, she materializes. To the rest, she's unseen. Except for Gurn, who comes in in that scene where the Sylphide puts on the tartan. Gurn can see her because she has materialized to James. He always sees her together with James, and when she is with James, then she is real.

"The marriage with Effy has been arranged by Anna [James's mother] because she knows that James is so absentminded. She thinks he needs a girl, and she has just the right girl for him, and that's Effy. Effy is very much in love with James. He thinks that she is a nice, sweet girl, and when he has his calm moments, he thinks that she is all right. But when he has his dreams, he thinks, 'Am I going to marry her, and she is twenty-two and I'm twenty-three or twenty-four, and we're going to live for fifty years together? Am I really going to do that?' So it's the two sides of it. But he likes his Effy. He likes her.

"When I produce the ballet now, I tell them that Anna is very important because she is the one who keeps an eye on things so that everything goes properly. She is the one who goes down to him and says, 'Don't forget that you have to give the tartan to her,' and 'Don't do this,' and 'Don't do that.' She wants him married. She wants him safe. She knows he's a dreamer and that he forgets things. That's why Effy has to be such a happy girl, a sanguine girl, one who will say, 'When we're married, he won't think about anything else.' Anna should be sure of this.

"I have always felt that from the first minute James sees Madge, he is frightened because he knows that she is a clever woman who can see into him. He is afraid that she knows his dreams. That's why he behaves so rudely, right away, almost before seeing her. He gets so frightened that he overreacts. Instead of asking her to leave, he takes her and he throws her out. He gets so upset that he almost can't calm himself down, until Effy gets him into a calmer way of being.

"But all the time, he is frightened. So when Effy asks, 'Can I have my fortune told?' he says, 'No, not you. Let the others.' He tries not to let Effy see what Madge says to the other girls. Then he thinks, 'That witch has been drinking two big vodkas, or *snaps*, or something, and she's telling nonsense to everybody, and she slaps the girl's hands.' And he thinks, 'Maybe she's not that dangerous.' So he lets Effy go. And this is Madge's chance."

One of the clearest examples of how Kronstam used his own fears and experiences—his illness—in a role came in these descriptions of James. Days when "everything is crashing in on him" and "having to calm himself down" were problems Kronstam wrestled with nearly daily.

"That whole wedding day is too much for James. The Sylphide materializes. He has to keep the house going. He has to do all the gifts with the young girls. And the Sylphide comes back again, and he's almost running into the forest, but he stops, and she takes the tartan and puts it on, and he's never seen anything as beautiful as that. And then the door bangs, and Effy comes down, and the Sylphide disappears to nowhere. Then suddenly there's an old fortune teller sitting there. And so it's as though everything is crashing down on him on that day. While he's been a dreamer before, this is too much.

"That may be a reason, too—Now I talk and talk and talk. That may be a reason, too, that he says, 'No, no, no. I must go. I must go away. This is too much.'

"I think that's the buildup for the Sylphide, and the buildup for James. Maybe his doubts are over. He just has one last 'No, I can't' and then he takes the chance. She goes on her knees and begs him—and he should see her eyes; he shouldn't see anything else. Her eyes beg him, and then he says, 'Damn, I do it.'"

Many men who dance the part make James melancholy throughout, seeming to confuse him with Siegfried, or a generic Romantic hero, not realizing that James and the Sylph are happy in the second act until the final few seconds of the ballet. But Kronstam always lived in the moment and danced as though, like James, he was experiencing the action for the first time. If James is happy and confident and sure of his future, the ending is much more of a shock and more of a tragedy.

"When James first comes into the forest, he's amazed at how many sylphides there are, but through their whole first dance, he's searching for *his* Sylphide, his only one. I think he is coming to a world that is a dream world for him. Wonderful, wonderful, wonderful, because it's a different look of people, a different sound. I don't think they talk, the sylphides. They don't chatter. They're so quiet, and so nice, and they behave nicely to him. He is very taken by it, that his Sylph is the queen of all these sylphides. She owns the trees, the water, everything.

"That second act is all happiness in the beginning, because they've been running through the forest, and she has been flying, and she has been having a wonderful time with him. She asks him, 'Do you love me?' And he says, 'I love you.' She says, 'Swear.' This is the first time he thinks, 'Well, I just told you so, but okay. I'll swear.' Then he thinks, 'Now, I can embrace her because I've sworn I love her.' So when she says, 'Me, you cannot touch me,' he doesn't understand. He is human, so he doesn't understand. He thinks, 'Why can't I touch her? I swore that I love her. I followed her. I left my home and everything, and yet I can't touch her.'

"So he goes and sits down, takes his hat off and sits down, and she takes the hat and she starts being very domestic. Oh, she takes the little berries and goes to him and she gives him the water to drink. He tries to embrace her again, until she sees the butterfly, and she catches it, and she is all light and girlish.

"Then she dances, and as he dances with her, he gets more and more flying. The first variation is down into the earth; it's still close to the Scottish dancing [of the first-act reel]. The second variation is a little more light. The third variation is all jumps, as though he's almost joining the sylphides, their world. And then it ends, and she disappears again, and he runs after her.

"After the little scene where Gurn comes in looking for James and then gets betrothed to Effy and they go off, then James comes in again. He has been running around after that Sylphide, and she has been jumping from tree to tree, and she's been flying around, and he can't find her. He is happy because it's a beautiful day and he wants to continue his searching. He is having a good time in the forest, but he is thinking, 'What can I do?' And then he has the happy moment that he sees the witch, and he thinks, 'This is wonderful.' He goes to her and he should show, really, that he is getting aggressive about this."

James, always impulsive and self-centered, assumes that Madge will help him. "He has forgotten that he had the argument with her earlier. All he thinks about is the veil now, and he'd do anything to get it. He kneels for her. He gives her money. He thinks that she is just an old witch, maybe she's a little bit dingding in her head. He thinks he is very sneaky, getting that veil, and the witch explains to him that if he puts the veil around the Sylphide she will be his. She tells him, 'You, with this veil will her embrace, and you will win her.' And he believes that, because what she has foretold before has come true, that he won't marry Effy, that he will be matched with somebody else. He believes in her because she is a witch. He thinks that now he has the means to get the Sylphide."

For a few ecstatic moments the power shifts from the Sylph to James. "Then the Sylphide comes back, and he plays with her. As she plays with him in the first act, he plays with her in the second act. He is not upset with her; he just pretends to be. So when he steps in front of her, he looks at her as though she is somebody that he has dropped from his life. And she doesn't understand. He asks her to come closer because he has the veil and he knows that he has her. He stands there, and then he says, 'Look at this.' And he takes out the veil.

"Then he dances with her and they dance with the veil. When she throws herself on her knees, this is his triumph. He doesn't know what he's doing. He just remembers what the witch has told him, and he takes her and puts the veil around her and embraces her, embraces her, embraces her, and kisses her— and the dream dies. The Sylphide dies from the kiss. From the embrace and the kiss, and from the human passion. She loses her strength, she becomes paralyzed by the veil; that's why he is able to embrace her. Otherwise she might be able to fly away and escape from him. And then, after he kisses her, this is just too much. Then her wings fall off. You can say, too, that she dies because he has touched his dream. He has gone too close to his dream. He's embraced it. He's kissed it. Anybody can put whatever they like into it.

"I think James dies in the end.[3] He dies from a heart attack. That's the way I produce it now. To me, he dies. His dream dies, so he dies. When I danced it, I died. I always died. I died in every ballet I could get."

Kronstam had three Sylphs: Margrethe Schanne, from his debut in 1956 until her retirement in 1965; Kirsten Simone during the 1960s; and Anna Lærkesen, from her debut in 1966 until Kronstam tore his Achilles tendon in 1970. In various conversations Kronstam seemed to prefer first one partner, then another but, on balance, he enjoyed dancing with all of them.

"Schanne and I opened all the festivals, all the different tours, with *La Sylph-ide*. She was nice to dance with because she gave a very professional performance; she had thought through in her brain what she was going to do. She had a magical presence on the stage. She was lovely and light, but she didn't care so much about who she was dancing with. She was the same with each partner.

"Maybe this is a little bit harsh to say, but Kirsten was a very human La Sylphide. She was a woman, a warm, loving woman, who was very feminine and very, very much in love. I was always very confident, as a James, with Kirsten. I was sure that we would live happily in the forest; no question about that. She just needed to be laid. That's all. Then she would come down from those trees, and we'd have a good time.'

"Then came Anna, and Anna was more dangerous because you couldn't explain exactly what she was, if she really was after him, or if she just wanted him to be after her. You never knew with Anna what it was going to be like. So

The death of the Sylph: with Kirsten Simone on British television in the 1960s.
Photo: A. John Cura. Private collection.

they were all different, but you can't say which one was the most interesting."

Kronstam's James jilted many brides, beginning with his childhood sweet-heart, Viveka Segerskog, but his most usual Effy was Arlette Weinreich, the outstanding interpreter of that role of her generation. Weinreich enjoyed danc-ing Effy with Kronstam because of the seriousness with which he approached his work and the commitment that he brought to it. "I had ten different Jameses: Rudi and Erik and Flemming and Peter and Peter and Flemming and Niels and Jørn and Bruce,[4] and Henning. Henning was the best. He was num-ber one." She remembered, with a laugh, that Kronstam had been so convinc-ing a lover in rehearsals that the line between ballet and real life became blurred and she fell in love with him for a time, an experience not uncommon among the young women of the Danish ballet. "At the beginning, I have to say that I was very much in love with him. The way he could touch you, the way he could look at you. He was really in love with you in rehearsal. So when I met him the next day in the hall, I blushed. I had kept the same feelings afterward, and he could see it. He started to laugh when he saw me because he could tell that it was a little more than just being on stage. But when you were together

The death of the Sylph: with Anna Lærkesen in Copenhagen, late 1960s. Photo: Mydtskov. Private collection.

with him on stage, you never held back. You always tried to go further. That's what I felt was so good about dancing with Henning. He inspired you. He made you try to come up to his level."

James's other "partner" in the ballet is the witch, and Kronstam danced with three different Madges. "I never had Gerda Karstens as Madge on stage. I only saw her Madge in mime class. She was very, very powerful. She was old when she did it last; she must have been in her sixties. I remember that she put so much strength into it that her husband would stand in the wings and she would run out and collapse in his arms.

"My first Madge in performance was Niels Bjørn Larsen. It was different to have a man do the role, but when Niels Bjørn got into the makeup, he was very good in it, very believable as a woman. He didn't try to play it like a woman. He was dressed like a woman, and he was made up, and, as he was a tiny little person, he could do it, but he didn't put any mannerisms into it. I had him as Madge for a very long time. He had a strong presence on stage, but it was hard to get anything from him. He was like an old oak tree.

"Then I had Lillian Jensen. She had been taught by Gerda Karstens, and she was very much like her. Lillian Jensen was a huge woman and her Madge was jealous of James's youth. She was jealous of the Sylphide's getting him because she wanted him, and she was jealous of both the Sylphide and Effy because they were young and she was old. She was very much a woman doing this. Then there was Lizzie Rode. I did it with her for a long time. We had learned it together because we were in the same group in the school.

"I think Madge should be played by a woman. I always cast it that way when I produced it. I like pitting the sexes against each other because I think that makes it more dramatic."

Kronstam stopped dancing James at the age of thirty-six, after his Achilles tendon tore in performance. His injury brought condolences from the King and headlines in the tabloids. "I did my last James, when I ripped the Achilles, with Anna. It happened at the end of the ballet, when we were dancing with the veil. It was on one of those push-offs [the deep plié a dancer makes before a jump], and I heard it snap. I rolled out into the wings, and Anna continued, took the veil herself, put it around her, went up, screamed for the girls, and did the whole death scene all alone. She was carried out. Niels Bjørn came in, did the death scene alone.

"I remember it happened on the day before the winter holiday [in 1970]. My family was in the Theatre and the King and the Queen were there that night too. The King came backstage to hear what had happened to me, which was very kind of him to do. I was sitting on the floor and I said, 'I think my Achilles has gone.' The King said, 'Oh, I hope not.' Then the King asked the doctor, and the doctor told him there was no problem. The doctor said to me, 'There's nothing wrong with that Achilles. Go home and put a cold bandage on it and you'll be able to dance tomorrow.' It was hanging down, so I knew. I went home—I had to hop up all those stairs—and the next day I went to Dr. Tomasson in Arhus. He operated, and I was in a cast for three months. So that was the end of James."

Kronstam's James changed in several ways over the years. Technically, he was equal to the role from the time of his debut, although, of course, his dancing grew stronger as he matured. An example of how he would take something from one ballet or rehearsal experience and incorporate it into another role is what happened after he began to coach the women of the corps de ballet in Harald Lander's *Etudes* in 1969. "For the Sylphides section, I had to teach the girls those soft arms, and I had to figure out how to do them myself so I could show them. One night I used the same arms for James, and after that performance Vera came to me and said, 'I see it's good for you to be working on *Etudes*. Your arms were different tonight.' I had always had a trauma about being masculine on stage. I used to try to look so macho when I danced, although Franz and Hugh Williams and people like that said, "Why are you doing that? Just be yourself." So I did, but I was afraid to make the arms so soft. But I thought they suited James, when he was in the woods with the Sylphide, and so I tried them."

Kronstam's characterization of James was initially shaped by his repertory on that first American tour. He was to dance the Poet in *La Sonnambula*, Romeo in *Romeo and Juliet*, and the Youth in *Chopiniana*, and he wanted to differentiate them. "I didn't want to come to New York and have them say, 'He played the same role in all the ballets.' So my James was different. Perhaps it was to Hans's surprise, but I was much more happy and much more angry with the Sylph, and I tried to be as different as I could be from Romeo. Later it changed and I became more Romantic.

"Of course James changed, but it changed naturally. It didn't change purposely. It's not as though I said, 'Now I have to do something else.' That's something Erik did. He would say, 'I want to give the audience a shock. I want to go down[5] and do something completely different.' I didn't think about it like that, but it did change.

"My dramatic range got bigger. I dared more. It had something to do with the new roles I got. After I'd done Cyrano de Bergerac, Apollo, they, too, helped me to change James into a different man. I was not so happy and so young any longer. I became more of a haunted man, one who sometimes turned to Effy and said, 'Oh, relief. You're here. Stay with me. Don't run away. Stay with me.' That became more and more apparent in the way I was doing it, and it came out of the other ballets I was doing. When you think about it, most of those heroes of Bournonville—and the Princes too—are all haunted by something, and they are in despair, never knowing where to go or who to turn to.

"The more you have lived, the more you have danced a role, the more you have fears, joys—all these things matter when you go on stage, if you give yourself completely into it. When I was dancing, I never thought, 'Now I have to do something very extraordinary.' I just lived. But I used everything that I knew of life."

Apollon Musagète is not Apollo Belvedere; he
is the wild, half-human youth who acquires
nobility through art.

—George Balanchine, Balanchine and Mason,
Stories

Eleven

Apollo: Balanchine's *Apollon Musagète*

For many of those who saw it, Henning Kronstam was indelibly associated
with the role of Apollo, which he danced for the first time in January 1957 at the
age of twenty-two. His exquisitely musical, athletic performance was in a totally different key from the Poet, Romeo, or James. In addition to the pleasure
of the role and the privilege of working with Balanchine, Apollo gave Kronstam his final breakthrough with the Danish critics. This was his first major
role that was not the Romantic Lover, and after Apollo, he was regarded as one
of the company's stars.

Although Kronstam met Balanchine and his Apollo in 1957, this was not the
first time *Apollon Musagète* had been danced by the Royal Danish Ballet. Balanchine first came to Copenhagen soon after Diaghilev's death and the collapse of the Ballets Russes at the invitation of the Royal Theatre. His tenure

was not an unqualified success, as Svend Kragh-Jacobsen explained: "He stayed only for six months and even though he did not make the impression his ability had promised, he managed as guest choreographer to produce six ballets in the period from August 1929 to January 1930: Fokine's *Scheherazade* and *Legend of Joseph;* Massine's *The Three-Cornered Hat* and *La Boutique Fantasque;* as well as his own *Apollon Musagète* and *Barabau.* His success with the audience was by no means absolute, but his stay had a great effect on the youth of the Ballet."[1] It may seem odd to think of Balanchine staging Fokine's and Massine's works, but he was only twenty-five, not yet a world-famous choreographer, and it was customary for choreographers to find work as ballet masters, as stagers of ballets. Whether Balanchine's stagings were faithful to the original, or more his choreography than Fokine's or Massine's, is still debated. Royal Theatre lore says that its very powerful conductor, Victor Schiøler, was interested in the music of these ballets and wanted to conduct their scores, and this determined the repertory.

Apollon Musagète was first given in January 1930 in its original sets and costumes by André Bauchant, on Balanchine's second program of ballets at the Royal Theatre. The cast included Leif Ørnberg (Apollo), Else Højgaard (Terpsichore), Gertrud Jensen (Polyhymnia), and Margot Florenz Gerhard, later Lander (Kalliope).[2] Ørnberg, although rather short and short limbed, was the company's Blond Youth of his generation, the Junker Ove in Bournonville's *A Folk Tale.* This is perhaps the reason why many of the Danish critics thought of Apollo as a "blond role" (several commented on Kronstam's "dark" Apollo) and thought that the ballet was about the Apollo Belvedere, although Balanchine has stated that this was not his intention: "Apollo is not the kind of ballet most people expect to see when they know its name. When the ballet was first performed, a French critic said that was not Apollo at all, that the choreographer had cultivated the deliberately odd, that Apollo would never have done this, or this, or this, etc. When the critic was asked how he knew what Apollo would have done, he had no answer. He was thinking of some familiar statue of Apollo, the Apollo Belvedere, perhaps, and imagined that a ballet about the god would personify sculptural representations. But Apollon Musagète is not Apollo Belvedere; he is the wild, half-human youth who acquires nobility through art."[3] The original Apollo had been Serge Lifar, not at all a Belvedere, whom Stravinsky described as "then still quite young, conscientious, natural, spontaneous, and full of serious enthusiasm for his art."[4]

Although several Danish critics wrote, at that time and later, that Erik Bruhn would have been an ideal Apollo, he never danced the role. Bruhn would have been the ideal Apollo Belvedere, but perhaps not the "wild, half-human youth." Later, it seems that Balanchine changed his mind about Apollo. Peter Martins, the dominant Apollo of the 1970s and early 1980s, was very much a Belvedere; subsequent notable Apollos, such as Ib Andersen and Mikhail Baryshnikov, were neither quite Belvedere nor quite wild and half-human. Since that time half the world has danced the role, and there are many different interpretations, but in 1957 it was a demi-caractère role, and Balanchine used images like "tiger," "black panther," and "wild boy" in rehearsals.

The story of Tanaquil Le Clercq's illness and how Balanchine came to stage *Apollo* in Copenhagen has often been told. Here is Kronstam's slightly more intimate version. "In 1956 we came back from the States and that was the evening that New York City Ballet closed their season at the Royal Theatre and the last evening that Tanaquil was dancing. We were at a party afterward at Christiansborg when rumors slowly started that she had been hospitalized. We didn't know what it was about at first. A couple of days later we heard that she had polio. And then Mr. B said, 'The company has to go on, continue the tour,' and there was a stage manager or something, people like that.

"He started cooking for Mme. Volkova, because what should he do? He couldn't do anything. He couldn't sit at the hospital. She couldn't do anything. He got so depressed. So he came to watch classes and he bought food and he cooked. And then one day Vera said to him, 'Why don't you do a couple of ballets for us while you are here?' And he said, 'I think I'll make *Apollo* for the tall, dark boy.' And he took [Kirsten] Simone and Kirsten Bundgaard and Mette Mollerup for the three Muses. And then he said, 'It's a pity for the older girls, because they don't have anything to do while I'm doing this, so maybe I should do *Serenade* at the same time?' He was a very disciplined man. He put Margrethe Schanne, Mona Vangsaae, and Inge Sand into *Serenade*. It was lovely. Mona was wonderful in the Russian dance, Inge Sand was doing the waltz, and Margrethe was doing the one with the jumps."

Kronstam's story of the first rehearsal has been told before as well, how Balanchine showed him Apollo's first solo, told him to work on it by himself, and then left for the hospital. "He came into the room and put the score on the piano [Bam!!!] and he said to the pianist, 'Please play this,' and he played the first variation. He showed me the steps and then he said, 'Now I have to go back to the hospital and I'll be back in three hours and I would like to see what you've got out of it.'" This must have been a disappointment for a young dancer who had looked forward to working with a master choreographer. Kronstam said, "I was scared to death! I wanted to scream. Of course, he wanted to see what he could get out of me for the next variation. All valid reasons, you know. This was his way of trying me out."

Left to his own devices in the rehearsal room, Kronstam worked with the pianist. "I counted the score out like I don't know what. That first one is a little bit tricky." Although Kronstam had a very good step memory, remembering a variation that he'd been shown only once, from a ballet that was totally unfamiliar to him, was not possible. "My version was different," as he put it. Balanchine didn't change anything when he returned to see what his young Apollo had managed to work out, and that version remained in the Danish repertory until 1993. "I later figured out that nobody had ever done that variation the way I did it," Kronstam said, "because I had something with that mandolin, getting around, where they do the jump. He just had me doing soutenu and turn around, soutenu and turn around. But apparently he was very happy because he wrote to Tanaquil that he had found a boy in Copenhagen who should be in Hollywood."[5]

Kronstam remembered that Balanchine had been "very kind to us," but "didn't really get interested in us until the end. He was turning Kirsten [Simone] inside out because she couldn't do [i.e., Balanchine wouldn't allow her to do] one pirouette from fourth position properly. Everything had to be en dedans, and with knees together. And for me, it was the same. We were too proper for him. He wanted to get us out of our fifteen years of training in a nice, Bournonville way."

The great lesson Kronstam learned from Balanchine, however, had nothing to do with technique, but with performance. "I had problems with the last pirouette, when the three girls go out. It's almost a frantic moment. And he said, 'Who cares? Turn on your heels. Don't think about that high arch. Turn on your heels. Just get around.' I learned from this. I used it a lot for dancers. I'd say, 'I know this is correct and you have to work on it, but when you get on the stage, the people who have paid for their ticket and are sitting in the theater after eating a nice meal don't care if you are two-thirds higher in your double tours or in your pirouettes, or anything like that. They don't care. They want to see a performance.'"

Balanchine was known for changing the steps in a ballet if they did not suit his cast, or if the dancers had trouble with the steps, but that was not the case in Copenhagen. Kronstam remembered the dancers had difficulties with the finale. "It doesn't seem difficult to me now, but at that time, in 1956, it was rhythmically difficult. He gave very short directions, and if anything didn't work on the stage, he would say, 'Well, you work on it.' It was nothing like, 'Well, try to do this, or try to do that.' Just, 'You work on it.' That is the way he worked with us. We were beautifully trained by Vera, so there was no problem technically. But he worked on us for our belief in ourselves on the stage.

"He had four very ambitious people. It was a beginning for all of us. Simone was a bit plump at that time; Mette Mollerup was more his favorite girl. She had feminine chic. She was more jazzy, too, and she was pretty. You could get into her by talking to her. Simone and Kirsten Bundgaard, they packed their little bags and they went home, but Mette would hang around the Theatre— not that there was any affair. I won't say that. She had a big success. It was the biggest success she had in her career, Mette Mollerup, was Terpsichore in *Apollo*."

Though both were known as musical choreographers, there was a marked difference between Ashton's sense of musicality and Balanchine's. "Balanchine goes on counts and Ashton goes on the melody. I can count the whole of *Apollo* for you. One and two, three four, and five, six. One, two, three, four, five, six. One and two and three and four, and one and two and three—that's how it goes. While Ashton was floating on the melody, on top of the rhythm. I don't mean there's anything wrong with it. Lander was counting too. We were always counting in his ballets. For me, the Ashton way was freer because you could move within the music, and it didn't matter if you were on one or four, as long as you had beautiful movements. But of course, then you have to have professional dancers. You cannot do that with people who can't hear the music. [For them] if they get the counts right, they'll look musical."

At times Kronstam seemed to think of Apollo only as a technical challenge: "You can continue to develop Apollo, continue to find new ways of doing it, finding new ways of being smoother in your pirouettes and smoother in your pliés, more stretch in the back, and all these things." But he also considered it a dramatic role: "It was a new way of moving, but it was, too, a new way of standing right in the middle of the stage all alone and starting a big variation and keeping the audience with you. I didn't want the audience to leave the Theatre and say, 'Well, what was that about?' I wanted them to know what I meant with that role. And I know that I made more of a role out of it. I made more the young child into the young god, into the walk to Olympus at the end of it, the one that leads the Muses up. I know I was putting more drama in it, but I couldn't stop that." Balanchine did not discourage this and "never complained. It was fun. It's a wonderful ballet, and I did it for a long time."

One of the comments often made by Americans about the Danish Ballet's dancing of contemporary works is that the dancing is too calm, too harmonious, too complacent; there is no visible energy. Danes might retort that the effort isn't supposed to be visible but rather, as Bournonville wrote so long ago, "all effort must be concealed under cover of harmonious calm." Photographs of those *Apollo* rehearsals, many with Balanchine present, show that he used the qualities of his dancers, including their innate sense of harmony. "Balanchine didn't want more energy," Kronstam said. "He wanted more fulfillment of every step. As I was taller than any of his former Apollos—I think only Jacques [D'Amboise] was almost as tall as I was—he really stretched me out, so I used the full stage for everything. They do it differently today. He changed it for Baryshnikov. Maybe he was a bit influenced by those old photographs of Fokine and Fokina in their little Greek costumes. I think it's a pity, because it's so beautiful with a big man on stage—let him fill it [he began dancing in his chair, moving his arms in wide, sweeping movements]. Let him fill the stage. I must say that Pat Neary [who staged the ballet in Copenhagen in 1992] agreed with me, because she had seen Jacques D'Amboise do it, and Jacques was doing it the same way I did. I learned it right around Christmas 1956, '57, and Jacques was just after that. Pat remembered it. When I saw what she was teaching them in 1993, I said, 'But Pat, it's never been like that here.' 'I know, I know. Mr. B wanted it like this, but if Peter [Martins] or Barbara Horgan comes, then they'll scream if I don't do it [the new way].'"

To the Danish critics the 1957 *Apollon Musagète* was not a new ballet but a revival. Many had seen the original production twenty-seven years earlier. However, in this instance, Kronstam didn't have to worry about being compared to his predecessor, as there was an unwritten ban on mentioning Leif Ørnberg because of his wartime activities. Any disappointments that were voiced involved the changes in sets and costumes. Anne Chaplin Hansen wrote:

But why, then, do we have to look at these boring, ungracious costumes for the Muses? Half track suit, half traditional tutu? And why put Apollo in black

tights with a stupid, short white piece of cloth, now that we have been looking
forward to the youthful, classical nakedness of Kronstam?

Henning Kronstam's god of fine art found shape in his handsome body, his
flexible arabesques. Is it all just a game in numerous variations between Apollo
and the Muses? Soon comes the solo of the god, his discovery of the inner being
of music, the union of the steps with soul and body. (*Kristeligt Dagblad*, January
1957)

Harald Engberg, writing in *Politiken*, was unusually satisfied with Kronstam's portrayal:

> It is always a delight to see Henning Kronstam give body and technical ability
> to a classical character, but furthermore, the young god that Balanchine has
> made of this young dancer has stage authority and at least he has the physiog-
> nomy. He used to have a tendency to open his mouth and droop his face a little
> in the heat of the dancing, but he now maintains it with dignity and mature
> mind, a beautiful young seriousness. His musicality is in complete accord with
> Balanchine's and his secure lightness makes even the most difficult and com-
> plicated steps look simple and easy.
>
> The audience at the premiere saluted Balanchine with thunderous applause
> and fantastic curtain calls, and the royal couple were the first to clap.

Svend Erichsen's review in *Social-Demokraten* indicates that Kronstam's
fears about that final pirouette were unjustified: "Apollo was danced by Henning Kronstam, who was in magnificent shape. He has never reached greater
heights in classical technique. His pirouettes had a precision that is rarely seen
on this stage, but his body is also used in the long, stretched movements with
wiry masculine power that reminds one of the young Lifar."

Nils Schiørring expressed the worry, common in the late 1950s, that Kronstam, now that he had had some successes, would leave the company: "And as
their leader, who gives them life and wit, Henning Kronstam grew from the
first scene's swaddling cloth and became a true god of dance. Apollo is the center point of the ballet. Balanchine has given him not only solos and has him be
the partner of the Muses, he is also the dominant part of the ensembles, not
merely a supporting character for the ladies there. Henning Kronstam carried
this Apollo ballet with all the maturity and technical élan he has gained in the
past few years. He is on his way to becoming—no, wait. Let us keep him here
at home for a little while longer."

And Svend Kragh-Jacobsen's review shows that at least one Danish critic understood the difference between Apollon Musagetes, as he is called in Danish, and Apollo Belvedere.

> Apollo also has to show the Muses his art at its most exquisite. With Henning Kronstam's great final solo, the ballet is crowned, and last night it became great dance art. His authority was as impressive as his ability. Every step was given full value. Every rhythm became one with the tones of the notes from the orchestra. It was the god of dance himself who showed himself on stage. During this dance, sublime classical purity is attained. The wild Apollo is purified until he, with Belvederic arms, walks around the stage.
>
> Balanchine's inspiration sparked something in the young, dark dancer. His own Romantic softness grew fully to the might of the god, so that Apollo stood whole and glorious at the center of the ballet. As the god of dance, Kronstam led his Muses, his mother, and the goddesses up to Olympus, while the applause cascaded toward the stage. It was dance and drama in the art of Apollo, created by Balanchine, and realized with beauty by Danish ballet youth. (*Berlingske Tidende*, January 10, 1957)

Kragh-Jacobsen's "young, dark dancer" comment is not a casual remark but a recognition of the difference between dark and fair that seems essential to the Danish way of looking at art. Many dancers made similar comments. Erling Eliasson, a dancer from Kronstam's time as ballet master who had seen Kronstam's *Apollo* when he was a teenager, put it very poetically: "I have a memory of dark poetry, a poetic presence, darkish, and therefore a little mystical. Peter Martins was bright, he was like a god of the Olympics, but there was a mystery to the way I remember Henning doing it."

Kronstam was the company's only Apollo for ten years. In 1967 he taught the role to Peter Martins, although he continued to dance the role, with Martins and Anna Lærkesen as second cast. Martins has written and spoken of his experience working with Kronstam several times, saying that Kronstam taught him to do the role exactly as he had danced it, yet, later, when he danced it for Balanchine, Balanchine's comment was, "You know, dear, you dance it all wrong," and Balanchine gave Martins many corrections that the dancer found extremely helpful, completely reshaping him in the role. In a 1996 interview for this book, Martins explained: "It was the wrong approach. It was the right steps, but the wrong thinking about it. Balanchine said to me, 'It's not a Prince. It's demi-caractère.' Balanchine almost made it ugly, grotesque. It was stylistically wrong, not the steps." Yet Kronstam did not dance Apollo as a danseur noble, and Martins did not dance it demi-caractère, so it is difficult to understand what happened.

Perceptions change over the years. In a monograph on Martins written in 1967, Arthur Todd makes several interesting comments about these early performances of *Apollo*.[6] Todd observed a rehearsal of *Apollo* in Copenhagen when Kronstam was preparing Martins for his debut: "It was highly interesting to note the great care and respect that Mr. Kronstam gave to every detail of movement in teaching it to Peter Martins, and I must add that Peter certainly was most perceptive and responsive." Martins is quoted as saying, "Henning was a very meticulous person and he taught me the role exactly as he had learned it. When I arrived in Edinburgh, Mr. Balanchine looked me over as though I were a thoroughbred horse. Then he put me into *Apollo* with Suzanne Farrell. Apparently, I was all right, because Mr. Balanchine invited me to be a guest with the New York City Ballet." There is no mention of Balanchine's saying Martins had danced the role "all wrong." In the same monograph, Martins says: "It's marvelous the way Balanchine's mind has changed over the years. *Apollo* has become completely different because Balanchine has simplified it and it has become clearer and purer."[7]

Allan Fridericia's review of a performance of Kronstam's staging concentrated more on that staging than the dancing.

> One of the most far-reaching initiatives for Danish ballet that Flemming Flindt as ballet master has made is to give the staging of Balanchine's works to Henning Kronstam.
>
> Henning Kronstam reveals himself as one of the few who thoroughly understands the choreography, manages to engrave character and rhythm into the dancers.
>
> Henning Kronstam is the greatest Balanchine producer I have ever experienced, including the master's own assistants.
>
> One can only hope that the Royal Theatre finds practical ways in which Kronstam can learn brand new Balanchine works that we otherwise would not have a chance to see.
>
> Last night *Apollon Musagète* once more strode over the stage, just as spotless as every time Kronstam has been in charge.

Kronstam later taught the role to Arne Villumsen, who looks as though he would have been a marvelous Apollo, but somehow was not. "At the time, he was a little bit too placid. He didn't have that go in him that I wanted. He

With Mette Mollerup, Kirsten Simone, and Kirsten Petersen (left to right). Photo: Mydtskov. Private collection.

With Mette Mollerup as Terpsichore. Photo: Mydtskov. The Royal Theatre, Copenhagen. By permission of Det kongelige Teaters bibliotek og arkiv.

became better, but it's not one of his great roles," Kronstam said of one of his favorite pupils. Kronstam also prepared Ib Andersen in the role but did not allow him to perform it because he felt that at the time (in the mid-1970s, when Andersen was in his very early twenties) Andersen was still too young for the role. Andersen did dance the role after he joined the New York City Ballet in 1980 (and later in Copenhagen as a guest), and said he used what he had learned from Kronstam. "My input for the ballet, in some ways, at least the essence of it, came from Henning more than Balanchine, John Taras, and those people I worked with. Because he was able to verbalize the story of it in a way that Balanchine never really did—not, at least, in the normal sense of the word. [Balanchine's approach] was more of the physical and musical aspect of the whole thing, where to Henning, it was a story from beginning to end, and that's how I approached the role too. Also, he had actually danced the role, and that made a difference."

The ballet went out of repertory after 1976 and was not revived until 1988, when Kronstam taught it to Nikolaj Hübbe and Lloyd Riggins; he later coached

As Apollo, 1957. Photo: Mydtskov. The Royal Theatre, Copenhagen. By permission of Det kongelige Teaters bibliotek og arkiv.

As Apollo, 1965, in performance in Los Angeles. Private collection.

Kenneth Greve, who had learned the role from Rudolf Nureyev in Vienna. There are people in Copenhagen who will say that some of the greatest performances of the late 1980s and early 1990s were in those rehearsals, with Kronstam dancing, often merely marking, Apollo. Ingryd Thorson, rehearsal pianist for many of these rehearsals, said, "What impressed me the most was working with him on *Apollo*. He used the music." She had not seen Kronstam perform the role as a dancer, but, from watching him in rehearsals, said: "I can never see Apollo without seeing him, and it had to do with phrasing. It had to do with that extrasensory perception that he had of what goes on behind the movement. At the end of *Apollo*, where he walks, Henning would look up and say, 'It's up there, Olympus.' And his whole being would radiate, and he would just stand, looking. And he'd wait. And if that note wasn't long enough, he'd be irritated because the note has to be long enough for him to express what was behind the movement."

The dancers who worked with him had a similar experience. As Nikolaj Hübbe put it, "Every time I stepped into the studio with him—for the first time in my life—I was intimidated by him. Every time he took a pose, I thought, 'Oh, God. What a pose. I can never do that.' For the first time in my life. Never happened before, never happened after. [In other ballets] there was always some kind of assumed, maybe from my part, connection. But with Apollo, there was this big gap, because I was too much in awe of him. Of his looks, and how old was he? Fifty something? And you thought, 'Well, why doesn't *he* do it? Why do I have to do it? You go down there and play that lute, Henning, and I'll watch you from the wings.'"

When the Prince dances, he dances slowly,
and in the grand manner.
—Henning Kronstam

Twelve

The Princes: Florimund, Siegfried, and Albrecht

Kronstam's career coincided with the beginning of a postwar interest in reviving the grand ballets of nineteenth-century Russia. While excerpts from these ballets had been danced by various Ballets Russes companies since the early years of the twentieth century, the older companies in Western Europe—in Paris, Milan,[1] Vienna, and Copenhagen—had their own repertories, and the younger, smaller companies lacked the resources to put on three- and four-act dance spectacles. It was the new companies who saw these ballets as an ideal core repertory. Extracted pas de deux or acts were danced by stars on gala programs and were sometimes included in regular repertory programs. They became a way to judge a dancer's technique and a company's dance power. Programming the full-length versions put a company and its dancers into the big leagues. In the 1950s and 1960s Petipa (or "after-Petipa") productions of the old master's ballets became the new international standard.

Sleeping Beauty

While Kronstam's first guest appearances were at the Aix-en-Provence festival, and in the new choreography of the stillborn Edinburgh International Ballet, he soon was on Europe's star circuit whenever he could get leave from the Royal Theatre. Male dancers at Kronstam's technical level were extremely rare in the mid-1950s, and his appearance and bearing made him the perfect classical Prince. He began his work in the classics with Ninette de Valois's production of *The Sleeping Beauty* in Copenhagen in the spring of 1957, working mostly with de Valois's assistant, Peggy van Praagh (who remained in Copenhagen to rehearse the dancers after de Valois returned to London) and Volkova. For many male stars, *Sleeping Beauty* is a bore because there is very little dancing for the Prince. He doesn't appear until halfway through the ballet, and, for those who only consider virtuosic dancing to be true dancing, he has only a single pas de deux and solo. However, Kronstam enjoyed dancing the role.

"The first Prince was Florimund in *Sleeping Beauty*, and there I was alone on it [he had no understudy or second cast], so I danced it with Margrethe [Schanne] and Kirsten [Simone]. I never had any difficulties with those Princes. He has spleen too, Florimund, in the hunting scene. And then in the third act, he just has to be brilliant and warm.

"I loved the walk through the hedge with the Lilac Fairy, getting to the castle. The music for that is so beautiful. We went into the boat and drove out, but then we walked, and there was a hedge, and another and another and another, and we had to walk all this way to that beautiful music.

"Florimund is the chosen one. He's the right man at the right time," he said with a laugh. "The Lilac Fairy must find someone who is so good-looking that Aurora will wake up and say, 'Ah.' So I don't think he's a dreamer who's been dreaming about a princess. It's when the Lilac Fairy comes to him, like an angel who comes and says, 'Jesus is born.' Here comes a beautiful fairy and she tells him that here in this castle is a beautiful princess, just waiting for you."

Productions in the West in the 1950s generally tried to be faithful to the original choreography. In de Valois's production there was no solo for the Prince in the second act. There was a full suite of court dances in which the

With Margrethe Schanne
in *Sleeping Beauty*, 1957.
Photo: Mydtskov. Private
collection.

Prince took part. In the third act Kronstam danced a variation that Ashton had
fashioned for Michael Somes a few years earlier. De Valois thought it suited
him because one of Kronstam's special steps was ronds de jambe.

"I did the Ashton variation, which was wonderful. It was not challenging for
me at all because it was all double ronds de jambe and piqué attitudes. Of
course the thing that was awkward about it was that you were walking around
in those high-heeled boots in the whole second act before the kiss. Then the
curtain goes down. You go out and change and there are all the fresh dancers
coming down: the pas de trois boy, the Bluebird boy, and they are all warm and
they all jump, and you stand there in the wings and you say, 'Oh, I'm never
going to get through it.' But when you're twenty-two, twenty-three, you have
the bounce in you.

"With Schanne, I had to be careful. She had the characterization, of course,
but she was not a good turner. But with Kirsten it was just fun because we had
been working on all those partnering steps since we were fifteen. It was one
pirouette, and one, two pirouettes. Then one, two, three, four, five, six, then let
go. She was so absolutely sure about what I was doing, and I knew what she

was doing. She turned like a devil. Her head was so wonderful. You never saw her neck. You always saw face, face, face, face, face."

Kronstam was not a natural turner and envied those who were. "Turning is a question of balance and of the shape of the legs and the holding of the body. If you have a high arch and a swayback leg, then you have to compensate up here [in the upper body] and that goes into the neck. If you are all square and you have loose thighs you don't have to do that. People who have a high arch are a little bit more frightened to get up there [on high demi-pointe] than if you have a very square, very straight foot. And then, of course, the height has something to do with it too. It's easier if you are shorter. The little ones, the small ones, could always turn beautifully."

To a young man brought up in the Bournonville style, the differences between the Russian and Danish ways of dancing were quite clear: "Everything had a deeper plié and a bigger stretch to it. I realized that later when I did *Swan Lake* with [Nina] Anisimova. Also, you have to walk in the Petipa ballets. After you've done your tricks you walk back and you start again, where in Bournonville, there are always steps in between.

"In *Sleeping Beauty* there weren't any walks [in the pas de deux]. We didn't even do the coda. The Three Ivans did the coda, which was very odd. [This was a change made by Bronislava Nijinska for the Diaghilev production in London that de Valois retained.] The Princess finishes her variation and you expect something else to happen, but she just walks out. Then we came back for the Polonaise. In the second year Vera took out the Three Ivans because we didn't have three boys who could dance on their knees, and then it was changed into a coda."

In 1962, Kronstam and Niels Kehlet were invited to dance with the de Cuevas Ballet on a tour to several European cities, Kronstam to dance the Prince and Kehlet the Bluebird. They replaced Rudolf Nureyev, who had danced both roles with de Cuevas, the only company that would hire him after he defected, because of political pressures placed on the national troupes. The company director, Raymundo de Larrain, had suggested to Nureyev that he go to Volkova in Copenhagen for polishing, then contacted Volkova to ask if there were any men there whom she could recommend. The company was in financial difficulties— it would fold halfway through the tour that Kronstam and Kehlet joined—and its fantastic production of *Sleeping Beauty*, which looked like something out of a Fellini film had Fellini been French, was its last gasp.

"It was Rosella Hightower's version. We had greenish costumes with ballet slippers, and green hair in the second act. I had pink hair for the last act. This is a French version, so—you know. When the whole production was together, everybody was so weird-looking that it was all right. But it was very elaborate, I must say. When I was there I also did *Suite en Blanc* with Daphne Dayle, and the *Nutcracker* pas de deux with Marilyn Jones, who is now ballet master in New Zealand."

Kronstam's Auroras were Génia Melikova and Marilyn Jones in Amsterdam and Yvette Chauviré, who joined the company in Athens. His first meeting with Chauviré and the subsequent negotiations to rehearse sound like something out of court life in the time of *Sleeping Beauty*.

"I had heard that I had to dance with her on opening night in Athens, and I wanted to rehearse. She came in and I was sitting waiting for her at a café across from the theater, and she just walked up to the hotel. I had one of the dancers go and ask if she wanted to rehearse. And the dancer came back and said, "Miss Chauviré wants to drink her tea first." So she had her tea, and then someone came to say, "Miss Chauviré would like to rehearse now."

"I went over and she talked through it. And I said, "Then the lifts are coming." And she said, "No, I don't want to be lifted. We'll wait for the lifts until we have to do the performance." So I did the lifts with her in Athens on the stage, just before the performance. But there was no problem. Melikova, I couldn't lift, so we did the other version with the arabesque—she was almost as tall as I was. That was one of the reasons they got me, because Marilyn Jones and Melikova were both very tall. I remember Melikova told me right away. 'Don't bother. Don't even try to lift me.'"

"I must say I always liked working with the French. Not so much Chauviré. She was very artistic, but she was so much older than I was. But Melikova, and Colette Marchand—their approach was so interesting. The way they would rehearse was different. It was, 'Well, we'll rehearse a little here. And then we'll rehearse a little there, and then we talk about it. And then we don't do it before tomorrow.' Except for Violette [Verdy]. She wanted to work, really work."

Kronstam had expected to dance the Ashton variation in the third act, not realizing it was set to different music than the variation in the de Cuevas production. When he began rehearsals he heard the unfamiliar music for the pas de deux and panicked, but one of the corps dancers, Floris Alexander, told him not to worry, that he could teach him the variation, as well as two variations in

With Anita Cardus in *Sleeping Beauty,* Act II, Stuttgart Ballet, 1965. Photo: Alo Storz. Private collection.

the second act that Kronstam thought were Nureyev's choreography. "It was [Nicholas] Beriosoff who taught me, but actually, it was Floris Alexander who said, 'Well, Rudolf was doing it like this.' Because Beriosoff couldn't care. I was the tenth Prince in that production."

Two years later Kronstam was invited by John Cranko to join the Stuttgart Ballet for a two-week festival, dancing several ballets, including *Sleeping Beauty*. He found the experience very rewarding, and it's interesting that he felt he learned more about this ballet from Cranko than from either de Valois or Volkova.

"The Stuttgart version was almost the same as the Royal Ballet version that I had done with Ninette. I didn't really get a proper coaching in *Sleeping Beauty* until I came to Stuttgart and worked with Marcia [Haydée]. She was very young at that time, and Cranko was there and he wanted the best for Marcia. It was there I started learning. I did *Beauty* there with Anita Cardus. I was working more intimately there because Marcia wanted to have everything out of John.

"So we spent more time in the rehearsal room and he was very interested. He had invited six foreign dancers for the festival we were doing. It was Attilio Labis and Arthur Mitchell and Violette [Verdy] and Antoinette Sibley and Marcia and me. We had to do the whole season. I did a couple of performances of Cranko's *Daphnis and Chloe,* with Marcia and with Violette, and two of *Sleeping Beauty* while we learned the other ballets. I did *Flower Festival* with Antoinette, and that was lovely; I always loved Antoinette. In one week John presented all his guests with his own company. It attracted a lot of critics and it was a good, strong period for me. It was in 1964 and I was thirty."

Kronstam kept what he referred to as "Rudolf's variation" for Stuttgart and also when he did the pas de deux on tour in America. "When I did just the pas de deux, I did Rudolf's variation, not the Ashton one. That was beautiful, but it had only the three steps in it. It had seven ronds de jambe, going all the way down, continuing [across the stage]. And then it had twice sort of a sissonne, assemblé, sissonne, assemblé, and an assemblé en tournant à sissonne—it all had to do with style. And to take it on an American tour, to all those small towns? No. The audience would say, "Well, who's this, continuing to do the same step?" And besides, those stages were so small, I would have ended up out in the wings. With the other variation I had double tours to fifth [position], and on a small stage I would go twice around, so it was more showy, better to do."

Kronstam received consistently good reviews in *Sleeping Beauty,* in Denmark and on tour. The Copenhagen production acquired a reputation of having been a critical and a popular failure, as in this review from Bent Schønberg:

> The principal dances from this three-act ballet are well known in Copenhagen, as for some years a version of *Aurora's Wedding* [staged by Hans Brenaa] has been in the Danish repertoire. Now that we have the three acts and prologue, the work is generally considered by the Danish people to be too long and too dull. Above all it was felt that if you are going to have brilliant choreography, which Petipa's undoubtedly is, then you must have brilliant dancers to execute it. Unfortunately, the particular qualities of the Danish dancers do not number extreme brilliance of technique among them. The designs of [André] Delfau were not in the best of taste and the orchestra never did full justice to Tchaikovsky's score. The lighting was poor and there never seemed to be enough people on the stage.
>
> Certainly [de Valois] is not to blame for the fact that she could not find the dancers she needed. Just how good an instructor she is could be seen in the dancing of Henning Kronstam, who gave a delightful performance as the Prince, which has been praised by everyone. (*Dance and Dancers,* June 1957)

While the costumes—stripes and pompoms by Delfau, who set the ballet in sixteenth-century Spain—were certainly disliked, and the Danes, who always put the story first, were bemused by three hours devoted to a fairy tale, some, at least, did appreciate the ballet's virtues. The headline for pinoc's review was "*Sleeping Beauty* Is a Beautiful Child": "The greatest performance of the evening was when Margrethe Schanne and Henning Kronstam threw themselves into their bravura variations. This was dancing that would become any stage in the world. . . . And in the end Sleeping Beauty and her Prince are united in the final scene, according to the best Tivoli pattern, surrounded by the good fairies, and there was no doubt that all had been a wonderful fairy tale. *Sleeping Beauty* is a beautiful child, the way she is danced here at Kongens Nytorv."

Jørgen Budtz-Jørgensen wrote in *Dagens Nyheder,* "Schanne's and Henning Kronstam's great pas de deux in the final tableau was a fairy-tale ending to this fairy-tale ballet. For Kronstam, *Sleeping Beauty* is a new great victory. One wonders if the solo that Ashton put in the last act has ever been danced so perfectly beautifully as he does. He is the one who is able to fulfill the demands of Petipa's demanding choreography with the most virtuosity."

In *Sleeping Beauty*, Act III, 1957. Photo: Mydtskov. Private collection.

And Svend Kragh-Jacobsen, in *Berlingske Tidende*, wrote as though the performance were a battle, as Danish critics of this time often did: "Once more this season, Henning Kronstam, who has shown astounding development [in his rise] to the top of the Danish ballet, conquered the stage completely when he was given it for his solo. His Prince Florimund was the victor of all of them that evening and this in spite of the fact that he doesn't come on till the third act and only has an opportunity to dance at the final wedding. But what a revenge in his brilliant pas de deux with the other star of the evening, Margrethe Schanne, where the security of his solo variation as well as his noble and gallant partnering of his Princess gave much support to his prima ballerina. No wonder the audience cheered the two."

Kirsten Simone scored her own triumph in the second cast, and she and Kronstam danced the pas de deux throughout their careers. The summer after the premiere, they danced the pas de deux from *Sleeping Beauty* twice a day for several weeks at Tivoli. Kronstam was asked by a reporter if he didn't find this boring, and his response—that it was a good experience for them and a chance to perfect their technique so that when the ballet came back into repertory it would be better for the audience—is typical of the way he understood his role as a servant of the company even at the age of twenty-three.

Swan Lake

Although Kronstam looked as though he had been created by Central Casting specifically for the role of Siegfried in *Swan Lake,* it was a role that did not particularly interest him. He never danced in a production that he felt made the story clear, and he was very much in line with the other male stars of the day in feeling that there wasn't enough for Siegfried to do. The fact that Kronstam liked and understood Junker Ove in *A Folk Tale,* an almost completely mime role, or Florimund's walk through the mists and hedges in *Sleeping Beauty,* says much about the sensibilities of this son of Bournonville. These Princes "had spleen"; that is, they had divided natures, a mixture of melancholy and sunniness. Siegfried he saw as simply weak. Kronstam's comments are very much the dancer's point of view. He never staged a *Swan Lake* (although he wanted to), and so never rethought the ballet from a director's perspective.

"I did my first Siegfried in Frank Schaufuss's one-act version two months after *Sleeping Beauty.* That didn't succeed, really, because there was no style to the ballet. A little bit was taken from [London's] Metropolitan Ballet, a little bit from what he had seen in Paris, a little bit from everywhere. But he didn't have the idea of getting it to be either dramatic or melancholic—I think the second act should be a very melancholic piece, but that didn't come out. There would be this little bit of drama in the beginning, with 'You must not touch me,' and all that business. But then that was forgotten and he just touched her. It didn't make any sense. So. Let it rest in peace. I enjoyed doing it with Mona [Vangsaae]. There was a variation [for Siegfried]; Frank made it. It's a waltz, probably one of the dances of the big swans, in a repeat.

"The next was the Russian one, staged by Nina Anisimova. She came with a teacher, Xenia Ter-Stepanova. Vera went to Stockholm to teach the company there, and Ter-Stepanova was here and taught us for two months, and then Anisimova—well. She was a real Russian.

"We had a bit of trouble because I was put in the first cast with Kirsten, and Anna [Lærkesen] was to do second cast with Eske Holm, but Anna wanted to dance with me as well and said she was not going to do the second cast if she didn't have me. So I had all the rehearsals and there I really learned to fly. We had classes with Anisimova in the morning and there were rehearsals all day,

As Siegfried. Photo:
Mogens von Haven.
Private collection.

and I learned how to stay up in the air in a jump. There are certain dancers who can do that. It's something you can do when you're in the air. You lift your legs instead of going down. It's something certain small dancers are born with, but for a tall dancer it was [difficult]. I didn't know that I could get it."[2]

Kronstam found Anisimova very demanding and he enjoyed that. "She said that that variation has to be danced so slowly, it must be so grand. She was not satisfied until she got the bigness of it, the grandeur. She said this is not the pas de trois. When the Prince dances, he dances slowly and in a grand manner."

Swan Lake had been changed a great deal since 1890. At mid-century, both Vladimir Bourmeister and Nicholas Beriosoff had staged revised versions, with a prologue showing that Odette was changed into a swan by Von Rothbart, and eliminated much of the mime. In addition, Benno, the Prince's noble friend, whose presence made the original White Swan pas de deux so distinctive, was often replaced in the first act by a jester.

"I had a jester. I don't see why there's a Benno, if you don't use him for anything. Sometimes they use him in the pas de trois, or in the pas de deux, just to catch Odette. I had Benno in the Frank Schaufuss version. But here, in the first act, I had a lot to do with the jester and, of course, the tutor as well. But otherwise it was very traditional, the tutor having the blindfold and all this business. If you have a prologue then everybody in the audience will understand the story because in the prologue Odette is changed [into a swan] and they can see that. If you don't have the prologue then you have to expect more from the audience's imagination than maybe you can get.

"Siegfried is infatuated with this creature when he sees her, sees that she is so fragile. He is rather rough in the beginning, the first time he puts his hands around her. But then he realizes that she is very delicate, and when she comes on and says, 'You, my little swans and me, shoot—no, don't do it,' then he's already said, 'No, I won't. I will never touch them.' The love pas de deux is nice to dance. It's so big and romantic. And you're warmed up because you've done all those lifts.

"He has fallen in love in that second act, and then in the third act he has five, six princesses and none of them interests him because he has this thing in his head. And then she comes and she looks so fantastic in her black. In the third act he does have doubts because he hadn't known, in the second act, that she could look at him like that. But then suddenly, when she sees that she has overdone, she goes back and pretends to be the White Swan. And then he thinks

In *Swan Lake,* with Kirsten Simone. Photo: Mydtskov. The Royal Theatre, Copenhagen. By permission of Det kongelige Teaters bibliotek og arkiv.

maybe it's because she is with her father that she dares to be a little bit stronger. But—he still swears."

For many Siegfrieds, the third act presents a problem because the Prince has to sit on a throne and watch the character dances while his muscles grow cold. "In Anisimova's version, I was sitting in the third act during all those dances, but in Flindt's version later, thank God, we changed that. So I went out and came on to do the Black Swan.

"Dancewise, the Black Swan pas de deux and coda is very interesting to do. So if you want to just dance, fine. But if you want to get something out of it, a more spiritual thing, this was hard for me, those Princes. It's just all told so plainly. There isn't much emotional depth to it, for me. There's the swearing, and the flame comes up, and then he comes out to the lake again, and she is unhappy and the whole thing is such . . . it is just not interesting for me."

Flemming Flindt did his own version of *Swan Lake* in 1968 and, despite Kronstam's appreciation for Anisimova and her coaching in Russian style, he preferred dancing the later production.

"The Flindt version was not bad. It had terrible costumes, but it was not bad. It was more interesting to do. First of all, I didn't have that stupid tutor in the first act. I had friends that danced with me in the big waltz. I had the jester—always Niels Kehlet. And we ran to the lake, and we didn't have all that about the Queen and the mother's tears, so I didn't have to listen to that. Otherwise, the second act was almost the same.

"The third act was four different countries that had sent their princesses, so there were different costumes. I came down and danced with them, within the character dances, so I moved, at least. And then there was the Black Swan. And in the fourth act, there was a very good fight scene with Rothbart, where he was dancing, too. That was Palle Jacobsen, and that was good.

"It's a ballet that exists in the music, but it's almost impossible to say anything, really, in choreography. But it is a big success with everybody, with all the companies that do it. I won't say that I have been in the best productions, not in the ones that are the most interesting." (Kronstam was probably thinking of John Neumeier's version, which weaves the history of Ludwig, "the mad king" of Bavaria who had a thing for swans, with the story. Arlette Weinreich was sitting with Kronstam when he first saw that production. "He loved it," she said. "He was nearly jumping out of his seat, he wanted so much to dance that boy.")

Although dancers felt that Kronstam was a marvelous Siegfried, his reviews in Copenhagen in *Swan Lake* were mixed to the point of confusion, as these examples, representative of the reviews generally, show:

Pia Nimb: "Once again, Henning Kronstam proved himself to be an outstanding partner. He performed the solo of the Prince with flying ease and elegance."

Allan Fridericia in *Information:* "The new ballet premiere was not an undisputed victory for Henning Kronstam either. Not for one minute did one believe the elevated love of this Prince Siegfried for this bewitched Princess. Unfortunately, one could say that, too, about his partnering."

Sigurd Berg: "As her partner, Henning Kronstam is the born ballet prince, blinding in technical brilliance and helped by his looks, which radiate this indefinable thing called poetry."

In the final analysis, Kronstam "didn't like Siegfried as a character. He is so negative. He was one of those figures who says no to everything. 'No, I don't want to.' 'No, I don't want to marry.' But you never get into why he doesn't want it. Then he sees this woman . . . well." Bored with the conversation, he thumped his fist on the table and said, "I don't believe in swans. I believe in sylphs."

Giselle

The role of Albrecht in *Giselle* was by far Kronstam's favorite of "the Princes."
Giselle has never been especially popular in Copenhagen. The first version was
staged in 1862 by Gustave Carey, who was ballet master when August Bournonville did a three-year stint at the Royal Swedish Ballet. Bournonville tossed it
out of repertory as soon as he was back, finding it sentimental. 'I always
heard," Kronstam said, as though Bournonville were a regular visitor to the
company coffee klatch, "that he didn't like it that the hero lied." The ballet
came back into the repertory in 1946 in a staging by Alexandre Volinine; in
subsequent seasons Kronstam was a huntsman as a teenager in that production. Erik Bruhn staged two versions and Anton Dolin one between 1959 and
1968. When Kronstam became director of the company in 1978, he brought
Bruhn in to stage a third version, and staged the ballet himself in 1990. This
meant that Kronstam was at the heart of Danish *Giselle*s in the twentieth century. It was a ballet he came to love, and Albrecht was a character for whom he
felt deep sympathy, but it took him several tries to come to grips with the ballet
and the character.

"Albrecht is the best of all the Princes to do because there's a meaning to the
role. He has spleen, the same as James. He's in love with a girl. It's not a sylph
but a real girl, a pretty girl who is happy, who loves to dance. She is sweet to her
mother, she is sweet to her friends, and he would just love to take her on a ride,
or something like that. But he's going to be married. And he forgets himself
because he doesn't think enough of that fiancée. He courts Giselle, without
thinking that he is harming her. Because if he knows that, it is impossible to do
the ending.

"He has seen her in the forest but this is the first time that he comes to see
her. This is the first time that he comes dressed as Loys [Albrecht's name in his
disguise as a peasant]. She is his chance to lead a normal life, away from his
life up there in the castle. He has no idea that Bathilde could come down there.
He is with the peasants and he just has a wonderful time. He has his Giselle,
they are happy. He thought about it when he ran away from the castle: 'I have
to get down there.' Now that I have produced it, I find that it's a relief for him
to go down to the village. All that artificiality of the court is stifling for him.

"My first version was with Schanne. She was fifteen years older, so that was
a bit hard. That's why I played it a little bit more as though I was toying with

As Albert (Albrecht) with Margrethe Schanne as Giselle and Kjeld Noack (center) as Hilarion. Photo: Mydtskov. The Royal Theatre, Copenhagen. By permission of Det kongelige Teaters bibliotek og arkiv

her. Until, of course, she rips the necklace off and falls to the floor. Then you change a bit. But otherwise it was fun to see how far you can go with her. But that's not my version of it now, when I produce it.

"The second act is wonderful. First of all, you get to come on the stage and you don't do too much, you just get to have the feeling of the stage, with all the assemblés from side to side, so you get in a dancing mood. And then you come out for the first variation and you're still fresh, so you can give the variation everything you've got in yourself. You are nicely warmed up, you've done the lifts, and then you give the variation everything you have and you can fall flat afterward. You don't need to finish with a bang bang bang, but just fall and breathe like a madman. And hopefully the audience will clap long enough for you to recover."

Beginning in the 1960s many choreographers inserted an additional solo for Albrecht in the second act at a point where he was usually offstage, supposedly to show that he was under the spell of Myrtha. The solo usually consisted of either thirty-two entrechat sixes, or a series of brisés. "I had the sixes in Dolin's version. This was something invented by the Russians, but Dolin had it too. I always thought they were a bit strange, the sixes. Strange that he would run after her and then stand in the middle of the stage and do the sixes. It didn't make sense to me, but it was nice to get to do all those sixes."

To Kronstam, Albrecht has been going to visit Giselle's grave for several nights before the night we see on stage. He has felt Giselle but not seen her until this night. "First, she is like a ghost. He lifts her—maybe he's going a little bit crazy because he is in such pain and such frustration that he has to go to that grave every night. But in the beginning of their first meeting in the second act, he just feels her. And she goes right through his arms.

"But then when she starts taking the flowers, then suddenly there's something real. Then she comes on with more flowers and gives them to him, and then she disappears again. But then he's got the flowers, and then there is something he can hang on to. He has a memory. And he runs around and around, but she's not there. What has happened? He's felt her before, but this

With Margrethe Schanne in *Giselle*, Act 2. Photo: Mydtskov. The Royal Theatre, Copenhagen. By permission of Det kongelige Teaters bibliotek og arkiv.

is the first time he's got those flowers, so he can see that there really is something there.

"And then she materializes. She points to the grave and they go to the grave together. And she dances, she starts the adage. And now she is real. At the end again, she disappears with the morning coming. She fades out. And then again there are the flowers so that he will know that she was real for him."

In the original production, Bathilde comes to the forest searching for Albrecht at the end of the ballet and forgives him. In later stagings, this ending was seen as too sentimental and was dropped. Kronstam's Albrecht could not have done that ending. Asked what happened to Albrecht after that last night in the woods, if it would have been possible for him to have married Bathilde, he said, very quietly after a long pause, during which he seemed to become Albrecht—the look of pain on his face was extreme—"I don't think he could have done that, because he is not a cold person."

Kronstam danced *Giselle* first with Margrethe Schanne, then with Kirsten Simone, then Anna Lærkesen. "They did it in different ways because Anna was more fragile. Kirsten was a little healthier, especially in the first act. While with Anna, you understood she was not in the fields, but the mother kept her in the house to serve wine and for her sewing.

"Schanne was wonderful in the second act because she jumped. She really flew. She was better in the second act. Then, she really had that mystery. And there was no big love scene. That was always very difficult to make between the two of us because we were very different people.

"Kirsten was very good in the second act, very good. But Anna had a period where she was playing Russian ballerina, and everything was like this [*mimes "droopy"*]. Like Ulanova, but Ulanova at fifty-five, and Anna was only twenty-five. But Anna had a beautiful adage. She was very slow, almost like not being right on the music, but playing with the music. But I enjoyed it with both of them."

While Kronstam's James was a fully formed portrait from the beginning, however much it changed over the years, his Albrecht grew more slowly. "The first one was probably a copy of Erik, because I'd seen Erik and Markova, and that was a great experience. They were wonderful. He wasn't Romantic, but they were so beautiful together, and I loved the beauty of his line, the beauty of his looks and of his dancing.

"But then with Dolin, I was the first cast with Anna, and that was something else completely. He used me more as a dramatic dancer too. When Erik came back again, then I already was that much further. I had been to Rome, where I did it with Carla [Fracci], and that was a completely different version."

In the photographs from the 1959 production, Kronstam's portrayal looks atypically external, as though the pain and the love are put on like a costume rather than developed from the inside. This may well be because of his youth, or simply because, as he said, he found it difficult to make love to Schanne on the stage. Later, with Simone and Lærkesen, his portrayal deepened.

For Lærkesen, he was a wonderful Albrecht: "He was a very handsome, charming, attractive man with some sort of secret in himself that made him a little more intriguing. A man, maybe, who had a darker side inside himself. Not a demonic other side but—more that he was torn.

"He was very much in love with Giselle. I also felt a lot of resentment and begging for forgiveness in the second act. He would really know that he had

With Anna Lærkesen in
Giselle, Act 1, 1966.
Private collection.

done something wrong. That really came forward because, as a person, Henning is so conscientious not to do anything wrong. That is what I remember. But then I will also say that in his character roles he could find something in himself that would come out that he didn't come out with in the classical roles, and that made it all the more interesting. It was as though he could let some side of himself go, in a way, in those character roles."

Carla Fracci invited Kronstam to dance *Giselle* in Rome with her. He enjoyed dancing with Fracci, but did not love Rome. "Rome Opera is impossible. I went there and I was greeted in the airport and they said, 'Sorry, we have a strike. So we don't know whether the performance is going to happen.' And I only had a one-month leave of absence." Kronstam hated being alone, so he phoned Kirsten Simone and asked if she wanted to come too. "She didn't have anything to do because I was away. We shared a room because we only had my salary. We walked around the city and we had a good time." Despite the strike and the uncertainty over whether the performance would happen, "We started rehearsals. We didn't know what was going to happen. The whole company was sort of sloppy because they thought the strike would go on. But at long last, suddenly the strike was over and we did it. I think I had about two weeks' rehearsal. I changed [the ballet] into the version that I had learned here in Copenhagen, and that was the version that Carla did with Erik later at ABT.

"As Giselle, Carla was very touching. And she was pretty and that was nice, because I danced with Schanne at that time. Carla was definitely prettier, and so that made it easier for me. Rose [Gad] has the same kind of style, the whole bearing of her body, the long balance in arabesque. Carla had enormously long arms. Her characterization was lovely. She was absolutely lovely. But it only came to one performance, after all the rehearsals."

For her part, Fracci found Kronstam "a beautiful dancer, so noble. So noble." Fracci's husband, filmmaker Beppe Menegatti, remembered their partnership well and said, in June 2001, "It is odd; I was just talking about Henning the other night. I always thought Kronstam was the true danseur noble. He and Carla went beautifully together, their bodies, their line."

The Danish reviews of Kronstam's Albrecht do show a clear picture; you can watch him develop through reading them. In an article called "The White Triumph," Harald Engberg, who often thought Kronstam unpleasantly weak in noble roles as a young dancer, found him completely satisfactory by the late 1960s:

With her great style, mastery of movement, her genius for dreamy un-approachability, more and more Anna Lærkesen unites her ability for tender-ness with a sort of sublimated eroticism that makes her Giselle something that should be seen all over the world. She didn't have to conjure up a partner. Henning Kronstam was completely at her level. He possessed lightness and tightness, a subtle elegance in his adoration, something beautifully tragic in his dance of death that made him appear rejuvenated in his dance while his sensitivity and sympathy as a partner has matured and been refined. It is now devoid of any and all attitudes.

Earlier performances had been more sketched in than filled out. Svend Kragh-Jacobsen described Kronstam's debut with Schanne (on the night that he and the other principals in the dancers' union had been fired, as part of the second Lander Scandal):

> For the first time, she had Henning Kronstam as Duke Albrecht last night, a role that he was destined to perform. He danced his steps very nicely, noble in style, with ease in his jumps, and he was secure and pure in each and every one of the difficult variations, quite a virtuoso in the variation of the second act.
>
> He looked excellent, the costume became him, and that which he still lacks, which Erik Bruhn had when we last saw him—and hopefully both of them will now alternate in the role—is the adult calm that can place Albert. Kronstam was like a young, fine boy to look at, a little shy in certain moments. In terms of mime, the part is very difficult, particularly in the first act, where he must let Giselle down in the decisive moment. Kronstam did it, but his expressions could have been used in any ballet. It was nice, but he missed the dramatic concept of the character.

By the 1960s Anne Chaplin Hansen, representative of others, would write: "A more handsome Duke Albert one has rarely seen. The most slim and proud young tree in the forest, and in the first scenes he displayed a tender and happy and subtle love, the most charming and humane he has done thus far. He can do it all now, in terms of both expression and content, and it is a great joy."

A review by Svend-Kragh Jacobsen, undated, but obviously after 1965, con-tains one of the first references to Kronstam's extraordinary range: "Kronstam unites his Duke Albert with true nobility—a nobleman of noble blood who is in deep despair because of the misfortune he causes. But also it is his perfect dancing in the night act that raises his part up among the exquisite pleasures of dance. And this after the fiery Romeo, the psychopath in *Enetime* [*The Les-son*] and the angry Toreador, to remember how different he can be."

Anton Dolin coaching
Anna Lærkesen and
Kronstam, 1966. Photo:
Jørgen Schiøttz. The
Royal Theatre, Copen-
hagen. By permission of
Det kongelige Teaters
bibliotek og arkiv.

The same moment in performance. Photo: Mydtskov. The Royal Theatre, Copenhagen. By permission of Det kongelige Teaters bibliotek og arkiv.

Unlike others of his generation, Kronstam did not consider the Princes to be his most important roles, although he did understand that they were used to judge and compare dancers, as the roles required a top level of technique. He was never a technical innovator, never invented a step nor inserted a bravura combination into a classical solo. That was not his interest, and he disliked anything that would interfere with the drama. But if another star, especially one in his firmament, like Bruhn or Nureyev, raised the technical bar, he would rise to meet it.

"When you get one of these big roles, and you know the whole company is watching you—Vera was always in the Theatre. Sometimes Erik was there, and Stanley was nearly always there, too—so you have a pride. You want it to be perfect. And you hate yourself when you miss, if anything goes wrong. There is a physical satisfaction in doing a four-act ballet and knowing that you got through it and everything has succeeded. It's like an athlete, the same thing. You can sit afterward and say, 'Ah! I got through the whole thing, and I didn't do anything wrong, and the doubles went, and everything was perfect.'

"That is another thing about the classics. You see movies. I saw [Nikolai] Fadeyechev do *Giselle* before I had ever touched it myself. I said, 'Oh, my dear, my dear, my dear. I want to do those steps too.' He had this wonderful plié and grandness in his dancing. In *Giselle,* when you see what can be done with the role—Erik changed after he had met Rudolf. The variations were getting more difficult, and they demanded that from me. And this was something that you had to live up to. Before, the variation was simple, simple cabriole. No doubles.

"In *Swan Lake* the variation is only a minute, but it has to be there. And Anisimova was no chicken. She wanted what she wanted. There were cabrioles, and landing in arabesque, stay. Double doubles. Doubles with arms over your head—all these things she demanded. And when it succeeded—and it didn't succeed every night—then there was a satisfaction, because you had been working on these things for such a long time in the classroom, so to do it on stage and have them work, and have the full orchestra playing and the audience. I was thinking last night, that I said I enjoyed the Bournonville and the modern ballets better, but I enjoyed, too, the physical demands that were made on me in these roles."

In his face a young and brilliant smile of victory has been lighted, and it becomes him.
— Jørgen Budtz-Jørgensen

Thirteen

The Knights: Nilas, Jason, and Don José

Kronstam's development as a great dance actor began in the ballets of Bournonville, Balanchine, and Ashton but matured in those of Roland Petit and
Birgit Cullberg. Working with these two choreographers broadened his range,
and he drew on these experiences throughout his career to enrich his characterizations in other ballets, both classical and modern. The ballets—*Carmen,
Moon Reindeer, Jason and Medea,* and *Miss Julie*—were not masterpieces, but
they gave not only Kronstam, but Bruhn, Schanne, Simone, and Flindt interesting, meaty roles and the Danish ballet many great performances.

Carmen, a one-act condensation of the opera set to a suite from the Bizet
score that Roland Petit had choreographed for himself and his wife, Renée
Jeanmaire, and that was a hit on Broadway in the late 1940s, came into the
repertory through Volkova. Kronstam had expected to dance Don José and was

stunned when Petit cast Flemming Flindt, who was two years Kronstam's junior, with Kirsten Simone in the leads, giving him a small character part.

"Of course, I was terribly disappointed because I was second cast on Don José, with Kirsten Bundgaard. But as it turned out, the Toreador was one of my great breakthroughs to a different way of performing because Roland demanded that I be nearly crazy fond of myself. He would say, 'Jump higher, use your teeth and use your hands and show your shoulders,' that kind of thing. He got the girls to fall on their knees when I was there. It was just that it was so short.

"I remember I told Franz, 'It's a very little part, and I just come in the very last act.' [In an earlier scene] there's this little man who comes walking over the stage and is knifed and falls down, and Franz thought that was me, and said, 'I must say, that is a little part.' But Roland loved me in it and asked me to come to Paris to do the film [Black Tights, in which Zizi and Petit are Carmen and Don José and Bjørnsson dances the red-haired thief]." The Toreador is an almost anti-Bournonville role, forceful, awkward, exhibitionist. Kronstam's performance is full of detail. His Toreador is so taken with himself that there is a

Kronstam as the Toreador in *Carmen*. performance shot, Los Angeles, 1965. Private collection.

moment, at the end of his solo, before the girls (marching after him, like the acolytes in Martha Graham's *Appalachian Spring*) swarm over him where he ends on one knee and, just for an instant, almost shudders with the pleasure of his own perfection.

Kronstam was also originally scheduled to dance in *The Devil in 24 Hours* with Cyd Charisse as part of *Black Tights,* but this did not work out. "She said I was too young for her," Kronstam said. "And she was not trained in the same way. I wanted to learn the whole ballet and then do it. And she wanted to learn it a little bit at a time and then we'd talk about it and we'd see. So we didn't really fit together. But I was paid for two weeks in Paris." While there, he asked Renée Jeanmaire which classes to take. She suggested Serge Peretti, whom Kronstam found "old, and really too like Bournonville." Jeanmaire then referred him to Michel Resnikoff. "I went to Resnikoff's classes and I met André Prokovsky for the first time. We had a competition in those classes because he liked to do doubles and big jumps, all those things, and not all the beauties that I had learned from Vera"—suggesting that Kronstam was not always the good boy; when away from the Theatre, he liked to explore.

Kronstam danced the Toreador, often on a double bill with James in *La Sylphide,* for several years, until he gave the role to Kjeld Noack. "It was really too much. I said, 'I cannot do the Toreador after *La Sylphide,* too.'"

Kronstam eventually got to dance Don José when the company needed a second cast for the 1960 American tour (with Mette Hønningen as Carmen.) He did not consider this one of his best roles, either technically or dramatically. The role was full of pirouettes and "Erik (who had taken over the role when Flindt left for Paris) was a turner, a beautiful turner. There was never one evening he missed. But if I had to junk just one pirouette, it was over for me. Also, if you don't get the part right away, if the choreographer says to you, 'You are not right for Don José. You are the Toreador. I made the Toreador for you,' then it's hard to go back and do Don José later on."

When Kronstam did learn the role, he learned it from Niels Bjørn Larsen. "He couldn't give me anything. There's never been anything from Niels Bjørn Larsen except keeping the ballets going, one ballet after another, but he never had any creative ideas. If he didn't have anything to say, he would say, 'Do the whole thing again.' That was it. And that didn't help a lot. You've got to get into it, and I didn't get really into it." A comparatively minor problem was that there is a scene where Don José smokes a cigarette. It's an after-sex cigarette, very suggestive, but Kronstam didn't smoke and choked when he tried it. He got through the scene by not inhaling.

Although he danced *Carmen* with both Hønningen and Bundgaard, his favorite partner in this role was Simone. He had admired her in it from the first, as much for her courage in going after the role as for her success in it. "Kirsten really developed her Carmen with Erik. Flemming was very good as Don José, but Erik was very strong in that part. And Kirsten wanted to get up to him [up to his level]. With Flemming it worked because there was a love-hate between them. But with Erik—Erik was always a principal dancer on the stage. But Kirsten wouldn't give him a damn. She was perfect. She was a very good Carmen."

Kronstam got very good reviews in *Carmen* on the American tour. Danish critics generally preferred either Flindt or Bruhn. Despite this, and despite Kronstam's misgivings about his performance, a brief film excerpt of two scenes in Kirsten Simone's collection shows an extraordinary performance. The first is a brief bit of dancing in a scene where Don José is outside Carmen's house. Kronstam, very sleek with those long legs, shows his passion in extremely controlled, strong, small steps, punctuated by five perfectly placed and executed pirouettes. The dancing smolders. The second scene in the film is the one in which Don José murders a man simply to please Carmen. The choreography contains a series of arm thrusts, practice stabs with a knife. Some dancers use the movement to build up enough adrenaline to commit the murder. With Kronstam, his conflict—his battle with his conscience and his self-loathing—is evident in the gesture, as well as his passion for Carmen. It's an example of how skilled he was in using a few seconds of action to show many layers of a character. After Kronstam's death Copenhagen's Ballet Club devoted an evening to his career, and this was one of the films shown. The dancers who attended, especially the younger ones who had never seen him dance the role on stage, mentioned Kronstam's Don José as being the performance that had most astounded them.

While Petit was a ballet choreographer, despite his fondness for cabaret, Birgit Cullberg was a modern dancer, a pupil of Mary Wigman. She was Swedish and not Danish, but Larsen was under pressure to stop using all those Britons, Frenchmen, Americans, and Russians and get someone who was at least Scandinavian. And so Birgit Cullberg came to Copenhagen and gave the Royal Danish Ballet several works that were extremely popular in the 1950s and 1960s. The first was *Moon Reindeer.*

"There was a Danish composer called Knud Riisager, who did the *Etudes* arrangements. And Niels Bjørn decided that Cullberg was coming on in Sweden, and I think he contacted her and asked her to do a ballet with Knud Riisager, and she wanted to do this story. So she went to Lapland and stayed there, watching the reindeer. She stayed for six weeks, just watching them.

"We did *Moon Reindeer* at the end of the 1955–56 season, right after we'd done *Romeo and Juliet*. It was the first time I worked with a female choreographer—and Cullberg is not a classical dancer. But she chose Mona Vangsaae and me, the two most classical ones. It was one of Mona's biggest successes, because she has such a lovely little face, and she was girlish. [Nilas] is a hunter. He doesn't like her as a girl, but he is crazy about her when she is the reindeer. She is a white reindeer, and he wants to hunt her. It would be so fantastic if he could bring that white reindeer back to the camp. She keeps changing. She changes into a reindeer, and then out of the reindeer and into the reindeer and out of the reindeer—and at the end, he breaks her neck and suddenly he realizes that the reindeer is a girl. And it's too late because she's dead. Mona did it beautifully. Then later I did it with Anna, who was perfect in it too.

"Cullberg worked very strangely because she can't do anything. She can't hear. She can sort of move, but she couldn't do anything with Mona's pointe work. She didn't know what to do with it. But she had ideas, and she'd been

As Nilas in *Moon Reindeer*. Photo: Mydtskov. The Royal Theatre, Copenhagen. By permission of Det kongelige Teaters bibliotek og arkiv.

With Anna Lærkesen in *Moon Reindeer*. Photo: Mydtskov. The Royal Theatre, Copenhagen. By permission of Det kongelige Teaters bibliotek og arkiv.

watching other performances that we had danced, and she said, 'I want the thing you do in that ballet. What is that step?' And we'd show the step, and then we'd put that in."

"She was not classical, and I was very young and brought up in a classical tradition, and I had no idea of what was going on. But it ended up being a very classical ballet. It has all these coupés jetés, all things that were typical of my jumps. It's perhaps a little too long. In Copenhagen choreographers are paid by the minute. That's how their royalties are figured, and sometimes ballets can be a little too long."

Cullberg did not come to the studio with the steps prepared in advance. "It was always, 'What's this step? I want something like this.' She would say things and then you'd have to do it, and then she would say, 'Yes, that's good.' She had the structure in her mind. She's a strong personality. She knew what she was going for, but she didn't know exactly how to get it, or even if it was possible."

Kronstam described one rehearsal where Vangsaae performed steps without the dramatic impetus behind them, in a scene suggestive of sexual intercourse. "[Cullberg] didn't care about the steps, not too much as long as she got the drama out of the dancers. At the end of the big pas de deux in *Moon Reindeer,* when Aili is a girl, before she changes back into the reindeer once again, the man is on the floor, and the girl is on full pointe in à la seconde. And she goes down on his arm. And she raises up. And she goes down on his arm and she raises up. And she goes down and he lifts her lower hip, and that we did a lot of times. I knew what it was about. But Mona was such a nice lady, and Birgit finally had to tell her, 'Have you any idea what this is about, Mona? Are you just doing à la seconde and plié and à la seconde and plié and à la seconde? Don't you know what it is?' So she didn't explain it, but she got upset when we didn't get it."

The Danish critics regarded Nilas as another breakthrough for Kronstam. This was his first "hero" role, and some seemed surprised that he could carry it off. Allan Fridericia in *Information* wrote: "Henning Kronstam performed the dance of Nilas without any difficulty. It will be very interesting to follow this gifted dancer as he develops in the role. If he manages to fight his way to a genuine mime performance as this man who is so alien to him, then Kronstam will be able to add something significant to the work."

Svend Kragh-Jacobsen: "Henning Kronstam blinds by his mastery, so pure is his dancing as Nilas, so secure is he in the way he portrays the character."

Jørgen Budtz-Jørgensen saw that the role had given the young dancer a new confidence: "Since Apollo he has not danced any part that liberates his talent to this degree. His excellent ability as a jumper and eminent mastery [of technique] leads him victoriously through solos and pas de deux. Furthermore, in his face, a young and brilliant smile of victory has been lighted, and it becomes him."

Kronstam's next Cullberg role was Jean in *Miss Julie,* in which he, as a butler, rapes his mistress and then goads her to suicide. It is based on a play by
Strindberg and, with *Carmen,* was probably the most popular ballet in the Danish repertory in the 1960s. Kirsten Simone and Erik Bruhn had danced the
premiere in Copenhagen. Both *Moon Reindeer* and *Miss Julie* were included on
the second North American tour, and Cullberg came to work with second casts
in both ballets. Flemming Flindt and Hanne Marie Ravn were the second cast
in *Moon Reindeer,* and Kronstam and Kirsten Bundgaard were given *Miss Julie.*

Again, Kronstam had to follow Bruhn in a role in which he was brilliant.
Kronstam was still quite young, only twenty-five, and Bruhn was a more experienced and mature performer. "Jean was a wonderful role. But I'd seen Erik
and I was so taken by them, by both of them, Kirsten and Erik, in that ballet
that I thought, 'Aaagh! Am I going to do Jean?' But then I made it into [some-
thing of] my own.

"I was meaner than Erik was. Erik was more correct. Dangerous, but very
correct. I was more straightforward, a wicked man that wanted her down. It
was as much revenge as lust because she was—when she does the first scene,
she's really throwing herself around with everybody, and her lover gets the
whip, and things like that. But when he sees her in the drunken scene, he decides—well, he's drunk himself—so he decides, 'I'm going to get her down.' It
was a class thing as much as lust.

"It's a classical role. Maybe because Erik had been doing it in Ballet Theatre,
it became a very classical role, all pirouettes and everything. Very square. So it
was challenging, both in the character and in the dancing."

It was the first ballet in which Kronstam had danced an antihero, not a good
man gone astray but a nasty man, and he enjoyed it. "He's not been planning
it, but because he is drunk he lets his anger get out. Because she is a castrating
lady. We don't know what she has been doing to him, but we know what she
does to her fiancé, and that's to whip him. And when she comes down and sees
this drunken brawl, and she's in her negligee, he sees her and says, 'What the
hell. I'm going to take her.'

"I think that's when it happens, but of course it's been in him. He's been
hating that little frustrated bitch. And then when he starts he can't stop. His
manhood is aroused and there's no way he can stop himself up. He resents
her. He wants to raise the classes. He wants to earn money, he wants to build
himself. But he doesn't kill her. He helps her kill herself.

Two moments from *Miss Julie*, both with Kirsten Simone. The good servant, but with an undercurrent of menace. Photo: Mogens von Hagen. Private collection.

Jean's subservience and his resentment. Photo: Mogens von Hagen. Private collection.

"I did it with the two Kirstens and with Toni Lander. Kirsten Simone was so touching in that last scene. She was so alone after he had raped her. She had been so proud in the beginning, but when she came into the drunken scene, she showed that she needed somebody. She was alone. After raping me, she was so sick at what she has done. There, she was so lovable. It was very pitiful, her performance.

"I only did two performances with Toni and she was rather cool in it. Kirsten and I, we had such a good relationship in these roles and we enjoyed doing them. Not by talking about it, but by doing it, certainly by doing something on the stage that will make her react. It was not wild things, but little different looks, different eyes, that will make her think, 'What is he going to do tonight?'"

Two reviews from Chicago critics provide details of his characterization. Thomas Willis wrote from home about the Danes' third American tour:

> As for the performance, the news, not surprisingly, was Henning Kronstam's Jean. The demi-bow of servility, roistering bout in the barn, drunken adulation, conquest, frowzy revulsion, and final surrender are outlined in the clearest dramatic terns. The high leaps, strong turns, and pointed brilliance mark him as one of the greatest technicians on the stage today. His layered dramatic skill, all too briefly demonstrated in this single appearance, may well put him at the top of the heap, for all of the certain dissent of Nureyev fans.
>
> Miss Simone is accomplished, as are all the Danes' solo corps, and prettier than some. Her Julie is as physically explicit in sexual play as her Carmen; both lack the impact of the prima ballerina personality. (November 1, 1965)

Roger Dettmer reported from Copenhagen:

> The main course was Birgit Cullberg's *Miss Julie,* after August Strindberg, danced with an emphatic and unblushing sexuality by these superbly disciplined Danes. Kirsten Simone was arguably too feminine in the title role until her seduction by Henning Kronstam as the footman, Jean, but her realization of repressed libido and sudden, brutal release during the midsummer revels was starkly conveyed. Kronstam is a premier danseur of extraordinary range and fanatical concentration, who seems ever to be airborne, and always better. (*Chicago American,* May 23, 1965)

A third Cullberg role was that of Jason in *Jason and Medea* (a ballet also in the New York City Ballet repertory). "I don't remember much about it, except that it was powerful music, Bartok. Schanne was Medea and Kirsten was Clytemnestra. The funny thing about Cullberg is, except for Jean and maybe *Moon Reindeer,* her choreography was not on the music. Usually the music is your cue. You think, 'Oh, the music starts,' and then you go 'Aha, this is it. Here we go.' But with Cullberg, she flowed around the music. You could just as well dance it with something else.

"Except for Jean. Jean was very much a part, right there, on the music. *Moon Reindeer* was loose. Jason—I couldn't remember a step if I heard the music today. It wasn't that she was unmusical, it was just her way of making choreography. She said, "The music is one thing, and the choreography is another thing," but it doesn't have to be exact. It was nothing like Lander, who was sitting there with his music, and the dancing steps hit everything: one, two, three, four, one, two, three, four. She felt that it could be in the audience's fantasy to put the two things together. So it wasn't that it was unmusical, but it was just not concrete enough. It was like—well, what modern dancers do." Whether Cullberg's musicality was a matter of aesthetics or anatomy is open to question. "She doesn't hear very well, so she has an ear trumpet. But sometimes she takes it out, and then she can't hear anything. And then we just do the steps and she doesn't hear whether you're on the music or not on the music. She is all her own."

Although Kronstam did not consider Jason one of his important roles, the Danish critics saw it as a major dramatic breakthrough for the young dancer, as the following excerpts from reviews show. Svend Erichsen, first noting that Birgit Cullberg is the "nearest we have in Scandinavia to an international-level choreographer," and that she's helping the dancers in drama, "to express with their bodies and not just their faces," wrote of Kronstam's performance: "Henning Kronstam, with his Jason, exploited his virtuosity with a tight sense of drama that was more intense than anything one had seen him do before. He, so to speak, lived through his soulful phases of drama with his body. His jumps gave sparkle to the action itself, not so much because of their perfection as because of what they expressed."

Allan Fridericia wrote in *Information*: "With Jason, Henning Kronstam creates his best Cullberg role this far. His dancing is fluid and his restrained mime is in accord with that of the weak Jason." This is one of the first reviews that does not confuse Kronstam's creation of a weak character with a weakness in his own personality.

Sigurd Berg wrote: "As the mythical hero Jason, it was easier for Henning

Kronstam. His balances on the night of the premiere were not perfect, but his looks gave the character the air of an easily influenced man with no thoughts for anything other than his own irresistibility. And he found several handsome expressions for his despair and helplessness toward his fate."

Svend Kragh-Jacobsen said in *Berlingske Tidende:* "As the handsome, masculine, and easily seduced Jason, Henning Kronstam is much advanced since he did Jean. He looked wonderful, a Patroklos on his way to becoming Achilles. He danced beautifully. Every step of Cullberg was given full value in his long, elongated lines and in his flying jumps. But it was new that alongside the ease of the rhythm of the movements there was also a male gravity to the character. Jason is the blue-eyed man [a naïf] who follows his senses without knowing the consequences. Kronstam's mime can easily acquire more richness, his acting at the end can have a more convincing sense of tragedy, but he did have the character right. It was his most surprising performance of the season."

One of the first things Kronstam said when discussing his career was, "I was never a classical dancer; that was Erik. I was really a character dancer." By this, he meant a dance-actor, not a mime or a dancer who specialized in Spanish or Russian character dance. In one sense he spoke truly. When he danced a Prince he was a classical dancer because the Prince was a classical dancer; that was the way that character would move. A sadistic butler, a hunter, a madman would move differently. At base Kronstam was always an actor, but an actor who preferred music and movement to words.

"I hate to just stand in fifth position. I get the greater satisfaction out of doing character roles—classical character roles, like James and Albrecht, or roles like *The Moor's Pavane* or *Bagage.* Of course, I wanted the challenge of doing *Apollo* and all these straight neoclassical and classical ballets too. *Giselle* was a dream that I had to do. When I was a young dancer I wanted to compete in the classical repertory. Definitely.

"But very early—in *Behind the Curtain* [Bag Tæppet, a ballet by Fredbjørn Bjørnsson], I didn't do one step. It was just my face [my expressions] that made Kirsten Ralov change from a dull dancer into a beautiful woman. This was when I was nineteen, so already they were using my imagination. And then *La Sonnambula,* when I was twenty. There were not many steps but there was a big difference between my pas de deux with the Coquette and the pas de deux with the Sleepwalker. And I died—I had a wonderful time."

Kronstam seemed to be unsure of his abilities and surprised that so many choreographers wanted to work with him. "They saw something, because I didn't know that I could do it. I didn't know that I could do *La Sonnambula*. I didn't know what it was about. I didn't know that I could do Romeo. I didn't know anything. I just went [into the studio] and I did what they said. And then I built it. You have it in you, somewhere. I had the nastiness for the later roles. I had the Romantic side but [the nasty roles are] are not so far from the white Romantics, really. Because a Romantic—not the sweet, sweet Romantic, but the other type, in the Verdi opera, or Puccini opera, that type of Romantic, the rich Romantic—it's not that far. And you can find a lot of those things in yourself, or I could, at least. So you find something inside yourself that you can use."

Many dancers who worked with him pointed out that one of the special things about Kronstam's performance style is that he managed to be both introspective and spontaneous, as though he had thoroughly thought through a role, and then would re-create it, as though living it for the first time at each performance. He felt he was more intuitive than intellectual in his approach.

"It happened in my bed, during the night, that I suddenly realized, that's how I had to do it. It comes in the morning in those times between dreaming and waking, and I think, 'Maybe I should try it this way.' And then I find something in me that I could use. And usually the producers or the directors were satisfied with it.

"I could sense the character building during the whole day. You think about doing the performance in the evening, and the character was already starting to build when I did my first class in the morning. That was in my mind. I did the class. I did everything that I was expected to do. I could rehearse other ballets, but I was still holding back the thing that I had to do in the evening. It was always there in the back of my head. He was a shadow behind me. I was doing everything that Vera wanted, or that Mrs. [Edite] Frandsen, or Stanley said, but I was holding something back because I knew that there was another character waiting for me. I couldn't explode in those classes. I would just do the steps and listen and work on my technique, but I couldn't—sometimes you give in class, you know, you just abandon yourself, when you're only yourself, and you don't need to think about a performance in the evening. If you have one of those big roles in the evening, there is something in the back of your head that's saying, 'Well, Romeo is there,' or 'Siegfried is there.' So you can rehearse everything, but you don't develop in the rehearsals on those days. When you're getting in costume and making up, sitting in the dressing room, then he is there right in me.

"But that's a ritual, this whole thing about coming to the Theatre at six o'clock and start your makeup, go to do your class. I always did about a forty-five-minute warm-up. And then having the hair set, putting on the costume, going on the stage, trying out the stage, that two hours. But then I was there. Completely. And that meant that it was a whole day of buildup. That's why it was troubling for me when I had to do La Sylphide one evening and Romeo the next evening, The Lesson the third evening, Carmen and Miss Julie the fourth evening. It just went like that and I constantly had to get the one role out and the other one in.

"If I had to do two roles on the same program it could be hard. That's why I had to stop doing Toreador after doing James. It was just too hard to get James out of me. And I would do Lifeguards and Lilac Garden on the same evening, and that was hard too because you knew that you were going to do these two parts and you had to separate them because there's such a difference between Du Puy [the hero of Livjægerne paa Amager], who is so easygoing, and then to be the nasty man in Lilac Garden."

Kronstam spoke about his character roles with such obvious pleasure, one might wonder if he were not a character dancer after all. But he admitted that this delight in acting roles was in retrospect. "When you're a young dancer," he said, "all you want to do is get out there and dance."

Part Three

The Mature Artist

Kronstam's Cyrano is one of the rarest ballet
performances in its phenomenal dancing as well
as in the emotion of the mime.
—Svend Kragh-Jacobsen, *Berlingske Tidende*, 1960

Cyrano

The years framed by the Royal Danish Ballet's second and third American
tours (1960–65) were full of temptations for Kronstam. While his first forays
abroad, to Aix-en-Provence and Edinburgh, had been arranged by John Taras,
by the 1960s his reputation had grown enough so that he got invitations on his
own—to Stuttgart, as well as other European companies and festivals, and to
the New York City Ballet, American Ballet Theatre, and Ruth Page's Chicago
Opera Ballet in the United States. His files are filled with telegrams saying,
"Could you come such-and-such date to do *Sleeping Beauty* pas de deux," and
more often than not, the response is an expression of regret, such as the telegram dated June 10, 1962: "Impossible to come. Repertoire changed here.
Sorry. Kronstam."

The Theatre was as accommodating as possible and, with notice, would work to arrange a repertory in which Kronstam was not cast or had an understudy. This too was a double-edged sword, because in a year in which Kronstam had many guest engagements scheduled, it meant that when he was home he didn't have as much to do. During those years he matured in his core repertory of James, Romeo, Apollo, Albrecht, and Jean and added a new role that he loved and that suited him perfectly—Roland Petit's Cyrano. He also widened his international reputation through two North American tours with the Danish Ballet and those guest and television appearances that he did accept.

In the fall of 1960 the company made its second tour of North America (August 12–October 21). They opened on the West Coast, in San Francisco, and continued to thirteen cities in the United States and Canada, bypassing New York for reasons that were never stated. Critics from New York (John Martin of the *Times* and Walter Terry of the *Herald Tribune*) traveled to see the company in Philadelphia, Washington, and Baltimore, grumbling a bit that they had to do so. The tour was again a critical success, but much of the repertory was foreign to audiences and critics outside New York, and performances did not always sell out. Several reviewers scolded their cities for not turning out a bigger audience for the Danes.

Kronstam's repertory included Romeo, the Poet, James, Apollo, Nilas, the Drummer, the Toreador, and Jean. He received very favorable reviews and was recognized as a dancer of international caliber, but the company still presented itself as an ensemble company—a fact remarked upon favorably everywhere— and neither Kronstam nor Flemming Flindt, who joined the company for this tour, were presented as stars.

The Royal Danish Ballet in general, and Kronstam in particular, did especially well in Chicago, which was known at the time as the only other real ballet town in the United States outside of New York. The city had several newspapers in the 1960s and some of the most interesting, and most feared, critics in America, including the *Chicago Tribune*'s Claudia Cassidy, a woman of sophisticated tastes and an acid tongue. Walter Todd, who worked with the Metropolitan Opera and became a friend and correspondent of Kronstam's, wrote him: "The review you got for Jean in Chicago from Claudia Cassidy was fantastic. She is a first class bitch and can be vicious, so it is a great compliment that you impressed her so much. Some of our singers refuse to go to Chicago because of what she has written about them."[1] Cassidy's review of the company's farewell performance in Chicago includes a glowing account of his Apollo:

> Typical of the company's generosity was that closing night performance of
> *Apollon Musagète* for its unique dancer, Henning Kronstam. . . . [*Apollo*] is a great
> part of ballet history, but I have never been convinced that it is a great ballet. Yet
> it is effective for Kronstam, who is the one Apollo I can remember who did not
> look a little foolish. There is no vanity in the man for all his gifts as a premier
> danseur noble, and there is a flick of wit at the heart of some of his most
> glorious dancing. Here as Apollo, who was created by light and is in the end
> claimed by light, symbol of Zeus the father, he puts candor in mystery, which in
> great dancing is no paradox. Nor was he too engrossed in becoming a god to
> partner the muses, who were Mette Mollerup, Kirsten Petersen, and Kirsten
> Simone.

Ann Barzel, dance critic for the *Chicago American* and less acid and more knowledgeable about technique than Cassidy, wrote of Kronstam in *Romeo and Juliet,* "Four years ago, I used superlatives in reporting on [Ashton's *Romeo and Juliet*]. Time has brought even more polish to the presentation, especially to the great performance by Henning Kronstam and Mona Vangsaae. Kronstam is the ideal romantic dancer. His manner is a blend of fervor and elegance, and he has a lyric movement quality underlined by strength. He has a meticulous technique and great taste."

The New York Ballet Club once again singled out Kronstam. One member (S.Z.B.) wrote in the November 1960 newsletter (which also welcomed eleven new members, including a young Arlene Croce):

> Sad to say, my favorite male dancer of the company, Henning Kronstam, only
> danced twice, and at that, the parts were not very large: the Drummer in *Grad
> Ball* and the Toreador in *Carmen.* The program did not list him at all for the first
> night, and a few other club members and I were so unhappy that we wanted to
> go home. Mme. Volkova, one of the Artistic Directors of the company, over-
> heard us and assured us that he would dance as a replacement in *Grad Ball.* She
> also said that she would tell Henning that three nice looking girls wanted their
> money back when they thought he was not going to dance. I must say that he
> played and danced the parts of the Drummer and the Toreador to the hilt.

When the company was in Philadelphia, Lincoln Kirstein came down from New York to see Kronstam and invite him to join the New York City Ballet, he said, at Balanchine's behest. Kronstam was pleased at the invitation and wanted to accept it. "There were so many good roles in that company," he said, but he ultimately had to turn down the offer. "When I got home, I spoke with my direction and they said, 'We can let you go for a month here, and three months there,' but Balanchine wanted me for a whole year, and that we couldn't do." Rather than resign, as others had when faced with such a choice, Kronstam stayed. "I was always leaving the Theatre," he said. "But I'd make a list of reasons to do it and reasons to stay, and always there were more reasons to stay. I had Vera, and I had Franz, and I had no rivals in my repertory here at home."

Although sorry that he missed out on so many good roles (one Balanchine ballet in particular that he longed to dance was *Bugaku*, "because it was so strange"), Kronstam accepted the situation philosophically. "It would have been interesting," he said. "There were some beautiful roles in that repertory and I could have gone into the Magallanes and Moncion roles. But what you've said no to, you've said no to. And besides, if I had gone there, I would have missed two-thirds of my career. I would have always been the pretty boy."

Back in Copenhagen, the 1960–61 season brought him one of his favorite, and finest, roles, that of Cyrano in Roland Petit's *Cyrano de Bergerac*. Petit had

With Kirsten Simone as Roxane in Roland Petit's *Cyrano de Bergerac*. The two cousins meet, and Cyrano is embarrassed by his deformity. Photo: Mydtskov. The Royal Theatre, Copenhagen. By permission of Det kongelige Teaters bibliotek og arkiv.

As Cyrano, expressing Christian's love for Roxane. Photo: Mydtskov. The Royal Theatre, Copenhagen. By permission of Det kongelige Teaters bibliotek og arkiv.

Cyrano mocked by the crowd. Photo: Mydtskov. The Royal Theatre, Copenhagen. By permission of Det kongelige Teaters bibliotek og arkiv.

created the title role himself the previous year in Paris and decided to stage the ballet in Copenhagen after the success of *Carmen*.

Petit's *Cyrano* was one of many flawed ballets that the Danes turned into a masterpiece through performance. The role of Roxane was another success for Kirsten Simone; Eske Holm, an up-and-coming star and future choreographer, was the young Christian; and there were dozens of small roles that great Danish artists turned into detailed characters. Cyrano was not only one of Kronstam's finest portrayals but one of the few that gave both acting and dancing equal measure. He led a dance of the knights, and there were several solos and pas de deux, as well as mime speeches. Cyrano was an extremely difficult role dramatically as well as technically, especially for a twenty-five-year-old, as he portrayed a knight, a lover, and, in the last scene, an old man.

Kronstam was ideally suited to the role of this poet-knight, and he was always drawn to stories of thwarted love. "The nose, the ugliness, is an insurmountable barrier," he said firmly, not allowing for an instant the notion that if only Cyrano had confessed his love to Roxane directly she might have accepted him. "No. That was never a possibility." In *Cyrano* deformity was destiny. There was a repeated gesture in the ballet, where Cyrano shyly shields his nose with his hand and turns his head, that dancers could sense Kronstam especially liked, from the way he approached it in rehearsals.

There was still interaction among members of the different branches of the Theatre. Kronstam said: "Poul Reumert, our great actor, who had just done Cyrano at the Comedie Française, came to me when he heard I was going to do the role and asked if I wanted help. But it didn't work because the ballet was so different from the play.

"Cyrano was an enormous role. I know that Walter Terry was angry that we didn't bring it to the States, because Kirsten was wonderful in it. It was perfect for this company, and there were gorgeous costumes by Yves Saint Laurent.

"I loved it even though I was almost killed in the last scene. It was so hard, and of course Roland, like the French, would not do it full out: elegantly, hands a little easy, and everything else. And I danced it like a bulldozer. I had a good time with it. When I came to the last scene, where she realized that it was me who has written all the letters and saying all the words, there I was—it was a very Roland Petit thing, you know, where he would do little changes of the feet, and I was lying in the wings before that scene getting a massage."

Danish critics liked the ballet; British ones (who saw it during the company's annual festival) admired Kronstam's performance but thought the work was a lightweight pastiche. Of Kronstam, Svend Kragh-Jacobsen wrote:

> The most excellent thing about the Danish performance was that in the title role, Kronstam surpassed even Petit's own interesting performance in Paris. If one could speak of soulful dancing, Kronstam managed to show it to us. Not when he was impressing us with his glorious steps, his proudest dancing, but in the silent moments, by looking at Roxane, freezing in a statuesque pose. It was a great victory for a dancer who has conquered us over the years by the beauty of his dancing and by his romantic and noble appearance. . . .
>
> The young Eske Holm was a handsome and noble Christian, a nobleman by blood, even if, as a dancer, he cannot compete with Kronstam. Nobody can in *Cyrano*.

The American historian and critic Lillian Moore, a frequent visitor to Copenhagen, wrote: "As Cyrano, Henning Kronstam is magnificent. It is a cruelly demanding role, but from the very first solo (the famous monologue of the nose) to the last poignant scene, he sustains it superbly." Noting that the ballet is weakest in parts where the play is strongest, and vice-versa, she continued: "*Cyrano* is a ballet-drama on a grandiose scale. In it, Denmark's celebrated male dancers really have a chance to shine, and Mr. Kronstam's Cyrano is not easily to be forgotten" (*New York Herald Tribune*, March 12, 1961).

The British critic A. V. Coton saw it as another example of Danish artistry transcending the Danish repertory. This would come to be the prevailing foreign view, although it is not a Danish one, as a ballet is not defined solely as choreography in Denmark:

> Some of the good modern works are being heavily misinterpreted and much good production and talent is thrown into foreign-made ballets of no great quality. This second point was illustrated with crushing emphasis in Roland Petit's version of *Cyrano de Bergerac*, shown in London two years ago and recently staged by him here.
>
> For a still young artist Henning Kronstam brings some powerfully precise acting to the leading role. As against Petit's own interpretation in Paris and London, Kronstam makes Cyrano more civilised and less bombastic; he is much more a worldly-wise man resigned to his ludicrous deformity. This interpretation sets the key to which the production is geared. Every role is performed with studied care and in mosaically minute detail. All of this merely emphasises the choreographic poverty of most of the work and leaves an impression of a vast expenditure of time, talent and energy on something

theatrically almost meaningless. The characterisation of Cyrano is simply impossible without the medium of words.[2]

Cyrano was given on the same night with a world premiere by Petit, *Chaloupée,* a pop piece for Erik Bruhn, home for a guest appearance, in which
Bruhn played an Elvis Presley–type figure. It was a totally new departure for
Bruhn and by all accounts he was brilliant in it. An incident immediately following the premiere illustrates a few differences and similarities between
Bruhn and Kronstam. Both were high-strung individuals, both were perfec-
tionists, both had trouble dealing with preperformance nerves. Any performer
has precurtain butterflies; pressures on star performers, however, are far
greater than on ordinary mortals, even dancers. It's as though each night is a
battle, or at least a prizefight—the star versus his image, or his past performances, or his rival, or all three. If a star has an off night, talk of "Is he beginning to slip?" begins to make the rounds.

Both men not only dealt with these pressures differently but expressed and
experienced their anxiety differently. Bruhn danced in extreme physical pain
for at least the last ten years of his classical career; he had an undiagnosed
ulcer, dismissed as "nerves" until it perforated in 1971. Kronstam experienced
anxiety attacks (often associated with manic-depression), the physical manifes-
tations of which included uncontrollably shaking hands and difficulty in sleeping. Both dancers overcame these handicaps and performed, but at great
physical and emotional cost. Bruhn had a reputation for missing premieres
from nerves, Kronstam did not. He managed the anxiety and his "ups and
downs" by planning. He had to know what was expected of him and then he
could manage his energies. He would know at the beginning of a season which
performances he would be dancing and plan for them. He devised a set routine—rising at a certain hour no matter how little sleep he'd gotten the night
before, a preperformance nap, specific meals at specific times—from which he
did not deviate. Any change would knock him off balance. With enough time
he could adjust and regain his balance, but change would always present a
difficult, sometimes frightening, challenge.

At the opening night party for *Cyrano* and *Chaloupée,* Henning Rohde, then
acting as "administrative leader" of the ballet, came up to Kronstam and told
him that they would need to repeat the program the next evening—an opera
had had to be postponed because it needed more rehearsal. Kronstam threw
everything into a role, every bit of emotion and energy. A ballet like *Cyrano* was

extremely taxing, and under ordinary circumstances he would need a day or two to recover. "He completely ruined the evening for me," Kronstam said. "He didn't understand what he was asking." Kronstam danced the next night; Bruhn, equally spent, could not, citing illness, and Jørn Madsen, his understudy, danced in his stead. This is not an isolated example, yet, curiously, Kronstam developed a reputation for being unable to handle stress because he was "weak," and Bruhn did not.

Another incident played havoc with Kronstam's nerves. After years of intrigues and attempted coups Harald Lander returned, without protest this time, to stage *Etudes* and create a new ballet for the company, *Les Amours de Victorine*. Nearly everyone in the company had a part in Lander's new ballet except Kronstam, and it seemed odd that he had not been cast in such a large work. "I was sick and couldn't do it," he said, adding when pressed, "I had my problems." Exactly why Lander's return was so upsetting to Kronstam is not clear, but it triggered a breakdown, the first known hospitalization for his "ups and downs." Kronstam had an injured foot, and that provided a cover for his trip to the hospital in Arhus. A letter from Volkova to him in the hospital dated only February 8 makes it clear that the hospitalization was not primarily for a physical injury. "I am relieved to hear that you have decided to go to hospital. *Now you have a chance to give your foot a real rest and to be looked after at the same time.* As I said, nothing of importance is going on in the Theatre at the moment" (emphasis added).

Whether or not there were previous hospitalizations is unknown, but this one was not the last. Kronstam was hospitalized many times during his life, although it is now impossible to determine dates or details because of Denmark's strict patient confidentiality laws. Kronstam's brother said on one occasion that he received Kronstam's medical records after his death and they included a dozen hospitalizations. In a second conversation he said he had been unable to obtain his brother's hospital records. One Danish psychologist who several people said had treated Kronstam was contacted, but he said he had not done so. Kronstam's longtime general practitioner retired the year before Kronstam died and moved "to the country" with no forwarding address. Both Kronstam's brother and Kirsten Simone said that there had been occasions when he took tranquilizers in order to be able to dance. Other dancers were not aware of this, but it is possible. There certainly were times when he was ballet master that he appeared to be extremely passive, which could have resulted from taking tranquilizers (or could have been a symptom of depression). Kronstam told friends outside the Theatre at several different times that a doctor had prescribed tranquilizers, but dates and doses are not verifiable. From 1962, at least, the ups and downs came more and more to the fore and were less and less easily controlled. By the mid-1960s his condition was noticed by foreign visitors to the company, who could be more objective about what they were seeing than those who had known him all his life and thought of it as artistic temperament, or moodiness, or "just the way Henning was."

A very different letter from Volkova to her husband, Hugh, a few months later gives an example of Kronstam's concern with company direction at the very early age of twenty-seven. There was a new staging of Ashton's *Romeo and Juliet* (without Ashton) that he found troubling. Larsen had notated the ballet and filmed it so that there would be a record. He was a conscientious director, though not an especially imaginative or inspiring one. Kronstam was disturbed by the casting. Mona Vangsaae would not dance Juliet this time; Kirsten Petersen, originally the second-cast Juliet, would dance the role to Kronstam's Romeo, and a new cast, Anna Lærkesen and Eske Holm, was added. Kronstam pressed for Kirsten Simone to dance Juliet, instead of Kirsten Petersen. Petersen, with her beautiful feet and line, was a lovely dancer but, Kronstam thought, had not matured emotionally. He felt that Simone, especially after her Roxane in *Cyrano*, would be more interesting in the role.

Kronstam's suggestions went beyond the casting of the leads. He felt that Larsen, who favored demi-caractère dancers generally, had cast classical roles with demi-caractère dancers to the ballet's detriment. Kronstam drew up a suggested cast list that he felt more clearly carried out Ashton's intentions. Volkova was very proud of this. In her letter she included Larsen's cast list and Henning's, presenting it as though it were a final exam that her pupil had passed with flying colors. Kronstam's ideas were not accepted, at least not in 1962, and Simone did not get to dance Juliet until the 1965 American tour, when she was acclaimed in the role.

Compared to his first few years as a solo dancer, Kronstam acquired few new roles during this period. Partly this was because he had already danced most of the leading roles in the repertory by this time, partly because although he always remained based in Copenhagen, he spent a great deal of time as a guest artist, and partly because as a director, Larsen preferred demi-caractère ballets and, as Kirsten Simone put it, "short, cute dancers." Kronstam once dismissed this with, "That's nonsense. We had plenty to dance," but on another occasion agreed, saying they had to look outside the company for new roles. Kronstam didn't miss out on any great roles by traveling. The new repertory in Copenhagen continued to be undistinguished, the new creations, often by Danish choreographers, negligible and lasting only a season or two.

New ballets in which he did dance included works by Kenneth MacMillan and Balanchine, as well as two minor works—Frank Schaufuss's *Garden Party,* in which he danced the Host, a role created on Erik Bruhn and thus a technical challenge, and Elsa Marianne von Rosen's *Irene Holm,* a ballet based on a Herman Bang story of an aging corps de ballet dancer forced from the Theatre and teaching in the provinces, in which he portrayed the ballet master.

MacMillan, at the time considered one of the most promising classical choreographers of the coming generation, came to stage a triple bill that used the company well. *Solitaire,* a playful work suited to young dancers, gave Anna Lærkesen one of her first star parts; *The Burrow,* a dark work about people hiding from the Nazis, provided terrific roles for some of the company's mimes, like Larsen and Bjørnsson; and *Danses Concertantes,* a pure-dance ballet, showcased the dancers' classical technique. Kronstam danced the leading male role in the latter, a part he found difficult (because it had been made for a small man) though not particularly interesting.

The new Balanchine evening was a different matter. The company revived *Symphony in C,* with Kronstam and Simone in the first movement (the "red movement," as it was known in Copenhagen); *The Prodigal Son,* for Flemming Flindt, who was home as a guest; and *The Four Temperaments.* "That was one of the few times in my career that I asked for a role," Kronstam said. "I went to Una Kai [who was staging the work for Balanchine] and said, 'Una, I would like to dance Phlegmatic, if you can use me.' I loved that role. It has such nice steps in it." Kai initially did not think Kronstam was suited to the role, which she considered demi-caractère, but he was in the first cast, garnering praise from both fellow dancers and critics. It's interesting to note that since Kronstam's performance as Phlegmatic, in New York, the role has often been danced by tall men, while Melancholic has become a "short-boy" role.

His appearance and his huge jump made Kronstam seem more suited to Melancholic, a role he later danced in an emergency, when the first-cast Melancholic (Jørn Madsen) was injured. Dancing a role without a formal rehearsal was unheard of in those days and warranted a news article. Kronstam was also

As Phlegmatic in Balanchine's *Four Temperaments*. Photo: Mydtskov. The Royal Theatre, Copenhagen. By permission of Det kongelige Teaters bibliotek og arkiv.

well received in this role but did not dance it often and did not discuss it easily. During the first session of interviews for this book, when he was in depression, he avoided questions about Melancholic, always steering the conversation back to Phlegmatic. A few months later, when his depression had lifted, he said, "You have never asked me about Melancholic," and talked quite happily of learning the role without a rehearsal, rather enjoying the fact that his efforts had been judged heroic.

The Danish reviews of this program are interesting on several counts. In the 1980s it was often said by Americans, and some expatriate Danish dancers, that the Danes neither liked nor understood Balanchine's work, but the critics of this generation certainly did, as these reviews show. A piece in *Berlingske*

Tidende entitled "Three Times Balanchine" (probably by Kragh-Jacobsen) pointed out the absurdity of programming *Symphony in C* as a middle ballet. It also chides Kronstam a bit for having incorporated some "Americanisms" from the recent tour, although he may have been trying to dance Balanchine in the American rather than European manner.

> It's obvious that *Bourée Fantasque,* following *Symphony in C,* is a choreographic anticlimax that serves none of the ballets. On the other hand, *Bourée Fantasque* was performed yesterday better than *Symphony in C,* so that the evening built. In the last ballet Kronstam was secure in his brilliant dancing, but without the previously seen warm charm [now replaced] by the hard style that they [Kronstam and Simone] have brought home from their American tour. What they have won in show glamour, they have lost in grace, but as dancers, they are still in our top rank. . . .
>
> Best in the whole ballet [*Four Temperaments*] was Henning Kronstam's wonderful dancing of the Phlegmatic part. Here his tightened dancing had been loosened.

In a review entitled "Music for the Eyes" (a phrase often used to describe Balanchine's ballets), Harald Engberg found Kronstam "outstanding in the Phlegmatic section." In a review of the repremiere (the very convenient Danish term for the first performance of a work when it reenters the repertory in a subsequent season) he praised Kronstam as both dancer and stager; Kronstam took over rehearsals of the Balanchine repertory, among other ballets, in 1966. Engberg also pointed out a problem of costuming for the women: Danish thighs and Balanchine black-and-white were not compatible. "After Jørn Madsen's fine performance in Melancholic we have Henning Kronstam's excellent immersion in the Phlegmatic section. . . . The rare and exquisite work looked beautiful at the repremiere, which gives great credit to Henning Kronstam and which he does proud. It is therefore OK to add that the sparse costuming, which doesn't give anything to anybody, is beginning to show that several of the dancers are not as graceful as they used to be. Balanchine's musical ballets in bathing suits make demands on the feminine shape as well as artistry. Very hard demands."

Kronstam was cast in Schaufuss's *The Garden Party* on very short notice. "*The Garden Party* was made for Erik and Anna, and it was all dancing, and using all Erik's virtuoso steps. There was a beautiful pas de deux with Anna. And then Erik left [without notice], as usual, and I was at the tailor—I remember that. I was at the tailor, having a fitting for Danilo [in Ruth Page's *The Merry Widow*, which he was about to dance in America for Page's Chicago Opera Ballet], and the phone rang and they said I had to come to the Theatre because I had to learn that role. And, as Vera said, it was good to take it because it was good exercise, to keep you in shape—because already they knew that Kirsten and I were going away for three months. They were doing a repertory that we would not be fitted into, so I didn't have that much to do."

Svend Kragh-Jacobsen described the ballet as: "Frank Schaufuss's step orgy *Garden Party* where Henning Kronstam has taken over the part of the host after Erik Bruhn. He gave it his most handsome dancing, his white elegance and his calm and exquisite partnering. He performed his first solo with great jumps, and was a lovely and calm partner for Anna Lærkesen in the adagio— the pas de deux, where his romantic appearance contributed to the atmosphere. And, of course, he had the brilliance, when Schaufuss, toward the finale, lets the white and the black couple meet."

Von Rosen's *Irene Holm* was another attempt to give the repertory a Danish story ballet, but Kronstam agreed with the prevailing opinion that it was too weak choreographically to last. "It's a beautiful story, a little human tragedy. She [Irene Holm, the aging dancer, danced by Schanne] tries to keep [her technique] up, and she is standing there by her bed and the peasants are looking through the keyhole, watching the old lady doing her exercises, holding onto the bed. But then she is thinking back, and then she remembers the ballet master, and she dreams about her time in the theater."

Kronstam played the ballet master at the theater in the city. "I gave class to the whole company on the stage. I picked on her all the time. She was not good enough, and things like that. She was thrown out. And then she started teaching and ended up teaching just to have a room somewhere. If there had been better choreography, it could have been a good ballet. Elsa Marianne is a nice lady, but she was always disturbed by her husband [the critic Allan Fridericia]. He had to have everything in it. He had to have every little word in the book presented. Instead of seeing what the main point of it was, and what was suitable for dancing."

The state of the repertory had been a consistent problem since the Lander Scandal, and the search for a Danish choreographer had been unflagging. In 1964, Danes thought they had found one. Flemming Flindt created a one-act ballet based on an Ionesco play, *The Private Lesson*, that suited the company.

Dramatic, with a dark subject matter, it was both Danish and not Danish and, with Lander's *Etudes*, it is the only twentieth-century Danish work to enter the international repertory. Flindt created it in Paris and danced the first performance; the ballet was staged for Danish television and, instead of dancing the role of the Dancing Master himself, Flindt gave the part to Kronstam.

The role of the dancing master who eventually kills his pupil (Flindt had to change the play a bit) was completely different from anything Kronstam had done. Kronstam was not yet thirty, and this twisted, gnarled, and knotted man was very far not only from the Princes, but also character parts like Jean or Cyrano. He had a triumph in the role and from that time forward he was more often described as a dramatic dancer than a Romantic one. *The Lesson* pointed a new path for Kronstam, which he would follow over the next decade. Svend Kragh-Jacobsen wrote of his performance:

> Henning Kronstam has built on this fancifully shaped and most sinister character. Not only did he suggest the insecurity of the professor, but by repeatedly touching his temples he also indicated the pain and something sickly. His mask was excellent, a vile, pale, meager being, perhaps somewhat too sinister as he makes his entry, causing the surprise of the violence to be revealed too soon. At the same time, however, this exterior, and Kronstam's subdued movements, kept the character in place, and in him we saw the whole development, the freedom of the movement as the teacher takes power over the student. In his fits of anger against the pianist, the scary temper of the dictator strikes like lightning. The pendulum between an inferiority complex and megalomania in the professor was [clearly delineated] and he naturally performed with admirable élan in terms of dancing. It is as if this particular danseur serieux, who performs his princes so beautifully on stage, has more bite when he is allowed to hide in character figures. Here, he definitely became the main character of *The Lesson*.

The Lesson was a triumph for Flindt. The 1960s were a time of artistic revolution in Denmark, as they were in the rest of the world. Pressures for a more modern repertory, a younger direction for the company, had been heard for some time. The classical side of the company, led by Volkova, was training the corps for *Swan Lake*, which also entered the repertory that season. *Swan Lake* and *The Lesson* represented a crossroads for the company. The former was the culmination of fifteen years of Volkova's hard work in bringing the Danish Ballet to international level as a classical company, the latter suited to the tastes of those in the new audience that Flindt was bringing to the Theatre, who

As the murderous teacher, with Mette Hønningen in Flindt's *The Lesson*. Photo: Fred
Fehl. University of Texas at Austin. By permission of University of Texas at Austin.

preferred realism to fairy tales or abstractions. The fact that *Swan Lake* and
The Lesson were diametrically opposed aesthetically and that a ballet company
would find it difficult to do justice to both branches of the art form did not seem
to trouble many people.

Kronstam danced Siegfried in this *Swan Lake* in 1964. Nina Anisimova
came from the Kirov to stage it, and Kronstam danced in both the first cast
(with Simone) and second (with Lærkesen). He enjoyed working with Anisimova, who pushed him technically. He said he got from her the "Russian trick"
of seeming to hover in midair during a jump.

Anisimova's production of *Swan Lake* was not very successful. During this
period Danish critics and audiences resisted Petipa, finding the ballets too
long and the dramaturgy not equal to Bournonville's. Critics also recognized
the problem that had plagued the company since Lander left: how to dance

non-Danish works in a Danish way. As the ballet world became more and more international, more influenced by Russian ballet, the Danish ballet was becoming hemmed in on its tiny island. It would either have to generate choreography compatible with its own style or abandon its style and fall in line with the rest of the world. It tried to find a compromise—dance foreign works in a way true to the work, and also true to the Danish style—but this is a conflict that has never been satisfactorily resolved.

During this period Kronstam made many guest appearances. One of the most interesting for him was to dance John Cranko's *Daphnis and Chloe*, which had been created for Erik Bruhn and Georgina Parkinson. Bruhn left the company suddenly, after dancing only two performances (Bruhn said in his autobiography that he had been so perfect at the second performance that "I was afraid I could not surpass myself"),[3] and Cranko needed a replacement on short notice. "This is the one where Erik left, and nobody could dance it," Kronstam remembered. "Taras sent me a telegram when I was in the States asking if I would join the company for the summer season and go to Edinburgh with it for their festival and do Daphnis, and then I should do the Prince in *Sleeping Beauty* too.

"Daphnis, I loved. I did it with Marcia [Haydée] and I did it with Violette [Verdy]. In the first act, first scene, he is just very nice. But then he had the competition dance, where Dorkon [his rival] dances first, and then Daphnis dances. He is not in the second act, but when he comes back there is a passionate pas de deux. Really passionate.

"It was very difficult. I had a shock at how hard it was, especially the variation in the competition. That had grand jetés where you'd have an extra tour in the air and land on one leg and things like that. And I said, 'My dear, my dear, my dear. Give me two weeks.' And I had only ten days to learn it.

"I did it about four times in Stuttgart and then three performances in Edinburgh. I was happy to go to Stuttgart. There was a wonderful atmosphere there. Cranko had a way of having everybody around him. I came alone and the first evening Ricky [Cragun] and Marcia took me out for dinner and everything went like that. Cranko was wonderful to work with. The rehearsal period is a wonderful time for a dancer because you can try things out. It doesn't matter if you fall down, or something like that. You can work on things." Cranko was beloved by dancers who worked with him, and his letter of invitation to Kronstam shows his warm and personal style.

12 May 1963

Dear Henning,

I am so happy that all seems to be working out O.K. Let me clarify. . . . In this week you will be dancing one *Sleeping Beauty* with our ballerina Anita Cardus. One *Daphnis,* and one *Flower Festival* pas de deux (I suggest with Antoinette Sibley, as she has already done it at Covent Garden and it will be less work for you).

Before the ballet week, there is only one performance of *Daphnis and Chloe,* as you couldn't get here earlier and we could not manage to shift the performances around. Therefore, if you could get to Stuttgart about the 28th of June, that would give you all week for *Daphnis* (with stage rehearsals) and then just over a week for *Beauty* and *Flower Festival.* The other guest artists arrive on the 1st of July. . . .

Henning, we are all looking forward so much to having you with us, it is a fun company, and I do so hope you will be happy with us.

Much love,

John

Kronstam danced *Flower Festival* at the gala, with Antoinette Sibley. "She had done it with Erik in London, so she knew it. We had to figure out what to do with it because I had a different version than she had. I liked her so much. She's very free, very open. I knew her from the Nervi Festival, when Kirsten and I danced there. Antoinette was there with David Blair and Svetlana [Beriosova], a little group. We worked very well together."

Kronstam also danced in *Sleeping Beauty* during his time in Stuttgart, with Anita Cardus; Sibley danced Princess Florine in the Bluebird pas de deux in that production. One German review of *Sleeping Beauty* singled out both dancers for similar reasons:

> Ballet is not the same as the circus, although we sometimes confuse the two when people applaud for the highest leaps, the X number of fouettés, etc. But the big quantities should never disturb the beauty of the flow.
>
> Two masters of this gave guest performances during the ballet week for *Sleeping Beauty:* Antoinette Sibley of the London Royal Ballet and Henning Kronstam of the Royal Danish Ballet in Copenhagen. Sibley, who danced the Bluebird this time, remains a great lady even in bravura passages, showing her culture, transforming the difficult into a play of lightness and joy and culture.
>
> So also, Henning Kronstam in his first appearance as the Prince. His entrance in the second act is unforgettable, although it is an ungrateful costume, with high boots, which don't permit him to dance much, only to mime, to seem

surprised, to run, and to lift a bit. Mediocre Princes are not up to this. Kronstam, without showing any effort, is simply there, at rest, but attentive, curious,
with small, restricted gestures, a bit of skepticism at the corners of his mouth.
He is, perhaps, Prince Hamlet. As he showed later, he's a wonderful dancer, of
fine-limbed elegance, intelligent, and with a nervous sensibility. Therefore it's
that much more of a joy when he finally smiles. He did succeed with his
partner, Anita Cardus, whose transformation from a small girl to a real diva was
very well done. They make a magical pair.

Back in Copenhagen the Theatre's administration was about to undergo a
major change. There had been problems after the 1960 tour, which had lost 1.2
million kroner. The company had made up this deficit by using a government
fund allocated for commerce. Arguments pressed by Niels Matthiasen, a

With Violette Verdy in John Cranko's *Daphnis and Chloe,* 1965. Photo: Alo Storz.
Private collection.

member of Parliament passionately devoted to the ballet, that the Danish ballet was as vital to the Danish economy as Danish bacon, won the day, but this
was another controversy that would often rear its head in succeeding decades.
Henning Brøndsted, who had been theater chief for more than twenty years,
resigned. The post had previously been an open-ended appointment. It would
now be a four-year appointment, and the first new theater chief was Per Gregaard, director of Copenhagen's Ny (New) Theatre, a man who would be expected to put drama ahead of opera and ballet in this theater of the three arts,
but a sensitive man who loved the arts.

Larsen resigned as ballet master. There was no scandal, but rather a sense
that it was time for new blood. He must have been sick of the dissension and
constant attacks by the press (although these had slowed after the second
Lander scandal), and his duties as director of the Pantomime Theatre were
proving to be a conflict. By unwritten Danish tradition, the post of ballet master descended through the male line. The company's leading principals were
asked, in order of seniority, first Bruhn, then Kronstam, both of whom turned
down the job. Flindt, next in line, only twenty-nine and a danseur étoile with
the Paris Opera Ballet, said yes. It was decidedly the beginning of a new era.

A rare photo of Kronstam
clowning on tour. Private
collection.

Larsen remained director until December 31, 1965, and agreed to lead the third American tour. This time, the company would dance in New York (at the State Theatre, part of the brand new Lincoln Center) and would be presented, not by Columbia Arts Management, but by Sol Hurok. This was not an incidental change. Columbia presented artists, Hurok made Stars! The difference between the press material for the first two tours and the third is quite stark, and the critics responded to it. While in 1956 and 1960 the Royal Danish Ballet was admired for its ensemble approach to dancing and was always reviewed as a company (many reviews not even mentioning the dancers' names), in 1965 it was a collection of stars. Erik Bruhn danced with the company, as did Toni Lander (both were stars with American Ballet Theatre and very popular with New York audiences) and Flemming Flindt.

Unfortunately, Kronstam's repertory for that tour did not include *Cyrano*. "I was always very sorry that Henning never got to do *Cyrano* in New York," Stanley Williams said. "They should have brought it in 1965. It would have made a big difference in his career. I told that to Niels Bjørn. I asked him to bring it, but he wouldn't do it. I don't know why." In New York most of the attention went to Flindt as the new young director. There were huge articles about Flindt in the *New York Times* by its new critic Clive Barnes, late of London. Both Bruhn and Kronstam were virtually ignored. Of course, Bruhn was established in New York by that time, but Kronstam was not and, despite generally excellent reviews and audience response, he was never in the spotlight.

Kronstam and Bruhn shared several roles and were often compared on this tour. Walter Arlen described a performance in Los Angeles:

> As her love [in *Moon Reindeer*], Henning Kronstam did some stunning work showing him to be a master of athleticism tempered by elegance and emotional projection of telling power which reached its climax in the dramatic final pas de deux.
>
> [In *Miss Julie*] if Kirsten Simone and Erik Bruhn did not quite have the flair and electricity to sustain it like their predecessors, they still made it an often breathtaking spectacle. (*Los Angeles Times,* November 15, 1965)

Walter Terry reviewed the New York performances:

> For the second *Carmen,* the stars were Henning Kronstam and Mette Hønningen and to them fell the difficult task of following Erik Bruhn and Kirsten Simone who had roused the audience to wild cheers the preceding night.
>
> Mr. Kronstam fared the better of the two, and by a long ways. He is, as all dance lovers know, one of the truly great premiers danseurs of our day and, in

the character assignment of Don José, he is both appealing, effective and, needless to say, technically brilliant.

Mr. Kronstam and Mr. Bruhn, within the basic outlines of Don José's character, approach the role quite differently. Mr. Bruhn is ferocious in his passion; Mr. Kronstam, impetuous. There is no need to carry the comparisons further, for although Mr. Bruhn's Don José is an unforgettable and, indeed, matchless portrayal, Mr. Kronstam's characterization of the tragic lover is both vital and valid. How splendid to have two contrasting interpretations of a challenging role! (*New York Herald Tribune*, December 6, 1965)

Clive Barnes wrote:

In Birgit Cullberg's melodramatic *Miss Julie*, the Strindbergian heroine, still powerfully played by Kirsten Simone, found a new victim tyrant in Henning Kronstam. In his own way, Mr. Kronstam's portrayal of Jean proved almost as compulsively powerful as that of Erik Bruhn's earlier in the week.

Mr. Bruhn's Jean was like a man touched by the devil; his eyes blazed graveyards. Mr. Kronstam has chosen to play the valet as a weak, sensual man swept by uncontrollable circumstances.

Not unexpectedly, Mr. Kronstam's dancing was remarkable. (*New York Times*, December 6, 1965)

Daniel Webster wrote about *Miss Julie* on opening night in Philadelphia:

Kirsten Simone in the title role made the central figure a confused girl, hard on the outside, deeply troubled within. Her characterization was somewhat prettier than that of, say, Maria Tallchief, but not as commanding or as stark.

Henning Kronstam, the butler Miss Julie seduces, has built his characterization to one of the finest in ballet. His steely leaps and spear-like figure propel him through the affair revealing flashes of savagery and subservience, gaiety and fear. His role in maintaining the sustained atmosphere of the work was stronger than his partner. (*Philadelphia Inquirer*, September 30, 1965)

Both Barnes and Terry admired Kronstam in *The Lesson*. Barnes would often write that it was "perhaps Kronstam's finest characterization," which galled Kronstam, as he did not consider it an important role. In a review entitled, "Flemming Flindt Work Has Debut Here," Barnes wrote, "Henning Kronstam as the psychopathic killer, victim of his own desires, wild-eyed and lost, every movement informed with a clinically observed madness, gives what is perhaps his finest characterization. He has placed everything at the disposal of the choreographer, and acts with a frenzied intensity that at times is almost embarrassing to witness" (*New York Times*, December 8, 1965). Terry's review includes a report on the audience's reaction: "Last night, Henning Kronstam, the company's leading male dancer, gave a tremendous performance—he was cheered to the rafters—of the ballet master, a portrayal in which sheer horror and a curious sense of pathos were intermingled by this superb artist" (*New York Herald Tribune*, December 8, 1965).

By 1965 the articles in the Danish press speculating about whether or not Kronstam would leave had stopped. After Flindt became ballet master, guest engagements were strictly curtailed. A few dancers left the company; Kronstam—now thirty and at the height of his powers—was appointed first solo dancer and stayed. There was much speculation as to why he stayed, but Kronstam never addressed it publicly. It never seemed to occur to anyone that Kronstam actually wanted to stay. For his part, Kronstam could never figure out why anyone would want to leave and invented endless reasons why they might, all linked to artistic rather than personal reasons, which provides a strong clue to his own reasoning.

A brief interview by "Fel" headlined "But Nevertheless, They Made It Home" (after Kronstam and Simone returned from a three-month guest appearance with Ruth Page) gives some of the reasons why Kronstam felt touring was necessary for his survival as an artist, but his total frame of reference here is the Royal Theatre:

> The Royal Theatre is unique in its way of discovering and developing talents. It has a brilliant school but there is a tendency to leave the ballet people alone on the top. And that serves no purpose. We have to get *out* to try our strengths in competition with equals.
>
> That is why I, more now than ever before, look at it this way: either the ballet has to go on frequent tours abroad to let us try our strength, or a practice must be set up that makes it possible for the soloists to go on tours separately three to four months every year. You cannot just sit in Copenhagen and say that we are just as good as the best abroad. You have to get out to find that out.
>
> In the ballet you operate, as it is known, with double casts for the different performances, and parts are assigned with a view to cancellations due to illness. Instead you probably ought to let this double casting make it possible for the dancers to go out and dance abroad. I think this is something quite important, just as it naturally is important that the Theatre shows that it *needs* us at home. (emphasis in original)

One has an empty feeling inside when one is
not used; one feels that one wastes too much
and too precious time doing nothing.
—Henning Kronstam, 1965

Ruth Page and Walt Disney

From 1962 to 1965, Kronstam joined Ruth Page's Chicago Opera Ballet for its
annual three-month tour of the United States. He had met Page in 1955 when
he went with John Taras to Page's villa on the Mediterranean. Page always
brought in guest stars for her tours. She had seen Kronstam dance, both at the
Aix-en-Provence festival and again when the Danes came to Chicago in 1960,
and invited him to join her company on its cross-country tours, at first suggesting that he dance with Sonia Arova, a frequent partner of Bruhn's.

Kronstam was interested in the invitation but wanted to bring his own partner, and he proposed that he dance with Kirsten Simone instead. There was an
exchange of letters. Page was not interested in Simone, at first saying that she
wasn't well enough known in America; later there were problems over salary.
Page suggested a number of other potential partners, as the following letters

from Kronstam's files show. Page's tone becomes successively more wheedling and a bit desperate, tossing out names of ballerinas who she thinks would be appropriate.

The first, from Tom Fisher (Page's husband, who handled the company's business affairs), is dated December 1, 1959. He begins by asking Kronstam to join the 1961 tour from January to April as the company's "first male star dancer." The letter continues:

> There will also be the question of who will be the first star ballerina for the 1961 tour. Ruth has asked Melissa Hayden to return in 1961 for her second tour. If Melissa is not available, which will depend somewhat on whether the NYCB [New York City Ballet] will be out of the U.S.A. at that time or not, there is a possibility that Marjorie Tallchief may want to return. Whoever is the female star, it will be one of the top dancers in Europe or this country.
>
> About the second ballerina, Ruth does not yet know whether Veronika Mlakar will return in 1961. . . . I mention the second ballerina because Ruth would like to know about how you feel regarding Kirsten Simone and whether you think she might be available.

However, Kronstam did not want Simone as the second ballerina but as his partner. Page responds to this nearly a year later, on November 27, 1960 (Kronstam did not retain any intervening letters or his responses):

> Was so disappointed that Kirsten Simone can't come as your partner, as I adore her, but Columbia just couldn't be persuaded to give her so much money. They like her very much, but they say she has no "name" as yet in this country. Inge Sand has a *much* bigger name because of that tour where she really was the star. Well, I'm really sorry about Kirsten, but maybe another time we can have her. (emphasis in original)

Kronstam did not dance with the company on that 1961 tour. On March 29, 1961, Page wrote suggesting several partners, again including Arova, as well as others. Money was still the sticking point, as Columbia refused to pay Simone the same salary as Kronstam. By this time, Page just wanted a ballerina, either someone Columbia would consider a star or, if not, a good dancer who would accept less money:

> Moira Shearer has been considering coming with us next season but she finally decided that all she can do is an occasional [illegible word] or television. I imagine from what I heard in Paris that she is not in very good dance form. Svetlana Beriosova wrote me that she would like very much to do the tour with

us, but she has to wait to get permission from Ninette de Valois. The latter apparently doesn't like to make up her mind long in advance, so whether we should wait for Ninette I don't know. I think Svetlana is a great dancer. My God, she was lovely when she danced in Chicago at Xmas Time. And she would be perfect for *you*.

I am very disappointed really not to have Kirsten Simone, as I think she is just the right type for my ballets. Unfortunately, Columbia does not consider her name big enough in this country to warrant paying her the price that she asks. I told them I felt sure she would make a big name. But I couldn't persuade them that she would be worth so much.

Is there anyone else in your company that you would particularly like to dance with who would be available? How about Inge Sand? She is already popular in this country. If there is no one else in the Danish ballet, is there anyone else in Europe you would like to suggest? (emphasis in original)

Two months later, in a letter of May 7, 1961, Page has still more suggestions:

I just received a letter from Yvette Chauviré from Paris that she would like to go on our tour starting in January. I was quite surprised as I thought she was completely tied up in France and Germany. I saw her dance in Berlin last year and I must say I think she is wonderful. Do you know her and would you like to dance with her? De Valois has not given Beriosova an answer yet. Of course, we already have Sonia Arova, who is absolutely first class, and I have a young new dancer, Patricia Klekovic, who stepped into Melissa Hayden's roles when the latter became pregnant and had to leave us. Patricia had a big success. Maria Tallchief says she would like to do some performances with us, but her husband is on the warpath and doesn't want her to go on any tours!

Bill Judd of Columbia keeps telling me about a wonderful young dancer in your company. I think her name is Marianne Walter or something like that. What about her? Columbia says we don't really need a "name" dancer but of course we want someone outstandingly good. Maybe Marianne (I hope I have the name right) could come for the whole tour and then we could have Maria when and if she could come. Same with Chauviré. Columbia hates to do this, but I know Maria can't do the whole tour, and not even half of it. Of course, Yvette said she would like to do the whole tour, but she is not young and used to the American tour, like Marjorie and George Skibine (who adore touring here) or Arova. Well, do let me know what your ideas are.

There's a postscript hint: "I think Inge Sand would make a delightful Merry Widow!"

But Kronstam held out for Simone and said that, as Columbia was adamant about money, he worked out an arrangement where extra money for Simone "was taken out of my salary." Simone was quite successful on the tours and certainly achieved a name big enough to satisfy Columbia.

Kronstam had pressed so hard for Simone not merely because they were friends, but because he knew he could rely on her, and because they had a rapport in rehearsals and on stage that he found with few other ballerinas. At the end of his life he had this to say about his most frequent partner:

"I knew her so well. We were in the school together, we were sitting on the same bench. We were the young couple. We had always worked together and she was always there. The first time I really saw that she was extraordinary was when she did *Miss Julie.* And then later came *Carmen,* and then she developed. Roland [Petit] came back and he did Roxane for her, and she was gorgeous as Roxane. She was so beautiful—Yves Saint Laurent did the costumes. And she loves good clothes. She has always been well dressed. That was a triumph for her, especially when Erik came. Carmen was one of her great roles. Carmen and Miss Julie, Roxane and Juliet, when she at last got that role. We had to go to New York in 1965 and Kirsten got her Juliet and she was lovely.

"We were living it when we were on stage together. Sometimes we sit together, Kirsten and I, and we say, 'Why are they just doing steps? Why don't they get into the roles and let themselves go?'

"We traveled a lot. First of all, we toured with Inge Sand's group through all of South America, doing *Sleeping Beauty,* pas de six in *Napoli,* pas de sept in *Folk Tale, Nutcracker* pas de deux, *Chopiniana.* And we went to all the cities: Buenos Aires, São Paulo, Rio de Janeiro, Santiago de Chile, Lima in Peru, Colombia, San Salvador. In seven weeks. We didn't know that much Spanish, but it was a nice tour. There were eight of us and they loved us. Especially the Danes. Some of them had traveled by horse for two days in order to come and see Danish dancers, because they were living in the pampas.

"As a person, Kirsten was a trouper. She never missed one performance. Never. We did three-month tours with performances every day, driving about three hundred miles and then doing a performance in the evening. And on her days, you know, when she had her days, she just took one drop of whiskey and that was it. But she danced. She always danced.

"I had an accident. It was my Achilles, I think, and we had to do a season in August. It was the 800th anniversary of Copenhagen, I think. Kirsten stayed home for the whole holiday to give me classes in order to get me back. We met

Two views of a partnership. *Left:* Kirsten Simone backstage. Private collection. *Above:* Kronstam and Simone in a friendlier mood. Private collection.

at the Theatre every day and she gave me classes, building them so I wouldn't do too much. She knew the importance of the slow training and the building up because she had had an operation on her knees. She had one knee that always was dropping out, and Dr. Thomasen took two tendons and crossed them over the kneecap. She stayed home for the whole holiday in order to do that. So as a person, she was warm, too. We were very much together. We went on holiday together—the three of us [Kronstam, Gerstenberg, and Simone]. We went to New York, I think about five times together. So it was a friendship as well as a partnership. I was the one that introduced her to the minister for cultural affairs [Niels Matthiasen], and she became his lady for going to parties, and then our relationship slowly dropped off."

"Then I became the chief of the ballet and that meant that I was her superior, and that was a difficult time. Flemming wasn't there any longer. I couldn't dance any longer, so there was no one suitable for her to dance with. And she was older and I had to take roles away from her. So there came a cold atmosphere between us—which is not there any longer. She still calls me. As a person, I can't say anything except good about her."

With the matter of Simone's participation solved, the letters turned to contracts. The first, from Tom Fisher (February 15, 1962), indicates that he was already aware that Kronstam read everything he signed very carefully and would question oddities, such as why on earth he would be required to bring toe shoes? It is also interesting to note the lengths to which Fisher and Page had to go in order to keep stars' salaries a secret from her regular dancers.

> Don't be bothered by Paragraph 6 of the Rider which talks about "toe shoes." In your case, you would naturally not get toe shoes, but regular shoes forming part of your costumes would naturally be furnished to you. Please bring some of your own shoes with you.
>
> Turning to the supplemental Agreement, it has two purposes. The first is to eliminate $150 per week from any claim of Federal income tax on your salary. The second purpose is to conceal from the other members of the company that you are actually receiving total compensation of $650 per week. You will understand that this is a higher salary than the regular stars of the company receive, and in order not to make trouble with them, we therefore pay you this additional $150 (plus the additional for traveling expense) entirely outside of the formal AGMA [American Guild of Musical Artists] printed contract.
>
> Our company managers have always tried to find out the total salaries which our top stars receive, and the fact is that we can never rely on their keeping this sort of information confidential. Therefore, we provide in Paragraph 3 of the Supplemental Agreement that our top stars shall not disclose to anyone in the company, *even* the company manager, the total amount of their compensation. (emphasis in original)

The years with Ruth Page were generally very happy ones for Kronstam. He liked women like Page, who was small, dark, and vivacious. She was a bit flamboyant and a bit eccentric, and this amused him. He remembered one of her visits to Copenhagen, when she asked to see some ballet. It was summer and the Theatre was dark, but the Bartholin Seminar (a summer program) was in progress and Kronstam took her there. Alexandra Danilova was teaching and when she saw Page, an old friend, the elegant Russian ballerina lay down on the floor, "flat on her back and began to kick," squealing; Page joined her and they acted like two schoolgirls. While Kronstam was always reserved himself, he was often delighted by exhibitionist behavior in others, and he found this incident extremely amusing. Not surprising, perhaps, of Page, but a delightful shock from Danilova.

He admired Page, even though he knew she was not a great choreographer: "She was tough too, but she was holding that company together for many years. She kept the same dancers in the company and she always had good dancers as guest artists." Other dancers who made the tours with Page over the years included Marjorie Tallchief and Skibine, Bruhn and Arova, and Flindt and Josette Amiel.

Page's lifestyle also fascinated Kronstam. Her husband had been the lawyer to Chicago's infamous gangster Al Capone—exotic enough to a European—and was rumored to have been rewarded with fabulous wealth. Fisher financed the company and was devoted to Page. It was, in a way, a vanity company, with a repertory made up mostly of Page's ballets. They were story ballets, danced versions of operas and operettas. But it was a fun company. "I liked the people," Kronstam said. The next several years, there were dozens of letters, mostly from Fisher, written in green ink with many underlinings, full of ballet gossip in between the pleas to sign contracts and "please answer this one and let us know when you can come."

Larry Long, one of the company's principals, remembered: "Ruth was a bit of a character and he knew exactly how to handle her, and yet he always handled her, as he did everybody, with great respect. He wasn't condescending. He was wonderful with her. He wasn't afraid to tell her what he thought about things. I think he liked Ruth. She adored them both [Kronstam and Simone]."

Ruth Page. Private collection.

The week after he finally signed a contract with Page, Kronstam got a letter from Lucia Chase asking him to dance with American Ballet Theatre. Chase's letter, handwritten and personal, is a good example of the informality of the era. Chase emphasized how friendly the company was before mentioning repertory, and didn't mention money. One of the roles she offered Kronstam was Nilas in *Moon Reindeer*, asking if he was familiar with the ballet. Although dancing with ABT at that time would have been a far shrewder career move—simply because, while it also made coast-to-coast tours in those days, the company was based in New York—he never considered going back on his word to Page. "I had told Ruth I would come," he said simply. His files contain several other telegrams to Chase, but he was never free when she needed him. Kronstam once wrote, apologetically, "I have no doubles [second casts, or understudies] in my repertory here and cannot get away."

Touring was grueling. The dancers (most of whom traveled by bus, the guest stars and two other principals by car) arrived in a strange city and a strange theater, often a high school auditorium with a concrete floor and inadequate dressing rooms. There was time for a run-through and a warm-up before the performance; afterward there would be a late dinner, a night in a strange hotel, and another day in a car traveling to the next city.

Other dancers in the company said that both Kronstam and Simone behaved beautifully, never expressing dismay, nor even surprise, at some of the odd places they found themselves dancing. The pair had a fondness for one performance given in a convent, where the nuns served as stagehands, running up and down ropes and ladders with their habits hiked up around their waists. Fred Konrad, a dancer with the company during this time, remembered one place with a single dressing room for all the men, no mirrors, and only one light. Konrad showed Kronstam how you could put on makeup by lying on your back on the floor under the light and holding a mirror. Often there was only one large room, and the dancers would hang a blanket or sheets down the middle of it to separate men's from women's changing areas. Larry Long remembered one special night in Leadville, Colorado: "We were in a high school and we hooked up all our lights, and then in the middle of the performance we were using so much electricity that the whole town blacked out. It was during *Nutcracker* and Henning and Kirsten were doing the grand pas de deux. The only light that was on the stage was the arc light, because it wasn't an electric light. So they danced the pas de deux in Leadville, Colorado, with an arc light, and they didn't dance it less than if they'd been in the Metropolitan Opera House. They didn't let it drop, and it made you go, 'Wow. If they don't, so can we.'"

Both dancers were very popular with the company regulars: "They were very, very gracious to everyone in the company. They were wonderful examples, both of them," Long said. "We had lots of guests. It was the wonderful thing about Ruth's company, because you got to see all these people dance, and if you were at all an astute kind of student, or even kind of a dense student, you couldn't help but observe them and see how they worked. We weren't in the biggest company in the world, we didn't have the greatest classical repertory, but we did have that. We did have wonderful dancers." Speaking of Kronstam's dancing, Long said: "Henning was just a mind boggler. This enormous, handsome, big, tall man, to move as beautifully and as gracefully as he did. It sounds funny, but he danced like a small man. One thinks of small dancers as being very quick and clean and sure and fast and bravura, and taller dancers as being perhaps a little more elegant, certainly, but also just a little bit more lyrical and less punch. But he was all of it." Patricia Klekovic, one of the Ruth Page ballerinas, said, "He had such a fluid way of moving, it was so beautiful to watch him. To watch him run was like watching a beautiful racehorse."

Long, a fine teacher in his own right, also observed Kronstam's teaching: "Henning gave his own warm-up class before performances, for himself and Simone, very quietly, off in a corner, and several other company members took it. I think he was a very, very thoughtful teacher. He admitted, and said as much, that he was very influenced by Volkova. He spoke more about Volkova than he did about Stanley [Williams]. Both he and Kirsten would talk often about the fact that they thought they owed almost as much to Volkova as they did to the Bournonville tradition." Klekovic took Kronstam's class and said, "One year he toured with us, I took his class a lot because it warmed me up. That was the first time I came back from tour and my teacher said, 'You didn't lose your strength.' And it wasn't a tricky, hard class, it just worked everything."

Both Klekovic and Long remember Kronstam as being very reserved but friendly and easy to like. "He would coach you, but you had to ask," said Klekovic. One season she was dancing Juliet in Page's version of *Romeo and Juliet*, to the Tchaikovsky suite. "Ruth could say she didn't like something but couldn't tell you how to fix it," Klekovic said, and she asked Kronstam for help. "He came and watched and talked to me about it, and he'd watch during the tour and would say things like, 'You should think about it this way.' He was primarily helping me put the choreography with the feelings of the story, or, 'Maybe you think you're doing something here, but it doesn't show.'"

Although the initial plan was for Kronstam and Simone to dance in several of Page's ballets, it was never possible because there wasn't enough time for rehearsals. They danced *Merry Widow* and classical pas de deux (usually *Sleeping Beauty* or *Don Quixote*). John Martin, in his biography of Page, explains the reason for this: "[The imported guest stars] were Kirsten Simone and Henning Kronstam, who proved themselves to be so excellent in *The Merry Widow* (among other things) as to make it virtually their own. Pas de deux, both Danish and "standard," were now a regular feature of the programs. This was partly because visiting stars knew them and did not require rehearsal time for them, and partly because provincial audiences were coming more and more to prefer the decorative acrobatics of the pas de deux to anything more demanding on their background and attention."[1]

In 1966, when Flemming Flindt became ballet master and curtailed guest appearances by Danish dancers, Kronstam and Simone could not get leave. Page suggested they now come every year for *Nutcracker,* thinking a month's leave would be more easily arranged, and a letter from Fisher dated January 10, 1966, shortly after Flindt took over shows how enterprising they were about arranging it:

> Since I assume that you will have to take this matter up with Flemming before you can definitely know if he will release you should you want to accept, I suppose I will have to talk to Flemming and find out his reaction without delay. I would hope that Flemming would be reluctant to prevent either of you from earning somewhere between $10,000 and $12,000 in this country next year, and, therefore, assuming that you want to come to this country I hope that you will be able to get Flemming's approval quickly.

Kronstam's reviews with the Page company tours were uniformly glowing, both from Chicago critics and throughout the country. Claudia Cassidy, who saw Kronstam many times with both the Royal Danish Ballet and Ruth Page's company, wrote:

> That Henning Kronstam moves in the proud line of succession of the great male dancers was established when he came to town with the Royal Danish Ballet. It was underscored yesterday when he and his partner Kirsten Simone returned to the Civic Opera house as guests of Ruth Page's Chicago Opera

With Kirsten Simone in Page's *The Merry Widow*. Private collection.

Ballet, a light-hearted, mostly light-footed, young troupe stemming out of Lyric Opera.

Kronstam is slender and dark, with the clarity of a rapier, an intuitive sense of style, and a dynamic brilliance that takes off at jet speed under perfect control. With Simone, who is blonde and fragile, and ideal for the artful innocence of the Bournonville ballets, he danced the most winning imaginable performance of the pas de deux from *Flower Festival in Genzano,* which can so easily turn cloddish and coy.

In the *Don Q,* which really did not suit Simone at all, he was Castilian to the bone, with a concentration of fire power, a dazzling technical bravura to set the house roaring. When you remember his *Apollo* and his mordant *Miss Julie* with Simone, 1964 seems a long time to wait for the return of the Royal Danish Ballet. (*Chicago Tribune,* 1963)

Barzel thought Kronstam the best of Page's Danilos:

Kronstam, the handsome lad the fans swooned over when he danced *Romeo* with the Danish ballet, is a superb dancer, with the beautiful masculine technique that is a specialty of Danish schooling. He also has the characteristic acting ability. The result was a Prince Danilo of aristocratic bearing and romantic presence, easily the best in a distinguished list of Danilos. (*Chicago American,* January 13, 1963)

The company was well received in other cities, as well. In Seattle, John Voorhees wrote:

Whatever reservations one may have concerning Ruth Page as a choreographer, one can certainly heartily applaud her shrewd decision to hire Kirsten Simone and Henning Kronstam as guest artists for her Chicago Opera Ballet tour this season.

The company made two appearances—Saturday night and yesterday afternoon—at the Moore Theater (to full houses) and Miss Simone and Kronstam were so splendid one could hardly wait to see the entire Royal Danish Ballet, with which the two handsome dancers appear regularly in Europe.

Miss Simone, a smashing beauty, and Kronstam, a marvelously masculine dancer, performed in the *Don Quixote* pas de deux on Saturday night, then took the roles of Sonia, the Merry Widow, and Prince Danilo in the ballet version of *The Merry Widow* danced yesterday.

Both are beautifully disciplined dancers, who do everything with that extra fillip of detail, poise and polish that set apart the great dancers from the merely good ones. The *Don Quixote* pas de deux was magnificently, electrically interpreted. It is a crowd pleaser and the two Danish dancers did it superbly. Miss

Simone's every movement has that marvelous kind of definition about it that is so rewarding to see on stage and Kronstam moves so well that it is a pleasure to see him even walk across the stage, let alone dance.

Both dancers seemed particularly attuned to the European atmosphere of *The Merry Widow*. He was every inch a prince, and she was believable as the flirtatious merry widow, teasing yet always proper and beguiling. (*Seattle Post-Intelligencer*, February 11, 1963)

Robert D. Oudal seemed a bit less familiar with ballet than Voorhees, but was impressed nevertheless: "I find words inadequate to express the precision and beauty of these two and even more the easy grace with which they carried off their difficult patterns. Every nuance of musical lines found visual expression in their dance (*Don Quixote* pas de deux). Phrases undulated and rippled through their bodies only to cadence in the flick of a fingertip. The virile efforts of Kronstam did much to support the thesis that there is real difference between male and female ballet dancers. His timing and leaps were awesome" (*Rochester [Minnesota] Post-Bulletin*, March 7, 1963).

In the *Don Quixote* pas de deux. Photo: Mydtskov. Private collection.

Kronstam was as reserved in America as he had been in Copenhagen. "He would go out to eat, he and Kirsten. Sometimes with Orrin and Neal [Kayan], or Patricia Klekovic and Ken Johnson, two other dancers in the company," Larry Long remembered. "He would go to company functions, when it was indicated that would be the thing to do. He wasn't unfriendly, he was just a very reserved person. In a way, Kirsten was much more open and gregarious than Henning was." Kronstam's self-imposed restriction about dalliances with other dancers also held only in Denmark. Dancing abroad, or on vacation in Europe, was a different matter. One night, there was a knock on Kronstam's hotel door. When he opened it, "Orrin was there, with a bottle of whiskey. He was very clever," Kronstam said with a smile. (He loved whiskey, but it was so expensive in Copenhagen that he rarely drank it at home. Whiskey was an American pleasure.)

Orrin Kayan was a dancer with the company and the brother of its conductor, Neal. There were dozens of photos of him in Kronstam's photo drawer, which disappeared after his death. They showed a young man with warm dark eyes and an easy grin. Kayan was very different from Kronstam. He didn't take ballet, nor much in life, very seriously, and was more interested in play than work. "We had such good times together," Kronstam said. By this time the relationship with Gerstenberg was that of uncle and nephew. As much as he needed the older man's steadying hand, and the structure he provided for his life, Kronstam wanted a lover and a playmate-companion. "We were nearly the same age. [Kayan was a year younger.] We would go to the beach together, go to movies," the kind of relationship that Kronstam had never really had. There's little question that the chance to be with Orrin was one of the main attractions of the Chicago Opera Ballet for Kronstam, and why he returned there for several seasons. Patricia Klekovic, who had known Kayan since high school, said, "Henning was a wonderful influence on Orrin, not only as a person but as a performer. He would say, 'There are things you have to do. Why don't you want to do that role? You'll never grow if you don't do that role. You can't just do things you want all the time.'"

Gerstenberg was aware of the relationship. Some described him as jealous and he may have been, although Kayan stayed at their home in Copenhagen and Kronstam invited him in the summers to take class with the company. Klekovic went to Kronstam's flat for dinner with Orrin one night (she remembered Kronstam had made a delicious oxtail soup) and thought that everything

Orrin Kayan. Private collection.

was very friendly. Gerstenberg had promised to guide Kronstam's career, to act as his father or older brother might have acted, and may well have been concerned that Kayan would lure Kronstam away from ballet or threaten his discipline. Whether Kronstam was ever really tempted to leave Gerstenberg for Kayan is not clear. He may have realized that Kayan's easygoing nature was not what he needed in the long term and that however pleasurable the relationship was, his career came first. Klekovic was certain that Kayan would have settled down with Kronstam but "realized that it was not going to happen." When Kronstam stopped dancing with the Page company, the relationship ended, not because it had run its course, but because it was impossible to maintain.

Otherwise, summer vacations were spent in the sun. Kronstam and Gerstenberg, sometimes with Simone, sometimes with their friend Margrethe Noyé, would go to Spain, Italy, or the south of France, spending most of their time sightseeing and swimming. One summer Kronstam was involved with much of the Italian navy, who convinced him to streak his hair because he was a "Nordic god" and should, therefore, be blond. Kronstam kept several letters from some of the young men he met on vacations, all hoping to sustain a relationship that had begun in a summer café. ("If you don't remember me, I'm the tall skinny one," one letter began.) There were also letters from friends outside Denmark, writing to introduce someone who would be coming to Copenhagen and asking Kronstam to show them the town, and there were thank you letters, indicating that he had done so. There are other letters indicating deeper friendships, with only first names or initials, like this one from "Donny" in 1960:

> My very dearest Henning,
>
> I accidentally met Franz, and decided to write a couple of words to you. The very first, I have to thank you so very much for your help when I was sick. I really appreciate that very much.
>
> I was so happy to hear that you had had specially very very good critics, and lots of success. I was very sure of that, as I think you really are wonderful, not only as a dancer, but as a personality, and that's the most important thing a dancer must have, to be clever and considerate in daily life.

As a teenager, Kronstam had had "head shots" made and, at the suggestion of Hugh Williams, sent them to an unspecified studio in Hollywood. He had been offered a screen test but decided not to pursue the matter. In 1965 he finally got to Hollywood, working on a Walt Disney movie called *Ballerina*. The finished film was shown in movie houses in Europe and on the Disney weekly television show in America. In *Ballerina*, Kronstam played "Henning Thorberg," the "primo ballerino," as he called him, of a nameless company, obviously intended to be the Royal Danish Ballet. The star of the movie was a young Danish ballerina, Mette Hønningen, whose movie mother doesn't want her to pursue a dancing career but to have a "more fulfilling" life as a housewife. (The film seems unintentionally funny in these postfeminist times. The mother gives heartfelt speeches about how she's worried her daughter will live an empty life, as she sets the table, bakes, and irons.) Mette has a mentor, Kirsten (Kirsten Simone), who, in one of the most unrealistic plot twists in any ballet movie, gives up a performance so that her young rival can have her Big Chance. Mette sprains her ankle an hour before curtain time, but her boyfriend brings in his soccer coach, who performs a miracle of massage and bandages so she can dance.

The film is hokey, even for Disney, but provides some interesting glimpses of backstage life. Mette herself is a mentor to a young student (Jenny Agutter) who comments on events until you want to smack her. In some ways, the film captures some of the most charming aspects of the old Royal Danish Ballet—the close ties of school and company, the coexistence of opera, drama, and ballet in one theater, the seriousness of the artists. The one thing *Ballerina* shares with *The Red Shoes* is the almost religious dedication of artists.

There are substantial dancing sequences. Simone and Kronstam dance an unnamed Spanish-flavored classical ballet and a very lovely White Swan pas de deux. There is a tantalizing glimpse of the reel in *La Sylphide,* but Kronstam isn't in it (both Flemming Ryberg and Peter Martins can be spotted in the corps). Unfortunately, the centerpiece ballet is *Coppelia,* and in a generic international version rather than the Royal Danish Ballet's gloriously idiosyncratic one. Kronstam dances two solos, wearing boots. These, as well as the nameless Spanish ballet (both by Norman Thompson), show his beautiful line and attest to the level of his technique, but nothing in the film shows his acting ability.

Kronstam was quite proud of the fact that his voice did not have to be dubbed, while Simone's did, but all the Danish actors—including the Royal Theatre's very fine stage actor Erik Mørk—seem stiff and overcareful. Kronstam's character is arrogant and totally driven, Simone's gracious to the point

On vacation with Kirsten Simone and Franz Gerstenberg in Majorca, 1969. Private collection.

On vacation, mid-1960s.
Private collection.

of sainthood. The film was not made in Copenhagen. There were a few days in Hollywood and the rest was shot in Helsinki. In California, Mette Hønningen remembered with gratitude that Kronstam saved her from several Hollywood "wolves."

A letter from Disney Studios dated May 21, 1964, gives another example of both Kronstam's patriotism and his attention to contractual details that's rather amusing. The contact about which he complained was not in his papers, but it probably contained phrases like "the German ballet":

> This is with reference to the Agreement made between Walt Disney Productions Ltd and you concerning the film with the tentative title "Copenhagen Ballet" dated May 12, 1964.
>
> It is hereby agreed that the words "Danish" are to be substituted for the words "German" in lines 5, 8, and 12 of Clause A of Paragraph 17 of said Agreement.

Kronstam was interviewed in a Danish popular magazine about the movie:

> In the film, Henning Kronstam is a young ballet dancer who lives and breathes for his dancing. Are you like that in real life?
>
> [Kronstam]: No, God save me. As a dancer at the Royal Theatre one has to

have a private life if you don't have one already—what else should one do then during the long interval when one does not perform? It's a weird feeling to come home from the American tour, where you performed six days a week, where you also had to drive every day for about 300 miles to get from place to place, and then suddenly come home with way too much spare time on your hands. One has an empty feeling inside when one is not used, one feels that one wastes too much and too precious time doing nothing.

Touring can give a dancer, tested in front of new audiences, new confidence. It can also introduce new faults; it can change him. There's more than a hint of wistfulness in Svend Kragh-Jacobsen's review of Kronstam and Simone in the *Don Quixote* pas de deux, "Bravura Homecoming." When Erik Bruhn performed this virtuoso display piece, with equal brilliance, he would leave and take his foreign bravura with him. It could be savored, but as an exotic delicacy, and the audience could return to its staple diet. Svend Kragh-Jacobsen is reacting to yet another aspect of the International Question. Yes, Kronstam and Simone were dancing the pas de deux correctly, but it wasn't . . . Danish. The pressures on the company and its dancers to be more international would increase in the coming decades. This review was written by someone who knew he was on the cusp of a precipice. He could admire what was happening, but he would never love it:

> We were happy to see that this couple still is our best. They do not seem to have learned anything new in the art of dancing while they were abroad, but on the other hand they do seem to have acquired more elegance in the way they serve these shining decorations [i.e., the bravura Russian pas de deux] that can always be used and that look good on a mixed ballet program. The newest thing about them was a slim line, especially his, that gave more accentuated expressions. Their dancing was shining and beautiful. . . .
>
> He seemed more serious than before and more self-conscious in his dancing. This is part of the genre. With usual brilliance, he gave us the difficult tours en l'air that are part of this solo and that he performed for the first time. The final jump to both knees was an especial surprise. Brilliantly performed, even if perhaps a bit contrived. Still, the way Henning Kronstam performed it is the way it's supposed to be done. No wonder the audience cheered him and Kirsten Simone, and may we now quickly get them back into the repertory that expects them. Among other things, it will be exciting to see him with the new, poetic Juliet of the Theatre [Anna Lærkesen].

In the long and, seen with international eyes, unique Danish tradition of brilliant male dancers from Bournonville to Nikolaj Hübbe, Henning Kronstam will stand out as the absolute number one.
—Ebbe Mørk, *Politiken*, 1995

With calculated publicity and launching, Kronstam could very quickly be developed into an international star.
—Walter Terry, *New York Herald Tribune*, 1965

The Swan in the Duck Pond

In many reviews, especially by American and British writers, Kronstam is consistently called "one of the greatest dancers of the day." In view of this, and the fact that he was so highly regarded by dancers and choreographers both in and out of Denmark, it is curious that he is so seldom mentioned in general accounts of the international ballet scene of the 1960s and is given only a passing mention in all but one of the several books specifically devoted to great male dancers. As the company's artistic director and instruktør, too, he is barely known outside Denmark and was not highly regarded in Copenhagen by many Danish critics. His career raises interesting questions about exactly what is meant by *international star*.

Perceptions of Kronstam among dancers vary by generation and seem to accurately describe his development as a dancer. Those closest to Kronstam in age who saw him dance in the 1950s say that his technique was the equal of anyone's, but that, although he was always a sensitive artist, at the beginning he was a bit bland on stage. Those who saw him dance at the height of his powers, in the 1960s, say that both his dancing and his acting were at the absolute top. Those who saw him in the 1970s and 1980s, when he performed mostly partnering and character roles, thought of him as a great artist, though not a great technician. Those outside the company had similar observations. As a young dancer, in the mid-1950s, Violette Verdy remembered Kronstam as "an absolutely beautiful dancer, one of the best I have ever seen by any standard, even with the Danes. Technically, he was able to do absolutely anything." Antoinette Sibley, who danced with Kronstam in the mid-1960s, agreed: "He was the perfect Danish Prince—with Erik Bruhn, of course."

Bruhn is the dancer to whom Kronstam is most often compared, presumably because they were both Danish; they had little else in common. They were very different physically and temperamentally. In Denmark, Bruhn was considered by nearly all the critics to be "our world dancer," while Kronstam was merely "our first dancer," meaning that Bruhn was an international star and Kronstam was not. The implication was that this was not merely in the sense of celebrity, but that Kronstam was inferior to Bruhn. Yet many Danish dancers felt that Kronstam was the greater artist, with a far broader range; others, that Bruhn and Kronstam were equals—as technicians or dancers or artists, however one defined *great*—and which dancer one preferred was simply a matter of personal taste.

No two dancers have exactly the same technique; each has different strengths. While Kronstam was not a natural turner, there were some steps—certain jumps, for example—that dancers felt he performed as well or better than anyone. He also had greater flexibility than other dancers, and he had a very high extension, especially for a man. Many dancers made the point that Kronstam's technique was deliberately very modulated, that he was the equal of the best of his generation, but that he would not show on stage what he could do in class unless it was appropriate to the ballet. "He wouldn't jump higher than the role allowed," as Verdy put it. Erling Eliasson spoke of the perfection of his turns: "He would be very graceful. He would do three pirouettes: one, two, three, like pearls on a string. You could see every single pirouette, and they would be just beautiful. It was done with grandeur."

Peter Martins, twelve years younger than Kronstam, said, "Henning was the great dancer who stayed behind. He was the great interpreter. He wasn't only a beautiful classical dancer—which he was; he was very clean in his positions—but he also was a wonderful actor in the Bournonville roles, and also in other things. Henning had this great stage presence and fantastic acting ability." Earlier, however, in his autobiography, *Far from Denmark,* Martins, writing of the dancers in the Theatre when he was growing up, said of Kronstam: "During my teens the three most important male dancers in Denmark were Henning Kronstam, Erik Bruhn, and Flemming Flindt. Though a first-rate dancer, Kronstam was thought to be the one with the smallest talent among these three, but his great gift was that he seemed the most sensitive, the most poetic in performance, what John Gielgud is considered as an actor. He was the dream prince, the romantic hero: Albrecht, James, Romeo. The audience loved Kronstam and everyone loved him too for being the one who stayed in Denmark, who stuck it out."[1] This assessment surprised many Danish dancers, who do not agree that this was the general perception. "Perhaps that was just among Peter and his friends," as one dancer put it. Arne Villumsen, slightly younger than Martins, also disagreed: "We all looked up to him. He was the hero. We all wanted to be like him. Henning always had something that Erik and Flemming didn't have. He was the artist, if you understand what I mean." Adam Lüders, another émigré Dane, said: "Henning was always highly regarded—as much as you can in the very Jantelov way. He was the model. He was in class every morning and was the model in class. There were other good dancers—Niels Kehlet, Erik came home a lot—but he [Kronstam] was highly regarded. I have thought about Henning nearly every day of my life, all twenty years in New York. Henning went through my head somehow every day: the way he was in class every day, regardless of snow, rain, whatever. Every day. That's not Erik, that's Henning."

Martins's comparison of Kronstam and Gielgud is an interesting one, as the two artists shared many qualities. The comparison raises another question. In appreciations written after Gielgud's death, he was considered by many to have been the greatest English-speaking actor, the greatest Hamlet. To the average theatergoer this must have seemed surprising, as in the popular imagination Laurence Olivier, another very great actor, is identified with Hamlet. Gielgud, who did not make movies until very late in his career, was not well known to the general public. "Ah, but now you're talking about fame," said Ralov, in a slightly different context, but appropriate here, "and that is something quite different."

Popular perceptions are formed by critics and journalists. Many dancers felt that Kronstam was undervalued by critics, especially in Denmark. The current generation of dancers blames this on Jantelov. Kenneth Greve, one of the few young Danish dancers who has experience dancing abroad, explained why. "The fact is that in Denmark, you cannot be allowed to be anybody. To be somebody, you have to go away and come back. Then when you're back, after six months, you're nobody again. That's the way it is. The moment you are away, you are a star. You are very interesting, and everybody wants to speak to you and hear about you. The moment you've been here six months, they don't care. It just goes on. And that's Denmark." There are many Danish dancers, of all generations, who felt that Kronstam was ranked under Bruhn at home not because he had a "smaller talent," but because he didn't leave. Whether it was done consciously or not, Bruhn's career-long practice of dancing in Copenhagen, leaving, always with a farewell performance and party, then returning for three months before leaving again, fit beautifully into the pattern that Greve described.

Peter Bo Bendixen, a Danish solo dancer who arranged a memorial performance for Kronstam two years after his death, spoke for many of his age group: "If you ask people that are older than me who has made a great impression on them, if they saw people dance in the 1960s and 1970s, the people they would mention are Erik, Nureyev, and Henning. And Henning accomplished that staying in Copenhagen, not going around, not guesting as much as the others. He didn't do his career in the same way as other dancers who were of the same caliber. He accomplished all that by staying here, and that's pretty amazing." Far from belittling Kronstam for not leaving, Bendixen's generation admired it. "He never took the easy way. He could have done James and Romeo and made a fortune on it. He could have danced with everyone."

Bruhn was asked, in his "Oral History," whether Kronstam could have had an international career. He replied: "Henning was, from the very beginning, a very, very talented boy, and turned out to be a magnificent artist, but his mentality was more designed for Danish living, or a Danish lifestyle. And he succeeded internationally only when he traveled with the Danish ballet. So he would have had possibilities if he had wanted to go. He could have probably made the same career, or a similar career, like some of us. But he chose to stay with the family in Denmark, and I don't think he was hurt any way by doing that, for he's the only one of [those who stayed] in Denmark that made it that big."[2]

Chicago Opera Ballet dancers, who watched all three over several seasons, felt, as Larry Long put it: "Henning Kronstam and Bruhn were real peers. They were at the same level, they were just very, very different. It's nonsense that Henning couldn't turn. He did it all. It was the question of the way he thought about dancing. It was not that he couldn't do it."

Not everyone agrees that Kronstam could have functioned on the international ballet circuit. Several dancers, especially those who had the experience of dancing with other companies, feel that Kronstam could not have functioned as well elsewhere because he had been so coddled in Copenhagen, where he basically had the run of the repertory and no real competition. Ib Andersen, who admired Kronstam and said, "Henning was the greatest dancer I ever saw, greater than Erik, greater than Rudolf," was one who thought that Kronstam would have had a difficult time of it outside Copenhagen. Andersen, who danced for a decade with the New York City Ballet, where no one is coddled, explained that Kronstam needed the kind of support he received in Denmark, referring to stage and orchestra rehearsals, working closely with a director, and so on. In essence the two views are merely different sides of the same coin. Whether Kronstam's remaining in Copenhagen and refusing to compromise was an act of courage or timidity, the fact remains that he chose not to compromise or put himself into a situation where he would have to compromise.

Kronstam's artistic integrity included his approach to technique, and that approach probably contributed to the perception by some that he was not a great technician. Kronstam didn't "sell" a performance, didn't telegraph how difficult the steps he was dancing were. Bruce Marks phrased it that "you had to cross the footlights to him"; Verdy, that "he did not jump into the lap of the audience." Because he made dancing look easy, many assumed that what he was doing was not difficult. One Danish dancer compared Kronstam and Flindt in this regard: "Flemming would make faces to show how hard it was, what he was doing, and so the audience and the critics thought he was better. He learned this in London. Henning had such a relaxed expression on his face and made everything look easy." Kronstam, for all his Russian training, was a living embodiment of one of the principles Bournonville wrote in his "Choreographic Credo," that "all effort must be concealed under cover of harmonious calm."

Once, speaking of dancing James in Paris, at the Paris Opera, Kronstam said how wonderful it had been to dance on such a large stage, that "finally, I could really fly there." He explained, "I was so big that I could never jump that high [in *La Sylphide* in Copenhagen] because it would be too big for our stage here," and too big for the proper Bournonville style. He added that the "critics here never understood that. You would think they could see it." A huge jump in *La Sylphide* would be a violation of the style. Yet Kronstam did jump very high in contemporary ballets, such as *Miss Julie* and *Medea*. Kronstam assumed that people would understand that if he jumped high in one ballet and not another, there was a reason for it. Like many intelligent people, he assumed that anything that was self-evident to him would be obvious to others as well.

Another dancer might have discussed this with critics—who would probably have been very grateful for the insight, for such things are not self-evident—but Kronstam did not. This was taken by some to be arrogance, but to Kronstam it was natural. It was how he had been brought up, both at home and at the Theatre. One was not told why one was not given a role, nor why one was taken off a part. The cast lists were posted on the board, the dancers read the lists, and it was up to each individual to figure out why certain people had been cast and others had not. One observed and analyzed the observations in some depth before reaching a conclusion. Kronstam seemed to think everyone was gifted with his powers of insight and analysis.

For critics outside Denmark, Kronstam was difficult to assess because he was so different in each role. One needed to see Kronstam in several roles— say, James, Romeo, Apollo, Albrecht, Cyrano, the Toreador, Jean, and the teacher in *The Lesson*—to begin to take his measure. Reviews in the early part of his career, especially, show that some writers are confused because Kronstam was so different from one role to another. Being a star is like having a brand name. To keep that brand name recognizable, one must dance everything in a similar fashion. There was never a question that Bruhn was noble, or that Nureyev was animalistic. But what was Kronstam?

A television appearance by Kronstam and Simone on the *Firestone Hour* dancing *The Sleeping Beauty* is a very good example of Kronstam's style. He dances the pas de deux as an excerpt from the ballet, not a concert number. There is only one glimpse of Kronstam, the Romantic Lover: a yearning backbend as he extends his hand to Aurora. Kronstam did not dance Florimund as a Romantic Lover, but as a Classical Prince. He is warm, there is a discernible personality, but it is understated. The dancing itself is very beautiful, very pure, but in a soft voice. One cannot help but notice the way his body relates to the music, the way the arms and torso are in counterpoint to the legs, creating a continuous arc of smooth movement so that the solo is danced in one seamless legato flow, and one begins to see what dancers saw. Kronstam had a strong stage presence, but he drew the eye without actively seeking attention. When you found Kronstam, you could not look away. But if you were looking for something else, you might never notice him.

Some dancers say that Kronstam "did not dance in New York enough," which gives a very interesting twist to the term *international star.* If the Royal Danish Ballet had danced in New York every year or two, and if he had been shown in a variety of roles, Kronstam may have been more highly regarded in America, but that would not have made him a greater dancer. One New York critic who did value Kronstam and understood very well the relationship between ballet politics and international ranking was Walter Terry, who wrote this account for the Danish newspaper *Politiken:*

> But Erik Bruhn alone does not make the Royal Danish Ballet, even if he is the greatest celebrity to come from it these days. On the male side, there is Henning Kronstam, a dancer of beautiful technique with a beautiful style and with remarkable dramatic ability. One only has to think how wide his range is, from the brash Toreador (a stupefying caricature in his gestures) in *Carmen* to the wonderful display of romance in *La Sylphide* (and Kronstam is possibly the finest romantic dancer of our time) to the two-faced, evil, sexy servant in *Miss Julie.* With calculated publicity and launching, Kronstam could very quickly be developed into an international star.

But Kronstam was not promoted by the company, and he did not promote himself.

Many dancers feel that Kronstam was undervalued by some critics because he didn't go to the parties, didn't socialize with, or befriend, the important critics, as many other stars did, and this is part of the International Question. In the 1960s, the Age of Nureyev, the height of the Ballet Boom, the ballet world was very glamorous, especially in New York and London. There were parties attended by society people, dancers, and critics; it was the way of the world. Critics expected to have social interaction with dancers, and Kronstam's refusal to take part in this world may well have caused him to be pushed aside, consciously or unconsciously, by some. He believed this had affected his reviews with at least one critic and told this story about the 1965 American tour: "Flemming [Flindt] was very kind to me because he told me that if I wanted to have success in New York, I would have to go out to dinner with Clive Barnes [the newly appointed dance and drama critic for the *New York Times*]. Flemming said I should come with him and Vivi to dinner. And I thought about it and at first I said yes, but then I thought I just couldn't go through with it. I had met Clive in Edinburgh. And I just could not sit there, night after night, with that man and flatter him and all that nonsense. So I didn't go."

For whatever reason, Flindt dominated the *Times*'s coverage of the Royal Danish Ballet's New York season, not only in profiles and interviews, but in reviews as well. It's not a matter of judgment—both Bruhn and Kronstam were reviewed fairly—but of the amount of space and the placement and tone of the comments.

Kronstam hated the games and the politics surrounding ballet and stubbornly refused to take part in them. The other major New York critic, Walter Terry, who wrote for the *Herald Tribune,* lavished praise on Kronstam and this embarrassed him, as he feared that people would think that he had befriended Terry to get good reviews. In Denmark too he kept his distance, especially from the critics who were near to him in age. Kronstam's rather jaundiced view of critics was based on his experience with and observation of the games, not whether one praised him and another did not. One critic that he did see socially was Svend Kragh-Jacobsen, a very knowledgeable and judicious reviewer, whom Kronstam described as a "friend of Franz," and who never skewered a dancer in print. Despite their friendship, Kragh-Jacobsen consistently wrote that Erik Bruhn was the great international star and Kronstam "led the home team," and Kronstam never complained about that assessment.

It wasn't until the notices for his sixtieth birthday that Danish critics gave him his due—quite probably because it was known he was ill, and these birthday pieces in the Danish press often serve as living obituaries—a fact that wasn't lost on Kronstam. "It was only after I retired that they started saying I was one of the top ones," he said, but this was the only time he let slip that he felt he had been undervalued.

It was Kronstam's fellow artists who consistently rated him highly. Some of the most interesting comments came from two foreign choreographers who worked with Kronstam, Eliot Feld and Glen Tetley. Feld, who created a ballet for Kronstam in the early 1970s, said, "I have never worked with an artist of greater stature, male or female. There is nobody of greater stature in my opinion, and maybe one or two in my entire career that I think come near him.

"It has to do in part with his artistry, but in part with the exquisiteness of his actual body. The length of the neck, the way the head sits on the neck. The volume of the thigh, and the proportion, the length of it. To me, it is the most beautiful male physique I've ever seen on a dancer. Not overly refined, and not—he is Michelangelo's ballet dancer. It's elegant, but it's masculine, as opposed to, say, Erik Bruhn, who had an extraordinary facility, but for me, Henning's physique has more to do with the volume of a male body.

"I think he could do anything. It was some combination of his actual physical ability, musicality, and his intuition, understanding, trying to get at where the furnace was that this movement was the symptom of. He always danced in the first person, and that's why his work for him was obsessive, because he was searching within his own imagination or experience for that which would make the movement true."

Glen Tetley, who worked with Kronstam both as dancer and artistic director, had worked with many of the international stars of the day, and made this assessment: "Henning never acted like a star. He was there just to work, if you wanted him. He was open. There was nothing demanding, there was nothing forbidding.

"Every time I saw him perform, he was of the first rank. He had the ability to transform himself in the roles he did. He was [not like the] international stars who transformed the role into their persona. They don't enter the role; they transform the role into their persona. Which Erik did. It was always Erik Bruhn. It was always Rudolf Nureyev. The international superstars, we're talking about.

"Henning, in every way, was a star, a first-class dancer, but he did not trade on the star persona. He did not insist on the star aura about him. What he achieved he did through his incredibly beautiful physicality and his very dark, smoldering, passionate physicality. I did not ever think of him as an exhibitionist dancer. He was not merely someone entertaining the eye alone. There was a soul there always, in what he did."

Tetley was one of many artists who did not understand why Kronstam was not more highly valued by the Danish critics: "I think there is a mental attitude that runs through a company like the Royal Danish Ballet. If you stay at home, you haven't really made it," which is another way of stating the Jantelov principles.

Feld had lived with the company for nearly two months, and sensed

Jantelov as well. Asked how he thought Kronstam was regarded by his fellow dancers, he said several things that might now seem prophetic: "I can't really be sure. I think that I felt he was separate. This was my impression, that he was a world unto himself. Now, this may have been much more my perception than some more objective reality."

Other people, especially visitors to the company, had sensed the same thing, saying that Kronstam was special, but Feld disagreed: "There's something coarse about that. I think there's something more subtle about what was different about him. I think that he was incorruptible, and I think that there is nothing more despised and frightening to people than somebody who is not corruptible, because they cannot be purchased, subtly, insidiously. They are a threat to the order of things because they will not negotiate in any way their position, which is one of purity. That's why Joan was burned at the stake. That's why Thomas More—it is endless. I perceived him to be isolated for reasons having more to do with that than that he was just 'special.' He has to be excised because his presence somehow assaults the commonness of the rest of us."

Feld sensed the dark side of the Danish ballet, the resentment artists felt toward someone who is special. While most of the dancers genuinely liked and respected Kronstam, several of those closest to him in age, who were rivals for roles or attention or both, seemed to harbor a long-hidden resentment. They tried to belittle him, tried to minimize his accomplishments, "couldn't remember" any of his roles, and were politely angry that someone was paying attention to him and not to them. It is likely that Kronstam survived as long as he did not only because he never "pushed himself forward"—the cardinal Danish sin—but because he was not singled out for special attention in the press.

Jantelov is much less about equality for all than power and status without regard to merit. It is a way for the mediocre to control the talented, the Rare Few. The first rule is not to think one is special. But that is not enough. He must not be treated as special, nor do anything that would cause him to be treated as special. The penalties for violation are harsh and they are inevitable. It is akin to a Japanese proverb, "The nail that sticks up gets hammered down." The nail sticks up, or is perceived to stick up, because it is so far above the level of the other nails.

Kronstam was the dominant dancer in the 1950s and 1960s and ultimately became the central artistic figure in the Royal Danish Ballet. He was very much the swan in the Royal Theatre's duck pond, admired by many, but also resented. As more and more swans flew away, he became more and more isolated. Swans and ducks live in harmony on the beautiful Copenhagen lakes, but one cannot help but notice how much more impressive the ducks seem when the swans are not in view.

He had a sense of gravity and he could not only escape gravity, he could give in to gravity, could give in to the floor.
—Glen Tetley

Seventeen

First Solo Dancer

On January 1, 1966, Flemming Flindt became ballet master. In a very real way this brought an end to the Lander Scandal, although it did not completely heal all the wounds. It provided an ironic triumph for the deposed ballet master, as Flindt, who had worked with Lander in Paris, was very much a Lander man. However, since Flindt wanted to choreograph himself, it was unlikely that he would return dozens of Lander ballets to the repertory. Hence, his appointment must have mollified Lander's ardent supporters, while removing the underlying objections of the anti-Lander forces. Lander, now in his late sixties, could be honored as a former ballet master, and there were some critics who would always refer to him as a great Danish choreographer. Underlying the cries for the return of Lander had been the need for a resident Danish choreographer; Flindt promised to fulfill that need. Like Lander, Flindt had been out in the world. A new era dawned on Kongens Nytorv.

If the old divides between Lander and anti-Lander factions, Danish and international repertory were sealed by Flindt, his appointment began a new one: classical ballet versus modern dance and dance theater. In the mid-1960s, the world was changing and classical ballet had fallen out of favor in many places. Some companies that had clamored to get on the ballet bandwagon in the immediate postwar years—at least partly in emulation of Britain's Royal Ballet, with its internationally renowned productions of *Sleeping Beauty* and *Swan Lake,* as well as tours to the West by the Kirov and Bolshoi ballets—began to look upon classical ballet as an outmoded style rather than an infinitely renewable language. This, coupled with the revolution in modern dance in America, with its emphasis on the ordinary, on found movement, on cooperative choreography—on everything ballet was not—would present a serious challenge to classical ballet.

New York and London were cities large enough to accommodate many tastes. There, small experimental companies catered to the modernists, and large classical institutions were dedicated to both preserving and expanding ballet. Copenhagen, a city of less than a million people in a country of five million, did not have that luxury. Questions began to be asked: what was the place of the Royal Theatre in Danish society? The old notion, that a country's national theater represented the best of the culture, began to be questioned. Whose notion of best? Who was the audience? The general population, who paid high taxes to support it, or the few Copenhageners to whose tastes it had always catered? What about the two-thirds of the country that never saw the Royal Danish Ballet? Denmark wasn't large enough to support more than one ballet company. The Royal Danish Ballet had to serve many masters.

In this new controversy between traditional ballet and newer dance forms, Kronstam was both gourmet and gourmand. His sensibilities, his personal aesthetic, were classical and his loyalty to Volkova and everything she stood for was unshakable. At the same time, as a dancer he wanted to dance everything that was available in his time, and his competitive nature made him want to continue to be chosen for new works, whether they were ballet or modern dance. Flindt would use Kronstam's classical sensibilities and gifts, but he also acquired several unusual modern or pantomime pieces that expanded his range.

Flindt named Kronstam assistant ballet master—a clever way to ensure that a dancer senior to him had a respected place in the company's hierarchy. In this position, Kronstam's duties would be to teach both children and company class, to work with visiting choreographers and rehearse their works in repertory after they had gone, and to head the school. This was the first time in the company's history that a person other than the company's ballet master had headed the school, and it was a matter of some controversy.

Initially it was announced that both Kronstam and Toni Lander would be Flindt's assistant ballet masters. Eventually Lander didn't accept the job and Inge Sand was then appointed as the other assistant. Sand was a solo dancer and had headed the Soloists of the Royal Danish Ballet for years. Her principal duty was to maintain the rehearsal schedules and attend administrative meetings when Flindt was unavailable; she was also responsible for rehearsing ballets.

Kronstam underwent a crisis of conscience during this period, but the details are irretrievable now. He was not overly fond of Flindt—they were never friends, and Kronstam did not admire what he considered Flindt's star attitude and technical sloppiness—and it may have simply been that he was worried about what the company, as well as his own career, would be like under Flindt's direction. Something happened at a rehearsal in New York during that 1965 American tour, but Kronstam never explained what it was. "I made up my mind to leave the company," he said. "I took all my notebooks for teaching and threw them away—Vera's classes and Stanley's classes and my classes." However, something changed his mind. "I decided I had to stay because somebody had to stay to take care of Vera," was all he would say. Although she remained in Copenhagen until her death, in 1975, Volkova's position in the company was now shaky; her influence was greatly diminished. Larsen had needed an artistic advisor; Flindt did not. Whether one agrees with his policies and the direction in which he guided the company or not, Flindt was an artist with definite ideas of what he wanted, and he had his own international contacts.

Exactly what was behind Kronstam's appointment as an assistant ballet master is not clear. In another conversation, asked if there was any important figure in his life who had not yet been discussed, he said, "We have not talked about my dear Per Gregaard [the new theater chief]. He made it possible for me to have that assistant directorship." Again, no details, but, he added, significantly, "Per Gregaard understood me because he had to go away to hospitals when he had breakdowns too."[1]

Back home in Copenhagen, Flindt, who had left the company at eighteen and made a career in London and Paris, clamped down on guest appearances by the dancers. Kronstam was given the title *første solodanser,* the only man in the company's history besides Børge Ralov so honored.[2] "It was because what we were doing was above the level of the others," Kronstam said, adding, practically, "and it meant more money." More important to Kronstam, Flindt gave him plenty of roles. "They came to him at the beginning of the season and asked him what he wanted to do," as Simone put it. Bruce Marks, who joined the company in the late 1960s, also observed that Kronstam was treated differently. "Everybody else was dealt with," Marks said. "Henning was handled," a characterization that seemed to delight Flindt. "I tried to listen to Henning," Flindt said. "I knew he would not come to me with a problem twice, so I had to get it right the first time."

Flindt created a full-length ballet for Kronstam his first season, *The Three Musketeers,* but it was not one of Kronstam's favorites. Flindt's ballet replaced his beloved *Cyrano,* which was dropped from the repertory, probably because Flindt's own work was so similar, Kronstam and other dancers believed. *The Three Musketeers* looks, on paper, to have been an inspired idea: a story ballet with lots of characters, an emphasis on male dancing—the perfect Danish work. On stage, however, it was less satisfactory.

Kronstam created the role of D'Artagnan and found the part technically difficult and dramatically unrewarding. "It was just a lot of tricks," he said. Although simplistic dramatically, the role was very tiring physically. "It was hard. I was dancing all the time. I was standing on my leg and my hands, and rolling over and things I'd never done before. And Flemming threw all those things out when he had to do it himself. *Cyrano* was a touching story. Very touching. It was French, and it had to be brassy, but there was something human and touching behind it. D'Artagnan was just a swashbuckler."

This was one occasion when Kronstam and the Danish critics agreed, as a review by Robert Naar indicates: "Henning Kronstam is D'Artagnan, hero of all boys. His eyes, set a little bit too close, and his long profile gave him a Spanish irony, and he was magnificent in his comic cheekiness. His erotic scene with Kirsten Simone's fabulously danced Milady had a lot more content than the comic tone of the ballet."

Other critics, like Herbert Steinthal, found something to like in the ballet: "Kronstam radiates his entire masculine self-awareness, which the part requires. You feel how the lust burns inside him but is suppressed in the calmly sliding pas de deux, which is so beautiful, and in the final advances it is sublimated in a straightforward moving way in a gentle kiss. There is something very beautiful and moving about Kronstam's forced calmness."

Kronstam's dislike of the ballet may also be at least tangentially related to the fact that it was the cause of a painful injury, duly reported in the Danish tabloids:

An entire season is wrecked for the Royal Theatre's leading dancer, Henning Kronstam. The exquisite ballet artist returned to his home this Saturday from Arhus, where Dr. Thomasen operated on his leg.[3]

The accident, which in a manner of speaking has spoiled Kronstam's season, happened on October 15. As D'Artagnan, after the love scene in ballet master Flemming Flindt's full-evening ballet *The Three Musketeers,* he jumps with a tiger leap down into the prompter's box to avoid his pursuers. That night his leg hit an edge just below the left knee and cut a gash three centimeters deep into his shinbone. He was patched up and treated at the Orthopedic Hospital.

"Only one thing about this makes me happy," says Henning Kronstam, "and that is that this year's festival has been postponed till August." (*BT,* April 24, 1967)

Kronstam's version is a bit more gruesome and sheds an unpleasant light, as do several of his medical experiences, on Danish health care. "At the end of the first act, I had to jump down into the prompter's box. It was open and I had to jump down into it. I had done it a million times. Niels Kehlet was my waiter, Planchet, but at that performance, I had the second-cast boy and he was used to Flemming [who alternated with Kronstam in this role]. He was standing there [in a different place from where Kehlet would be]. So instead of jumping straight down, I had to jump so I caught the iron on the corner of the box. I had an open gash here. They put a plaster on it, and I danced the whole second act with it, but the blood was running down my leg.

"The next day it was getting blue and awful, and I called the hospital and told them what had happened and said, 'Can't you send an ambulance, because I can't walk.' And they said, 'No, we can't. You can take a taxi.'

"So I went, and I was sitting in the place in the hospital where they would do operations. The doctor came out—he was all bloody and everything—and said, "What's that?" and he just took a needle and sewed it together. So. I continued dancing. I went to the States. We did three months of touring. I came back and it was still hurting and I didn't understand why. I was taking this electric treatment, ultrasonic.

"I went to Dr. Thomasen and said, "Can I come up to you?" And he took an X ray and there was a piece of the bone sitting inside there that had been cut off, and I had been dancing with it all that time. So he operated. So that leg was not so good, for a period."

As nearly always happens when a new director takes over, there were dancers who left the company and dancers who were encouraged to leave. Almost as soon as he became director, Flindt asked Margrethe Schanne, now forty-six, what she would like for her farewell performance. Schanne was very popular and a favorite of several important critics. However, she also belonged to an older time. She chose *La Sylphide* as her farewell performance, dancing it with Flindt.

Kronstam at first thought that he would now be regularly paired with Simone, but that was not to be. Although Flindt and Simone did not get along, Flindt took her for his partner and Kronstam usually danced with Anna Lærkesen, the company's newest ballerina, a very gifted, sensitive, and rather willful artist. Kronstam said that Flindt's mother, whom Flindt adored, liked seeing Flindt with Simone, and that may be partially the reason, but they were also physically well matched, both fairly short and solid in build, while Lærkesen and Kronstam were both Romantic dancers, with long lines.

Kronstam's next role, which he had learned in New York on the 1965 tour, was the male lead in Jerome Robbins's *Afternoon of a Faun*. "Vera was always out for good things. We went to see his rehearsals of *Les Noces*. And then she said, 'Why don't you teach some of our dancers *Faun*.'" As was Robbins's custom, five couples rehearsed the ballet. "We learned it first and then we did it couple by couple. We worked for about a week with him to learn it. And then he told Francisco Moncion, 'Go to Copenhagen and you use Henning and Kirsten in the first cast and Dinna [Bjørn] and Arne [Bech] in the second cast, and the rest you don't bother with.'"

Kronstam enjoyed dancing *Faun*. He was presented with a portrait of the opening scene, minus Simone, which hung in his living room. "It was very interesting to do. Francisco Moncion came here to work with us. It was made on him, and a thing that's made on you, you can always do. He was a sweet man. He had very quiet rehearsals, and then the last three days he said to me, 'Now, a little more animal.' So that was another help, to understand the role. Because Kirsten was so pure in it, so he wanted me to be [a contrast]." Kronstam's animal was introverted, with the expectant stillness of a woodland creature. "And wait for something to happen. And something did happen because she came in. I loved that ballet. I really did."

Danish critics were divided on his performance. Some thought Kronstam and Simone, both thirty, too old for the ballet; some expected to see something more literally animal, as Knud Voeler wrote in *Aktuelt*: "Henning Kronstam and Kirsten Simone danced the Faun and the Nymph at the premiere. The atmosphere of infatuation made an impact during the curious semiconscious, but sensitively obsessed meeting, between the two beings. So soft, so spiritual, danced by both with much grace and beauty, without, however, the feeling that a demonically ferocious inner spark was present. But it did become an impression of beauty of a most captivating nature." Svend Kragh-Jacobsen saw the ballet as being about dancers, not animals: "Henning Kronstam has never more brilliantly proven his position as the Royal Ballet's top dancer than this Saturday night, when, without a sound, he met the strict aesthetic requirements demanded of the dancer who is only wearing black tights. He was a complete dancer—not some naughty faun—and he gave us every difficult step with effortless ease" (*Berlingske Tidende,* March 14, 1966).

The next season Kronstam had his first experience with modern dance and the only ballet in which he felt completely dissatisfied with his performance: Paul Taylor's *Aureole*. He was the first ballet dancer to dance Taylor's part. This ballet blanc of modern dance, to music Handel had written for a ballet, all lightness, bounce, and joy, seems an ideal way to introduce modern dance into the Danish repertory, but modern dance was much more foreign to Danish dancers than it would have been to Americans in 1965. Kronstam had seen very little and had never taken a class.

Aureole presented Kronstam with the only role he ever danced that he could not turn into a character. He had to be himself, and he felt inadequate, he said, mostly because he felt too small for it. Kronstam was tall but still, at that time, extremely thin; Taylor was much more muscular. There is a bit of rehearsal tape extant that shows Kronstam dancing the solo wearing thick, fuzzy leg warmers, obviously trying to give himself bulk. "When he started on that variation, that slow one, the adage one, his own, I said, 'What?' Because it was so against everything that I could do, or had done. It was all flexed feet, all sorts of crazy pliés and crazy jumps, and I don't know what going on. I enjoyed the pas de deux and I thought the finale was fun. But I had trouble with that adage because I couldn't find something to hold onto, like I did with Phlegmatic or Apollo. There I knew that this was something I had to express. But with Paul Taylor, I didn't know what to do. We had no training, no preparation for it. All of a sudden he was here, and he watched class, and he picked us, and then we had to dance in bare feet. He was very nice to me, very encouraging."

In Paul Taylor's solo from
Aureole, 1967. Photo:
Mydtskov. The Royal
Theatre, Copenhagen.
By permission of Det
kongelige Teaters
bibliotek og arkiv.

Taylor worked with the dancers for eight days and later wrote, "As aped by the
great Danes, the steps came out looking like those of an ostrich with lumbago."[4]
Kronstam remembered that the rehearsals had been barefoot (painful and
difficult for ballet dancers, whose feet had not built up the calluses of modern
dancers), although Taylor wrote that Inge Sand had said that "dancing without
ballet shoes is also verboten," and he had rehearsed the dancers in ballet slippers; it was they who came, at the end, and asked to dance it in bare feet. Taylor
also wrote that he did not know the names or status of the dancers before he
watched class, but dancers at the time felt that was unlikely. He picked Kronstam, Vivi Flindt (wife of the director), and Anne Sonnerup (wife of the television producer), along with Sorella Englund and Aage Poulsen, whom dancers
remember as Taylor's favorite, because of his bouncy jump and muscular body.

With Vivi Flindt in the
duet from *Aureole*. Pri-
vate collection.

Kronstam found Taylor's musicality quite different from what he was used
to. "It's beautiful music, but I just thought that the steps didn't fill out the
music. I was standing and waiting for the music to continue, and then you did
another little step, and you did one other crazy thing, and the music was going
on and you said, 'Well, here I am. Everybody is watching and I am doing nothing.'" (Kronstam said he finally understood Taylor when he saw squadrons of
Chinese citizens performing Tai Chi exercises on his first trip to China.)

In his autobiography, *Private Domain*, Taylor speaks rather disparagingly of
the Danish Ballet and seems conflicted about setting the work for the company
and accepting money for it. Ballet and modern dance were still very polarized,
and working with a ballet company was, in a way, "selling out." His account of
the rehearsals, which dancers cast in *Aureole* often missed because of scheduling conflicts, includes a comment on Kronstam: "To make up for it, I call in my
company's *Aureole* cast to help teach, assigning each dancer to his counterpart
while I concentrate on Henning. He's musical, or at least able to count, and a

speedy learner, but his dancing looks like a series of still pictures rather than a flow of movement."[5]

Aureole was televised in 1969, with Kronstam in Taylor's role (it was later televised with Nureyev in that role). It's hard to see what is unmusical about Kronstam's performance, although there are certainly other things that can be criticized. He doesn't have Taylor's playfulness; he's overcareful. By instinct, although it's doubtful he knew the music's history, he dances the solo like an eighteenth-century danseur noble wearing a very strange costume (a white unitard). Allan Fridericia wrote: "It was an experiment in itself to let the first solo dancer of the Royal Danish Ballet, Henning Kronstam, appear in this consciously unpretentious scene. He, whose personality and physique are so different from Taylor, has been given the choreographer's role. At the premiere one felt that Kronstam had managed to give something new to the part. Exciting steps were unfolded with exquisite adagio" (*Information*, May 27, 1968).

Ebbe Mørk, who, with Erik Aschengreen, was one of the new young critics who began to write in the mid-1960s, wrote kindly of the experiment: "Henning Kronstam does not get quite as much pleasure out of the attempt in bare feet. The exquisite dancer hardly feels at home with Taylor, and does not have the distinguished assurance that he normally provides. It is hard to manage pirouettes and balance without shoes. Kronstam, however, contributes to the overall impression of beauty, not least with his waving arms and beautiful lines."

"I did my best, and it was the best he could get," Kronstam said. "But about two years later Bruce [Marks, trained in modern dance] came in. My name was just crossed out. Nobody told me. I didn't miss it, but I thought they should have told me." There was no one with the company at that time that rivaled Kronstam in classical roles, but what he learned from *Aureole* is that if he were going to maintain his position as the company's leading male dancer, he would have to learn to adapt to other styles. Unbeknownst to his colleagues, Kronstam began to take jazz dance classes in the summers in Cologne, where he taught at a summer institute.

Kronstam's next big role was the title part in Elsa Marianne von Rosen's *Don Juan*, which he danced with Simone. The ballet was another disappointment, both for Kronstam and the audience. It was in what was by now beginning to be an old-fashioned style, a story with classical variations, and it premiered on the same night as Flindt's new-style theater piece *The Young Man Must Marry*, which was hailed as bold and new.

With Bettie de Jong, rehearsing *Aureole*. Paul Taylor is in the background. Photo: Mydtskov. The Royal Theatre, Copenhagen. By permission of Det kongelige Teaters bibliotek og arkiv.

Again, Kronstam felt that von Rosen was unduly influenced by Fridericia, who choreographed through his wife, giving her suggestions that Kronstam felt were overintellectual and undertheatrical. Don Juan was a case in point. Kronstam felt he was given absolutely nothing of the character by von Rosen. He was familiar with Mozart's opera—one of the most important in the Danish repertory since the nineteenth century—and read about the Don Juan legend as well.

"I remember very little about it. Just a couple of variations, very tough, very awkward. I read that Don Juan really didn't like women. He used them, but he didn't like them. It was just a ritual he had to do. So I used that in the role. I think I had eleven girls and ended up with Kirsten [Simone]."

Don Juan received mixed notices, although Kronstam was praised. Svend Kragh-Jacobsen wrote, "Henning Kronstam is Don Juan—brilliant in looks, mightily costumed in changing colors. In terms of mime, he's at the peak of his form. He still has passion in his eyes and a noble elegance in every movement that may deny the jester in his blood, but he gives the manner of a gentleman (*Berlingske Tidende*, October 17, 1967). Harald Engberg's review was wittily entitled "Two Don Juans, and One You Don't Take," but he liked Kronstam: "Henning Kronstam's Don Juan is a man strong of limb. He is endearingly lighthearted in his many erotic conquests; he's at the height of his manhood, facing his hardest and most beautiful prey—Tadea, brilliantly danced by Kirsten Simone as the fate of a man for good and evil."

In 1968 the company revived *Petrushka*, which had originally entered the repertory when Fokine worked with the company in the 1920s. Kronstam, Flindt, and Fredbjørn Bjørnsson were announced in the title role. In some ways it seems ridiculous to have a tall, skinny Petrushka, but Fokine's sad little sawdust clown was very much Kronstam's character, if not his physicality. The story appealed to him—rejection, the heartless ballerina doll, the aggressive Blackamoor, the evil, manipulative Charlatan, the ultimate triumph of the spirit—but he withdrew after a few rehearsals. "I was tried out on *Petrushka* too, but didn't dare do it. I'd rather do something new that nobody has seen in that context, and I needed more support. Again, it was Niels Bjørn Larsen that was producing it. He just said, 'You do it again, do that scene. Do it again. Do it again.' I

Conducting a rehearsal of *Etudes*. Vera Volkova is behind Kronstam. Photo: Photo: Mydtskov. Private collection.

know that Jerome Robbins wanted to do *Petrushka* with me. He wanted to come and stage *Petrushka*, not his own version, but a real *Petrushka*. That would have been something interesting." This is the first time Kronstam mentioned withdrawing from a role. Although he was always insecure, until this point he had always taken risks. Whether this change was because Volkova had less power in the company and hence Kronstam had less support, or because his illness was beginning to worsen after the breakdown in 1960, is unclear.

There was a three-day tour to Covent Garden in 1968. Oleg Kerensky, writing in the *New Statesman* in May 1968, called the company "backward looking and escapist," although he praised the male dancing, saying that Kronstam "seems to have gained in personality and dramatic strength without losing his elevation and agility." The British press, almost to a man, laughed at *La Sylphide*, finding it hopelessly silly and old-fashioned.

Nicholas Dromgoole wrote, "The plot, creaking forward in jerks of antiquated mime, is as bad as they come. . . . The music is undistinguished, the dances only pretty-pretty in an old-fashioned way, and what once was living theater has somehow become little more than a museum exhibit. Two acts of it seemed awfully long, and Anna Lærkesen, who danced the Sylphide, seemed, in those frozen arabesques, a cold statue obstinately refusing to come to life. Henning Kronstam was as good as anyone could have been in the circumstances." In contrast, he found Flindt's *Miraculous Mandarin* "straightforward, inventive and theatrically effective" (*Sunday Telegraph,* May 1968). Alexander Bland agreed: "*La Sylphide* is such an outrageously old-fashioned ballet that it always skates along the edge of absurdity. The new production seems blithely unaware of this danger. It runs along in its jerky old way and the dancing is always quick and lively" (*Observer,* May 5, 1968).

While Kronstam certainly didn't agree that *Miraculous Mandarin* was a superior ballet to *La Sylphide,* he did agree with these reviews in the larger sense. "It was a bad production," he said. There is a television broadcast of the *La Sylphide* of this era, and it *was* a bad production. Although newly staged by Brenaa and Flindt (with Brenaa very much under Flindt's thumb, according to both Kronstam and Jens Brenaa), it looked thrown on, all the attention paid to the dancing and little to the staging. The seamless flow of miming and dancing we like to think of as Bournonville is nowhere to be seen; the ballet is a succession of numbers, like a musical. There are some good performances, but no dramatic flow.

Kronstam had more luck with his second modern-dance role than his first. Glen Tetley cast him as Brighella, the dark clown, in his *Pierrot Lunaire,* another part that used his acting skills. The Royal Danish Ballet was the second company to perform *Pierrot Lunaire,* considered a major work in the 1960s and 1970s. Tetley was a hot choreographer, in demand in Europe and America, and acquiring the ballet was quite a coup. Tetley's way of combining ballet and modern dance fit in well with Flindt's plan for the company, and *Pierrot Lunaire* was stark enough, and sexy enough, to titillate the Danish critics and public and coax the new, younger audience that Flindt was beginning to attract to the Royal Theatre.

In a curious way, *Pierrot Lunaire* has Danish roots. Tetley had visited Copenhagen a few years earlier and was enchanted, with the old Commedia dell'arte ballets performed at Tivoli's Pantomime Theatre. (A group of Commedia players, traveling since time began, came to Copenhagen to perform one summer nearly 200 years ago and never left.) Tetley became very interested in the commedia and read about it when he got home.

Kronstam liked the role and gained much from working with Tetley. "I enjoyed doing Brighella. There was meaning there, that he was a devil, and that he would influence Colombine, and they would seduce Pierrot and take his virginity away from him. I enjoyed that. So Brighella I understood—and Brighella had shoes on." Kronstam found Tetley, who was accustomed to working with ballet dancers, easier to work with than Taylor. "Glen talked about it. He didn't just give you the steps. He talked, and explained why we were doing this. He was a very nice man. Very nice."

Tetley also found working with Kronstam productive. He began by speaking of Bruhn, to illustrate their differences. Tetley was a good friend, and admirer, of Bruhn, with whom he had worked at American Ballet Theatre. "Erik had an inherent elegant classicism and he was, in every essence, a Prince. I never felt that Erik was right for, or comfortable in, anything that had any contemporary quality to it. His physicality was not right. It's the muscles. It's the muscle language. And Erik did not have the weight. He did not have the off-center quality or the breadth of contemporary dancing. He had the poised stillness and the lift of classical dance, and it was beautiful. But the other, he did not have. But from the beginning when I saw Henning, I saw that, in physical language, Henning could do both. He had a sense of gravity and he could not only escape gravity, he could give in to gravity, could give in to the floor, and he could put weight into his movement. This was not just acting with the mind, or creating a character, this was moving in this other sphere."

Tetley provided an interesting account of how Kronstam worked: "When you were in the studio with Henning, you never felt that he was sizing up the part, how much he was going to do or whatever. He was totally, 100 percent concentrated. Total concentration. Total bond between you, as choreographer, with Henning as dancer. It was great. There was never a moment when he was sorting out the technical differences. In Pierrot I use quite a bit of contemporary dance technique, and elements of Graham technique, and I know that Henning immediately got the quality of the spine of this animal, the back that is not held just erect, as one does in classical dance, or in the antigravity figure of Pierrot. He had this curved cat's back. I kept saying, 'You have to be half-cat, half-snake,' and he understood that."

Pierrot Lunaire was much admired in Copenhagen. Allan Fridericia saw something of Bournonville in Kronstam's Brighella: "Henning Kronstam is awkward, a sort of Loke, probably like the one old Bournonville had dreamed of in *Thrymskviden* [The Lay of Thrym]. He was as blindingly captivating in his theatricality as he was intended to be."[6] Another writer, Mogens Gade, noticed that Kronstam had less difficulty with *Pierrot* than he had had with *Aureole:* "Kronstam looks more at home than usual in modern ballet, no matter how much his very great talent makes up for his less than relaxed relationship with different rhythms, and he gives Brighella a provocative character. Vivi Gelker [later Vivi Flindt] stands—and lies down—in the right way as the sexy Colombine." The comment on Kronstam's "less-than-relaxed relationship with different rhythms" is worth noting. His was a melodic rather than rhythmic musicality and he always felt uncomfortable with a score he couldn't sing.

Although Kronstam enjoyed dancing Brighella, it was a costly role. "It was on the same program as *Donizetti* [Balanchine's *Donizetti Variations*], and that's how I got my prolapsed disc. I had to be restrained in the *Donizetti* first, and I was a little tired. Then I had to go down and do all these contractions and I had Vivi Flindt to lift and carry around and I told her that she weighed a ton! And you know, Colombine, she goes and jumps on you and you lift her, and I was warm from *Donizetti*. Maybe I should have said, 'Well, let's take it a little easy here.' But I didn't.

"My back had already troubled me. There was a period when Frank Schaufuss was teaching men's class, and he decided that Kirsten and I should do

In Balanchine's *Donizetti Variations,* with (left to right) Sorella Englund, Dinna Bjørn, Annemarie Dybdal, Eva Evdokimova, Anita Søby, and Gerre Cimino. Photo: Mydtskov. The Royal Theatre, Copenhagen. By permission of Det kongelige Teaters bibliotek og arkiv.

As Brighella (left) in Glen Tetley's *Pierrot Lunaire*. Niels Kehlet is Pierrot. Photo: Mydtskov. Private collection.

Nutcracker, and he took us out right after the barre to do the *Nutcracker* pas de deux. There's a lot of lifting in the *Nutcracker* pas de deux, the one we did then. The first time, I had a little ping of the back. And I had to go and have a massage. But I didn't think much about it.

"But then when I did the program with *Pierrot Lunaire,* then suddenly there was another crash from the back. And right after that I should have done *Etudes,* one of the leading boys, and I was writing it down at the same time because I would be taking over [the rehearsals] after Lander left. I was sitting with woolen blankets around me, and then one day I just couldn't move my left foot.

"I went up to Dr. Thomasen and had an operation on the spine. And he took out a vertebra. It had crashed, and the inside was touching the nerve and making the whole leg useless."

In 1969, Kronstam finally made his peace with Harald Lander. Lander returned to stage *Etudes* for Danish television. Because of scheduling conflicts and injury Kronstam had rehearsed, but never danced, either of the two leading male roles in that ballet. He did not expect to be in the telecast because he was on tour in America. Bruhn and Flindt, with Toni Lander, would be the leading dancers. Lander asked for Kronstam as rehearsal master, and he ended up dancing the Sylphide pas de deux, now a separate danseur noble role.

Kronstam got along very well with Lander, who discussed his casting choices with the man who had been both his protégé and his opponent. Kronstam thought the casting for the corps "perfect" but disagreed with his choice of Anna Lærkesen over Simone in the ballerina role. Simone was an unstoppable turner, Lærkesen was nervous about the fouettés. Kronstam also worked with Lander to restage *Qarrtsiluni,* his Nordic *Rite of Spring,* which had had an extraordinary solo for Niels Bjørn Larsen that dancers still talked about. *Qarrtsiluni* was a ballet that the Danish public remained curious about, but the revival was not a hit. It was felt that its time had passed.[7]

Kronstam had begun rehearsing ballets from Flindt's first season. He replaced Larsen, who, as ballet master, had rehearsed most of the repertory (Kronstam's view of Larsen as an uncreative and dry director was shared by many dancers). The first ballet he was given to work on was Robbins's *Fanfare,* in which he had never danced, and he had to go to Larsen for his notes and films. Another man might have made things difficult for him, but Larsen was very kind and cooperative. "Niels Bjørn was always completely professional," Kronstam said.

One of the roles for which Kronstam was most grateful to Flindt was *Bagage,* a ballet pantomime by the Polish mime artist Henryk Tomaszewski. Flindt had seen the piece performed and thought it would suit the company. Although both Flindt and Peter Martins also danced the leading role, it became one of Kronstam's biggest successes.

The story for the ballet came from one of Denmark's greatest writers, Herman Bang. Kronstam, who always read anything he could get his hands on in preparing for a ballet, developed an abiding interest in Bang's works after *Bagage,* which tells the story of Franz Pander, an idealist longing for beauty who comes to work as a porter in a grand hotel, where he is repeatedly seduced, bedazzled, and betrayed by beauty. Intercut with his sufferings are memories of his dead mother, the only pure beauty Franz Pander would ever know. During the course of the forty-five-minute pantomime, Pander experiences nearly every human emotion, from infatuation to passion to humiliation and despair. Disillusioned, he hangs himself at the end. It was absolutely perfect for Kronstam.

"It was all about his losing his dreams," he said. "He has a poor mother who has saved up so that he could have a good position, and he becomes a porter in the hotel. And he thinks everything is going to be beautiful. But when the evening comes and they're all finished their work, the other waiters and waitresses and the maids try to rape him. And this is his first shock.

"It's the story of the disillusionment that the world is not what you have expected, and it was so satisfying to do. I loved doing it. It was an hour in hell. I was completely destroyed afterward.

"It was a very specific mime style, and Tomaszewski gave four hours of class a day. You do it with your whole body. You don't do it with your face alone or with the gestures. It was very strange. I don't think I ever had so great a response, letters, than I had with that. I did it on tour in Denmark and people in the provinces just loved it. And here in the Theatre there was a group of fifteen young people who came to all the performances, every single performance, and would write me afterward.

"It was one of those extraordinary things. I couldn't do a step from it now. It's all forgotten. We tried to get it back for my Jubilee [in 1976], but Flemming wrote to Poland and they said, 'This person does not exist.'"

Bagage was considered by almost everyone to be one of Kronstam's greatest roles. Svend Kragh-Jacobsen, who remained very open to contemporary work despite his classical leanings, wrote:

Arlette Weinreich as the Whore, smelling the blood from Franz's shirt. Photo: Mydtskov. The Royal Theatre, Copenhagen. By permission of Det kongelige Teaters bibliotek og arkiv.

In *Bagage* Franz Pander (Kronstam) torments the old woman (Inge Jensen). Photo: Mydtskov. The Royal Theatre, Copenhagen. By permission of Det kongelige Teaters bibliotek og arkiv.

In *Bagage*. Kronstam and
Arlette Weinreich, mocked
by the clown (Tage Wendt).
Photo: Mydtskov. The Royal
Theatre, Copenhagen. By
permission of Det kongelige
Teaters bibliotek og arkiv.

In *Bagage*. Photo: Mydtskov.
The Royal Theatre, Copen-
hagen. By permission of Det
kongelige Teaters bibliotek
og arkiv.

The greatest experience of the evening in *Bagage* was Henning Kronstam's profoundly touching creation of Franz. Not as the misunderstood servant of reality but as the suffering person. What was admirable was that at no time did Kronstam enlarge the figure more than he, in his own emotions and expressions, could validate. The crucifixion scene seemed more discrete than in earlier variations. Franz's pain became more common. As Cyrano Kronstam had already shown what an important ballet actor he is. Here he surrendered his brilliance as a dancer completely in favor of mimic intensity that made him the touching center of this Passion pantomime. He was genuine both as a servant in livery exposed to temptation and as the victim exposed to the trials of life. The set's suggestion of a cathedral, with its floating palms, alluded to the Restoration, and the revolving doors in the background sometimes seemed like confessionals or altars that enhanced the Passion style of the pantomime. This image was strong in itself, yet it was just the frame of the nightmare on the stage, as people come tumbling out when everything passes through Franz's memory.

Despite his gratitude to Flindt the director for *Bagage,* Kronstam was never quite reconciled to Flindt the choreographer. One work he especially disliked was *Galla-Variationer* (Gala Variations). A photograph of the pas de deux from *Gala Variations* shows Simone collapsed like a pocketknife on Kronstam's shoulders; both look miserable. Simone has a film of his variation as well. There's a section where Kronstam takes an arabesque, grabs the extended foot, holds it, and hops.

"*Gala Variations.* That was [Knud] Riisager. It was his seventy-fifth birthday celebration. Flemming wanted to do something new, and he wanted to do *Moon Reindeer* [for which Riisager wrote the score] on the same evening. And he asked me, 'Would you rather do *Moon Reindeer* or would you like to do the new ballet?' And I said, 'Well, everybody has seen me do *Moon Reindeer,* so I think I should do the new ballet.' And we came to rehearsal, Kirsten Simone and I, doing all these strange things. On the premiere night—I knew it was awful, and I didn't understand the music. I had a variation that was very difficult and I danced it very fast. And I finished it, and the music was still going on. I thought, 'Oh, God. You've done it too fast.' Flemming didn't mind at all. He came to me and said, 'It was very exciting.' Nobody noticed because it was so awkward."

That summer Kronstam's father died of cancer. He had been ill for several years and was living with friends in the country who looked after him. "A man to talk to and a woman to cook the meals," as Kronstam put it. Kronstam had been on friendly terms with his father since his mother's death twelve years earlier, but they never became very close. Still, the death affected him. His father's funeral was on a Saturday morning; he had to dance *La Ventana* that afternoon and he did not withdraw from the performance. Critics wrote that he was "unusually glum." "Well, I would be, wouldn't I?" Kronstam said, sarcastically; the funeral notice had been in the newspapers and he probably expected the critics to have read that and understood his situation. His family did not understand his leaving the funeral reception to go dance. "The Theatre has always been very much the way I sustained myself," Kronstam said.

His next role was another clown ballet, John Cranko's *Lady and the Fool*. Kronstam and Simone had danced the pas de deux from this ballet with Inge Sand's Copenhagen Theatre Ballet several years earlier. It was a sentimental story about a woman (La Capricciosa) who turns down three princes because she loves a clown [Moondog]. Kronstam had been injured when the ballet received its Danish premiere but danced the last few performances of the season.

"That's one of my crying ballets," he said, meaning that the audience cried, not the dancers. "It's so sad. She didn't want the prince. All she wanted was a clown, but he didn't feel up to it. He was out on the streets and he had a friend, a second clown [Bootface], and they had a good time, but she wanted him. I think it ended happily. She went off with both of us. It was a very sentimental ballet." Emte Stag's review indicates there was a burlesque juxtaposition to the sentimentality: "Henning Kronstam gave a touching characterization of Moondog the clown. At first, in a totally burlesque dance with his friend and fellow clown Bootface, danced by Hans Jakob Kølgaard, only to later reach helpless love in La Capricciosa. The great pas de deux at the end became one of the real highlights of the evening, so truly and brightly performed."

In December 1970, Kronstam injured his Achilles tendon on stage, which ended his career as a classical dancer at the age of thirty-six. A tabloid account, headlined "First Solo Dancer Collapses during Performance," gave the grim details:

> The First Dancer of the Royal Ballet, Henning Kronstam, 36, has had an accident that is the worst nightmare of a dancer. He collapsed on stage with a torn Achilles tendon. The excellent dancer experienced this tragedy shortly before the ballet went on holiday. *La Sylphide* was almost ending when the accident happened. Kronstam had danced the part of James, the Scotsman,

grandly and was in unusual form and had the interest of the audience. When in the second act, in the scene in the forest, he wanted to please Anna Lærkesen with the witch's lethal veil, he collapsed with a strong pain in his right foot. He rolled into the wings, where he was assisted by those of his friends who were not on stage. Anna Lærkesen and Niels Bjørn Larsen performed the rest of the ballet without James.

The King was in the Theatre, and afterward went on stage to ask about the unfortunate dancer. Kronstam had a sense that it was the Achilles tendon that was the problem, but was hoping that perhaps it was just a serious sprain.

Sunday morning he flew to Professor Thomasen at the orthopedic hospital in Arhus.

Henning is completely in shape again after his illness.

This last comment seems ludicrous and sounds suspiciously like the work of Gerstenberg, who occasionally leaked news items to the papers. Kronstam was not at all "completely in shape." He was in a cast for three months and did not consider himself a classical dancer after this injury.

Kronstam thought the injury was the result of the prolapsed disk; his left leg had remained weak after that operation. "So I worked on the right leg for a year and a half. I did *La Sylphide* again, and I did everything on that foot. But I overworked that leg. So on the fourth of January, two years later, the Achilles on the right leg went. And that meant that I was finished with classical roles. I was in a cast for three months and when the cast came off the leg was nothing, only a big knee and big ankles because all the muscles go, and they go so fast, the minute you're not using them."

In another company such an injury would have ended his career completely, but Kronstam continued in dramatic and character roles for more than a decade.

Even when he was in deep despair, his dancing
came out of joy, out of the sun.
—Nikolaj Hübbe

Eighteen

Dark and Fair

Along with employ, there is another division in Danish ballet, one so ancient
that no one really knows the origins; it's buried deep in Nordic myth, or perhaps before. This is the distinction between the Blond Youth, the hero, and the
Dark One, who has been, variously, the villain, the pagan, the passionate
yearning youth, and, in the twentieth century, the Outsider. There is a difference in musculature between the two as well as in coloring: the erect, statu-
esque Nordic blond in opposition to the more supple Mediterranean body.

Kronstam had medium coloring, often darkened for the stage, and open,
even features. He was dark, with a flexible musculature, but he was also fair,
both in the sense of being pleasant to look at and with a light heart. Some
blond Danish dancers have such a heroic carriage that they seem made of
marble. Despite his perfect placement and soldier's back, in contrast, Kron-

stam seemed made of wax, molten and mutable. He had a muscular and skeletal flexibility as well as an emotional one. In Bournonvillean terms, he was both dark and fair.

In recent years Danish critics have written that Kronstam was not a Bournonville specialist, nor even a particularly good Bournonville dancer. This is a revisionist view; during the 1950s and 1960s critics consistently rate him as an excellent Bournonville dancer. The later opinion is perhaps because of the notion that Bournonville can only be danced well by very small dancers. During the Lander and Larsen years, when the perceptions of the critics who were active during Kronstam's performing years were formed, short dancers and the demi-caractère genre dominated at the Royal Theatre and became the standard.

Bournonville was five foot eight,[1] considerably taller than the "ideal" Bournonville dancers of the 1950s and 1960s. To dance Bournonville, a dancer needs speed, to be fleet of foot, able to change directions in the blink of an eye, a trait unusual in very tall dancers unless they're trained in the Bournonville style. Kronstam had that training. American dancers were always surprised at his speed. "He danced like a small man," as Larry Long put it, not in the sense that he looked small on stage, but that he moved quickly and lightly, as a much smaller man would. Back home, Kronstam went through a period in the mid-1960s when he seemed to be trying to dance in the Russian manner. But there is also film of him dancing *Flower Festival*, where he surprises with his sweetness, lightness, speed, and ballon.

Kronstam danced a few Bournonville roles as a young dancer, but only a few: James; Wilhelm in *Far from Denmark*, a mime role, and the Chinese dance, a dancing role; and the pas de trois in *La Ventana*. He danced all the pas de deux and pas de trois at galas or on tour with Inge Sand's group (center boy in the *Folk Tale* pas de sept, the third solo in *Napoli* Act III, the "yellow pas de deux" in *Kermesse*, and the *Wilhelm Tell* pas de deux at a special performance to open SAS's new route to Japan). He would have to wait until his thirties to dance Gennaro, Junker Ove, the Señor in *La Ventana*, and the Dancing Master in *Konservatoriet*; Flindt saw him as a Bournonville dancer, Larsen had not. In his late thirties and forties Kronstam danced some of the great mime parts in the repertory—Edouard in *The King's Volunteers on Amager*; Don Alvar, the villain in *Far from Denmark*; Peppo, the troublemaking lemonade seller in *Napoli*; and a quasi-Bournonville role, Mr. William in Flindt's reworking of a lost Bournonville ballet, *The Toreador*. He never danced Madge, although he would take the part in rehearsals, and dancers say they begged him to do it on stage. (He thought he was too big to be convincing, and he didn't approve of men taking women's roles, especially this one, because "the chemistry isn't right.")

Kronstam learned James, Gennaro, Wilhelm, and Ove, as well as Diderik (the nasty troll) in *A Folk Tale* in Gerda Karstens's mime class. "And I was doing Geert in *Kermesse*. Without having the nose, of course." (Noses are another division in Danish employ. Long, straight noses for serious parts, turned-up noses for comic ones—a bone of contention for ambitious dancers with pug noses. Having a nose job was considered cheating; one dances with the nose one is born with.)

"After Gerda Karstens, I owe all the Bournonville roles to Hans Brenaa. Gerda Karstens was first to show me the repertory and teach me all the mime scenes, and Hans would come in and, as I knew the mime scenes, he was just—he was very fumbly in his way of working, but he knew what he was talking about. And he had charm in his ballets."

Like almost every dancer who worked with him, Kronstam adored Brenaa. "Hans was not a Bournonville dancer really. He learned the repertory, yes, naturally, but he went to Egorova in Paris, and he loved the French, and the Russian styles. The first thing he did in the Theatre as a director was *Aurora's Wedding*." Brenaa became interested in staging and teaching Bournonville "because he suddenly saw that nobody cared about the Bournonville ballets," Kronstam said, adding passionately, "And thank God he had the memory."

Brenaa did not teach strict Bournonville, nor strict Egorova: "He was teaching free. But when Vera came and we had the influence of a foreigner in the company, then he got more and more strict, that he would teach the Danish Bournonville style and only that one. He gave us a barre that was free, and then after the barre he said, 'Well now, today is Wednesday, and we're doing it [Wednesday class].'"

The Bournonville barre "could be done in twenty minutes. There's only the grand plié, the tendu, the jeté, the ronds de jambe, fondus, ronds de jambe en l'air, petits battements, and grands battements (thirty-two). And sometimes an adage."

Twenty minutes is not considered time enough for a dancer to warm up thoroughly. "You can do anything when you're fifteen or sixteen. I wouldn't say we looked the greatest when we went out into the middle of the room [for the center practice that follows the barre], but the body can get used to a lot of

things. Mrs. Frandsen [from Riga, a Vaganova dancer] also gave a barre sometimes of fifteen minutes."

In any grand old company older dancers offer advice to younger ones trying
out a big role for the first time; Kronstam certainly did (and it was usually wel-
come). But as a dancer he listened only to himself and the person staging the
ballet. In his "Oral History," when asked (in reference to the role of James),
"Did anyone offer you any advice?" Kronstam replied: "Usually only the people
who have produced me in those ballets. You know, there are so many different
opinions, and if you start going to other people and ask them—because they
mostly tell you what they did themselves. And very few will say, 'Well, I think
that *you* should do like that, because you are different.' I think that only the
man who is in charge of directing or producing that ballet is the one that you
can ask and say, 'What would you think about it if I did like this and like that
because *I* feel like that,' and then that man can say yes or no. But asking a lot of
people . . . if you start listening to that, you'll break the character completely.
And the worst thing is if they come to me and say, 'This place is just so beautiful. You're doing that so wonderfully.'—[Snaps fingers]—ruined for me. I can
never do it again. When I come to it the next time, I say, 'Well, this is where I
am beautiful.' I have to change it and find another movement, another way to
stand, or another thing to think about, because that ruined me."[2]

In Kronstam's day the Bournonville repertory had roles for the dancers
from the time they entered the school until they retired at the mandatory state
age of seventy. He discussed his roles, the various productions in which he
took part as a dancer, as always weaving in second thoughts and refinements
he realized when he began to stage the ballets himself (*La Sylphide*, *Napoli* Acts
I and III, and *Konservatoriet;* he also coached principals in *A Folk Tale*, *Far from
Denmark*, and *The King's Volunteers on Amager*).

Napoli

Like every Danish child, Kronstam stood on the bridge in *Napoli*. He was first
an altar boy, then a fisher boy, running around and playing in the first act, and
he got to sit on the top of the cart and wave the flag in the last. His first adult part
was the Dandy, whose tips of the hat and flirtations are strictly choreographed.
"He is right on the music. That is where he has to be. When you cast it—well,
first, you have to find a man that you know won't stand like a wooden statue."

Kronstam was never cast in the pas de six during Larsen's time. He was most suited to the third variation, and this was "owned" by Svend Erik Jensen through the 1950s and 1960s. Kronstam performed it only if Jensen was ill or injured. He danced the third variation (now called Gennaro's variation, although originally Gennaro danced only in the tarantella) on the Inge Sand tours and "on special occasions here."

Brenaa did a new staging of *Napoli* (with Flindt) for Kronstam and Simone in 1967. The third act was changed to be more similar to Petipa ballets in several ways. Previously, Teresina and Gennaro had not danced in the pas de six, just in the tarantella. "It's out of relation with his role, that he [Gennaro] suddenly should stand up and dance a classical solo. The fisherman says [after the pas de six], 'What's with this craziness? Let's get on with the dancing,' and to him, that's the tarantella," observed Kronstam, an indication of how sophisticated and sure his dramatic instincts were.

That was Kronstam the instruktør talking; as a dancer, he enjoyed the third variation. "It's a wonderful variation. It sways, it's so off-center. The second one, it's hard to get anything out of it because it's all very much in the middle. It doesn't show anything really, except that deep plié. That's a hard one. The first one is always a success."

In *Napoli*, Act III, in performance. Photo: James O'Callaghan. Private collection.

Of his characterization he said, "I was very influenced by Børge Ralov, whom I'd seen for ten years. He was brilliant. That was one of his great roles. He was a wonderful Gennaro. Fredbjørn did it after Ralov, and he was a happy boy."

Napoli has the last surviving mime monologue in the Bournonville repertory. In it Gennaro—in an outpouring of anger and grief that would have, in Bournonville's time, been considered typically Italian—mourns his fiancée, who he believes has drowned. "It's wonderful to do. If you are in the mood—of course, you have to get in the mood. It is your job, as a professional, to bring yourself in the mood to do it. It's impossible to do it in the foyer [the little room where the dancers often warmed up before going down to the stage] with a mirror and things like that. Forget it. You just go through it and be on the music. But you've got to be in the set, on the stage, with the orchestra and everything. And then you can do it. Of course it has to be rehearsed so it is exactly on the music, because otherwise, it just disturbs you."

He clarified: "It has to be absolutely correctly produced or directed. After you do it on the stage you've got to be so sure about it that you can go free and you can go wild. Because he is going mad. The words are in the book. He is asking the earth, the sea, the Heavens, the moon, 'Give me back my Teresina.' It's absolutely set.

"It's a wonderful role. And wonderful, too, to come into [the Grotto in] the boat in the second act. Because if you've seen it before, you know yourself how extraordinary it is suddenly to see the little boat coming through that hole. I always felt that was a beautiful thought, that whole scene." Kronstam and Gerstenberg spent part of their vacation in Naples and Capri the summer before he danced the role. He wanted to paddle through the Blue Grotto and see the religious processions as well as drink in the sights and smells of Italy. His characterization of Gennaro surprised and disappointed some of the critics. Kronstam felt they had expected him to be Romantic, but that wasn't his reading of the role, and he danced Gennaro as a leader, a lover, and an adventurer.

In Brenaa's version the second act was very short. "You only came in, walked around, found the guitar, played the guitar, and there was Teresina. 'You with me, out there go.'[3] And then she does bourrée. . . . 'Why should I do that?' You walk forward, see the ring. 'Don't you remember this? I gave you out there?' 'You gave me out there?' 'Put your hand on your heart. Feel it [beating].' And she feels the heart, and she starts—It's when they are kneeling and he doesn't know what to do. And then he shows her the medallion, and that's what makes her blood start flowing again; the warmth comes back into her. It's a very Christian story. You must believe in Christ and in the Devil. You have to believe it.

"People used to go to Brønnums [a restaurant across the street from the Theatre; the building still exists, but it is now a Chinese restaurant] in the second act. It was so long. And people used to go, especially the men. And they would say, "Oh, we will have a glass of port." And then your wife could sit in the Theatre and see all that nonsense, and then you would come back for the third act. It's all changed now [referring to Dinna Bjørn's second act for the 1992 production]."

Kronstam thought the third act's tarantella was fun to do. "If you know your partner—and I must say, by that time I knew Kirsten—then you can play with it. So it is fun."

In his "Oral History," Kronstam sounded uncomfortable talking about Gennaro. "That wasn't one of my successes," he said. Pressed to say why, he answered, "I don't know. I don't know if it didn't suit me or what it was. I had some performances that were good—it was very spread when I got it, you know, very spread [meaning there were gaps between performances]. So I didn't get into, you know, sort of having it run, like in three or four months I'd do like ten or something. I did my first one that festival we had in August that year with the centenary of Copenhagen, seven hundred [years] or something like that, and we did a festival, and I did my first Gennaro there. And then I didn't do it for three months, and then I did one Gennaro more, and then I did another, you know. So it didn't get into my wings [?] the same way as the other Bournonville ballets have done."[4] One is left with the impression that he wasn't satisfied with his performance. However, in 1994, Ebbe Mørk, writing an appreciation in *Politiken* for Kronstam's sixtieth birthday, mentioned Gennaro as one of his finest roles and thereafter Kronstam spoke more confidently of his Gennaro. "I think it was just that the critics wanted me to be Romantic, but Gennaro isn't a Romantic man. He is a passionate man, but he has no spleen."

A 1967 review from Mørk indicates that his appreciation of Kronstam's Gennaro was a later development and reflects the prevailing view at the time: "The Fisherman and his Bride was performed for the first time by Kirsten Simone and Henning Kronstam, neither of whom seems to have been born for these lively, youthful Neapolitans, and they did not bring to the ballet the coyness and charm that Niels Kehlet and Anette Amand had done before."

Erik Aschengreen also found Kronstam unsuited to the role but saw things that Kronstam brought to it: "New in the roles in the evening were Kirsten Simone and Henning Kronstam. He doesn't seem a natural for the part of a fisher youth from Naples, and from time to time the illusion didn't work. But as an artist he is so great that he also manages to bring something beautiful to this part, especially to the scene where he thinks Teresina has drowned, and where he was more than touching without breaking the frame of the ballet."

Allan Fridericia found Kronstam's Bournonville dancing excellent. He also chided "Uncle Hans" for the new, Russian-style pas de deux:

> The part of the fisherman Gennaro had been given to Henning Kronstam. In his dramatic interpretation he showed a less personal touch than his counterparts; this Gennaro has not caught many fish in his life and his forceful emotional outburst could belong in a large number of ballets. Kronstam, however, has one great advantage—he possesses an exquisite sense of Bournonville style.
>
> It thus became due to Kronstam that you did not react more violently against the rash attempt [to revise the ballet]. Hans Brenaa has tried to improve the perfect pas de six with a pas de deux, which as regards content seemed like Uncle Hans's serious dinner talk to the young newly married couple and which, as regards step composition, was not in the spirit of Danish romance, but on the contrary seemed a Petipa pastiche. If you are going to add a pas de deux in the last act for the first time, it must be with an unfailing sense of style. It would be extremely hard to place—perhaps it could make up the couple's entrance.

In 1978, Kronstam danced Peppo, the lemonade seller who has his eye on Teresina, with Fredbjørn Bjørnsson as Giacomo, purveyor of fine macaroni. "That's another naughty one, like Alvar in *Far from Denmark*. We had fun with that. [Yuri] Grigorovich saw it, and that's why he said we had to do Don Quixote and Sancho, because he had seen us in *Napoli*. Fredbjørn played it as though he didn't really understand what I meant, but, 'Oh, good idea. Great idea.' I was really sneaky about everything and it worked very well that way. And I pushed him to do dirty things, too. I didn't do [Peppo] very often. I did it for one and a half seasons, or something like that, but we had fun."

Kronstam gave more details in his "Oral History" about how he and Bjørnsson worked: "The fun of Peppo and Giacomo is, of course, that we play together, that we know what we are doing. . . . I must say, I make a little—cheat him a little bit sometimes. I make him a little bit nervous." He explained: "By whispering in the other ear than the one I whispered in last time, or something like that. That always makes him confused and Fredbjørn is very sensitive on the stage, and in the kind of role that I do like, as the Lemonade Seller, I can be as nasty as I want to be. . . . I don't like him [Peppo and Giacomo are rivals], so I can do anything."

Tobi Tobias (the interviewer for the "Oral History") interjected, "From the look on your face, you seem to love this part." "I love it. I'm very—well, he responds to it, of course, Fredbjørn, because Fredbjørn's such a sincere artist, you know, so he can, right away—[*Snaps fingers*]—react to me. But to me, the Lemonade Seller is the one that puts all the things in, through, you know. All the nasty things in the first act is him. . . . And Kirsten Ralov, who staged the production, thought it was fine, you know, that I was the one that confused him and irritated him and still was very sure about my own cleverness."[5]

Even though Peppo was a comparatively small role, Kronstam thought him through with the same thoroughness he applied to James. Asked in his "Oral History" if he thought he had a chance to wed Teresina, he replied: "Well, he thinks that he is rich. And maybe he is rich, too, by Napoli standards, and maybe he thinks that money can do it. He knows that he has to go through the mother [i.e., Teresina's mother, Veronica], and he tells her that he has got a lot of money, and he tries to hold the mother on that she's promised Teresina to him. But he is not that unhappy. He is—he's just having a good time being vicious."[6]

Konservatoriet

In *Konservatoriet*, Bournonville's tribute to Auguste Vestris's Paris classes, Kronstam had danced with the children when he was ten. He hadn't felt special to be chosen, "We were so few boys that there was nothing special about it. They didn't have anybody else. But to do these fondus on the one leg, and the ronds de jambe—that was difficult." Six years later he danced one of the corps de ballet boys.

"Then it rested for a long time and Hans brought it back. Fredbjørn had been doing it, and Stanley was doing it, and [Flemming] Ryberg was doing it, and then Hans decided now he wanted to see a new cast, and he put me [as the ballet master], Mette Hønningen and Anna Lærkesen in it.

"It's a role from a special period because it was made just after the French

Revolution. The ballet master is not a strict ballet master, because that never would have happened. He would be [mimes "guillotined"]. So he has to be kind. He has to be nice to the pupils. This is something I know from Allan Fridericia. He told me about it when he knew I was going to get it. He called me. He said, 'Remember the years when that was happening in Paris.' So the ballet master is not all that glorious. He is on the level with everybody else. But he has to be the best dancer of course.

"So I saw it as a period piece. It's a difficult role, dancewise. The jeté en tournant into attitude, and then the other way around—it's so hard. Of course it can't look hard. It should look like it's the easiest thing in the world. He is the ballet master, so he just does it, and he says, "Well, please, now you do it."

The mime in the ballet master's part is not set. "You walk around with the stick. You can choose if you want to call the dancers forward, or you could choose—[as a stager] I always said that you should have the feeling that the ballet master is in complete control, so he knows which dancer is going to do what, and he knows the violinist is sitting there. But it is not written down. That was something you have to figure out. And then you have that little story that he is actually in love with one of the ballerinas, so it has an extra little kiss, and a little following her around, and like that.

"It's small. It's small. But it's a lovely ballet. Without the style, it is nothing. It's the style that makes it."

Svend Kragh-Jacobsen wrote: "For the first time, Henning Kronstam was the teacher, who, with exquisite authority, directs the dances, gives little nods and in the decisive moments, joins the principal dancers as an elegant and superior and supportive partner in these small, but characteristic, pas de deux that are created with Bournonville's sense of both feminine and masculine dance" (Berlingske Tidende, September 2, 1968).

The Kermesse in Bruges

In The Kermesse in Bruges, Kronstam danced the clog dance in the first act as a boy and the second solo in the divertissement as a gala number. "Later I did the whole divertissement with Eva Evdokimova. The whole divertissement, two variations, and the coda and everything. I didn't do anything else. Carelis, I never touched. That was Fredbjørn's role."

He disliked the divertissement. "That's terrible to do. I hated it. It wasn't in the Bournonville version originally. It was put in later from another ballet. Maybe they were trying to make it longer, but it interrupts the story.

"That variation, the second variation for the man, was made for Hans Beck. It's nice to do in a dancing room. It's a nice variation. But on the stage you get so cramped, because it's really difficult. You have to do double tours down to arabesque plié, right away, right and left. And it has to be perfect. And that you will try out in the studio and it goes wonderfully and you have a good time with it, but on the stage there is the one to the right, and then one to the left, and if they're not there, then the evening is ruined."

La Ventana

La Ventana is also a divertissement, one of the ballets of local color that so delighted nineteenth-century audiences. Hans Brenaa tightened the ballet to make it look more contemporary, a "pure dance" ballet. *La Ventana* was not taught in the mime class because there are no mime scenes. "It's just a leading couple, her image in the mirror, and then six couples, corps de ballet, and then the pas de trois." Kronstam learned the pas de trois, the center boy in *Napoli's* first act ballabile, and James for the first American tour in 1956. The pas de trois in *La Ventana* is considered by many to be very difficult, but Kronstam found it easy. "For anybody else, it may be difficult, but for us who were brought up in the style, I don't think it's difficult at all."

What he did find difficult, as he did with any divertissement, is that there's no chance to warm up, not only the muscles, but as a performer. "You had to be warm. You had to know where you were [before you started]. It's not like coming down and getting into the role. You had to be there. This is one of the things I have been doing in the later years. I ask the young people [who would often not warm up on their own before a performance], 'Why do you think people buy tickets, if you don't do it full out?' You cannot go down on stage and think, 'Well, now it's going to come.' They bought their tickets maybe three weeks in advance to see this."

He danced the pas de trois with Kirsten Ralov and Inge Sand when he was very young. "They were jumpers, and they were really selling the goods, especially Inge. And then later, when I did the Señor, it was with Vivi."

"She has this little mirror dance first and then she has a variation. And then she throws her veil around her and she runs out and her room opens and you go right into the male variation. And then the corps de ballet [*sings and dances with hands*]. And when that's finished, you go back and in comes the pas de trois, coda, and in comes the Señorita. And that gets into a sort of *Don Quichotte* pas de deux—the one from the first act, a very melting pas de deux. And when that is over, then comes the finale. It's a divertissement. And the fun of it was, of course, that he [Bournonville] did [the mirror dance] for two sisters. We have done it with Viveka and Agneta Segerskog, two sisters, too.

"We haven't done it in years now. I thought it was a pity that Frank [Andersen] didn't bring it back for the [1992] festival. Of course, it's not the finest ballet in the world, but give it a chance."

In a review entitled "*La Ventana* after Being Tightened," Nils Schiørring wrote, "Truly there was carriage in Henning Kronstam's typical Bournonville male solo and in his seguedilla with Kirsten Petersen. Those were the most beautiful and joyful ballet moments of the evening. Here and in the final solo

As the Señor in *La Ventana*. Photo: Mogens von Haven. Private collection.

of the first scene, Kirsten Petersen showed her confidence and her sweetness as a dancer in beautiful motion."

The King's Volunteers on Amager

The King's Volunteers on Amager had been out of repertory for nearly thirty years when Hans Brenaa revived the ballet in 1971.[7] Kronstam had danced the hoop dance in the second act divertissement as a child. "I don't think we did *Lifeguards* [in the mime class] either, because the funny thing is, there's not that much mime in *Lifeguards*. It's very simple, what's happening, but you can't take [the mime] out and say, 'This is a full scene.' Because suddenly you dance, and then you stop.

"*Lifeguards* was one of the joys for me because when first I knew that I was going to do it, I started reading about Edouard Du Puy and found out that he was both a charmer and a bit of a villain. So I thought he was fun to make. I don't think anyone had done it the way I did it before because I made him more French."

In his "Oral History" Kronstam spoke in detail about Edouard: "I read about him because nobody explained anything. Just said, 'Well, this is Du Puy in *Lifeguards*. Here you are.' So I had to dig down and find out who, what was he, and who was he, and what did he do, and was he successful. . . . He was a composer, a musician, and he taught piano lessons to the king's daughter. She fell in love with him. His wife is in love with him. A countess in Jutland was in love with him—or in Funen was in love with him. The whole city was at his feet, you know. Now, all the rich and wealthy people were playing soldiers at that time, and there was an invasion from the English or the Swedish; I don't know what it was. And of course, he had to join the wealthy men's little army, and he, right away, became a løjtnant [lieutenant]. He was a very lucky man all the way through, but he was a little [bit] of a flirt."[8]

In the ballet's second act there is a party, set up by Edouard's wife, Louise, to teach her philandering husband a lesson. In this scene Edouard sits at the side of the stage for a time, surrounded by his equerries, who continuously bring him girls. "The whole male corps de ballet, all the soldiers, we had such life going on while I was sitting in the chair on the side and getting all those young soldiers to bring the girls down to me. All these kinds of things—we just figured out ourselves [the choreography was not set; some think this was because

As Edouard in *The King's Volunteers on Amager,* with Anne Marie Vessel and Vibeke Roland. Edouard plays a song of his own composition that reminds him of his wife, Louise. Photo: John Johnsen. The Royal Theatre, Copenhagen. By permission of Det kongelige Teaters bibliotek og arkiv.

Edouard flirts with the two Amager girls (Vibeke Roland and Anne Marie Vessel) before going off to war. Photo: John Johnsen. The Royal Theatre, Copenhagen. By permission of Det kongelige Teaters bibliotek og arkiv.

In the second-act divertissement, Edouard is enchanted by a masked woman (Vivi Flindt) whom he does not recognize as his wife. Photo: John Johnsen. The Royal Theatre, Copenhagen. By permission of Det kongelige Teaters bibliotek og arkiv.

Unmasked, Louise forgives Edouard, who swears his wife is his *only* true love. Photo: John Johnsen. The Royal Theatre, Copenhagen. By permission of Det kongelige Teaters bibliotek og arkiv.

Brenaa could not remember it, and it was not written down in the Notebooks.]
In a way, we created this with Hans, because it had been away for such a long
time."

The divertissements in the second act are danced by the ballet's characters.
Edouard dances the central man in a reel, with two men and four women. "You
can't do it if you don't put yourself in the spirit. You've got to put yourself in the
spirit of it, because if you're not having the spirit, building yourself up to it, it's
kind of silly to do all this stuff. But if you put yourself into it and have fun—
now, I had Mie [Anne Marie Vessel] and Vibeke Roland, and they were very
silly, funny girls, so we always had great joy doing it."

Edouard did not originally dance the reel; Emil, one of the young soldiers,
had this part. Hans Beck danced Emil as a young man and was very popular in
the reel; and when he took over Edouard, he kept that dance.[9] This had not
been explained to Kronstam, who said that in the 1970s Brenaa really didn't
give very much background instruction; he had to figure things out for himself. "I never understood why he changed costume, except that I thought it was
because he wanted to enjoy the party and have fun," he said. This may account
for Kronstam's slightly distant air in the reel. In a performance televised in the
mid-1970s, he dances it objectively rather than immediately, the way one
might expect him to do a sailor dance. It's the way a member of the upper
classes would have acted in those days, at such a party at a provincial inn, dancing with peasants. He does their dance, but he is not one of them.

Kronstam was especially effective in the final scene, when, tricked into ex-
changing favors with the enticing stranger he does not recognize as his wife, he
is forced to confront his misdeeds. Kronstam believed that, in the final analysis,
Bournonville's Du Puy loved his wife. "He says he does. And I think he—well,
when I played the role, I loved my wife. At the moment of truth, where Du Puy
says to her—she asks him, actually, 'Do you really love me?' And he says, with
only one finger, 'The only one [i.e., You are the only one].' That has always been
very true for me, when I said that. . . . always that minute—because it even now
gives me goose pimples because I think, it's such a simple—but she is asking
him, 'Are you really?' and he just does [i.e., mimes], 'You alone. All the rest is
just!'—because she has seen him with all the girls and everything, and that's
all he says. 'You are the only one.' So he believes—I believe—that he loves
his wife."[10]

A small detail indicates how thoroughly Kronstam worked through a character. Louise wears a very small mask, and it's difficult to believe that a man as intelligent as Du Puy would not guess her true identity. "You've got to use your imagination and think the mask is bigger than it is," he said. "Because all she's wearing is just a little thing. You've got to believe in your head that she is masked so he can't see her face. And the only time he really touches her is when he goes down to her and takes her waist, and then she disappears."

The King's Volunteers on Amager was a ballet that had been out of repertory for nearly thirty years. Hans Brenaa revived it, quite literally saving it from extinction. It's one of Bournonville's vaudeville ballets,[11] and sadly it is not highly regarded by contemporary Danes, although it is a mature work, dramatically and structurally perfect.

Edouard was the first of Kronstam's great Bournonville character roles. It was a deft portrayal of the perfect nineteenth-century gentleman-soldier. Kronstam made Du Puy seem contemporary by giving him an internal life—one could see him think, and sense what he was thinking—while staying absolutely true to the period of the ballet. He entered Du Puy's world and made it live. One of the most detailed reviews of Kronstam's Edouard was by Ulla Bjerre, one of the Danish critics who consistently valued Kronstam's artistry. While her review covers an evening when Kronstam did not dance, her account of what she found missing says more about Kronstam's performance in this work than many reviews of his actual performance:

> Some weeks ago Henning Kronstam injured his leg on stage and the night's performance had to be danced to its end without him. The accident happened just before the ballet staff's winter holiday and it was hoped that Kronstam would be well again when it was over. But instead he underwent surgery and *Livjægerne på Amager* was suddenly without a lieutenant to lead the jolly Shrovetide fun during the billeting at Farmer Tønnes's.
>
> On Monday night Flemming Flindt danced the part for the third time, and when it comes to the dancing everything was very good, even though the jolly sailor reel still lacks a little turn of the hips. But the elegant lieutenant, who according to Theatre history also was leader of the orchestra at the Danish Theatre, has to be so French and a charmer par excellence—a gentleman who can draw his sword, dance, and compose a serenade—and he must furthermore be a bold philanderer who can make the girls fall into a swoon of ecstasy. Flindt's Du Puy had not enough of all of this. The figure is still too loose in its outline and he lacks the warmth and fieriness in his look that Kronstam had and that made him so convincing and right for the part.

Far from Denmark

Far from Denmark is one Bournonville ballet that many wish had not been saved; it is not a favorite in Denmark. But Kronstam liked it. "I think it's fun," he said in his "Oral History." "And if you really look at the way he has constructed it, with a very short, twenty minutes, opening scene where you get the whole story absolutely clear in your eyes, you know what's going on, and then he has all the dancing in the second act."[12]

Kronstam danced two roles in *Far from Denmark,* the young Danish lieutenant, Wilhelm [a Du Puy in training], as a very young dancer, and Wilhelm's Latin rival, Don Alvar, when he was in his early forties. "Wilhelm was not as fun as Alvarez. He's so Spanish!" Kronstam said.

In a story that supports some dancers' contention that Kronstam was asked what he wanted to do and pretty much got his own way at this point in his career, Kronstam continued: "Brenaa had wanted me to do the captain on the ship, but I said, 'Never. Not in my life. When I just walk on with the other ones? Never.' And so he said, 'What do you want to do, then?' And I said, 'I want to do Alvar.' 'Okay. So you can do Alvar.'

Kronstam, with Brenaa's blessing, changed the role into a slightly comic one. "It hadn't been like that before, but I couldn't stand it. I had to make fun of it. You know, the whole plot, the whole ballet, is so idiotic, that you had to do something so that the audience at least has a sense of fun.

"He's a very vain man. And this is fun to do. Somebody that is always thinking, 'How do I look?' and 'How do I speak?' And the servants thrown around. And it's fun to play. And then of course, I had Vivi Flindt, and she was fun. She is so flirtious."[13]

A Folk Tale

With James, the Bournonville role to which Kronstam seemed most suited was Junker Ove in *A Folk Tale.* He got the role late in his career, as the ballet had been out of repertory for twenty years. *A Folk Tale* is no children's story but a very deep work that deals with the question of heredity versus environment—does one behave as one is brought up or as one is born? When the two natures are in conflict, how does that affect behavior?

"It's a typical Danish story, a Hamlet story, in a way. He [Ove] hopes that he can work it out with Birthe [his ill-tempered fiancée], but she is really too much. She and I together?—I just don't believe it." Kronstam's Birthe was Vivi Flindt, who he said, in his "Oral History"—quite happily—was "a sexual witch." "Vivi was very likable in that role. Of course, she had her changes of mood all the time, but at the same time, you know, I tried—playing the role, I tried only to see her when she was at her best and sort of ignore her when she had her bad moments. But at the same time, of course, he is concerned, you know. He thinks that, This can't work, you know. She gets worse and worse during that first act, and at the end, when he sits down, he just thinks, Well, maybe I have to skip the whole thing and just live alone."[14]

In 1995, watching a video of his performance (with Sorella Englund as Hilda and Vivi Flindt as Birthe), Kronstam described the action: "He takes the shoulders of the nurse and walks a little upstage and says, 'You go. I want to stay here.' He is not a dramatic person. I thought that the role was very close to a Hamlet person, a typical Danish melancholic man. He will be happy if only the sun would shine."

Alone in the woods, Ove feels the ground shake under his feet. A hill opens and he sees the troll family surrounding a beautiful maiden who is holding a golden cup. She comes forward to tempt him with it, offering him a drink. "He looks at the cup. He is a little worried. He says, 'No, I don't want to drink it' [Ove turns the cup over, emptying its contents onto the ground.] And then the flame comes. And then he says, 'You shouldn't have done that.'" In Kronstam's performance in the 1977 televised production, the clenched fist that he raises to Hilda is turned inward, and there's a measured righteousness in the gesture's rhythm that has archaic authenticity and force. Asked whether the gesture was remembered from a predecessor's performance or something the production's director had shown him, Kronstam answered, "No, that is how I learned it from Gerda Karstens back in 1950.

"He keeps [the cup] because it is a memory of her. Maybe she will come to him again. In their pas de deux—she's not looking at him so much as she is looking at that cup. So as long as he has the cup, he thinks she'll stay with him. He keeps it in his hands because Muri [the troll mother] says, 'Give it to me.' And he says, 'No, never.' And she calls all the elfins [elf maidens]. So now, that is another thing. He holds on to it during that whole elfin dance.

"What's difficult is the start of the third act, where he's half-mad. Because you've been hanging around during the whole second act. All the trolls are on the stage. Then comes the third act, and the curtain comes up, and right away

As Junker Ove, with
Hilda (Sorella Englund)
in the first act pas
d'action of Bournon-
ville's *A Folk Tale*. Photo:
John Johnsen. The Royal
Theatre, Copenhagen.
By permission of Det
kongelige Teaters
bibliotek og arkiv.

after the first dance you have to come on with your mind still [in the mood of]
the first act."

One of *A Folk Tale*'s difficulties for any Ove is to remain in the mood
through that long second act, where he is not on stage. "Professional people
will do that. But it's hard because you've always got to keep in your mind the
person you were in the first act. As far as Ove is concerned, no time has passed.
He is coming straight out—this is the night where the elfins have come, all
those girls in their dresses. This is the night, and then in the morning, the next
morning, then he comes. But you have to be the same, so the audience can
understand what has happened.

"He hasn't slept all night at all. He's met a girl that's completely different
from everybody else. He has been through that night with the elfins. He's seen
the whole earth raised up and little trolls running around. He's been dancing
with the elfins. So he is—he is not mad, but he is blurred.

"What used to happen in the old version is that he came forward in the third act, then one of the young peasant girls came toward him and said, 'Good morning.' And he got so scared, because he can't see. He thinks the girls are the elfins again. All of them. It's the holy water [to which Hilda, now free of the trolls, leads him] that helps him to get his brain back. He is all in a turmoil."

Junker Ove is almost completely a mime role, a true danseur noble role. It's all walking, with very little dancing. Others who have danced the role say that this is what makes it so difficult. But to Kronstam, walking to music was dancing. "It never bothered me. Never. I wouldn't say it's the most enjoyable role to do, especially that long second act [where Ove is not on stage but "sitting up in his room waiting to go down and do the third act"].

"In the last act, that was so beautiful, because I loved Sorella. I tell you. She looked at me like I was the god for her. And we were holding hands all the time, all through, sitting there—not on big thrones, as they do now, but on two little chairs, just holding each other. We really were in love. I had chills when she came in with the wedding dress. She was so pure."

Fredbjørn Bjørnsson, as Viderik, is heartbroken, as Junker Ove and Hilda (Anna Lærkesen) pledge their troth. Photo: John Johnsen. The Royal Theatre, Copenhagen. By permission of Det kongelige Teaters bibliotek og arkiv.

With Sorella Englund in the third act's wedding waltz. Photo: John Johnsen. Private collection.

Ove may be melancholic but he is not a Romantic hero. He is not searching for anything outside his world; he recognizes a foreign force within his world and flees from it, and, despite her allure, he rejects the dangerous choice—Birthe—for the noble, though enchanted, Hilda. "Don't you think that it's meant that he feels that she is a pure person? Not mischievous, just serene. Instead of playing all the games that Birthe plays, there is one who is straightforward. Good. And he instinctively knows that."

Of the productions he saw, or danced in, Kronstam admired Brenaa's the most. "Hans's production was much more lyrical. It had charm and was alive." He thought the one Kirsten Ralov had done under his directorship was "historical [accurate], but maybe not very dramatic."

Nothing Kronstam said is a better guide to how the Bournonville repertory was kept so long and so well, and how it could be revived after periodic lulls, than this: "Some of these roles are just taught to you and then you figure out what you do yourself. Hans Brenaa didn't produce me in it. I learned it from Gerda Karstens. There, I learned the mad scene, and I learned the first act, where Birthe is flirtious. And with Hans I just learned a little bit of dancing, and there it was."

Of Brenaa's 1969 revival of *A Folk Tale* (on a double bill with Balanchine's *Serenade*), Svend Kragh-Jacobsen, perhaps the last Danish critic to see the ballet as centered on Hilda and Junker Ove and not the trolls, wrote,

> The most important thing, however, is Hilda and Junker Ove. Henning Kronstam performed the latter with stylish noblesse, but there isn't much for him to do. However, in the healing scene by the spring there were expressions that spoke beautifully.
>
> Kronstam and Lærkesen looked like the blue Prince and Princess of the fairy tale.[15] That made us forget that there are, in fact, more beautiful colors and more warmth in a Danish midsummer than in the surrounding scene here. The Royal Theatre has a new ballet performance of old art that can give joy to both children and grownups who care about Bournonville's romantic danced fairy tale and Balanchine's music for the eye.

When Hans Brenaa left the company, Kirsten Ralov took over this production. It is this version that was filmed for Danish television. Ralov made no changes in the production at first; she staged her own version in 1979. Yet in a rather rude review called "Belittled Bournonville," Henning Jørgensen wrote:

> Bournonville's *Et Folkesagn* [*A Folk Tale*] should, I suppose, rightly be the ballet repertoire's national Romantic classic at the Royal Theatre. But if you, as the director, Kirsten Ralov, not as much handle as market Bournonville as musical standard goods, the tradition muddles along and belittles the work, dramatically as well as choreographically. . . .
>
> Kronstam was in pure control, poetically inspired in every expression, every movement, with mime and with dance, and sublime in the true scene of madness.

In the next decade Kronstam would be sublime in many true scenes of madness, as he began to dance more dark parts.

At first I thought he was just snobby. Then I
thought he was frightened. Then I thought he
was psychotic and then I finally realized that he
was many things, and very different from day
to day. He did not have a façade. He was one of
those people who did not have a public face. I
think one of the reasons he could be many
faces is that he had no public face.
—Bruce Marks

Nineteen

Dreamland

Kronstam was out most of the 1970–71 season, and when he returned it was to
two roles that wouldn't hurt his back or his leg: Edouard in Bournonville's *The
King's Volunteers [Lifeguards] on Amager* and the Man She Must Marry in
Antony Tudor's *Jardin aux Lilas*. While few would consider the latter a starring
role, Kronstam's performance is still talked about in Copenhagen.

Lifeguards was given on the same bill with *Jardin*—a brilliant piece of programming, as both ballets deal, in very different ways, with marriage and convention—and one of the most enthusiastic tributes to Kronstam comes from
Eliot Feld, who saw this program in Copenhagen.

The first ballet was *The Lifeguards of Amager*. There was this man who was
this kind of Errol Flynn, swashbuckling character, with great panache. He was
wonderful. And after the ballet, I asked a dancer in the company who I knew,

and she said, "Oh, that's Henning Kronstam." And I said, "Boy, what a wonderful, what élan, what"—he was extraordinary.

The next ballet was *Lilac Garden*. I had always thought that *Lilac Garden* was the best ballet ever made, although I had never seen a performance I'd liked. The curtain went up and there was the old man with Caroline, and it was—from the get-go it was just fantastic. She was disheveled, and her makeup was screwed up, her costume was torn. You had come in in the middle of a drama. You felt so much had preceded it, and the ballet went on to be extraordinary. It was an amazing performance. And after it was over, I was speaking to the same person again and I said, "Who played the older man?" And she said, "That was Henning Kronstam." I said, "Henning Kronstam was in the first ballet, but who was that?" And she said, "Henning Kronstam." To this day—I was standing forty feet from him, and it's a small theater—I was absolutely stunned.

Tudor staged *Jardin* himself and had a dream cast: Anna Lærkesen as Caroline (in what Kronstam thought was one of her greatest roles), Flemming Ryberg was Her Lover, Sorella Englund, only eighteen, was the Episode in His Past.

The Man She Must Marry is by no means a romantic hero. "That man was cold and a little bit mean," Kronstam said. "He is not up to her standards socially. That's what Tudor told me. He is nouveau riche. She is getting poorer and poorer, but she is from a noble family. And he buys her, and he owns her, and so he feels that he can do anything. He couldn't care less about anything. She just has to belong to him, and he'll pay.

"It's a little pearl of a ballet, but you have to have a very good cast. It's all little—little looks and little touches—and so you really have to be very much into it. Anna was very good in it."

Kronstam found the role very satisfying. "It was such small things; there were no big movements. It was just touching. The pas de deux with Sorella is a little stronger [than his moments with Caroline], because he still is in love with her and she wants to keep him. But he has to push her away because he's got other ideas. He wants an entrée into high society." It was these "small things" that dancers remember, especially the final gesture, when Kronstam took Lærkesen's arm and led her out. Everything about their relationship and their future together was in that gesture.

Tudor was "very precise, but sarcastic sometimes. That was usually with the corps de ballet, not too much with the principals." Kronstam would work with Tudor again, inviting him to stage two ballets for the company when he later

As the Man She Must Marry in Tudor's *Jardin aux Lilas,* with Anna Lærkesen as Caroline. Photo: John Johnsen. The Royal Theatre, Copenhagen. By permission of Det kongelige Teaters bibliotek og arkiv.

The last moments of *Jardin.* Flemming Ryberg is the Lover. Photo: John Johnsen. The Royal Theatre, Copenhagen. By permission of Det kongelige Teaters bibliotek og arkiv.

became ballet master. "He was a nice man. He wrote to me when he heard that I had retired as ballet master and said he was very sad to hear it, but he hoped that I would stay with the company as a guardian angel. You wouldn't think that that cold man could write something like that."

Sorella Englund remembered one rehearsal where she had to run and jump into Kronstam's arms, and she was very young and rather timid. Tudor goaded her: "He stopped me [in mid-run] in front of everybody on the stage and said, 'Is that the way you love a man?' So then I said, 'I'll show you how I love a man.'" She laughed at the memory. "He [Tudor] said this was the best cast he ever had, so it was a great compliment. Maybe he just said it, but he usually didn't say anything he didn't mean." Tudor was unusually generous with his praise in Copenhagen. After the premiere, Kronstam said Tudor, standing in the wings, told him, "And I thought *I* was the best in that ballet."[1]

Danish critics admired *Jardin* for its delicacy and its subtle and cruel psychological subtexts. One review suggested an interesting future for the unhappy couple: "Kronstam is again, with his whole psychological superiority and sense of occasion, powerful as her cold husband-to-be. . . . The erotic tensions are entirely left to the scent of the lilacs. When Lærkesen and Kronstam exit the stage, a certainty has been created in a brief quarter hour that they exit to a tragedy that will last as long as they can bear it." Of Kronstam, Svend Kragh-Jacobsen wrote: "Most secure of them all stood Henning Kronstam as the man who has chosen sides and cynically controls his feelings."

That season was Flindt's high-water mark as a choreographer and artistic director, with his theater piece called *The Triumph of Death*. It was very popular, especially with young people, many of whom came to hear the rock music. Although some critics questioned the artistic value of the work, Flindt was praised for bringing a new audience to the Theatre. It could be argued that what he was bringing them in to see wasn't ballet, however, and this would have repercussions in the next decade. *Triumph of Death* became the kind of piece the public expected from Flindt, and theater pieces rather than ballets would dominate the repertory.

In the 1971–72 season Flindt prevailed upon Kronstam to dance the Prince in his new production of *The Nutcracker*. Kronstam said he had not wanted to do it because he didn't think he should still perform classical parts. "Flemming said I had to do it because I was the only one who could run on stage," he said, and he agreed to do the role. He was afraid of the lifts, after his back injury, but

"Flemming promised me there wouldn't be any lifts, and then the whole thing was lifts, and I had Vivi as the Snow Queen." He was always uncomfortable dancing in the ballet and flatly refused to perform it in Moscow. "That version? In Moscow? In May? Never. So Bruce had to do it." (Bruce Marks, now married to Toni Lander, had joined the company, the first foreigner to dance with the Royal Danish Ballet as a solo dancer.)

Kronstam thought Marks had been responsible for giving him his next major role, one that suited him perfectly and that he loved doing: the Friend in José Limón's *The Moor's Pavane*. "I think it was Bruce who gave Flemming the idea," Kronstam said, "because he had danced it at ABT. Bruce and Toni knew it when Limón came, and it was Bruce who said, 'Henning should do Iago.' Bruce was a very big fan of mine at that time. And he thought Vivi should do Emilia. And afterward, Limón said it was the best cast he ever had."

The Moor's Pavane was performed by many ballet companies in the 1970s;

As the Moor's Friend in *The Moor's Pavane*. Photo: John Johnsen. The Royal Theatre, Copenhagen. By permission of Det kongelige Teaters bibliotek og arkiv.

With Vivi Flindt in *The Moor's Pavane*. Photo: John Johnsen. The Royal Theatre, Copenhagen. By permission of Det kongelige Teaters bibliotek og arkiv.

Nureyev and Bruhn both danced the Moor. It became a gala number, to the distress of many modern dance purists. There was a controversy, too, at the way ballet dancers performed the ballet, as many of the men who danced either the Moor or His Friend [Kronstam's part] changed turns into pirouettes, altering the very nature of the work, which was based on Limón technique, not classical ballet. Kronstam said that in Copenhagen this was done with Limón's blessing.

"Limón came and he had his friend, his Iago [Lucas Hoving], with him, because he was at an age where he couldn't show all the steps. We learned it in a very short time. It was a joy to do. I was so mean. I just loved it. I could get everything out of it—and Vivi was wonderful in it.

"It was fun, but it was hard. Thank God we had moments where we stood still, where you could get your breath back. I was doing it on a level so high that I used all my energy in it. So when I stood still, I had to turn my head to breathe. We were all doing it at a very high level, because I got Bruce up, and Bruce got me up. He was so suited to the role too, that it was perfect."

By this time Kronstam had danced enough modern dance roles to be more comfortable with the movement. "I didn't find it strange at all, because it had all the proper jetés—maybe when he [Limón] saw what I was like, he changed it. He let me do pirouettes and jumps and things like that because he thought it was in the character." Kronstam liked Limón. "He was a very warm man. Lucas would show the steps and Limón was just sitting there. 'I think it's good what you are doing, so let's just do it.' And Lucas would say, 'This is not the way we're supposed to do it.' And Limón would say, 'But I like what he is doing.'"

Limón didn't discuss the characterization, but Kronstam needed no further instruction. "It's all really in the choreography, the whispering and all that. I knew it from the play, and I knew it from reading. Iago is jealous. He envies that Moor. He's a racist, too. He hates it that the Moor should be a general, and that he should have a white, beautiful girl. He is against him. He feels superior to the Moor because he is a white man. So he wants to break him, to show him—that's what I felt. At the end, he feels no guilt, just 'Triumph. I [Iago] was right!'"

Kronstam always enjoyed playing unheroic characters. "You've got different sides in yourself, everybody's got that—jealousy and envy, all those things. You have to find it somewhere in yourself. It wasn't difficult." He laughed, then said, seriously, though it was whistling in the dark, "Maybe that's why I never had these breakdowns, like some people have had, because I've not just stayed being nice and kind on the stage."

The Moor's Friend was another of Kronstam's most admired roles during this period. Ulla Bjerre wrote, "Henning Kronstam's Iago is a court puppet. Every movement is meaningful, there is something sinister about his pointing fingers and affable attitudes, and the strong rhythmic emphasis that he adds to his dance brings back memories of Mephisto. His mime is without any discordant elements. He is most powerful in the passages without music, where the lead is all his."

Kronstam danced the ballet for about two and a half years, until Marks and Toni Lander left for Salt Lake City. Nureyev wanted to dance the ballet in Copenhagen, with Kronstam as Iago, but Kronstam backed out of that cast, feigning injury. Dancers say that everybody in the Theatre knew he wasn't really injured, and there was much speculation as to why, the most usual suggestion being that Kronstam was afraid of the competition. Without knowing that, he gave this account: "I knew the way Rudolf worked and I knew I couldn't deal with it. He had to change everything. He would never do what was set." Vivi Flindt thought it was more that Kronstam knew that Nureyev would not work well in an ensemble cast, that he would change the balance of the work. "Rudi never changed steps when he was here," she said. "He couldn't get away with it here like he could in London or New York."

Kronstam created roles in two new ballets by American choreographers for which he retained affection. The first was Eliot Feld's *Winter's Court,* which Kronstam described as a cross between *The Moor's Pavane* and *Lilac Garden.* Kronstam's wife in the ballet was Mette Hønningen, with whom he would often dance in the 1970s. "Mette is very vulnerable. At the same time, she stands on her rights. I have produced her in *Etudes* and other things. If she believes in you she will do the most gorgeous things. Alvin [Ailey] loved her. Glen Tetley loved her. But if she had a choreographer that didn't, or that thought she was mediocre, then she couldn't do anything. She had to have support all the time. She was one of the last of Volkova's pupils. She was a beautiful, beautiful dancer."

In *Winter's Court,* "I was a King, or a Lord. It started very nicely, but then I was so occupied with my hunting bird. My poor wife was sitting alone and then she fell for Johnny Eliasen, one of the courtiers. So it ended tragically. Nobody killed anybody—I don't think. I don't remember that. We just left each other. I went with my bird, she went with Johnny."

The hunting bird was problematic for the ballet as well as the marriage. Feld's original idea had been to have a live falcon, but Danish law forbade it and he had to settle for a mechanical bird, which proved stubborn and temperamental and made dancing the ballet very tense for Kronstam, who was always afraid that the bird wouldn't work and would spoil the performance. Feld told a story that is probably amusing only in retrospect: "This goddamned bird was worked by some kind of remote, so that its wings and its head could be manipulated from a little remote offstage. On opening night, the young dancer who was assigned to make the bird animate got involved with the music and had his hands on the dials, so here was the bird on the perch, pecking its head in absolute time to the music. I thought I would drop dead. If the bird could have been snapping its fingers, it couldn't have been funnier."

Aside from the bird, Kronstam liked the ballet. "Eliot was very kind to me. We got him at a high point in his career. I think the first half of the ballet was genius. The second half—he realized that it wouldn't work, so the second half was a letdown. Maybe the company didn't live up to him. But the choreography for the first half of the ballet had fantastic imagination."

Feld recounted one incident during the rehearsals that reveals an interesting aspect of Kronstam's personality and what he needed to work successfully: "I was working with him for a week or two, and one day Bruce Marks came to the rehearsal, because Bruce was going to do the second cast for this. And Henning was acting strangely on this day. Something was bothering him. After the rehearsal, I went to his dressing room and I said, 'Henning, something is the matter. Did I do something, or did something happen?' And he was very tense and very removed, and said, 'No, no, no, no.'

"And I said, 'I came here because of you. I am here only because of you. Something is the matter. I sense it. You must tell me, because we have to change this.' And he said, 'I can't talk about it.' I said, 'You must talk about it.' And he pulled himself physically into a tighter unit and said, 'I cannot share your attention. When I work with you, I bring everything to the studio. I must have all of you, as you have all of me.'

"And I said, 'Yes. Yes, I understand. I apologize. How stupid of me.' What he was saying is that 'I'm in a fit of passion, and I thought that that was mutual, and you are attentive to others. It is unacceptable.' And I thought, 'That's exactly like me. How could I have been so stupid as to think that I might cast an eye, however momentarily, on someone else?' That absolutely is the truth.

It is at the very center. It is an obsession that one shares with somebody. That's why he was a great, great, great artist. It was a moment that has stayed with me always, because I realized that somebody else felt as I felt, that his survival depended on the fulfillment of these moments. It wasn't his job. It was his actual being, his identity, his everything. It was a very extraordinary moment."

Feld also gives a very clear picture of Kronstam's perfectionism: "I remember him working endlessly when he couldn't get a certain shape, or a certain connection from one step to the other, or he couldn't find the melody in space, the geometry that steps made in a volume of space, in three-dimensional space, when he couldn't find the tune of it. And working endlessly and obsessively so that it was integrated for him in a way that made sense."

Another ballet Kronstam enjoyed doing was Bruce Marks's first work, *Dichterliebe*. "*Dichterliebe* was a beautiful ballet. I think that was the best that Bruce did. He had a good cast for it. I was Schumann and he was Heine, and Mette was Heine's grown love, and Sorella was mine." Told that Marks had indicated it was the other way around, Kronstam shrugged. "Well, if he knows that, then he knows that. But I think I was Schumann. I read Heine, but I definitely think I was Schumann. Bruce did a very beautiful ballet. I had many letters from people in the conservatory of music writing that it was so beautiful to have a singer singing all the songs. And then I had Sorella. I died in Sorella's arms. I was so happy with that." (Sorella Englund remembered *Dichterliebe* as "all happiness" and several dancers feel that it is a ballet worth reviving.)

"There were lots of duets, and at the same time, there was a connection between the two men," Kronstam said. "Heine and Schumann. I liked that ballet. Flemming didn't like it. It was too pretty. The audience liked it."

Marks also had an affection for *Dichterliebe*. "In doing my first ballet, I certainly wanted Henning there, and what I did in *Dichterliebe* was make us two parts of the same person. So he was Heine and I was Schumann, or vice versa, depending on how you wanted to look at it, but we were mirror images of the same person. I'm not sure how good a ballet it was, but it was certainly fun to do. And he read Heine for weeks before, and I'd catch him with his books of poetry and his investigation of this life. At the end of the ballet he was tremendously touching."

Kronstam got another meaty character role from Rudi van Dantzig, who came to stage *Monument for a Dead Boy* for the company. Van Dantzig remembered that when he first came he wanted Ib Andersen, then only sixteen, in the leading role, and Kronstam resisted the idea, saying that although Andersen was extremely talented, he had not yet done a leading role and might not have the experience to carry a ballet. Kronstam seemed very reluctant to change the casting, specifying another dancer for the part. Van Dantzig mistakenly believed that Kronstam was the company's director (he thought Flindt, who was away at the time, was merely the resident choreographer) and so thought Kronstam was being timid, afraid to take a chance on a young dancer. It is likely that Kronstam had been left in charge by Flindt with instructions on casting and did not feel he had the right to change it without Flindt's approval. But Van Dantzig insisted and Andersen got the role—and handled it very well.

Kronstam did not mention this, saying only, "Rudi van Dantzig came and he chose, first, Ib for the young boy, and Linda [Hindberg] for his dream girl, and Lis Jeppesen, who was very young at that time, for the little girl in white, the innocent. Johnny [Eliasen] was the homosexual school friend, I was the father, and Jette Buchwald was the mother. I was really common, down to

As the Father, Kronstam, with Jette Buchwald (the Mother), drags Ib Andersen (the Boy) in Dantzig's *Monument for a Dead Boy*. Photo: John Johnsen. The Royal Theatre, Copenhagen. By permission of Det kongelige Teaters bibliotek og arkiv.

scratching my arm pits and being really ugly. When the boy looks at his parents, that's all he sees. He sees a father who was a drunkard, dirty. He never takes a shower. And whenever he needs it, he just takes his wife and throws her dress up and fucks her. That's what the boy remembers of marriage, and this is why he turns to the schoolboy instead of to Linda.

"But at the end, when the boy gets really frightened, he runs to the father, and then the father is sort of a Christ figure, all dressed up. The boy comes to him because he is lost. The father is kind to him then. At the first point, when he sees the father and mother, it's a very low, common family. But after he's been through—it's not a story about the father, it's a story about the boy—when he's been through all the difficulties in the world, he turns again to this father. Then the father is kind of a Christ figure that he can hang on to.

"I enjoyed that one too. I had a good time with him because he was such a dirty old man. Franz hated it. He said, 'You look exactly like your father would if he was living in the dirt.' Because I was bald, gray-haired, dirty, old whiskers."

Van Dantzig told another story that is absolutely unique, though quite credible. Kronstam invited him out for a meal. They talked shop, and during the conversation Kronstam revealed fears about working in the studio that he does not seem to have shared with any other colleague. Kronstam talked of being afraid of working with the dancers, saying that sometimes he would come to the Theatre but be too afraid to go inside. "Sometimes I am so frightened by the way they look at me that I can't get enough courage to walk in the room," he said. Several dancers mentioned that there were times when Kronstam would pause outside the room, take a deep breath, and physically pull himself together—"pull himself into a physically tighter unit," as Feld had described in another context—before entering the room. This is an indication of the fear Kronstam had to face and overcome during a large part of his working life.

In February and March the Royal Danish Ballet made its first tour to the Soviet Union, dancing in both Leningrad and Moscow. It was a very "sweet time" for Kronstam, as Volkova was returning to her country for the first time since she had left it nearly fifty years before, and he went with her for a tour of the city, seeing all the places she had loved. "There were still people at the theater that remembered her," he said. "The dressmakers, some of the old dancers. It was beautiful to see."

Volkova, always enterprising, managed to get them tickets to see *Don Quixote*

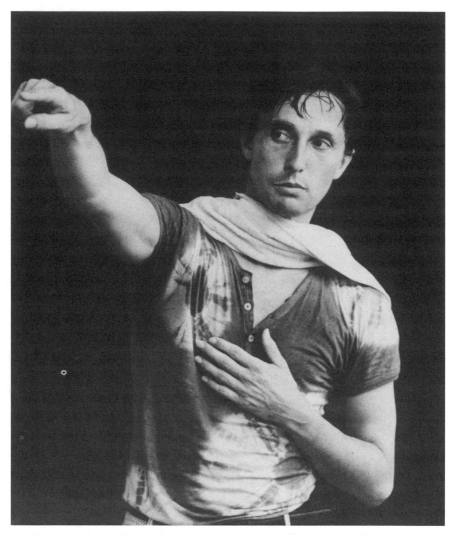

Teaching in Cologne during the summer. Photo: A. Löffler. Private collection.

in Leningrad—seats in what was once the czar's box, and then reserved for top Communist Party officials. Kronstam said that everyone stood when they entered the box, assuming that they were important guests of the state, which greatly amused them. He was not very impressed with *Don Quixote*. He thought the mimes didn't understand what they were doing, and he liked only "Misha's [Mikhail Baryshnikov's] solo in the last act, because that was absolutely extraordinary." Kronstam took a class with Alexander Pushkin when he was there, but he found the great teacher "very old," and also, at that time, Kronstam had had so many injuries that he preferred to take Volkova's class, which accommodated them.

Back home in Copenhagen, Kronstam danced two roles in a program of new choreography, one in a ballet by Eske Holm, another by Marks. It was a very dark, very difficult program emotionally.

In Holm's *Kronike* he played a priest, and his only instruction was to sit at the side of the stage and watch the action (a series of violent, tragic, or depraved events) until the very end of the ballet. Holm was a dancer with an interesting personality, though not a strong technician. He eventually left the Theatre to work in modern dance, where he remains a strong and controversial force on the Copenhagen dance scene.

"*Kronike* was the one where I was sitting in a chair on the side of the stage and seeing all the vulgar things going on. At the end I walked over, and I was standing on top of that girl, praying for her. I didn't do much. I walked over the stage at the end of the ballet. Then I had to go down and do *Asylum* immediately.

"Can I say something strange?" Kronstam said, which always meant that he was about to say something that some might consider too revealing or egotistical. "I did that myself. It was forty-five minutes. The whole ballet went through my mind while I was sitting, and I reacted to everything in it, the girl who was raped, everything. There was a spot[light] on me all the time. I had the agony of how people live, how children die, things like that. Then I had to walk over the stage and look at the little girl who had been raped. And maybe he [the priest] wanted to do it himself. It was not a bore to do because I had lived the story."

To perform *Asylum,* Bruce Marks's second ballet and one of the strangest, and certainly most challenging, roles Kronstam ever had, immediately afterward must have been extremely difficult, because he would not have had much time to get himself into the mood. That may have been a good thing. "That was a very strange ballet," was the general comment. "Humph," sniffed one dancer when looking over Kronstam's role list. "Did he ever tell you this was the *worst* ballet he ever had to be in?"

Asylum was very controversial among the dancers. Marks said that this ballet about mental illness was suggested by memories of visiting his schizophrenic grandmother in a mental institution when he was a child. Dancers, asked to do what they considered very invasive, personal things on stage, felt that Marks was trying to strike back at them because he had never been really accepted in Denmark. At the beginning of rehearsals, Marks asked the dancers in the cast to write down their greatest fear. They did. Then Marks literally choreographed those fears. Someone afraid of dying of drink was in the asylum because she was an alcoholic. Someone afraid of losing a child was there because she lost a child. Fairly or not, the dancers took this personally, and the atmosphere in the rehearsals was extremely uncomfortable. Several dancers dropped out of the ballet.

Kronstam was not asked to write down his greatest fear, which probably made him feel even more insecure, as he knew everyone else had been asked. Dancers felt that Marks pushed Kronstam very hard psychologically in rehearsals. Kronstam played a man who raped two children, a boy and a girl, went mad, was institutionalized, and was castrated in the end.

As the Priest in Eske Holm's *Kronike,* with Inge Jensen. Private collection.

In Bruce Marks's *Asylum*. Photo: John Johnsen. The Royal Theatre, Copenhagen. By permission of Det kongelige Teaters bibliotek og arkiv.

"I didn't realize how far he would go," Kronstam said. "Bruce sent letters to the people he wanted and asked them what was their biggest fear in the world. To Lis, it was to be raped. And I raped her in the ballet, of course. *Asylum* was something where I had to go out of myself completely." He found it much more difficult than *Bagage*, for example. "In *Bagage*, I was a person. *Asylum*, this was just an idea of Bruce's."

Marks said that he intended for Kronstam to be him (Marks) in the ballet. Kronstam realized that "only later. I am the one who hasn't been asked about my fears. I must be Bruce. It was dangerous, really. It was very far out psychologically. I don't think he knew how far he could go."

Marks's account was more benign: "In my second ballet, Henning was the protagonist. I had wanted to do a ballet about my experiences in childhood with my grandmother, who was schizophrenic. I started going to asylums when I was six years old and had vivid, nightmarish memories of these places. And I wanted to do something about that and wondered how I could make a group piece about it. I asked the dancers to write down their worst fears. I didn't ask Henning to do that, and I knew I should not do that. Henning's nightmare was my nightmare because I was Henning in the ballet, and I choreographed it for him so that I could be him.

"I wondered, really, how far I could go with him, and go with the whole thing of the—he thought it was emasculation. It was never my intention for it to be about that. It was really about the duality of this man/woman person. I made it about a man who, because of his confused sexuality, was a pedophile. Because it was clear that [Lis] Jeppesen and [Thomas] Berentzen were children. I put a sheet on them and had them stand one on top of each other to make a tall person [Jeppesen stood on Berentzen's shoulders]. And the central figure, Henning, danced a kind of mad waltz with this tall person, and he indeed did rape them. I made them two people, a boy and a girl, instead of having it just be a boy. It ended up having him locked up. They come out and they put this straitjacket on him, and he does the last solo in a straitjacket. And they do an adagio. And they finally pull down—the straitjacket has a roll here, and it becomes a dress. And I thought, 'This guy is never going to get through this ballet. He will refuse to do this.'

"Well, he did it. The solo in the straitjacket was so hard. You had to do all this jumping, and beats, kind of frantic beating things, without the use of your arms. And he did it and he was amazing in it. He was frightening.

"Throughout the process I was so frightened that he would leave, and I would have no ballet if this man left." Marks did not discuss anything with Kronstam in rehearsal. "I did it through the movement. I didn't do it through words about who this person was. I was convinced that he knew who he was, that if anyone knew what they were doing [it was he]. All the other people had to be told, 'This is a scream here.' But not Henning.

"He was amazing and he pulled it through. Other people asked to be taken out of it because it was too personal or too painful. I tried to use older dancers too, something one didn't do, and they got very excited about doing this, and then when they found out what it was, so many of them probably had connections to this kind of activity that they said, 'No, I don't want to be in this.' It is the ballet I've loved most, and that I felt absolutely injured by people not being moved by it."

Marks gave an interesting portrait of Kronstam at this time, and of his position within the social framework of the company. He, like Tetley, thought Kronstam was separate in some way from the others. "There was everybody, and then there was Henning. Henning was apart from everyone; he was on a different level. You used to take the measure of Henning from twenty feet before you decided whether you were just going to say, 'Goddag' or if you were going to try and talk to him. Henning created a distance. He was what he wanted to be, or had to be at the moment. If he had to be totally uncommunicative to protect himself, he would do that. If he wanted to make small talk, he did. If he felt good after a performance—you could always go by his room. He always had visitors. Franz would come with one lady friend of theirs [Jytte Abildgaard] and you could tell, as you passed the room, what the feeling was coming out of the room, as to whether you—you were never invited in—but whether you could come in and, in a sense, celebrate—he had passed the hurdle."

Shortly after *Kronike* and *Asylum*, Kronstam danced in another ballet about death, Flemming Flindt's *Dreamland*. "*Dreamland* was a beautiful ballet Flemming did for me. It was a man in a happy marriage and the wife dies. I had a suffering variation, and then I met them, I met my children and my wife, my father and my mother, in another world. The children had died too. They had all died. That was about the time when Flemming lost his mother, whom he was very attached to. That was a suffering ballet. This was one of the beautiful things Flemming did for me."

Ebbe Mørk wrote of Kronstam's performance: "[He is] the man with dreams.

His dramatic expression has grown into the very rare, and in *Dreamland* he appears as a romantic Albrecht from *Giselle* but rooted in another time and in other expressions. Mette Hønningen is his love—dead and alive—and the two of them make an exceptional couple, especially in their great pas de deux, where Flindt is closest to the best of his talent" (May 20, 1974).

When Kronstam spoke about his roles, unless he had staged the ballet himself, he did not analyze them as he would as ballet master but as he remembered them as a dancer. He unconsciously put himself back in the time and mindset that he had had at the time he danced the role. The dancer of the 1970s seems a very different man from that of the 1950s and 1960s. While "I had to make something of that" is a common thread throughout, the younger man took chances constantly and would never turn down a role. As he matured Kronstam seemed to gain confidence in some ways and to lose it in others. In his late thirties he did turn down roles, and several times he gave up a role because he didn't feel able to maintain it himself. This may be one reason why dancers of different generations had different opinions of how Kronstam would function outside the Royal Danish Ballet. The Kronstam of the 1950s and 1960s flew to foreign companies, partnered foreign ballerinas, and danced difficult roles on only a few days notice with little coaching. The Kronstam of the 1970s does not seem to have been able to do that. As he grew older, as his range grew, he sometimes could not draw on his own resources. Perhaps this was because he did not believe in himself and needed someone to say he could do a role. Flindt seems to have sensed this and was very helpful in this way, not only giving Kronstam opportunities but prodding him to accept them.

Perhaps Kronstam's confidence as a younger man had been grounded in his technique—something over which he had control. Perhaps his reticence was rooted in experience. He had worked with this choreographer or that coach and knew that the person would not be able to give him what he needed. Perhaps his standards had been raised too high, or perhaps his self-confidence was eroding from within, as the "ups and downs" began to worsen, with corrosive effects. Whatever the reason, shortly after *Dreamland,* and shortly before his fortieth birthday—a difficult birthday for any dancer—Kronstam had reached a breaking point. "There comes a certain time when you can't dance to the music, your knees go, your ankles are going wrong and everything. And we go mad, because it's a long, long life in the Theatre, and we do *Asylum* and all these crazy things. And that takes a lot out of you."

With Mette Hønningen in Flemming Flindt's *Dreamland*. Photo: John Johnsen. Private collection.

"I took every pill we had in the house," he said. "I wanted to do it." Kronstam had neither talked about suicide nor given any indication that he was planning it. "I came home one night with all my problems, and Franz was there with all these people. He was going to start a political party. And I went into my room and took pills."

After the guests had left, Gerstenberg went to Kronstam's room to say good-night and realized what had happened. He called his cousin to come and take care of the dogs, and then called Jytte Abildgaard to take them to the hospital. He probably didn't call an ambulance because he wanted to keep the incident out of the papers. Kronstam was unconscious for three days. "When I woke up, Franz was there, sitting there, feeding me soup," something Kronstam mentioned often in the weeks following Gerstenberg's death, as though this was one tangible proof he had that the older man really had cared for him.

When he left the hospital, Kronstam went back to the company and offered no explanation for his absence. "I think Vera knew, because she asked me if I was all right and I said yes. But when I was teaching I said, 'Boys, you're going to have to let me take it easy for a few days.'" Characteristically, he was simultaneously stoic and needy. "Not one of them asked how I was or what was wrong with me," he said, although he would have been very embarrassed if they had, because it would have meant that his façade had cracked. He certainly wouldn't have told the dancers if he had not told Volkova, as the two were very close by that time.

Neither Flindt nor any of the dancers, even those close to Kronstam, ever suspected what had happened. This suggests that by this time they were used to seeing Kronstam come to the Theatre looking very down, and being quiet and withdrawn. The season ended, Kronstam and Gerstenberg went on vacation, and he returned the next season as though nothing had happened, although photographs of him during this period show him as more fragile, looking a bit lost and wispy.

"I wanted to get out. Simply get out. I didn't care. You're forty. You start feeling that you cannot do everything. I thought, Now this is it. I might just as well leave. But then I had the teaching to do and suddenly those parts came back. Flemming used me a lot in his ballets.

"I probably have gotten into something else that made me stay. Vera was still here, and I enjoyed teaching very much. I taught the children first and then company class. Sometimes I did afternoon classes too, and I danced in the evening." When Kronstam said, "I might just as well leave" in this context it was not clear whether he was talking about leaving life or leaving the Theatre. For him, they were always much the same thing.

You're lost before you enter [the stage] in the
big roles. You're very alone, this excitement and
this anxiety—this breathlessness. . . . I accept
the mystique in the art of ballet because it is
there. Not the purely technical and the basics—
that's something you work on—but those who
suddenly transform all this knowledge to an
experience. It is mystical, it is something that's
built into the talent. . . . presence, that's what
you buy the ticket for, to see it. Otherwise you
might as well watch television or go to the
movies and see the same movie every night.
But what we long for is the unexpected.
—Henning Kronstam, *Politiken,* 1977

This Breathlessness

The years between 1974 and 1977, between the time that his dancing career
slowed and when he finally agreed to become artistic director of the Royal Danish Ballet, was one of the few periods when Kronstam's private life took, if not
center stage, at least a bow. In the mid 1960s, Kronstam and Gerstenberg had
moved to a five-story apartment building on Peblinge Dossering, on the north
banks of one of Copenhagen's lakes. They bought the building, and another on
the other side of town. Gerstenberg managed the real estate, as he managed
their other investments. While Kronstam seldom socialized with dancers at
this point in his life, he made friends with several neighbors, most of whom he
met while walking his dogs.

Gerstenberg had bought a basset hound, which he named Winston, in the
early 1970s, but the puppy was lonely and howled. They thought they should

get another to keep him company, and so Iago entered the family (named, of course, for Kronstam's role in *The Moor's Pavane*). "And so they howled together," Kronstam said. Dancers remember one evening when Kronstam took the dogs to the Theatre and left them in his dressing room, and they wailed so loudly that everyone in the Theatre could hear them.

The banks of the lakes are a wonderful place for dog walkers; at dusk one can see dozens of dogs and their owners. In the autumn of 1973 Kronstam met a young woman, Lene Schrøder-Hansen, walking her dog, Totte. Schrøder-Hansen would be a close friend until the end of his life. She and her mother lived in a few houses away on the same street and they became Kronstam's second family.

"In the beginning it was an informal thing," Schrøder-Hansen remembered. "The first time he came here, I think he came into the garden when we were sitting out on the porch and he was walking by. Then, when he was walking the dogs, he would come by and sit, and perhaps he would have a beer, or a

Lene Schrøder-Hansen
in the 1970s. Private
collection.

cup of coffee. My mother was always a polite person, asking, 'What can I get you?' That would probably be on Sundays or a summer evening when he wasn't working. So that was the beginning. I don't remember when Franz came into the picture, when he started coming here too. He probably came with Henning.

"Then it got more formal—not more formal, but we'd talk on the phone and say, 'Won't you come to dinner tomorrow?' or something like that. But also, often either Franz or Henning would come by and just come in. Later, Franz would come here alone, if Henning was in the Theatre working. Then Franz would come here, with the dogs and so on. Or if he thought he needed a beer and could have one for free."

Schrøder-Hansen, then in her early twenties, said that Kronstam "had great respect for my mother. They talked about music—my mother loved music. He insisted on calling her *De* [the Danish formal form of *you*]. He said that the people he had respected the most and loved the most, he always said De to them. He wanted her to say *du* to him [the informal form], but he wanted to say De to her, and she wasn't the type of person who would do that." So they remained on formal terms. Kronstam was always drawn to older women, especially mothers. He had been very close to Agnes Gerstenberg, as well as Jytte Abildgaard's mother. Now, Elly Schrøder-Hansen became another mother in his life.

Lene Schrøder-Hansen and Margrethe Noyé are among a very few people who regularly saw Kronstam in relaxed, social situations in the last twenty years of his life.[1] While there were certainly dancers whom he liked and with whom he was close professionally, there was always a barrier between Kronstam and his colleagues. With Noyé (who shared a house in Spain with Kronstam and Gerstenberg)[2] and Schrøder-Hansen, Kronstam was more relaxed than he was at the Theatre.

It is easy to see why Kronstam was drawn to Lene Schrøder-Hansen. She is an intelligent woman with a sense of humor who seems able to see the good in everyone—a rare combination—and is very levelheaded. She began her interview with a decisive: "You must not exaggerate my importance." She had been a ballet fan since girlhood and had admired Kronstam before she knew him. The friendship deepened over time, and she probably saw him more frequently than anyone during the last twenty years of his life. "I think I was his chance to live a normal life, away from all his problems at the Theatre," she said, not knowing that this was exactly how Kronstam had described Albrecht's attraction to Giselle.

"We'd see each other, sometimes several times a week, and some weeks we wouldn't even meet. But almost every Saturday we would meet, because we would go shopping together in the morning. We would usually walk in [to Kongens Nytorv] and do the shopping on the way. So I would see him most Saturdays, and several times, when he had the dogs, we would take a stroll with the dogs in the evening. My offices were very close to Kongens Nytorv, so I would often see him in the morning. On weekdays we would take the bus in—not every day, because he would have different times at the Theatre." Kronstam and Gerstenberg would come once or twice a month for dinner. "But he might come here more than that. He might come just when he was taking a walk. Just walking the dogs, he could simply drop in. Sometimes they would call me and say, 'Can you come over to discuss this and that?'" Kronstam would also take Lene to the ballet. "The first time was in 1976, I think, when Nureyev was dancing here. I remember it quite vividly. We met a lot of people that night," people who knew Kronstam and approached him in the Theatre for a brief chat. Once, as a "birthday treat," Kronstam took Schrøder-Hansen backstage and introduced her to some of the dancers.

Although Lene Schrøder-Hansen and her mother were invited to Kronstam's flat, it was never for a meal, nor were they taken out for dinner. "I think Henning took me out to dinner once. I don't think it was more than once. But before the theater or after the theater, we'd go to D'Angleterre or to Brønnum's to have something to drink, and he would pay. So he was able to pay. But he wouldn't say no if I said, 'No, tonight it's my treat.'"

Schrøder-Hansen provides an interesting picture of Kronstam as his neighbors saw him. "If you talk to people around here, the people who lived close to him, they all miss him, and they love him a lot. When he was out of the Theatre he was just a simple, gentle person." Kronstam was generally kind to strangers, she said, but only if they approached him. On their walks through town she observed him interact with his fans. "There were always people who wanted to get to know him and to talk to him. One time a ballet had been on television. I remember the following day going with him and people stopped him and said, 'Oh, we saw you on the television yesterday,' and 'Oh, it was so good,' and so on. And he would always be very kind. He would never just nod and walk away. He would always talk to them."

During the period when Kronstam was ballet master, the two fell into the habit of doing Saturday morning shopping together. He was very careful with money and tried to avoid situations where he would be tempted to spend it. "He wouldn't walk on Strøget[3] because he said there were too many stores and he wanted to buy everything. He was very sensible about money. He wasn't a big spender. The few times he bought me presents—I bought a trench coat, and I remember saying to him, 'How could I buy this thing? The color is no good for me, and it's so dull, and how did I do that?' And then shortly after was my birthday and he came with a scarf in red and some other colors. He had actually gone to a store and bought it for me."

This was a rare event. Kronstam did not often give presents. This was not because he was ungenerous, Schrøder-Hansen thought, but because all his life he had been the one receiving presents; that was his role. "Henning was so used to being the one having all the attention and being spoiled. People would look up to him and admire him. He was the one who was usually fêted. He was accustomed to people having him as their guest and being the star of the party, so he wasn't used to the fact that it could go the other way round, that he could do something for other people. I think it wasn't lack of will or ability, it was simply not thinking.

"I would remind him of my mother's birthday because I knew how much he liked her, and I knew how much she would appreciate him remembering her. So I would always, a few days earlier, tell him, 'She is having a birthday,' or, 'Won't you come?' for instance. He was here several times on her birthday. So he would remember her more than he would remember me because I wouldn't say to him, 'Oh, it's my birthday.' He would bring her flowers and he was always so happy to see that people were happy to receive his gifts."

When Kronstam came to dinner or dropped in on Friday nights, when Fru Schrøder-Hansen held an open house and served tea and cold cuts to friends who dropped by, they would discuss "everything. Books, music, people we knew. He read a lot. Mostly fiction, new fiction, mostly serious fiction, but in the traditional way, nothing experimental. And biographies. We would exchange books. We had a common love in Herman Bang. When he made *Bagage,* he read all of Herman Bang's books, not just that short story. He loved to read and he loved music. He was interested in art. He wouldn't go to museums very often—he would when he was abroad, but not so often here. But he was interested in all kinds of art.

"He would not often talk about the Theatre. I would talk about my work to him a bit.[4] He was very patient with me. So when I had one of my fits, when I was angry or sad or irritated, he could always say something that would make me laugh. He would always have an ironic remark."

Although it is difficult to find a dancer with anything good to say about Franz Gerstenberg, both Schrøder-Hansen and Noyé liked the older man, who could be charming and amusing. Noyé had known Gerstenberg since he was a teenager and knew how to handle him. He could be a bully and, like all bullies, retreated when challenged. Then, she said, he would turn childlike and ask for forgiveness. She felt that Gerstenberg was devoted to Kronstam to the exclusion of anyone or anything else, and that his frequent outbursts of temper, or just plain nastiness, to dancers and other Theatre people were deliberate, a way to keep them away from Kronstam. Gerstenberg was the watchdog, but there was another side to him as well. "I wouldn't have spent so many vacations with him if he were a monster," as Noyé put it.

Schrøder-Hansen also had a more balanced view of Gerstenberg. "I always said we were best enemies. Franz could be kinder and more generous than Henning in many ways. He would always remember birthdays, for example. But one thing I did not like is that he would tell Henning that people didn't like him. I remember Henning calling and saying they couldn't come for dinner because Franz was ill, and I said, 'Oh, then can't *you* come?' because we would rather have had Henning than Franz, and he seemed very surprised that we would want him to come on his own." Gerstenberg could be irascible and bossy. He would call dancers at the Theatre and curse at them on occasion, especially young men to whom he thought Kronstam might be attracted. Dancers naturally assumed this was the way Gerstenberg treated Kronstam at home. Schrøder-Hansen saw no evidence of that, although she, too, had felt Gerstenberg's tongue and been a party to several uncomfortable scenes. When Gerstenberg was in one of his nasty moods, Kronstam would not intervene, she said, but would simply leave the room.

Although it was never discussed, Schrøder-Hansen understood that Kronstam was homosexual and, as she put it dryly, "I didn't have any dreams." This is probably one of the reasons Kronstam trusted her. Too often, women had mistaken friendship, or the expressions of love that seemed so sincere in the studio or on stage, for something more. Kronstam was very masculine with women. "He was always 'the man,' when we went out," Schrøder-Hansen said, "always the one in control." There was a persistent rumor at the Theatre that Kronstam was really heterosexual and that Franz had effectively kidnapped him and kept him away from women. Kronstam had given them reason to believe this. As a young man, he had gone to parties with the other dancers where he enjoyed kissing the girls. Arlette Weinreich remembered that at her sister's twenty-fifth birthday party, Kronstam took the sister upstairs, where they made out passionately in a corner until discovered by another of the company's women, who reacted with jealousy; there are several similar stories.

The only important regret of Kronstam's life was that he never had children. "He was good with children," Schrøder-Hansen said. "He liked to talk to them. He loved Torben's [his nephew's] children. When he was in China, he bought a gold chain with a Chinese letter that means 'love and happiness' for the christening of Line Kronstam [Torben's first child]." Perhaps he thought now that his career as a dancer was coming to a close he should marry and have a family. Sometime in the 1970s, Kronstam had an affair and became engaged briefly to a friend of Jytte Abildgaard's, a charming and high-spirited young woman named Anna. Abildgaard has a photograph of the two of them on holiday. Anna is small, dark, and very pretty. Kronstam looks absolutely enchanted with her.[5] They eventually decided not to marry, they told friends, because Anna thought she was not ready to settle down. Kronstam too may have had second thoughts. What he said in describing his role in Cranko's *Lady and the Fool* seems significant here. "He was not up to it [marrying La Capricciosa]. He was happy being down in the street with his friend." In the last years of his life Kronstam often mentioned his regret at not having children to many people, but he could not take care of a wife and children and have a career at the Theatre. The idea of marriage and children lingered for a while. Shortly after he resigned as ballet master—Schrøder-Hansen couldn't remember if it was in 1985 or 1986—he announced, without warning, "I think it's time that Lene and I got married." "Franz took some pills the next day," Schrøder-Hansen said, "and that was the last we heard of that." In 1989, when Denmark enacted domestic partners legislation, Kronstam and Gerstenberg got married. "We waited for about ten days because everybody was going down to the town hall, looking at all the gays and lesbians. But when all that died down, we went in, and there was a nice woman and she said, 'Now, you must promise to take care of each other,' and I said, 'But that's what we've been doing all our lives.'"

In the 1974–75 season, Kronstam had only one new role, that of Lord Capulet in John Neumeier's *Romeo and Juliet*. Neumeier, who enjoyed a very high reputation in Europe as a dramatic choreographer, had long ties to the Danish ballet. He, too, had been a pupil of Volkova, coming to Copenhagen as a teenager one summer to take classes with her. "Those classes were extraordinary," he said, as the other dancers in class with him were Bruhn, Kronstam, and Nureyev. Neumeier also had long talks about ballet and choreography with Volkova, who was very encouraging. From his student days, Neumeier had wanted to be a choreographer, one in the line of Noverre and Bournonville. Ib Andersen, who was the first Romeo in Neumeier's production in Copenhagen, remembered him as an exacting director. "After the first stage rehearsal he gave us forty-five minutes of notes. Forty-five minutes. He was so detailed in what he wanted." Dancers often mention this attention to detail and the care Neumeier takes with his productions—and with dancers—and it is one of the reasons why Neumeier is so respected by them.

Romeo and Juliet was a hit with dancers, critics, and the audience. Critics thought it an example of the kind of ballet the company should commission or create and it remained in repertory for more than twenty-five years. "Neumeier had done it in Frankfurt, and then he came here and he got a lot of money and had Jürgen Rose to do the sets, which were gorgeous," Kronstam said.

Kronstam assisted Neumeier on *Romeo and Juliet*. He learned the ballet and directed it, maintaining those extremely complicated musical and dramatic details, until he left the Theatre. He retained affection for the Ashton version, but he thought the Neumeier was better suited to the Danish audience. He liked its drama, although he said reluctantly, "Well, the choreography is a little bit awkward." In 1995, when Kronstam thought he would return to the Theatre and work with Peter Schaufuss on reviving the Ashton *Romeo*, he worried, "The audience will think that Ashton's is too clean and too nice for our audience."

That season was the end of an era at the Royal Danish Ballet. In the spring Hans Brenaa left the Theatre after a fight with Flindt over casting. "He walked out on a rehearsal with *Konservatoriet*. Mette [Hønningen] and Anna [Lærkesen] were doing the two leading girls. And on one of the last rehearsals, Mette was sick and Hans said to Inge Jensen, who had done it before, 'You do that role.' Then Flemming came down in the theater and he said, 'What is that girl doing there?' to Hans. And he said, 'That girl is Inge Jensen. She has done it before, and Mette is sick.' Flemming said, 'I specifically said to you that I didn't want her to do it.' And then Hans rose up, left the theater, went down to Mr.

Rohde, and said, 'I've had an argument with Flemming Flindt and I want to tear up my contract.' And Rohde said, 'You can't. You don't have a contract.' And he left." This meant that, as Kronstam put it, "Hans had been the one in the Theatre who was screaming for Bournonville, and now there was nobody to do that."

At the end of the season, in May, Vera Volkova died. She had been ill with cancer for months, and Kronstam had visited her regularly in the hospital, the last time the evening before she died. Her funeral took place when some of the dancers, including Kirsten Simone, had left for vacation. Kronstam thought that Simone should have stayed for the funeral. "Vera made Kirsten's career, and for the teacher who made your career, you go to her funeral," he said emphatically. At the funeral, Kronstam took the chair next to her husband, Hugh Williams, and saved the chair next to him for Simone, but she did not come. Shortly before the funeral was ready to start he went to Mette Hønningen, Volkova's last pupil, who was sitting in the back, and asked her to sit in Simone's chair. Hønningen didn't feel it was appropriate and the chair remained empty. Kronstam mentioned this incident several times in the first months after Gerstenberg's death, when funerals were much on his mind.

In the next season Kronstam took on the mime role of Peppo, a role that Niels Bjørn Larsen had danced for over thirty years, when Kirsten Ralov, who had taken over Hans Brenaa's ballets, staged a new production of *Napoli*. Kronstam, wishing to set an example for other dancers by not holding onto roles, only danced the part for two seasons, and he abandoned it with some regret. He always loved being "naughty" on stage, and Peppo is very naughty. Bjørnsson was his sidekick, Giacomo. Ralov remembered those rehearsals with pleasure, saying, "Working with those two guys was like a kiss."

And then, out of the blue, came a modern dance role that Kronstam considered the final breakthrough in his career, the last time he was confronted with, and conquered, something totally outside his range. It started in the dressing rooms. All Danish dancers, whether principals or corps, share a dressing room. Kronstam's last dressing room mate had been Flemming Halby, and when Halby left the company, Flindt did not move anyone else into Kronstam's room. "Flemming said I should take the foreigners when they came and I didn't mind. I had Neumeier there. And suddenly, I had Murray [Louis] there. He was a funny little man. He said, 'You should have some plants here.' And I said, 'They have to be watered and I have no time for that.' So the next day the room was filled with plants in little saucers and he was watering them, and there were plants all over—plants in the windows, all over.

"He started working on *Hoopla*. Flemming had seen it at the Falkoner Center and took it in for Niels [Kehlet]. Murray watched class [in preparation for casting the ballet], and he was fast in his eyes, and seeing what people could do."

Hoopla was about a clown in a circus and was one of Louis's most personal roles. Louis was a small, light, quick dancer, which is undoubtedly why Flindt thought that the role would be a good one for Kehlet. Kronstam said the role came to him gradually. "You know, every morning you talk. You say, 'How is it going?' out of politeness. And one day he said, 'Why don't you come and see?' so I came and saw, because I was always interested in what was going on.

"Then one day Murray said, 'Why don't you try it in the back.' It was in bare feet too, and it was very far away from what I could do, especially in the finale number, the solo with the silver balls [a juggling solo]. All in silver leotards.

"So I was trying it in the back and then he said, 'In case anything happens to Niels, I think you should have a couple of stage rehearsals on it.' And then

With Murray Louis, rehearsing *Hoopla*. Photo: John Johnsen. The Royal Theatre, Copenhagen. By permission of Det kongelige Teaters bibliotek og arkiv.

came the general rehearsal, which was Niels, because he was going to do the premiere, and afterward Murray and Flemming came up and said they had to talk to me, and Flemming said, 'Murray is not going to let us do it if you don't do the premiere tomorrow.'[6] I needed two more weeks of rehearsals. But I thought, 'Well, it's so far out for me, that I may just as well jump on it, go right down and get it over with.' So I said, 'Give me a rehearsal tomorrow during the day, and then I'll do it in the evening.'

"At that time I still had my back injury, and my left leg was almost paralyzed, but he didn't know that. The beginning is all balances, where you have to stand on the left leg. Murray saw that was a problem and he changed it to the right leg.

"So I did it, and that was another time when I went out of my skin, because it was circus music, and I was doing the maddest things in the world. I was changing costumes all the time in the wings." The ballet consisted of a series of numbers. First Kronstam, as a clown, advertised the circus. Then there was a solo, "very slow, about what-it's-going-to-be-like, the natural fear that all performers have." There were circus tricks, he slept, he knitted, he cleaned the floor. "I was doing a lot of crazy things. I had a hand puppet—this was all just so wonderful. I was all alone [on stage] for three or four minutes, doing all those crazy things.

"The next number was the clowning, where Ib [Andersen, as the rival young clown] always got the spotlight. Whenever I started doing something, I looked at the audience and clapped, and the light went away. And Ib was standing in the bright light. So I ran to get to the light and I did another spectacular thing, whatever it was, and the light went away. Then there was a golden pas de trois, an acrobatic sort of thing, and then in my last variation, which was with silver balls, there were a lot of pirouettes on the heel and it was all jazzy."

By all accounts, Kronstam gave an outstanding performance at the premiere, one that he felt he never equaled. "It was such a rush suddenly to be down and do it with the audience. But then I couldn't get back the same feeling. It was supposed to open the next season and I said, 'If Murray isn't coming, then I'm not going to do it.' Because it was Niels Bjørn who was taking the rehearsals. So I only did it for half a year." Kronstam's performance in *Hoopla* stunned the other dancers, as it was so far from his usual range. "I was one of the snakes in *Hoopla*," said Heidi Ryom, "and I remember looking up at him and saying, 'My God, can he do this too?'"

Ulla Bjerre wrote, "The recurring figure that holds this 'crazy comedy' to-gether is Henning Kronstam. He has a rare comic talent—you saw it a few years back in the Toreador's small part in *Carmen*—and in *Hoopla* it really comes out of its shell. His clown is both comic and glum. The despair that is said to hide behind all clowns' white mask Kronstam expresses with his naked torso bending deeper and deeper, accompanied by a quick trumpet solo and heavy hammer strokes. The Silver man's solo is the finest part of the perfor-mance, because here Kronstam unites ability with a strange depraved perfor-mance that brought back memories of the compère in *Cabaret*" (October 10, 1975). Others must have made the same connection, because Kronstam was offered this role when the drama department took *Cabaret* into the repertory, but he turned it down "because I can't sing."

Several critics had reviewed the general rehearsal rather than the opening-night performance, a tactic sometimes used to cope with early deadlines that was exposed, in this instance, by the last-minute cast change. Viggo Sørensen, a poet who occasionally also wrote dance criticism, described the differences between the two:

> It can be problematic having to review a performance on the basis of the dress rehearsal. As for instance the other day at the Royal Theatre when the Murray Louis ballet *Hoopla* appeared as a rather dull and not very funny parody of the circus environment. But on opening night it seemed a totally different work, whose fine, pointed humor became a success and where silent moments of poetic seriousness captured an enthusiastic audience. Yet another exciting night of ballet on Kongens Nytorv was saved at the last second.
>
> In my previous review I wrote that it is hard to be more fun than a skillful clown, but not for Henning Kronstam. He was the comically moving center-piece in which the gracefully comic is united with the humanly tragic. His immersion in the play with the doll was very beautiful, and when he looks a little like a fool in his struggle against the quickly growing flower, we under-stand his misfortune, too.

Ironically, one of the qualities that made Kronstam so successful in modern dance late in his career was the sense of weight that Volkova had given him years ago in remaking him from a too-tall demi-caractère dancer into a danseur noble. Louis notes this weightedness in what is one of the clearest descriptions of Kronstam as a dancer: "When I knew him, he had a certain weight—and I don't mean heaviness. I mean solidity. When he walked on the ground, he walked. He didn't skitter, he didn't float. And for me, as a contemporary choreographer, that was terribly important. I wanted somebody whose movement came out of the ground, whose foot could press into the ground and pull the movement out through the body and up.

"He had bearing. He was at ease with himself. This may sound too general, but he knew how to lift his arm. He knew how to use space in terms of demonstrating the proportions of his body. He knew the weight of the space around him; he moved through the weight of the space. He had a marvelous face. He could confront any direction and you knew where he was going. He was not evasive. He had a totality. The whole body moved as a unit into where and what he was doing. He had the wonderful gift of being professional, to relax the audience and say, 'Now I'm taking over. Just sit back and I'll show you.' I was never once worried when he was on stage because he knew intuitively how to reassure me, whatever he did.

"When I got him he was not emaciated. He looked rich and full—not heavy. He looked gorgeous. He looked like a kid. Great physique. I thought he was fabulous."

In March 1976, Kronstam celebrated his jubilee, the twenty-fifth anniversary of his debut. Jubilees are one of the loveliest of the Royal Theatre's customs. The dancer to be saluted is given an evening with a repertory of his choosing—Kronstam danced *The Moor's Pavane* and *La Sonnambula,* and gave the third repertory slot to his pupil Arne Villumsen, in *Apollo.* This was very typical of Kronstam: he would be celebrated, but he would also share. After the performance there are speeches from not only the ballet but all the other branches of the Theatre—the actors, the stagehands, the opera chorus, the musicians. Flowers and huge bottles of champagne, jugs of champagne, are presented. But once again, Kronstam had to be coaxed.

"I didn't want to be celebrated, but Flemming wanted it. So at last I said, 'Well, okay.' The whole day was so extraordinary. Flowers were coming in like I don't know what, and telegrams and everything. So you were sort of in a blur." Ulla Bjerre wrote of the atmosphere in the Theatre: "It was a happy, glad, and grateful person celebrating his jubilee who received a storm of applause for ten minutes, a giant crown with laurels from the ballet master, and hugged a lot of chairmen from different factions within the Theatre. Finally, when the spotlight was put on the audience, everybody got up, the orchestra gave a flourish, and the applause would never end. For a brief moment Kronstam was

Taking a curtain call at his
25th-year Jubilee, 1976.
Photo: Claus Poulsen,
Private collection

moved, his eyes and firmly closed mouth testified to that, but then his face lit
up again in a radiant and warm smile. Salute in honor of Henning Kronstam."

Afterward, of course, Kronstam was glad that he'd done it. "And I said so to
Arne [Villumsen, when his turn came, twenty years later], because he didn't
want to do it either. I called him, and I said, 'Well, you've got to do it, Arne,
because you will be happy afterward, and your wife will be happy, and you will
be very sorry later on in your life if you don't do it.' And he had five minutes'
applause, with the audience standing, full light [with the house lights up]. And
all the flowers and everything. He was scared of it, like I was. Because you have
scary thoughts. You think maybe nobody is coming. Maybe the house will be
empty. And then there's speeches."

Kronstam didn't make a speech—"I didn't have to, because Flemming made a beautiful speech for me"—but he did something almost as extraordinary: he gave a party. For nearly everyone in the company, it was the only time they ever visited Kronstam at home. "We had a hundred people here. Our press agent from the Theatre was living over there [across the hall], and he opened his house too, so we had both apartments. It was an amazing party. It lasted until next day. I was absolutely out.

"I have a picture of it. This whole window and this whole [wall of the dining room] was filled with bottles of red wine and champagne and I don't know what. And some clever people sent me a bicycle, which was nice. I have it in the country house now." There was an entire photo album with snapshots of this party. Bruhn came, and Stanley Williams and Peter Martins; the album is full of snapshots of the guests.[7]

At the end of the 1975–76 season, the company made its first U.S. tour in a decade, this time only to Washington, D.C., and New York. In Washington, Kronstam danced Edouard in *The King's Volunteers on Amager;* in New York, he danced Edouard and Lord Capulet in *Romeo and Juliet.*

The next season Murray Louis came back to do a full-evening work for the company, mainly for Vivi Flindt: *Cleopatra.* This was not as happy an occasion as *Hoopla.* The dancers could sense that the ballet wasn't working, and rehearsals were difficult. "Murray got so interested in the company and in Vivi, and Flemming got so interested in him, that they thought about doing a full-evening *Cleopatra.* The idea was fine enough, but I don't think it succeeded. It was really a series of numbers more than a ballet. That worked for *Hoopla,* but not here."

Kronstam had an odd double role, that of High Priest and Caesar. It was always difficult for him to have to try to make sense of something that he thought nonsensical. "It was strange to do. First, I was the High Priest, giving her the blessing to be queen. Then I changed into Caesar, where she had her first love affair with Caesar. And then he went mad, and I had all the girls—Heidi and Lis and Benedikte [Paaske] and all—wearing masks, and frightening me. That was the first act. I was not in the second act, because then Tommy [Frishøi] was Marcus Antonius, and she had a big affair with him, and there was an orgy with a lot of dancing going on. That was where the girls had to be on pointe for ten minutes. When they came out their ankles were just jelly. They were lying on the floor. And then Marcus Antonius left too, and then Vivi was alone and she got dramatic."

Louis didn't explain the role. "I just wondered why I should be the High Priest *and* the Caesar. It didn't make sense to me. And I didn't like the costume [which was quite skimpy]. I didn't want to go onstage in those little gold pants."

Kronstam hid his feelings well. Louis, who had found the company difficult to work with on this occasion and the dancers undisciplined, said that Kronstam had been very helpful in rehearsals, where he acted as a leader. "He could silence them with a look," Louis said. "We got along well. I trusted him. I depended on him. He came through for me in every respect. He knew what I was doing and he appreciated what I was trying to bring to that company. He saw me struggling with those people. He saw my exasperation and he also saw me maintaining my temper. He saw me push a work through that never really should have come to life because the obstructions were so numerous. How we ever reached that opening night, I'll never know."

The next season, Flindt made a wonderful comic role for Kronstam (and one for Niels Kehlet) in his revision of Bournonville's *The Toreador.* Flindt retained Bournonville's story, but completely rechoreographed it. It's a complicated story with many subplots, but the central one is the love story of a dancer and a middle-aged English tourist. Bournonville often created roles in pairs to show contrast; there were two English tourists. In the original, Mr. William was the short tubby one who got the girl, Mr. Arthur, the tall skinny one who didn't. Flindt kept the names, but switched the descriptions. Kronstam did Mr. William, Kehlet, Mr. Arthur. Both Kehlet and Kronstam said they had a grand time. Kehlet remembered that they clowned so much in rehearsals that Flindt had to tell them to pare back some of their improvisations. It was a perfect role for Kronstam at this age and it's difficult to imagine anyone else carrying it off. Mr. William was a bit ridiculous—pompous, not an easy traveler, he went about with a handkerchief tied over his head to protect him from the sun. But at the end, when he declared his love, he had to be romantic, and Kronstam did both parts of the role beautifully.

It was a controversial revival. Brenaa had worked for a long time trying to revive both *Toreador* and *The Wedding Festival at Hardanger* (Bournonville's Norwegian ballet) in the original choreography, calling in older dancers to see what they could remember. When Brenaa left the company the project was abandoned and Flindt decided to choreograph *Toreador* himself (he would later mount a similar revival of *Hardanger* in Norway). This meant that it would be highly unlikely for Brenaa's project ever to come to fruition, and Brenaa was

As Mr. William in Flemming Flindt's *The Toreador*, with Thomas Berentzen. Photo: John Johnsen. The Royal Theatre, Copenhagen. By permission of Det kongelige Teaters bibliotek og arkiv.

very upset about it. Flindt's side was that they had tried to revive the original but the dancers could not remember it; Brenaa always maintained that they could.

Kronstam's work in the studio during this period was at least as important as his work on stage. Allan Fridericia wrote about Kronstam's sensitive direction several times over the years. In "Again *Serenade*," a review from the late 1960s, he was upset that Inge Sand had taken over rehearsals of the ballet. "At the Royal Theatre it seems that they do not realize the importance of whom they ask to set a work by Balanchine. Over the years several people have been tried out, but as far as I can see only one has succeeded. This is more than most European theaters can do. An important Balanchine stager is a rare commodity. Why on earth have they stopped Henning Kronstam's work in this field? Why do they continue on what one can, with no exaggeration, call the path of mediocrity?" Fridericia wrote that Sand did not have the right musicality, and ended, "One has no idea how great the work is after having seen it staged by her."

He wrote again, in October 1974, in a piece called "Guardian of Culture" (Fridericia's reviews were often editorials):

> Why do the politicians talk about art if they want to make cuts? Why do they remain silent when a group takes Danish cultural traditions through a critical situation and also shows that cultural tradition is synonymous with showing new, topical ideas?
>
> Henning Kronstam is a fine stager. He has shown us this in connection with Balanchine and works by Harald Lander. The staging of *Fanfare* confirms this impression. As a whole, this small, festive story about the instruments of the orchestra in the shape of dancers seems even more fresh than when it was first premiered. Kronstam had a cast list that underlies the youth and talent of the ensemble.
>
> The woodwinds and the strings have all the names that will soon carry the repertory. Kronstam has captured the musicality and the accents of the composition, but he has also made *Fanfare* more lovely.

In the same year, John Percival had noticed a difference in *Etudes* when the company visited London.

> First things first: it is not often that the corps de ballet deserves to start a notice, before one so much as mentions the principals. However, in the Royal Danish Ballet's opening programme at the Coliseum last night it was the ensemble that deserved the highest praise.
>
> . . . I am sure we have not seen the group dances in *Etudes* done so exhilaratingly before. . . .
>
> Some of the credit for this must go to Henning Kronstam, who is listed as the producer of Harald Lander's ballet. To get such careful finish to the exercises at the barre in the opening scene must be difficult enough; to maintain this standard when the men are soaring in big jumps or the whole cast is whizzing at high speed in diagonals across a stage lit only by two beams must be even harder. (*London Times,* April 2, 1974)

In 1976, Flemming Flindt announced that he would resign at the end of his current contract. Flindt went to Kronstam before he resigned, asking if he wanted the job. The dancers, and other unions in the Theatre, also asked Kronstam to take it. He was under enormous pressure to take the job. Niels Matthiasen, who had asked him in 1964 and pressed him in 1968, when there began to be doubts about Flindt's stewardship of the company, was especially persistent.

"And then came the long struggle, because the company wanted me, and the minister of culture wanted me to do it. Mr. Rohde [now theater chief] wanted me. And I still said no. I said to Niels Matthiasen, 'Why don't you ask Neumeier'—because he was out of contract in Hamburg—'because I don't want to do it.' And Niels said, 'We've never had a foreigner. We want a Dane. I couldn't get it through.' But we talked about it, and then he said, 'Can't you get Neumeier to be chief choreographer?' I called John and John said, 'If I'm not in charge of the whole thing, I won't come.'" Neumeier enjoyed working with the Danish dancers but was not interested in a position of resident choreographer. "I wanted to start my own tradition," he said, and was more interested in that than in maintaining another one. Although it was long a dream of Danish critics for Neumeier to come and revise the Bournonville ballets, that never interested him. "I would not have given up the shaping of a company to be a permanent choreographer somewhere. For me, there was no question about the importance of the Bournonville repertoire, and the fact that I was certainly not the person to take care of that," Neumeier said. Kronstam suggested Kirsten Ralov for the job, but Niels Matthiasen said, 'Kirsten Ralov is not going to be ballet master.' He told me she would be named acting director until they found somebody else."

Matthiasen then changed his tactics, asking Kronstam what he would want if he did take the job. "I said, 'Okay. Then I would need money for the school.' Because that was the big problem at the time. Vera had died. Mrs. Frandsen had gone to Vienna, Johnny [Eliasen] had left the company, and I was the last experienced teacher. I knew how to teach, but I didn't know how to teach others how to teach. So I said, 'We have to develop new teachers. I have to have money for that.' I could never get money from Flemming for that. It all went to his productions. The young teachers could give a class, but if there was a problem, they didn't know how to deal with it. So that's why I had to have that money."

Although Kronstam and Matthiasen had been friends for nearly twenty years, there is no reason to believe that the minister of culture wanted Kronstam to be ballet master because of cronyism. The two had had many discussions about ballet and the company over those years and had similar ideals and ideas about ballet and what the Royal Danish Ballet should be. Several other Danes have said that they were offered the job at this time, and this may well be true during the months when Kronstam insisted he was not interested in the position, but Kronstam was not only the first choice but the insistent choice of Matthiasen, the Theatre, and the dancers. Kronstam said, "Niels believed that it should be, first of all, a classical company again, and then he believed in my artistic ideas."

Kronstam also wanted assurance that the ballet could have three full-evening productions a year, and this he got. "Nobody had that in their contract before, but I said I wanted it in my contract. It might be three small ballets, or one full-length, on each evening, but three evenings."

The final sticking point was that Kronstam wanted Kirsten Ralov as his assistant director. Ralov had held the job for a short time in the early 1960s. "She was somebody who was administrative and artistic, of course, but who liked the office work, the scheduling, and dealing with all the meetings with the economic department. Flemming had Lizzie Rode to do that and Lizzie Rode left. I knew Kirsten could deal with [the budget director]. So that was one of the things I said to Niels: 'I'm not going to do it if I don't get somebody who can fight.'" Why Niels Matthiasen was so against Ralov is a mystery. She was a strong woman who made her opinions known, and she undoubtedly had ruffled some feathers at the Theatre, but she was an ideal candidate for the number two slot: loyal, honest, and a fighter. Whether Kronstam convinced Matthiasen that Ralov was really ideal for the job, or whether Matthiasen wanted Kronstam so badly that he gave in, is not known, but Ralov did become Kronstam's assistant, with the new title—a salute to her stature and experience—of vice ballet master.

Sensing that Kronstam seemed to be beginning to be resigned to the fact that he would have to take the job, Matthiasen began to press Gerstenberg. There must be something Kronstam wasn't telling him. "Well, Henning has this problem," the answer finally came. Niels Matthiasen had been a trusted friend for a long time. He could be told that Kronstam was manic-depressive and would need time away from the Theatre after periods of extreme stress. Another problem was that Kronstam was terrified of speaking in public. Kronstam would say, "I'm a dancer. I don't talk," but it was more than this. He had a fear of being stared at, and that fear and anticipation could trigger anxiety attacks. His hands would shake. He would lose his balance and fall. He sometimes took tranquilizers to control this, but that was not a permanent solution. "Well, that's no problem," Niels Matthiasen said, and volunteered to make all the speeches. It was then that Kronstam said he would take the job, although he always emphasized that it was the support of the dancers that gave him the courage to do it.

The summer before Kronstam took over as ballet master, he gave a very long interview to *Politiken's* Ninka, one of the most interesting and respected Danish journalists, in which he outlined his philosophy and his plans for the company. Substantial excerpts are reproduced here. It is the longest interview Kronstam ever gave and he said things that he never said elsewhere.[8]

Ninka began by setting the scene. The interview took place at Kronstam's summerhouse:

> In the garden up north in Asserbo, tomatoes, potatoes, and parsley are grown with the same excitement as Bournonville's ballets are grown on Kongens Nytorv, even if the ballet master admits that his green thumb is probably not as talented as his stretched toes. During this summer's small vacation Kronstam has been walking up and down his huge grounds—the possibilities of the company, from the principal down to the youngest ballet child, have been analyzed over and over again.
>
> In one year the dancing begins and it is in Kronstam's nature that it will happen in style. In this way both the days and the short summer nights have

With Winston and Iago at the summerhouse. This photo accompanied the Ninka interview in *Politiken*. Photo: Erik Petersen for *Politiken*. Private collection. By permission of Polfoto.

been sacrificed to planning. But today, on a sunny afternoon, the voice is happy and eager and the smiles come more often than his basic reserve normally allows. It is an expectant ballet master who shows his cards. With warmth he starts telling you:

Happy and relaxed?—no, that I am not. . . . it is a huge challenge, isn't it?—what I'm feeling . . . is the responsibility for the company.

Kronstam spoke of why he had turned down the job when it was offered to him previously (in 1964 and 1968) and why he accepted it now:

Remember, ten years ago I had my dancing to think of, and in the meantime one has probably learned a whole lot, about dancing, but also about one's fellow human beings and about oneself—what you can deal with, what you can't deal with, and as time passed and the different people that were sought out [after I turned down the position] had to be given up one by one, then it became almost a pressure for me to know that everyone was almost disappointed in me, and the fact that I knew I had the whole company behind me, and the fact that Kirsten Ralov was ready to come on board as assistant artistic director . . . that was a deciding factor, that she was ready to do that.

The rest of the problems were purely personal. I have been a very closed person, but lately I have met a lot more openness than I ever thought possible, so I tried to reevaluate the way I see things. That is something I have had to do—open up more. Flemming and Vivi [Flindt] have had many social engagements and really have given the company lots of good publicity . . . but I don't like public life, so I'm hoping that, apart from the strictly necessary, very quickly, through my repertory, it will be the dancers that will become interesting, it will be the dancers that are shown off.

My most important job will be to animate the corps to like dancing, to feel that dancing is not just a job; it is their own personal responsibility, because they have chosen it themselves. During my time the company will not be run as if it's my company [as was Flindt's style]. It's the company's company and they themselves will have to take responsibility for what they have started—and then it will be my responsibility to inspire them and make them happy as much as I possibly can. Now, this summer, I have traveled quite a bit and there are many companies at a high level—we need to hurry a bit.

Kronstam described what he felt was special about the Danish ballet, and why it was necessary to return the company to a more Danish, rather than international, orientation:

We have an unbelievable bonus in our Bournonville repertory, and that has something to do with the Danish temperament in these ballets—because it is very special that all of us are Danish. If you take almost any company abroad, the dancers all come from different places. And the Danish temperament— there's a certain joie de vivre in our way of dancing, a certain robustness, and at the same time I have to say that our girls are very Nordic and fresh looking, whereas in some companies they can seem anemic . . . the grace in our girls is something special in the Danish company. And then we have the big advantage that we are able to tell stories, we are able to fill the Bournonville repertory with all its quirky characters.

After praising Flindt for creating a "big and diverse repertory," he noted:

At the same time, [throughout Flindt's tenure] the manifesto has been that we can't take any more of the classical ballets. I feel that if you have educated a classical dancer and they have come so far technically, then they should be allowed to try out these [classical] parts. I think it would be a great pity for such wonderful ballerinas as Mette Hønningen and Sorella Englund if their careers would end without doing these parts that belong to a classical ballerina.

We educate classical dancers and we are supported by the state and we have all the facilities—and then we don't really use them for what they were educated to do for many years. Our classes are not mandatory,[9] and if you want to demand of the dancers that they should show up in the afternoon [for class as well as in the morning] to polish a technique they have absolutely no use for on stage—how can you ask that of anyone? It is a fact that the really big classical parts demand a completely spotless technique plus a personal talent or presence in that technique. This doesn't mean that I don't think we should do modern ballets, and I think it is great that Eske Holm [modern choreographer] receives support [from the state], that we would have that alternative to our company.

Kronstam's first priority would be to reinvigorate the school: "One of the first things we need to do is to educate teachers. At the moment we're all half-taught thieves, but we ought to have, sometime in the future, something that would be known as the Danish school, and all should know what that was. The motto is: Prepare the next generation!"

Another important theme in his directorship was to use the entire company: "The modern choreographers we have had all use the same ten to twelve dancers—altogether I guess there are about thirty dancers that are used so much they run into themselves in the wings."

He also, of course, would have to develop dancers. Ninka asked, "Do you have the ability to spot a talent?"

Not until I started directing ballets eight years ago. Only when you sit down there [in the audience] and look up at the stage, only then do you see what really catches the eye. Some [dancers] are called "a dancer's dancer," where everything is perfect, when we can all see: oh my, how spotless it is! Then we [dancers] sometimes wonder why this dancer isn't being as celebrated by the audience as is deserved. And then there are the others who catch the eye on a stage, and with time I have become more taken by them, those who catch the eye. . . . the personality, the talent on a stage, that is something the audience will always recognize.

Kronstam outlined more specific plans:

I would very much like to direct the *The Kermesse in Bruges*. Three new productions are allocated to the ballet company each year and that's enough—but then the question is how many revivals you can manage. What I would love to bring back is the Ballet Festival, if not in its old form, then at least do one or two "Ballet Weeks" [where the company dances every night, and presents its best ballets and casts]. And if the Theatre can't afford it, then maybe we could do it in Tivoli. We have to move in there anyway for a year and a half while the Theatre is being renovated. Ballet weeks would be inspiring for our dancers, just as it has been inspiring to see the big international ballet companies in Tivoli this summer. What I wish is for our dancers and our company to reach that level. We have the resources.

The most surprising part of the interview is its ending. Ninka's final question was, "What is the result of, so far, thirty-four hard and good years in ballet?"

Few would have predicted Kronstam's answer: "In the end it is probably that you have been good to the people around you—that you have had compassion. And the times when you didn't, that is actually what has been the hardest. . . ."

Part four

The Ballet Master

It is time for classical dancing on Kongens
Nytorv and time to uphold the old traditions.
It is not a moment too soon.
—Erik Aschengreen, *Berlingske Tidende*, 1978

You don't fight for ten years of your life to
become a classical dancer to spend the rest
of it rolling around on the floor.
— Henning Kronstam

Twenty-one

Priorities and Challenges

When Kronstam became ballet master of the Royal Danish Ballet, the Danish
audience and critics were divided about not only its future but its very nature.
Some wanted the company to preserve and build upon the Bournonville tradition, remaining a classical ballet company; others demanded a more contemporary, even modern-dance, repertory. Kronstam would have to please, and
appease, both audiences. The city was too small to support more than one ballet
company, and there were no modern-dance troupes in Copenhagen at the time.

The idea of having a second Danish ballet company, a small contemporary
troupe to supplement the larger one at Kongens Nytorv, had been suggested
during the previous decade by those worried about the direction in which
Flindt was taking the company. It was thought that an ideal compromise would
be to have two ballet companies, one small experimental one, directed by

Flindt, and the traditional Royal Danish Ballet, directed by someone else. This is an interesting suggestion, and it was probably scuttled because of lack of money, but it would have solved many problems. By supporting only one company, the government ensured a continuing controversy. If a director like Flindt were in charge, he would be constantly under fire for neglecting the classical tradition, while someone with Kronstam's sensibilities would be seen as too old-fashioned. Flindt did form a small company when he left the Theatre, taking with him a handful of dancers, but it could not survive as a private enterprise.

Kronstam believed he had a responsibility to his audience, but he also believed his main task was to guard the Theatre's resources, both its repertory and its dancers, and he had made his main objectives quite clear: he wanted to return the Royal Danish Ballet to its classical base. Because of this, some saw Kronstam as too conservative, confusing his classicism for timidity and lack of creativity. It was likely not an accident that the photograph accompanying his announcement as ballet master in one of the major papers was in his role as Phlegmatic, in Balanchine's *The Four Temperaments*.

For Kronstam, "getting the company dancing again," as he put it, meant returning it to its Bournonville roots—surprising to some, as Kronstam had never been seen as a Bournonville man. As was often the case, this was more a matter of perception than reality. Although he never announced himself as a Bournonville expert, Kronstam believed that Bournonville was at the heart of the Danish tradition and that his ballets needed to be danced regularly in refreshed traditional stagings rather than revising them along then popular pseudo-Freudian lines. The dancers generally supported Kronstam's ideas. "It was a very big relief when Henning became ballet master," as ballerina Mette-Ida Kirk put it, "because he changed the repertory from Flindt completely and it was a much higher quality. He invited very good choreographers to Copenhagen, brought in much more Balanchine, and he took Hans Brenaa again for the Bournonville, so there were a lot of things to work with."

In order to have the best Bournonville productions possible, the first thing Kronstam did was to ask Hans Brenaa to return to the company. Kronstam had immense respect for Brenaa, not only for his knowledge of the repertory, but for the way he inspired the dancers with his "liveliness." Brenaa accepted immediately. "He said, 'If you are there, Henning, I will be there, and if you ask me to do anything, I'll do it.' So he did *Lifeguards* that year, and he did *Kermesse*."

It is worth noting that Kronstam had said in the Ninka interview that he had wanted to stage a *Kermesse* himself, but he ceded this to Brenaa. He felt the older man was key to restoring the repertory, and that the stagings Brenaa did after his return to the company were superior to those before he left it. Kronstam said this was because when Brenaa was away, working with people who had not grown up in the tradition, he had had to rethink the ballets and discover how to explain them. Brenaa's son, Jens, agreed, but added that Kronstam had given his father a free rein, especially in matters of casting, which Flindt had not, and that this had made a significant difference. Kronstam sometimes disagreed with Brenaa's casting, especially at the beginning, but let the older man have his way and learned his reasoning.[1] Kronstam always gave his instruktørs and choreographers a free hand. "I allow the producer—I can give a hint. 'If you don't mind, would you mind maybe teaching that role to this and that person,' or 'If you think about next time we cast it, maybe she can do it,' something like that," he said in his "Oral History." "But I won't demand it of him, because if a producer has a certain person in his mind, or in her mind, for that role, it will never go well. It's better. Let them have their own ideas, let them do it. Of course, if it's ridiculous, I would say, 'Well, it's not possible.' But otherwise, I will not interfere."[2]

Work on the Bournonville repertory began immediately in the first season, with revivals of *The King's Volunteers on Amager* and *The Kermesse in Bruges* (a major restaging by Brenaa). The *Flower Festival* pas de deux, *Konservatoriet,* and *Napoli* were also part of the repertory, as was Flemming Flindt's *Toreador.*[3] Kronstam's often stated desire to fill the repertory with large-cast ballets, ballets "that use the whole company," was not merely to make everyone feel well employed but to mold the company into a corps again. The repertory of the past few years had been so geared to small-cast modern-dance and theater pieces that the corps was undisciplined and out of shape. In the speech a new ballet master traditionally makes to the company at the start of his first season, Kronstam stressed that the emphasis would be on classical dancing. "I told them, 'No more *Triumph of Death,'*" he said, referring to Flindt's big hit from earlier in the decade, a theater piece to a rock score that did not use the dancers' classical technique. This, as much as taste, was at the root of Kronstam's choice of repertory. If ballet dancers do not dance classical ballets regularly, they will lose their technique, and Kronstam wanted to acquire ballets that would provide dancing roles for as many dancers as possible.

Kronstam also immediately began to make changes at the school, changes that he had long wanted to make. Although he had been nominally in charge of the school since 1966, he had not had a completely free hand in hiring teachers, nor an adequate budget for training them, and new teachers were badly needed. Volkova had died in 1975, no teacher had ever replaced Stanley Williams, and Edite Frandsen—the teacher of Linda Hindberg, Lis Jeppesen, Mette-Ida Kirk, Benedikte Paaske, and Heidi Ryom—had left for Vienna a few years earlier. During his tenure Kronstam hired teachers who had a background in Cecchetti, if not Volkova or Bournonville (the schools share, among other things, a similarity in their use of music), and rehired Frandsen.[4] He also expanded the number of grades from three to five—also a matter of money, as he needed to hire two additional teachers to do this.

The Danish ballet had never had a syllabus—a systematic method of teaching, noting which steps would be taught grade by grade—nor a codified vocabulary. Beck's Bournonville Schools were not intended to be a syllabus, but a method of keeping Bournonville's enchainements in the dancers' bodies and maintaining a high classical standard until another teacher of genius came to renew the vocabulary. That had been Volkova, and Kronstam kept her way of melding Bournonville steps with steps from the broader vocabulary. "I don't think there's anything missing in the Bournonville training," he said in his "Oral History." "It's the teachers that we had in the Bournonville training [when he was growing up] that didn't know what to do with it. Because if you just give the Bournonville steps without explaining how and why and don't build the class, if you just take the whole Wednesday Class and go through it and say, 'Well, this is how we start and this is how we end, and now an hour is over, and good-by,' you don't learn to dance that way."[5] During Kronstam's directorship, there were separate Bournonville company classes, given by Hans Brenaa, Fredbjørn Bjørnsson, and Flemming Ryberg. Anne Marie Vessel taught Bournonville classes in the school and Kirsten Ralov had special afternoon classes for the older pupils. Kronstam did not teach Bournonville classes. "I never taught strictly Bournonville," he said, and this was deliberate. He did not wish to restrict the company to Bournonville, nor to isolate Bournonville as something separate and apart from the dancers' usual fare.

Kronstam went to New York the summer before he took over to look at schools. At Erik Bruhn's invitation he also went to Toronto, where Betty Oliphant had established a system of training at the National Ballet School there.

Bruhn was enthusiastic about Oliphant's methods. He had had success with them in Stockholm, where he had directed the Royal Swedish Ballet a decade earlier, and he urged Kronstam to adopt them. Kronstam invited Oliphant to come to Copenhagen and she picked three dancers—Johnny Eliasen, Ulla Skow, and Anne Marie Vessel—to go to Toronto for training. Oliphant also suggested that some of the present teachers be replaced, and Kronstam agreed with her choices.

Ulla Skow, one of the teachers sent to Canada, gained a lot from the experience: "Here in Denmark, when you have a tradition for such a long time, you never question it. You just do as you've always been doing, whether it's good or bad, and that was what Henning wanted to try to change. They always say 'the Canadian system.' What we were trying to do here has nothing to do with the Canadian system. It was just we learned some good things about what they were doing. In Canada, they talked to me about the Danish jump, for example, and so I had to figure out what were we doing. And I found out a lot of things that they didn't do there that we were doing, so I came up with a solution for that, so that was quite interesting also."

Kronstam's changes to the school were, and remain, controversial. Some felt that Oliphant's methods were too foreign; Kirsten Ralov wanted to develop a Bournonville-based syllabus. Teachers say that many of Oliphant's ideas were sound, but others simply did not work and were eventually discarded.

Kronstam also had to develop dancers. The company was thin at the top when he took over. There was a big generation gap, caused by illness, emigration, and natural attrition. Some principals were in their late thirties or early forties, while the new generation—all pupils from Kronstam's tenure as head of the school—was in its early twenties. From Flindt, Kronstam inherited several fine young dancers who had been dancing solo parts since their teens, and he built the company on them: Ib Andersen and Arne Villumsen, two very different, but extraordinarily talented dancers, equal to the best anywhere in the world, among the men; and four women: Linda Hindberg (already a principal) and Mette-Ida Kirk, Lis Jeppesen, and Heidi Ryom, each of whom Kronstam would promote to solo dancer in that order.[6]

Kronstam's philosophy of life was to play the cards he was dealt. Turning the cards back to the dealer would be cheating; the challenge was making the best of what you had. He had inherited several dancers whom he would probably not have chosen or promoted and a corps de ballet with a disproportionate

Ib Andersen and Mette-
Ida Kirk in *Romeo and
Juliet*. Photo: Bent Mort-
ensen. Private collection.

number of women in their thirties, a result of the high-spending 1960s, when
the company was expanded. Kronstam did not prune; he used who and what
he had. He closed the company again to all but Danish dancers trained in the
school. This was not simply out of patriotism, although Kronstam was not the
only Dane who felt that the Danish repertory required a peculiarly Danish
sense of humanity to perform well. There was also a social contract between
the company and the dancers, who had a stake in the traditional ballets because they knew there were good roles awaiting them in middle age. Bringing
in foreigners not trained in the school would introduce not only many different styles—different ways of holding the hands, a naturally straightened rather
than curled back extended leg, and the like—but transient dancers who would
stay for only a year or two, with no interest or stake in the traditional repertory.

Closing the company took considerable courage and for a time seemed a
gamble. For several years few dancers were taken into the company from the
school, leading to much second-guessing of Kronstam's policies. Kronstam al-

ways had his eye on the future. "At times when I am tired or uninspired, I always go and watch the children," he often said, and he saw in them the company's renewal. As it turned out, Kronstam was the last director able to field a completely Danish company.

Restoring the repertory would be more difficult than restoring the school. It is one of the unfortunate ironies, for both Niels Matthiasen and Kronstam, that Kongens Nytorv finally got its classical ballet master at a time when new classical choreography was nearly extinct. Kronstam was in the same position as nearly every other artistic director in the world at that time; he had to scrabble for repertory. Like any artistic director, Kronstam drew on contacts from his dancing days. The major classical choreographers whom he knew and with whom he had worked—Ashton, Balanchine, MacMillan, Robbins, and Tudor—were directing, or had strong ties to, other companies and did not need to seek work outside. The choreographers with whom he had worked in the 1970s worked in modern dance. During his tenure Kronstam revived or added ballets

Lis Jeppesen and Arne Villumsen rehearsing the death scene in *La Sylphide*. Photo: Erik Petersen for *Politiken*. Private collection. By permission of Polfoto.

by Ashton, Balanchine, and Tudor. He acquired ballets from the few younger neoclassical choreographers then working, such as Hans van Manen and Rudi van Dantzig. He also acquired or commissioned works from contemporary or modern dance choreographers such as Alvin Ailey, Richard Alston, Christopher Bruce, John Neumeier, Robert North, Paul Taylor and Glen Tetley. He often chose a work because it suited a particular dancer or dancers or would stretch them, technically or emotionally.

There were suggestions by both émigré Danes and American critics when Kronstam assumed the directorship that he should acquire a large number of Balanchine ballets. Kronstam programmed one Balanchine work each season because he admired them and because he thought they were good for the dancers, but "I didn't want to do so many ballets from one choreographer," he said. "I had *Divertimento* [*No. 15*] and *Serenade* and *Four Temperaments* and *Concerto Barocco* and *Symphony in C*."[7] He wanted several Robbins ballets, including *In the Night* and *Dances at a Gathering*, but Robbins would not let him have them. ("I think he just didn't want to work here," Kronstam said, perhaps referring to the problems many visiting choreographers had with Danish union rules.) This was a competitive age, and companies often did not want works they considered signature pieces to go to other companies. Kronstam asked Ashton for *A Month in the Country*, but was told it belonged to Anthony Dowell, then director of the Royal Ballet. Kronstam said Dowell refused permission, saying it would be like the Royal asking Kronstam for *Napoli*.

Kronstam inherited something from Flindt's time that would prove less easy to work with: the critics. Flindt choreographed for a broad public, using big themes and broad strokes. He was rightly credited with bringing in a new audience to the Theatre, but that new audience was, of course, attracted by the new ballets, and the repertory trained that audience's eye, as repertories always do. The younger generation of critics did not seem as interested in choreography or classical style as in theme and dramatic content; some, at least, had a marked preference for realism over abstraction. (A few older female critics who did appreciate classical ballet were considered old-fashioned and dubbed "the aunties.") Reviews primarily dealt with character and psychological motivation. Kronstam was aware of this. "They [the critics] don't really see, somehow. I don't think they see that the style is there. They can see it when it's good dancing, but they are more interested in the drama."

Other challenges included the Theatre's subscription system, which allowed a new work to remain in repertory only two years before resting, and the fact that there was no true ballet audience in Copenhagen. Danes went to theater, opera, *and* ballet, and that was the way most subscriptions were arranged. Drama was the central art. In ballet, the audience too preferred drama or comedy. Of course there were some people who loved ballet and were primarily interested in the dancing, but not nearly enough to fill the house.

1978–79

Kronstam's first program of *Serenade,* the *Flower Festival in Genzano* pas de deux, and *The King's Volunteers on Amager* certainly fulfilled his stated intentions to get the company dancing again, to use the whole company, and to begin restoration of the Bournonville repertory. The casting was a mixture of generations, of soloists and corps dancers. *Serenade* was led by Mette Hønningen, Linda Hindberg, Eva Kloborg, Arne Villumsen, and Palle Jacobsen; *Flower Festival,* staged by Kirsten Ralov, was danced by Ib Andersen and Dinna Bjørn; and *King's Volunteers on Amager* starred Kirsten Simone as Louise, with Tommy Frishøi in Kronstam's old role as Edouard. Erik Aschengreen recognized the significance of the evening: "It can, I assume, almost be considered a program statement that Henning Kronstam opens his first season as ballet master for the Royal Ballet with Balanchine and Bournonville. It is time for classical dancing on Kongens Nytorv and time to uphold the old traditions. It is not a moment too soon."

Kronstam's second program was completely different and a bit of a shock. He had asked Glen Tetley to stage an evening of three ballets. Tetley's trademark was a blend of modern dance and ballet. He melded ballet's sleek look and virtuosity with modern dance's flexibility and contracted torso, a blend of turnout and turn-in that he used to express emotions traditionally reserved, in ballet, for mime. Kronstam had spent a good deal of time traveling in the months before he took over looking at other companies' repertories and had seen Tetley's *Rite of Spring* performed by American Ballet Theatre. He thought it would be a good role for Ib Andersen, who had so far been cast primarily in lyrical roles. Kronstam sensed a Dionysian quality in Andersen and wanted to bring it out. There were other dancers from Flindt's period who were more suited to crossover or modern dance than classical roles. "I knew Glen would get them moving," he said. In addition, a Tetley evening would be an ideal bridge for both dancers and audience between the old and the new regimes. And so Kronstam came to New York and met with Tetley.

"I was working with American Ballet Theatre and Henning came to New York and asked to meet with me," said Tetley. "He said, 'I want you to come and I want you to do a full evening. I want you to do three ballets.' I was quite stunned at that, and I thought, 'My God. That's going to be an enormous job.' But Henning said, 'I know your work and I feel there is a group of dancers in the company that I think will be able, in terms of the solo roles in your work, to do what you want to do.' We talked about it, and I agreed to do *Greening*, which I had created for the Stuttgart Ballet and Birgit Keil; and *Voluntaries*, which I had created also for Stuttgart—Marcia Haydée and [Richard] Cragun and Birgit [Kiel]; and to do *The Rite of Spring*."

It was an expensive undertaking, as Tetley wanted to bring his staff with him, including Mary Hinkson, a former Graham dancer and excellent teacher, as well as Bronwen Curry, his choreologist and assistant. "I was going to have to do a lot of coaching in terms of movement. And Henning said, 'You can be assured I will give you everything you need.'" An example of how Kronstam fulfilled this promise is the way he handled union and scheduling problems. Tetley preferred to work all day without a break. Union regulations required that the dancers be given a break after a certain number of hours of rehearsals on nights they had to perform. Late afternoon rehearsals could be scheduled on overtime (not time and a half, as is the American custom, but a nominal amount). Kronstam solved the problem by dividing the dancers into groups so that each could have its required break, but at least one group would always be available to Tetley and his team.

Tetley came to teach for a month before rehearsals began so that he and the company could get used to each other. Tommy Frishøi, who worked as an assistant to Tetley during this time, noted how strange it seemed that Kronstam, who had been so disapproving of Flindt's use of modern-dance choreographers, had not only brought one into the company but required the dancers to take Tetley's classes. "And he took them too, got down on the floor with the dancers." Kronstam explained, "If they're going to have to do it, I thought they might as well learn how to do it properly." Kronstam's objection to Flindt's repertory had not been anti–modern dance, per se; he felt it could have a place in a ballet company, if the company's identity was strongly classical. He had objected to the prominence of modern dance in the repertory, the exclusion of new classical productions, and the fact that dancers were confronted with modern dance without proper preparation.

Tetley was very pleased with the dancers. "Henning's instinct about the dancers was right. There was Mette Hønningen. There was Linda [Hindberg], whom I loved too. And I had Arne Villumsen, and Torben Jeppesen, and Ib Andersen. Mette and Torben did the central roles in *Greening* and Mette—she also did *Voluntaries,* but Linda and Arne were the first cast in *Voluntaries* and were quite beautiful in it. Arne had a beautiful way of moving, and he had weight. And speed, and elegance. He also could be lazy. I wanted to stick pins in him.

"But the revelation was Ib Andersen, who was brilliant in *The Rite of Spring* because there was a vulnerable quality about him. He had the brilliance of movement, and there was an almost ecstatic quality about it, along with an uncertainness, a vulnerability. He brought a quality that nobody else had at that point to *The Rite of Spring.* You understood why suddenly everyone in the ballet picked him as the sacrificial figure.

"It was an enormous amount of work, and certainly the soloists were open and up to it. I had a bit of trouble with some of the corps, especially the men. They had problems with the lifts and the partnering [in *Voluntaries*]. They were not used to doing overhead lifts. But the boys were very good in *The Rite of Spring,* because they do jump wonderfully."

Ib Andersen gave a dancer's view of working with Tetley: "I think, after the Flemming years, that really pushed the company. Henning gambled very, very big, I would say, but he did win. It could have been a big failure. It could have been that we could not do that kind of ballet. It was a different language, and you didn't know whether we would master it or not. And during the rehearsal period, I would say there were some big question marks about that.

"During Flemming's time there were not many ballets that required technical feats from the whole company, and these ballets really did, so it was a shock for a lot of dancers that they really had to work, but Tetley would not have it any other way, and for Henning to start in that way, he won big. *Sacre* [*The Rite of Spring*] was a very important work for me in every way. It challenged me in a way that I had not been challenged before, and I loved dancing it. While I was doing it I actually didn't think it was a good ballet, but I loved doing it because it was so all the way, totally, 1,000 percent there. Wild—and the physicality of it, and dancing to that music."

Kronstam had been worried that the Tetley works would cause injuries, and he had Tetley and his assistants teach so that the dancers would be properly prepared. "Those kind of ballets are not dangerous if you know how to do them, but it is a different way of dancing," said Andersen. "A lot of the technique is based in Graham, so it's a very different center and a very different way of using your body. I think for a lot of the dancers, it gave a different dimension to their dancing that they could use for anything. That was definitely the case for me, because after that ballet I got much more controlled, much more upper body, because you use tremendous upper body in every possible way, and it only helps your classical dancing, and especially dancing Bournonville, where your upper body is so still.

"*Sacre* was the hardest ballet I've ever done. I've never done a ballet that required a stamina and a physicality like that. I don't think Tetley started to trust what I could do until after about two months. There was one rehearsal that was a breakthrough for me, when I plugged into the right energy of the piece, because that piece is about energy, and if you don't have that wild, explosive energy, it won't work."

Tetley found Kronstam extremely helpful, whether dealing with dancers, bureaucrats, or stagehands. "Whenever I had a problem I went directly to Henning, and he was immediate and strong, and he handled it with the wisdom of someone who knew how to handle people." One of Tetley's stories is especially worth noting in light of subsequent events. "I remember for the set of *Greening*, there's a very beautiful tree which is made out of metal. It was from a photograph I found of a tree in the middle of a desert, and the tree had not one leaf on it. Nadine [Baylis] translated it into this very shimmering metallic structure. And without conferring with her, the stage construction people made it out of rattan.

"It looked like one of those fantasy Puerto Rican bedsteads. It was so—*awful*. I ran up and I got Henning, and I said, 'Henning, this is an abomination. This has got to be thrown out. I don't care if they have to work forty-eight hours nonstop.' And they were saying, 'No, we have no time. It's too close to the premiere.' Henning was marvelous. He told them, "Well, you have to make time." He went into a fury with them, a fury, and demanded that they change it. So I always found whatever I wanted, Henning would do, and he would fight for it, right down to the last element."

The program was a hit with both the audience and the critics. Ebbe Mørk wrote: "It is an outstanding beginning for Henning Kronstam as ballet master. He has demanded that the ballet perform a fantastically demanding assignment that it hopefully will be able to fulfill even when Glen Tetley has left town. All the manpower and talent of the Royal Ballet will be needed, not least on the classical front when, next year, the world will see that Denmark is in the world elite, with a Bournonville festival. It is extremely demanding to be a classical company with challenges ranging from Bournonville to Tetley. But this is also what makes it exciting to be in the audience" (*Politiken,* December 15, 1978).

The day of the general rehearsal for the Tetley program, Kronstam resigned. He had been ballet master for six months. "I was overtired," he said. He seems to have taken Lander as a model, and tried to do what Lander, in a much less complicated time, had done: teach company class daily and conduct rehearsals. On top of this, he had to handle contracts and other financial and business matters and serve as producer for every ballet in repertory, not only those he was rehearsing, which meant dealing with costumes, lighting, and other production details. His nature was such that he felt responsible for everything; he could delegate administrative, but not artistic, work. As he had feared, the stress was too much for his nervous system and he had a crash. He wrote a letter of resignation and retreated to the summerhouse with Gerstenberg. The Theatre moved quickly to get him back. The head of the dancers' union, Ingrid Glindemann, and the theater chief went to his summerhouse to try to persuade him to stay. Gerstenberg told them, "He doesn't have the nerves for the job," but both Matthiasen and Henning Rohde believed that if they gave Kronstam more administrative help it would be possible for him to continue. Rohde's handwritten letter, from Henning to Henning, is a very touching testament to the regard in which the Theatre held Kronstam:

December 16

Dear Henning,

I have with great sorrow read your letter and the motivation for your resignation. I understand your motivation. I, myself, know what it means to have to administrate with difficulty and have way too few personnel to help you.

It is no secret that the analysts feel that the artistic departments have to be

strengthened with artistic administrative personnel. Therefore, I have to immediately, before anything else, ask you, were I able to strengthen your administrative artistic personnel, if your decision would still stand.

Dear Henning, I have been happy to work with you. I am aware of the
difficulties, but just think. I don't believe the ballet ever before has had a ballet
master whom everybody backed 100 percent, as has been the case this season.
Therefore, this letter for your consideration,
Henning

Kronstam's resignation and the attempts to get him to stay were thoroughly
covered in the press. Some used the situation to attack the current administration, especially two people, Max Sørensen, the Theatre's economics chief, and
Jørgen Mydtskov, its technical director. An article by Per Jensen in *Politiken*
(December 21, 1975) entitled "Minister [of Culture] Holds Kronstam Back" included an interview with Matthiasen: "'It is a precarious situation,' says Niels
Matthiasen to *Politiken*. 'I will try to solve the problem by relieving the ballet
master of administrative duties. It is true that no other ballet master in the
world has administrative duties similar to those of the master of the Royal Ballet [who not only was head of both company and school but served as general
manager]. The situation is even more precarious because the ballet is just
about to rediscover its lost self-confidence. And it is Kronstam who has given
the ballet its self-confidence back.'"

Much of the article is an attack on Jørgen Mydtskov, blaming him for Kronstam's resignation and explaining backstage politics in great detail, claiming,
in the subhead, that the "Technical director is really running the Theatre." This
was a time of what is often euphemistically referred to as fiscal restraint. "Cuts
in the budget and heavy administration have made it hard to concentrate on art
on the national stage on Kongens Nytorv," the article continued. "Internal
fights at the top of the Theatre's administration have not made it any easier."

Jensen quotes unnamed stage technicians who claimed that "Jørgen Mydtskov has worked a lot through the years at theaters, but he never learned
anything." Mydtskov, as technical director, would have been ultimately responsible for that rattan tree. He was not loved. "Internally he's called Jørgen Svingarm [lit., Jørgen Swing-Arm; it rhymes in Danish] because he always opens
his arms and says, 'Oh, we'll take care of that.' And then, the theater's technical
personnel say, nothing happens."

Kronstam never mentioned Mydtskov. He did say several times, however, that Max Sørensen "hated me" and made things very difficult for him. The *Politiken* article has some unkind words for Sørensen as well, saying he has "responsibility for the treasure chest, and he is sitting very tightly on it. Every paper clip is being picked up off the floor for fear that it will explode the budget if it is lost."

The incident of the rattan tree may have been the trigger, but it's unlikely that Jørgen "Svingarm" was wholly to blame for Kronstam's resignation. In an interview in America in 1982, Kronstam said: "I'd like to know which ballet masters really know what the job entails before they start doing it. Of course, you want to be concerned with the artistic side—planning repertoire, overseeing rehearsals and classes. Then suddenly you realize you have to attend meetings, endless meetings. Not that much happens, you just go and sit there and listen—but if you don't, you learn the hard way that you should have been there."[8] What Kronstam did not like was, as Kirsten Ralov put it, "the nonsense": the bureaucracy, the endless meetings with people in various departments, which he thought were often a complete waste of time, the turf fights, the constant flattery and game playing that were necessary if one were to get around the bureaucrats. Kronstam had no difficulty in dealing with dancers, guest choreographers, musicians, or backstage personnel and was highly respected by the technical people—stagehands, painters, carpenters, and the like.

After discussions with Matthiasen, Rohde, and Henrik Bering Liisberg, Kronstam was persuaded to stay on as director. He insisted on two changes. First, that he be given control over his budget, and second, that he be given a secretary to administer that budget. Until his tenure, the ballet's budget was merely a part of the Theatre's budget. The ballet director would propose a production but could always be told, "Oh, we don't have the money for that" at any point in the season. "We were always fighting with the opera for money," Kronstam said (a situation the Danish ballet shared with other European companies). If the ballet had control over its budget, if a specific amount of money were allocated to it for each season, the ballet master could plan productions to fit within that budget. There would be no substitution of a Puerto Rican fantasy bedstead for a metallic tree to save money. This was a significant change that gave the ballet an autonomy it had never had, and Kronstam used his political capital to get it.

It may have been at this time that Kronstam sought professional help for "the problem with the nerves." Certainly he must have had coaching in stress

management, at least, for he had developed a repertoire of strategies for dealing with stress that it is unlikely he could have come up with on his own. At
first he tried smoking. He didn't like the taste and could never inhale without
choking, so he gave it up after a month. He found tea soothing and began to
drink that instead of coffee. He would drink it in a glass during classes and
rehearsals, as well as meetings. He also took mints and chewed gum. If none
of these worked, for some meetings or occasions where he had to meet with
the press, he would take a tranquilizer. During the times he had trouble sleeping he would drink wine before retiring, and if that did not calm him suffi-
ciently, he would take a prescription sleeping pill. He said that no matter how
little sleep he'd gotten the night before, he woke at 7:30 A.M. every day of his
life. As he got older, however, the sleepless nights showed more and more in
his face and he often looked drained and exhausted. When the nerves were
especially raw, his hands shook. Bering Liisberg, who was to take over the
management of the Theatre the following season but who had come on board
early to get a feel for the place, was a bit wary of Kronstam's stability but was
assured by Rohde that it was nothing to worry about. Rohde, who had known
Kronstam since he was a boy, knew that all Kronstam needed was a few days'
rest and he would be fine.

If not quite fine, he was at least back at work. Kronstam presented another
new program: Balanchine's *Divertimento No. 15* paired with Bournonville's *The
Kermesse in Bruges,* a major revival. He had planned to get *Allegro Brillante,* but
fell in love with *Divertimento* the first time he saw it. "As soon as I got home, I
wrote Mr. Balanchine a letter," he said. "I said, 'I know I had asked for *Allegro
Brillante,* but I have just seen your beautiful *Divertimento No. 15* and I would
love to have that for the company.'" Balanchine consented, and the two works
went together beautifully, the Mozartian purity of *Divertimento* complement-
ing Brenaa's masterful, yet delicate, staging of *Kermesse.*

The previous production of *Kermesse,* from the 1960s, had not been successful, and many felt that the ballet was too old-fashioned to be revived and was a
negligible work at that. But Brenaa breathed new life into it. He saved *Kermesse,*
at least for a generation, as he had saved *Lifeguards.* Brenaa's production used
almost the entire company: Mette-Ida Kirk and Ib Andersen danced the young
lovers, Niels Kehlet and Johnny Eliasen the hero's brothers, and Kirsten
Simone, in an entirely new interpretation of the rich widow who falls for the

bumpkin brother, had a great success in what she had made, with Brenaa's encouragement, a star turn.

Svend Kragh-Jacobsen's review was headlined "The Ballet in Joyous Growth":

> It is a great pleasure to see how our ballet grows—almost from night to night—with the difficult and very different tasks it has been given this season. The first new program was Balanchine and Bournonville, which went well. Then came the big Tetley night, which brought a number of young names in focus. Finally, a week ago, the two Bs who constantly inspire our dancers, namely Balanchine and Bournonville.
>
> A number of new dancers had tried the parts on the second night, but this Saturday, at their second chance, they settled down so that the performance held its own compared to the first cast, thus assuring Henning Kronstam's third success this season. For the new program—like the previous ones—the red light [signifying a sold-out house] shone out over the icy Kongens Nytorv. (*Berlingske Tidende*, August 7, 1979)

The season finished with a new production of *Giselle* by Bruhn. Kronstam wanted Bruhn not only because he had produced *Giselle* for the company several times before, but because he knew Bruhn would be an inspiration to the dancers. In the Ninka interview, Kronstam had said he wanted to get the big classical ballets for Mette Hønningen and Sorella Englund, but both were ill when *Giselle* entered the repertory. Instead, two young ballerinas danced the title part: Ann-Kristin Hauge (with Ib Andersen) and Lis Jeppesen (with Arne Villumsen). Kronstam took the small role of the Duke of Courland in this production because, he said, "None of the boys knew how to walk on the stage and present a woman, and I wanted to show them an example."

One unfortunate by-product of *Giselle* was that it precipitated a breach between Kronstam and Kirsten Simone. Simone, his old friend and partner, had not fared well under Flindt. Both she and Anna Lærkesen had been essentially benched in the 1970s in favor of Flindt's wife, Vivi, and Mette Hønningen—not from personal favoritism, but because as Flindt's interests turned more and more to modern dance, he wanted dancers suited to that repertory. By the time Kronstam took over, Simone was forty-four, as was he, and had not been dancing classical ballets regularly for several years. Ballerinas elsewhere often continue dancing *Giselle*, or *La Sylphide*, well into their fifties, but that had never been the practice in Copenhagen. Kronstam also felt that there was no suitable partner for Simone now that he and Flindt were no longer dancing. "The hardest thing I had to do," he said about his directorship, "was to keep going to Kirsten and saying, 'No, you're not going to dance that role. Mette is going to dance it.'"

Instead, he gave Simone roles that were appropriate to her age, and two of them—Fru von Everdingen in *Kermesse* and Louise in *Lifeguards*—were special successes. He also had her teaching and assigned her to assist Bruhn in rehearsals of *Giselle*. Unfortunately, this did not prove successful and Bruhn asked that she be taken off the production, explaining in a letter to her what the problems were. The issue was not her knowledge but her manner, which the dancers found condescending, and Bruhn thought this was having a negative effect on the rehearsals.[9] Kronstam agreed with Bruhn, and replaced Simone.

This further damaged their relationship, and the fact that Kronstam withdrew from the company socially when he was ballet master caused them to grow further apart. According to Simone, she did not visit Kronstam at his home from this point until after Gerstenberg died, fifteen years later, in 1994. The breach was eventually healed, or at least patched over, but, perhaps understandably, some resentment remained. Perhaps because of this, perhaps because she wanted to think of her childhood friend only as her partner, Simone seemed unable to accept the fact that Kronstam's career had developed in ways that her own had not. While other dancers would speak of the excellence of Kronstam's productions and his skills as an instruktør, Simone was dismissive of this aspect of his career. Because she was so often turned to by those interested in the company's history or what was going on backstage, and because she was generally considered Kronstam's closest friend within the company (which in many ways she was) her view of him as an ineffectual ballet master, as well as some inaccurate characterizations of several aspects of his personal life, were accepted by many as fact.

Other early experiments in using older dancers did not work out well either. Kronstam invited Margrethe Schanne to teach the aspirants' mime class for a month. "I thought she might be able to give the girls something interesting," he said, but found she was unable to communicate what she knew. He never invited her back. Kronstam would not sit down with someone and say, "This is what I think you're doing wrong, and that's why I'm taking this action" unless he thought the problem was correctable. This often caused hurt feelings and misunderstandings. One of his most frequent expressions was, "But that's the way she is," by which he meant he tried to understand someone's nature and act accordingly. He did not believe in trying to change a person's basic personality. When dancers asked why they did not get this or that role, his answers could be terse to the point of being cryptic. "Not the way you are dancing," he told one ballerina, which could mean that she did not have the technique for that role at that time, or that he felt her unsuited, by personality or type, to the role. "Because Arne is the man I want to see on stage," was the response to a dancer who demanded to know why he was often second cast to Arne Villumsen, a response that could be interpreted, and probably was, that Kronstam simply liked Villumsen better, but really meant that Kronstam's first rule of casting was to serve the needs of the ballet. If Villumsen were the dancer most suited to five leading roles that season, then he would dance at all five premieres. "I always felt that, since I wasn't a choreographer, the casting must be done very carefully," Kronstam said, "so that the dancers who weren't cast would understand." This was probably a bit optimistic, but despite the resentments that exist in any ballet company, Kronstam's artistic integrity was always highly respected.

Astonishment preceded delight and awe. None of the public, not even Danes, suspected that there was so much variety, such depth as well as charm, nor did we know beforehand the full value of the mime. One wondered where these pieces had been all one's life, and believed that this single week had opened a wider window on the past than all the hours we'd ever spent at classical ballet.
—George Jackson, "Falling in Love Again"

We are happy about Bournonville, but he is a Devil.
—Henning Kronstam, qtd. by Dunning in the *New York Times*, June 13, 1980

Twenty-two

The Bournonville Festival and *The Firebird*

November 30, 1979, would be the 100th anniversary of the death of August Bournonville, and Kronstam decided to use this opportunity to revive and refresh as many of his ballets as possible. Restoring the ballets and dancing the entire Bournonville repertory in a concentrated period of time would also return the dancers to their roots, and to classical ballet, in a way that changing teachers or company classes alone would not do. Kronstam had begun planning the festival in 1977. "I thought we had to do one evening—only one evening. That was all I thought about, in the beginning," he said. "Then during that season there was a week where Stanley Williams was teaching here and Lynn Seymour was taking his classes, and we spent a lot of time talking. And she said, 'If I ever could see all the Bournonville ballets in one week, I would come to Copenhagen.'" Kronstam kept that in the back of his mind.

"In 1978, I started thinking about the Bournonville—not a festival, but the Bournonville gala performance—and I talked about it to Kirsten Ralov and she said, 'Well, we could maybe do three ballets.'" Then Hans Brenaa returned to the company. "He was, at that time, about seventy and I thought, 'Let me get as much out of Brenaa as possible.' So I said, 'How many ballets can you do?' He thought he could do everything. He was very energetic. And he said, 'Okay, I can do *Lifeguards*. I can do *Far from Denmark*. I can do *Kermesse*, and I can do *La Sylphide*.'

"So we started, Kirsten Ralov and I, slowly to say, 'Well, we've got more and more ballets.' We went to the minister of culture [Niels Matthiasen] and said, 'We can do all these ballets'—it was about nine at the time. He said, 'We have to negotiate with the people from the National Museum of Art.' [The art museum presented a major Bournonville exhibition during the festival.] We called for a big meeting in the Ministry of Culture, and everybody got very excited about the idea. The marketing and public relations were given to Søren Dyssegaard [an avid ballet fan who was very knowledgeable about Bournonville, borrowed from the Foreign Ministry]."

Most of the ballets presented at the festival were not in active repertory. Kronstam had only fifteen months to restage, refresh, and restore the seven full ballets and two fragments presented. There was not time enough to do this in the regular seasons at Kongens Nytorv. "We used everything. In order to get *Folk Tale* into the repertory, we had to do it in Tivoli." Kronstam had run into Niels-Jørgen Kaiser, the director of Tivoli Gardens and a ballet fan who presented ballet companies in his concert hall. Kaiser congratulated him on becoming ballet master and said they must do something together. Kronstam proposed a new production of *A Folk Tale* and got Tivoli to pay half the costs. Peter Martins, reportedly Kaiser's favorite dancer, flew home to dance Junker Ove. Kronstam said Kaiser had not insisted on that but that "it was his wish."

Kronstam had not expected that the festival would attract so much attention. 'It was something only for here in the Theatre," he said, "but then the art museum and the Court Theatre began to get involved, and there were books, too. Allan Fridericia wrote a book about Bournonville. Walter Terry wrote a book about Bournonville. Everybody got interested in the idea and suddenly it opened like a flower."[1]

Lifeguards and *Kermesse* had been brought back in the 1978–79 season. "We did *Folk Tale* in August [1979] in Tivoli, and then up to November we did all the rest of them. *Napoli* was the one that was not so forgotten, so Kirsten Ralov did *Napoli* and *Flower Festival* pas de deux. Flemming Ryberg did *Konservatoriet* and Hans Brenaa did the rest." Brenaa was doing so much that Kronstam asked to work with the new cast in *La Sylphide* (Lis Jeppesen and Arne Villumsen, with Sorella Englund as Madge), and he is listed as instruktør in the 1979 program for that production. He had had the dancers in the mime class as aspirants and had taught them the ballet there, as Gerda Karstens had taught him. Lis Jeppesen also went to Margrethe Schanne at her summerhouse for help. Stagings during this period were very collaborative. Kronstam often coached dancers taking on his former roles—he worked with Tommy Frishøi on Edouard in *Lifeguards* and Alvar in *Far from Denmark,* and with Arne Villumsen on James—and he oversaw all the productions, often making suggestions to the stagers and the dancers.

Brenaa would have been happy to stage all the ballets, but Kirsten Ralov had taken over *Folk Tale* and *Napoli* during Brenaa's self-imposed absence, and Kronstam would not take them away from her. Kronstam knew that Brenaa's stagings were more theatrically alive than Ralov's but probably reasoned that it would have been dangerous to have entrusted the entire repertory to a single stager. Ralov was as knowledgeable as Brenaa about Bournonville technique and an excellent coach. She was not up to his level as a director, and the Danish critics' complaints about her productions as being inferior to prior ones is apt, but her stagings were acceptable. Compared with what was to follow, they were brilliant.

1979–80

During Kronstam's first season, there were seventy-five performances of Bournonville ballets (not counting thirteen of Flindt's *Toreador*), compared to an average of twenty-five to thirty per year during Flindt's tenure. The 1979–80 season, excluding tours, included 161 performances of Bournonville works. "It was almost too much, it was so much Bournonville," Ib Andersen said, twenty years after the festival. "But we knew it was going for something more and it was on such a high level. That was the last time when the ballets were rehearsed by people who actually had a connection to the past. You could not do it today." The concentration on Bournonville was another gamble that paid off. As several critics noted, the company seemed to dance Bournonville better the more it danced him. There were new productions of *Far from Denmark* (another ballet long out of repertory) and *La Ventana*, and two new productions that were also major restorations, though not revisions: *La Sylphide* and *A Folk Tale*. The only new ballets were *Gærdesanger under Kunstig Stjernehimmel*, an experimental work by a dancer, Inge Jensen; Hans van Manen's *Song without Words;* and the divertissement from *William Tell*, which may or not be by Bournonville. Kronstam thought not and so it was not included in the festival.

In September the company made a brief visit to Düsseldorf, dancing *Kermesse in Bruges* and *Napoli* Act III. One critic, Frank Pauli, was a bit condescending to Bournonville, and his view is not unlike the typical Danish one: "Simple sugar, this short visit from Copenhagen. Color, joy, merriment reigned, and the ballets of Bournonville always let God be a good person. Everything always ends for the best. The dancers, therefore, can leap as much as they want, full of the joy of life. The world is healthy and the audience gives its approval." But he also noted the depth of the performances: "The lightness in these works is not treated in a light manner. There's care and that's why we care about what happens on stage, and the effect is a deep one." He credited the company's unity of style to the fact that there was little turnover and that it was obvious that they were all Danes.[2]

Several events shortly before and around the time of the festival served as its harbingers and helped to stir interest in Bournonville far from Denmark. Patricia McAndrew, an American who had seen the company in 1966 and had become so interested in Bournonville that she learned Danish, translated Bournonville's *Mit Teaterliv* into English. *My Theatre Life* was published in 1979, as well as McAndrew's translations of the Bournonville libretti in the scholarly journal *Dance Chronicle*. For English-speaking critics and historians, these translations were tremendously important, as there was very little material in English about Bournonville at that time.

For ballet fans as well as critics, Stanley Williams's production of *Bournonville Divertissements* by the New York City Ballet in the spring of 1977 was also important. For some critics, this gave Bournonville Balanchine's imprimatur. For fans it was a surprise to see how difficult the century-old choreography was, and how much fun. The lightness and speed were dazzling. Suddenly, Bournonville was contemporary, a "hot" choreographer.

Perhaps inspired by the new interest in Bournonville in America, that summer two young Danish dancers, Frank Andersen and Dinna Bjørn, independently came up with the idea of starting a touring company modeled on Inge Sand's Soloists of the Royal Danish Ballet, which had been very successful in America. The two joined forces with several Danish dancers, and the group jointly put up the money to get the venture off the ground. Andersen served as coordinator and Bjørn used the troupe as a laboratory to revive lost pieces of Bournonville choreography. Hans Brenaa also worked with the company, which was a private enterprise. It had no official connection to the Theatre and was not a branch of the Royal Danish Ballet, as many supposed, a point on which Kronstam was adamant for several reasons. As dancers, neither Andersen nor Bjørn represented the standard of Bournonville dancing Kronstam (and Brenaa and Ralov) wanted for the company. In addition, several of the dancers were not solo dancers, and Kronstam did not want people to think that they were Royal Danish Ballet principals. Perhaps most important, Kronstam disliked seeing the Bournonville repertory reduced to gala programs of virtuoso pas de deux and feared that those for whom this was an introduction to Bournonville would be disappointed when they saw the full ballets, with their long passages of mime and folk dancing.

The Bournonville group was very popular in America, performing at City Center in the spring of 1978 and, for the duration of Kronstam's tenure as director, every summer at performance parks in America. As such, it did much to keep alive the interest in Bournonville here. At home, the effects were not uniformly sanguine, as the group's constant touring around Denmark interfered with the company's schedule and overworked the dancers, causing injuries. Abroad too, some of the revivals of long lost Bournonville ballets were such literal renderings from the skeletal notation that they seemed very different from what was seen in the full ballets in repertory, leading some to surmise that what had survived could not really be by Bournonville at all but must be the work of later generations. Many feel that Bjørn's revivals lacked the emendations a Brenaa would know how to make.

It was the Bournonville Festival itself—eight days in the gray, dreary Copenhagen November—that revived both Danish and international interest in Bournonville and in the company as a major classical institution. "It was a tremendous event that week and the end of it was festive, like we've never seen in this Theatre. All the young dancers said, 'Oh, this is different.' The house was full every night and people just got blown away," Kronstam said.[3] Over 200 critics from around the world came, as well as many ballet fans. The festival opened November 24 with *Konservatoriet, Flower Festival* pas de deux, and *Far from Denmark*. Sunday was a day off, possibly so that foreigners could recover from *Far from Denmark*. The next week the programming was as follows: November 26, *Napoli;* November 27, *La Ventana, Far from Denmark, Lifeguards;* November 28, *La Ventana, Kermesse en Bruges;* November 29, *Konservatoriet, A Folk Tale;* November 30, *La Sylphide, Napoli* Act III.

Kronstam invited company directors from around the world, as well as dancers he had known through his long career, among them Galina Ulanova,[4] Yvette Chauviré, Serge Lifar, Robert Joffrey, and Ruth Page. Lifar gave his Nijinsky Prize that year to Ib Andersen, the Pavlova Prize to Lis Jeppesen, and special Nijinsky Prizes to both Brenaa and Kronstam. The festival was covered extensively in both the Danish and the American press. Reviews were overwhelmingly favorable, from old friends of Bournonville—Mary Clark and Clement Crisp of London, Clive Barnes and Walter Terry of New York—to a younger generation of critics new to Bournonville—Deborah Jowitt and Marcia Siegel, Arlene Croce and Tobi Tobias all fell under his spell. By the late 1970s the Danish way of dancing was so different from that in the rest of the ballet world— more gentle, more harmonious, more fluid, more precise—that foreigners had to look at it hard to see it. The festival made them do so. "The way the Danes dance Bournonville is not the way it is done in New York," Croce noted. "But whether the style is 'historic' or 'anachronistic' it is lucid on its home ground. The age of a theatre, the tempo of a city, the scale of its architecture prepare an ambience. To see the Royal Danish Ballet at home is to see it plain. One can still dissent from its style, but the pleasure of a clear and consistent vision is such that one doesn't. It just feels better not to."[5]

For many Americans, the most intriguing ballet was *A Folk Tale,* which eyes brought up on *Swan Lake* and *Sleeping Beauty* saw as a classical ballet. Ralov's production included a very ingenious updating, one that did not damage the fabric of the ballet. Rather than having the trolls portrayed as charming storybook characters, as in previous productions, she made them creatures who aped human behavior, a very contemporary approach that many Americans took to be Bournonville's—and may have been. Costume sketches for the original production show very humanoid trolls, in simple peasant garb. George Jackson wrote:

> *A Folk Tale* is the most haunting of Bournonville's ballets. Who can resist the droll hobbling and hammering of its dwarfs, the irrepressible spasms that

bring disorder into the dancing of the troll changeling, or the human changeling's sentimentally lyric yearnings for love and faith—feelings that are just as irrepressible as her opposite's tantrums?

Those snotty children, besotted women and mean men at the troll party are, at one and the same time, outrageous caricatures and severe indictments of the irreligious, of unwashed bohemians and of the undeserving poor. Only one other dance work has a similar philosophic scope and realistic viewpoint: *Don Quixote* by Balanchine.[6]

Audience response throughout the festival was so overwhelming that many observers said the dancers did not know what to do during the many curtain calls or how to handle the flowers tossed to them from the audience. On the final evening, after *Napoli* Act III, everyone in the company took a final call, each dressed in a costume from one of the ballets, so all Bournonville's characters could take a bow. Ulla Bjerre wrote of the festival's closing night: "It was brilliant to see the Theatre's big audience in gala [the proscenium rimmed with flowers], to stand up in the lit auditorium and hear the cheers, clapping so that your hands burned, and to see the Royal Orchestra's musicians in gala facing the stage and giving a flourish. Our ballet has done its duty with clear joy and has danced Bournonville's name to great honor, and ballet master Henning Kronstam has also, from the highest place, received personal thanks for the fine outcome of the Bournonville week" (December 5, 1979).

There was one unpleasant by-product of the festival for Kronstam. In connection with the festival, a film had been made called *Dancing Bournonville*. It included footage of Kronstam, Bruhn, Fredbjørn Bjørnsson, and Flemming Ryberg teaching, as well as some of Brenaa and Ralov coaching Bournonville excerpts, and scenes from *Kermesse en Bruges* and the third act of *Napoli*. The film was successful and there was the possibility to make a companion. According to Kronstam, Ebbe Mørk, a critic involved with the film, suggested they make a second film out of the unused footage. Kronstam replied that he had looked at all the footage and selected the best sequences for the original film and that there wasn't enough good material left to make another. Mørk tried to persuade him, arguing that there was plenty of acceptable footage, and besides, no one would notice if there were a few less than perfect shots, but Kronstam said, "I could not do that to the dancers" and refused.

Bournonville had written in *My Theatre Life*, explaining why certain people had been omitted from his book, "My friends I will not smuggle in, and my

Curtain call on the last night of the Bournonville Festival, 1979. Kronstam is in the center, holding wreaths. Kirsten Ralov is to his right, Hans Brenaa to his left. Private collection.

enemies I consign to oblivion."[7] This is, perhaps, a Danish theatrical tradition. Mørk had been assigned to write a history of the company for the festival's souvenir program and in it he consigned Kronstam to oblivion. Kronstam was mentioned only twice in an article that stretched over seven pages (one of which was completely devoted to Flindt): in a list of Vera Volkova's pupils and, very briefly in the final paragraph, as the current director. Roles identified with Kronstam were discussed in performances by the dancers in subsequent casts. To Kronstam this was an example of the pettiness he had more than occasionally experienced from critics. "He was angry because there would have been money in it," he said. Kronstam never again took Mørk, a very intelligent writer, seriously, believing what he wrote was personally motivated, and much of what he wrote after this incident is quite harsh.

After the festival, to ensure that the Bournonville ballets would be well kept, or at least easily revived if some mishap befell them, Kronstam had each of the extant ballets videotaped twice, once in practice clothes so the steps and gestures could be clearly seen by future stagers, and a second time in costume. He kept the ballets in repertory in rotation throughout his seven years as ballet master, believing that Bournonville should make up a third of the repertory and that no ballet should be out of repertory too long, lest the dancers lose touch with it.

Because of the festival's success and the subsequent interest in Bournonville, the company was suddenly in demand around the world, but presenters only wanted to see the Bournonville ballets. Kronstam fought this because he did not want to become a Nordic D'Oyly Carte. Also, as interest in Bournonville burgeoned, many people came with suggestions for revivals of Bournonville ballets. Because of the nature of ballet, and these ballets in particular, someone wanting to revive a Bournonville ballet almost of necessity had to come to Copenhagen for both the company's financial and human resources. Kronstam rejected all of them, either because he did not think the stagers could carry it off or because he did not think there was enough material remaining to permit revival and, as he put it, "I hate pastiche." Kronstam did take the proposals seriously enough to investigate them. One scholar presented several notated variations that he thought might be worth reviving. "Hans and I took them into a studio and we tried to dance them," Kronstam said, "but if you're brought up in the style, you know when something is not right, and these were not right."

A few months after the festival, in March 1980, Niels Matthiasen died suddenly of a stroke. Danish classical ballet and the Bournonville tradition lost not only its champion but one of the very few people who understood what it took to maintain that tradition and who had the will and the power to make it possible. For Kronstam it meant that he had lost not only a longtime friend but also his backup, in a political as well as a very practical sense. Matthiasen had promised him many things—a theater for when the company had to vacate the Royal Theatre during a period of renovation that was about to take place and enough money to acquire the repertory he wanted. In the years that followed, Lene Schrøder-Hansen remembers Kronstam saying several times, "If Niels were still alive, this wouldn't be happening." Without Matthiasen's support, Kronstam was not able to get as much money as he had in the first two seasons to spend on new ballets, and this, as well as the move to Tivoli, is why he had to turn to the small-scale, cheaply acquired, and cheaply mounted works he had wanted to avoid. After Matthiasen, the minister of culture position became a political plum and has never been filled by anyone as knowledgeable about and committed to Danish culture. Kronstam continued to have a good relationship with Bering Liisberg, and the two men shared the same vision for the company, but Bering Liisberg had lost his backup as well.

There were other losses. Around this time, Svend Kragh-Jacobsen retired. Although there were able writers who followed, there would never again be one so steeped in classical tradition that he could write of a young dancer, "He is a Patroklos on his way to becoming an Achilles," or who was as sensitive to ballet's subtleties until the generation of critics whose eye and taste had been trained by Kronstam began writing in the 1990s.

At the end of the 1979–80 season Ib Andersen left the company to join the New York City Ballet. Andersen said he had intended to leave Denmark from the time he was about sixteen and had gone to Kronstam when it was announced that Kronstam was to take over as ballet master to advise him of his intention. "He told me," Kronstam said, "and I said to him, 'Don't you leave during my first season,' and he didn't. He gave me two." Andersen's departure was a blow, though Kronstam minimized it, saying there were so many talented dancers it opened up new chances for them. There were dancers with some of Andersen's lightness and charm in the coming years, but none with his hidden fire and technical virtuosity, and his absence not only created a hole but also left Arne Villumsen, a velvet technician who could be both lyrical and dramatic, to carry the classical repertory nearly alone. In addition to principals on the verge of retirement, at least as classical dancers (Niels Kehlet, Flemming Ryberg, and Palle Jacobsen), there were two other principal men— Johnny Eliasen, the leading man in many of Flindt's ballets, a character and modern dancer, although Kronstam occasionally cast him in classical roles, and Frank Andersen, a demi-caractère dancer, charming in roles like Franz in *Coppelia* or Geert (the uncouth brother) in *Kermesse in Bruges*—but neither had the range or artistry of Ib Andersen and Villumsen. Coming up were Bjarne Hecht, who danced many leading roles during Kronstam's directorship and whom the American critic Tobi Tobias described as "he of the elfin face and dazzling footwork";[8] Torben Jeppesen, who Kronstam said was "perhaps not so interesting as a technician, but with a very masculine quality onstage"; and Erling Eliasson and Lars Damsgaard, two very tall men frequently cast in the contemporary repertory.

Mette Hønningen, who excelled in classical as well as modern dance roles, and Sorella Englund, a romantic dancer who could be both Sylph and Coquette, were both fully developed artists when Kronstam took over. Both, unfortunately, were sick or injured often during much of this period. Among the younger women, Linda Hindberg had been dancing virtuoso roles—*Etudes, Swan Lake*—from a very early age and had been promoted by Flindt. Three of her classmates became principals under Kronstam: Mette-Ida Kirk, Lis Jeppesen, and Heidi Ryom. By Danish employ, Kirk was the Hilda and Myrtha, Jeppesen the Sylph, and Ryom the Svanilda of their generation, although each extended her range and their repertories often overlapped.

Kirk was the first dancer Kronstam promoted, and she told an interesting story about one of the few times Kronstam seems to have contacted a dancer privately, and that says much about the reticent Danish psyche. "It was a big change for me and it took me some years to figure out why I was a principal," she said. "It was because, I think, to be in the corps de ballet, and at the same time do principal things, as you do before you get to be principal, and then suddenly you are a principal, it's a little lonely. You're not in the corps any more, doing all these things with the other girls. You are suddenly all on your own and it's your responsibility, because you are in the center, you are in the main role. And it took some years for me to find out how to become easy with that, and I know that Henning couldn't understand that. We were living quite close to each other at the time and one night Henning came and knocked on my door, and I was very surprised because he never did things like that. He came in and asked if he could talk with me, and he said that he did not understand why I was so shy, why I was so afraid to show myself a little more and take what he thought belonged to me and go for it, and really be more aggressive, in a sense. And I knew what he said, and I understood what he said, but at the same time I needed a lot of help at that time, some kind of guidance, to know how. Because of course there was a lot of pressure from other colleagues, and I was not that secure at the time. Why am I the one who should have all the roles? Maybe they should have a chance too."

In June the company took the Bournonville Festival to Chicago at the invitation of Geraldine Freund, a wealthy patroness who presented a festival each year. "She said, 'I want to buy the whole Bournonville Festival and then I want one piece only for myself,'" Kronstam said. "So I did *William Tell*, too, because that hadn't been done at the Bournonville Festival." Freund also demanded guest stars—Peter Schaufuss and Peter Martins—not a popular move with the company, although Kronstam presented the guests in the second casts.

Freund was said to have lost money on her festival, which was estimated to have cost a million dollars.[9] The *Chicago Sun Times* called it "the ballet happening of 1980" and noted with some pride that the Brooklyn Academy of Music had wanted to present the festival too but that the Danes had chosen Chicago. Freund wanted them to come back in 1982, but "The Danes are reluctant to become a touring company."[10]

In addition to performances, there was a lecture on Bournonville by Erik Aschengreen, a demonstration of Bournonville technique by Kirsten Ralov, and a panel on Bournonville reconstructions moderated by Walter Terry. Reviews contain interesting details of the state of the company. Mary Kerner noted: "There's none of the star system buffoonery that besets so many American companies—i.e., you're apt to see last night's Sylphide in tonight's pas de trois—which means no scrimping on the quality of the performance that every single dance segment gets in every ballet. You can count on a septet receiving the same careful attention the leading roles do. It's almost a redundancy of treasures" (*Christian Science Monitor*, July 17, 1980).

Lewis Segal wrote an analysis of Bournonville as a choreographer, as a teller of stories through steps:

> When the Danes danced, Chicago was an international ballet center, the only city outside Copenhagen to present the Bournonville festival, and dance consciousness here became almost a civic responsibility. Bournonville mime is not the sterile, conventionalized sign language we all endure in the Russian warhorses, but far closer to silent film acting, vigorous, individualized, detailed and musical, too.
>
> Even today, no choreographer besides Ashton has so wide a stretch and Bournonville not only mastered every genre, he combined them for telling dramatic purposes. For instance, he gave nasty Birthe (the troll baby, grown to womanhood) a lyrical pointe solo in which she tries to display her grace and refinement. However, her troll nature won't stay suppressed. It bursts through the veneer of classicism in claw like spasms of the hands and gnarled jumps that alarm her but are funny to everyone else. (*Los Angeles Times*, August 10, 1980)

Chicago critic Ann Barzel answered some of the questions about the company that had been raised in intermission and postperformance chats. During this period American critics often condescended to the Danes as technicians, writing that they really weren't up to international standard and were only suited to the Bournonville repertory, and Barzel tackled this directly:

Then there are the scores of questions about the unfamiliar ballets and the fallacies in evaluating the unfamiliar. Mention has been made of the lack of virtuosity. Danish dancers, whose schooling includes modern technical innovations, are terrific dancers.

Audiences were conscious of the airiness of the dancing but not aware that the jumps were as high as those of the more flamboyant Russians. Danes don't stop the flow to take a deliberate preparation that announces, Here comes a hard one. Our box-office great, male superstars rarely dash off the rare entrechat huit, the many crossings of the feet in a high jump. At least a dozen young Danes whipped them off without fuss in ballet after ballet.

I heard a murmur of lack of Flamenco verve in the Spanish-flavored and utterly charming *La Ventana*. The fact is Flamenco dancing did not emerge from the gypsy caves until late in the 19th century. The Spanish dance of Bournonville's time was the romantic type, which the choreographer balleticized further in his romantic pieces.

Then there was the remark that the Danish dancers were not as good in slow movements as in quick steps. Not so. Bournonville often set "promenades" in which the dancer on one flat foot revolves slowly, pushing himself with a slight shoving of the heel. That cannot be as smooth as whirling on the toe, and the slight waver does not mean inept execution. (*Chicago American*, July 3, 1980)

1980–81

In his third season, Kronstam presented John Neumeier's *A Midsummer Night's Dream*, which was so popular that for the first time in the Theatre's history tickets had to be restricted to only four per patron. Kronstam had seen the ballet in Hamburg "and right away I knew it was the right ballet for our audience," he said. The designs were beautiful, it was magical yet contemporary, comic and lyrical, and it had good roles for many dancers. Kronstam said that Violette Verdy, then director of the Paris Opera Ballet, was in the audience. He could sense that she was interested as well, and he was eager to get to Neumeier ahead of her. He coveted a tiny role, that of Button the Tailor, for himself "because it was the silliest part in the world," and insisted that it be written into the contract that he could perform the role. *A Midsummer Night's Dream* uses Mendelssohn's suite of the same name, with the music of György Ligeti added in the dream sequences. "That hurdy-gurdy music," Kronstam said with a sigh. "The only time in my life I ever fell asleep at the Theatre was during *Midsummer*. It was too long. The next day I called John and said, 'You're going to have to cut it.'"

The ballet had been scheduled for the preceding season, but a strike by the costume department forced its postponement. When it finally received its premiere, the ballet was a critical as well as a popular success. Neumeier has always been highly regarded in Copenhagen and, of course, Hamburg, where he directs the Hamburg Ballet, though not in America. In a rare pro-Neumeier review by an American, Peter Rosenwald, in *Dance News* (December 1980), wrote that under the new direction, the Danes had "continued to build back their strength as a company, and look better than ever."

If Balanchine's version could be called "minimalist," Neumeier's creation is definitely "maximalist." There is nothing wrong in that. Neumeier shows a strong sense of theater and has created a rich and delightful ballet, full of action and humor as well as a very sympathetic understanding of Shakespeare's original with not a little inspirational help from British theater director Peter Brooks, whose *Midsummer Night's Dream* for the Royal Shakespeare Company was a landmark production. He has been brilliantly assisted by sets and costumes by Jürgen Rose. The Danes have obviously taken to the work with joy and gusto and the result is a fine ballet, finely danced.

The second program of new works was a mixed bill of works by Alvin Ailey, Rudi van Dantzig, and Hans van Manen. "The only time that Henrik [Bering Liisberg, now theater chief] gave me a suggestion was when we did Alvin Ailey's *Memoria*. And the company was screaming. They said, 'Oh, we can't do that. It's impossible.' They were scared of it because they'd never done anything like that," Kronstam said. The Ailey company had been dancing at Tivoli and had one of the biggest successes of any dance company in Denmark. Kronstam liked Ailey and thought a ballet by him would be good for both the dancers and the audience. "*Memoria* was new. I heard that he used the full company with seven principals and the leading girl. And he came in and he chose Mette Hønningen right away," Kronstam said.

"Alvin loved the dancers and he liked the atmosphere of the company. Later he came back to do *The River* and then he came back to do an evening of two new ballets. And he knew exactly—he wrote to me, the casting and everything, because he knew the dancers." When Ailey returned to do *The River,* Kronstam said that during one of the stage rehearsals he suddenly "became very inspired by the dancers," and stopped the rehearsal because he no longer wanted to do *The River*—he wanted to stage a full-length production of *Swan Lake* for them!

Soon, the company would be dancing at Tivoli Concert Hall, because the

Theatre's long-needed renovation was ready to begin. The renovation would be primarily of the backstage areas, which had been barely touched in the twentieth century, although the stage and orchestra pit would be enlarged as well. The lighting apparatus was so primitive that lighting was basically either day (on) or night (off), for example. Kronstam had been sitting, glumly, in planning meetings for months. "There were about 152 architects, I think," he said. At Tivoli Gardens' concert hall, the only suitable theater available, the company would have to dance on a long and shallow stage, and it would have a very different audience.

1981–82

For three seasons Kronstam had had one critical and popular success after another, but this was about to change abruptly. Kronstam had invited Glen Tetley back to create a work for the company. "I had always wanted to do the full score, the original score written for Fokine for *Firebird*," Tetley said, "and I suggested that to Henning, which he loved, and I knew that in Mette Hønningen I had found somebody that I thought I could really create on."

Kronstam remembered it differently, saying he had not been thrilled with Tetley's suggestion of *Firebird*. "Eske Holm had done a *Firebird* about two years before. I knew that the press here would hate it because I brought a foreigner in to do a ballet that was done by a Danish choreographer a couple of years before.[11] But Glen said, 'Well, if it's not *Firebird*, then it's nothing,' so I said all right. He was very fascinated by Mette. And it was a beautiful, beautiful ballet. The Danes hated it. The New Yorkers loved it. It was very interesting. It was not *The Firebird* [the Fokine version] at all. It was a long story about a girl being loosened up from convention. And then she flew out and became a woman. There was a long pas de deux with Torben [Jeppesen] and Mette. At the end they became human again and there was a celebration—not a marriage, but a celebration."

Firebird was not popular with either the audience or the critics, and this was a shock to the dancers. Bjarne Hecht remembered that the rehearsals had gone very well, and "all of us were convinced that Tetley was making a masterpiece. You could feel it in the atmosphere. On opening night, when the curtain came down, there was absolute silence from the audience. And we looked at each other and said, 'It was that good!'—because sometimes people can be so stunned and they won't applaud right away. But the applause never came. It was really a shock."

Another evening of new work, by two young British choreographers, was also unpopular. Critics found Christopher Bruce's *Nat Med Blegnende Måne* (*Night of the Waning Moon*), a dark ballet that was thought to be too similar, and inferior, to Tetley's *Pierrot Lunaire*. Richard Alston, a modern-dance choreographer whom many British critics saw as having classical sensibilities, created an interesting experiment. Kronstam had seen a videotape of an Alston dance that he thought would suit the company, but Alston wanted to make a new work, a classical ballet rather than a modern-dance piece, on the company instead. Margaret Mercier remembered that this was the only time she was aware of complaints from dancers about the repertory. As Cullberg had done years ago, Alston kept asking the dancers if they could do this step or that—he had never worked with dancers on pointe before—and they were not happy with the experiment.

Alston used a suite of dances from Benjamin Britten's ballet, *The Prince of the Pagodas,* and created a set of dances to it (which he named *Kingdom of the Pagodas*). Lis Jeppesen and Bjarne Hecht, as two young lovers in a lyrical pas de deux, had a personal success, but the ballet as a whole was not liked. The British critic John Percival saw something in the work, but his was a lone voice.

> *Kingdom of the Pagodas* proves satisfying as well as stirring. It is a fine example of how pure dance reinforced by good music, can exhilarate by its sheer physical display and, at the same time, create its own imaginative mood. . . . *Kingdom of the Pagodas* is a great stride forward for Alston, showing that he can work on a scale and in a style he has not tackled before. How odd that it should need a foreign company to spot his potential and take the risk; and how sad that so enjoyable a work, to the only score written by Britten exclusively for dancing, should not be in a British repertory. (*London Times,* April 26, 1982)

Another experimental evening had a limited success. This was a workshop performed at the Gråbrødrescenen (Gray Friars' stage, an alternative space a few blocks from the Theatre). Kronstam revived Samuel Beckett's *Act without Words*—considered a play, although it is completely a pantomime, a tragicomic work about a man who is such a failure he can't even successfully kill himself—for Niels Bjørn Larsen and Fredbjørn Bjørnsson. There was a new ballet by Palle Jacobsen in traditional style called *Styx,* to music of Chopin; and then a theater piece, an intriguing retake on the Orpheus myth, by Arlette Weinreich, a dancer who was assuming increasing responsibilities as a rehearsal mistress and wanted to try her hand at choreography. Called *Brev til Orfeus* (Letter to Orpheus) and subtitled "a drama for two persons," it portrayed Orpheus as a self-absorbed choreographer so fascinated by his own thoughts and the music he hears through his Walkman that he never looks at his wife, Eurydice, danced by Jette Buchwald, one of the company's most interesting character dancers. The ballet had a script, delivered by voice-over, commenting on and advancing the action. Kronstam danced Orpheus; it was his last created role. "I knew for my first ballet I wanted Henning," said Weinreich, "because if you asked him, 'Would you show your soul in your face,' he would do it."

At the end of the season Ebbe Mørk wrote one of the earliest attacks on Kronstam's directorship:

> The audience of the opera has taken the matter into their own hands, rebelling against the anemic repertoire of the Royal Theatre. It cannot be long before one can imagine a similar situation on the ballet front. Anemic repertoires have characterized the time of ballet master Henning Kronstam. He has concentrated very much on elevating the corps to the technical heights where you rightly can demand to find it when it is supposed to count, on the great international stage. There is a colossal amount of talent in the Royal Ballet right now, but unfortunately not a lot to use it on.
>
> When the repertoire looks the way it does, it is due to some undeserved bad luck, but also to a somewhat indefinable repertoire policy this season. *Napoli* failed and it is a pure disaster that Bournonville is brought to other places in the world while his legacy stagnates through hesitation and lack of fantasy here in Denmark, where he belongs. Glen Tetley was the man they counted on, and it was here that the bad luck struck. Tetley is the international choreographer who has had the most influence on the Royal Ballet's repertoire over the last couple of years and with his best things like *Pierrot Lunaire*, *Le Sacre du Printemps*, and *Voluntaries* he has given us alternatives to the classics. It could not be predicted that his version of *Firebird* would fail and become a faint reflection of what this work offers solely through the music of Stravinsky. (*Politiken*, April 16, 1982)

Kronstam's three-year honeymoon with the Danish press was over.

In my last seasons, I had very bad critics.
—Henning Kronstam

 Twenty-three

Tivoli and Tours

During Kronstam's tenure as ballet master, and especially after the company had moved into Tivoli Gardens, the Royal Danish Ballet toured extensively. Kronstam knew that it would be impossible to keep a uniformly high standard of dancing at Tivoli because of logistical challenges and that there would likely be morale problems. One of his solutions was to tour as much as possible. "I wanted to keep the dancers' minds off what was happening at home," he explained. "It wasn't very nice being in Tivoli," as Johnny Eliasen put it. "It wasn't nice for Henning and it wasn't nice for any of us. It was like going on a camping trip in a tent. He made the best of a very bad situation."

Touring is both exhilarating and stressful to performers. Each new city, each new theater, is unpredictable. If a dancer becomes ill, a carefully prepared repertory can be endangered, and there are difficulties dealing with unfamiliar theaters and backstage personnel. For Kronstam personally, touring held special terrors, as he was alone for long periods of time, which always caused him tremendous anxiety, not because he was lonely but because solitude can in itself trigger an anxiety attack.[1] Yet, "I wanted the dancers to feel they got to dance on the big stages," he said, and during Kronstam's directorship, the Royal Danish Ballet danced in Berlin, Chicago, Brussels, New York, Tel Aviv, Wiesbaden, Paris, Lausanne, Washington, D.C., Dresden, Bergen, Singapore, Beijing, Shanghai, Tokyo, Hiroshima, and Osaka.

In the spring of 1982 the company made its fifth American tour, spending two weeks at Washington's Kennedy Center and one at New York's Metropolitan Opera House. Kronstam brought a repertory tailor-made for American critics to hate: Glen Tetley's *Firebird,* Alvin Ailey's *Memoria,* Arlette Weinreich's *Letter to Orpheus,* and Galeotti's *Whims of Cupid and the Ballet Master.*[2] *Coppelia* and the two Bournonville programs shown in Washington only (*Kermesse in Bruges/Napoli* Act III and *A Folk Tale*) were another gamble, as they were so different from usual ballet fare. On this tour, Søren Dyssegaard, now stationed at the embassy in Washington, was an immensely helpful "advance man," preparing theater press people and critics for what they were about to see.

The company received excellent reviews in both cities, which is all the more astounding as injuries caused last-minute cast changes. Kronstam had brought *Firebird* and *Memoria* to New York partially to showcase Mette Hønningen, but she and her partner in those ballets, Torben Jeppesen, were both injured and could not dance. Mette-Ida Kirk, fondly remembered for her Hilda at the Bournonville Festival, and Erling Eliasson (a tall young Prince and sensitive artist) were to dance *Folk Tale,* but they were also injured and a new cast had to be prepared on very short notice (Heidi Ryom and Bjarne Hecht, both of whom were judged quite successful). On top of this, Lis Jeppesen came down with the flu and had to be hospitalized briefly.

Several critics noted significant differences from the way the company had looked on its 1976 tour and credited Kronstam for those changes. Alan M. Kriegsman explained the renewed Danish ballet in a *Washington Post* Sunday preview piece, which began with his consideration of the Royal Danish Ballet as one of the top six companies in the world:

> Now, as ten years ago, these troupes are American Ballet Theatre and the New York City Ballet in this country; England's Royal Ballet; the Bolshoi and the Kirov in Russia; and finally, the Royal Danish Ballet.
>
> [This visit] is bound to become, by its very nature, a landmark event, one that

will be remembered and discussed for years afterward. This is especially so since nearly everything about the troupe has altered radically since its last appearance here—though many of the dancers are the same, there'll be lots of new faces and rankings; the artistic directorship, the esthetic orientation, and very largely the repertory all have changed.

Those who remember the company's 1976 performances here may remember the considerable furor over the programming and policies of then-director Flemming Flindt. Though the programs made their inevitable bow toward August Bournonville, the 19th century patron saint of Danish ballet, the repertory in general seemed drastically tilted towards the flamboyantly theatrical and belligerently contemporary work of Flindt himself.

Flindt was succeeded in 1978 by Kronstam (with Kirsten Ralov, a noted Bournonville authority, as his associate director) and a readjustment of plan and image ensued. . . . Stylistic diversity and contemporaneity have retained their place in the Royal Danish Ballet palette, but a renewed dedication to bedrock traditions under the Kronstam regime has again bestowed a sense of balance upon the repertory and with it, a sense of rebirth and reaffirmation upon the company as a whole. (May 30, 1982)

Kriegsman's long and rich reviews over the next two weeks give one of the most detailed pictures of the company during this period:

Ever since its first appearances in this country almost three decades ago, the Royal Danish Ballet has had a reputation for a special brand of bright-eyed bristling zest—a combination of joie de vivre and joie de danser. . . . Pervading the atmosphere during last night's program was a sense of joy, of vigor, of warmth and conviviality; the dancers' eagerness to share the pleasures of their art seemed a tangible entity. (June 2, 1982)

Of *Folk Tale,* Kriegsman wrote:

In repeat performances . . . the Royal Danish Ballet shuffled its . . . casts around in sundry ways. The ballet retained its singular charm and radiance throughout the permutations. What was more amazing was the way the various roles kept their identity and their relation to the dramatic whole in the face of these rotations, and this, despite the considerable variation in appearance and characteristics. The wonderful homogeneity of the Danish tradition and training seems to insure stylistic integrity at the same time that it enfranchises a broad latitude for individual interpretation. (June 7, 1982)

Kriegsman was especially delighted with *Coppelia,* which he described as "a corker," and with Lis Jeppesen, whom he saw as a ballerina of international caliber:

The bewitching Jeppesen, with her saucer-eyed child-woman look, is not only an ideal Hilda, but, as becomes more evident each time she takes the stage, a consummate artist in point of phrasing, line, rubato, and poetic sensibility. She is, in short, one of the most remarkable dancers one can see anywhere these days. (June 2, 1982)

He also admired the modern program and understood its virtues:

After a week devoted exclusively to ballets by August Bournonville, the sovereign choreographer of their 19th century tradition, we were treated to a program anchored at one end by the U.S. premiere of Glen Tetley's *The Firebird* and at the other by the first American performance by the Royal Danish Ballet of Alvin Ailey's *Memoria*. Coals to Newcastle? Maybe. But the point was securely made. Though a Danish accent in the dancing of these ballets by American choreographers was plainly perceptible—the more so in the Ailey, for good reason—these were brilliant, gripping, virtuosic performances, thoroughly sensitive to the stylistic idiosyncrasies both works entail. (June 9, 1982)

New York magazine's Tobi Tobias, who had been so interested in the Bournonville tradition after the 1979 festival that she had begun a mammoth oral history project, interviewing Danish dancers about their training and performances in the Bournonville tradition, traveled to Washington see the Bournonville program and wrote:

The Washington performances of *Kermesse* were extraordinary, perhaps most for the detail, rhythm, and radiant spirit of the ensemble playing. No other ballet company can equal it. Each character, down to the merest walk-on, seems to have a history, an immediate intent, and a clearly defined relationship to his fellows. In the marvelous self-contained world of a Bournonville ballet, as the Danes perform it, even a star is only part of the mosaic.[3]

The company was highly praised in New York as well. *New York Times* critic Anna Kisselgoff pointed out one of the chief attractions of the Danish ballet to foreigners: "The special aspect about the Royal Danish Ballet that never ceases to amaze is the attention paid to the most minor of nondancing roles in its productions. It is one of the few ballet companies that retains its mature artists and puts them to work. A classical dancer often develops artistically when he or she must retire from dancing. Yet the artistry acquired at this point can be used in other ways—which is why the Royal Danes have so many star performances in mime roles" (June 24, 1982).

Two New York critics even liked *Firebird*. The *Wall Street Journal*'s Peter Rosenwald wrote:

> The Danes are extraordinarily engaging and handsome, technically brilliant, yet never letting technique get in the way of their art. They are a true ensemble. . . .
>
> This combination of strength and warmth must have inspired Tetley in his creation of a new *Firebird*, which received its New York premiere. The ballet is Tetley's best. Using the entire Stravinsky score, it has a richness of invention and conception distancing it from any of the more familiar renderings of the firebird legend. If at first it appears to be a dark Victorian tale of repression and angst, it quickly becomes a beautifully measured love story in which Arne Villumsen as the lover, and the lyrical Linda Hindberg as the Firebird, triumph over all the obstacles to their love. (June 22, 1982)

Clive Barnes, now writing for the *New York Post*, echoed the general opinion that it seemed odd for the Danes to dance an American modern-dance work dedicated to an American teacher, but he wrote an interesting defense of *Firebird:*

> It is admirable that this company—true-blue classicist through and through—should dance the Ailey so well. But why it was thought worth demonstrating this fact in New York is beyond reason.
>
> Tetley's *Firebird* is altogether a different matter—and it is terrific. A genuine rethinking of the Stravinsky score and Fokine scenario, and replete with stunningly sensuous and richly emotional choreography. When premiered at the end of last year in Copenhagen, the European critics were strongly disapproving.
>
> It is a disapproval I cannot share—this is the best large-scale work Tetley has ever created, light years ahead of his much praised *Rite of Spring*. (June 22, 1982)

Jennifer Dunning wrote an advance piece about Weinreich's *Letter to Orpheus*, which would provide the occasion for Kronstam's last performance in New York:

> The ballet [*Orpheus*] came about when Mr. Kronstam, eager to develop new choreographic talent from within the company, announced that the dancers were welcome to participate in a workshop project, using company members and the theater's third performing space, a 180-seat basement house for experimental programs.

"None of us dares to make a ballet," Mr. Kronstam said. "How could we challenge this man, this Bournonville? And what can a young choreographer do when he comes to me with an idea for a ballet, and I must tell him, 'I think we'll have space and time in 1984.' But it is important that people who want to explore can do it, and do it with good lighting and sound. They must know about other things besides choreography." (*New York Times*, June 18, 1982)

1982–83

This would be the company's last season at Kongens Nytorv for two years, and it was a truncated one: only sixty-one performances. Yet Kronstam had programmed one Russian classic and two triple bills that mixed new ballets by company members with ballets by Ashton (*La Valse*) and Tudor (*Judgment of Paris*). *La Valse* is a swirl of dancing to the Ravel score, a corps piece rather than a star vehicle. It's one of the rare classical ballets that uses a large male corps as well as a female corps, and it is difficult both musically and in its extensive use of épaulement. Besides, Kronstam said, he liked the costumes. "We had been having all these Dutch ballets, drab, brown, and I wanted the girls to wear those

Kronstam and Jette Buchwald in Arlette Weinreich's *Letter to Orpheus*. Photo: Erik Petersen for *Politiken*. Private collection. By permission of Polfoto.

ball dresses. I remember Lise Stripp came to me opening night and said how nice it was to be able to put on a dress and a tiara and go down and dance."

La Valse was not popular and Kronstam blamed himself for its failure. "That was my fault," he said. "That whole evening was a very strange mixture of ballets. It was one modern, and then a classical pas de deux [*Le Corsaire*, probably to help get the principals in the mood for *Don Quixote*], and *La Valse*." It hadn't been planned to be a "strange mixture." What ended up being "the modern work" had been planned as a classical ballet by a company member, Ann-Kristin Hauge, but it turned out differently from what Kronstam had expected. "It was about Bluebeard, the one who kills all his wives. It started out classical, but then she chose Johnny [Eliasen] as Bluebeard, and it didn't develop to be classical." Kronstam did not consider going to Hauge and suggesting changes. "I think it is very difficult to say, 'I don't think you should do that. I think you should do something else.' It was her first ballet. She wasn't so experienced that she could say, 'Okay, then I have another idea.' It might take her a year to find out what she wanted to do." Hauge had found the experience a positive one. "I approached him with the idea, and he was extremely supportive. It was my first piece, and you could say it should not have been done, because I had practically no experience and I was working with a composer. It was a wonderful experience, I must say, and Henning gave me the best rehearsal situation I could get. I got all the rehearsals I wanted and all the overtime I wanted and I was just treated fabulously."

Kronstam believed that he had to let people make their own mistakes and let them see their ideas play out. He gave several dancers chances—three that season alone—and was especially encouraging to anyone who wanted to try to make a dramatic ballet. He usually gave someone more than one chance if he saw any promise. Hauge was scheduled to do another ballet the following season but was ill and couldn't complete the work. She suggested the company bring in Robert North to stage his *Mellem to Vande* [usually given with its Spanish title, *Entre Dos Aguas*], a work for a small cast that could be put on quickly. The ballets created by company members in Kronstam's time went from "the curtain could go up on it" to "disasters. And I had some disasters," he said. "Lise la Cour did a terrible ballet. One critic said, 'It looks like the ballet that goes on in *Oklahoma!* in the back [of the main action], and here it was in the front.' And that was right. It looked like what was going on in those '40s musicals." This was *Gry* [Dawn], a Western with Linda Hindberg as a sheriff.

Ashton's *La Valse*. Left to right: Lis Jeppesen and Bjarne Hecht, Annemarie Dybdal and Torben Jeppesen, Lise Stripp and Mogens Boesen. Photo: John Johnsen. The Royal Theatre, Copenhagen. By permission of Det kongelige Teaters bibliotek og arkiv.

"It wasn't the cast that was the problem," said Kronstam, who did not always disagree with critics. "The leads were Linda and Arne, and they were fine. It was the ballet that was the problem."

Gry was on a program with Arlette Weinreich's second ballet, *Kombinationer* (*Combinations*), a drama for four women and a man based on characters from a television show about Danish life in the 1930s. Tudor's *Judgment of Paris* was a comic character ballet. "I asked him to do his Bertolt Brecht ballet with the three whores," Kronstam said, "and he [rehearsed] it in 1982 when we were in New York. It was fun. I'd seen it with Ballet Rambert. But I think I was the only one who thought it was fun, because the audience was not too wild about it." Kronstam thought the ballet would be perfect for Jette Buchwald. "She was wonderful in the rehearsals, but when we came home to Copenhagen she said, 'I'm sorry. I'm pregnant.' And they had those awful costumes, so she couldn't do it in pregnancy. So we had to do with another girl, and that was a pity, because Jette had that sense of humor that it needed."

For the third new program that season, Bolshoi choreographer Yuri Grigorovich set his production of *Don Quixote* on the company for Annemarie Dybdal, a strong technician in the Russian mold, and Johnny Eliasen; Linda Hindberg and Arne Villumsen led the second cast. "I had written through the minister of culture, through the Soviet embassy, because I knew we were going to be at Tivoli and I wanted to do one of the classics there, because the girls had to do their fouettés and all that business, to keep them in shape. We couldn't do *Swan Lake* in Tivoli. We couldn't do *Sleeping Beauty* in Tivoli [because of the size and shape of the stage]. And I'd seen *Don Quichotte* at the Bolshoi and I thought, 'Well, that one we could do.' So Grigorovich came with Rimma Karelskaya,[4] who everybody loved, and a character dancer to do the character work. Of course, the press didn't understand why I did *Don Quichotte*—silly story, and things like that. But they admired Dybdal [as Kitri] and I didn't want to explain that it would be silly to bring in another *Swan Lake* or *Sleeping Beauty* in the last season. They should have had enough imagination to figure that out."

While the company enjoyed working with the Russians, their mime style came as a shock. "They didn't want any sort of a natural, easy way of doing it. They really want it like a big opera, you know. You have to see it all the way out in the Bolshoi house," Kronstam said in his "Oral History." "So in the beginning, we were all a little embarrassed and saying, 'Ah, they don't—no, they don't mean that.' But of course, as we came into the production and got the costumes on and everything, we could see that that was the way you had to do it. But in the beginning we laughed."[5]

Kronstam had a secret yearning to dance the Torcador and learned it at Grigorovich's insistence, but he declined to do it on stage. "I told him I was too old. He said, 'You must do the Toreador,' but I wanted it for my young dancers. So I lied a little. I said, 'I can't. I'm fifty.'" He did, however, take the role of the Don, with Bjørnsson as his Sancho Panza. It was his last great role. Even the critics who found the ballet trivial and questioned Kronstam's judgment in bringing it into the repertory admired his Don.

Allan Fridericia, the devotee of Soviet ballet, wrote: "It is the first time I have seen Don Quixote rightly carry his title. . . . Henning Kronstam's performance at the opening was unforgettable. He was Quixote in tinplate, weakened by age, serious and involuntarily comical" (*Søndags Aktuelt*, March 15, 1983).

In a review entitled "Superficial, Royal Show Dance," Viggo Sørensen wrote:

> Nevertheless, thanks to one performance on the greatest expressive level, there are moments of moving humanity in all this sumptuous superficiality. On

the dramatically weakest imaginable basis Henning Kronstam creates a figure of great and sincere poetry out of the mimic title part. A great stage artist manages here to turn the giant fool into something else and far more than a comic act, because Henning Kronstam makes the tragedy behind blind idealism's futile fight against a prosaic world comprehensible for everybody, while Fredbjørn Bjørnsson is moving as the knight's ever faithful and pathetically simple squire.

Henrik Lundgren, a young, rather brash critic who often wrote with an acid pen, attacked not only *Don Quixote* but the entire season:

> Ballet master Henning Kronstam gambled all on one card. And lost. The '82–83 season was a game of chance—with subsequent resounding failure. The introduction included only minor matters. A couple of British semiclassics (*Judgment of Paris, La Valse*), a brilliant pas de deux without brilliance, and three Danish novelties, of which one (*Dawn*) was cheap variety and the two others (*Combinations, To Bluebeard*), had their positive parts smothered by the way-too-heavy Royal machine. Left was *Don Quixote* as the all or nothing gamble. A manifestation at the eleventh hour could have explained away the preceding season as a pure attempt—or an artistic defeat—while the opening on Friday demonstrates the repertoire's inadequacy in no uncertain terms. (March 13, 1983)

Kronstam was attacked so harshly and so quickly it seems as though some critics, at least, had been waiting for the first possible opportunity to do so. There was no consideration that he was working during a time of limited budgets and that his repertory choices must be made with an eye to the years at Tivoli and all the restraints that implied. Kronstam well understood the need for new, good choreographers but, as he said in his "Oral History," "You do not dig them up from the earth."[6]

Erik Aschengreen wrote a long state-of-the-company piece called "Fateful Years for The Royal Ballet" at the beginning of the 1983–84 season.[7] In many ways, he defended the company against its more strident critics and explained some of those things that Kronstam thought "the critics should have enough imagination to understand." He pointed out, for example, that it "was not unreasonable" for the Royal Danish Ballet, a classical ballet company, to acquire classical ballets, like *Don Quixote*. Aschengreen began with an assessment of the company, using the temporary move to Tivoli as the opportunity to "reevaluate its repertory, its level, and all its glorious tradition." Although Aschengreen was more reasoned in his arguments than others, he agreed with his colleagues who felt that Kronstam was too conservative and that his direction was timid.

> So far it seems as if the company's administration first and foremost has seen it as its job to make sure the dancers survive, and that is important. When Henning Kronstam last month published the plans for the coming season, he stressed that he had chosen a repertory that would have as many dancers dancing as possible. A wise policy, but of course it is not without importance what they will be dancing.
>
> It is as important to think of the audience as of the dancers, and this season's repertory is not colored by any vision or new ways of thinking. *The Leaves Are Fading* by Antony Tudor from 1975 and *Verklärte Nacht* (Transfigured Night) by Jiri Kylian from same year are the news of the season. These are beautiful ballets but not pieces that excite us with anticipation.

Aschengreen also raised one of the main problems between Kronstam and the critics, which is that Kronstam did not discuss his ideas with them or ask for their advice. This was quite deliberate and not merely out of shyness. "Critics don't really want to know what you are doing," Kronstam said. "They want to give you their advice, and if you don't take it, they never forgive you for it." Kronstam's reluctance to become chums with the Danish critics at the time would cost him dearly, and it also lost him a chance to explain his program to people who would have been genuinely interested in his reasoning.

Aschengreen noted the American success, but urged the company not to rest on its laurels but to engage in discussion. "The company returned with the biggest U.S.A. success to date, which should not be seen in opposition to the problems at home. The facts are not that abroad they love our company while we at home simply are critical and pouty, and it would be unfortunate if the Royal Ballet saw the situation this way and thereby cut itself off from a discussion that can bring forward wishes and ideas and in this way help to bring the company onward."

Another point of disagreement between Kronstam and the critics was how to deal with the Bournonville tradition. "Because of the international excitement over Bournonville and because of a lot of exploration into Bournonville during the past ten years, we now have a lot of new experience and knowledge that ought to be mirrored in new productions, and a responsible administration has a duty to think forward, to think about renewal, and to think about the next generation."

Aschengreen then asks "a couple of nagging questions":

> Why won't the Theatre ask Elsa Marianne von Rosen or Peter Schaufuss to do
> a Bournonville production? They have done stagings with success in Leningrad,
> London, Berlin, and Toronto that it would be exciting for a Danish audience to
> see. The Theatre probably doesn't like this question but it has to be asked,
> because it is what we ask each other out here. And actually, we don't understand.
>
> You could let an intelligent director from the acting department meet with
> one of our Bournonville experts for a new production. Or let John Neumeier
> turn *Napoli* upside down. Since the status quo is kept on video and in writing,
> nothing will be lost by taking a daring step, and if the Bournonville tradition
> cannot stand a little meddling here and there it isn't worth much.

All these ideas, except for Neumeier turning *Napoli* upside down, were tried
in the late 1990s with unfortunate results, and there are some who hold the
critics of this period responsible for much of the upheaval that befell the company after 1992. The idea of having "an intelligent director from the drama
department" was often raised and was particularly insulting, as the clear implication was that there were no intelligent directors in the ballet department.[8] It
is a hard criticism to understand, especially of Brenaa and Kronstam. This was
one of several sentences in Kronstam's copy of the Aschengreen article that
were underlined, very deliberately, as though with a ruler. He obviously took the
piece seriously, yet he did not respond himself. Kirsten Ralov gave an interview
to *Berlingske Tidende*'s Else Cornelius, which may have not only underscored
the general impression that she was really running the company but also probably deepened the perception that Kronstam was too arrogant to speak with the
press.[9]

Ralov answered Aschengreen's comments point for point, but the most interesting, perhaps, are her remarks on revising Bournonville:

> Peter Schaufuss has put some variations in *Napoli* and in *Folk Tale,* which I
> haven't seen, but I suppose he did it to make the performances longer and to get
> more dancing for himself. He most likely has that against Bournonville, that
> there is too much mime and too little dance, and so he's seeking to create a
> different balance, but that wasn't Bournonville's intention. His ballets are built
> on the mimical tradition, which our dancers have been educated to fill out. It is
> funny that you are ready to change Bournonville, while nobody would ever
> dream about changing the ballets of other great choreographers. Just think if
> you said about Fokine's *Chopiniana,* that there was too much dancing for

women, so it was probably better to put in a couple more variations for men. Or if you put in a few more dances in Balanchine's *Apollo,* there would be screaming.

Several observers of Copenhagen's ballet scene during this time think that what was at the root of all the fuss was that some wanted Peter Schaufuss, a friend and favorite of several critics, to be director of the company, or at the very least that his productions of Bournonville ballets should be danced at the Royal Theatre. However, the notion that Bournonville ballets needed to be changed can be traced to the émigré Danish dancers, beginning with Erik Bruhn, who gave frequent interviews about how backward the Royal Danish Ballet was (otherwise, why would they have left it?) and their complaints were taken very seriously by many critics and scholars. Unfortunately, depending on dancers—even great and intelligent dancers—for information about ballets can be misleading. Both Bruhn and Schaufuss, for example, held to the view that in one of the Act II solos in *La Sylphide,* James does a one-and-three-quarter air turn rather than a complete double air turn because early Jameses didn't have the technique to complete a double tour en l'air. This is not correct, however. Not only could Bournonville do double air turns, but having James finish his turn in that position puts him facing the Sylph, for whom he is dancing, and not the audience. It was a deliberate choreographic choice on Bournonville's part. This was one of the many changes made or suggested by the "new thinkers" that Kronstam and Brenaa were well aware of, but rejected not only because they were inauthentic—not in the notebooks and a violation of tradition—but because the change violated Bournonville's principles.

Emigré Danes also often complained that the Danish productions were old-fashioned, both in technique and directorial approach. While it is true that there had been directors who told dancers to do something because that's the way it had always been done, this approach was outmoded by the time of Kronstam's directorship. Brenaa and especially Kronstam certainly had a thorough knowledge of technique and of trends in contemporary ballet. They rejected changes they felt were counter to Bournonville's aesthetic. Yet from the time Schaufuss's production was shown in Tivoli in 1979, it became a rallying cry not only for critics but for other Danes who seemed fed up with Bournonville. Kirsten Ralov was accosted one night at Tivoli by Max Sørensen, who asked rather forcefully why he could not see that production at Kongens Nytorv.[10] It must be difficult to maintain one's artistic integrity in such an environment. "You just go on and do it," Kronstam said. "You have to believe in what you are doing; then it doesn't matter what people say."

Of the divide over whether Bournonville should be presented in traditional stagings or revisionist ones, Bering Liisberg explained the popular Danish point of view: "In Denmark people say, 'Oh, *Napoli. Napoli,* third act? Oh, God.' That's what ordinary people would say. They've seen it. They don't realize that that tradition is important outside Denmark, and it's always a discussion you have in a small country. I can understand the discussion, 'Why should we always come up with Hans Christian Andersen, Søren Kierkegaard, and the Royal Ballet? It's boring, when we have to send our culture abroad.' We also have younger artists in many fields who feel they are good and should be productive, and that's true too. But you can't do without Hans Christian Andersen, Bournonville, and Søren Kierkegaard. They're there. They're important persons and creative in our culture, and that's why I can't understand [this position]."

While it's understandable, perhaps, that audiences would feel this way, it may seem a bit surprising that critics would share the popular view rather than explain the artistic position. However, this was a period when the choreographer was king; no one, anywhere in the world, was looking at the role of an artistic director in any depth, and this should be borne in mind when reading some of the Danish reviews. To dancers, choreographers, and teachers, it's only common sense that if a company is going to continue to be a classical company it must dance classical works; it cannot be a modern-dance company for six months of the year and then drag out a few old ballets to put on a festival. But this is not self-evident to everyone, and some thought of ballets as pies that can be put in a freezer and brought out and reheated when needed.

1983–84

Working at Tivoli was a logistical nightmare. "It was almost impossible to have classes at the Theatre and the beginning of the rehearsal there, and then later to go by bus into Tivoli to have the stage rehearsals there, and a bus back to the Theatre, change again, and then get to Tivoli in the evening and have our dressing rooms there. So that was a mess." Kronstam was very proud of the fact that he didn't lose a single dancer during the renovation. During this time, the company also danced at other venues, the most successful being a theater, the Gas Works.[11] It was an informal space, a theater in the round, and drew young people who might be reluctant to go to Kongens Nytorv or Tivoli.

"That was Frank [Andersen]'s idea," Kronstam said. "There was an actor who had rented it and Frank came to me and said, 'Henning, we can have it for two weeks. Can you find a repertory for it?' The first year we did not have the best repertory. The second year, we did a good repertory. I know we brought *Five Tangos* [by Hans van Manen], and I think we did *Song without Words* there.

"The next year we did *Memoria,* which was a great success there. The whole company was dancing, and the audience loved it. We had full houses every night. *Memoria* and *Arden Court.* And that looked marvelous out there, too. It's a big, round—it's like a circus, and the people are sitting up above looking down. *Memoria* looked quite different there. I wanted to do *Apollo* out there too because it would have been interesting to see it in that space.

"We did the jazz ballet, the Spanish ballet that Robert North did for us [*Mellem to Vande*]. He did it for Mette [Hønningen], and then Linda [Hindberg], and Annemari Vingård and Ann-Kristin Hauge took it over. At the Gas Works we had to repeat it, the audience liked it so much. I had to do all these things because we were out of the Theatre. So I had to go strange places. Linda [Hindberg] and Arne [Villumsen] danced the *Don Q* pas de deux. All the young people went wild—that was at the time when Linda did one, two, three pirouettes, and then a double and a triple, and things like that."

In December of the company's second Tivoli season there was a strike, the second in Kronstam's directorship. "We had a premiere, an evening of *Leaves Are Fading, Verklärte Nacht,* and *Etudes.* And the last rehearsal went beautifully, and everything was perfect. Henrik [Bering Liisberg] and I went to Malmö to see a workshop and we got a call from Copenhagen that the stagehands had gone on strike."

Kronstam thought of canceling the performance but decided against it. "I should have said no. But then we would have had to wait five weeks and start all the rehearsals again. The Finnish lady [Ari Hynninen] who does the Tudor ballets had to leave because her contract was out. Toni's contract was out. [Toni Lander had staged *Etudes.*] And *Verklärte Nacht*—they were all engaged until the premiere and then they had other projects."

Kronstam decided to go ahead with the performance using the stage manager and chief lighting manager to work the lights. "And it worked, more or

Heidi Ryom and Arne Villumsen in *The Leaves Are Fading*. Photo: John Johnsen. The Royal Theatre, Copenhagen. By permission of Det kongelige Teaters bibliotek og arkiv.

less, it worked for *Leaves Are Fading* and *Verklärte Nacht*. But *Etudes* was impossible because there are spots here, and spots there, and spots there, and the barre, and then change, and spots and spots, and all that backlighting. So I was creeping down there. Hiding. I was crawling out of the Theatre."

That night, Kronstam called a journalist and said he would resign. "And this time," he said, "I meant it."

He was very shy of power.
—Henrik Bering Liisberg

Twenty-four

The Search for a Successor

Kronstam's resignation was in one way a spontaneous decision, but in another, a quite calculated one. The strike was merely the final blow. "I had told Niels Matthiasen I would give him four years," he said. "I had signed a contract for four years. Then I just continued because we had to go to Tivoli, and Henrik said, 'Well, you've got to stay because otherwise the company will split up, and some of the dancers will leave.' So I stayed. I knew that if I left, Kirsten [Ralov] would leave too. So what was there to do?"

It seemed out of character for Kronstam, whose dealings with people were generally considerate and honorable, to resign suddenly without first alerting Bering Liisberg and, especially, Kirsten Ralov. Both of them learned of it, with the rest of Copenhagen, from the newspaper the next day. However, Kronstam readily admitted that this is what had happened. "There was a party with the

Canadian ambassador with a lot of our dancers, and I told them then—but not the whole company. Kirsten Ralov wasn't there. I was afraid that they would persuade me to stay, so that's why I had to call a paper and say it," he explained. There was a pervasive rumor that Gerstenberg, who often phoned dancers saying how lonely he was and how Kronstam only cared about the Theatre, had forced Kronstam to resign, but he did not discuss it with Gerstenberg either. There was also an assumption, mentioned in several press accounts, that Kronstam had been driven out by the harsh reviews, but this is unlikely. The reviews may have hurt Kronstam or made him angry or sick, but he would have kept on doing what he felt was right as long as it was physically possible.

Kronstam had never wanted the job, and nothing that had happened in the preceding five and a half years made him like it any better. "As ballet master, you sit in your office and people come in and complain. And you read letters and you dictate letters. And you go into the rehearsal room and you look around, and then you have a little meeting. You don't get into anything artistic," Kronstam said. The months at Tivoli exacerbated the situation. "I hated to see it on stage when you knew it wasn't what you knew it should be. In *Midsummer Night's Dream,* there's about twenty-two elfins [fairies], and I had to cut it down because they just simply couldn't bourrée over the stage without crashing into each other. So I had to cut it down, but I knew how it should look. The audience loved it still. They still came. But I could see it, and I hated it. So it was sitting and watching and having to go up and say, 'Well, you should do it different,' and all of those things, but at the same time, inside you were crying."

Bering Liisberg sent Kronstam a cable the day after his resignation:

14 December 1983

Dear Henning,

Sad news for a flight—very sad news after so many good years of collaboration and such beautiful artistic results on your side.

I do understand and respect your decision and hope very much that your [successor] will be just as keen on employing your artistic quality and inspiration as I have been. But I implore you to reconsider postponing your retirement another year so that we can celebrate it with the performances at the Met in May 1986.

If we try to place *Manon* in the spring of '86, after the Neumeier premiere in November '85, I will do almost anything within my reach to take the responsibility off your shoulders that last year.

I feel sure that we can find a solution so that I and somebody else can do all the tiring and boring work that year in order to let you concentrate on the artistic inspiration and direction that has been so important to all of us since you took over.

I implore you as your personal friend to reconsider this—in the spirit of our [mutual] friend Niels—with the hope that we can discuss it between Christmas and the New Year.

And I thank you for your fantastic inspiration and quality in our years together. I hope you realize that one of the most decisive factors for my taking over the Royal Theatre was your acceptance of Niels's proposal to you at that time. It was equally important to me as it was to Niels—and still is to me.

Best wishes from New York.

Your friend,

Henrik

Shortly after the New Year, Kronstam wrote Bering Liisberg, "I have thoroughly considered my situation and I have reached the decision that at present I am unable to undertake any obligations apart from my job as first solo dancer from the end of the '84–85 season. It's a hard decision, but necessary for the Royal Ballet." This may have been because Kronstam was so exhausted and ill that he could not imagine continuing, even as a teacher or instruktør, but it is more likely because he was trying to bow out so that he would not stand in the way of his successor.

The dancers, and probably the Theatre administration, thought that Kronstam could be persuaded to change his mind, but he stuck to his guns. The problem, as everyone in the company knew, was that there was no obvious successor, which is why they had tried so hard to keep Kronstam in the position. The names always tossed around in the press—John Neumeier, Peter Martins, Peter Schaufuss—weren't possible. All had their own companies or were uninterested for other reasons. The ballet master must be Danish, or at least from the Danish tradition, which narrowed the field considerably.

At first it seemed that the company had found a surprise, though ideal, candidate, in Helgi Tomasson, just winding down his dancing career at the New York City Ballet. Tomasson was an Icelander and hence had not been allowed to join the company, which had been closed to foreigners when he was a young man. But his teachers had been Danes and his dancing style and sensibilities were in accord with those at Kongens Nytorv. He understood and respected the Bournonville tradition and he had begun to choreograph. It seemed like a good match.

Tomasson was interested in the job, the dancers supported him, and for several months everyone assumed he would become ballet master. At first Tomasson said he was a bit worried that, as often happened, the former ballet master would never quite give up the job. However, Tomasson talked with Kronstam and was reassured that this would not be a problem. "He really didn't want it," Tomasson said. He would be happy to have the older man continue as teacher and instruktør and Kronstam, for his part, liked Tomasson and felt he would have no trouble working with him. But Tomasson and the Theatre were never able to come to terms on two matters. One was the salary, which by international standards was very low, especially when the high Danish taxes were taken into account. The other barrier is interesting in light of subsequent events. Tomasson said he would have to fire many of the dancers, especially many of the older corps women, to be able to dance the repertory he wanted to bring to the company. He was told by Bering Liisberg that this would be impossible because of union regulations. Tomasson said that this is what ultimately led him, after many months, to decide against taking the job.

The negotiations with Tomasson had gone on for so long that the company was now in a difficult situation. Kronstam was asked again to reconsider, and again he said no. Attention then turned to Toni Lander. There were other applicants, three from within the company (Frank Andersen, Dinna Bjørn, and Johnny Eliasen.) The dancers' union voted on all the candidates and gave Lander overwhelming support.[1] There was justice in Lander's appointment as well, for returning a Lander to the company was the final resolution of that ancient scandal.

Bering Liisberg went to New York to give Lander her contract to sign. She signed it, then handed it back to him and said she could not serve. She had gone for a physical exam and had been diagnosed with terminal lung cancer.[2] Bering Liisberg flew home immediately. That weekend there was a meeting of the Theatre administration to decide what to do; neither Kronstam nor Ralov were present. On Monday the dancers were told that Lander could not accept the position and why and, with barely a pause, that the Theatre had decided to name Frank Andersen as the new ballet master. Dancers remember that there was utter silence in the room. The dancers were of course stunned and saddened at the news of Toni Lander's illness. But they were also stunned at the selection of Andersen, only twenty-nine years old, who was not well regarded within the company as a dancer and who did not teach, choreograph, or stage ballets. His only experience had been coordinating a small touring company of less than a dozen dancers that performed during summer vacations and on weekends, a very different matter from managing a large ballet company throughout a full season.

Why Andersen was chosen is still a mystery. At the time it was said that the Theatre felt they could not do another search and had to choose from among the remaining candidates, but they could have named Kirsten Ralov acting director and continued the search, or named Bering Liisberg as a general manager, with Kronstam and Ralov continuing the artistic work of the company, as had been done with Henning Rohde and Volkova two decades earlier. Many dancers blamed Kronstam for Andersen's appointment, thinking that the younger man was the elder's handpicked successor. Several thought that Kronstam had urged Andersen's appointment because, as Andersen could not do the artistic work, Kronstam would be able to stay and work in the studio, whereas an artist with his own strong vision and capabilities might find him in the way. But Kronstam had very willingly agreed to step aside, and he did not choose Andersen.

Ralov said that Andersen had "a friend in the government" intervene on his behalf. Kronstam too said that there had been nothing he could do about Andersen's appointment "because he had the government backing." While Andersen is at least as good at public relations as anyone in the ballet world and, especially considering Kronstam's problems with the press, that was certainly a valuable asset, there remained the problem of who would teach company class, choose the repertory, coach and develop dancers, stage productions—and handle administrative matters, as Andersen was inexperienced in that area as well. The solution seemed to be to ask Kronstam to serve as artistic advisor, a new title (Volkova had served the same function for Larsen, but was never given the title) and continue to work as instruktør and teacher, and he agreed. Ralov, very reluctantly as she did not approve of Andersen's selection and thought it would lead to trouble, agreed to stay in her job as vice ballet master "as long as I could stand it." The role Kronstam was expected to play in the company is reflected in the fact that his salary was not reduced.[3]

The dancers' objections about Andersen were not based on personal animosity but artistic considerations. Usually in a ballet company there are divergent views, but in this instance opinions are remarkably monolithic. Ask a Danish dancer, or the choreographers and the foreign artists who worked with the company during this period, what the difference between the two men is, and the answer will contain some variant of: "Henning was the artist and Frank was the salesman." The two men were polar opposites and their ideas of how to direct a company were very different, from repertory and casting choices to planning and building a season.

What is also always said about Andersen is that he is extremely energetic and ambitious. He never became one of the company's stars. His best roles were Gurn in *La Sylphide*, Geert in *Kermesse in Bruges*, Franz in *Coppelia*, and Puck in Neumeier's *A Midsummer Night's Dream*. However, he wanted more serious parts, parts for which Kronstam, Ralov, and Brenaa thought him unsuited. Many dancers felt that Andersen's unfulfilled ambitions as a dancer colored his directorship. As Alexander Kølpin, one of the leading dancers during Andersen's tenure, put it: "Frank tried to get the international fame he didn't get as a dancer on the back of the company."

Because there had been so many conflicts with Andersen and Bjørn's little touring group, Kronstam had made Andersen an assistant instruktør the previous season. "I thought if he had to look at the whole company instead of just his eight people, he would understand," he said. Unfortunately, it turned out that Andersen did not have a talent for staging, either. "The first thing he did was take over Flindt's *Nutcracker*. Flemming was here to do *Nutcracker* in Tivoli and he had Frank as assistant. And then he came back the next year and Frank started rehearsals. Flemming came to me and said, 'Not Frank. I don't want it.' So Mie [Anne Marie Vessel] took it over."

Andersen's approach to coaching is illustrated by a story told by Bjarne Hecht, one of the most popular dancers in the touring company, about his first season with the Bournonville group. It is a good example of why the dancers did not admire Andersen as an artist and could not accept him as their leader. Hecht, only nineteen, had been thrilled to be invited to join the group but soon felt that Andersen had recruited him because he was trying to build a base of young dancers loyal to him.[4] Andersen tried to help Hecht with his dancing. "I remember I had trouble with the landing after a double air tour," Hecht said. "And Frank was working with me, and he said, 'Don't worry about it. When you land, just give a big smile and open your arms and the audience will never see your feet.' I knew that wasn't the kind of coaching I needed. Niels [Kehlet] saw I was having trouble and worked with me until I learned how to do [the step]."

There are many stories like this, and dancers trained by Volkova, Kronstam, or Brenaa found his ways "circus" and "in bad taste."

It was for all these reasons that Kronstam was asked to stay as artistic advisor and Ralov as vice ballet master. A letter that Bering Liisberg wrote to Kronstam at the end of his last season as ballet master indicates the role Kronstam was expected to continue to play:

> . . . it's a comfort and joy for me that this is not a good-bye, nor the end of a good collaboration, but merely a structural and positional change that in the future gives us the possibility of collaboration and, most important, gives the Theatre the opportunity to benefit from your indispensable artistic sense of quality and your power of inspiration.
>
> It made me immensely happy when you consented to continue as an artistic advisor for the ballet and as such secured both Frank and me the confidence and support in the artistic judgment and the continuity that I think is essential for the further development of the entire ballet.

Although Andersen drew on Kronstam's experience and international contacts, and many dancers felt that, at least at the beginning, he sought and took the older man's advice, his public statements seldom, if ever, made mention of Kronstam's role in the company. In America, especially, Andersen presented himself as completely in charge, and this became the generally accepted perception. Andersen's intelligence is often unfairly underestimated. He was extremely shrewd in public relations, and grasped the central fact that it didn't matter what one did as much as what a few people wrote that one had done. To this end he expended an enormous amount of time and energy courting critics of the major newspapers and magazines in New York, London, and Copenhagen, and he did it brilliantly, handling news cycles and mastering the art of spin as well, if not better, than many politicians.

Andersen's concentration on the short term and media attention during his tenure—premieres, galas, celebrations, and awards ceremonies—were the opposite of the patient, long-term building that Kronstam had done, and it is highly likely that Kronstam was put in the position of artistic advisor to serve as a brake to Andersen's enthusiasm and ambitions. Kronstam could have exerted much more power and influence than he did, but he seemed to try to let Andersen make his own way. "Frank would come to me at the beginning of the season and say, 'This is what I have planned. What do you think?' and I would

Frank Andersen, his
official photograph in the
company's souvenir book
for the 1992 Bournon-
ville Festival. Photo:
Mydtskov. Private collec-
tion.

tell him what I thought," was Kronstam's only comment on their relationship,
and it sounds very characteristic of Kronstam to make his opinion known but
not to try to push his ideas on Andersen. Either the younger man would take
his advice or he would not. These tensions would eventually come to a head,
but at the time Kronstam and Brenaa, according to several people, felt that the
collaboration might work. The thought was that the two men's strengths would
complement each other, that Andersen's energy, enthusiasm, and public relations skills would serve the company well and would free Kronstam to work in
the studio. What no one seems to have considered is that the artistic director is
the one who chooses repertory and makes casting and other artistic personnel
decisions, and that is what, in the end, decides the direction and artistic health
of a ballet company.

1984–85

In his last season Kronstam scheduled a Stravinsky evening (Robbins's *Circus Polka,* Balanchine's *Rubies,* Birgit Cullberg's *Pulcinella and Pimpinella,* and Nils Christe's *Symphony in Three Movements*), a program of very different styles of ballets unified by a single composer. Kronstam had originally wanted *Agon* as the Balanchine selection, but "[John] Taras was in Copenhagen then and he told me, 'Henning, you are going to have a hell, because you're going to have to rehearse it every time it is going on stage. And since you are going to have a difficult time in Tivoli, take *Rubies.*'" Balanchine's works remained a bit foreign at least to some. After a performance of *The Four Temperaments* at Tivoli, one of the retired ballerinas came to Kronstam at the interval and gently chided him for having the girls in such "unpretty" costumes (Balanchine's practice clothes uniform of black leotard and pink tights). "You should have them in little pink-checked dresses," she told him, and, rather than having their hair pulled back into the standard-issue ballerina bun, "have them wear it in little curls."

That season the company did its first work by Choo-San Goh. This was the one work brought into the company on Kirsten Ralov's suggestion. She had seen some of his ballets, and Kronstam watched a tape of Goh's work when the company was in Washington in 1982. "He came, and he looked at the company, and he said he would do *In the Glow of the Night.* And it went all right. Not more." Kronstam also revived *Petrushka,* which suited Niels Kehlet, who was now in his forties, perfectly.

Kronstam's last act as ballet master was to lead the company on a tour to China and Japan. He told a story about planning this tour that was the only specific complaint he made about Theatre intrigues. "There was a meeting to set the repertory," he said, "and I sent Kirsten [Ralov], and then I found out later that Max Sørensen [the Theatre's economics director, whom Kronstam mentioned several times as giving him difficulties] had set the repertory and Kirsten wasn't able to stop him. And of course he picked all the wrong things, so I had to fight about that." This is perhaps why he gave a brief newspaper interview before the tour, which included, among other ballets, *La Sylphide* and *Coppelia.*

> Kronstam is confident that the ballets that the Chinese are going to see are the right choices.

They have asked for history ballets, something with action. They look very much forward to seeing something from H. C. Andersen's country and emphasize that Bournonville and H. C. Andersen lived at the same time. They like fairy tales, poetry, and grace and that is what they get with Bournonville. There is a big interest in other classical schools than the strict Russian one, which used to dominate the Chinese ballet school.

I visited the Central Ballet's school and was impressed. Unfortunately some classes are missing because there was no teaching of classical ballet under the Cultural Revolution, just heroic steps. But what I saw was superb. When the Chinese train their elite, it is very purposeful. I saw, for instance, a performance with dancing, acrobatics, and singing, and I must tell you that my spirit was lifted.

Kronstam left the tour early, coming back with Kirsten Simone, who had broken her wrist while performing Madge. He was exhausted. "Sometimes I look back and I wonder if it was so nice for him," Ingrid Glindemann reflected. "It was great for us for some years, but it was too tough a time for him, as a human being." She was right. The directorship had taken a toll on his health.

This is the one aspect of Kronstam's life that was misunderstood by nearly everyone who knew him. It was obvious that he had great difficulty in handling stress, and it was widely assumed that this was because he was weak—not physically weak, but having a weak character. Kronstam had exerted an enormous amount of energy, as well as his considerable craft as an actor, to hide the fact that he was manic-depressive and seems to have been extremely successful at it; it was, perhaps, his greatest role. Dancers and others in the ballet world erroneously assumed that Kronstam was an alcoholic—although it must be noted that all but three of the dancers interviewed for this book put this in context by saying something like, "Of course we all knew Henning was an alcoholic, but he is such a great artist it doesn't matter, and besides, he always kept it away from the Theatre." Kronstam's image became that of the tortured artist who drank partly for his art and partly because he was trapped in a miserable relationship. Since the dancers had no interaction with Kronstam outside the Theatre, and since no one would dream of going up to him and saying, "I notice you look a bit tired this morning and people say you've been drinking; is that true?" the stories persisted, usually bubbling harmlessly below the surface, but occasionally erupting and eventually causing great harm.[5]

Kronstam had always been known as a man who liked to drink. He probably liked that reputation and did nothing to discourage it; it was manly; it made him one of the boys. During the years he socialized with the company, he was often one of the group who went out for a beer after performances or enjoyed the room parties that dancers have on tour. "He was a drinker but not a drunk," was how Bjarne Hecht put it, an opinion shared by many, and is probably the most accurate assessment. He was a social but not a problem drinker. The problems that people sensed stemmed from other causes.

Lene Schrøder-Hansen, one of the few people who saw Kronstam socially from the early 1970s until his death, said that there were times when he was not himself. "Once, twice, sometimes three times a year, I would know that he had had a few days off where I thought he had been drinking. And we wouldn't see him, and then he would come and ask for coffee or tea instead of a beer. He would be rather quiet, and this would last for a few days until he began to drink normally again," which, she explained, was "a beer with dinner or wine with dinner, nothing more." Margrethe Noyé, who knew of Kronstam's condition and said "he was different from morning to night," observed similar behavior, saying it was three times a year, usually in March (which several dancers noticed as well) and "in July, but that the dancers never saw." Another time, Schrøder-Hansen remembered Kronstam talking much more than was his wont, and Gerstenberg volunteering, though no one had questioned it, "There's nothing wrong with him. He's not been drinking or taking pills or anything," but offering no further explanation.

She never asked what was wrong. "Henning had this way about him. You couldn't ask him anything. You couldn't say, 'What is this about?' He wouldn't allow you to. He would close down immediately." Nor did she ask Gerstenberg. "I don't think I could, but I wouldn't, because I wouldn't intimidate Henning by talking to Franz about him. You see, Franz would call me and say things about Henning and say, 'Now you must take over. I can cope no more,' or things like that. Or, 'Oh, he's hopeless and I'm so tired of this, and now I'm going to Spain and I want to live in Spain forever,' but Henning didn't want to leave the Theatre."

Many manic-depressives use either drugs or alcohol to manage the illness—what psychologists call self-medication—if they are otherwise untreated. It is almost certain that the periods Schrøder-Hansen describes (which match descriptions by dancers and Theatre personnel), where Kronstam would disappear for a few days, were a time of clinical depression, and almost certainly he would drink very heavily during those periods. Depression is such a hideous and painful illness that its victims drink for oblivion—to lose consciousness until the mood changes. Being in the light becomes physically painful; Kronstam's bedroom had specially made blinds that would completely blot out light. He would retreat here until the tour, as he called his depressive periods, was over.

The mania was less debilitating. There are no indications of severe mania, with violent outbursts or extreme risk taking, though there were mild examples of such behavior. During Kronstam's manic phases he would talk much more than was normal, his thoughts would fly faster than he could express them, and his sense of mischief would come to the fore. During the intense periods of mania, also of two or three days' duration, he would drink to "calm himself down."[6] In this state, he could drink large quantities of wine without showing any effect; it took a bottle or two before he seemed normal. The amount decreased, day by day, until the manic episode was over. Then, as Schrøder-Hansen observed, he would "drink normally" again. To complicate matters further, when manic, Kronstam's behavior made him appear to be drunk even if he hadn't been drinking, and he would seem sober after a glass or two of wine had "calmed him down."[7]

After Kronstam withdrew from the company socially, the dancers had no contact with him except on tours, where he was always under great stress and where he often attended the company room parties, and there was at least one instance when he drank more than was advisable. When the company was in New York in 1982, Gerstenberg and Jytte Abildgaard showed up suddenly. The three went to lunch; Kronstam, who had probably been drinking, fell when leaving the restaurant, cutting his ear. The news quickly spread through the company and later stories about Kronstam's drinking often start with "but he was drunk in New York." Because he was presumed to be an alcoholic, if someone saw him in a bar or drinking a beer at dinner, it was assumed he was off the wagon; conversely, if he drank water for lunch he was "not drinking." This became the context in which many came to view Kronstam.

Bering Liisberg, who accompanied Kronstam on the foreign tours to make the speeches Kronstam couldn't make (which Niels Matthiasen had promised, and had expected, to do), ended up spending a great deal of time with his ballet master. Bering Liisberg's observations are the clearest and most objective anyone from the Theatre made about Kronstam. Rather than start with rumors, he observed, and he analyzed what he saw.

"I was never told that he had a disease of any sort, but I gathered that he had some mental problem. I don't know the diagnosis, but it certainly wasn't drinking that was his problem, as most people said, because when he seemed drunk, he hadn't had much to drink. He seemed to me, at least, to have drinking connected with something else—medication and so forth.

"It was my impression that he was manic-depressive. I think there were times when he was low, but then we didn't walk into that room that day. We were very much together on the tours, and he never drank very much—that I saw. There is a difference between a drunkard's behavior and somebody with a mental problem, so I always saw that there was something more to it than just a glass of wine or a glass of beer.

"On one occasion, we were walking in Washington. He was certainly not in a good shape, and he was walking very straight. He wouldn't have been able to do that if he were drunk. When you see a real drunk person, even if he tries to behave, he is not able to walk straight. He is not even able to stand up for a long time." When Kronstam had an anxiety attack and was afraid of falling, he would, as Bering Liisberg had observed, hold himself "very straight" and take very small steps, like an old man walking on ice. Few others made the same deductions, and in the future, when people would see Kronstam look shaky or walk very straight or seem overtired or withdrawn, most assumed that the problem stemmed from drinking.

It was concern for his health, as much as anything, that caused Kronstam to resign. In 1994 he said of this time, "If I had continued for four more years [a third term] I would have been in the earth." The stress of the job was exacerbating the illness, an illness that he used his professional discipline, willpower, and considerable abilities as an actor to cover up. When he would withdraw into himself, when most people sensed that it would be wrong to go near him, he was "having a down." When he was a bit giddy or overconfident, or had interesting-to-bizarre ideas for casting, he was having an "up." Most of the dancers thought of this as "artistic temperament"—"Henning can change any minute," as Alexander Kølpin put it. "One day he's happy and up and funny, and the next day he's really sharp and bitchy and 'I want it like this.' He's changing a lot, but that's because he's not just dull Henning, sitting there again and again. It has an edge, and I think that's very good." Kronstam had a particular look that the bravest person would not challenge, a way of holding himself and willing observers to think there was nothing wrong with him that he used successfully for most of his career. About a month before he died he was about to leave his apartment and tried to pull himself together, to turn into Kronstam—he was broken then; he walked with a stumble and his hands shook constantly. He suddenly sat down and said, "I just can't do it any more. They are going to have to take me as I am." The stigma of mental illness is very severe in Denmark, and the stress of never being able to be himself, of always hiding that illness, took a terrible toll.

At the end of Kronstam's seven years, although his own health was a wreck, the company was in far better shape than it had been when he took over. There are many in Denmark who feel that the company had never looked better than during his first three years, and that was certainly the impression foreigners had as well, not only at the 1979 festival, but from the company's appearances in Chicago in 1980 and the 1982 American tour and the tours in Europe. He maintained the company as well as possible during the years at Tivoli and on tour, and it is a shame that he could not have continued for a few years more after the company moved back to Kongens Nytorv, where he'd planned a repertory of *Swan Lake* and *Sleeping Beauty*, as well as MacMillan's *Manon* and a full-length ballet commissioned from Neumeier—both of which would have silenced the Danish critics' complaints about the repertory.

Kronstam received many royal and state decorations during his career. He was knighted in 1964 and awarded a first-class knighthood in 1975. His foreign honors included Commander of the Finnish Order of the White Rose, Honorary Officer of the Order of the British Empire, Commander of the Order of Civil Merit of Spain, Grand Knight Cross of the Icelandic Order of the Falcon, and Commander of the Order of Civil Merit of France. Although the Danish knighthoods especially meant a great deal to him, the sweetest honor was the unstinting respect of the Danish dancers.

While Kronstam did not accomplish all the things he wanted to do, he laid a solid foundation for the future. The dancers who were aspirants when he resigned became the stars of the next decade (Alexander Kølpin, Nikolaj Hübbe, Lloyd Riggins, Peter Bo Bendixen, Rose Gad, Silja Schandorff chief among them) and all credit Kronstam with being of primary importance in their development. He did not follow the trend of the times to have a handful of stars and an anonymous corps de ballet but kept to the Danish tradition of giving everyone in the company a place and using his or her special gifts. In addition to the stars he developed, there were a number of dancers in the corps who were giving beautiful performances in solo roles—Bjarne Hecht and Ann-Kristin

Hauge most prominent among them, but also Torben Jeppesen, Erling Elias-son, Mogens Boesen, Niels Balle, and a bevy of young women: Tina Hollman, Marianne Rindholt, Karina Elver, and Benedikte Paaske.

Although it was often pointed out that Kronstam disliked the administrative part of his job, he did it well. Vibeke Paulsen, his secretary (and Flemming Flindt's previously), who was considered extremely efficient and often served as a hostess of small dinner parties for visiting choreographers, said, "He was reluctant to take over, yes, but then when you go for it, you go for it—and he did go for it. He worked from nine in the morning until nearly midnight, every day. He wasn't in the office all day—why should he be? The artistic director should be in the studios. He delegated work and we all worked well as a team, but when he needed to be here, he was here."

Among the administrative and artistic personnel at the Theatre, Kronstam was both respected and liked. Peter Ernst Lassen, a leading Danish conductor, spoke of how easy it was to work with him and how seriously he treated the musical side of the ballet. "He would come to me and ask how much rehearsal time I needed, and I always got it," was one example. Lassen's wife, Anne Grethe Lassen, who worked at the Theatre for twenty-five years, said that Kron-stam had been the best of the department chiefs—including opera and drama—during her time there. "There were never any surprises with Henning. Whatever he said he would do, he would do," she said. Bering Liisberg, the only person who has both a practical as well as artistically analytical assessment of Kronstam's tenure, had this to say:

"He was very inventive and creative. He could easily catch an idea and then develop it further, if he was in that world. He had his own mind, but that doesn't say that he didn't want to listen. You could ask him an artistic question, as a question, and not get the answer you expected. Mostly he had his own reasons and could explain why am I doing this or that. We could always discuss [artistic matters]. I could always talk to Henning and he could talk to me. And many times he explained a lot of things to me. I was happy—I got more and more interested in the ballet.

"His strength was his artistic *integrity*, if I could say one word, both the per-sonal choices and in the way he carried them out. That was always the main thing, to reach the quality he felt was the right thing, with his experience. He was as able to compromise as anyone else. We always have to do that in the theater because things are happening from the outside that you can't control.

"As an artist, I can't say that there were any weaknesses. All artists have their own way, but with a person with his artistic background, you accept that that will be the leading factor in what he's doing. Of course, you could say that a person who takes on a position that is partly administrative has a weakness in not liking conflicts. But on the other hand, his capacity in artistic matters way overcame that."

Bering Liisberg saw Kronstam's dislike of conflict "as part of his illness. There are degrees of being shy towards conflicts, and he was, to a large degree. But not when it came down to artistic questions. He could face it and argue for his position, not in many words, but so that you knew that there was a reason behind it. It was all the other conflicts that he didn't want to get into, and I think that was because they stressed him too much and took his forces out of him, the forces he wanted to spend on artistic matters.

"If too many factors from the outside at the same time were against what he wanted to do, there was a conflict. But there were also conflicts with persons, of course. An emotional person hates to be obnoxious to somebody, and I think he didn't want to do that. And that made him very closed sometimes, too."

Bering Liisberg also understood why the Danish critics did not understand Kronstam's importance to the company. "I think, generally speaking, that they were looking too much for a choreographer and didn't recognize his qualities enough. I think they recognized his artistic power, but of course, critics don't work in the ballet world and they don't see the inspiration we talked about earlier. That, a critic will normally not come close to, and because of that, they couldn't evaluate him well enough. And then, as a person, he didn't talk much to the press. He was not part of the little ballet circle in Copenhagen. He wasn't a person who relied on dialogue, even within the Theatre. But there he could explain it with his eyes and his gestures. That you cannot do to a critic on the phone."

To most of the Danish critics, Kronstam was judged merely to be a hardworking, though not creative, figure who kept the company running without adding to its luster. To artists—both the dancers who worked with him and the musicians, teachers, and choreographers with whom he had contact—he was held in the highest esteem. Perhaps Kronstam's greatest weakness was that he could not sell himself as a director and allowed others to define him. For the next nine years, Kronstam made magic in the studios of Kongens Nytorv, yet despite occasional mentions of this in interviews with the dancers, few others seemed to notice.

His spirit gave you energy. He had a tremendous ability to make everybody believe they could do more than they could do. He made you believe in yourself, at the same time that he was asking everything of you.
—Sorella Englund

You had huge respect. Huge respect. You wouldn't even have to look when he entered the room. You could feel it. There was something there that you can't buy and you can't learn.
—Silja Schandorff

Twenty-five

The Red Thread

It was only after he had resigned his position as ballet master that Kronstam could finally devote himself to actually being a ballet master. Now he could do what he most enjoyed doing, next to being on stage himself, which was to work with dancers in the studio. The first few months of Andersen's tenure were rocky, however, and Kronstam was still burdened with Theatre problems.

"Frank started in August, and by December or January he hadn't done anything in rehearsals. He hadn't given any classes. He was on the telephones in the Theatre, calling New York or Japan for his group [a bone of contention for both Kronstam and Ralov, as they saw it as using the Theatre's resources for Andersen's private enterprise]. I went down to Henrik [Bering Liisberg] and said, 'This is absolutely wrong. The man is only working for his own little group.' Henrik said, 'Would you please come down with Frank tomorrow and tell him straight to his face?' I'd already had complaints from other people in the company. So I said, 'Frank, you've got to work with the company. You can't just sit in your office.' So he started to give classes, but that he stopped very fast. He came with his book and gave steps, but he was so mechanical." The Theatre did stop Andersen's work with the group, however.

There were other, much more serious problems that first year. Andersen tried to fire several dancers who were ill or who performed only mime roles. He wanted to replace them with dancers trained outside the school, primarily (of necessity) foreigners. This immediately got him into trouble with the dancers' union, as he had fired the dancers without the mandated administrative hearing.[1] Among these was Sorella Englund, one of the most admired artists in the Theatre, whose Madge (in *La Sylphide*) was one of the Danish Ballet's main attractions. Englund was only thirty but was able to perform only mime roles because her fragile health no longer permitted her to dance on pointe. At one meeting, when Andersen was pressed to defend his decision, he said that he could find no artistic justification to keep Englund on the roster, which became emblematic of what the dancers called "Frank's bad taste." The dispute grew into the biggest fight between the dancers' union and the Theatre since the second Lander scandal in the late 1950s. There were many meetings; both Andersen and the dancers stood their respective grounds. Although they were forbidden to strike, the dancers found that if a union meeting happened to be scheduled at the same time as a performance, the performance had to be postponed until the meeting was over. One meeting ran (deliberately) so long that a performance had to be canceled, and the audience, which understood the reason, cheered.

The dancers eventually gave Andersen a vote of no confidence, the first in the history of the company. By custom, in any union workplace such a vote means that the recipient must resign, but Andersen did not and the Theatre management did not, or could not, force him to do so. The Theatre did back away from the fight, however, and the dancers were not fired. Who or what was behind the attempted firings is not clear. Some dancers had the impression that Andersen had been ordered to fire the dancers, yet if this were so, why was Tomasson told that such an action was impossible only the year before?

The vote of no confidence was never rescinded. During every year of Andersen's directorship, the question of whether or not to lift the vote was raised at the first meeting of the dancers' union, and every year the dancers voted to leave it in place. Kirsten Ralov remained as vice ballet master for a year and a half, then resigned, after several attempts. She said the reason was because "I couldn't stand that bad taste," but also because "I couldn't work any longer with someone so dishonest in the way he dealt with people."[2] Andersen appointed Lise la Cour to replace her.

During all this Kronstam continued teaching company class and rehearsing ballets. He became the principal instruktør, but that does not quite explain his importance to the Danish ballet. After his death several dancers, asked to describe Kronstam's role in the company during Andersen's directorship, said, "He was the red thread of the ballet." This refers to one of the most beautiful of the old Norse legends that concerns the fabric of a person's life, a cloth woven by the Fates. Running through the fabric is a red thread; it is the thread that connects and sustains the cloth. When the Fates are tired of weaving the thread is cut. It is, of course, the blood-red thread of life. Kronstam was the last of a long line, and when he left the Theatre, that continuity was severed, as well as, many feel, the company's international standing. "He was the glue that held the company together. He was the reason it maintained its international reputation as long as it did," as Ib Andersen put it. If there is to be hope of piecing together the red thread of the Royal Danish Ballet, it is important to understand not only why Kronstam was so highly regarded by the last three generations of Danish dancers, but some of the things he taught them.[3]

First and foremost, Kronstam had an overview of the company, watching over all the dancers, from the children in the school to the stars, and the ballets, from the rehearsal studio to the technical departments. He was the walking aesthetic of the Danish ballet, its moral force. "He was the éminence grise," as Nikolaj Hübbe put it. "He taught us that you have to have a sense of responsibility. You have to avoid this Danish leniency, the institutionalized art of the Royal Theatre. You have to challenge yourself and stay on a high artistic level. You have to develop. You have to do your utmost. You can't just be comfortable."

Kronstam always led by example, never making speeches, but a word or a look would indicate that a dancer had crossed some invisible artistic line and offended his sense of taste. Kenneth Greve remembered, "The very first thing we worked on was *Nutcracker* when I came as a guest here. I had just done *Nutcracker* in Vienna, and I said, 'Henning, what do you think? Could I do this coda, because it's a bit more thrilling?' He just looked at me and said, 'I

Kronstam with Lis Jeppesen and Nikolaj Hübbe, rehearsing *Giselle*. Photo: David Amzallag. Private collection.

wouldn't do that.' Well, after that, there was no way I would do that, and I didn't."

Many dancers have stories of Kronstam watching them when they were children, giving them their first chances by casting them as understudies in a big ballet as fourteen- or fifteen-year-olds, and making sure they got on stage as early as possible. He made everyone feel a part of the production, "from the principals down to the smallest child," as Mogens Boesen put it. "I remember when I was a child and was cast in the premiere of *Romeo and Juliet*. I was working in the Capulets' house, holding the door, and nobody had the time to work with me, and I thought, you know, "I will just do my best." But Henning came to me and gave me the instruction, with the music, and wrote down for me when I had to push the door, how far, how fast. I was fourteen, fifteen, something like that, and he made it seem as though it was the most important part in *Romeo and Juliet*."

"I think he could always get [his intentions] across, because what he did was so well thought out," said Ib Andersen, who was that production's Romeo and directs Ballet Arizona. "Even though Henning was such an intuitive dancer, he gave so much thought to what he did. He probably taught what he had learned from Volkova, that to do anything it has to make sense to you. You must understand why you are doing something, whether it's something specific or more abstract. It has to have a purpose, because if it doesn't, it won't be interesting."

It was the combination of having a clear vision of the whole, as well as a keen eye for detail, and his ability to communicate his vision to the dancers that struck people as extraordinary. Kronstam was the one everyone wanted to work with, and he coached both men and women. "The incredible thing about Henning is that he knows everything in a ballet. He knows the technique, he knows how a woman has to look on the stage—and that's very difficult for a man," said Heidi Ryom, who worked with Kronstam on nearly every important role in her career. "You can meet Henning in the hall and say, 'I can't figure out what count I go out on in the last part of the second act,' and he will think about two seconds and say, 'Seven, eight, and out.'"

Kronstam often taught company class from the 1960s until 1992; when he wasn't teaching, he usually took class with the dancers and did barre, at least, until 1992 as well. He very much set the company's style, and since he taught what he had learned from Volkova, this is why the company's style was so consistent for more than forty years, despite a variety of ballet masters and a multi-choreographer repertory. "I've never had a better teacher; he really made us fly," said Lis Jeppesen, the great Bournonville ballerina of her generation. "Henning could put joy for dance in the classes and we miss that so much now. Everybody talks about how we should be hard and tough, and you forget about the joy of dancing. I think that is the main thing for Bournonville, where you really show the spontaneity of dancing, but you could put that in anywhere—you could put it in Balanchine. Without it, when you go see a performance, you're seeing a class."

Although Kronstam's base was Volkova, he incorporated what he had learned from working with choreographers as well. Stephen Pier, a modern dancer by training, saw the effects of Kronstam's work in modern dance in his classes: "He approached it more like a lot of modern dancers approach their work. It had to have daring. It had to have risk in it. It had to communicate something, and he worked on that in class, to really get it past what you assumed your boundaries were, and that was unusual for Denmark. Everybody else was trying to be correct and be "true to the style"—whatever that is; nobody can define it—but he was more interested in getting it all to *move*. Very intent on what was proper when he was rehearsing Bournonville things, but that wasn't the main interest. It had to move, and you had to be moved by it."

The importance of finding the meaning in a movement, the idea that dancing was a personal act, an expression of feelings and emotions, was very much a part of Kronstam's classes. "The way he did the partnering classes was a big help for me," said Mette-Ida Kirk, who took that class as an aspirant, "because he always made sure that there was time to explain, time to go over things, and there was the feeling that your inner statements had to be shown in the movement. He emphasized the connection between your feelings and the way you danced, so that everything was an expression for your feelings. And he created a good atmosphere, so that I felt safe and was not afraid to be clumsy."

Some dancers, especially those who had left Denmark, felt that Kronstam had not developed, had not changed his teaching when a more quantitative technical approach began to dominate ballet in the late 1970s. Others, while

Kronstam with Mette-Ida Kirk in rehearsal. Photo: David Amzallag. Private collection.

agreeing that Kronstam kept to what he learned from Volkova and Williams, saw this not as a lack of development but a choice and understood the reasons for it. Adam Lüders, now a teacher himself, said, "He was a very good teacher. He didn't develop the way Stanley [Williams] did. Henning remained old-fashioned, very simple. He didn't incorporate all the new Russian things. But Henning had other things, like the importance of the torso, and he had a different feeling behind it that Stanley doesn't pay attention to." Erling Eliasson, a very musical dancer with an eye for style, said, "I can still see him in the studio showing a movement. There is a big difference in the way he would move and the way they move today [three years after Kronstam had left the Theatre] because today they want to show extremes. The legs have to be up. Of course, Henning could lift the leg high, but with Henning, he had the rounded movements. The legs went backward and the body went forward; it wasn't a question of showing the leg up very high. To me, that's much more beautiful because it makes the dancer three-dimensional."

Every dancer who worked with Kronstam mentions his extraordinarily sensitive musicality. Kronstam was not a musician; his musical training consisted of those two years of piano lessons in childhood. However, he had an instinctive sense of both rhythm and melody. Julian Thurber, one of the company's rehearsal pianists who played for Kronstam for more than twenty years (and with his wife, Ingryd Thorson, also a rehearsal pianist, is a concert musician in his own right) described one aspect of Kronstam's musicality: "There's a connection between breath and dance. You can dance with a fixed diaphragm, where you sort of hop around, and probably do it all right, but where nothing happens, or you can dance with a free diaphragm, where certain things happen, and where you remain up in the air for longer periods, and where certain movements suddenly become worth something. That is the breath, and that breath is also a musical thing. He would choose slow tempi to work with until he got the breath inside the movement, and then he would work it." Thorson spoke of Kronstam's way of responding to music and how this was linked to the action in a dramatic ballet. "He pulls the tempi back when you're rehearsing with him. Where James first feels the Sylph coming in the window, Henning hears the music and responds to that, so it's like the music comes first, and then the response comes, and then the feeling that something is there, and then he moves. He doesn't move on the music, which normally people do. It's a response."

Many Danish dancers refer to this as "dancing through the music." Lis Jeppesen described it as a natural rather than regimented musicality: "The whole corps doesn't have to be on the beat, like soldiers," and added: "In one sense, it is singing the dance. You have to hear the music, and what is the soul of the music and what is the melody. And then you have to transfer the melody to your movements. The other thing you do is to extend the movement out as long as you can before you go further, and that is the phrasing." Arne Villumsen, the great James of his generation who, with Jeppesen, shared Kronstam's sense of musicality, said: "Henning is very musical. That you could see when learning the steps, because he knew exactly how to move [with the music]. In *Sylphide,* for example, you could think about what you were saying. You could see it before you say it. It's not *on* the music. It has to be within a certain limit, but you could do it how you were feeling, expressing yourself. It's almost more moving through the music instead of on the beat. We had rehearsals, just walking rehearsals, on the stage. 'Not on the music. Try not to go on the music,' he would say. Today when I see them walk on the music, I say, 'Don't walk on the music,' because it looks stupid."

Sometimes Kronstam would count in rehearsals, sometimes not. Nikolaj Hübbe, also a very musical dancer, said, "I never counted anything that I learned from Henning because he would show me musically how it was and then we would do it until I learned it." "If you have to count when you're on stage," said Ann-Kristin Hauge, "then you don't have it in your body and in your soul."

All these elements went into Kronstam's way of coaching and staging a ballet. When he had been artistic director, Kronstam had staged few ballets for lack of time. He oversaw what others were doing and made corrections and suggestions and often coached soloists, but he worked on comparatively few productions himself. "He was always very inspiring," said Mette-Ida Kirk, "and it is hard to explain how he gave that spirit, because when he was ballet master he didn't work that much with people." During Frank Andersen's tenure, however, freed from meetings, Kronstam directed or rehearsed most of the important ballets in the repertory; he was directly responsible for much of what one saw on stage, and what made him the red thread was that he carried through what he had learned, adapting it to his own times and making it live for the dancers.

Kronstam had started coaching at a very early age. "I could see that the Theatre needed producers," he said. "I thought I had a good memory, and Niels Bjørn had already used me when he had to revive, but that was usually my own roles. He would call me down and say, 'Is this right?' because he couldn't show it. So that I started in the early '60s. I was in everything and I was not leaving the room when I was not involved. I was always seeing the whole ballet. I was always listening to what they were saying. And sometimes I knew the next year I would have to do it, and I would have to remember, not only the steps but what was said about it. I already felt at that time, in '65, that we needed classical producers because of the way Flemming was going."

Although he learned everything he could from the choreographers with whom he worked (good, bad, and indifferent), Kronstam especially learned from watching, and later working with, Hans Brenaa. One of the most important lessons he learned from Brenaa was the art of casting. In a small company like the Danish ballet, which had always been made up of individuals with distinct theatrical personalities and uneven technical abilities, casting—putting the right person in the right role—was key. The Royal Danish Ballet was very much an ensemble company, and the whole was always greater than the sum of its parts.

During the periodic flowerings in this century, casting has often approached wizardry, not only making the company's ballets as perfect as possible, but developing dancers and expanding their range as well. Hans Beck was a casting genius, as was Harald Lander, although they had different sensibilities. Hans Brenaa and Henning Kronstam were the last of this line. Their approaches were very different—they were products of different eras and had had different careers and experiences as dancers—but how Brenaa made the type system work long after it had died out elsewhere, and how Kronstam modulated from the old, external to the newer, more internal way of acting is probably the most important reason the ballets they directed looked contemporary. This kind of incisive casting was very much a part of the Danish way of ballet mastering, of the way the dancers were taught the ballets and the way the ballets were maintained. The results were not always understood by dancers, audiences, or critics. There were situations in which a dancer of relatively limited gifts would be so perfectly cast and brilliantly coached that the dancer would give a star performance and many would wonder why he or she wasn't cast in every leading role. The reason was because the dancer wasn't appropriate for every leading role, perhaps not even any other leading role. Brenaa would say a dancer wasn't the right type; Kronstam would say, "It is not in his character." When ballets were cast and staged with as much care as they once were in Copenhagen, dancers who would seem extremely ordinary if left on their own often gave remarkable performances.

In Kronstam's day, ballets were staged from the ground up each time they reentered the repertory. Because of the subscription system, a new ballet was usually in the repertory for two seasons only. Then it was rested for a season or two before, if it was popular enough, it could be brought back. When a ballet reentered the repertory (called a repremiere) it was treated like a new work. Roles were "called back" after the end of the season (meaning that the ballet could be recast) and the ballet was staged as though new. A ballet was taught, scene by scene and role by role, by the instruktør, from memory. Brenaa became custodian of the Bournonville repertory because he knew the ballets, having committed them to memory, minute by minute and role by role, as was necessary in the days before video and notation. In fact, one might argue that video and notation are needed only when a company does not have a Brenaa or a Kronstam. One must be able to see detail in order to memorize it; the two skills are inextricably linked. Although both video and notation can be valuable tools—Kronstam used both as aids, to check his memory or clarify a point—if the stager relies on them completely, telling dancers to "do it just like it is on the video," without being able to provide additional information or infuse the scene with dramatic cogency, the results will not match the video. The common practice elsewhere (outside of Paris or St. Petersburg) was to teach the variations separately, and then, if there was time, work on mime and characterization. In contrast, Kronstam (as Brenaa and Lander had before him) taught a role's steps, gestures, musicality, and character motivations simultaneously.

Kronstam would say or sing the action of the particular segment he was teaching as he showed the steps so they would be welded together in the dancer's mind. "He would do different voices for the different characters," said Rose Gad. "He would say the line [of the mime] out loud as people were doing it. I remember more what he said than what he showed me. It was wonderful what he could do—he could do any character." As Hübbe noted, if Kronstam considered a dancer musical he did not give counts, unless the score was unusually complex. If the dancer was not naturally musical, he would sing the counts to the melody of the score, as though trying to force the dancer's body to inhabit the music. In some ways, Kronstam worked the way a conductor would work with an orchestra. He would begin rehearsals at a much slower tempo than he would want to see on stage, so that the dancers would learn the parts thoroughly and perform them cleanly. As rehearsals progressed, he would tighten the ballet by tightening the musicality, speeding up the tempo. Sometimes the ballet would not be a tempo by opening night, but it would be clear; tightening and polishing was a continuous process, and his productions improved the longer they remained in repertory. "Henning gave you time," as Lloyd Riggins put it. "We get so much into the premieres, the big performance, and after that, you know, rehearse? It's not important. But Henning understood that it takes time to develop these roles."

In Bournonville mime sequences the musicality is especially key. Stephen Pier, who was part of a conversation among five people in the first act of Kronstam's 1992 production of *Napoli* (in the role of the Friar) gave an example of how Kronstam could be implacable and not allow a dancer any leeway in his interpretation. In this instance, Pier had been instructed to turn and deliver his mime gesture on one count, but he wanted to take three counts to do the gesture and had what sounded like a perfectly reasonable dramatic explanation for it. This was not allowed, and no explanation was offered, but the reason was clear in performance, for when the five characters' gestures were put together they were so tightly interwoven with the music that the small scene became the climax of that segment, exploding with the force of a firecracker, pulling taut the texture. This is not an isolated example of Kronstam's insistence that a role be done in exactly one way; there are other examples, though, of how much latitude he would give a dancer, and his approach probably depended on both the dancer and the role.

There are many views on this subject. Silja Schandorff felt that: "Henning would try and push, but he would never try to change. I always felt that whenever I worked with him he encouraged me so much. He would push me as much as he could, but he would never try and make me into something else." But other dancers, like Mette-Ida Kirk, sometimes felt that Kronstam was trying to make her copy him and often "felt ridiculous" until she found a way of working out the role her own way. "I discussed that with him," she said, "and asked if he would just let me work things out for myself, and then I felt much better, much more relaxed."

Lis Jeppesen said that in working with Kronstam, "You have to be modeling clay, and then you have this wonderful person, and he is molding you. So you

throw yourself in his arms and say, 'Do what you want! I'll do anything!'"
Jeppesen felt that Kronstam encouraged dancers to change the roles as they
got older. "He'd say, 'You are in that period now, so you have to do it that way.'
If you're older, maybe you're not innocent any more, so you change it. And
sometimes you give your own thing to it, and he'd say, 'Now that's not working.
Do it the other way.'" Heidi Ryom had a similar experience: "When you did
something new, he'd say, 'That's very good. I like it. Keep that.' Even if it's impulsive, do it. That's the great thing with Henning. He keeps you loose. He
knows, 'She's got it. Now it's hers. Now she can build on it.'"

Lloyd Riggins enjoyed the variety of approaches Kronstam brought to rehearsals: "He is different every time. I don't know if he plans it, or if it's inspiration, like a choreographer. With me, it was more watching him. He'd give me
a sense of what he wanted by what he did, and then he'd sit down and he'd
watch me. And then he would manipulate it a little bit, mold it a little bit, or
give me clues. He never made it apparent. You always had to think, which I
like, and there was never the fear of making mistakes. You could see how he
did it and you just saw it was right, but he never said, 'Do it exactly as I do it
because I am Henning Kronstam.' It was never like that. He did it that way,
and it looked so good on him because it was so pure, it was so real for him. And
what he wanted you to do, I felt, was to make it real for you.

"The things he would give you were so clear. They talk about the Danish
danseur noble's simplicity? That's how he was as a coach, too. It was so clear
that you could find your own identity in it. He would give you a box and let you
open it and do what you would with it. It was as if he trusted you. And you
trusted him. It was so fantastic."

Niels Balle, Hilarion in Kronstam's production of *Giselle,* said, "He would
guide you within a frame. He would want it to be inside that frame, but you
could have a little slide on each side. He would get you to make it look like what
he wanted, and then he would give you the freedom to create it in your own
way." Kronstam had decided ideas of what that frame was, and how much a
dancer could "slide." Mogens Boesen remembered a time when, working with
Kronstam on *Etudes,* he felt uncomfortable with one of the set arm positions
and was a bit miffed at first that Kronstam wouldn't allow him to change it. "He
saw it as a picture, and maybe I would be more comfortable, but it wouldn't
look right."

Kronstam did see ballets as pictures, and had a sense not only of detail, but of composition; what was going on in the back of the stage must relate to what was going on in the front, as the dancer's arm and head must complement his leg. He also had a sense of color and texture, and when he cast he used the dancers almost as paints, matching or contrasting them not only by coloring but by weight and line. "When I did *Folk Tale,* Henning came to me and said, 'The way I did *Folk Tale* and the way Erik did *Folk Tale* were different. I was very determined in what I was doing, and Erik had the blond hair, the light features,'" said Lloyd Riggins, himself a pale blond. "Henning said, 'I think it would probably be better for you to do it the way Erik did it, to be a weaker character in the first act, to let things happen to you, not to be decisive. It's not, 'I'm staying here because I want to.' It's, 'I'm staying here because I don't know what to do.'"

The dancers came to expect this kind of detailed coaching, and were dismissive of more superficial approaches. "Henning came to me after my debut in *Sleeping Beauty,*" Kenneth Greve remembered, "and said, 'That was a nice performance, Kenneth,' and it was like gold. It was like Nureyev said something to me. Henning very rarely—after one *Apollo,* he said, 'Today, I saw you see the mountains when you look out.' That was another difference between Henning and Frank. Henning would come to you and say, 'I couldn't see you tonight, Kenneth. I couldn't see your eyes,' and then one or two technical corrections, but that didn't mean as much. And then Frank would come up and say, 'Your hair looked nice.'"

Some dancers, at least, sharpened their own perception skills by watching Kronstam's rehearsals. "When I think back and remember Henning watching rehearsals, he would express Juliet, or Romeo. If he was looking at the people, he would be a part of it himself," said Thomas Lund. "I remember that, especially coming up as a young kid, and it's not like he's putting on an act. You can see it's so honest that he really feels for the work, and for the particular role that he's watching. You could see how it went deep inside his heart. He would actually be acting together with the person who was doing it, but then he would also stop and say, 'No, no. Don't do this. Try and do that instead,' and that was quite amazing."

Kronstam was noted for having an inexhaustible supply of ideas, and he would work to find something that made each dancer understand a role. "Henning had great images and he gave me everything that he had. In that sense, he was totally generous. Completely. Any little clue, any little idea," said Nikolaj

Hübbe, speaking of working with Kronstam on the role of James. While working on the scene at the end of the first act, where James is torn between the Sylph and his soon-to-be-bride, his reaction to his betrothal ring shows the state of his heart and conscience. "He would say, 'Sometimes, the ring is burning. The metal of the ring is burning a scar into your finger, and it burns so hard, it's like cattle being seared.' And: 'Sometimes the ring is heavy. It's so heavy. It's like a chain. You can't get it off. It's just so heavy. It hurts. It's so heavy.' You could choose the image you wanted, but he said all these things to give you the choice."

Nearly every dancer had an example of how Kronstam would insist on finding the meaning behind the movement: "You should feel that you are at one with the part you are doing. With Henning, I never felt that I should be trying to do the steps and do a character," said Alexander Kølpin. "He would always make you understand that this character is not dancing this variation to show off his beats. He is showing the love for the Sylph—or whatever. He felt that when you are a dancer, you are a human being, and the steps are your tool to express feelings. Henning was always good at encouraging people to feel emotionally involved with what they're doing. The whole atmosphere makes the character. It's not that everybody can do James the same way."

With some dancers Kronstam was more directive, pushing them rather than offering choices. Others needed a shove: "He got things out of me," said Arne Villumsen. "He said, 'You have to do it.' And he had to do that, because I was not the type who worked very hard myself. I had to be beat up a little bit— and he knew that. He was always pushing me." But Kronstam knew when to push and when to hold back, and he made it clear he expected the dancers to maintain a high standard of professionalism. "If there was something technically demanding and you got frazzled about it, he would get really furious," said Hübbe. "Because he thought you cannot let it affect you that way. It's up to you to work it out. You have to dissect it, and then through dissecting it and through making it logical, then you will be able to do it. He'd say, 'You have to work. You can't just assume that it will be there, especially if you have a problem with it.' So he would make you go over things a million times until you got it, and until it was in your body technically."

Alexander Kølpin also noted how Kronstam matched his approach to each dancer: "It's not enough to rehearse and rehearse and rehearse. It's a psychological thing to make people feel good about themselves, and when people feel good about themselves, they produce better. In that way, Henning was very much ahead of his time because in the old days you would just do it again and again and again, and that's a very old-fashioned way of being a leader. But the way you get the best out of people is to make them feel good and happy. And he knows that this is what makes Alexander happy, this makes Heidi work harder, this gets more out of Nikolaj, and when you can see that, you can take people so much further than just rehearse and rehearse and rehearse, because that just makes you tired."

For Villumsen, "Henning has a good way of saying things so people can understand them. He doesn't just go down and give something. He's really thinking about things and thinking about the roles. And what he learned from the role, he told us. He showed the steps. Then, when I learned all the steps, we could start pulling things from each other.

"It was about the feelings. He would want to get you to do the exact expression in your body and your face. He could come with a little story: 'Think of it like that and then you might get to it.' And that makes you wonder to yourself about the story, and how you want to do the role. He made you do things you couldn't believe you could do. He believed in the roles. And when you have seen him do a role, seen him do it with that belief, you do the same, and then you believe in it yourself."

To help a dancer attain that self-confidence, Kronstam would use any opportunity to open his or her eyes to a role. Lloyd Riggins remembered, "The month before we started working on *Apollo* we had a tour to Athens, and we danced in Herodes Atticus. Henning came up to me and he said, 'Look at this.' And we were in a 5,000-seat theatre and there is the Parthenon up there, and a crystal blue sky. And he said, 'Remember this, and remember this feeling.' That first movement in the second solo in *Apollo,* you're standing in this amphitheater, with the Parthenon there, and you're holding up the sky. It just sets your posture."

Silja Schandorff told a story that showed the intensity, but also the fun, of rehearsals in Copenhagen in the 1980s and early 1990s. "Sometimes he would get up and dance with you. When I learned *Apollo,* I remember doing almost the whole pas de deux—not the lifts, but he would do all the turning around and the looking, and I felt so strongly when he looked at me that he was in love with me. Not because he was in love with *me,* but he was doing Apollo and I was Terpsichore. It was the weirdest feeling. It was one of those things you can't really explain. It was as though he gave you his whole soul. It was as if I could look at him, right through his eyes. He would draw you and you would be so drawn by it that you would just follow."

When they rehearsed *Theme and Variations,* "We always went into *lille nye* [little new, the studio] with the beautiful view. And we would just do these steps over and over again. And he would say, "More, more, more." I remember once, I was absolutely dripping wet. I was soaked. And there were girls sitting outside. And Henning opened the door [like the teacher in Flindt's *The Lesson,*] and said, "Next! So who wants to come in?" And they were all looking at me like, "What happened?" And I was having the best time. It was fantastic. We always did the opening together. It's such a beautiful pas de deux. He really worked on that ballet. He took so much care of it."

Schandorff also gave an example of the difference between working with Kronstam and working with those who followed him: "For [MacMillan's] *Concerto* Henning would show how you would walk in, and how you would sense a man on the other side of the stage, and how you would listen to the music, and how the first time you touch him, it's just by the hand, and how you would put your hand in his hand. It was really important for him.

"Other people would say, 'You go in, and you stand here, and you wait for eight counts, and then you have another four, and then you go point point, and then you give him your hand.'"

"Today coaching has become more and more specific," said Rose Gad, "because some people just completely get off reality and they say, "Oh, you know, you have to use that muscle in between there," and they go down to such nitty-gritty things, and in the end you can't move. Henning gave very specific technical corrections, but he was never like that."

Kronstam was often said to take good care of the dancers, and Gad gave an example of this. "He was so good at arranging things, and I can say this because I have now learned that it is not that easy. You would never have any worries whether you would get rehearsals. All the things were just fixed. You had enough rehearsal, your costume would be ready, and you would have a rehearsal with everybody before you went into a new part. Things were just taken care of, because Henning demanded that. All you had to do is worry about doing your part."

All the meticulous attention to detail had but one purpose: that what was happening on stage would be interesting to the audience. Probably the most

Silja Schandorff and Kenneth Greve rehearsing Kenneth MacMillan's *Concerto*. Photo: David Amzallag. Private collection.

important thing Kronstam taught his dancers was stagecraft. "He would always say: 'They pay. You have to do something. I don't care what you do, but you have to do *something*. Don't just stand, look. If you're going to stand and look, then *stand* and *look*,'" said Hübbe. "Everything with Henning was having a lesson in how to perform, how to make things alive. In that sense, I think he was Old World, and I think that's good. 'It's art. It's art. But we have to live [make a living] from it.'"

When I was sitting in the Theatre, I would see
him, like a shadow coming in, and I wanted to
know what was in his mind, sitting in the
darkness, looking at his own life up there.
—Anne Wivel

Twenty-six

Life and Art

By the end of the decade Kronstam had decided, very quietly, to stop dancing.
"There was no one left who could get anything out of me," he said. The impetus was more specific: *Abdallah,* a reconstruction of a long-lost Bournonville
ballet by Bruce Marks and Toni Lander that Andersen had acquired. Kronstam
did not like the ballet, which he felt was an unconvincing pastiche. He played
the Sheik, a small role with only two scenes, but one that needed a powerful
personality. He felt the role did not make sense, although he never articulated
the reasons clearly. "Well, they couldn't tell me why it was three or seven or
five," was one of his more inscrutable comments. He was offered the role of
Odin in Allan Fridericia and Elsa Marianne von Rosen's reconstruction of *The
Lay of Thrym* (which he had turned down when he was director and which
proved to be a failure), but he declined. "I had worked with them before," he

said. Rather than continually saying no it was better to stop. Kronstam said he thought his last performance had been as Don Quixote. At the end of the performance, "I asked the dancers to leave me alone for a minute on stage. I knelt down and kissed the stage and thanked God for giving me so many good years in this beautiful Theatre."

Another likely reason for Kronstam's decision, or at least its timing, was the death of Hans Brenaa in the spring of 1988. Brenaa had been ill for several years and was preparing a revival of *The Kermesse in Bruges* when he suddenly weakened. He spent the last week of his life on a cot in the studio, coaching dancers in a ballet he had both loved and resurrected. Brenaa was seventy-seven when he died. Kirsten Ralov, an excellent coach of the Bournonville style but without Brenaa's theatrical flair, was nearly seventy. The future of the Bournonville repertory was now unsettled.

Brenaa had two assistants at the end of his life, Arlette Weinreich and Anne Marie Vessel, both of whom had been fine Bournonville dancers. Weinreich has an excellent eye for detail—which she said she had learned by watching both Brenaa and Kronstam over the years, learning to see what they were seeing, constantly refining her own perceptions; Vessel had enormous energy and was a spirited mime. Kronstam had also worked with Brenaa, of course, and the older man had made a speech at his seventy-fifth birthday in which, Nikolaj Hübbe remembered, "he passed the torch to Henning." Kronstam was expected to take over *La Sylphide*, which he did. Weinreich had worked with Brenaa on *Kermesse* but after his death Andersen assigned that production to Vessel. Andersen and Vessel immediately took over Brenaa's production of *Coppelia*, and the results pointed the way to the future. As Bent Schønberg, Brenaa's biographer, wrote, it was

> a catastrophic version of *Coppelia*. This light and gay ballet has been danced at the Royal Theatre since 1896. The Beck-Lander version, later continued by Hans Brenaa, was, in my opinion, the best in the world. Not so any more. Anne Marie Vessel, who with Arlette Weinreich was brought up by Brenaa as his Crown Princesses for preserving the Bournonville repertory (and *Coppelia*) intact, codirected this Delibes charmer with Frank Andersen. . . . All the magic had disappeared. All the humour had gone as well. The same with the lightness, the flirtations, the whimsy, which usually pervade the ballet.

Schønberg also noted that the dancers "played to the audience much more than to each other" and, of one cast, "From their interpretations, no one would guess they were in love with each other! They were simply two rather good, sympathetic dancers who simply did not understand their roles and obviously had received no coaching."

Andersen's approach to directing was, as his dancing had been, emphatic, unmusical, and lacking dynamics; everything was at the same, highly energetic, level. Dancers said, in his rehearsals, they were constantly exhorted to do "more, more, more!" or sometimes, simply, "Smile!" As Andersen and Vessel began to take over the Bournonville repertory the two competing aesthetics within the company became more obvious. Dancers danced differently Tuesday night, in Andersen and Vessel's *Coppelia,* than they did Thursday night, in Kronstam's *Giselle.*

It seemed that Andersen was attempting to make the company more international, which really meant making it more to American taste. "He's going the American way," said Yuri Possokhov, the Bolshoi star who danced with the company from 1992 through 1994, "and that's the wrong way for this Theatre," a statement with which most Danish dancers would agree. Dancers say, at least since the days of the Bournonville group, that Andersen had always been "very oriented to America," as Bjarne Hecht put it, and looked to American reviews and American reviewers for approval, as the standard on artistic matters.

Between Andersen's international course for the company and the Danish way of dancing stood Kronstam with all his gentle might. It is not that Andersen and Kronstam were at loggerheads—tensions were very much below the surface in the early 1990s. Kronstam liked Andersen and said, at the end of his life, that "it was not a bad relationship"—but that the dancers saw Kronstam as their artistic leader and looked to him, rather than Andersen, for guidance. When Sylvie Guillem appeared as a guest in 1990, for example, her trademark high extensions drove the audience wild but, rather than trying to emulate them, the company's women thought them in bad taste. Kronstam's ideas were very much in sync with those of the theatre chief, but that too was about to change.

In 1989, Bering Liisberg was forced to resign as theater chief after a political brouhaha over how the Theatre had been managed. Like arts institutions all over the world, the Danish Royal Theatre ran at a loss, and some politicians used this as an issue in the elections of that year. A new theater chief, Boël Jürgensen, a provost at the University of Roskilde with no managerial background in theater, was appointed to succeed him. The relationship between Kronstam and Andersen began to change dramatically almost immediately after Bering Liisberg's departure. Andersen made wholesale changes in personnel, replacing people who had been part of Kronstam's staff and had stayed on to work with him, including Vibeke Paulsen, the company's secretary (who had also been Flindt's secretary); Arne Bech, Kronstam's stage manager; and Arlette Weinreich, who was eventually succeeded as instruktør by Andersen's wife, Eva Kloborg. Kirsten Ralov, then the company's senior Bournonville stager and a teacher of inestimable value, would soon lose both her productions—*A Folk Tale* and *Napoli*—to Andersen.

In 1990, Boël Jürgensen renewed Andersen's contract, which was due to expire, despite the vote of no confidence renewed annually by the dancers. The head of the dancers' union, Benedikte Paaske, protested this vigorously but had not learned of the reappointment until after it was a fait accompli. Kronstam was still to hold the position of artistic advisor. Jürgensen respected Kronstam and understood his importance to the company, but Kronstam had lost his backing. Bering Liisberg's successors did not have his knowledge of ballet or background in theater and did not understand the ramifications of some of Andersen's policies.

For the next two years, Kronstam continued much as he had before, staging the big ballets (*Don Quixote, Romeo and Juliet, Onegin, La Sylphide,* and the company's Balanchine repertory). He began making subtle changes in *La Sylphide* when he took over the production after Brenaa's death. ("He stepped in and didn't miss a beat," said Nikolaj Hübbe, who took part in those rehearsals.) Two of these minor changes indicate how Kronstam worked. One was a change of tempo and dynamic in the first act's reel. Kronstam's direction gave the dancing a fierce, almost wild, and very masculine quality, presenting a stronger contrast to the quiet, feminine world of the Sylph and her sisters. It was a musical reflection of the claustrophobic atmosphere of the first act, helping to make the contrast with the second act more distinct. The second tiny change involved casting. Kronstam had learned from Brenaa the secret of changing the way a role was danced by simply changing the dancer. In the fortune-telling scene, Kronstam thought that the dancer playing the role of the girl who learns she may be pregnant was a little too broad, the humor a bit too obvious. What was being done suited the dancer then in the role, but he wanted another coloration, so he began to experiment. He first cast one of the company's most alluring dancers, and although the broadness disappeared the moment wasn't as funny because the girl was such an obvious flirt. His next choice solved the problem. He put a dancer in the role whose open face and youth made her look not only innocent but absolutely naive, "as though she could be tricked into doing anything," he said. It worked. The bit was funny again, but in a more delicate way. Kronstam's patience in fine-tuning a ballet moment by moment was one of the reasons his productions were so extraordinary.

Kronstam built on what Brenaa had done, as Brenaa had brought clarity and life to the stagings of the prior generation. "We all loved Hans," said Ib Andersen. "He had a phenomenal memory and he was able to be simple and direct without anything extra; it was just right on—an unusual gift. Where Henning, I would say, was much more intelligent in a way, and because of that, I think he saw many more things. Henning was more a man of detail—not that Hans was not, but they had very, very different minds. When Henning staged the first act of *Napoli* [in 1992], what he did there was more detailed and functioned better than Hans's staging. Henning would also make more sense out of it in terms of your character. It would be much more rich."

Kronstam had direct charge of *La Sylphide* for only four years. During that time he worked with dancers who had learned their roles from Brenaa, such as Lis Jeppesen and Arne Villumsen, Rose Gad and Alexander Kølpin. He also worked with guest artists, such as Bolshoi ballerina Nina Ananiashvili, in 1991. Kronstam said that Ananiashvili had learned the role from the video before she came, "So I had to say, right away, forget all that. Because the video she had seen was Lis [Jeppesen] and Nina was nothing like Lis." Bolshoi style—big and free—is nothing like Danish style either, and Kronstam said that he had to make Ananiashvili feel comfortable being smaller. "We would do it a little day by day. I would bring her in [reduce the scale of her dancing], and then the next day say, 'That's good, but today we'll try it a little smaller.'"

Ananiashvili was at first skeptical about learning a role from a man but soon realized what Kronstam could give her. "He is so fantastic and good in this part. He knows everything, every step, every movement. And also, it was very interesting for me, because he brought all these notebooks where some ballerina had written everything down, and he'd check these things and show me, 'Now, you see, this is what they are writing.'

"When Henning showed me every step, he explained why, why I had to do

Nina Ananiashvili and Kronstam embrace as Peter Bo Bendixen looks on. Photo: David Amzallag. Private collection.

this, and why I'm looking here, and why I'm thinking this. Any small detail, he would explain. He is a great, great artist." Ananiashvili sent Kronstam a photograph after these rehearsals and wrote him impulsively that she never wanted to be coached by anyone else. She said that the only coach she had ever worked with who was on his level was her Bolshoi coach, the great ballerina Marina Semyonova. (Yuri Possokhov made the same comparison, adding to Semyonova his own teacher at the Bolshoi, Nikolai Simachev, a great character dancer and coach, and saying, "Nobody there [in Copenhagen] was on the same level as Henning," a point on which dancers, both visitors and resident, were in agreement.)

Kronstam did not stage a production of his own until the 1989–90 season, when Frank Andersen asked him to revive *Giselle*. Kronstam had danced in every twentieth-century production of this ballet in the Danish repertory, and bits of all these productions, from the "very dramatic atmosphere" of the 1946

Volonine version to two dramatic details from Bruhn's 1978 production, were woven into Kronstam's. He worked with Arlette Weinreich for a year, watching videotapes and reading about the ballet. "We had a great time," Weinreich said. "We were stealing from everywhere." Kronstam kept the designs from the 1978 production because he liked them, and doing so saved money. He did not care for the second act in the Bruhn production, a bit of which was taken from one version and a bit from another, and he asked Rimma Karelskaya to teach the Kirov's production to two dancers who, in turn, taught it to the corps. One Danish detail—that the Wilis cross their arms over their chests instead of extending an arm in arabesque during the second-act "Wilis' hop"—was retained, and the entire second act had Kronstam's softness and legato phrasing. Kronstam also put the current Kirov peasant pas de deux in the first act. The three Albrechts—Nikolaj Hübbe, Lloyd Riggins, and Peter Bo Bendixen— were all quite young and "very different," as he put it, and he made accommodations for each in their second-act solos.

The fashion of the times was for someone staging a nineteenth-century ballet to make an obvious dramatic change, "to put one's stamp on" the production, as many dancers put it, or add a solo or pas de deux. Doing this entitled one to be called a choreographer. Kronstam, however, did not want to change *Giselle,* but to tell the story clearly, to enliven the first act and bathe the second in moonlight and poetry. He kept two elements Bruhn had added that he thought worked. The first was the addition of two characters to the first act, an older couple, supposedly Albrecht's old nanny and her husband, who have been pensioned off to the village and live in the house across the square from Giselle. This gives Albrecht a reason to go to the village as well as a logical place in which to change clothes. It also answers a question *Giselle*'s original audience probably never asked, but that a contemporary one will, namely, How did Albrecht get that cottage? Bruhn had also imported a detail he had learned in America from Anton Dolin—making Bathilde and Myrtha a double role, danced by the same ballerina.

Kronstam, thinking as a dancer, believed that the second act was a dream. "There is a time when Albrecht is kneeling with his head in his hand, at the beginning, and Giselle comes and stands behind him. And then at the end of the act there is the exact same pose. And I always felt that in between those two moments it is all a dream." Kronstam the director could not ignore the Wilis and their dance (a later emendation by Petipa that, though beautiful, breaks up

Lis Jeppesen and Nikolaj Hübbe in *Giselle*. Photo: David Amzallag. Private collection.

the action and that Kronstam felt got in the way of the story, as did the first act's peasant pas de deux). Kronstam did not try to make the idea of Albrecht's dream obvious but implied. "I wanted to leave it ambiguous," he said, "but as a possibility, in case someone can't follow the story." Mette-Ida Kirk, who danced Myrtha/Bathilde at the premiere, added two interesting insights. She didn't see it as unusual that Bathilde would turn up in the second act as Myrtha because "all of the peasant girls in the first act are Wilis in the second act," which is literally true. Kirk, who danced the role like a small, vengeful demon, also said it helped her dramatically because, as Myrtha, "I already have a relationship with Albrecht."

The original ending, in which Bathilde comes to the forest and forgives Albrecht, had been dropped long ago, as it was thought too sentimental and old-fashioned; Ashton tried to restore it in the production for the Royal Ballet he staged with Tamara Karsavina in the 1960s, without success. There is a point to it, however, in that ballets of this time had, if not a happy ending, at least a final resolution. One of the common experiences of grief is for the bereaved to have a dream in which he is reconciled with the person who has died. Kronstam, who had had so much experience with grief and guilt, understood this. Making the second act a dream is an abstraction of this emotion and provides a resolution, without having all the characters left alive traipsing into the forest at dawn, which would be unacceptable to most contemporary audiences.

Kronstam also changed the character of Hilarion slightly, making him aggressively masculine and inarticulate (his miming is coarse), in strong contrast to Albrecht, with his smooth manners. "Hilarion lacked Albrecht's noblesse," as Niels Balle, who danced Hilarion at the premiere, put it. In the mad scene, Kronstam had Hilarion, who never understood Giselle, grabbing her and kissing her, as if to say, "See? Now that I've exposed him and told you the truth, everything will be all right, and I will love you." Kronstam made another dramatic point simply through casting: mismatching Giselle and her mother. A lyrical, introspective dancer (Sorella Englund) was mother to the much more down-to-earth Heidi Ryom. Mette Hønningen, who portrayed the mother as solid and sensible, was mother to the more poetic Lis Jeppesen. Without having to add a program note, Kronstam got across the idea that the mother and daughter never understood each other. He also brought out the drama simply by finding elements in the choreography that other producers ignore, most notably a theme of games and play, underscoring the danger of Albrecht's philandering—"it's a flirtation that goes bad," as Kronstam put it. The dances in

Heidi Ryom and Lloyd Riggins in *Giselle*. Photo: David Amzallag. Private collection.

Rose Gad in *Giselle*. Photo: David Amzallag. Private collection.

the first act, especially, recall the danced games of the Middle Ages and under-line this aspect of the story, rather than serving merely as filler.

One of Kronstam's most personal touches was in the mad scene. Except for Hilarion's brief intrusion, he did not change a step or a gesture but made the scene one of trying to maintain sanity rather than losing it, an idea that un-doubtedly came from his own experience. According to Rose Gad, his young-est Giselle, "He said that she didn't die because she was crazy. She died of a broken heart. Of course, maybe she has a bad heart, but because she has this broken heart, she can't cope any more. So it's not something that she does on purpose, but she distances herself from reality. She is so hurt that she loses her senses. She is fighting to get her balance back, the last time around. And then he said, 'The moment you see the mother, you are back to yourself, normal.' So he actually wanted us to come out of it again, so when we would die we would be ourselves. So of course it would be even more heartbreaking, as she dies."

Kronstam expected Weinreich to work with him in rehearsals. However, when going over assignments with Andersen the spring before the premiere, he was told that Lise la Cour (now Andersen's vice ballet master) had wanted to work with the corps, and Andersen had taken Weinreich off the production and

With Arlette Weinreich, backstage at the Royal Theatre, planning. Private collection.

substituted la Cour as Kronstam's assistant. Kronstam had always liked la Cour, but had no illusions about her skills as a rehearsal mistress, and also felt this was unfair to Weinreich. He told Andersen, "Then there will be no *Giselle,*" and Weinreich was put back on the production. The next season, however, Weinreich was offered only a partial contract (a way of getting rid of people without actually firing them), and left the Theatre. It seemed obvious that "financial reasons" were a poor cover, as Weinreich was immediately offered work in the Theatre's opera department, and the amount of money involved would barely cover two transatlantic airfares. Weinreich had stood up to Andersen on several artistic matters and always spoke her mind, but she was, as Bent Schønberg had written, "one of Hans Brenaa's Crown Princesses." She had an extraordinary memory and a clear eye for detail, and her departure was a blow to the Bournonville repertory and to Kronstam personally. "Arlette was always very helpful to me," he said several times.

Rehearsals for *Giselle,* of course, were as much about technique as drama. All three of Kronstam's Albrechts were very young and new to the role. Riggins was a demi-caractère dancer, and Kronstam had to work to give him the necessary weight for the role. His method for turning a "bouncing ball," as Riggins described himself, into a young nobleman sounds simple: "Well, you just calm them down and stretch them out," he said.

"I remember in *Giselle,* I would throw in little hop-skadoodle things before running to the corner," said Riggins. "And he would say, 'No. Keep it heavy.' The whole solo is—you're down. You're trying to save your energy because you know you have a long night ahead of you." The key to weight, as Kronstam had learned from Volkova, was the plié, something Riggins said he lacked at the time. "*Giselle* was one of the first ballets where I really had to try out—I learned it basically in *Onegin,* the adagio solo in the second act. If you're up like this (on high demi-pointe), you can't do it. And that's where he really taught me to get down into my plié, down into my heels, use my whole foot, get on the floor, get the weight." Kronstam also worked on weight with Ryom, a very light dancer. In the second act he had her "go more down into the ground," be weighty, to serve as a contrast to the jumps.

Kronstam also worked on style. "He is so classical," said Hübbe. "In the second act, I remember, I'd do: step step, double cabriole, assemblé dah-dah; step step, double cabriole. But he would say, '*Glissade. Glissade,* double cabriole. This is classical ballet. *Glissade,* double cabriole.' He was very clean and clear. His hands and arms were so expressive, and they always would cross his body. Always. They would always cross his body, and he would make beautiful big, round shapes. The little finger was always showing. 'When you go up, when your arm and your hand and your elbow go up, you go up, but your back goes down and your shoulders go down,' so it's a two-way thing. It's a movement which has a pull and a stretch. In that way, he's not what I think the Brits would call pure, but to me, 'pure' is academic, and that's not ballet. His arms are always over the head. It's a frame. He would say, 'À la couronne, à la couronne, like a crown, like a crown.' He was always after me about my arms because they're so long and flaky. When I came home for *Romeo and Juliet,* he said, 'Your arms, Nikolaj, your arms! You know, the lower department is really working well now since you went to America, but your top. My God.' Then he laughed."

Kronstam also worked with Hübbe on walking, one of the most difficult things for a dancer to do. "I remember Henning screaming at me in the beginning because I was so weird. Walking in with the cape. He said, 'No, it's wrong. It's wrong.' He took me out to the corner and said, 'It's like this.' He would walk it and put the flowers on Giselle's grave, and we did that so many times. I couldn't get it. He said, 'You have to switch your brain off. Just do it. Don't act. Just listen to the music.'"

Kronstam's *Giselle* did not find favor with the Danish critics, who wanted something more dramatic. Many saw it merely as a restaging of Erik Bruhn's production and said, quite openly, that Kronstam should have given Bruhn credit. Erik Aschengreen was one:

> There is unfortunately a lot in the Royal Theatre's new version that lacks meaning. Henning Kronstam is in charge of the production, but the version is so similar to Erik Bruhn's production from 1979 that this ought to have been mentioned. It also makes use of the same scenography from Desmond Heeley. It had thus been better if Henning Kronstam, with his style and ability, had created his own version. . . .
>
> This staging of *Giselle* is a performance divided into two parts. Henning Kronstam has worked with the main characters and it is wonderful what he and they have achieved. For their sake you can see the performance again and again. Lis Jeppesen and Nikolaj Hübbe are a romantic, beautiful couple whose like you do not see on many stages today. They bring romance to life. When they dance we believe in another world, and in their interpretation love is victorious—the love that makes Albrecht able to continue to live. There is thus a beautifully thorough idea in their dance and play. It is a shame that so much around them is unclearly thought out and manifested. This ought to be remedied.

A different view was offered by Anne Chaplin Hansen:

> Henning Kronstam's staging of the old ballet renews itself through a return to forgotten true feelings. In *Giselle* poetry becomes passion, pain the purest spirituality and redemption; beauty and aesthetics unveil other realities.
>
> How the Royal Ballet, one of the leading in the world, has been able to be without such a significant piece in its repertoire, one does not understand. It has been more than ten years since we last saw it, but now it is just a question of rejoicing together with the international audience that, pointedly, immediately crowds to the theatre.

Anne Wivel, one of Denmark's leading filmmakers, had wanted to make a film about Kronstam for some time and decided that *Giselle* would provide a good opportunity. "He was a Romantic person," she said, "a person for whom art is a Romantic thing, and I wanted to do a film of him working on a Romantic ballet." She called it *Of Dreams and Discipline,* an apt summary of Kronstam's life in the Theatre. Wivel's film follows Heidi Ryom and Lloyd Riggins through the rehearsals of *Giselle* to their first performance on stage. Wivel shot all the rehearsals but said she decided to use this cast rather than the first cast, of Lis Jeppesen and Nikolaj Hübbe, because Jeppesen had danced the role before and Wivel wanted to film someone actually learning the role.

Wivel's film is a fascinating glimpse of the world backstage, of how a ballet is staged and how Kronstam worked. She understood Kronstam as a creature of that Theatre, and the film has a sense of discovery, looking first at the Theatre—from its oldest character dancer, Niels Bjørn Larsen doing his character barre, to the smallest children in the school—then almost casually filming a rehearsal, and then, as though the camera became fascinated with Kronstam, focusing in on him until he becomes the center of the film. Wivel said that Kronstam had been very open with her and did exactly what she had wanted of him: to behave naturally and not be self-conscious of the cameras. The only problem had been that the script called for Kronstam to sit in rehearsals looking thoughtful and commenting on the ballet, "Two people, madness, love." He had not felt comfortable doing this and they thought of doing a voice-over with someone else saying the words. Kronstam did not like that idea either and so agreed to do the voice-overs.

Wivel found Kronstam easy to work with. She noticed a difference in energy from day to day, and, watching the film, it is possible to make a very good guess which day is an "up" and which (more usually) was a "down." The film received mostly favorable reviews in Denmark and won two video prizes in Europe. Wivel, and several of the dancers, felt that Andersen was not happy about the film because it concentrated on Kronstam so completely. The Theatre has a table where books and videos are sold and, despite Wivel's efforts, she said the video was never sold there.

In December 1991, Kronstam and Gerstenberg spent the Christmas holidays in Spain, relaxing and, for Kronstam, preparing for a new production of *Napoli* and new casts of *La Sylphide*. The weather in Spain's southern mountains was warm during the day, but the nights were bitter cold. Decades of heavy smoking had weakened Gerstenberg's lungs, and respiratory infection was a danger.

On the afternoon of January 4, 1992, Gerstenberg fell down, unconscious. Kronstam couldn't revive him. The two men were alone in a house without a phone, sixty miles from the nearest hospital. Kronstam ran to ask neighbors to call an ambulance. The trip to the hospital seemed endless. At the hospital doctors told Kronstam that his old friend was dead. Kronstam's Castilian Spanish wasn't good enough to communicate with the Andalusian doctors. He took a cab to the house of a Danish friend whom he had known in Copenhagen, Jonna Jerlang, who lived not far away. "I was screaming," he said. "I was running and I was drowning myself in the sea." Jerlang calmed him and called the hospital to find out what had happened. Two hours later a doctor found Gerstenberg in the morgue, still alive and in a diabetic coma. Gerstenberg never fully recovered from the illness; Kronstam never fully recovered from the shock.

Gerstenberg was in a coma for several days; he emerged with pneumonia. Seventy-two and frail, he was too ill to be moved. Kronstam called the Theatre and told them he would not be able to return until Gerstenberg was able to travel and asked that Anne Marie Vessel Schlüter begin the rehearsals of *La Sylphide*. After a month, Gerstenberg was well enough to travel, if accompanied by a doctor, but there was no doctor in Spain who would make the trip. In desperation, Kronstam called Vessel Schlüter, whose husband, Poul Schlüter, was then prime minister of Denmark. Schlüter arranged for a Danish physician to fly to Spain to bring Gerstenberg and Kronstam home, a kindness Kronstam always remembered with gratitude and spoke of often. Gerstenberg was hospitalized in Denmark for about two months. During this period, Kronstam spent his evenings at the Schrøder-Hansens. He was usually exhausted, and Lene remembered he would fall asleep in a chair in the living room before dinner.

As he had done all his life, Kronstam pushed his problems aside and, through discipline, managed to stage three ballets in two months. For *Konservatoriet* he had only two weeks. Julian Thurber, Kronstam's usual rehearsal pianist, who had worked with him for years, remembered that his hands were shaking badly from nerves. "Julian would always tell me, 'Henning, you are a worrier.'" When presented as a one-act ballet *Konservatoriet* has become an exposition of Bournonville's style. It was to open a second Bournonville festival that Andersen had planned for late March. Kronstam used his favorite dancers for *Konservatoriet;* Heidi Ryom, Lis Jeppesen, and Nikolaj Hübbe were in the first cast; Rose Gad, Christina Olsson, and Lloyd Riggins in the second. The production reflected Kronstam's elegance, musicality, and sense of style, but he also brought out the drama. Ingryd Thorson, who also played for those rehearsals, remembered: "It was so precise. The two ballerinas, Victorine and Eliza, he actually differentiated their characters. He was very precise about how they should be. Niels Bjørn [Larsen, in the revival of the full ballet a few seasons later] didn't do that."

Kronstam then began work on *La Sylphide* with a new James, Lloyd Riggins. Riggins remembers the rehearsals being very intense. "He danced all the parts for me. He was Effie, Madge, Gurn, the Sylphide, the mother, everybody," he said.

The festival would revolve around the 150th anniversary of *Napoli*. Andersen asked Kronstam to work on a new production of that ballet. Kronstam, with Andersen, would stage the first and third acts; Dinna Bjørn would rechoreograph the second act. Kronstam remembered several mime sequences that had disappeared from *Napoli* in recent years. "Frank came over on Sundays and we played the record and he would say, "Come on, Henning, what else can you remember?" and we'd act out the mime scenes," Kronstam said. "I knew he only wanted to get everything out of me that he could so that he could get rid of me, because he thought he could stage it himself from the video, but I didn't care. We had a good time."

By this time, Kronstam had begun to see the writing on the wall. There had been trouble the previous season during the rehearsals for Andersen and Vessel Schlüter's production of *A Folk Tale*. Several of the production's principals (Lloyd Riggins, Peter Bo Bendixen, and Silja Schandorff) had gone to Kronstam for coaching, as they were not getting what they needed in rehearsals. This put Kronstam in an uncomfortable situation. "I told them what I knew, and then I went to Frank and Mie and told them what I had done," he said, "and then I said I think it's best I go away for a week." This had taken place a week before the premiere, and Kronstam was afraid if he stayed there would be more requests for coaching. In fact, dancers did go to others—Anna Lærkesen, Sorella Englund—for help on this and other ballets now that Andersen, la Cour, and Vessel Schlüter had begun to work in the studio. Perhaps because he had been so sharply criticized for not doing enough of the artistic work of the company, perhaps because he had long harbored dreams of staging ballets, Andersen seemed very serious about becoming a ballet master in the traditional sense of the term. He wanted to be recognized as an artist, but he did not measure up to what the dancers knew from Kronstam and his predecessors.

Dancers differed on what happened in the rehearsals of *Napoli*. Some didn't remember Andersen taking part in the rehearsals at all but could only remember Kronstam. Others thought, as Lloyd Riggins put it, "It was a very good rehearsal period. Everybody really got into it and it brought a new life into that ballet." Of Kronstam and Andersen's working relationship, Riggins said, "They seemed to work well together. I remember Henning taught me the mad scene and Frank watched," which may be the common link among these varying perceptions. "They worked together quite well," said Lis Jeppesen, "because Frank wasn't saying anything, because he didn't have anything to say. Frank was very energetic, and that is all I can say about Frank, but he couldn't see artistically." Others had sensed tension and said that, although Andersen and Kronstam never argued in front of them, one would set something and the other would change it later (this was usually a matter of dynamics and musicality rather than steps). Stephen Pier gave the outsider's view: "If Frank did enter into something, no one would ever really listen to it as long as Henning was in the room. Which gives some insight into what happened later and why Frank had to get rid of him, because he didn't stand a chance. He was looked at like a joke."

The story of the young, overconfident director getting rid of an older artist who stands between him and the sun is as old as ballet, but it is hard to find an example where the difference between the two was as stark as between Andersen and Kronstam. Because Kronstam was so highly regarded, it would have been impossible to move against him directly, but political circumstances, in the broader sense, would change this. Early in 1992, a new board of directors (the first in the Theatre's history), headed by Niels-Jørgen Kaiser, director of Tivoli Gardens, was established. Kaiser immediately fired Boël Jürgensen and appointed as theater chief Michael Christiansen, who had formerly held the highest civil service, rather than political, position in the Ministry of Defense, a man with no background in theater administration, whose charge, like Jürgensen's, was to reorganize union contracts and sort out the Theatre's finances, which he did swiftly and surely. Christiansen was unversed in the ways of the theater, but he was not expected to interfere in artistic affairs. Kaiser, whose familiarity with ballet was as a presenter rather than an administrator, wanted each of the Theatre's three branches to be headed by someone whom he considered a great international star—in the case of ballet, Peter Martins or Peter Schaufuss—and most thought Andersen's days were numbered from the moment Kaiser took over. However, at the time, Andersen, ever the optimist, seemed certain that he would be reappointed and continued to establish himself as an instruktør, supported by Lise la Cour (who soon became a good friend of the new theater chief), Anne Marie Vessel Schlüter, and Eva Kloborg (Andersen's wife). He also seemed to be trying to assume Brenaa's mantle as the principal Bournonville stager and would often say in the next few years, "Bournonville is safe as long as I am here," which made many outside the Theatre think of him as Bournonville's only guardian.

The 1992 Bournonville Festival was a success; critics had come to celebrate Bournonville, and troublesome productions of several of the ballets were overlooked in most reviews, although they prompted informal conversation and questions during the festival. It would not have been possible to duplicate the first Bournonville Festival, with its element of surprise and discovery, but Andersen turned the 1992 festival into a personal triumph. To Kronstam, the festival exemplified what he considered the problems in Andersen's director-ship: the inferior level of several ballets, casting that had been arranged to give leading roles to as many people as possible rather than show each ballet at its best, and the calculated way the festival had been pitched to the international press. The dancers seemed to have caught Andersen's sense of urgency about the importance of the festival for their careers. Kronstam was so disturbed after one performance, which he said "was a humiliation for me because the dancers forgot everything they had been taught and were dancing for New York," that he decided not to attend the closing-night gala, where he was supposed to stand on the stage, along with the rest of the instruktørs and teachers. He had invited Lene Schrøder-Hansen to the gala but called her to say he wouldn't go. She had been looking forward to the performance, and they had a spat. Kronstam ended the conversation by saying, "I'm sorry, but I cannot stand on the stage and let people think I support what that man is doing to the company."

The photograph taken of Kronstam for the 1992 souvenir book but not used. Photo: Mydtskov. Private collection.

In the spring of 1992, immediately after the festival, in which his productions (*La Sylphide, Napoli,* and *Konservatoriet*) were the ones that had measured up to, or surpassed, past productions, Kronstam was removed from teaching and Andersen informed him that he would no longer direct *Onegin*. Nor would he direct *Apollo* in the 1992–93 season, but instead would serve as assistant to Patricia Neary. Along with *La Sylphide, Apollo* and *Onegin* were the ballets that meant the most to Kronstam, and their loss was a blow. He had been responsible for *Apollo* since 1965 with the knowledge and approval of Balanchine. Kronstam had kept the production in the same version that Balanchine had staged down to the last eyelash, as the dancers would often say, making only a few changes that dancers who'd left the company to join the New York City Ballet suggested when they came home as guest artists. As for *Onegin,* Kronstam said he was told merely, "We think this is too much for you to do, and so Lise [la Cour] will do it." *Onegin* had been scheduled to follow *Romeo and Juliet,* another ballet for which Kronstam was responsible. When he told Andersen he thought he could do both ballets if he knew in advance and could plan for it, he was told, "No, Lise wants to do it."

At the end of the 1992 season Andersen was finally able to get rid of the company's senior dancers. The pension age was lowered from forty-six to forty, and about eighteen dancers over that age were fired. A very few senior dancers were retained, now dubbed "character principals," but several of the company's finest mimes left the Theatre. Acting, the very essence of Danish ballet, was now structurally separated from dancing. The fired dancers would be replaced by foreigners, as the school could not possibly produce eighteen new dancers in one year,[1] and this action left the Bournonville ballets denuded; there were not enough mature dancers to fill out the character parts, which would now be danced by young people with cotton-stuffed cheeks, just like everywhere else. Many of the dancers fired in the purge of '92 were those who had been close to Kronstam, and their removal affected him deeply. Most of the dancers who had any personal connection with Kronstam, or who knew him from his years as a dancer and director, were gone. He was now very isolated, and among the artistic staff, at least, Kronstam was now the only swan in the duck pond.

Harmony, love, and humanity you have to find inside yourself. People are not as warm and understanding toward each other as they should be. It may be due to our society, a society I personally do not think has given me special possibilities, but I have succeeded very well nevertheless. Some people are fantastically loyal to me and I am very happy about that. It is a quality that my own generation, especially, displays and I hope it is a quality that young people will also learn to possess—after all we are all more or less dependent on each other in our work and in our private life—aren't we?
—Henning Kronstam, 1977

Twenty-seven

Night Shadows

In addition to coping with the political intrigues, which shook his always fragile nerves, Kronstam also had to act as a nurse to Gerstenberg, who was now home. "The doctor told me if I left him in the nursing home he would die," Kronstam said simply, "so I brought him home." Gerstenberg needed more care and attention than Kronstam could give him and, at the advice of his doctor, they hired a new housekeeper, a woman who had been a hospital night nurse. She came in two mornings a week and tended to Gerstenberg in addition to cooking and cleaning duties. Kronstam tried desperately to arrange home care. "I was on the phone every day, screaming for help," he said, and finally was able to have home health nurses come in twice daily. Gerstenberg was mending slowly and, in addition to the diabetes, suffered from dementia. He slept irregularly, demanded nearly constant attention, and was occasionally violent. The combination of stress and sleeplessness made Kronstam's illness worse. By the autumn of 1992 the strain began to take its toll, and he suffered several bouts of depression. Partly this was undoubtedly due to Gerstenberg's condition, but it was also partly due to events at the Theatre as well.

It was well known that Kronstam, especially when under stress, found it difficult to deal with sudden change. The 1992–93 season was full of last-minute changes in scheduling, casting, and other things that affected his productions. Once when Kronstam came in prepared to begin rehearsing *Konservatoriet* he found a notice on the bulletin board that the rehearsals had been postponed until later in the season. He had not been notified. Preparing for rehearsals for Kronstam was no casual matter, and weeks of mental preparation were wiped away. This precipitated a minor crash.

At the beginning of the season the dancers entered a new vote of no confidence against Frank Andersen on artistic grounds, among them dissatisfaction with his repertory and with the level of coaching. Kronstam was still nominally Andersen's artistic advisor, but he had virtually no power. He was replaced as instruktør on ballet after ballet, and this caused problems with the dancers. In the *Apollo* rehearsals, the men made it clear they did not want to work with Pat Neary, whom Andersen had brought in to rehearse a number of Balanchine ballets, and insisted they work with Kronstam. A compromise was worked out in which Kronstam worked with the Apollos and Neary worked with the women. Kronstam did not fight or complain about the people brought in to replace him; "I liked Pat," he said, adding that they worked well together. Kronstam did not have to be in charge to satisfy his ego. He was happy to work in concert with people if they were working for a common goal. Heidi Ryom thought that he had been a bit upset at first in the *Apollo* rehearsals, but then pushed that aside and worked, as he always did, to get the best production possible onto the stage.

A more difficult situation occurred during rehearsals for a revival of *La Sonnambula,* staged by John Taras. The dancers questioned Taras's memory and considered him an uninspiring coach. Those who had seen former productions say that the steps and phrasing he set were not accurate, and many were puzzled, even dismayed, that Kronstam didn't take over the rehearsals. Kronstam didn't interfere because he had been instructed by Andersen not to change anything set by anyone from the Balanchine Trust.

Silja Schandorff, one of the Sleepwalkers in this production, gave this account: "*Sonnambula* was very difficult. Maybe we were spoiled, because we were used to something very different here. With Henning you had a man who really knew what it was about and who wanted to give everything, and he couldn't. He was not allowed to." Her description comports with that of the other dancers in *Sonnambula*. Lis Jeppesen, who danced the Sleepwalker at a gala to honor the tenth anniversary of Balanchine's death, said: "Then for the first time I had Henning alone, and that was very nice. I had gotten it all wrong because I had had John Taras before, and it was not in the music." Taras, perhaps sensing something was wrong, eventually turned the production over to Kronstam. "John said he had to go to Paris for a few days to find his notebooks," Kronstam said, "and told me to take over, but by that time it was too late. There was only a week and I couldn't save it." Ib Andersen, who danced the Poet in New York and has staged the ballet himself, saw *La Sonnambula* on a visit to Copenhagen and understood the problems: "When I did *Sonnambula*, Henning was my inspiration—totally, totally, totally. So for me to see that production, and remembering what I had seen over so many years there—it was appalling. And knowing that the best Poet and the man who actually made the ballet was right there, yet was not able to do something, and so you see not even a ghost of a ballet, but basically an awful ballet."

In the fall of 1992, when it came time to discuss his contract for the 1993–94 season, Kronstam was informed he would only direct *Romeo and Juliet, La Sylphide,* and *Etudes*. Every production that had once been his responsibility had been crammed into a two-month period in the autumn, so that he could not possibly have rehearsed them. He was not even to direct *Napoli;* Frank Andersen and Kloborg would take over that ballet. Kronstam signed that contract, dated December 8, for the 1993–94 season. He said nothing to the dancers about what was happening.

At home the situation was becoming equally unbearable. On New Year's Day, Gerstenberg took an overdose of pills. "He would call," said Lene Schrøder-Hansen, "and say, 'Oh, I've done something stupid.'" This was not an unusual occurrence and Gerstenberg never took enough to do harm, although the threat of suicide could always be counted on to terrify Kronstam. In mid-January, Kronstam had a crash and was hospitalized for a few days; on January 27, Gerstenberg made another suicide threat, calling Schrøder-Hansen to say that he couldn't cope with Kronstam any longer. Not knowing of Kronstam's condition, she dismissed this as just more of Gerstenberg's complaining. What was behind the suicide attempts is not known. On February 7, 1993, Orrin Kayan died. Three other old friends were seriously ill—Fredbjørn Bjørnsson, Kirsten Ralov, and Elly Schrøder-Hansen. He was surrounded by illness and death, and he knew his days at the Theatre were numbered.

In February and March 1993, Kronstam directed John Neumeier's *Romeo and Juliet,* a ballet that had been his responsibility for twenty-five years. There were difficulties from the beginning because there was a major last-minute cast change after Kronstam had already prepared the ballet in his mind, and because he felt that some of the dancers in one of the casts he was assigned were unsuited to their roles.

About a month before he died, Kronstam said several times, "It was *Romeo and Juliet* that killed me." He had to prepare "three and a half casts," as he put it: three Juliets and four Romeos, several of them new to the roles, as well as new Capulets and Montagues of various ranks and conditions. Gerstenberg was now very ill, very frightened, and very difficult. Kronstam seldom slept through the night. He had trouble sleeping during rehearsal periods in the best of times because his mind would race with ideas. "You come home and

At home, September 1992. The captain's table behind Kronstam was a gift of Frederick Ashton. Private collection.

In the studio, spring 1993. Private collection.

think about what happened during that day and how you didn't reach a dancer, and you try to think of what other thing you could do or say that would be better," he said. Now he was under a stress load that would have been too much for a well man. Yet there were also pleasures. Lloyd Riggins was one of the Romeos, and Kronstam enjoyed working with Colleen Neary, cast as Lady Capulet. Neary interested him enough for him to rethink that role. He was reading a biography of Michelangelo at the time and found in it ideas about the role of women during the Renaissance.

Kronstam had had a free hand with *Romeo and Juliet* for twenty-five years. Even when there were new casts, he had prepared them. He served the ballet as director rather than repetiteur. This season, however, Neumeier sent Ilse Weidmann, a ballet mistress with the Hamburg Ballet, to supervise the staging and incorporate changes that Neumeier had made in the production over the years that he now wanted brought to Denmark. Kronstam disliked some of them, particularly changes in tempo. Several dancers say that Neumeier had actually preferred the Danish version and would come back to Hamburg after seeing the ballet in Copenhagen and instruct his dancers to "do it the way they do it in Denmark," yet this season he wanted the changes he had made in Hamburg transferred to the Danish production. Neumeier said that he had been very happy with the way Kronstam had maintained the ballet, but that he wanted to update it. "When we did it there was a great deal of Renaissance detail—three women embroidering on the balcony at a certain point," Neumeier said. "Every time I went back, those women were embroidering on the same music, with the same concentration, the same involvement, from the day we set it, and this is extraordinary. The way the ballet was preserved was quite incredible. But time had not stopped for me as a choreographer, or for the ballet. And living, for me, means I'm going to see the performance tonight and if I don't like something, I'm going to try another way." To Kronstam, who believed that ballets were enlivened through performance and that text was sacred, and who saw ballets as wholes rather than parts, this disturbed not only his eye and ear but the very way he looked at and thought about the ballet.

Kronstam was ill during at least some of the *Romeo and Juliet* rehearsals. The exhaustion and a drop in energy noticed by several dancers during this period was likely the result of lack of sleep and the strain of tending to Gerstenberg. During the early spring of 1993, Kronstam was found asleep on the stairs several times, and he occasionally napped in his dressing room between rehearsals. Many of the *Romeo and Juliet* rehearsals were scheduled in the very late afternoon, at four o'clock. Kronstam complained to several people about the way rehearsals had been scheduled. As he rose at 7:30 every morning, in an attempt to "keep the rhythm of the day," as he put it, by four in the afternoon he would have been desperate for sleep. Yuri Possokhov, who danced Mercutio in this production, said of the *Romeo and Juliet* rehearsals: "I thought he devoted himself to work with *Romeo and Juliet*. I saw it in his eyes. It was a part of him. He came, he dedicated himself from the first rehearsal to the end. Maybe it exhausted him because this kind of person, he is so dedicated he works to the end. He didn't leave anything inside himself, always out, out, out."

Suddenly, rumors that Kronstam was drinking heavily, even coming to the Theatre drunk, began to surface. The rumors have grown over the years, but at the time, the first indication that there was a problem was during the rehearsals of *Romeo and Juliet*. Dancers differ as to what the problems were, some saying he seemed drunk, others that he was "low in energy," still others that he just seemed very tired. According to Lene Schrøder-Hansen's diary for this period, Kronstam seemed stressed, but otherwise normal. She spoke with him frequently on the phone and met him in the street, noting only that "he looked stressed from the Theatre, but otherwise all right." After the premiere Kronstam called to invite her to a performance of *Romeo and Juliet*, and they attended a matinee.

There was one incident, however, witnessed by several people, that seemed to confirm the rumors. Neumeier came to take the final rehearsals and one day, in a small rehearsal room with a half dozen people present, there was a blowup. Neumeier made a correction and Kronstam protested, saying, "It has never been that way. Show him the way we do it, Heidi." Kronstam was obviously so upset that, in the interests of getting the ballet on the stage, Neumeier did not argue. "It was clear that you couldn't reason with him," he said. When asked to describe Kronstam's behavior rather than characterize it, Neumeier said his impression was that Kronstam had been very disturbed, agitated. Neumeier, who was a friend of Andersen's and spoke to him frequently during that period, had heard that Kronstam had been drinking heavily and suggested that Ilse Weidmann could verify Kronstam's condition. However, asked if she had been aware of any problems during the *Romeo and Juliet* rehearsals, Weidmann's first response was "that there were problems with Frank, that I knew," but she said she had seen no signs of inebriation. "I heard that too, but when I was there, and he was sitting by my side, I wouldn't say he was drunk. I only saw that he was more sick in some way. But that doesn't mean that he was not good doing steps or knowing how Juliet should be." Weidmann had heard the stories that Kronstam had been drunk at these rehearsals but said, "That must have happened after I left," and added, "I don't like to hear too much what people say, especially when everyone says something different."

As has previously been mentioned, Kronstam suffered a collapse once or twice a season, after staging a big production. "Whenever he had a big production, you knew from day one that he would see it through, he would be there to the end," said Silja Schandorff. "Then sometimes he would go away for a week, or maybe two, and then come back all rested and tanned," she added, a description similar to that of several other dancers and hardly consistent with a man returning from an alcoholic binge.

The boys of *Romeo and Juliet:* left to right, Johan Kobborg, Lloyd Riggins, and Alexander Kølpin. Photo: Martin Mydtskov Rønne. Private collection.

Shortly after the premiere of *Romeo and Juliet,* after the second cast had made their debuts, Kronstam had one of his "tours" and collapsed. He called in sick but was told that he must come in to begin rehearsals of *Konservatoriet.* Kronstam said he was too ill to work and asked that Eva Kloborg, assigned to assist him on this production, start the rehearsals. He was told that was not possible and that he must come in and work if he wanted to keep his job. Kronstam spoke of this several times shortly before his death, always in the form of questions: "Why would they do this? Why did they make me come in? Why wouldn't they give me the leave of absence?"[1] Despite his condition, Kronstam came to the Theatre to work on *Konservatoriet,* the ballet that had been rescheduled from earlier in the season.

By all accounts, Kronstam's appearance that day shocked the dancers, especially those who had never seen anyone in a severe clinical depression; everyone seems to have assumed he was drunk. Kronstam tried to explain what was wrong, but the clues he gave weren't understood. For example, he passed Margaret Mercier in the hall and said, "I get this from my mother, you know." During the rehearsal, Kronstam told Niels Balle, who was dancing the role of the ballet master, "You must listen to what I am saying. I won't be here much

longer. There must be someone here who knows what to do when I am gone."
This must have seemed, at the time, like nonsense, an expression of Kronstam's insecurity.

Eventually he was sent home. The dancers asked what was wrong and were
told that Kronstam was drunk, that this was a continuing problem, that everything possible had been done to help him throughout the season, but he had
refused help. There is no evidence to support this and much to dispute it. His
friends and family did not notice that anything was wrong until several months
later, in July 1993, after he had left the Theatre. It had never occurred to either
his friends or family that Kronstam was an alcoholic. Margrethe Noyé had
heard some of the rumors but put them down to Theatre gossip. Lene
Schrøder-Hansen, who "didn't move in Theatre circles," as she put it, had heard
no rumors and the only abnormal behavior she had observed in Kronstam were
the curious times when he would withdraw, two or three times a year.

The season would end in early May, the dancers were off to Japan, taking
Kronstam's productions of *Konservatoriet* and *La Sylphide*. When Kronstam
came in to take a *La Sylphide* rehearsal the last week in April, he couldn't find
the room—the rehearsal schedule had been moved to a different bulletin board.
The usual rehearsal rooms were empty; the *Sylphide* rehearsal had been scheduled in a small room (Studio K) at the very top of the house, above Store Ny.[2]

He climbed the stairs slowly; there was obviously something wrong. He
walked and talked as if he were running on slow speed. Andersen, coming
down the stairs at the same time, seemed surprised to see him and asked, in
English, in very solicitous tones, "Henning, are you all right?" Kronstam
growled like a wounded bear and pulled away. Once at the top, he stopped off in
Store Ny to watch the end of Mercier's aspirant class and a few minutes of a
private *Onegin* rehearsal that the dancers had scheduled for themselves. The
ambivalence he was feeling—part resignation to what was going on, part total
involvement with the Theatre and thinking of the future—was evident in his
actions and comments. "Do you see that little one in the corner?" he said, nod-
ding at Saskia Beskow [now in the corps of the New York City Ballet]. "She will
be the Sylph in three years' time." He literally shivered: "Oh, it has been so long
since we have had one so delicate."

But, "I have no energy any more, and I cry all the time now," he volunteered
a moment later—totally out of character, to say something so revealing to a
writer he barely knew. He then turned his attention to Alexander Kølpin and

Kronstam and Heidi Ryom hug after a performance of *La Sylphide*. Photo: Marianne
Grøndahl. Private collection.

Helen Saunders, who were rehearsing a pas de deux from *Onegin*. "Alexander,
do you mind if I make a suggestion?" he asked. When his help was requested,
he gave a few comments on how to do the lift. "Use your own weight more, not
hers," he said. "That lift must look absolutely unique." This was Saunders's
debut and her first big role, and she was nervous. When she was about to leave,
Kronstam stood and took her hands: "Helen, you are beautiful. It is a wonderful role and you are beautiful in it. Go down on that stage and have fun."
Saunders looked at him for a moment as though trying to decide if he really
meant it; there was no doubting his sincerity and she visibly brightened, relaxed, and left the room as though she had received a blessing.

The *La Sylphide* rehearsal was friendly and relaxed. Kronstam joked with the
dancers, and there was a running commentary throughout the hour on past
Sylphs: You needed calves like Schanne's to do those jumps, Ulla Poulsen had
done this step that way; dancers had been kept alive for generations through
just such afternoons. Kronstam commented on Riggins's solo: "It doesn't look
like anything," he said. "Show the back leg more and it will look brilliant."

When it came to the final scene, he took the witch's part and spat out the curses with a pain and anger that was uncomfortably real.

Throughout that week there were other inexplicable administrative snafus affecting Kronstam's rehearsals. Two days in a row, for example, he had no rehearsal pianist. Through all this, rather than cracking at these small disturbances, as might be expected, Kronstam seemed almost preternaturally calm.

He was also unusually talkative, and one afternoon in the canteen after rehearsals he spoke about his plans and hinted at problems. "Do you know that next season will be my last at the Theatre?" he asked. "I am one of the old ones now, and they don't need me any more because they have the videos. I will come next year and stage *Etudes,* out of respect for Mr. Lander, and then I am gone." He spoke briefly of "an old friend" who had been ill but was getting better now and they were going to travel, perhaps to India, which he had never seen. He also spoke about the recent changes at the Theatre and seemed the most disturbed about the mass retirement of many of the older dancers the previous year. "I love those people. I've known them since they were little children, and I loved them. It's all the interesting ones he got rid of," he said, "and many of them were still good dancers." He listed the names, as though now talking to himself. He seemed like a man in the middle of a breakdown. He wore the same clothes every day, clipped his keys to his belt as though he couldn't trust himself to keep track of them, and often repeated sentences over and over, especially, "He fell down [referring to Gerstenberg's illness in Spain, now sixteen months in the past]. He didn't die; he fell down."

The only open indication of rebellion occurred in a rehearsal for *La Sonnambula,* which Kronstam was preparing for a Balanchine gala that would take place on April 30. The dancers were rehearsing the pas de deux of the Poet and the Sleepwalker, the part where the Poet bends over the Sleepwalker and they almost kiss. Possokhov, who was dancing the Poet to Schandorff's Sleepwalker, was troubled by the phrasing. He asked Kronstam if what he had been told to do was really correct, because it didn't feel right. Interested, Kronstam responded, "What do you think it should be?" Possokhov showed him, indicating that the bend should be more with the music, that the Poet should lean forward, the bend deepening as the music crested, the tension in his body matching the tension in the score. Possokhov had sensed this intuitively. Ignoring his instruction to follow the Balanchine Trust stagers to the letter, Kronstam agreed. "Yes, it was always like that. It was changed this last time. You are right, Yuri. Do it that way."

Two days later, in planning when and how to begin work on what was then to be a book about his roles, Kronstam said, "I can talk to you any day but Monday. On Monday I am coming in to clean out my office because I am leaving the Theatre." He elaborated: "I have just been given a new contract for only three months and then you have your pension. Ffft, out" (see appendix 2). He made a dismissive gesture, more weary and sad than angry. That was a Friday afternoon, April 30, a few hours before a gala commemorating the tenth anniversary of Balanchine's death. Kronstam had agreed appear on stage with the other instruktørs during a final curtain call to please Gerstenberg. "This is my last night in the Theatre, and he wants to see me on stage once more," he explained.

At his home that afternoon, he seemed quite normal. Gerstenberg, who had been out for a walk, spoke eagerly of getting his strength back and began to talk about how unfairly Andersen was treating Kronstam, but Kronstam quickly silenced him. They talked about going to Spain for the summer as well as some past visits, including the one when Gerstenberg had nearly died. Kronstam got out some old photographs, had some questions about the book, and then said he needed to sleep for a few hours before going to the Theatre. On the way to his flat, Kronstam had said, "You will forgive me, but I am a little bit depressed about the situation at the Theatre." At the door he again referred to the problems there, saying quite evenly, "They are doing this now because they know I am weak because Franz is ill, and I don't have the strength to fight them."

That evening, Kronstam and Gerstenberg watched from the wings as guests Darci Kistler and Nilas Martins danced *Duo Concertant* and the company performed several Balanchine ballets.[5] When it came time for the final curtain call, Kronstam said he was feeling unsteady, was afraid of falling, and didn't want to go out on stage. According to dancers who had been backstage, Anne Marie Vessel Schlüter took his arm, saying she wouldn't let him fall, and led him on stage.[4]

During the curtain calls, Andersen came out with several roses, one for each instruktør. He gave Kronstam a rose and then hugged him, with a huge smile. Kronstam pulled away, paused for a moment, and walked, very deliberately, to the middle of the stage, where he gave his rose to Heidi Ryom, who, with the rest of the company, had been lined up behind the two guests, something that Kronstam thought an insult to the Danish dancers. He hugged Ryom for a very long minute, then walked back—again with his "old man on ice walk"—to stand next to Vessel Schlüter.

The fact that "a drunk couldn't walk that straight" apparently occurred to no one, and within minutes rumors were flying that Kronstam had been drunk on stage and, since he had been in the Queen's presence, he would be fired. However, backstage, Queen Margrethe spoke to Kronstam, even asking to be introduced to Gerstenberg. "That meant so much to him," Kronstam said later. "It was so kind of her. All those years, I could never bring him to parties." The Queen's unusual action might also be read as an indication that she had not been offended by Kronstam's behavior. (One of the more outrageous rumors that later made the rounds was that Kronstam was fired because he had tried to attack the Queen at the party.) In any event, he was not fired that night. He did not stay long at the party and was walking quite normally when he left the Theatre.

Kronstam and Andersen had exchanged angry words backstage after the performance and Andersen was still smarting from it the next afternoon. Asked what was wrong with Kronstam, Andersen replied that he was drunk and had been for five weeks, that his behavior could not be tolerated, and that he was frightening the little girls in the hall. ("Oh, please put that in your book," Kronstam said when he was told this, two years later. "It will do wonders for my reputation!") Andersen described some of the problems he had had with Kronstam that season, saying that Kronstam would call every night and either "Eva or Lise or I will have to go over to his house and sit and listen to him and hold his hand while he cries and drinks," a statement that is not credible. Andersen also said that Kronstam would get a letter from the theater chief saying he could not come to the Theatre when he was drunk, adding, "He is my best friend, my idol. This is the hardest thing I've ever had to do." That there were other reasons was evident, however, by another comment: "Besides, he still thinks he's in charge here, and he's not."[5] Whether Andersen really believed Kronstam was drunk is an open question. In two subsequent conversations he backed off the idea very quickly when challenged. In one of these, asked directly whether he thought it was alcohol or tranquilizers (that Kronstam was bipolar had not yet been established), Andersen responded, "What difference does it make?"[6]

Kronstam conducted what was to be his last rehearsal as a ballet master at the Royal Theatre the next Monday, the day he had said he intended to clear out his room. It was of *La Sylphide*. The atmosphere was oppressive. Kronstam's depression was as thick as smoke; the sadness poured from him, yet his corrections were clear eyed and keen. The last was to Riggins. It was the second act, the part where James runs on, having momentarily lost the Sylphide.

"Lloyd, why are you so unhappy? This is a beautiful day. The sun is shining and you are having a wonderful time with the sylph. You know she is there, you just can't find her. So you run on and say, 'Oh, where oh where is my beautiful Sylphide?' There's no reason to look so miserable about it."

After the rehearsal (the last of the day), Kronstam went to the canteen and fell asleep after drinking two glasses of wine. One of the dancers tried to wake him and when he couldn't, became alarmed and called Andersen. The exact timing of the events that followed is not clear, but eventually Andersen, or la Cour, or both, took Kronstam to an alcohol treatment clinic recommended by a former dancer who had been a patient there. Kronstam was kept sitting in the stage door area while Christiansen and Kaiser were called from home to come to the Theatre to see him. Neither Kronstam's family nor his doctor were consulted. His sister, whom Kronstam had listed as his next of kin, learned of his hospitalization only after she received a letter from the clinic. When he got home Kronstam said that he had been taken to the clinic against his will. The only report of his condition at the clinic seems consistent with depression. At the time Anne Marie Vessel Schlüter said she'd been told that "he lies on his bed all day and cries because of all the emotion." She said the doctors had asked if Andersen would come up, because Kronstam was very worried about the situation at the Theatre, and that Andersen would go up and reassure him.[7] It is quite possible that Vessel Schlüter did not know then that Kronstam had already been fired, but Christiansen had written him a letter of dismissal the day after he had been taken to the clinic and sent it to him at the clinic.

The day after Kronstam was fired, the newspapers reported that Andersen's contract would not be renewed.

The dancers left for Japan, thinking that Kronstam had been sent to the clinic by a caring Theatre administration and would be back in the fall. Kenneth Greve had asked Andersen if he should call or go up to see him and was told it would be better to wait until after the tour. Kronstam left the clinic after four days. He received a bill for the entire month (the clinic's standard practice) and sent it to the Theatre with a letter saying he had not wanted to go there and would not be responsible for the charges. The bill was returned by Christiansen with a letter saying that the Theatre would not pay it. "So I sent it to Frank," Kronstam said.

Gerstenberg contacted a lawyer, Paul Rolf Meurs-Gerken, and asked him to intervene. Meurs-Gerken was the husband of Ulla Skow and so was aware of

Kronstam's importance to the Theatre. He first called Andersen, who "tried to say we have all admired Henning and we have all been looking up to him, but he has been creating many problems." Meurs-Gerken continued: "My feeling at that time was that, in fact, the problem that Frank had against Henning was that Henning was an artist, which Frank was not." Andersen told Meurs-Gerken that Kronstam "took up all the space." "He felt that people are concentrating on Henning instead of concentrating on the others. It takes too much attention from other people when he is there."

Meurs-Gerken then contacted Michael Christiansen. "He had been shocked by seeing Henning behave in a way that he felt absolutely shocking and unacceptable, and he said he would never come back to the Theatre. We can't have such a person." Meurs-Gerken, realizing that Christiansen didn't understand theatrical people, attempted to reason with him. "I tried to say that the Theatre, where people have given their heart, their life, is not like in an ordinary job," adding that Kronstam was a unique and invaluable artist. "And he said, 'Yes, that may be right, but I cannot have such a person here.' I don't know how much he had known about Henning's situation, because this depends, of course, on what he had been told by his ballet master."

When Kronstam came home from the clinic, Meurs-Gerken went to him and told him, "I'm sorry, Henning, but nothing can be done." Yet in his closing-night speech on the tour, according to Kirsten Simone, Andersen said that he would now go home "and take care of our dear friend, Henning." This was in May 1993. Except for a chance meeting in the street in the fall of that year, Andersen had no further contact with Kronstam until June 1994.

Kronstam and Gerstenberg left for Spain, spending a few weeks there and a few more in the summerhouse. They returned to Copenhagen in mid-July. Kronstam had been told he must be out of the Theatre by July 31, when his contract expired, and came in to clear out his dressing room. He found that the room had already been emptied out; Anne Marie Vessel Schlüter had moved in. Kronstam's belongings had been stuffed into paper bags and put out in the hall. Kronstam had written down many of Volkova's and Stanley Williams's classes; these notebooks, as well as several containing his own classes, were missing and were never recovered.

"I went to Lise [la Cour, who was responsible for dressing room assignments] and asked her why she had done this. She said that Mie hadn't wanted to wait. I took a few things out of the bags, threw my keys on the desk, and came home. I threw away all my dancing things. It was then that I gave up," he said.

This time, Kronstam was unable to fight off the depression, or perhaps he no longer had the will to struggle. He had a major crash and completely collapsed. Schrøder-Hansen, alarmed, asked Gerstenberg what was wrong and was told, "He doesn't have a job at the Theatre next year," but she dismissed this as implausible. "At that time, Franz Gerstenberg would be totally normal one moment," she said, "and then say something that made no sense the next moment. He had dementia. I thought what he was saying was nonsense."

Kronstam never told the dancers what had happened. He probably would not have wanted to upset them a few days before they left for a tour. It is likely, too, that he remembered the Lander affair and its devastating effects on the company and kept silent so as not to force the dancers to take sides. Gerstenberg wanted to call the tabloids but Kronstam, fearing a scandal, stopped him and did not contact any of the Danish journalists or critics, most of whom seemed sympathetic to Andersen, believing his version of events. No one investigated, or contacted Kronstam to ask what had happened.

In the fall of 1993 the dancers were told that if Kronstam agreed to go through an alcohol treatment program, for which the Theatre would pay, he would be welcomed back to the company. The dancers did not question this. "I think maybe we let him down," said Benedikte Paaske, then head of the dancers' union, "but we didn't know. I remember being angry with him, thinking, why does he love that bottle more than he loves us?" a sentiment many dancers probably shared at the beginning of the 1993–94 season when Kronstam didn't return. Others believed that Kronstam was going through a traumatic time in his personal life and thought the best thing to do was to leave him alone to solve his problems; they felt sure that he would eventually return, and they thought the decision to return was his. Kenneth Greve is apparently the only dancer who contacted Kronstam at this time. He did not ask about the past but rather expressed concern and asked if there was anything he could do to help, offering Kronstam the services of his agent. Greve ended the conversation by saying that he had always wanted to be coached by Kronstam, and if Kronstam ever wanted to do that, to please get in touch with him. Greve kept an eye on Kronstam indirectly, through their mutual friend Jytte Abildgaard.

In August, at the beginning of the 1993–94 season, the dancers sent Kronstam a bouquet of balloons. Many of them wrote cards and letters saying how much he meant to them and hoping that he would get well soon. "You can't leave," wrote Victor Alvarez, a young Prix de Lausanne winner from Spain. "You haven't finished teaching me everything yet." These messages must have been bittersweet, as Kronstam knew that his return to the Theatre was not in his control. "I know the dancers don't know about the contract. They think it is the illness," he said in January 1994, then unaware that "the illness" was assumed to be alcoholism. A few weeks before he died, he stated quite firmly that he had never come to the Theatre drunk. "I know the dancers think I was drunk at the Theatre, but I really wasn't," he said. "And I don't understand how they could think that of me, when I have been all my life so disciplined." He quickly added, "I don't want anyone to think that I was ever angry with the dancers."

Niels Balle, reflecting on what had happened two years after Kronstam's death, said, "Maybe he was *too* private," and Balle is probably right. In his effort to keep his private life out of the Theatre, Kronstam had left himself completely unprotected. Since no one at the Theatre knew, or at least understood, what Kronstam's medical condition was, it was possible to use the rumors that had swirled around him for years to deflect scrutiny from the canceled contracts, and why, if Kronstam had been considered fit enough for three months, he had not been engaged for the whole season. Any discussion of Kronstam's contract, or any other facet of these incidents, inevitably leads, usually very quickly, to the rumors and away from contracts. After Kronstam's death, one of the retired dancers was at a party where Kronstam's situation came up. "I heard that Henning was coming to the Theatre drunk every day," one man said. "Does that sound like Henning?" asked the dancer. "No, it doesn't," the man replied, and that ended the discussion. But in the spring of 1993, the dancers who would have known to ask such questions were no longer at the Theatre.

As Kronstam did not know what the dancers had been told, he wondered why they did not press for his return and, thus, what he had done to fail them. He believed he must have failed as an artist in some way because he could not comprehend firing anyone who was still useful as an artist. For the next eighteen months he would go over and over the last few years, criticizing every production, every artistic decision he had made. While he waited for the dancers to call him back to work with them, the dancers waited for him to "sober up" and walk back into the Theatre.

Right from the beginning, you could feel
the hole that he left. He was the inspiration.
We missed him. We felt it right away.
—Lloyd Riggins

Now that Henning is not here any more,
we have lost the identity that we had. Now
we are just a bad copy of what everybody
else does better.
—Rose Gad

Twenty-eight

The Terrible Year

Gerstenberg had long been urging Kronstam to retire to the house in the mountains of Spain that the two men had bought in partnership with their old friend, Margrethe Noyé, when Kronstam had been named ballet master. Kronstam would not agree to that, but the two men had discussed traveling more, if and when Kronstam ever retired. Now, it seemed, at least until Andersen's replacement took office,[1] that this would be a possibility. Gerstenberg had been gaining strength after his illness that winter but continued to have respiratory problems. Then, sometime in the late summer or early fall of 1993, Gerstenberg was diagnosed with lung cancer. He continued smoking his unfiltered Players, which he bought in hundred-packet lots and kept in a basket by his chair at the living room table by the window, but traveling was no longer possible.

Kronstam had no contact with the Theatre until October, when Arne Villumsen invited him to his twenty-fifth-anniversary jubilee and sent him a ticket. Kronstam was immensely touched by this and attended not only the performance but the party afterward. He must have been worried about his reception, but the dancers greeted him warmly and asked him when he was coming back. "I told them, 'You'll have to speak to your management,'" he said, still thinking that they knew what had happened.

Throughout that autumn, rumors about Kronstam's condition grew in Copenhagen's ballet circles like mad yeast. Those rumors could fill an appendix as long as this book, but one example will suffice. A dancer who was friendly with Kronstam and could be expected to be in contact with him was asked how he was. She replied with great drama, "He has been drunk every day since he left the Theatre." A week later, someone outside the Theatre saw Kronstam walking along the lakes, looking very sad, but quite sober. Contacted again, the person reiterated her story about Kronstam's condition, but when asked how many times she had seen him, replied none. Had she spoken to him on the phone? Yes, once or twice. This is a very typical example of what happened when rumors were checked.

During the first session of interviews for this book, in January 1994, Kronstam seemed, especially on the first day, extremely anxious. Gerstenberg said he had been so nervous that they had had to call a doctor in the middle of the night to come and give him an injection, an example of the lengths to which Kronstam would go in order to fulfill a responsibility. During the two-week interview session, Kronstam was different from day to day. For one or two days, he seemed well; the next day he would be very withdrawn. The city's modern-dance house called and asked if he would teach ballet there; at first he said yes but called the next day and withdrew. He had phoned his doctor, he said. "He said I wasn't ready. He said it would take two years," Kronstam said. Anne Marie Vessel Schlüter had kept in touch with him and arranged an invitation for him to teach at a summer program in England the coming summer, and he also turned that down, not only because of his own health but because of Gerstenberg's illness.

Ten days into the sessions, Kronstam called early in the morning and said, sounding perfectly well, "We have had a bad night here. I'm sorry, I can't work today. Please come tomorrow." The next day, he was unrecognizable. His face was flushed, nearly purple. He was bent and could not straighten. He had dif-

ficulty picking up objects and would drop things. Yet he spoke perfectly normally. "I could manage it better when I was younger somehow," he said, as
though it was obvious what was wrong with him. He was oddly, foggily cheerful. "I'll be fine in a few days," he said. "I know my tours."

The interviews continued in weekly phone conversations. Always, Gerstenberg would answer the telephone. On three occasions he said that Kronstam
couldn't talk that day, to call back the next day or, once, the next week. No reason was ever given, but once Gerstenberg said, "There is nothing I can do. The
Theatre has treated him so abominably." Gerstenberg himself was failing rapidly. He had taken (or been given) no treatment for the lung cancer but drank
several bottles of very strong *snaps* every day for the pain. Kronstam was worried about that and said he'd asked their housekeeper, the former night nurse,
if he should stop it. She said to let him drink, as it no longer mattered. Gerstenberg began going to an adult day care center every Tuesday to give Kronstam a
break. He hated it and fought going. Dancers learned that it was possible to call
Kronstam on Tuesdays and get through, and, slowly, began to call. Sometimes
they got him on a good day, more often on a bad one. He seemed often depressed during this period.

On Easter Sunday, Kronstam answered the phone himself. He sounded very
shaken. Gerstenberg had fallen down again and was in the hospital. Kronstam
was no longer able to care for him but seemed unable to face that fact. He felt
obligated to keep Gerstenberg home, saying several times that he had his
mother's death on his conscience, "and I cannot go to God with one more death
on my soul."[2]

Peter Schaufuss, who would assume the directorship in August 1994, had
visited Kronstam the previous Tuesday. They talked about repertory, and what,
if anything, Kronstam could do at the Theatre. Nothing had been resolved.
Schaufuss planned to replace Kronstam's major productions—*La Sylphide* and
Giselle—with his own; Ashton's *Romeo and Juliet* would replace the Neumeier
version. Schaufuss was not prepared for Kronstam's altered appearance; he
had gained weight in the early fall and looked defeated and disheveled. What
Schaufuss saw seems most probably a manic episode—Kronstam spoke rapidly and did not make sense; sentences did not follow each other logically. At
one point he led Schaufuss into Gerstenberg's room and spoke to the younger
man about his old friend as though Gerstenberg were lying on the empty bed.

Gerstenberg did come home, though only for a few weeks. On the first

Monday in May, exactly one year after Kronstam's last day at the Theatre, Gerstenberg's morning nurse found Kronstam lying unconscious on the kitchen floor. Gerstenberg was sitting at the table in the living room, drinking *snaps*. When Kronstam was revived, he asked to be taken to the hospital. Perhaps because he was so afraid he would be given shock treatments, Kronstam seemed unable to hospitalize himself but would faint, hoping that someone else would do it, something not uncommon with mental patients. He was admitted to the psychiatric ward of the State Hospital. Gerstenberg remained in their flat for a few days but was then hospitalized as well.

Kronstam later talked about this hospitalization in some detail. For the first week he did not have a room but was kept in a hallway with other patients—bad enough for someone with a physical illness, but for someone suffering from anxiety and depression it must have been unbearable. Kronstam was only assigned a room because one young patient crawled into bed with him. "There were screams," he said, referring to the staff's reaction, "and they found me a room." His roommate was a man who was receiving shock treatments, Kronstam's lifelong fear. He also seemed fascinated by it. "He was so sad. He would go every morning and come back and laugh and laugh and be so happy," Kronstam said, adding as though touching wood, "They haven't tried that with me."

Kronstam said he only saw a psychiatrist twice during the two weeks he was hospitalized and received no treatment other than the medication (probably tranquilizers). "They did nothing for me. Nothing," he said, one of the few times he spoke with anger. He was taken off medication for his shaking hands. He had a new doctor who told him it was better for him to shake.[3]

He was allowed to visit Gerstenberg, now in another part of the hospital, for much of the day. When he was in the psychiatric ward, he spent most of his time talking to the anorexic girls. They interested him more than his roommate, who talked about his conquests of women all day long. He learned their stories—one had been hospitalized for a year and a half—and was curious about their ingenious ways of hiding food.

On Friday, May 13, Kronstam checked himself out of the hospital and went to visit Gerstenberg. The old man was obviously failing. That Sunday, Gerstenberg told him, "Henning, I think I have to leave now," and began to apologize for past wrongs. Kronstam stopped him, saying, "Don't think about any of that now. Think about all the wonderful times we had on Capri and Majorca." They talked of happy things for awhile, then Kronstam went home to sleep. He got a call at four o'clock in the morning to come quickly, for Gerstenberg was dying. "I was there in ten minutes, but he was already gone," he said. "I had missed him. He was still warm and I could feel his spirit in the room. I went to talk to the nurses, and when I came back, he was cold. He was gone."

The funeral was that Friday. Gerstenberg's young cousins sang an English hymn that Gerstenberg had liked; Inge Jensen's husband, Lasse, a cellist with the Royal Theatre's orchestra, played the death scene from *La Sylphide*. Kronstam always took attendance at funerals; he knew who came and who didn't. His family attended, which meant a lot to him. Kirsten Simone was there, dressed in white, and Kronstam's brother-in-law, who remembered her from their confirmation so long ago, told him, "Henning, she's still the most beautiful woman in the room." Many of his neighbors came, and so did some of the men he had dallied with forty years ago, before he'd met Gerstenberg. Kronstam made a speech, standing with his hand on the white coffin, calling, he said, on all his years as a performer. Both Lene Schrøder-Hansen and Margrethe Noyé said he handled the funeral beautifully, not only the eulogy, but the reception afterward, when he had a few friends over to his flat for coffee.

Kronstam seemed fine for several weeks after the funeral and then began to be shaky. This was the first time that Schrøder-Hansen observed him drinking too much, although that too varied from day to day. "He would come here and ask for a glass of port, and he would drain the glass, a huge glass. I asked him if he thought he should really do this, and he said, 'I need it to cope.' And then the next night he wouldn't drink at all, or maybe just one glass of wine," she said. For the next month, Kronstam spent much of his time at the Schrøder-Hansens. Elly Schrøder-Hansen, Lene's mother, was in the final phase of her long illness now, and Kronstam often came over to read to her or make her tea and talk. "He'd call me and say, 'Guess where I am?' He seemed a bit proud of himself, I must say," said Lene.

As soon as the death notice ("For my best friend, Franz Gerstenberg") appeared in the papers, Kronstam started to receive phone calls from old friends, old flames, and potential new ones. For the first time in his life he didn't have Gerstenberg to screen the callers, and he made some mistakes. Some of the callers who seemed so solicitous were after his money, which Gerstenberg had invested wisely; a few were women who hoped, or even expected, to marry him and pursued him rather aggressively.

For the first time, too, Kronstam had to take care of business matters. He had never signed a check, never paid a bill. He called his brother and asked him to look over his finances and was told that Gerstenberg had managed things very well and he had nothing to worry about. Kronstam tried to maintain contact with his family, but relations between the two brothers had never been easy and did not improve. His brother had never tried to hide his dislike of Gerstenberg and showed no patience with Kronstam's need to grieve. Kronstam had always been hurt by his brother's refusal to accept Gerstenberg as an important part of his life. This was a breach that was never fully healed, although the brothers had resumed speaking to each other, at least, before Kronstam died.

Kronstam was in closer contact with his sister, Jessie, a kindly woman thirteen years his senior who had been his second mother when he was a child, and they spoke fairly often on the phone. His nephew, Torben, visited him and occasionally invited him home to family gatherings. He got along very well with Torben's wife, Janne, and their two children. He also maintained contact with Gerstenberg's cousin (really the wife of a third cousin, a very distant relative, but the only one Gerstenberg had), who had been very helpful in the last months of Gerstenberg's illness, driving him to the hospital. He was not without companionship, but there was no one with him in the huge apartment, which was resoundingly empty, especially after dark. Always in the past he had been able to push problems aside, but as he had said after his father's death, "the Theatre has always sustained me," and that sustenance was gone. He was not only cut off from everyone he loved but from the daily routine that had given his life its structure and its meaning. Because it was his habit when in depression to push anything away from him that would exacerbate the depression, he could not listen to the music he loved, nor watch ballet videos, as both reminded him of the Theatre. All that was left to him was reading. Often, however, he would not have enough concentration for reading and would sit for hours, looking out the window at the lakes and the people passing by.

Shortly after Gerstenberg's death, Kronstam received a call from Frank Andersen expressing condolences and asking if he could pay a call. When he came, he told Kronstam that what happened at the Theatre had been all Michael Christiansen's doing. Kronstam believed him at the time and said after their meeting: "I understand why he did it. He was just trying to keep his job." This visit shows the complicated nature of their relationship. Andersen also discussed his own situation, how he had not had his contract renewed, and how he had not yet found another job. Kronstam was very sympathetic, saying, "He is too young and has too much energy to be like this [meaning, as he was]." He seemed to bear Andersen no resentment. "It is just the way he is," he explained. A year later, Kronstam would say, "You can't hate someone all your life. It is wrong. Frank is one of my children and there will always be a chair for him in this house."

Kronstam was very nervous about his sixtieth birthday, which was at the end of June. By Danish custom people who have held important positions are given appreciations, rather like pre-obituaries, in the paper on major birthdays. What would these notices say? Would they mention that he had been fired? Would there be any at all? And so he approached his sixtieth birthday, which would have been a difficult one anyway, with dread.

The night before his birthday, on June 28, Elly Schrøder-Hansen died. "I called him and he came right away," said Lene. She in turn came over the morning of his birthday, as she had promised him. It was a terribly difficult period for both of them. As a measure of how totally drained of strength he was, Kronstam did not attend Fru Schrøder-Hansen's funeral. He called Lene afterward to apologize, saying he just couldn't handle it. She undoubtedly sympathized but had been caring for her mother for ten years and was not feeling very strong either, certainly not strong enough to take on yet another sick person.

There were indeed sixtieth-birthday pieces in the paper, and very kind ones. "My old friend Erik [Aschengreen] was very nice, very nice indeed," Kronstam said, adding with a laugh, "Even my dear old enemy Ebbe Mørk was very kind to me." Queen Margrethe sent a birthday telegram, which meant a great deal to him; he was not in disgrace after all.

Aside from the loneliness and the grief, Kronstam was trying to adjust to the fact that he would never return to the Theatre while, at the same time, at least half-expecting that Schaufuss would call him to work. The one person who stood up for him was Flemming Flindt, who reportedly had stormed into Christiansen's office and berated him, saying, "That was the stupidest thing you could have done," and that if Christiansen wanted to have a classical ballet company, he had to get Kronstam back. But nothing came of it. "The way they handled that was, I think, inexcusable," said Flindt. "When you have a person like Henning Kronstam, who really gave his life to the Royal Danish Ballet and to the Royal Theatre—something that both Erik Bruhn and I, we never did; we went out and did our own thing. But Henning gave his life to that Theatre, and so whatever happens, you have to get psychiatrists, or doctors, or whatever it is, and not say they can't come here, because then you kill people."

Flindt then tried another tack, calling Kronstam and asking him to take the part of the old man in a planned revival of *The Triumph of Death*. Flindt said when he telephoned and announced himself, Kronstam repeated his name, as though in a fog, "Flemming Flindt?" and thanked him very much for thinking of him but said that he wouldn't be up to it. Vivi Flindt tried to persuade him as well. "We thought this was a way to get him back to the Theatre," she said. Kronstam must have considered the offer seriously, because he said several times he was worried that his partner in the revival would be Elsa Marianne von Rosen. The part called for the old man to throw the old woman off the roof. Kronstam said, quite seriously, that he couldn't do that with von Rosen. "It would have to be somebody who meant something to me, like Kirsten [Simone] or Sorella [Englund]." But he also knew he was not yet ready to bear the stress of performing. And, as much as he wanted to work again, he doubted that he would be able. "I don't have my safety net," he said, referring to Gerstenberg. "I don't have my backup."

Several dancers visited him during this period, including Heidi Ryom, who brought her new baby, which delighted him. In August, Nikolaj Hübbe, home to dance, paid a call, which meant a great deal to Kronstam. "Losing Nikolaj [to the New York City Ballet] was like losing a son," he said, and there had been some misunderstandings resulting in a coolness between them. Hübbe's visit washed that away, and Kronstam spoke of it happily for weeks.

Schaufuss had begun staging his production of *La Sylphide*, which the Danish critics had been demanding for the past fifteen years. Kronstam began hearing stories about problems with it, and problems with working with Schaufuss and Johnny Eliasen, who had brought their own version of international standards into the Royal Theatre. The production was being set by a notator, and some of the notations may have been attempts to give the non-Danish dancers on whom the ballet had originally been staged external cues for certain scenes, but these cues were resented in Copenhagen. Lloyd Riggins gave one example, "Raise your left eyebrow on the count of five," an instruction that any Danish dancer of this time would have considered an insult. Schaufuss did work intensively with some of the dancers, but the coaching was centered completely on technique, "as in, what is your inner thigh doing," as one dancer put it. The dancers also felt that the production was inaccurate choreographically and musically—not only in the passages that Schaufuss added, but in the supposedly traditional portions of the ballet.

Hearing these stories and others, Kronstam half-hoped Schaufuss would ask him back to help sort things out. When it became evident that this would not happen, he was sure that the Danish critics who had written so nicely of his importance to the Theatre in the birthday notices would realize that the new production wasn't as good as the old one and say so. The new *La Sylphide* had its premiere and received mixed reviews. Still, there was no call from the Theatre and several weeks into the season Kronstam collapsed completely.

During the autumn of 1994, Kronstam seemed to be on a rapid, unpredictable cycle of ups and downs. He would be very depressed for two weeks, then normal (though very sad) for another two, then seem agitated and even overconfident for a spell. A few dancers called from time to time; Kirsten Simone kept in touch, and Kronstam began calling some of the older dancers who were no longer with the Theatre and meeting them occasionally. There were other visitors. Hugh Williams, now over 90, came to see him. A Danish critic and archivist, Majbrit Hjelmsbo, began working at Kronstam's flat every Tuesday to put his files of clippings in better order. In late September, Frank Andersen suddenly called, inviting Kronstam to come to dinner and, when Kronstam said he wasn't up to going out, insisted on bringing dinner to him. Afterward, there were persistent stories that this was a regular occurrence and that Andersen was "taking care of Henning," but the dinner was an isolated instance.

In October and November, there were times when Kronstam was drinking heavily. His drinking buddies were new friends, rather rough men who lived in the neighborhood. They seemed to drag his mood further down. Kronstam frequently talked of suicide—only once referring to himself, more usually to people he had known who had killed themselves, not only his mother, but several dancers and friends who had died by their own hand. Only twice during those months was he ever obviously sorry for himself. On one occasion he spoke of how he knew he would never work again, and it was obvious how painful that realization was. "I don't know why I can't at least look at them," he said. "Why can't I just go to the Theatre and look at my dancers?" Shortly before Christmas he said he knew why none of the dancers called him. "It's because I used to be beautiful," he said, "and now I'm not, and no one can stand to look at me."

Usually, however, Kronstam tried to make the most of things. When he wasn't in depression he was terribly bored and rearranged the furniture, turning Gerstenberg's bedroom into an office and giving away Gerstenberg's clothes and papers. He sold the summerhouse because he said he would never be able to spend another day there. There were too many memories.

He had gone to a psychologist, at Lene Schrøder-Hansen's urging, in the summer. She felt he needed help dealing with grief—still unaware of his situation at the Theatre—and was worried that he was drinking too much; their doctor was concerned as well, asking her "to give Henning a kick for me."[4] Kronstam did not feel comfortable with the man and did not return. But he knew he needed help, first to cope with Gerstenberg's death, second to deal with "the illness," although he was always frightened of seeing a doctor for that.

Kronstam's lifelong habit of dealing with stress by planning and measuring his energies failed him now. "How long does it take to get over this?" he asked one day. If he knew that a period of mourning would last one year, two years, even five years, he could steel himself for that. But everyone said, "It depends on the person. Everyone's different," and that provided no guidance. He continued to seek help, however. He next saw a psychiatrist, thinking that might make a difference. After the first visit, he was very excited. He liked the doctor immensely and thought she understood him. "It's better with a woman," he said. "She knows. She said, 'You've still got a knot in the pit of your stomach.'" But his second appointment was scheduled for three weeks away. At that time, he was neither depressed nor manic, and when he was in a balanced state he didn't think he needed help. He always thought he could control the illness through willpower, the same way he had conquered those other tours—pirouettes.

By Christmas, Kronstam seemed to be getting better. The cloud was beginning to lift. He was quite rational about accepting Christmas invitations. One dancer called and invited him to a gløgg party, but he decided against it. He was torn between accepting every invitation he received and trying not to overdo. His old friend Margrethe Noyé, who still saw him regularly, called and invited him for lunch. He wanted to go but had to go to his family that night, "and I

At home with Margrethe Noyé, January 1995. The portrait of Kronstam in Robbins's *Afternoon of a Faun* hangs on the wall behind him. Private collection.

wanted to keep my head clear for my family," so he called and canceled. He had not been seeing Lene Schrøder-Hansen—she disapproved of his new drinking buddies and had said so—but for Christmas he sent her a bouquet of flowers, and after Christmas he improved rapidly. On New Year's Day, he sounded like a different man. The depression was gone.

> I must have something to do
> with my imagination.
> —Henning Kronstam

Twenty-nine

The Ashton Solo

In January, Kronstam began taking walks along the lakes and having dinner at Lene Schrøder-Hansen's again. He also went to the Theatre to see a play, *Angels in America*. "I'm tired of sitting here. I want to get out," he said. The play was an American import that dealt with AIDS, and Kronstam found it very moving. He admired the acting, but he also liked its frank and sympathetic treatment of homosexuality. The experience seemed to break down some wall within him, and he began to be more open in speaking of his own homosexuality around this time. He was very positive during this period, saw visitors, and actually telephoned a few people, something he had not been able to do for months.

In February, Alexander Meinertz, a twenty-five-year-old university student who also wrote about dance, visited Kronstam to interview him about *Etudes*.

Meinertz was interested in the thread of classical ballet on Kongens Nytorv, in Volkova and Lander. He had met Kronstam through Hugh Williams, Volkova's husband, with whom he had been working, going through Volkova's papers and correspondence. Meinertz spoke with Kronstam for an hour and felt, in that brief time, Kronstam's artistry and thought he should be doing something more than sitting in his living room.

Kronstam was to have staged *Etudes* the previous season, but since he was no longer at the Theatre, the French ballerina Josette Amiel had been brought in. She knew a slightly different version from Paris, and both Kronstam and Meinertz had been hearing stories of how terrible the new production was. "I can remember it very clearly, although it sounds like nothing," Meinertz said. "We were watching a video of *Etudes*. It was the Paris version, the one Josette Amiel staged, and he liked it. And he was supposed not to like it, because it had replaced his, but he was really impressed by it. And he knew that he was supposed to not like it. He was saying, 'This is not bad.' And as it progressed, he said, 'This is very good. And I don't understand it. People are saying it's very bad, this new version.'

"I think watching ballet with him made you have a deeper understanding of the art form. It was like being in the presence of a spiritual master gently guiding you. Not that he was lecturing in any way; he was very simply sharing his knowledge and this seemingly never-ending sense of discovery. The latter was very important, I think. It was his way of seeing, which was very open, positive, and very special in that he picked up on the power and special atmosphere of every dancer. I remember seeing excerpts of *Etudes* that I was not really appreciative of, where he changed my perception completely, very much by his exactness. My opinion of the performance of a certain solo was related to a certain set of general standards, mostly aspects of the technique. He, however, instead instantly saw what was unique in that particular moment. Also, he saw potential, which was quite fascinating and which is a real gift. So it wasn't anything explanatory; it was witnessing his experience, which reached depths mine didn't by itself. I hope I have learned from it."

Meinertz had spoken with several dancers and knew that Kronstam was missed at the Theatre. He and a friend, Ralf Friedrichsen, one of the dressers at the Theatre, decided to have a dinner party and invite a young dancer who they thought might be persuaded to call Kronstam and ask him for coaching. "I remember the dinner being organized specifically to get Thomas [Lund] in a situation so that we could propose to him to do this," Meinertz said. Meinertz was curious about the Ashton solo from *Sleeping Beauty* solo that Kronstam had danced. "I must have talked to Kronstam about it before talking to Thomas, not mentioning it as a real possibility, but just asking him about the solo, and other things that he remembered, and he remembered some little pieces of choreography that are not seen any more. The Lander *Nutcracker* was one of them." Meinertz thought it might be possible to make a commercial video of Kronstam coaching these lost excerpts and began looking for funding, which he quickly found.

The dinner party was informal; Meinertz was cooking and Lund offered to help. When Lund began to talk about "how he was a little bit frustrated that he didn't feel that he was developing very much and learning things," Meinertz suggested that it might be possible to get coaching outside the Theatre and asked if he'd ever thought of asking Kronstam to work with him. "Thomas is a very thoughtful person," Meinertz said. "He takes it and then he reacts a little bit later. He was very interested, and later in the evening he kept coming back to it, and how could it be done. And I said, 'I guess you should call him and ask, and if you can't find a studio at the Theatre, I'm sure I can help you find a studio.' And I guess that's what happened."

Lund, then nineteen, was nervous about calling Kronstam, but he remembered a chance meeting he had had with the ballet master shortly after Kronstam left the Theatre that gave him the courage to call. They had both been at the physical therapist, and Kronstam called to him when Lund was leaving: "Please come and say good-bye to me, because we may not see each other again, and I wanted you to know that you were one of the ones I was looking forward to working with."

It took two weeks to arrange the session. In the meantime Kronstam had to be persuaded to do it. He was terrified of going into a studio again, convinced he was no longer able to work. There were other reasons as well. "They don't want me. I'm old, nobody wants to work with me," he said, and then, later, "I have killed that part of me and I cannot bring it back to life again just for one solo." When he learned that Meinertz had found funding for a video and that there was a real possibility that there would be more than one solo, he agreed, but he was still convinced that he couldn't do it. Kronstam invited Lund and Meinertz to come that weekend for coffee and then realized "it might not be proper" to have two "young boys" in the house with him unchaperoned, so he called Kirsten Simone to come too, expecting that she would serve the coffee. ("I served the coffee," Meinertz said.)

Kronstam agreed to work with Lund on the solo if the logistics could be arranged. At first Meinertz had thought of trying to find a studio in one of Copenhagen's dance schools, as it did not seem likely that Schaufuss would want, or be able, to have Kronstam at the Theatre. But matters had to be dealt with openly, as Simone told Lund he should write Schaufuss a letter asking for permission to work with Kronstam.

This could have derailed the project, but it was a time when all the constellations were aligned in Kronstam's favor. Meinertz arranged to interview Schaufuss. They spoke of *Romeo and Juliet* and the conversation led naturally to Ashton. "I remember talking about Ashton," Meinertz said, "and I asked Schaufuss, 'Do you know there is an Ashton solo that Kronstam knows, and that nobody else knows, and he's going to work with Thomas Lund on it?' And he got really excited. 'Oh, really? What, and where?' And I said, 'I don't know whether it's going to be in the Theatre or outside.' And he said, 'No, of course it will have to be here, and we'll get him a pianist. There's no problem.' That was how easy it was. It was so not complicated."

Schaufuss did not ask Michael Christiansen for permission to allow Kronstam to work in the Theatre, but Christiansen knew about it. The matter was raised at a weekly administrative meeting, the minutes of which were posted on the company bulletin board. He did not object and he did not try to stop it.

The week that Kronstam was supposed to begin working with Thomas, he had a crash. Fortunately, the rehearsals had to be postponed, as Lund was sent as a last-minute substitute to represent Denmark at the Erik Bruhn Competition in Canada. The day of the first rehearsal, Kronstam was obviously under great stress. He had slept badly and his hands were shaking. Schaufuss met him at the stage door and could not have been kinder or more gracious. He took Kronstam through the administrative offices and introduced him to the new people. The dressing rooms and backstage space had been rearranged slightly, and Schaufuss gave Kronstam a tour before taking him down to the old studio, Gamle B. Schaufuss also arranged for Kronstam to have Julian Thurber as the pianist, which delighted him. Thurber had worked with Kronstam so long that they had a real partnership. That evening Kronstam's remarks indicated how stressed he had been: "It went fine! It was just like I'd never been away from the studio! I didn't think I could do it, but it went fine."

Lund, who had never before worked with Kronstam in a one-on-one situation, was surprised at the depth of the coaching. Before he danced a step, Kronstam stopped him with a correction: "This is not the Bluebird. This is the
Prince. You have the palace, you have the Princess, and there you are running
up to the corner. People are going to wait for you. Take your time."

"I hadn't thought about that," said Lund. "The variation is so short and there
are so many technical things to remember. As I walked up to the corner that's
what I was thinking about," he explained. "When Henning said, 'Stop,' and
gave me that speech, he made me get into the role. With Henning, it's never
just the steps. There has to be a spirit behind everything you do."

At the second rehearsal, Meinertz came with a video camera (partly to make
a record, partly to have something concrete to counteract the incessant rumors). Kronstam was, again, very shaky and had trouble keeping his balance,
"but when he would get up to show Thomas, it would stop; he would be so into
it," Meinertz said. After that rehearsal, Kronstam went out to dinner with Meinertz, Lund, and Margaret Mercier. They stayed for hours because there was a
blackout in the city that night. It reminded Kronstam of the city during the war
and the young men began asking him questions about those days. Kronstam
began, slowly, going out more after this. He kept in touch with several older
dancers no longer at the Theatre and went to the pensioners' monthly meeting.
He even called the Theatre and asked if he could come and see the new production of *Sleeping Beauty,* which had been staged by Helgi Tomasson, asking for
tickets to the night Silja Schandorff was dancing.

Tomasson was in the audience that night and the two old friends spoke.
Tomasson asked Kronstam what had happened; Kronstam said simply that he
had been in the canteen drinking a beer and was so tired he fell asleep and they
fired him. Tomasson had spoken to Andersen about Kronstam the year before,
when he had been in Copenhagen to stage *Sleeping Beauty.* He had expected
that Kronstam would coach the principals and questioned why this had not
happened. Tomasson was told the usual story, that Kronstam was an alcoholic
and could not be allowed to work at the Theatre. Tomasson, who knew Kronstam was manic-depressive, although he couldn't remember how he had
learned it, questioned this, saying, as so many people had, that Kronstam was
so important to the Theatre, surely something could be done? "But—well, it
was obvious that they weren't going to do anything," Tomasson said.

Kronstam suddenly decided he had to go to Spain over Easter. Noyé, who owned a dress shop, could get away for a week and they would go to the house in Spain. He was afraid to be left alone over Easter again. He had a wonderful time in Spain and "saw all the people I needed to see." On Easter Sunday, when he returned, he was very relaxed and seemed a totally different person. He was almost gregarious; he went for walks, lunched at the café next door, where the people were all very kind to him and he could be himself, and every time he ran into a neighbor he stopped and talked. He knew every baby on the block, knew which husbands were out of work, knew who had just had the flu.

He was very talkative and very open. "I have a problem with my nerves," he said the first day, and his openness solved many mysteries. "Please don't look at my hands. When you do, they shake." Schaufuss had suggested that on the last night of the season all the former ballet masters would come on stage—Niels Bjørn Larsen; his father, Frank Schaufuss; Flemming Flindt; Kronstam; Andersen; and himself. Kronstam didn't want to do it because he was afraid he would fall down. He would lose his balance when people stared at him, he said.

Kronstam had another two rehearsals with Lund, who learned a great deal from the older man in these few weeks. "Henning said that Ashton didn't like smiling. He would prefer to have a polite face, and a mild face. He said, 'Look at the mirror and try to make happy eyes.' And how do you make happy eyes? So you really have to go home and think about it. And then things like that suddenly make sense. It's not like you put on a mask. It's so it becomes natural.

"Just from working with him on that one variation I could feel a very strong difference, because now I have only Peter and Johnny, and they only look at the technique and the steps, and they don't put any feelings into it. I could really feel a big difference, from working with Henning on that one thing—and I'm going to try and get further with it whenever I go on stage. You have to—not sell it, but you have to have a spirit behind whatever you do. It's not just technique. It has to be—of course, in a certain way it has to be technique, but then you have to also work on your face. Like an actor.

"He said, 'Your legs are the rhythm and your arms are the melody.' Things like that, which you never hear these days. It's like pieces of gold, and you swallow them, and they taste so good. I had days when I came home and just sat down and I was just thinking about those things, small things, and it's just one small phrase, and it makes so much sense."

Working with Lund was important to Kronstam. Asked how the rehearsals were going, he said simply, "It keeps me alive."

Lene Schrøder-Hansen also noticed a change in Kronstam after the coaching sessions began. "Working with Thomas really meant a lot to Henning. He was happy working again and it occupied his thoughts. I remember one time where he could not wait for Thomas to come home after the rehearsal because he wanted to call him. He had taught Thomas a wrong detail and was anxious to tell him so."

Schaufuss had scheduled a workshop on the Old Stage, devoted to male dancing for a Sunday afternoon near the end of the season, and Lund would dance the solo at that workshop. The Friday before the performance there was a general run-through, to which Kronstam had been invited. At the rehearsal Kronstam asked Schaufuss if he could give corrections, and Schaufuss said, "Yes, that's why I invited you," at which point, the dancers say, he took over the rehearsal. Kronstam thought it was a test on Schaufuss's part to see if he could still work. That is unlikely; Schaufuss was probably simply being polite. Dancers at that rehearsal thought that Schaufuss and Eliasen, especially the latter, were not pleased with Kronstam's actions. Several of the men said that Kronstam made, in that one hour, every correction to *La Sylphide* that the dancers had been fighting for all season, saying, for example, "What are you doing? Those arms have never been in *La Sylphide*. That's something Rudolf put in in 1974." It was obvious that he still had the respect of the company. Even the new dancers, the foreigners, listened to him—and kept his corrections.

At the workshop Schaufuss introduced Kronstam, sitting in the balcony with Johnny Eliasen, and thanked him for his work. It was a very gracious speech, but there was no hint in it that Kronstam would be coming back to the Theatre. Kronstam realized that he had made one mistake during the run-through, given one step incorrectly, and he was sure that was why Schaufuss didn't call him to come back to work. Leaving the workshop, he said he had to go home and calm down—he looked very calm, but said he was not. Then he said, 'I think I have given them a Prince." It was the first time he had ever said "they" and not "we" when speaking about the Theatre.

Kronstam seemed of two minds during those weeks. In one way, he was obviously getting better and was adjusting very well to Gerstenberg's death. He seemed embarrassed that people were still solicitous of him, asking him how he was doing, saying, "This is just something you have to get through in your life." "Franz told me I wouldn't outlive him by a year," he said once, as that anniversary approached, obviously delighted to prove his old friend wrong. At other times, he seemed to think there was something medically wrong with him and would make statements that began, "If you hear I have died." Then, ten minutes later, he would be planning for the future. He knew he would not be able to direct a full production again, at least not for a while, but thought he might be able to advise younger dancers, teach them how to stage a production, teach them what he had learned from Brenaa and all the choreographers with whom he worked.

Kronstam said he was taking Fontex (Prozac) but never said when he had started taking it. The drug may well have accounted for his elevated mood. Fontex is an antidepressant, not a mood stabilizer, and thus is not usually prescribed to manic-depressives. The Fontex exacerbated his manic phases. He couldn't sleep, he couldn't concentrate. He would do strange things. One evening he called up a critic and railed at him for things he had written—and some things he had not—which was totally out of character and as close as he came to a manic's characteristic obnoxious behavior. He went to the Theatre one night to see *Etudes* and *Konservatoriet*. The performance exhilarated him. He debated with himself over who was the night's ballerina—Christina Olsson, whom he felt had shown a new softness in the Sylphide section in *Etudes*, or Rose Gad, with her beautifully musical dancing in *Konservatoriet*—and decided on Gad. "I wanted to call them all right away, but I knew I probably shouldn't call them that night," he said, so he stayed up all night, thinking about what he would say to the dancers, and began calling them early in the morning. One by one, dancers who had not spoken to Kronstam in two years were called and given a technical correction or a compliment, or most likely both.

He remembered that Kenneth Greve had asked him for coaching months earlier, and he called Greve, telling him that this would now be possible. Greve saw Kronstam several times in the next month and was very kind to the older man, running errands for him. Kronstam called him once and asked him to buy him an electric razor, explaining that his hands shook so that he had difficulty shaving. Greve, who had danced in New York, Paris, and Vienna, was one of the few Danish dancers at the Theatre then with international experience, and the two swapped war stories.

Kronstam began to talk about what he might possibly do at the Theatre. He seemed to be trying to find a place that no one else wanted. The Ashton solo gave him the idea that perhaps he should revive ballets that no one else knew. He wanted to teach the Black Swan solo that Anisimova had taught him to

Greve. After that, he would show Lund the solo from *Nutcracker* that Lander had made for Bruhn and that only Bruhn and Kronstam had performed on stage. He remembered another Lander solo, a woman's solo from the pas de trois in Lander's staging of *Swan Lake,* Act II. Kirsten Ralov had danced it; Kronstam could remember most of it, but not the ending. He called Ralov; she too was excited about reviving it, about working with him again.

May 16 was the first anniversary of Gerstenberg's death and Kronstam received many flowers and phone calls. That evening he went to the Theatre with Schrøder-Hansen to see the second part of *Angels in America* because, as he said, "I'm not going to sit at home in my chair and cry." He was disappointed and thought the second part inferior to the first, which he still called one of the most powerful evenings he'd ever experienced in the Theatre. He called and made an appointment for Thursday to visit a doctor recommended by a friend, a neurologist who she said could give him pills to stop the shaking in his hands.

He did not keep the appointment. He never said why. On Friday morning, he was talking to Doris, his housekeeper, in the hall between the kitchen and the dining room. He said "good-bye" to her in a strange voice, turned, and fell down. When he regained consciousness he could not move his left arm and had no feeling in it. They feared he had suffered a stroke, and he went to the hospital. There he was given a brain scan and, he said, advised there was nothing wrong with him and told to go home. There was a nurse's strike and the hospital was taking emergency cases only. Kronstam protested, saying he couldn't go home, as he couldn't move his arm and he lived alone, and he was admitted to the psychiatric ward.[1]

Majbrit Hjelmsbo visited him the next morning and happened to be there when they transferred him from the regular hospital to the psychiatric wing. He seemed frightened and unsteady, walking very slowly, his arm dangling uselessly. By chance, Boel Jørgensen was there, visiting her husband, and Kronstam told her that he had suffered a blood clot, but there is no indication that he received either treatment or medication for blood clots. "He seemed to be trying to convince himself that it wasn't a blood clot," said Janne Kronstam (his nephew's wife), who visited him later. His arm was beginning to swell. Feeling was returning, too, and he could move his fingers; the fear of paralysis seemed unfounded. The hospital was threatening to send him home, and Jytte Abildgaard suggested he transfer to a private hospital. She would send a car for him and drive him anywhere he wanted to go. Kronstam seemed to take the suggestion seriously. He was afraid to go home alone, afraid of falling again, although he insisted that the doctors had said there was nothing wrong.

If it hadn't been for the pain and fear, Kronstam would have had a wonderful time in the hospital. He liked being around people. He talked to the anorexic girls, some of whom he remembered from his previous stays. He played cards with the other patients. Tuesday morning, he was called out of a meeting at eleven o'clock ("We had formed a group to talk about improving conditions at the hospital," he said, ever the leader), told there was nothing the hospital could do for him, and sent home. "The doctor there said I did not need a psychiatrist," he said rather proudly that afternoon. He had decided against going to the private hospital. It would cost too much money, and Gerstenberg had warned him to save his money for his old age. "You never know what will happen," he said. He was in very good spirits and seemed somehow relieved. He had had several tests in the hospital, and whatever fears he had had about his health seem to have been assuaged. He was in balance, and as always, he thought he would be able to function on his own. If he only tried harder, if he were only a little stronger, he would yet conquer the tours.

His arm was in a sling and still useless. His housekeeper, Doris, came every day to fix food and help him with his clothes. He said he could manage everything but his pants. Kenneth Greve came for a visit, got a tour of the apartment, and a good chat. Kronstam agreed to coach Greve in *Swan Lake* for guest appearances with the Kirov in New York and London; they would start work the following Monday.

Kronstam went to see his regular doctor, who told him the arm injury was the result of a pinched nerve and sent him to a physical therapist. The swelling was going down, he said, the bruise wasn't as ugly, and there was some tingling in his fingers. He saw the physical therapist on Friday. She confirmed the pinched-nerve diagnosis and gave him some exercises to do. The next day, when describing the exercises—which he didn't like, but faithfully performed—he said, "It will take a long time to heal. At least a month. But that's all right. I've got plenty of time."[2]

Sunday morning, when Doris came, Kronstam called to her that he couldn't open the door. He had had another embolism. Kronstam had slept in his chair by the window, as he often did. Doris went for help, recruiting a young man who lived on the first floor to help her move Kronstam from the chair. He took a few steps and collapsed. Doris called an ambulance, but Kronstam died before he got to the hospital. He was pronounced dead at 10:38 A.M., May 28, 1995, in Rigshospitalet. As is the Danish custom, no cause of death was given.[3]

Kronstam's obituaries would have pleased him. The most beautiful, perhaps, was written by Erik Aschengreen. After summarizing Kronstam's career, Aschengreen wrote:

> He loved the children in the ballet school, which he directed nobly and with authority. When, in 1978, he took over as artistic director after Flemming Flindt, he saw it as his most distinguished task to protect the classical ballet that he considered to be the cornerstone of the Danish ballet. The triumph during his directorship was the Bournonville Festival in 1979, which cemented the international reputation that the Danish ballet had built up over the past twenty-five years, a reputation that today is being debated.
>
> Personally Henning Kronstam was shy. It was not in his nature to lead but he did so for seven years because he felt responsibility toward the Theatre that was his home and that now needed him in that position. When Frank Andersen took over the directorship, Henning Kronstam continued as the gray eminence backstage. His knowledge and expertise could not be done without and the dancers loved working with him. Film director Anne Wivel's beautiful film *Giselle* from 1991 became very much a portrait of Henning Kronstam as ballet director. Two years ago illness forced him to take a break, but he was happily on his way back to the Theatre and work when death unexpectedly caught up with him. A few months ago he turned up in the Royal Theatre at the opening night of *Konservatoriet* and *Etudes* and just a couple of weeks ago he came to a matinee to see the young Thomas Lund, who became the last dancer Henning Kronstam worked with when he taught him the Frederick Ashton variation from *Sleeping Beauty* he himself had learned in 1957.
>
> Those of us who saw him during the great dancing years are forever thankful to an artist who night after night lifted us toward the sublime, the true, the deep. And in ballet history he stands as the one who through his whole varied career perhaps had the greatest influence on the Danish ballet in the second half of this century.

Allan Kronstam took over the funeral arrangements and planned a completely private funeral.[4] One of the retired dancers, Karin Vikelgaard, called him several times, urging him to change his mind and make the funeral public. She finally prevailed. Kronstam had made no arrangements for his own funeral, so the family thought the best thing to do was to make a copy of Gerstenberg's. Vikelgaard made the arrangements with the musicians. At the funeral there was no eulogy. Allan Kronstam merely stood up, introduced himself and the rest of the family, and said that his brother had been a modest man and would want no fuss. Although it was the end of the season and many dancers were away, the funeral hall was packed. Many said they had never seen so many people at a dancer's funeral in Copenhagen.

Henriette Muus expressed the views of many dancers when she said, a year after Kronstam's death, "I miss having such an artist to work with. We haven't had it for years now, and because I've tried it, maybe I feel it even more. Now I feel I just go down on stage and do some steps. But because I had Henning I think I'm also lucky because I remember his way of working and his ideas. If you have to go down and do a role where you have absolutely no help, you can go back and think about how Henning would have helped. So in a way, even though he is dead, he still helps me, somewhere."

On June 1, 1997, the dancers gave Kronstam an evening of remembrance, organized by Peter Bo Bendixen, who planned the evening and convinced the Theatre's administration to allow it to take place. The gala was arranged to have the dancers whom Kronstam had coached dance the major roles of his career, beginning with Drummer Boy. Included on the program were Thomas Lund, dancing the Ashton solo, and the first attempt to revive the traditional *La Sylphide* (by Dinna Bjørn) in which Lis Jeppesen danced the Sylph. The Theatre was packed, not only with ballet fans and dancers, but the city's musicians, actors, and artists.

The most emotional moments came during that part of the evening devoted to *Giselle*. A five-minute clip from Anne Wivel's film gave the shock of suddenly seeing Kronstam again, of hearing his voice come out of the Theatre's darkness. The clip ended with a close up of Kronstam watching the dancing, with all the characters' emotions flickering across his face: Giselle's love, and Albrecht's guilt, and both their passions. His feelings were so deep and so naked that they drew from the audience a sound halfway between a gasp and a groan. Immediately after the film Lloyd Riggins and Heidi Ryom danced excerpts from the last act of *Giselle* in perceptible pain. Riggins, who had come from Hamburg especially for this evening, wore Kronstam's jacket from his *Giselle* performances in the 1960s. Ryom was dancing her last performance and she danced it beautifully. The ending, when Giselle must return to her grave and Albrecht tries to stop her, was almost unbearable. Riggins's desperate anguish as he stood between Ryom and oblivion, spreading his arms in a gesture of "no," yet knowing he was helpless to combat both death and fate, was layered with so many meanings—Riggins's return, Ryom's farewell, Kronstam's death, and all that was and all that should have been—that the ballet was extraordinarily poignant and a more appropriate symbol of the evening than its planners could have anticipated.

The program ended with the tarantella from *Napoli*. After many calls for the dancers and much stomping on the wooden floor, the curtain closed as an enormous photograph of Kronstam as Romeo at twenty was lowered in front of it. The beauty of the image and the finality of the moment took the audience's breath and caused a few seconds of silence. Then everyone stood and there was a deliberate, sustained applause that would not stop, as if the audience were saying thank you.

To Hugh Williams, who had known Kronstam since he was a boy and watched his entire career, what was most admirable about Kronstam was the way he had kept the respect of the audience, and the dancers, until the end. "It was a remarkable performance," he said. And it was.

Afterword

Ellen G. Levine, M.D.

People often use the word *depression* synonymously with "feeling low," "being out of sorts," "the blues" as a generic term for sadness. It is important that the mental health professional be able to distinguish depression from major depression. To a mental health professional, depression often connotes transient feelings, which may or may not be easily linked to a causative factor. These episodes are part of the human condition; they represent and express real feelings of disappointment and loss in the essential experiences of living: love and work. They would not be regarded as major depression. They are not accompanied by a host of concomitant psychic symptoms on which the professional focuses. A mental health professional will look not only at the feelings but will explore in depth coexisting signs and symptoms.

Bipolar, or manic-depressive, illness is an affective mood disorder with a broad complex of symptoms. It is characterized by episodes of major depression alternating with episodes of mania. It is sometimes confused with major depression because the symptoms of a major depressive episode are identical with the depressive phase of bipolar illness. It is critical to make an accurate diagnosis since bipolar patients cannot be successfully treated over time without mood-stabilizing medications, such as lithium or Depakote. The symptoms of major depression are: depressed mood, fatigue, lethargy, hopelessness, impaired memory and concentration, insomnia or hypersomnia, feel-ings of worthlessness, and suicidal ideation.

The symptoms of mania include distinct periods of abnormally elevated, expansive, or irritable mood, and are characterized by grandiosity, inflated self-esteem, and a decreased need for sleep (at times a reversal of night for day), pressure to keep talking, flight of ideas, and distractibility. Extreme involve-ment in pleasurable activities with a high potential for painful consequences, such as unrestrained buying sprees and sexually indiscreet behavior, can also characterize a full-blown manic episode.

However, the diagnosis of bipolar illness can be quite challenging and elu-sive because patients in mania feel good, rarely see themselves as ill, and do not ask for help; so the physician usually sees them during a depressive epi-sode. Manic episodes are frequently not full-blown or can be "mixed," in which moods alternate rapidly within a day's time and the disorganization of think-ing, even psychotic thinking, may be overshadowed by agitation or evident anxiety. Without a diagnosis and treatment with mood-stabilizing medica-tions, the physician most frequently sees a profoundly depressed patient and, without a clear-cut history, usually from someone other than the patient, is unable to assess bipolarity without the presence of mania. The wide-ranging symptomatology of bipolar illness can mimic other psychiatric disorders and a high index of suspicion is often necessary to diagnose the condition.

At times, treatment with an antidepressant medication can precipitate a manic or mixed episode. Self-medication with alcohol or drugs to control pain-ful symptoms can also precipitate manic episodes, and comorbidity (simulta-neous existence of two distinctive health conditions) with these substances is present in a high percentage of untreated bipolar patients. The life history of bipolar illness without treatment is a downhill one in which the mood swings tend to escalate or deepen or both. Using alcohol and, at times, tranquilizers, such as benzodiazepines (e.g., Valium, Xanax, and others) or even barbitu-rates, to gain some measure of control over these worsening symptoms varies, but with the deterioration of symptoms, the need to self-medicate usually in-creases.

In my opinion, Henning Kronstam had bipolar illness. He had recurrent depressive episodes starting in adolescence. At age twenty-six he was hospital-ized for the first time. Although there is scant information about that hospital-ization, it is probably significant, as a particular stoicism typifies medical treatment in Denmark, and a depressive episode requiring hospitalization must have been quite severe and particularly striking to the treating doctors. These episodes persisted throughout his life, alternating with periods of intense creativity, decreased need for sleep, pressure to talk and interact with others, and irritability. These episodes were often followed by periods of collapse and great suffering; his instability of mood could be sudden and dramatic. Kronstam was probably treated with tranquilizers, perhaps antipsychotic medications, but there is no evidence whatsoever that he was treated with mood stabilizers. Treatment with the antidepressant medications may have reduced the severity of his depressive symptoms but may also have precipitated manic as well as mixed episodes.

Kronstam's mother was known to be bipolar; her "ups and downs" required hospitalizations and electroconvulsive therapy. Ultimately she killed herself at age sixty. A family history of major affective disorder, but especially bipolar illness, is a frequent finding in making the diagnosis. Major affective disorder occurs in 20 to 30 percent of first-degree relatives.

Psychiatrists speak of a patient's story holding together. By this they mean there are unifying threads of internal consistency in the story of a life. Kronstam's story, as presented in this biography, holds together for me. Clearly a gifted person, he was vulnerable from the start, not only from his genetic constitution (bipolar illness), but also from the early repeated abandonments he sustained from his mother's severe mood changes, withdrawals, repeated hospitalizations, and eventual suicide. Throughout his life he continued to be extremely vulnerable to loss and abandonment, whether imagined or real. His devotion to his art, with its rigorous demands, to the Royal Theatre, and to his relationship with Franz, were ways of warding off feelings of losing control. Bipolar patients almost always struggle with feeling out of control. The mood swings are in large measure dictated by biochemical changes over which the patient has no control; simultaneously, external stressors can precipitate the mood changes, so that these patients feel extraordinarily vulnerable. In fact, they are extraordinarily vulnerable and, without treatment with mood-stabilizing medications, feelings of desperation often lead to suicidal thoughts or acting-out behavior.

There were many factors that conspired against Kronstam's accepting his illness in a way that might have led to his actively seeking treatment. Shame and embarrassment and a sense of weakness that was at odds with the Danish ethos regarding illness were paramount. I believe that he would have seen seeking help as a defect in character and personality and, given his reticence and modesty about his homosexuality, would have distanced himself from being identified with his sick mother.

Franz's maturity (he was fourteen years older) and worldliness were deeply valued by Kronstam even as he chafed at the restrictions imposed by the relationship. Bipolar patients have notorious difficulty managing money and remaining in control, especially during manic episodes. Throughout the decades of their relationship, Kronstam turned his money over to Franz, who managed their combined resources. He could be quite dictatorial to Kronstam about spending. Volkova recognized Kronstam's need for external stability and Franz's meeting this need. She encouraged the continuation of their relationship a number of times, running interference with his family and supporting Franz's nurturance. Most striking is Kronstam's recognition and appreciation of Franz's value and worthiness. His loyalty to those he loved—Franz and Vera Volkova, for example—ran very deep.

Despite the lure of companies, choreographers, and countries, Kronstam remained in Denmark. He may have felt too vulnerable because of his illness and unconsciously sensed that he could not leave Denmark. He tolerated many indignities in the company, especially near the end of his life, in order to meet expectations he had of himself.

When evaluating any particular action, it is necessary to consider the person's personality, character style, the illness itself, and whatever is going on externally. It speaks to his strength of character that, despite terrible losses in the last few years of his life, Kronstam's loyalty and devotion to the company remained unchanged. He was eager to continue staging those ballets he loved, even as his illness progressed.

In his last year, he had become increasingly irritable. He was sleep deprived because of the living situation with Franz, but also from a breakdown in his typical sleep cycle, which is often the presenting symptom of mania. The irritability and exhaustion were observed by his dancers and others and interpreted as alcoholism. Other observers who spent more sustained time with him saw his exhaustion, catnapping, scattered and racing thoughts, and poor judgment, as well as his use of alcohol and occasional overindulgences, but also how relatively infrequently or frequently he actually drank. In reviewing this anecdotal information, the preponderance of evidence leads me to conclude that his episodic overindulgences were not due to alcoholism but rather fit in with his own cultural norms and resulted from attempts to hide his anxiety. His tremor and "old man on ice" gait probably reflected that anxiety as well as anxiety over being revealed as a "sick" man. It is important to remember the role of vanity and appearance in a dancer's life.

Proper diagnosis and appropriate treatment could have ameliorated or even prevented his eventual deterioration. In the last years of his life, as the borders of his existence broke down, both personally and professionally, his struggle to fulfill his expectations of himself were valiant indeed.

Appendix 1

Henning Kronstam's Roles

It is the Danish custom to list every role, including children's and corps parts. However, the American custom, which I have followed here, lists soloist and principal parts only. A single asterisk (*) indicates that Kronstam danced the premiere of an acquired work or a major revival. Two asterisks (**) indicate a role that was created for him.

1951–52
The Drummer, *Graduation Ball* (David Lichine)

1953–54
Pas de deux, *The Nutcracker* (Harald Lander)

1954–55
The Poet,* *La Sonnambula* (George Balanchine)
Bag Tæppet (Behind the Curtain)** (Fredbjørn Bjørnsson)
June, *Tolv med Posten* (Twelve with the Mail Coach) (Børge Ralov)
Harlekin, *Lunefulde Lucinda* (Capricious Lucinda)* (Niels Bjørn Larsen)
Neptune,* *Lunefulde Lucinda* (Larsen)
Romeo,** *Romeo and Juliet* (Frederick Ashton)
Orpheus,** *Orpheus and Eurydice* (John Taras)
Divertissement,** *Marriage of Figaro* (Taras)
Pas de deux, *William Tell* (after August Bournonville)
Zouave galop, *Drømmebilleder* (Dream Pictures) (Emilie Walbom)
Pas de trois, *La Ventana* (Bournonville)

1955–56
Wilhelm, *Far from Denmark* (Bournonville)

Chinese dance, *Far from Denmark* (Bournonville)
Quaker dance, *The Whims of Cupid and the Ballet Master* (Galeotti)
James, *La Sylphide* (Bournonville)
Ballabile center boy, *Napoli* (Bournonville)
Poet, *Chopiniana* (Fokine)
The Husband,** *Secrets* (John Cranko)
*Octet*** (Taras)

1956–57
Apollo,* *Apollon Musagète* (Balanchine)
Orpheus,** *Myte* (Ole Palle Hansen)
Prince Desiré,* *The Sleeping Beauty* (Petipa, Ninette de Valois)
Prince Siegfried,* *Swan Lake*, Act II (Petipa, Frank Schaufuss)
*Platée*** (Taras)

1957–58
Divertissement, *The Kermesse in Bruges* (Bournonville)
Nilas,** *Moon Reindeer* (Birgit Cullberg)
*Opus 13*** (Frank Schaufuss)
*Spektrum*** (Mona Vangsaae)

1958–59
Jean, *Miss Julie* (Cullberg)
Albert,* *Giselle* (staged by Erik Bruhn)
Jason,* *Medea* (Cullberg)

Bus Driver,** *Lykke paa Reise* (The
  Happy Journey) (Bjørnsson)
Symphony in C, first movement (Bal-
  anchine)
Symphony in C, second movement
  (Balanchine)

1959–60
The Toreador,* *Carmen* (Roland Petit)
Don José, *Carmen* (Petit)
*The Shadow*** (Birger Bartholin)
The Bridegroom,* *Blood Wedding* (Alfred
  Rodrigues)
Third solo, *Napoli,* Act III (Bournonville)
Pas de sept, *A Folk Tale* (Bournonville,
  with Inge Sand group only)
Pas de deux, *Flower Festival in Genzano*
  (Bournonville, with Inge Sand group
  only)

1960–61
Cyrano,* *Cyrano de Bergerac* (Petit)

1961–62
*Danses Concertantes** (Kenneth MacMil-
  lan)
The Sailor, *Lady from the Sea* (Cullberg)

1962–63
*Bourée Fantasque,** second movement
  (Balanchine)
Phlegmatic,* *The Four Temperaments*
  (Balanchine)
Melancholic, *The Four Temperaments*
  (Balanchine)
Prince Desiré, *The Sleeping Beauty*
  (Petipa, Rosella Hightower)

1963–64
The Host, *Garden Party* (Frank Schau-
  fuss)
The Ballet Master,** *Irene Holm* (Elsa
  Marianne von Rosen)

Stemninger (Moods)** (Hans Brenaa)
Danilo, *The Merry Widow* (Ruth Page)
Pas de deux, *Don Quixote*

1964–65
The Ballet Master,* *The Lesson* (Flemming
  Flindt)
Prince Siegfried,* *Swan Lake* (Petipa,
  Nina Anisimova)
Daphnis, *Daphnis and Chloe* (Cranko)
Prince Florimund, *The Sleeping Beauty*
  (Petipa, Cranko)

1965–66
*Afternoon of a Faun** (Jerome Robbins)
D'Artagnan,** *The Three Musketeers*
  (Flindt)

1966–67
Galla Variationer (Gala Variations)**
  (Flindt)
*Aimez-vous Bach?** (Brian MacDonald)
Prince Siegfried,* *Swan Lake* (Flindt)

1967–68
*Aureole** (Paul Taylor)
Don Juan,** *Don Juan* (Elsa Marianne
  von Rosen)
Albrecht,* *Giselle* (staged by Anton
  Dolin)
Gennaro,* *Napoli* (Bournonville)

1968–69
*Donizetti Variations** (Balanchine)
Brighella,* *Pierrot Lunaire* (Glen Tetley)
Kalkbillede (Chalk Pictures)** (Nini
  Theilade)
The Señor, *La Ventana* (Bournonville)

1969–70
Franz Pander,* *Bagage* (Henryk Tomaszewski)

Junker Ove,* *A Folk Tale* (Bournonville)
The Prince,* *Etudes* (Harald Lander)

1970–71
Edouard,* *The King's Volunteers on Amager* (Bournonville)
Moondog, *The Lady and the Fool* (Cranko)
The Man She Must Marry,* *Jardin aux Lilas* (Antony Tudor)
The Ballet Master, *Konservatoriet* (Bournonville)

1971–72
The Prince,** *The Nutcracker* (Flindt)
His Friend,* *The Moor's Pavane* (José Limón)
*Prisme*** (Hans Jacob Kølgård)
*Winter's Court*** (Eliot Feld)

1972–73
*Dichterliebe*** (Bruce Marks)
The Father,* *Monument for a Dead Boy* (Rudi van Dantzig)

1973–74
*Asylum*** (Bruce Marks)
*Dreamland*** (Flindt)
The Priest,** *Kronike* (Chronicles) (Eske Holm)

1974–75
Lord Capulet,* *Romeo and Juliet* (John Neumeier)

1975–76
*Hoopla*** (Murray Louis)

1976–77
Antony and the High Priest,** *Cleopatra* (Louis)

1977–78
Mr. William,** *The Toreador* (Bournonville, Flindt)
Cardinal Richelieu, *The Three Musketeers* (Flindt)

1978–79
Peppo, *Napoli* (Bournonville)
Alvarez, *Far from Denmark* (Bournonville)
Courland, *Giselle* (staged by Erik Bruhn)

1980–81
Button the Tailor,* *A Midsummer Night's Dream* (Neumeier)

1981–82
Orpheus,** *Letter to Orpheus* (Arlette Weinreich)

1983–84
Don Quixote,* *Don Quixote* (staged by Yuri Grigorovich)

1986–87
The Sheik,* *Abdallah* (after Bournonville)

Appendix 2

Kronstam's 1993 Contract

Balletinstruktør
Henning Kronstam
Peblinge Dossering 14, 3.
2200 Kbh. N.

1/3: H.K.
HJ/bb
23.4.1993

Kære Henning Kronstam,

Du tilbydes herved kontrakt som instruktør og kunstnerisk konsulent for balletmesteren for perioden 1. august 1993 til 31. oktober 1993.

Lønnen andrager kr. 42.000,- pr. måned. Lønnen, der er ureguleret, udbetales månedsvis forud.

Lønnen omfatter også eventuel undervisning af skoler efter nærmere aftale med balletmesteren.

Som bekendt sker der månedligt et fradrag i ovennævnte løn svarende til den gennem Statens Centrale Lønanvisning anviste pension.

Kontraktbrev af 3.12.1992 annulleres hermed.

Til formel bekræftelse på, at du er enig i ovennævnte, bedes du venligst returnere genparten i underskreven stand.

Med venlig hilsen

Michael Christiansen

Indforstået:

_____
  Henning Kronstam

This is a standard contract. Its extraordinary parts are the late date (April 23, 1993), the short term (August 1 through October 31) and, especially, the line written in bold in the original. An English translation of the body of the contract follows:

Dear Henning Kronstam,

We hereby offer you a contract as instruktør and artistic consultant to the balletmaster for the period of 1. August 1993 to 31. October 1993.

The salary comes to Danish kroner 42,000 per month. The salary, which has not been regulated, is paid every month and in advance.

The salary also includes potential teaching of classes by appointment with the balletmaster.

As you will know a part of the above mentioned salary is deducted every month in accordance with pension rules set out by the State's Central Payment Office.

Your contract of 3. December 1992 is hereby canceled.

For your formal confirmation of agreement with the above, please sign and return the copy enclosed.

Yours sincerely,

Michael Christiansen

Notes

Chapter 1. Henning Kronstam and His World

1. The other two are the Paris Opera Ballet and St. Petersburg's Maryinsky Ballet (known as the Kirov Ballet during the Soviet era). There were dozens of ballet companies in eighteenth-century Europe, but the rest either were founded or achieved prominence at a later date, or withered in the late eighteenth and early twentieth centuries.

2. Kongens Nytorv was a market square in the fifteenth century. It was once ringed with huge old elms, but they were cut down in 1998 after Dutch elm disease ravaged the city's trees. The Royal Theatre is on the square, across from the great Hotel D'Angleterre, a few stores, and a former palace that is now home to the Royal College of Art.

3. "The leap with which Bournonville, in his role of Mephistopheles, always enters and bounds into a motionless pose is commendable. This leap is an element which ought to be noted in an understanding of the demonic. The demonic is, namely, the sudden." Søren Kierkegaard, *Journals*, 1843.

4. Kierkegaard used ballet imagery in both *Fear and Trembling* and *Repetition;* a draft title page for *Fear and Trembling* had *Between Each Other* as the initial title and, in the margin, "Movements and Positions." The author was to be "Simon Stylita, Solo Dancer and Private Individual" (*Fear and Trembling; Repetition,* 243). While Simon Stylita was a Syrian hermit, not a Danish dancer, "solo dancer" was the title held by leading dancers at the Royal Theatre. The use of the word *positions* is significant because ballet enchainements (step combinations) are constructed by having the dancer move among the five set positions of the feet. The feet must clearly touch down in a position before the dancer can move to another position. Kierkegaard wrote, "It is supposed to be the most difficult

feat for a ballet dancer to leap into a specific posture in such a way that he never once strains for the posture but in the very leap assumes the posture" (*Fear and Trembling*, 41). Similarly: "The little dancer who last time had enchanted me with her gracefulness, who, so to speak, was on the verge of a leap, had already made the leap" (*Repetition*, 170). In thinking about movement so literally, the precise and artificial, thus quantifiable, movement of ballet dancers whom he would have seen at the Royal Theatre would have served as a model. It is more than possible that Kierkegaard was using dance quite literally as a metaphor for his famous assertion of the "leap of faith." The grand jeté en avant (big jump to the front) is a signature step of Bournonville's choreography and was used to punctuate a phrase of smoother, quick, side-to-side movements. Bournonville was not only the Royal Theatre's ballet master during Kierkegaard's day, he was its first solo dancer.

5. Instead of being known as stage left and stage right, the two sides of the house are known as the King's side and Lady's side. It is impossible to confuse them—from onstage, backstage, or orchestra—as *King's side* refers to the royal box, placed on the left, as one sits in the audience, and *Lady's side* refers to a box for the ladies-in-waiting, located on the opposite side of the stage.

6. The Theatre seated around 1,400 before the renovation of its backstage area and enlargement of the orchestra pit (1982–85).

7. Sandemose was a Danish-born Norwegian writer who wrote in Norwegian after 1930. *En flyktning krysser sit spor* (1933), published in America as *A Fugitive Crosses His Tracks* (Knopf, 1936), is about the oppressive nature of small-town life and includes the Ten Laws of Jante.

8. The moat was turned into several small lakes in the closing years of the nineteenth century, when Copenhagen's leaders thought that Europe had become civilized and they would never again have to worry about an invasion from Germany. Kronstam lived on the banks known as Peblinge Dossering.

Chapter 2. A Wartime Childhood

1. Anker (a Christian name) and Wad (a surname) were both from the Swedish branch of the family, although Kronstam did not know their significance.

2. The family previously lived at Thomas Laubsgade 10 (1931–33), Lyngbyvej 48 (1934–35), and Langvej (1936–38).

3. Kronstam said that his grandfather "was one of those people who went around to people's houses making things, a craftsman." His sister, Jessie, described her grandfather as an importer in later life.

4. Kronstam accepted the word *excitable* as a descriptor, but it is not his. On several occasions when speaking of himself as a child, he would use a gesture—waving his hands in the air, as though his hands were birds disturbed by a tossed pebble—while babbling a few nonsense syllables. He would describe his brother, Allan, by making his face perfectly expressionless, cocking his head to the side and pursing his lips, his hands miming the use of a calculator. In the interviews for this book he never used a

word to describe either himself or Allan as children, nor used gesture alone to describe anyone else.

5. Of Copenhagen's 7,500 Jews, 7,000 survived the war. A Danish Nazi tipped off the Resistance that a roundup was planned; neighbor helped neighbor and nearly all of Copenhagen's Jewish population was smuggled in fishing boats over the sea to neutral Sweden.

6. Kronstam often used the word *screaming* in the interviews for this book. Danes in general, and Kronstam in particular, are very quiet and do not often scream. The use of the word probably indicates Kronstam's mental state at the time. Although outwardly he adjusted to many blows, inside he was screaming.

7. After the war it was learned that the Nazis had dithered over whether to bomb Tivoli Gardens (the charming center city amusement park) or the Royal Theatre to punish Copenhageners for the General Strike in August 1943. They chose Tivoli.

8. Interview with Jessie Birger-Christensen, August 1996.

9. Kronstam, "Oral History," cassette 1, side 1.

10. The Deer Park is the royal hunt forest on the outskirts of Copenhagen; Helsingør [Elsinore], home of Hamlet and his castle, is thirty miles up the coastal road.

11. While Kronstam minimized this, his nephew, Torben, thought that Meta Kronstam had been hospitalized "most of the time" during the last decade of her life. This would have been when Kronstam was between the ages of twelve and twenty-two. Allan Kronstam remembered that there was a nanny who took care of them after their sister married, sending them off to school with lunches labeled "For the little gentlemen."

12. United States Surgeon General's Report on Mental Health, 1999.

Chapter 3. The Boy Who Practiced Dying

1. In European ballet companies the term *ballet master* referred to the man who choreographed the ballets, taught the classes, planned the repertory, and generally ran the ballet division of the opera house or theater. In America, where ballet companies have rarely been attached to a larger organization, the person who runs the company— hires the dancers, plans, and often casts, the repertory—is called the artistic director; a ballet master is a dancer, often retired, who teaches company class and rehearses the ballets in the repertory in the choreographers' absence. It is the European sense of the term *ballet master* that is used throughout this book.

2. Literally "grade book"; a compilation of report cards. A student's grades for each school year are recorded on two pages. The left-hand page has a list of the subjects taught in the Reading School and four grading columns, one for each of three terms and a final exam. The right-hand page has two columns, one for the teacher's comments on academic progress, the other for comments about the student's dancing. The highest grade is *ug* (*udmærket godt;* excellent) and is given 8 points. There is *mg* (*meget godt;* very good), 7; *g* (*godt;* good), 5; and so on, down to *slet* (poor, but with the secondary meaning of wicked), which deducts 23 points.

3. Ranks for dancers have varied widely in Denmark over the years. When Kronstam

entered the Theatre there were only two ranks: *danser* and *solodanser,* except for the very rarely given rank of *første solodanser,* which is the literal Danish translation of *premier danseur,* or *primo ballerino.* Børge Ralov, as noted, was accorded this title, as Kronstam would be in 1966. The company's leading female dancer (the Danish word is *danserinde;* there is no such concept as "male dancer" in Danish), Margot Lander, was the *første solodanserinde.*

4. Although Merrild taught the Bournonville Schools, he did not use Bournonville's barre. That was dropped in the 1930s. Like Balanchine's 150 years later, Bournonville's barre was short and brusque and was not deemed sufficient for training purposes. Teachers constructed their own barres and used the Bournonville classes for center work and jumps.

5. A character in a company of characters, Christian Christiansen had been a virtuoso demi-caractère dancer in the late 1900s, and a stick-wielding terror of a teacher in the first third of the twentieth century.

6. Kronstam, "Oral History," cassette 1, side 1.

7. In Copenhagen, this is written without the accent.

8. Valborg Borchsenius (1872–1949) had been Hans Beck's partner and assisted Harald Lander (1905–1971), the company's ballet master, in staging the Bournonville ballets in the 1930s. She was considered the guardian of the Bournonville style. The theater chief, or the director of the Theatre, was Henning Brøndsted.

9. Interview with Nikolaj Hübbe, December 1995.

10. The costume department pins pieces of paper with the assigned dancer's name printed on it so that members of the corps de ballet can quickly find which of the identical-looking costumes to put on. Often the names are left in from generation to generation. Kronstam was referring to this and meant that he had looked at the costumes and found the famous names of dancers of the teens or twenties.

11. This is confirmed by other dancers. Kronstam was not considered a sissy as a child. As Flemming Flindt, one of the most masculine dancers in a company of macho men, said, "He was never a girlish person, never effeminate."

12. He watched and he remembered what he saw. Before the company's first postwar tour (to Paris in 1948), all the pirouettes in *Napoli* were taken on half-toe. "In Paris they were all shocked, and the critics wrote that the Danish women couldn't dance on pointe. So when they got back, Mr. Lander changed it and put all the pirouettes on pointe."

13. Kronstam mimed this in an interview with the author, Copenhagen, August 1994.

14. Kronstam, "Oral History," cassette 2, side 1.

15. There is an interesting parallel here between Kronstam's career and Bournonville's. Bournonville also had his first important part in a play, Adam Oehlenschläger's Norse saga *Lagertha.* Bournonville was eight and he too played a murdered son. Like Kronstam, who read *Macbeth* so he could see how his character fit into the whole play, Bournonville read *Lagertha.* Unfortunately, Lagertha had *two* sons, and no one could, or would, tell Bournonville which of the sons he was supposed to be, much to the child's distress.

16. A Theatre tradition, it seems. Nikolaj Hübbe remembered that in the late seventies, when he was about ten, his teacher, Hans Brenaa, would sometimes give him a few kroner and tell him, "Go down to the canteen and get me a glass of milk from the black cow."

Chapter 4. The Lander Years

1. Emilie Walbom was a dancer of Hans Beck's generation who choreographed at least two successful ballets, both Danish adaptations of Russian works: *Harlekins Millioner* (Harlequin's Millions, 1906) and *Drømmebilleder* (Dream Pictures, 1915).

2. The first flowering occurred in the eighteenth century, two generations before Bournonville, when the Danish ballet enjoyed the services of an Italian ballet master, Vincenzo Galeotti; only one of his ballets is still danced, too.

3. Henrik Lundgren, "Bournonville i Danmark og udlandet, 1879–1980" (Bournonville in Denmark and Abroad), 462.

4. Kronstam, "Oral History," cassette 1, side 2.

Chapter 5. Vera Volkova and the Making of a Dancer

1. Cultural and artistic affairs was part of the Church Ministry. A separate ministry, the Ministry of Cultural Affairs, was a later development.

2. Spotting is a trick invented by the Italians in the last century. By focusing the eyes on an object during turns, a dancer is able to perform multiple pirouettes without becoming dizzy. Bournonville hated multiple pirouettes.

3. Kronstam, "Oral History," cassette 1, side 1.

4. Ibid.

5. Confirming or denying all the rumors about Kronstam would require a book in itself, but a few must be addressed. Williams and Kronstam went to Copenhagen's gay bars together and roomed together when the company toured, and there are fairly pervasive rumors dating from the late 1960s and early 1970s that they were lovers. This is untrue; they were friends.

6. "Theater Types," which are discussed more fully in chapter 18, were a way of allocating roles to dancers according to physical characteristics and personality that persisted, at least in vestigial form, well into Kronstam's day. Romantic Lover, Fool, and Prince are examples, and these words are capitalized in the text.

7. The exact date of this, and of the following incident, is unknown and cannot be reconstructed, as the only people who know are now dead. Kronstam said the murder charge incident happened when he was sixteen, so it must have occurred between May 4 and June 29, 1950. The company toured to a small city outside Copenhagen a few days after Kronstam and Gerstenberg met, and Gerstenberg went up to see those performances, so it is likely that this is when the dancers realized that Kronstam was gay. Everyone from that period remembers "Franz in that little red car," and Henning riding with him in that car.

8. Again, the date is unknown. Kronstam said this was when he was seventeen, so it

is likely this was during the 1951–52 season. Other dancers were aware of Kronstam's being called out of rehearsal but could not remember the month.

9. Interview with Kirsten Simone, January 1994.

10. Royal Danish Ballet, souvenir program book, September–October, 1956.

11. Dates of Kronstam's performances were determined by his own collection of theater programs.

12. Interview with Nikolaj Hübbe, August 1994.

13. The interview, "Ballettens ungdom" (Youth of the Ballet), was by Christian Fribert and was found in Kronstam's scrapbook; the date and publication were not noted. The other young dancers interviewed were Jonna Frank, Mette Mollerup, Viveka Segerskog, Elisabeth Envoldsen, and Anker Ørskov.

14. This story was confirmed by Hugh Williams.

Chapter 6. The Pepper Boy in the Sugar Bowl

1. There has been a controversy in Denmark over Volkova's role in the company. As recently as 1995, Henning Rohde, a Theatre administrator who was a Lander man and remained anti-Volkova during their many years of working together, published a memoir that said Volkova had been unsuccessful in bringing foreign choreographers to Copenhagen. Kronstam (and others) had no doubt that Volkova was directly responsible for bringing Balanchine, Ashton, Robbins, and Roland Petit to work with the company.

2. Kronstam, "Oral History," cassette 1, side 1.

3. Aschengreen, Der går dans, 81.

4. The old "genres" Noverre laid out in the eighteenth century still apply in ballet, as dancers still generally fall into these body types. The danseur noble, who was tall (around six feet), elegant, and classically proportioned (the waist bisects the body), portrayed kings and gods and danced the slowest measures; the demi-caractère dancer was a bit shorter (five-seven to five-nine), elegant, with long legs, and usually danced the quicker measures and portrayed pastoral characters; and the grotesque, shorter still, more muscular than elegant, portrayed demons. In the nineteenth century, this changed to accommodate the new repertory. The danseur noble, with his plumed helmet and adagio movements, nearly disappeared. A new genre, the semi-caractère classique, which combined elements of the danseur noble and the demi-caractère, took its place; this was the genre of human heroes, James and Albrecht. The demi-caractère moved more to the comic roles, and the grotesque became what is now called the character dancer. Bournonville listed a simplified layman's directory of the types in his Letters on Dance and Choreography: the noble, the light, the comic, and the strong (what we would now call a bravura dancer, or virtuoso), ingeniously combining physical attributes with personality. Nearly all the male dancers considered danseurs nobles today would have been classified as semicharacter classical in Bournonville's day. Kronstam, at six foot one, was a rare danseur noble in the original definition of the term.

5. Kronstam's collection of dance books was not systematic and, especially after about 1960, seemed to contain only books that had been given to him, usually by their authors and usually inscribed.

6. Interview with Hugh Williams, January 1994.

7. Gruen, *Erik Bruhn, Danseur Noble*, 52.

8. Aschengreen, *Der går dans*, 95.

9. Ibid., 101.

10. Unsigned newspaper article, dated April 1956, "Et flot tilbud til Henning Kronstam" (A generous offer for Henning Kronstam), Kronstam's collection.

11. In Copenhagen the ballet is called *Chopiniana*, not *Les Sylphides*, to avoid confusion with *La Sylphide*. In Danish the comparison would be *Sylfiderne* and *Sylfiden*.

12. August Bournonville, *My Theatre Life*, 279.

13. Kronstam, "Oral History," cassette 1, side 2.

14. At this time, the Danish company had only two regular ranks: dancer and solo dancer. The rank of solo dancer was equivalent to that of principal dancer, not soloist, although this was often misunderstood. The very rarely given rank of first solo dancer, which Børge Ralov had at this time and Kronstam would be given later, was something beyond a principal dancer, the equivalent of the old rank of primo ballerino.

15. New York, Boston, Hartford (Conn.), East Lansing (Mich.), Detroit, Toronto, Rochester (N.Y.), Philadelphia, Washington (D.C.), Baltimore, Newark (N.J.), and Brooklyn.

Chapter 7. Firestorms and Breakthroughs

1. Interview with Nikolaj Hübbe, August 1994, recalling what Kronstam had told him during *Apollo* rehearsals.

2. *Apollo* was referred to as *Apollon Musagetes* in Copenhagen; the more usual spelling is *Apollon Musagète*.

3. What exactly is meant by "new solo" is obscure. Kronstam did not remember being given any new choreography. He danced the third male variation, the one danced by Gennaro in the full version.

4. Bruhn would later dance *La Sonnambula* with the New York City Ballet.

5. Frank Schaufuss was appointed ballet master in his own right at the beginning of the 1958–59 season.

6. Conversation with Hugh Williams, January 1994.

7. Aschengreen, *Der går dans*, 139–43.

8. This letter is undated but was probably written in 1961, when Kronstam was twenty-six.

9. Aschengreen, *Der går dans*, 143.

10. Ibid., 136.

Chapter 8. The Poet

1. Erik Aschengreen, *Der går dans*, 628–37.

Chapter 9. Romeo

1. Hugh Williams, unpublished biography of Vera Volkova.

2. The core ballets in the Royal Danish Ballet's repertory date from the Romantic era, and Kronstam was the Romantic Lover of his generation. *Romantic Lover* is used to denote a specific theater type (the Fool, the Boy, the Blond Youth, the Prince) in Danish theatrical tradition. *Romantic* also refers to a specific style of ballet. Romantic, as opposed to classical, dancers have a longer, more attenuated line, a lowered upper body, rounded arms, and in Denmark, a curved back leg in jumps or in arabesque. Kronstam used Romantic line and style when dancing Romantic roles, yet had a back straight as a soldier's and the erect carriage of a classical Prince when dancing those roles. To say Kronstam was a Romantic dancer is analogous to saying a singer is a Wagnerian tenor; it does not mean he is the company's matinee idol or soap opera star, although there were critics during this period who confused the two, and Kronstam was criticized by some critics in some roles for bringing out the dangerous elements of Romanticism— the impetuous adventurer of a Byron or a Heathcliff—and by others, in other roles, for being too lyrical or poetic, which they misread as effeminacy.

3. "Pinoc," short for "Pinocchio," a wonderful name for a critic, is one of the pen names of Erik O. Hansson (1905–1980), who wrote about culture and theater in the newspaper *Aktuelt*.

4. Aschengreen, *Der går dans*, 628–33.

5. Interview with Niels Bjørn Larsen, August 1994.

Chapter 10. James

1. Kronstam, "Oral History." When Kronstam first danced James, the first act variations were danced by two soloists, as they had been in Bournonville's original production. During the 1960s this changed so that the first variation was danced by Gurn, the second by James. Kronstam said that in the version where James does not dance, he walks around the edges of the room, greeting guests and thanking them for their gifts. He said, as much as he liked the solo, that it had never felt dramatically right to dance it because it intruded on James's thoughts. He was considering going back to the original way the next time he staged the ballet. Interview with author, April 1995.

2. The internal quotations are the exact words of the mime speeches (unless they are used with the phrases "He thinks" or "He says to himself.")

3. In Bournonville's original libretto James fainted. Both endings have been acceptable in Danish tradition.

4. Rudolf Nureyev, Erik Bruhn, Flemming Flindt, Peter Martins, Peter Schaufuss, Flemming Ryberg, Niels Kehlet, Jørn Madsen, and Bruce Marks.

5. Kronstam often uses the phrase "go down and do a role" or just "go down." His dressing room was on the fourth floor, and he literally went down several flights of stairs to get to the stage.

Chapter 11. Apollo

1. Kragh-Jacobsen, *The Royal Danish Ballet*, 52.
2. Kragh-Jacobsen and Krogh, eds., *Den Kongelige Danske Ballet* (The Royal Danish Ballet), 392.
3. Balanchine and Mason, *Stories* (Garden City, N.Y.: Doubleday, 1977), 26.
4. Quoted in ibid., 27.
5. B. H. Haggin, *Discovering Balanchine*, 34. The wife in question was Tanaquil Le Clercq, then in a Copenhagen hospital after falling ill with polio on the last night of a New York City Ballet European tour. She reported that Balanchine was staging *Serenade* and *Apollo* for the Royal Danish Ballet and had found an Apollo whom he described as "beautiful boy, good face, could be movie star, Tarzan, you know, [Johnny] Weismuller."
6. Todd, *Peter Martins*, 8.
7. There are many Apollo mysteries. Several dancers suggested that Balanchine (well known for changing his ballets to fit different dancers) changed the role later on. Martins, who certainly knows the ballet well, disagreed: "Ever since 1967, when I first encountered Apollo, until the day he died in 1983, he never tampered with that ballet. In *Apollo* he never accommodated anybody." Ib Andersen, however, saw the Danish production in the 1980s and said, "There is a lot in that Danish version that is very, very different from what I learned. I mean, really different." (There seems to be a consensus that Kronstam kept exactly what Balanchine staged there in 1956–57.) And Johnny Eliasen, who also learned the role from Kronstam, remembered that when he later worked with Pat Neary in London he "said a few things to her and she said, 'That's right. I've forgotten that.'"

Chapter 12. The Princes

1. Milan (La Scala) had two fairly authentic versions of *Sleeping Beauty* that were not rechoreographed but credited to Marius Petipa—in 1896 (Petipa, staged by Giorgio Saracco) and 1939–40 (Nives Poli after Petipa)—but these were exceptions.
2. This seems to be an element of technique that was once known by Danes, as well as Russians, but became lost on Kongens Nytorv. Gudrun Bojesen, a young Danish soloist interviewed in January 2000 by the author, is the niece of Edel Pedersen, a dancer from Hans Beck's time. Pedersen told Bojesen of a trick that would allow a dancer to hover in midair: It's as though you have a balloon in your stomach, and you let the air out at the top of a jump.

Chapter 14. Cyrano

1. Todd to Kronstam, December 3, 1961.
2. Coton, Walker, and Haddakin, eds., *Writings on Dance*, 111.
3. Gruen, *Erik Bruhn*, 126.

Chapter 15. Ruth Page and Walt Disney

1. John Joseph Martin, *Ruth Page*, 217.

Chapter 16. The Swan in the Duck Pond

1. Martins, with Cornfield, *Far from Denmark*, 19.
2. Bruhn, "Oral History," cassette 12, side 23.

Chapter 17. First Solo Dancer

1. Kronstam did not explain further and was not pressed to do so. He was not able to discuss in any detail either past or present problems he had had with the Royal Theatre during the period of these interviews.

2. Kirsten Simone and Anna Lærkesen were named første solodanserinde, a title heretofore unique to Margot Lander. Kronstam gave the første solodanser title to Arne Villumsen when he was director, and for the same reasons he had been given it. Villumsen was not only the company's star but its workhorse during the 1980s and Kronstam wanted to recognize this, but the appointment was never made public and remained an internal accounting matter. Villumsen's reticence makes Kronstam look pushy. When he assumed the company's directorship in 1985, Frank Andersen appointed himself første solodanser. Andersen later changed the company's rankings from its unique Danish nomenclature of dancer and solo dancer to principal, soloist, and corps de ballet and the title is, hence, obsolete.

3. There are as many spellings of Thomasen as there are dancers whom he treated. This spelling has been used throughout.

4. Taylor, *Private Domain*, 301.

5. Ibid.

6. It is quite possible that Fridericia began to think of reviving *Thrymskviden* at this time. He approached Kronstam with the idea when Kronstam was director, proposing that he dance the role of Loke. Kronstam rejected the proposal, as he did not think the reconstruction would be stageworthy.

7. *Qarrtsiluni* was televised and it may well live again. It's a very well-structured ballet. It needs a stronger lead in the man's solo than the company had at the time in Aage Poulsen, but it may well be worth reviving. Kronstam had saved his notes from working with Lander, but they were among the papers that mysteriously disappeared from his apartment after his death.

Chapter 18. Dark and Fair

1. Jürgensen, *The Bournonville Tradition*, 19.

2. Kronstam, "Oral History," cassette 2, side 3.

3. In the Borchsenius notebooks, the mime speeches are written in French and the order of the gestures matches the French word order. When Kronstam spoke the words

of these mime speeches, he did so in the order in which the dancer delivers the mime.

4. Kronstam, "Oral History," cassette 3, side 6.

5. Ibid., cassette 2, side 3.

6. Ibid.

7. The "Life Guards" were volunteer soldiers who protected the king, literally guarded his life. The best translation for *Livjægerne på Amager* is "The King's Volunteers on Amager." The dancer's nickname for it is *Livjægerne*, or *Lifeguards*, and that is how it is referred to in this narrative.

8. Kronstam, "Oral History," cassette 2, side 3.

9. Knud Arne Jürgensen, *The Bournonville Ballets*, 171.

10. Kronstam, "Oral History," cassette 2, side 3.

11. This is not vaudeville in the American hoofers-and-hooks sense of the term, but refers to an early-nineteenth-century category of French theater. Vaudevilles were light entertainments that used popular songs to carry the action. Heiberg, the theater chief during much of Bournonville's time, programmed vaudevilles to attract audiences (planning to offer them weightier fare later). Bournonville's vaudevilles used popular songs in the score to cue the audience in to what was happening.

12. Kronstam, "Oral History," cassette 3, side 5.

13. Kronstam always said "flirtious" when he meant "flirtatious." He probably just liked the sound of it.

14. Kronstam, "Oral History," cassette 3, side 6.

15. The reference to color is not merely to the costumes of this production, but to a more ancient color symbolism, once central to European theater but now virtually lost. The hero and heroine wore blue, the color of nobility. The term *blue Prince* is still used in Russia to describe a danseur noble.

Chapter 19. Dreamland

1. This could not be verified with Tudor, but one of his biographers, Judith Chazin-Bennahum, said the quote "sounded exactly like something Tudor would say," and that Tudor had mentioned Kronstam among the dancers he had thought the best in his ballets.

Chapter 20. This Breathlessness

1. There were other friends, but they either could not be found or declined to be interviewed for this book. Many people who knew Kronstam simply could not believe he would consent to being the subject of a biography, as he had been such a private person. There are friends known by sight or nickname who could never be found. One man, a lover of Gerstenberg's who lived with Kronstam and Gerstenberg for several years during the 1960s, at first said, through a friend, he would be interviewed, then apparently changed his mind. Another friend of Gerstenberg's from the period when Kronstam was director died before he could be interviewed.

2. Agnes Gerstenberg had willed her summerhouse to Kronstam. Around the time

that Kronstam became ballet master, Gerstenberg found a house in the mountains of Spain, near Malaga. He, Kronstam, and Noyé bought it together; the three were equal financial partners.

3. The Pedestrian Street, a mile-and-a-half street full of shops that would have been part of the most direct route from Kronstam's home to the Theatre.

4. Schrøder-Hansen is a legal secretary. Once Kronstam spoke of this very proudly, saying, "Lene is a legal secretary, so she is not dumb."

5. Kenneth Greve, who had known Anna, spent considerable effort to find her. She was known to have married and moved from Copenhagen and had several surnames over the years. Greve finally tracked her down, but she did not wish to be interviewed. She confirmed that she and Kronstam had had a relationship, that they were engaged but broke it off; she said that it was a beautiful time in her life but that she did not wish to discuss it. Kronstam never mentioned her.

6. They had thought Kehlet not quite ready; he danced the part later in the season.

7. This is one of the items that could not be found after Kronstam's death.

8. Kronstam, "Det er ikke min balle" (It's Not My Company), interview with Ninka, translated by Bjarne Hecht, *Politiken*, August 21, 1977.

9. Morning class was given every day but the dancers were not required to take it. Their contracts stated that they had to be warmed up and ready to rehearse at 11:30. Dancers often only did the barre and left classes during the center work. This is often cited as an example of Danish dancers' inherent laziness, but the arrangement to exclude company class from the dancers' normal workday was an accommodation to strict Danish labor regulations.

Chapter 21. Priorities and Challenges

1. From some of the casting choices Kronstam would have made, it is likely that he was influenced by his memory of dancers during the Lander era, while Brenaa's memory stretched back much earlier. Lander had favored demi-caractère dancers in many roles that once had been classique, and Brenaa restored the older casting he remembered from *his* childhood.

2. Kronstam, "Oral History," cassette 2, side 4.

3. A few works from Flindt's repertory were retained for a season as part of the Theatre's custom of keeping new works in repertory for two years. In addition to *Toreador*, Kronstam programmed Inge Jensen's *Eurydike Tøver* (Eurydice Hesitates), Lar Lubovich's *Les Noces*, and Hans van Manen's *Septet Extra*, and he would revive each of these works save *Toreador* later in his directorship when the company danced at Tivoli during the Theatre's renovation.

4. Frandsen was a controversial teacher. Although dancers of the 1950s and 1960s had adored her, the young dancers she taught in the 1970s thought her strict to the point of cruelty and were disappointed, even angry, that Kronstam did not seem to take their complaints seriously. Everyone agrees, however, that Frandsen was a superb teacher.

5. Kronstam, "Oral History," cassette 2, side 4.

6. A strange story emerged after Kronstam's death, presented in the television program *Balletten danser: Temaaften on den kgl. ballet,* November 1999, that Kronstam had passed over a talented group of young dancers (Anne Marie Vessel, Inge Jensen, Eva Kloborg, and Lise la Cour) in order to push forward his own favorites, but this is not true. The four dancers named were already in their early thirties; if anyone had promoted them it would have been Flindt, five to ten years earlier. Several of the dancers Flindt had promoted—Mette Hønningen, Ib Andersen, Arne Villumsen, and Linda Hindberg—were mainstays of Kronstam's tenure as well, and several of the slightly younger dancers Kronstam promoted (Mette-Ida Kirk, Lis Jeppesen, and Heidi Ryom) had begun their careers under Flindt.

7. Kronstam had in his possession a list of ballets in the repertory of the New York City Ballet with notes written in English and Danish of the ones Balanchine would allow him to have. The decision seems to be based on the works' popularity, not complexity (Robbins's *Requiem Canticles* and several unsuccessful works from the 1972 Stravinsky Festival were among them).

8. Kriegsman, "The Return of the Danes, Tradition, Flamboyance and the Royal Danish Ballet," *Washington Post,* May 30, 1982.

9. Bruhn, "Oral History," cassette 6, side 12.

Chapter 22. The Bournonville Festival and *The Firebird*

1. Tomalonis, "How the Festivals Happened," 12.

2. At this time only Sorella Englund, one of the greatest Royal Danish artists, was not Danish born.

3. Tomalonis, "How the Festivals Happened," 14.

4. Kronstam had never danced with Ulanova but said she had asked to dance with him in *Romeo and Juliet* (presumably the Lavrovsky version) after seeing him in the Ashton; this had not been possible to arrange.

5. Croce, "The Romantic Ballet in Copenhagen," 233.

6. Jackson, "The Bournonville Caper."

7. Bournonville, *My Theatre Life,* 5.

8. Tobi Tobias, "Troll Fever."

9. Valerie Scher, "The Bournonville Festival: Afterglow after the Curtain." *Chicago Sun Times,* June 22, 1980.

10. Ibid.

11. It is just as possible that the critics retained affection for Holm's *Firebird* because it was very sexy, with the pirates dressed in black leather.

Chapter 23. Tivoli and Tours

Author's Note: The word *critics* is often used by Danes to mean reviews, but the double meaning is not inapt.

1. One story illustrates how difficult touring was for Kronstam. When the company was in Paris in 1980, he was at a party with several dancers. When the group got up to

go to another party, Annemarie Vingård, thinking that Kronstam needed to rest, suggested that he go home. "Not unless you will stay with me," he said, something that seemed totally out of character. Gerstenberg and Jytte Abildgaard had been staying with him but had left, and he was afraid to be alone. Vingård spent the night with Kronstam, and said they had talked for quite awhile, Kronstam telling her the story of Gerstenberg's saving him from the murder charge so long ago.

2. Tetley was not as popular in New York as he was in Europe; Ailey's *Memoria* had been choreographed in memory of Joyce Trisler, and many Americans wondered why the Danish Ballet wanted to memorialize an American modern dancer with no connection to Denmark; *Letter to Orpheus* was an experimental theater piece; and while the Danes were once congratulated for having saved *Whims of Cupid*, the world's oldest surviving ballet, it was now considered too racist to be performed and audiences were uncomfortable watching its blackface dances.

3. Tobias, "Troll Fever."

4. Kronstam admired Karelskaya as a teacher, saying that she was the closest he'd ever seen to Volkova, and wrote down some of her classes, incorporating material into his own.

5. Kronstam, "Oral History," cassette 1, side 2.

6. Ibid., cassette 2, side 4.

7. Erik Aschengreen, "Skæbneår for den Kongelige Ballet" (Fateful Year for the Royal Ballet), trans. Bjarne Hecht.

8. Arguably the worst production of a Bournonville ballet in the past fifty years was the result of a collaboration with "an intelligent director from the drama department," the 2000 production of *Kermesse in Bruges*.

9. Throughout his piece Aschengreen wrote as though Kronstam and Ralov were joint directors, a common misperception, perhaps because Kronstam often said "Kirsten Ralov and I," which he did out of respect for her and out of his natural instinct to include others and not take sole credit for himself. Ralov was Kronstam's assistant and performed the same duties as first Inge Sand and later Lizzie Rode had during Flemming Flindt's tenure, yet no one ever wrote that the company was directed by Flindt and Rode. Kronstam selected the repertory, chose and promoted the dancers, made the day-to-day decisions on running the company, and represented the ballet department at administrative meetings. Ralov's responsibilities included scheduling rehearsals and attending administrative meetings, as had Sand's and Rode's. Ralov also had several projects of her own independent of her duties, the most important of which was compiling the Bournonville Schools, which were published with Benesh and Labanotation and piano scores. Both Kronstam and Ralov worked in the studios, rehearsing ballets, and Kronstam often taught company class.

10. Schaufuss's production was brought in when he became director in 1994 but was not successful and was soon dropped.

11. The theater was built in a huge stone tank once used to store natural gas. Gas Works is a literal translation and it's how Danes refer to this theater when speaking in English, but a better translation would be "gas tank."

Chapter 24. The Search for a Successor

1. There was a third possibility, at least as far as the dancers were concerned, a non-Dane who had worked with the company on occasion. The dancers were told that this person would not be considered, for unspecified reasons.

2. Toni Lander died May 19, 1985.

3. Kronstam said of the salary negotiations that he was paid 425,000 kroner a year (about $70,000 at that time), and that this amount included his stipend as first solo dancer, as well as artistic director and head of the school. After a meeting with Andersen, his lawyer, and the theater chief, Kronstam said that Bering Liisberg suggested that they pay Andersen 400,000, but Kronstam said, "If I have 425,000, you've got to give him a little more, because otherwise there will be trouble. So he got 25,000 more." To reach this salary, Andersen was given the rank of first solo dancer—although this was not announced and Kronstam said it was merely an administrative matter—and made head of the school. Their salaries were unequal only because, like every other teacher, Kronstam received an extra payment when he taught company class. He received neither extra compensation for staging ballets nor royalties for his productions, as did others. "That was part of my salary," he said.

4. Tetley noted this as well when he was there to stage *Firebird*, observing that Andersen seemed to be trying to turn dancers against Kronstam and assert himself as a leader. Some dancers had a similar perception, but Kronstam said he was unaware of this.

5. A medical description and analysis of Kronstam's condition, as well as an explanation of the difference between the way words like *anxiety* and *depression* are used in common parlance and by clinicians can be found in Dr. Ellen Levine's afterword.

6. The comments on Kronstam's manic phases are based on conversations with several people, as well as the author's observations of a severe manic phase Kronstam suffered in April 1995.

7. Danish and American standards of what is normal drinking are very different. To Danes, especially those of Kronstam's generation, a beer or two at lunch and several glasses of wine at dinner, on a daily basis, is normal. The test is not the amount, but whether the drinker can control the drinking. When it's out of control, then it is considered a problem. However, Danes are extremely wary of any drugs—nothing, not even an aspirin, is available on supermarket shelves, and the American idea that taking a pill will make everything better is a notion at which most self-respecting Danes would scoff.

Chapter 25. The Red Thread

1. There may have been justification for firing several of the dancers, dancers who were ill or had not been performing for several years, and in these cases the union's action was taken because the firings had been done without administrative hearing.

2. One example of this and, by its timing, quite possibly the impetus for Ralov's resignation, was this story from Hecht, who had taken a leave of absence to dance with

the then London Festival Ballet, directed by Peter Schaufuss, a year after Andersen took over the company. Hecht was trying to decide whether or not to extend the leave and had scheduled a meeting with Andersen to discuss his repertory. "Kirsten's office was right before Frank's. And when I was on my way to his office, Kirsten was standing in her doorway and motioned for me to come in. She had never done anything like this before. She was so loyal. She was very upset. She closed the door and said, 'I feel I must tell you this. He is going to tell you that you are to dance James in *La Sylphide* next season. But there are only two performances scheduled and you are in the third cast, so you will not get to dance it.'" This, in fact, is what happened in the meeting with Andersen. Hecht, told that he would not be given another leave of absence, resigned. Later, stories circulated that Hecht had resigned because Andersen had not promoted him to solo dancer, but this is not accurate.

3. Most of the interviews from which the following comments have been excerpted took place from the year after Kronstam's ouster from the Theatre until five years after his death. The tenses (he is, he was) are therefore inconsistent and reflect the time of the interviews.

Chapter 26. Life and Art

1. Andersen had reduced the number of pupils in the school by about 25 percent in 1990, most probably, according to teachers and administrators, including Kronstam and Ralov, to pave the way for opening the company to foreigners. He had already brought in about a dozen foreign dancers during his tenure. The combination of a reduced school and eighteen vacancies all in one year fundamentally changed the company's composition. Andersen's successor, Peter Schaufuss, further reduced the size of the school and brought in more foreign dancers, including several foreign principals.

Chapter 27. Night Shadows

Author's Note: The epigraph is from an undated interview found among Kronstam's clippings; there is no identifying information. It is likely the interview took place shortly before he became ballet master. The sentiment is similar to one expressed in the Ninka interview in the summer of 1977.

1. A year after Kronstam's death, Ib Andersen, on a visit to Copenhagen, asked Christiansen what had happened and was told that Kronstam had come to the Theatre drunk and that he had not been allowed to stay home, saying, "We had to do what we did so the dancers would see him as he really was and understand why we were going to do what we had to do."

2. The observations for the remainder of this chapter are the author's, unless otherwise noted.

3. Nilas Martins, son of Peter Martins and his first wife, Lise la Cour, had attended the Royal Danish Ballet School but was let go at the end of his first aspirant year. He was considered difficult, with what might be called an attitude problem. Both parents had

been upset by this, especially la Cour, who, until then, had been on friendly terms with Kronstam.

4. The events in this paragraph are not from the author's personal observations but from interviews. The author's observations continue in the next paragraph.

5. This conversation took place in Andersen's office Saturday, May 1. It was not a formal interview, but Andersen was asked, "What is happening with Henning? And before you answer, you should know that I will be writing a book with him about his roles." Andersen received six letters asking for an interview. At first he agreed, but ultimately he declined to be interviewed, in person or by telephone. Michael Christiansen also declined two requests for an interview.

6. Telephone conversation with the author, January 1994.

7. Conversation with the author, May 5, 1993.

Chapter 28. The Terrible Year

1. Peter Schaufuss was appointed to succeed Frank Andersen as artistic director of the Royal Danish Ballet. Schaufuss was released from his contract after one year. After an interim period when Johnny Eliasen served as acting artistic director, Maina Gielgud was appointed director in 1996. She was succeeded by Aage Thordal Christensen in 1998. Frank Andersen was again appointed director in 2001 and will take office in 2002.

2. Kronstam was thought to be an atheist, but this is not true. He had a very simple Christian faith—probably not changed a bit since his confirmation classes—and still said evening prayers when he was sixty. He was antichurch, however, disturbed by the Danish Lutheran Church's antihomosexual stance. Gerstenberg was an atheist, but Kronstam was not.

3. At least by this time, Kronstam had probably been diagnosed as manic-depressive and his condition was known to doctors at this hospital. Danish doctors may not discuss patients with writers, but they apparently have no such compunction when it comes to friends and relatives, and more than one person interviewed for this book had been told by a doctor they knew, or by someone who knew a doctor, that Kronstam was manic-depressive.

4. Schrøder-Hansen and Kronstam saw the same general practitioner. The date is significant, because this is the first time that Kronstam's physician expressed concern about his drinking, and it corroborates Schrøder-Hansen's and Noyé's observations.

Chapter 29. The Ashton Solo

1. It is possible that the doctors thought Kronstam had suffered an anxiety attack and did not look further. In a phone conversation on his third day at the hospital, Kronstam said he had been given a strong sedative, and he chanted the daily dosages, "Two and two and two and two, then two and one and two and one, and today one and one and one and one," indicating that this was a usual occurrence and the decrease in dosage meant he was getting better.

2. Telephone conversation with the author, Saturday, May 27, 1994. Arlette Wein-reich came over that afternoon for a visit. She was the last person with a connection to the Theatre to see Kronstam.

3. Even Kronstam's death was clouded by rumor. Several people thought, assumed, or were told that he had taken pills. The family insists that they did not allow an autopsy. However, there were two separate reports from very different people that there had been an autopsy, and both reports were very similar: that there had been very little in the stomach, the only medications were a pain pill and a vitamin, that Kronstam's heart and liver were in good condition, and that he had died of a pulmonary embolism.

4. Allan Kronstam initially served as his brother's executor. There were problems with the will, which Kronstam had not changed since Gerstenberg's death, and his nephew, Torben, assumed the burden of handling Kronstam's papers. When he began going through Kronstam's effects, several things were missing, including all of Kron-stam's notebooks, the books where he had written down his own productions, as well as two books of Gerda Karstens's (*Giselle* and *La Sylphide*) that had been given him after her death. Whether they were thrown out in error or taken by someone who visited the apartment or retained by Allan Kronstam is not known.

Bibliography

Anderson, Jack. "The Great World and the Small: Reflections on the Bournonville Festival." *Dance Chronicle* 3, 4 (1980): 275–84.

Aschengreen, Erik. *Balletbogen* (Ballet book). Copenhagen: Gyldendal, 1982.

———. *Ballettens digter: Tre Bournonville-essays* (Ballet's Poet: Three Bournonville essays). Copenhagen: Rhodos, 1977.

———. "The Beautiful Danger." *Dance Perspectives* 58 (June 1974): 36.

———. "Bournonville: Yesterday, Today, and Tomorrow." Trans. Henry Godfrey. *Dance Chronicle* 3, 2 (1980): 102–51.

———. *Der går dans: Den Kongelige Ballet 1948–1968* (There is dancing: The Royal Ballet). Copenhagen: Gyldendal, 1998.

———. "Skæbneår for den Kongelige Ballet" (Fateful year for the Royal Ballet). *Berlingske Tidende*, September 24, 1983.

Aschengreen, Erik, Marianne Hallar, and Jørgen Heiner, eds. *Perspektiv på Bournonville* (Perspectives on Bournonville). Copenhagen: Arnold Busck, 1980.

Balanchine, George, and Francis Mason. *Balanchine's Complete Stories of the Great Ballets*. Garden City, N.Y.: Doubleday, 1977.

Beck, Hans. *Fra livet og dansen* (From the life and the dance). Copenhagen: H. Hirschsprungs Forlag, 1944.

Berger, Diane, and Lisa Berger. *We Heard the Angels of Madness*. New York: Morrow, 1980.

Bournonville, August. "The Ballet Poems." Trans. Patricia McAndrew. *Dance Chronicle* 4–7 (1980–83).

———. *Letters on Dance and Choreography*. Trans. and annot. Knud Arne Jürgensen. London: Dance Books, 1999.

———. *My Theatre Life*. Trans. Patricia McAndrew. Middletown, Conn.: Wesleyan University Press, 1979.

———. *Raad og leveregler fra en ældre til en yngre ven* (Advice and rules for living from an older to a younger friend). Copenhagen: Gyldendal, 1989.

Bournonville, Charlotte. *August Bournonville: Spredte minder i anledning af hundrerdaarsdagen* (Scattered reflections on the occasion of the hundredth anniversary). Copenhagen: Gyldendal, 1905.

———. *Erindringer fra hjemmet og fra scenen* (Memories from the home and the stage). Copenhagen: Gyldendal, 1903.

Bruhn, Erik. "Beyond Technique." *Dance Perspectives* 36 (Winter 1968).

Bruhn, Erik, and Lillian Moore. *Bournonville and Ballet Technique: Studies and Comments on August Bournonville's* Etudes chorégraphiques. London: Adam and Charles Black, 1961.

Bruhn, Erik, and Tobi Tobias. "An Oral History of the Royal Danish Ballet and Its Bournonville Tradition." Library of the Royal Theatre, Copenhagen, 1982.

Buckle, Richard. "Denmark." In *Buckle at the Ballet*. New York: Atheneum, 1980.

Buckle, Richard, in collaboration with John Taras. *George Balanchine, Ballet Master*. New York: Random House, 1988.

Cavling, Viggo. *Ballettens bog: Balletkunstens udvikling fortalt i billeder* (The ballet book: Ballet art developed and told in pictures). Copenhagen: Alfred G. Hassings Forlag, 1941.

Coton, A. V., Kathrine Sorley Walker, and Lilian Haddakin, eds. *Writings on Dance, 1938–68*. London: Dance Books, 1975.

Croce, Arlene. "Home to Bournonville." In *Afterimages*, 231–38. New York: Knopf, 1977.

———. "Out of Denmark." In *Going to the Dance*, 190–96. New York: Knopf, 1982.

———. "The Romantic Ballet in Copenhagen." In *Going to the Dance*, 228–32. New York: Knopf, 1982.

Dru, Alexandre, ed. *The Journals of Søren Kierkegaard*. London: Oxford University Press, 1938.

Fenger, Henning, and Frederick J. Marker. *The Heibergs*. New York: Twayne, 1971.

Fog, Dan. *The Royal Danish Ballet, 1760–1958 and August Bournonville*. A chronological catalogue of the Ballets and Ballet-Divertissements performed at the Royal Theatres of Copenhagen and a catalogue of August Bournonville's works with a musical bibliography. Copenhagen: Dan Fog, 1961.

Fraker, Mary. "Russian Influences on the Danish Ballet, 1915–1923." *Dance Chronicles* 4, 3 (1980): 22–35.

Fridericia, Allan. *August Bournonville*. Copenhagen: Forlaget Rhodos, 1979.

———. "Bournonvilles koreografi" (Bournonville's choreography). In *Perspektiv på Bournonville* (Perspectives on Bournonville), ed. Erik Aschengreen, Marianne Hallar, and Jørgen Heiner. Copenhagen: Arnold Busck, 1980.

———. *Harald Lander og hans balletter* (Harald Lander and his ballets). Copenhagen: Arnold Busck, 1951.

———. "*Thrymskviden:* Idé og iscenesaettelse" (*The Lay of Thrym*, idea and staging). Program of Det Kongelige Teater, 1990.

Garafola, Lynn, ed. *Rethinking the Sylph: New Perspectives on the Romantic Ballet*. Hanover, N.H.: Wesleyan University Press, 1997.

García-Márquez, Vicente. *Massine: A Biography*. New York: Knopf, 1995.

Gautier, Théophile. 1988. *A History of Romanticism*. New York: Howard Fertig, 1995.

Goodwin, Frederick K., and Kay Redfield Jamison. *Manic-Depressive Illness*. New York: Oxford University Press, 1990.

Gosse, Edmund. *Northern Studies*. London: Walter Scott Publishing, 1890.

Greenway, John L. *The Golden Horns: Mythic Imagination and the Nordic Past*. Athens: University of Georgia Press, 1977.

Grønbech, Bo. *Hans Christian Andersen*. Boston: Twayne, 1980.

Gruen, John. *Erik Bruhn, Danseur Noble*. New York: Viking, 1979.

Haggin, B. H. *Discovering Balanchine*. Photos by Martha Swope. New York: Horizon Press, 1981.

Hallar, Marianne, and Alette Scavenius, eds. Trans. Gaye Kypoch. *Bournonvilleana*. Copenhagen: Royal Theatre, in cooperation with Rhodos, 1992.

Haslam, Henley. "Preserving the Bournonville Style and Technique." *Dance Chronicles* 4, 3 (1980): 220–24.

Haven, Mogens von. *Balletten danser ud: Billeder fra Den Kongelige Danske Ballet* (The ballet comes out: Pictures from the Royal Danish Ballet). Copenhagen: Gyldendal, 1961.

Hershman, D. Jablow, and Julian Lieb, M.D. *The Key to Genius: Manic-Depression and the Creative Life*. Buffalo: Prometheus Books, 1988.

Himmelheber, George. *Biedermeier*. New York: Praeger, 1990.

Hude, Elisabeth. *Johanne Luise Heiberg som brevskriver* (Johanne Luise Heiberg as a letter writer). Copenhagen: G.E.C. Gads Forlag, 1964.

Jackson, George. "The Bournonville Caper." *Washington DanceView* 1, 3 (January–February 1980).

———. "Falling in Love Again." *DanceView* 9, 1–4 (special ed. for 2d Bournonville Festival) (June 1992): 36–40.

Jacoby, Jan. "A Survey of Art Music." In *Music in Denmark*, ed. Knud Ketting. Copenhagen: Danske Selskab, 1987.

Jamison, Kay Redfield. *Touched with Fire: Manic-Depressive Illness and the Artistic Temperament*. New York: Free Press, 1993.

Jürgensen, Knud Arne. *The Bournonville Ballets: A Photographic Record, 1844–1933*. London: Dance Books, 1987.

———. *The Bournonville Tradition: The First Fifty Years, 1829–1879*. 2 vols. London: Dance Books, 1997.

Kaplan, Larry. *Prodigal Son: Dancing for Balanchine*. New York: Simon and Schuster, 1992.

Kavanaugh, Julie. *Secret Muses: The Life of Frederick Ashton*. New York: Random House, 1996.

Kierkegaard, Søren. *Fear and Trembling; Repetition*. Ed. and trans. Howard V. Hong and Edna H. Hong. Princeton: Princeton University Press, 1983.

Kirmmse, Bruce H. *Kierkegaard in Golden Age Denmark*. Bloomington: Indiana University Press, 1990.

Kisselgoff, Anna. "Danish Attention to Nondancing Roles." *New York Times*, June 24, 1982.

Kragh-Jacobsen, Svend. *Margot Lander: En balletkunstners baggrund, udvikling, og blomstring* (A ballet artist's background, development, and flowering.) Copenhagen: Rasmus Navers Forlag, 1948.

———. *The Royal Danish Ballet: An Old Tradition and a Living Present*. Copenhagen: Danske Selskab, 1955.

———. *Twenty Solodancers of the Royal Danish Ballet*. Copenhagen: Danish Ministry of Foreign Affairs, 1965.

———. *Vor sidste Sylfide* (Our last Sylphide). Copenhagen: Thejls Bogtryk, 1966.

Kragh-Jacobsen, Svend, and Torben Krogh, eds. *Den Kongelige Danske Ballet* (The Royal Danish Ballet). Copenhagen: Selskabet til Udgivelse af Kulturskrifter, 1956.

Kronstam, Henning. "Det er ikke min ballet" (It's Not My Company). Interview with Ninka. *Politiken*, August 21, 1977.

Kronstam, Henning, and Tobi Tobias. "An Oral History of the Royal Danish Ballet and Its Bournonville Tradition." Library of the Royal Theatre, Copenhagen, 1982.

LaPointe, Janice Deane. "August Bournonville's *A Folk Tale*, 1854." Ph.D. dissertation, Texas Women's University, 1980.

Lauring, Palle. *Ei blot til lyst: Det Kongelige Teater 1874–1974* (Not for pleasure only: The Royal Theatre). Copenhagen: Forum, 1974.

Lundgren, Henrik. "Bournonville i Danmark og udlandet, 1879–1980" (Bournonville in Denmark and abroad). In *Perspektiv på Bournonville* (Perspectives on Bournonville), ed. Erik Aschengreen, Marianne Hallar, and Jørgen Heiner. Copenhagen: Arnold Busck, 1980.

Marker, Frederick J., and Lise-Lone Marker. *The Scandinavian Theatre: A Short History*. Oxford: Basil Blackwell, 1965.

Martin, John Joseph. *Ruth Page: An Intimate Biography*. New York: M. Dekker, 1977.

Martin, John Stanley. *Ragnarok: An Investigation into Old Norse Concepts of the Fate of the Gods*. Assen, Netherlands: Van Gorcum, 1972.

Martins, Peter, with Robert Cornfield. *Far from Denmark*. Boston: Little, Brown, 1982.

Mason, Francis, ed. *I Remember Balanchine: Recollections of the Ballet Master by Those Who Knew Him*. New York: Doubleday, 1991.

Mørk, Ebbe, and Niels Bjørn Larsen. *Bag mange masker: Niels Bjørn Larsen fortæller* (Behind many masks: Niels Bjørn Larsen speaks). Copenhagen: Lindhardt og Ringhof, 1977.

Neiiendam, Klaus. *Bournonville på scenen set gennem Edv. Lehmanns streg* (Bournonville on the stage as seen in Edvard Lehmann's drawings). Copenhagen: Teatermuseet, 1979.

Nørlyng, Ole, and Henning Urup. *Bournonville: Tradition, Rekonstruktion*. Copenhagen: C. A. Reitzels Forlag, 1989.

Oakley, Stewart. *A Short History of Denmark*. New York: Praeger, 1972.

Poulsen, Vagn. *Danish Painting and Sculpture*. Copenhagen: Danske Selskab, 1976.

Schønberg, Bent. *Hans Brenaa: Danish Ballet Master*. London: Dance Books, 1990.

Taper, Bernard. *Balanchine*. New York: Macmillan, 1974.

Taylor, Paul. *Private Domain*. San Francisco: North Point Press, 1988.

Tobias, Tobi. "Troll Fever." *New York* magazine, June 21, 1982.

Todd, Arthur. *Peter Martins*. Photos by Martha Swope. Brooklyn: Dance Horizons, 1975.

Vaughan, David. *Frederick Ashton and His Ballets*. New York: Knopf, 1977.

Veale, Tom G. "The Dancing Prices of Denmark." *Dance Perspectives* 11 (1961).

Wilson, James D. *The Romantic Heroic Ideal*. Baton Rouge: Louisiana State University Press, 1982.

Index

Alexandra Tomalonis has been a dance critic for over twenty years. She is the editor of *DanceView* and *Ballet Alert!*, has written criticism for the *Washington Post* and *Dance* magazine since 1979, and has been an adjunct professor of dance at George Washington University and George Mason University.